Kenneth John Angus is a senior project manager in the oil and gas Industry. Born in Teesside, he lives with his family in Newcastle, Britain. He served in the British Army Royal Engineers for nine years and has worked throughout the world, including many countries within the Middle East for 35 years. He has always had a natural interest in history and engineering and believes they are symbiotic.

I would like to say, "Thank you to my wife and children for their support," but that would be a lie. I would like to say, "In loving memory of my dogs," but they are not dead.

So I'll say, "Thank you, dogs, for your support!"

Kenneth John Angus

The Start:
Origin of Civilisation

AUSTIN MACAULEY PUBLISHERS™
LONDON • CAMBRIDGE • NEW YORK • SHARJAH

Copyright © Kenneth John Angus 2022

The right of Kenneth John Angus to be identified as author of this work has been asserted by the author in accordance with section 77 and 78 of the Copyright, Designs and Patents Act 1988.

All rights reserved. No part of this publication may be reproduced, stored in a retrieval system, or transmitted in any form or by any means, electronic, mechanical, photocopying, recording, or otherwise, without the prior permission of the publishers.

Any person who commits any unauthorised act in relation to this publication may be liable to criminal prosecution and civil claims for damages.

The story, experiences, and words are the author's alone.

A CIP catalogue record for this title is available from the British Library.

ISBN 9781398457034 (Paperback)
ISBN 9781398457041 (ePub e-book)

www.austinmacauley.com

First Published 2022
Austin Macauley Publishers Ltd®
1 Canada Square
Canary Wharf
London
E14 5AA

Standing on the shoulders of giants has become an overused statement and no longer used in its correct context. But this book could not have been written without the hard work and due diligence of people such as Leonard Woolley. Ur Excavation and The Royal Cemetery. A report on the Predynastic and Sargonid Graves excavated between 1926 and 1931. Also, Robert Carters knowledge on the Arabian Neolithic of the sixth–fifth millennia BC. Arabian Archaeology and Epigraphy. Which are the corner stones of this book. The irrepressible Klaus Schmidt, and his discoveries in Göbekli Tepe would have left the story untold if it hadn't been for these amazing discoveries in the last 20 years. Samuel Noah Kramer and is breath taking knowledge of Sumer

John Kutzbach's understanding of seasonal rainfall changes in the Middle East during the Last Interglacial Period which simply makes the understanding of the region so simple. Whilst Jeffery Rose's work New Light on Human lit my internal light on this amazing subject.

If Kathleen Kenyon had not carried out such exhaustive excavations at Jericho. Then it would have been impossible to place the puzzle together. To me Kathleen is the beacon of all good research and accuracy. Understanding the living world of Sumer, it would be hard to not acknowledge Thomas Van De Velde on his work of Black Magic Bitumen., Thomas's work opened my eyes to what could be achieved in the ancient world of travel and engineering

Mansfield, Daniel F and Wildberger, work on the Plimpton 322 exact Sexagesimal Trigonometry is like opening Pandoras box and many more questions than answers have now been raised. This simply led into the work carried-out by Hans Helbaek on Samarran Irrigation Agriculture at Choga Mami in Iraq as an engineer this work is so fascinating. Bernard Geyer, and Jean-Yves Monchambert work on Canals and water supply in the lower Euphrates valley ties perfectly into Plimpton 322 and Hans Helbaek's work.

Even Pedro Teixeira the Portuguese explorer of 1603 and Pietro Della Vallei 1625 have helped me appreciate that the land we see today wasn't the same yesteryear. Even Sir Alec John Jeffreys, an English geneticist who developed techniques for genetic fingerprinting and DNA profiling has helped clarify the situation.

Table of Contents

The Start The Origin of Civilisation	**23**
Introduction	**24**
A Chance Encounter 1625 AD	*24*
Finding the Sumerians	*26*
Understanding the Climate	*29*
Cognitive Homo Sapiens	*30*
Out of Africa	*31*
Into the Gulf Oasis	*34*
Flooding of the Gulf Oasis, the End of Last Glacial Maximum (LGM) 9,500 Years Ago, the First LGM Migration	*36*
9,000-9,200 Years Ago, the Second Last Glacial Maximum (LGM) Migration	*37*
Between 9,000 and 8,200 Years Ago, the Third LGM Migration	*38*
8,000 Years Ago, the Final Migration	*39*
Engineering of Sumer	*40*
The Lack of Building Materials	*42*
A Brief Overview of the Development of Human Activity	*44*
Changing Water Courses	*44*
Farming	*45*
The Start of the City States	*47*

A Word to the Learned:

    The Imperfect Historical Record   48

    Historical Bias   48

    Bias in Historical Writing   49

    Preservation of Middle Eastern Culture   50

Chapter 1: The Search for Accurate Information   **52**

    Searching for Sumerian Origins   52

    Root Cause Analysis   53

    Something Never Comes from Nothing and Changing People's Perceptions   54

    Eight Techniques   57

    Reason Behind the Madness   62

    Understanding the Dates and Terminology of Early History   62

1. Paleo Climatology and Post Glacial Sea Level Rise   **64**

    Understanding the Earth's Cycle and Effect on Weather   64

    Regional Weather Effects   65

    A Refuge During Hyper-Aridity of Surrounding Arabian Peninsula   67

    The Various Dates of Indigenous Habitation of Southern Arabia   70

    No Return to Africa   70

    Further Climatological Disasters   71

    The 4.2k Akkad Climatological Disaster   72

    Post Glacial Sea Level Rise   73

    Gulf Oasis Becomes the Persian Gulf   74

    Timeline of the Post Glacial Sea Level Rise Versus the Demise of the Gulf Oasis   78

    Conclusion   82

2. Migration Patterns and Archaeogenetic Data — 85

MIS Tracing Archaeogenetic Data — 86

1st Migration Out of Africa into Southern Arabia and Levant Region — 87

1 X 2nd Migration Out of Africa and into the Southern Arabia and Gulf Oasis Region and Beyond, Including the Return Back to Africa and Back Out Again — 87

2 X 2nd Migration Out of Africa and into the Levant Region South West Mediterranean — 88

3rd Migration Back Out of Africa and Back into the Levant — 89

Migration Via Afghanistan and the Caucasus into the Middle East and Converging with Local Populace Expansion from the Levant Region — 91

The First LGM Migration Event 9,500 Years Ago, Migration of People Once the Indian Ocean Encroached the Gulf Oasis — 91

The Second LGM Migration Event 9,000 Years Ago, Migration of People from the Gulf Oasis into Northern Mesopotamia (Levant Region and Taurus Mountain Region) — 92

The Third and Final LGM Migration Event 8,200 Years Ago, People from the Gulf Oasis into Southern Mesopotamia — 94

Migration 8,000 Years Ago from Levant and Taurus Mountain Region to Southern Mesopotamia: A Return of the 2nd LMG Migrants from Gulf Oasis — 94

Migration 8,000 Years Ago from Levant and Taurus Mountain Region to Egypt — 95

Conclusion on the Refugees of the 2nd LGM Migration Event 9,000 Years Ago from the Gulf Oasis — 95

Fertile Crescent Conduit — 96

3. DNA — 99

DNA Testing — 99

Dates of Marine Isotope Stages (MIS) — 10f

DNA Horn of Africa	*100*
Genetics of Early Farmers: Palaeogenetics	*102*
DNA Marsh Arabs (Madan) Link to the Sumerians	*105*
DNA of Bovine	*111*
4. Language	**114**
Brief History of the Sumerian Language	*114*
Data Mining the Sumerian Vocabulary	*115*
Proto-Euphratic	*116*
Sumerian Language is Known to Have Had Two Main Dialects	*116*
Words with Unknown Origins	*117*
The Sumerian Grammar	*119*
Sumerian Tamil Connection	*119*
Language Isolate?	*122*
5. Geology	**123**
In and Around the Persian Gulf: Gulf Oasis	*123*
Portuguese Explorer Pedro Teixeira	*124*
The Facts Outweigh the Theory	*124*
6. Archaeology	**127**
Discovering the Past	*127*
Middle Holocene (8,326 to 4,200 Years Ago) Settlement Activity in Eastern Arabia	*128*
Chronology of Pottery Neolithic	*129*
Conclusion to the Dating of Pottery	*130*
Farming Archaeology	*131*
7. Social Evolution in the Gulf Oasis	**135**
Shift from Hunter-Gathering	*135*

8. Historical Myths, Legends and Religious Material — 143

- Historical Hypothesis — *143*
- Dilmun and Its Place in Sumerian Mythology — *144*
- Dilmun Modern Day Name Bahrain — *147*
- The Great Flood — *147*
- Black Sea Flood — *150*
- Gulf Oasis Flood — *152*
- The Gilgamesh Flood Epic — *152*

Chapter 2: The Start of the Neolithic Revolution in Northern Mesopotamia — 155

- The Development of Agriculture — *155*
- Understanding of the Transition from Hunter-Gatherers to Farmers — *158*
- Time Periods (Levantine, Anatolian and Mesopotamian Broad Dates BCE) — *159*
- Natufian Culture — *160*
- Göbekli Tepe — *162*
- The Megaliths of Göbekli Tepe — *163*
- The King is Dead, Long Live the King — *165*
- An Organised or Stratified Society? — *166*
- Similar Sites in the Area — *168*
- Tell Qaramel — *168*
- The Start of the Neolithic Age 10000 BC-4500 BC — *169*
- Neolithic Advances in the Northern Powerhouse of Mesopotamia
- Jericho and Its Surrounding Area — *169*
- The Watch Tower of Jericho — *171*
- The Wall and the Tower of Jericho — *172*
- The Fall of Jericho: Death and Destruction

The Status Quo Gone!	174
Çatalhöyük	181
Artwork of Çatalhöyük	183
As I Look at the Dates of Habitation, the Real Standout Dates, they are the Beginning and the End and what drove the change	185
The Neolithic Revolution: From hunter-gatherer to Agriculturalist Competing Theories	186
Village Life Begins and a Population Growth	189
Early Agricultural Village Sites	189
Later Agricultural Cities	190
Effects of the Neolithic Revolution on Society	191
Effects of the Neolithic Revolution on Health	192
Overall Impact of the Neolithic Revolution on Modern Life	193
Regional Chronologies	193
Chapter 3: Pre-Start of Southern Mesopotamia	**195**
Rivalry Meaning	195
Mountains, Plains and Rivers of Mesopotamia	195
The Land of Sumer: The First Hydraulic Civilisation	197
Hydraulic Empires	198
Water Scarcity Today and the Same Problems Faced in Southern Mesopotamia	200
North South Divide of Mesopotamia	200
The Need for Irrigation in Southern Mesopotamia	201
Understanding Southern Mesopotamia	202
The First Civilisations	202
The Rise of a New Population During the Pre-Ubaid and Ubaid Period Throughout the Gulf	204

Finally Settling on Very Dry Land	*206*
The Start of the City States	*210*
Growth of the City States	*212*
The Urban Revolution: The Ubaid Period, 6500-3800 BC	*214*
Ready Steady Go	*215*
Dating of the Ubaid Period	*216*
Ubaid Culture	*218*
Elites and Social Stratification	*219*
Trade by River and Sea	*221*
The Five Cities Prior to the Flood	*223*
Conclusion	*225*
Chapter 4: Sumerian Engineering and Agriculture	**228**
Introduction	*228*
So, What Did the Sumerians Ever Do for Us?	*230*
Sumerian Sexagesimal (Also Known as Base 60 or Sexagenary)	*232*
Trigonometry and the Need in Ancient Building Projects	*233*
Plimpton 322	*234*
Understanding the Forces in Trigonometry	*235*
Reasons for Trigonometry in Construction	*236*
Trigonometry Used in Navigation	*237*
The Need to Supply Fields with Large Amounts of Water for Cultivation	*237*
Irrigation by the Sumerians, Akkadians and Regions Throughout Mesopotamia: 2900-2004 BC	*238*
Civilisation of the Region	*240*
Choga Mami Irrigation System	*245*
Mari Canal System	*246*

Sumerians, Akkadians and People of the Fertile Crescent	248
Fertile Crescent and Persian Gulf Trade Routes	250
Resources Required for Starting a Project	251
Required Teams	252
Layout of an Agricultural Cell in Southern Mesopotamia	253
Irrigation Canals	257
Sluice Gate	259
Ancient Reservoir	260
Regulator of Nina-Gena Canal	260
The Sumerian Irrigation Canal System	263
Water Disputes	264
Improvements in Farming and Irrigation	268

Chapter 5: Eridu: The First City in the World — 276

Introduction	276
Eridu Period 5400-4700 BC: The First City in the World	280
Eridu and Its Significance	280
Surviving on Terra Firma	282
Two Cultures Colliding	284
The Land of Firsts	285
Walking with the Gods	285
Living Together, Religion and Laws	287
Discovering Eridu, Its Location and Size	289
Water and Religion	293
Producing Surplus and the Starting of Trade	296
Boat Model and Actual Boats	296
Reed Boats	298
Conclusion	302

Ubaid and Sumerian Trade	303
Increasing in Early Trade Throughout the Gulf	303
Creation of Persian Gulf Trading Partners, Dilmun	305
Later Expansion of Mesopotamia Trade and Its Outposts	305
Eridu's Temples and Ziggurat, Berossus the Tower of Babel?	306
Magic and Myths of Eridu	310
Magic and Myths Passed on Through Time	311
Ishtar and Easter	312
Inanna and the Resurrection Story	312
Pre-Flood King List	313
Early Dynastic Eridu	314
Enki, Local God of Eridu	315
The Eridu Genesis	317
The Creator Goddess Thinks About Humankind (1)	321
Creation of Kingship (3)	321
The First cities Before the Flood (4)	322
Ziusudra's Vision (7)	323
Enki's Advice	323
The Flood (9)	324
Ziusudra's Sacrifice (10)	324
Reward of Ziusudra (11)	324
The Demise of Eridu	324
Passing the Baton to Uruk	325
Chapter 6: Strong-Walled Uruk: "The Venice of the Desert"	**327**
Introduction	327
Archaeological Levels of Uruk	329
Discovering Uruk, Its Location and Size	330

The Start of Inventions	332
The Two Most Important Inventions in the Uruk Period	333
Uruk Period (Largest Urban Area)	334
The Greatest Gift to Humanity	335
The Written Word	336
Bullae	337
The Stamp Seal	338
The Cylinder Seals	339
Intricacy of the Seals	341
Manufacture	341
Pictographs	345
Logogram	348
Rebus	348
Standardising Cuneiform	352
Cuneiform Script 2,500 BC	353
Assyrian and Babylonian are Members of the Semitic Language Family	355
Deciphering the Lost Writing of Cuneiform	355
History Revealed Due to Cuneiform	356
Conclusion	357
Uruk Art and Architecture	357
Sumerian Science	359
Sumerian Culture	359
Uruk City, Districts and Gods	360
Anu District	362
Eanna District	363
Uruk's Importance and Long Decline	365

The Rise of the King, Smoke and Mirrors:

The Sumerian King List — 369

Chapter 7: The Epic of Gilgamesh — **376**

Source of Gilgamesh Information — 376

Gilgamesh King in Uruk — 377

The Coming of Enkidu — 378

The Forest Journey — 383

Ishtar and Gilgamesh, and the Death of Enkidu — 393

The Search for Everlasting Life — 401

The Story of the Flood — 408

The Return — 412

The Death of Gilgamesh — 415

Gilgamesh Conclusion — 416

Chapter 8: Trade Routes of Southern Mesopotamia — **419**

Trade — 419

The Socioeconomic Control of Surplus — 423

Feeding the Elite Consumption with Gemstones and Precious Metals — 425

Importance of Trade Links with Bitumen — 426

Explosion of the Bronze Age and the Search for Tin — 428

The Rise of Sumer's Ancient Indus Trading Partner — 430

Indian Communities that Settled in the Land of Sumer 3rd Millennium BC — 435

The Indus Valley: the Land of the Socialist, Peaceful, Clean Harappa — 437

High Quality and High Skill Levels — 441

Trade Disruption Between Indus Valley and Mesopotamia — 442

The Decline of the Indus Valley Civilisation	445
The Climate Change Theory 1,800-1,500 BC	448
Chapter 9: A Time for Change and the Shift in Power	**449**
Early Dynastic Period of Mesopotamia Inclusive of Sumer	449
Shuruppak	450
Early Dynastic Period, 2,900-2,334 BC	452
Early Dynastic I, 2,900-2,800 BC	454
Early Dynastic II, 2,800-2,600 BC	455
Early Dynastic III Growth of the First Empire 2,600-2,334 BC	458
The City of Ur, 5,000-500 BC	459
Ubaid Cemetery at Ur	460
The Ziggurat of Ur	462
Sumerian Power Struggles and Chaos	463
Rise of Kish	464
Checkmate: The Rise of Sargon	465
The Akkadian Period	467
The Propaganda Hero-Kings of Akkad and Birth of Legends	468
End of the World's First Empire Due to Climate Change	469
The Sudden Collapse of the Akkadian Empire	474
The Gutians	475
Third Dynasty of Ur 2,047-1,750 BC: Ur-Nammu and Shulgi	477
The Disappearance and Rediscovery of Ur	478
Chapter 10: Akkadian and Sumerian Legacy	**480**
The Assyrians	480
The Rise of the First Babylonian Dynasty	482
Stele of Hammurabi Rediscovered	484
Hammurabi's Code of Laws	485

Hammurabi's Code	*486*
Trial by Ordeal	*487*
Minimum Wage	*487*
The Social Classes	*488*
Women's Rights	*488*
Babylonian Culture	*488*
Art and Architecture	*488*
Astronomy	*489*
Medicine	*489*
Literature	*490*
Philosophy	*490*
Warning	*491*
End Notes	**492**

The Start
The Origin of Civilisation

Even though the rich history and culture of the Middle East is well known throughout the world, very few know its true identity. The origins of the world's first civilisations run far deeper and closer than thought imaginable. So close you can almost touch it. The Origins of Civilisation were born within sight of the ancient relics that have stood abandoned and forlorn for many millennia, baking in the sands of the Middle Eastern desert, still holding on too many secrets of the past. An indigenous populace who inhabited the Middle East for 70,000 years before climatic changes started forcing people to make alternative arrangements and which changed the world we live in today.

Introduction

A Chance Encounter 1625 AD

During the European Renaissance in the year 1625 AD, an Italian composer and author Pietro Della Vallei was once again on his travels of discovery. He was born into affluence, a nobleman who was well educated, he read Italian, Latin, Greek, Turkish and a little Arabic. He also read classic mythology and the Bible. In his life, he travelled to the Holy Land, North Africa, India and extensively throughout the Middle East. Whilst he was on a vanity pilgrimage of curiosity in the Middle East, he married an Assyrian Christian Princess called Sitti Maani Gioerida in Baghdad. The two continued on their voyage of discovery together.

In later life, he became a remarkable man, a composer and author who made one of the first modern records on the location of Babylon and providing the first extremely accurate description of the site. Journeying by camel and accompanied by local guides, in a region made dangerous in the midst of the Ottoman-Persian wars fought over who would rule in Baghdad. The local bandits took advantage of the chaos to prey on unfortunate curious travellers.

He also visited the site of Nineveh, the original capital of the Assyrian Empire now forgotten, which later held the key to a land not known about during the Renaissance, the land of Sumer. But it was 18th June 1625 AD when he made his greatest discovery to date. He left India via Muscat and entered Basra. Della Valle had decided to take the Syro-Arabian desert route to Aleppo to avoid the Ottomans. The travellers spotted a distant group of tribesmen on the horizon. The guides decided that they might be in danger and searched for a place to hide. In the distance, they spotted a looming mass of a series of enormous ruins. As Della Valle later wrote in his memoirs:

Being suspicious to some Arabian vagrants or vagabonds, for more security we moved a mile further and took up our station under a little hill near some ruins of buildings which we saw from far away.

Della Valle's group waited for several nights while their guides negotiated with the local ruler for safe passage. During the day, under the baking Mesopotamian sun, Della Valle passed his time by walking amongst the monumental ruins and sketching the site for prosperity.

Our removal hence still being deferred. I went in the forenoon to take a more diligent view of the ruin of the above said ancient building. What it had been, I could not understand, but I had found it to have been built with very good bricks, most of which were stamped with certain unknown letters which appeared very ancient. I observed that they had been cemented together, not with lime but with bitumen or pitch.

In 1621 AD, Della Valle had stopped off at Persepolis in Persia copying and later publishing the first Cuneiform inscriptions. Once again, he was fascinated by the broken fragments of writing that littered the ground of this ruined place. He explored further and wrote down some of the symbols that he saw again and again, stamped into both the stone and pieces of clay brick.

Surveying the ruins again, I found on the ground some pieces of black marble, hard and fine, engraved with the same letters as the bricks which seemed to me to be a kind of seal. Amongst other symbols which I discovered in that short time, two I found in many places. One was like a pyramid, and the other resembled a star of eight points.

Della Valle and his wife had accidently stumbled across the ruins of Ur. One of the major cities of the first civilisation in the world. This society was known as the Sumerians and was where so much of the world we know today first began. Eventually the negotiations collapsed, and Della Valle's guides no longer felt safe camped out amongst the ruins. They departed in the dead of night and fled to safety across the desert. In Della Valle's bags were a few of the clay tablets he had found scattered among the ruins of Ur.

These were the first examples ever seen in Europe of a language that had been dead and forgotten for thousands of years. No-one in the West had suspected anything existed in these inhospitable scorching deserts. Della Valle may have wondered who had built these enormous buildings where no water existed in such a lifeless desert. If this had once been a great city as it seemed to be, what ever happened to it? Who witnessed its demise and why doesn't anyone else not know of its existence? How could something so large be forgotten and not known to the West. The ruins rediscovered by Della Valle represented one of the cities that formed a blueprint of the cities we inhabit today.

Writing, mathematics and the wheel are but a few of the inventions attributed to this civilisation but most of all, intensive farming, on a scale still not witnessed in the Middle East today, and certainly not in any arid region of the World. The success of farming allowed other new ideas to be pursued and the invention of commerce, the true birth of any civilisation.[1] I want to explore where this civilisation originated from and what course of events lead them to this place. How, in such a harsh unforgiving place, did life not just exist, but flourish beyond our wildest dreams.

If you thought you knew how great they were, guess again, you still don't come close to understanding how technologically advanced and how well organised these people were, the me and you of yesteryear. The urban landscape that they built has now vanished below the harsh desert sands and changed beyond all recognition, leaving it virtually impossible to imagine how inspiring it must have looked when travellers first saw these lands of Sumer at its pinnacle over 6,000 years ago.

Finding the Sumerians

The main focus of this book is predominantly within the Fertile Crescent with Southern Mesopotamia taking centre stage which was home to the first culturally advanced people called the Sumerians who had a supporting *caste*[2] that lays much further afield both North and South of the main arena. Historical and cultural events which had massive impacts on the world we live in today,

---

[1] *These ideas are fully described in Will Durant's "The Story of Civilisation"; also, the "The Ascent of Money" by Niall Ferguson speaking of commerce.*
[2] *Caste is deliberate play on words due to the ethnic diversity of the trade that aided the rise of the Sumerians.*

some of which we know, but some we take for granted without realising the original origins. The word *Mesopotamia* is formed from the ancient Greek words Mesos (Middle) and Potamos (River). *The Land Between the Rivers*.

Forming a swathe of land, this is more commonly known as the Fertile Crescent. This fertile swathe of land lies between two of the worlds most renowned rivers, the Tigris, and the Euphrates. The vast flood plains of these two rivers are situated in the modern Iraq. The deltas feed onto the shore of Northern Kuwait and the source of these two systems starts in Turkey, Syria, and Armenia. The Tigris and the Euphrates run parallel for nearly 2,000 Km (1,240 miles).

The weather hasn't changed in Southern Mesopotamia (Modern Southern Iraq and Northern Kuwait) for 11,700 years since the end of the Pleistocene. Which is the end of the Last Glacial Maximum (LGM). The summers are long, sweltering, arid and clear, only when the winds decide to abate. In winter, the nights are far more biting than you would first expect, with a touch of ground frost but predominantly dry, with pleasant daytime temperatures. But wintertime also brings the rains; when they come, they come in style, they are short and ferocious, wreaking havoc in its path. There is no hiding place, the raindrops are the size of bullets, with sand incarcerated within each globule. Smashing onto everything you own and leaving a streak of sand in its wake as the rainwater physically pours off you, nothing spared.

The modern drainage systems of the region simply can't cope with this deluge, dry hot sand blown in every direction have clogged up the drains for 9 straight months. The local people fighting a losing battle year in year out. It's constantly windy with no respite with sandstorms thrown in for fun. Over the course of the year, the temperature typically varies from 08°C to 46°C throughout the year but it is not uncommon for the heat to rise to 56°C. An average rainfall of just 107mm per year. This land is not for the faint-hearted.

Even today, with our vast array of technology and mechanisation, the land is still extremely unforgiving and seems impossible for modern people to yoke this inhospitable corner of the globe. Yet these are the same lands of the ancient Sumerians who ruled preeminent in the region for over 4,000 years. Apart from the weather, what makes this story even more remarkable, the land of Sumer possessed little in the way of what would be classed as normal construction materials such as wood or stone, no steep gullied ravines with dense forests, that could build homes or build barricades for protection. No plentiful supply of wildlife that could support tens of thousands of people that would eventually live within many city state walls. No thick-grassed savanna plains crying out to be tiled. A sun high in the sky, that would bake rather than aid cultivation.

The flat basin between these two rivers was a quagmire in the flood season, thick mud and impossible to traverse. The climate is harsh and the area devoid of all normal habitats that you would normally expect to see in a thriving metropolis that reigned far longer than any other civilisation the world has ever seen. It reigned supreme for thousands of years and predates all other known civilisations of the world. It is the land of firsts and Sumer is the cradle of civilisation. The reason for writing this book isn't just in the recounting of this cultural phenomenon but in discovering where these people actually came from, and why they chose this unforgiving, baking sand dune. How did they manage to get a foothold when the cards were so heavily stacked against them? How could this unforgiving landscape be shackled and tamed by so-called primitive hunter-gatherers of the Neolithic Age?

These people succeeded in the region when modern attempts have continued to fail. I want to highlight that these ancient people simply worked for the greater good of the community rather and any individual aspirations working closely as a single unit to overcome adversity. These newcomers were able to achieve the most remarkable and ground-breaking results. It clearly shows the sum is much greater than the individuals and further highlights that the people of yesteryear where equal to you and me. They are the same, no difference, same drive, the same ambitions, the same humour and exactly the same problem-solving skills we all possess today but used the adversity of their surroundings as a driving force for unbelievable collective success.

The purpose of this book is to understand where the people of Ancient Sumeria originally came from and why Sumerians became so advanced so quickly and what the contributing factors were for its growth and sustainability. What were the driving factors throughout their prolonged period of dominance in the area? The European Renaissance lasted for approximately 300 years, the Sumerian Renaissance continued, unabated, for 3,000 years. From the first physical evidence discovered by archaeologists to written accounts of the time and its demise. Because of the Sumerians, nothing on our planet would ever be the same again, the impact is still felt today, and we carry out our daily activities without realising the significance of the historical impact first provided by the first civilisation on Earth—*The Sumerians*.

We know the end of Sumer, it's written down, the Sumerians were kind enough to invent that for us! Subsequent Empires used variations of this same invention and described their particular role in history. Unfortunately, people quickly realised that early writing could be manipulated just like accounting, which was the driving force behind the written word. Some of the earliest written words on clay tablets in style called cuneiform were not always an accurate depiction of events.

Since modern humans have an eye for devilment and spinning a yarn for self enhancement, no more so than at the very start of writing itself. If it's written down and lasts a modicum of time, then the lie starts to manifest itself into fact and quickly embellished by future generations, who may also have a vested interest, to a point when fiction is believed to be truth. The passing down of the crown to their heirs and successors. It certainly wouldn't have been in the interest of the King or Queen to tell the truth by undermining their own authority.

It would be impossible to search for the beginning of Sumeria if we didn't carry out due diligence and start from the beginning of prehistory. It doesn't mean we have to go back to the Big Bang. Therefore, we can dispense with a few billion years and pick up the trail further on up the line. I believe the majority of people believe we came out of Africa, give or take a few arguments, and in my opinion a good starting point.

What we need to understand as the backdrop to this new starting point is to understand Mother Earth, as it is the initiating factor for the majority of events that are described in this book. Modern humans made the choices from known environmental situations. The decisions made by those individuals at the time cannot be deemed right or wrong because the majority of choices were made for the longevity and prosperity of the clan. To ensure they survived another hunting season.

Understanding the Climate

The Earth is not a static entity anchored in time and place. It is constantly moving and wobbling on its axis. It has an elliptical orbit around the Sun and being further distorted by both Saturn and Jupiter. What gives us our seasons is the fact that the Earth's rotational axis is tilted from its orbital axis, at present is around 23.4deg but slowly swaying back and forth overtime. It's not just 365 days a year cycle to get back to the exact same coordination to start again; it's closer to 125,000 years (even the Sumerian understood this concept of change).

Even then it's not quite the same, similar but changing. Mother Earth's core is also continually in a state of flux and changing the surface of the planet. For the first time in the long history of our planet, an unknown quantum has appeared on the horizon, that could offset the cyclic nature of our planet, Modern Humans. But fortunately, for the purposes of this book, the human impact on the planet during the period of time I am discussing is of minimal concern, but climatic events are the bookends to this book and instrumental in all the major events described.

Cognitive Homo Sapiens

The Cognitive Revolution[3] is well established to have started approximately 70,000 years ago and once again the time had come when humans could once again leave the womb of East Africa, which was the natural jump off point for expansion into the rest of the World. The forefathers of modern humans had already migrated out of Africa hundreds of thousands of years before. Eventually, spanning all four corners of the globe one footstep at a time. Homo Rudolfensis, Homo Erectus, Homo Neanderthalensis, plus a multitude of variants which all found various habitats to live in, making their home and adapted.

Over time, the new surroundings of these Homo's invariably enhanced various physical attributes aided early humans in their quest to survive. This wasn't the first time, and won't be the last, a variant of Homo had left Africa, but it was the first time that the people who were following the migrating herds where exactly like me and you, Cognitive Homo Sapiens. These direct ancestors were probably a little bit smarter than you and me. You might read this last statement whilst sitting in your air-conditioned room, listening to some music, in a nice soft chair with a cup of tea and scoff at such a seemingly irrational statement. These ancient people only had spears, stone tools and sat around campfires.

My retort to that would be, we had to start somewhere and standing on the shoulders of giants, springs to mind. We didn't get where we are today without having a solid foundation. These cognitive Homo Sapiens of 70,000 years ago had to manage so many variables throughout the year with the changing seasons,

---

[3] *Yuval Noah Harari describes in his Book "Sapiens" the genetic mutation and cognitive revolution of imagination and exceptionalism 70,000 years ago.*

migrating herds and various timings for plants bearing fruits and berries. The analytical skills required to survive, with no Marks and Spencer's, Walmart or Carrefour in sight. Yes, we are in a more favourable position as a whole.

But thankfully, Charles Darwin has by far the best response: *It is not the most intellectual of the species that survives; but the species that survives is the one that is able best to adapt and adjust to the changing environment in which it finds itself.*[i] To also clarify another point, that Homo Neanderthalensis had a much larger brain, so invariably we as Homo Sapiens shouldn't be sat reading this book, it should be a distant relative of ours Mrs Nancy Neanderthal. Due to her much larger brain, modern anthropogony understands the reason why. Nancy Neanderthal had an expanded brain size due to the larger visual cortex that was required for seeing in the snow. Simple equation Homo + Adapt = Survive*. * denotes unless it comes across different, more aggressive and tactically astute type of Homo.

Out of Africa

The dispersal of Cognitive Homo Sapiens population is dynamically linked with the changing climate and environmental conditions of Arabia[ii]. Many of all early theories have suggested that the propagation out of Africa and into the surrounding areas was predominantly via the Levant Valley. Numerous excavations have taken place in the Levant with breath taking discoveries on how and when early people first moved into the region and the transition from nomadic hunter-gatherers to being more sedentary pastoral early farmers. But academic opinion over the last half century has also started to reveal that the Northern dispersal wasn't necessarily the only route out of Africa but also via the Arabian Peninsula now seems to have been a more favourable route for the first Cognitive Homo Sapiens out of Africa.

Although Arabia is now an arid expanse, at times the vast Arabian deserts were transformed for thousands of years at a time into landscapes littered with freshwater lakes and active river systems. These became perfect grazing for a multitude of animals including gazelle, zebra, buffalo, antelope, ostriches and lions. With the ice caps still reaching down as far as modern-day Berlin this episode helped to dramatically increase rainfall in the region. Due to the difference in weather conditions, we witness today. The expanded ice caps resulted in an intensification and northward displacement of the Indian Ocean monsoon.

The Indian Monsoons we know today were the Saudi Arabian Monsoons 125,000-30,000 years ago, which caused rainfall to reach across much of the Arabian Peninsula. (Monsoon is a term derived from an Arabic word *Mausim*, meaning weather.) The dramatic change from desert to pasture lands is still seen very briefly today with the winter rainfall. The monsoon movement is affected by several contributing factors which includes tectonic plate movement, changes in the atmospheric CO_2 concentration, changes in Earth's orbit and also the changes in extent of ice caps.

Evidence from the Alluvial Fan records from Southeast Arabia indicates that the region was tropical with subtropical deserts due to high sun angles and a lack of cloud coverage which allowed for maximum solar radiation. Therefore, the increased monsoon rainfall led to the widespread activation of drainage systems, improved fresh water supply, expansion of vegetation and grassland development throughout the region. This aided an easy passage out of Africa for the dispersal of Cognitive Homo Sapiens populations. These grasslands supported the ideal hunter-gatherer landscape.

It should be noted that so few Homo Sapiens lived on the planet at this time, it wasn't a scene from the 1889 AD Oklahoma Land Rush, probably far less than the 50,000 in 1889 and stretched over several thousand years. These hunter-gatherers didn't have an exit strategy but lived on the balance of probability and with such resources available it really wasn't a hard decision to make. The only real decision was turn left to the Levant or right onto the Arabian Savanna Plains and the open fertile plains of the South would have been extremely inviting. Whereas the early migration out of Africa heading for the Levant was still home to Homo Neanderthalensis.

A recent theory has proposed that the lack of movement out of Africa for Cognitive Homo Sapiens prior to 125,000 years ago may have been due to resistance from Homo Neanderthalensis. Until a point in time when the less physical Cognitive Homo Sapiens had been able to plan grouped resistance and eventually remove Neanderthal from the newly acquired region of the Levant. But somebody else more capable can write about that hypothesis. It is unclear if Homo Neanderthalensis has ever been found in the warmer lower regions of the Arabian Peninsula which could have hindered migration of Homo Sapiens.

New research describes a dynamic climate and vegetation model that explains when regions across Africa, areas of the Middle East, and the Mediterranean were either wetter or drier than presently witnessed, and how the plant composition changed in tandem opening up conducive migration corridors. It should also be noted that the sea levels during this period of time were 120 metres lower than we see today. The landforms that are now a vast distance apart were a lot closer with lowered sea levels. This meant the physical water barriers were reduced. The Red Sea wasn't such a daunting obstacle and easily crossed. It was still very deep, but its neck narrowed to an achievable crossing.

The model used by scientists also provides research evidence concerning the relationships between Earth's climate and its orbit, greenhouse gas concentrations, and its ice sheets. The model shows that around 125,000 and 70,000 years ago both Northern Africa and the Arabian Peninsula experienced increased and more Northerly-reaching summer monsoon rainfall. That led to narrowing of the Saharan and Arabian deserts due to increased grassland.

At the same time, in the Mediterranean and the Levant (an area that includes Syria, Lebanon, Jordan, Israel and Palestine), winter storm track rainfall also increased. These changes were driven by the Earth's position relative to the sun. The Northern Hemisphere at the time was as close as possible to the sun during the summer, and as far away as possible during the winter. This resulted in warm, wet summers and very cold winters. With a stronger summer rainfall in both the (now) Savanna Sahara and Savanna Arabian areas and heavy winter rains in the Mediterranean.

At school we were all taught that Neanderthals prefer the cold. At this climatic change in history, the Mediterranean had a more temperate climate when Cognitive Homo Sapiens moved into the Levant Region and beyond. Archaeological evidence has shown that both Cognitive Homo Sapiens and Neanderthals lived in close proximity to each other for over 10,000 years they were neighbours with cave dwellings only 300 metres apart. It is not necessarily a case of Homo Sapiens meets Neanderthals, Homo Sapiens kill Neanderthals, Homo Sapiens are the rulers! We have between 1-4% Neanderthal DNA, so obviously something happened; even if it wasn't anatomically possible, somebody somewhere succeeded.

We also have evidence that Neanderthals burial rituals were eventually copied by Homo Sapiens, so some interaction had to have occurred. It's too simple and neat to say they didn't get on…they did, and for a significant period of time. Something happened as a trigger point, it could have been disease, but if I was a betting man, I would wager a lot on Homo Sapiens being heavily involved and acting as the coup de grace to the existence of Neanderthals.

It's not as if we are unaware of such atrocities. Many people reading this book will have gone through similar events and have first-hand experience of how Aryan Cognitive Homo Sapiens can act. The thought that these variations of Homo were competing for a finite resource with the inability of Neanderthal's to adapt doesn't stack up, due to the sparse populations that lived in these areas.

Now, Cognitive Homo Sapiens had reached the rest of the world and left Africa for good (maybe). The wider world had seen this all before, on a regular basis. But it hadn't. That is why the word Cognitive has been used extensively throughout the opening of this book. These *Humans* could converse accurately explain everything in detail, nothing lost in translation. If humans could discuss everything in detail, they could plan in detail. Nothing could defeat them now, apart from Mother Earth and the climate, but everything else on terra firma and in the oceans were in for a shock awakening.

Into the Gulf Oasis

By using various methods of research, we will be able to put together a picture of how events unfolded in the Middle East and the surrounding regions including the area that is now the Persian Gulf. This holds the key to events in world history and which predate all Civilisation. 10,000 years ago, the current Persian Gulf was empty, dry land, hard to imagine, but fact. Sea levels of the world where a lot lower than you see today, 120 metres lower.[iii] The migrating Cognitive Homo Sapiens of 70,000 years ago would have travelled extensively throughout the Arabian Savanna plains.

Weather oscillated over thousands of years. As climatic conditions started to deteriorate in the region, Homo Sapiens were forced further South to warmer climes for longer periods. Cocooned within an area that housed a dry lush Gulf was an oasis that would be home to the first Cognitive Homo Sapiens seen out of Africa who would eventually become the forefathers of the Sumerian people. This Gulf Oasis cossetted and protected these first Homo Sapiens for over 60,000 years and let them flourish and develop. During this time of habitation in the Gulf Oasis, the climate continued to oscillate. Weather conditions deteriorated, yet this Gulf Oasis seemed to be a perfect base for these new migrants.

Over many millennia, the weather became colder and wetter, whereas other Homo Sapiens who had migrated out of Africa and set up base in the Levant Region in the Northern area of the Middle East seem to have retreated back to Africa, until the weather improved. Once again leaving the Neanderthal all alone in the Levant to continue unmolested. The Gulf Oasis migrants had no intention of doing likewise they became the indigenous population of the region. The Gulf Oasis gave sufficient refuge from external surrounding climatic conditions which seemed less harsh and far more forgiving than first assumed by anthropologists. An area with an abundance of food sources, mango trees, date palms which are rich in calcium.

Many basics lay at the hands of its new thriving populace, clean drinking water, gazelles, pigs, freshwater fish, seawater fish, mussels, berries. Everything needed to support a more sedentary hunter-gatherers lifestyle. In an environment that would allow for close interaction with other clans and perfect for learning new social skills. The populace will have expanded as different hunter-gatherer groups interacted much more frequently than previously experienced due to physically living in closer proximity of each group than they had experienced on the Savanna Plains of Africa and for a shorter period on the Arabian Savanna Plains.

With time on their hands, the groups will have expanded and created the first embryonic stratified society that we all live in today. Unfortunately for the indigenous people of the Gulf Oasis, those days were numbered. 9,500 years ago, the people of the Gulf Oasis were forced for the first time to head on another untrodden path in History. With a rise in global temperatures and an end of the last ice Age (Last Glacial Maximum). Sea levels around the world started to rise to the levels we recognise today. Forcibly evicting the indigenous population of the Gulf Oasis from their lands and made to rethink their future and to find refuge elsewhere in the wider world. A world that was also changing and developing but not at the rate as seen in the Gulf Oasis.

These totally separate entities from the Gulf Oasis who had avoided any mainstream interaction with the larger external world were about to have a date with destiny a lot sooner than they envisaged. We will discuss where the indigenous population of the Gulf Oasis went and to what degree of impact these refugees had in the wider world. We will discover that some groups had an immediate impact on surrounding groups who were also starting to grow and culturally understand the changes afoot.

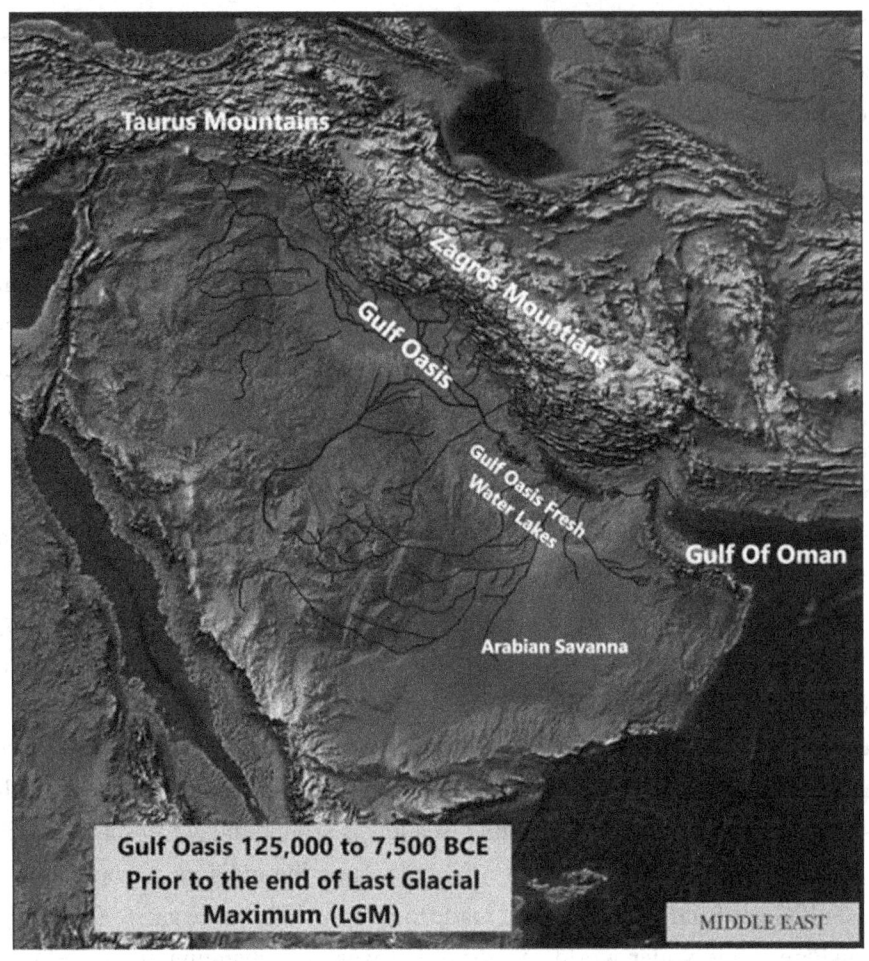

Gulf Oasis 125,000 to 7,500 BCE
Prior to the end of Last Glacial Maximum (LGM)

MIDDLE EAST

Flooding of the Gulf Oasis, the End of Last Glacial Maximum (LGM) 9,500 Years Ago, the First LGM Migration

The first critical decision by the populace of the Gulf Oasis had to be made.[iv] The sea levels of the world had been rising at an alarming rate for 4,800 years. But this sea rise hadn't affected the indigenous population. In fact, it had helped the indigenous people of the coastline as the ocean was a lot closer so they could fish the waters more efficiently. But now a decision had to be made, the land bridge between the Gulf Oasis and the Indian Subcontinent was about to be closed forever. People could actually see the marked difference in height and realised the rise in sea level wasn't stopping.

The first migration was imminent, people had to decide if they would stay in the present location or move to the Indus Valley region along the land bridge that traversed along the continental shelf of the Northern shore of the Indian Ocean before it was permanently cut off by the rising sea. The inhabitants of the coastal region of the Gulf Oasis had three options:

a) Move to higher ground, currently modern Oman.
b) Move further inland, thus encroaching on other clan's land, which may cause conflict disturbing the hunting and farming lands of their neighbours.
c) Separate from the main group of the Gulf Oasis and move to the Indus Valley Region and be permanently cut off from the rest of the family members once the land bridge had been consumed.

All three options would have been taken by various clan members, but one thing was common, they had to move, the sea level was continuing to rise.

9,000-9,200 Years Ago, the Second Last Glacial Maximum (LGM) Migration

The sea level continues its destructive encroachment into the Gulf Oasis. This becomes the main tipping point for life in the Gulf Oasis. The largest freshwater lake 11,000 Km² in size within the Gulf Oasis is now consumed with Seawater, instantly spoiling the natural supporting ecosystem. The Oasis had supported human habitation for tens of thousands of years and is known to have been extremely fertile due to its abundance of fauna and wildlife. The lake providing fresh drinking water, irrigation water for food production and a drinking hole for all mammals, this land eventually became the Persian Gulf.

The indigenous population of this area were quickly displaced with the rapidly encroaching sea waters, destroying all before it. Over 250,000 Km² of land disappeared in less than a thousand years. The spoiling of the fresh waters and the mass migration from the Gulf Oasis approximately 7,200 BC coincided with archaeological evidence unearthed of dramatic cultural changes in the northern areas of the Fertile Crescent, especially around the Near East in Jericho and the modern Turkish plains of Konya where many ancient mounds still lay with no archaeological work carried out. This may be able to provide evidence of were these displaced people of the Gulf Oasis settled or conquered similar to Catalhoyuk.

The new inhabitants in the Northern region in 7000 BC show advanced agricultural techniques and animal husbandry whilst showing levels of stratification which hasn't been seen in any previous archaeological evidence anywhere until this sudden advancement appeared overnight in the Northern region. A Tell on land is an artificially raised area of ground due to long-term habitation of a specific area, the building of one structure on top of the next for thousands of years.

In the Gulf Oasis, which was consumed by the Indian Ocean, we may be able to be identified and record similar ocean bed Tell. Possibly a good source for future subsea exploration to understand what life was like before the sea levels rose. If we have Tells on land, why shouldn't we be able to witness a similar scenario within the Gulf Oasis? If any evidence can be unearthed from the shallow depths of the Persian Gulf that correspond with land excavations in the Levant, then world history can be rewritten. Archaeologists clearly noticed a step change in social development.

These new inhabitants of Jericho showed signs of having a well-structured, stratified society. If this is the case, are we able to pinpoint these sites that maybe excavated in the near future. The indigenous people of the Gulf Oasis who were supported by the main 11,000 Km^2 freshwater lake, had very few options. Move to higher ground which will have already been taken or follow the rivers up stream and see what suitable land could be found elsewhere. During the research I believe that this second wave of migration are the lynch pin to all future events throughout the development of the Middle East, Egypt, Indus Valley and Sumeria and further natural events that took place in 6000 BC that aided the development of all future civilisations.

Between 9,000 and 8,200 Years Ago, the Third LGM Migration

The remaining people within the Gulf Oasis weren't reliant upon the Central Great Freshwater Lake that had been spoilt with the ingress of seawater. These remaining people lived further North along the Gulf Oasis soon found areas of habitation consumed by an ever-advancing saltwater ocean. World sea levels continued to rise by 2.5 centimetres (1 inch) yearly. The remaining refugees adapted to their ever-changing surroundings by moving to slightly higher ground which became a premium along the newly formed coastlines. Which continued to be pushed further back for a further 800 years until the sea levels finally levelled out in 6,200 BC. Or during the slow flooding of the land, some of the indigenous people of the Gulf Oasis simply built reed islands and floated at the edge of the freshwater and seawater margins moving very slowly further up the submerged Oasis.

The floating refugees finally came to rest in the freshwater estuaries of the Tigris, Karun, and Euphrates Rivers. These are the people who settled close to the future Sumerian cities not yet built of Uruk, Ur, Lagash, Umma, and Eridu. Being the direct descendants of the Marsh Arabs of Southern Iraq. The surrounding land was climatically inhospitable which lacked natural resources and for a time the people supported themselves with living on the reed islands and evidence found that the surrounding land was starting to be manipulated, which helped support the Marsh Arabs continued way of life in the marshes. Until 6,000 BC when the world for these people changed once again, but for the better.

8,000 Years Ago, the Final Migration

People from the Gulf Oasis had finally settled and started to thrive and prosper all along the fertile crescent and into the Plains of Konya (Turkey) for 1,000 years. The last migration from the Near East and the Konya plains acted as the catalyst for the entire region and its future development. When the Euxine had been breached via the Dardanelles from the Mediterranean in 6,000 BC. This huge flooding event created what we now know as the Black Sea. This cataclysmic event shocked everyone in the region and physically made the people in the region leave everything behind and seek a safer place to live. To the land of Sumer and also Egypt.

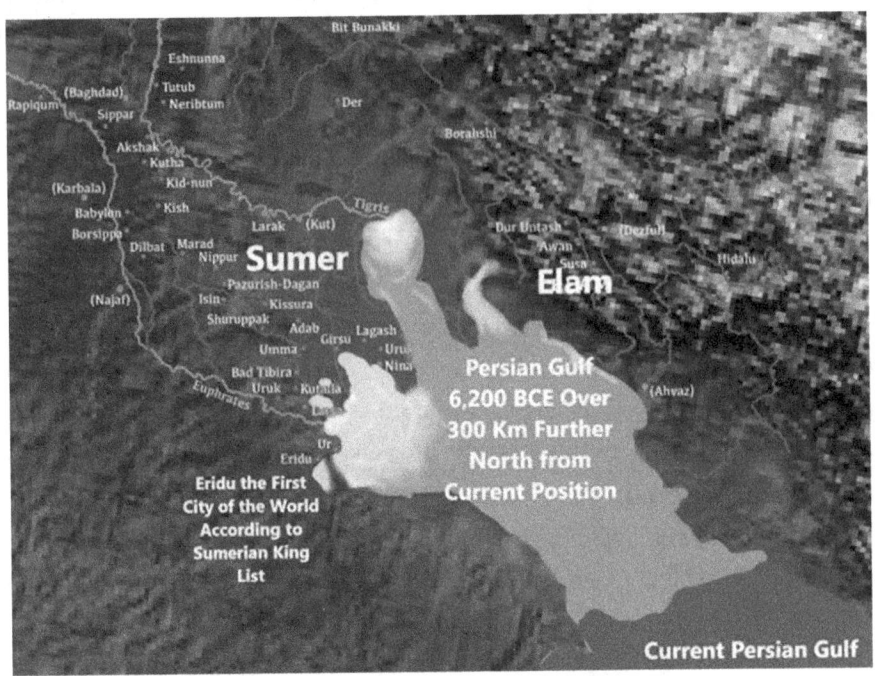

Engineering of Sumer

Historians have continually failed to answer the basic questions that need to be answered and avert their gaze to this thorny issue. The historian will discuss what they can answer without impacting their career. I am presenting the available facts and piecing together the story of the past, whilst letting the reader decide if facts reside within these pages. What surprises me more than all this, is the lack of knowledge the general public have shown to the ancient builders of Sumer and their achievements.

Throughout the book, we will look at the engineering prowess of the Sumerians and their untouchable skills of invention. These achievements of Sumer would not be surpassed for another 7,800 Years until the start of the Industrial Revolution of the 18th Century AD. I have struggled to understand why the engineering achievements of the Sumerians has been bypassed by historians and a lack of recognition awarded. My core skill is engineering and as an engineer, I feel it is only correct to raise the profile of these Sumerian achievements.

The Pyramid of Giza in Egypt is rightly lorded the world over as an engineering marvel, but physical volume is still a drop in the ocean compared to a single Sumerian canal system, of the hundreds built in Middle and Southern Mesopotamia region. Yet no laurels have been laid at the base of the people who built these phenomenal feats of engineering. A pyramid does not serve the population any purpose, it is a narcissistic extravagance, but a canal system serves all the people of the region.

If the reader can appreciate the physical size and complexity of these structures and canal systems and the volume of water that they could deliver. We could finally be on our way to appreciating the realistic levels of crop production that would be been achieved in ancient times. It is also capable of carrying out a time and motion study to appreciate how many and how long something took to build. If you can accurately predict the size of the fields and its yield, then you know the size of that workforce required to maintain it. The types of calculations are known and will also have been known during the construction phase of each canal project.

These people didn't just do the work, they invented it, and invented the tools to carry out the work. They discussed it in detail and had a plan of action, not just a plan, but a long-term strategy. *If someone's sitting in the shade today, it's because somebody planted a tree a long time ago[4]*. These people were no different from the hunter-gatherers who came out of Africa between 125,000 and 70,000 years ago and they are no different from us today. We need to remove the notion that we are more evolved, that nothing of yesteryear was better than today's achievements.

The land prospered under the Sumerians to a far greater degree than today. Evolution is over millions of years, not tens of thousands of years. We adapt and overcome quickly, but we don't evolve quickly. We pride ourselves with Newton and Einstein, the Newtons and the Einstein's will have existed in yesteryear. During and after the Sumerian reign but their names have been lost to the sands of time, just like the city states of Sumer disappeared for thousands of years. Once you get like-minded people in close company, then ideas flow and the one thing that no other animal on the planet has (that we know of)—imagination.

I believe imagination can also be used as a tool for *planning for the future*, you are setting goals that are currently unachievable, it'll take planning and new inventions to reach the objective of your imagination once writing was invented these thoughts could be wrote down and retained for further adaptation and

---

[4] *Warren Buffet; CEO of Berkshire Hathaway, one of the most successful investors in the world.*

improvement. The start of writing was used as an aid to accountancy and calculations a perfect tool for any engineer. It would have been impossible for the Engineers of Pre-Sumerian history to have survived in Southern Mesopotamia with a large populace without the aid of mathematics, which had its origins in the heavens which in turn was an aid to navigation, which in turn opened distant trade routes, simple cause and effect.

By using modern scientific methods, I hope to answer all the questions that have been asked for over a hundred years, without a conclusion: *Where did the people come from? How did they manage, not to survive, but to prosper beyond all comprehension? How did this wasteland become the epicentre of all culture and steer the world to new heights and expectations?* So, if this region has given so much to the world, why do so few people know of its place in the history books and know virtually nothing of its beginnings and its engineering exploits.

I have constantly found that Greek Classical Period educated people believe that the mythological tales written by the Greeks stemmed from their own imagination or *influenced* by the Egyptians, without ever investigating the root of these tales which lay within walking distance, albeit a long walk in Mesopotamia. Why, until nearly 400 years ago, nobody knew Sumer ever existed and a chance encounter by Pietro Della Valle in 1625 revealed it for the first time in many millennia. An area of civilisation forgotten and lost through the sands of time that vanished without a murmur.

The Lack of Building Materials

In a normal habitat throughout the world, the local materials at hand are what you build your home with. It is only very recently those notions have been forgotten. If you were in the Black Forest of Germany, you would have built your home of wood; if you had built your home in Yorkshire in England, you would have used local sandstone that seems to appear on every hillside. Therefore, the people of Southern Mesopotamia had to somewhat think outside of the box as they had very limited materials to build with.

The region has a natural abundance of reeds that form in the Deltas of the Tigris, Karun and the Euphrates. These ancient Marsh lands, with its dense thickets of reeds growing so tall you can't see over the tops. Now populated with Buffalo, wild boar, and marshland birds. The people of this region, the Marsh Arabs, have continued to build their homes from the surrounding reeds in the same stile since first arriving in the Marsh Deltas in 6,200 BC. Reed islands sit lazily on the water which haven't changed in design for many millennia.

Maybe when the Gulf Oasis had started to flood some of the people decided after a period of time to build these reedbed rafts and decided to float on the water rather than constantly moving keeping ahead of the rising, incoming waters. These reedbed rafts gently punting the 3rd set of refugees as far up the Oasis/Persian Gulf until the ice caps finally stopped after 1,000 years filling up by the world's oceans.

The final place of rest is now the present home of the Marsh Arabs still residing in the same manner as the refugees 8,200 years before. The people who decided to set-up home along the shores at the Delta of the Tigris and Euphrates Rivers, had to use some ingenuity in building homes. Reed Homes in the Marshes and as the people tentatively moved ashore, they shaped the mud that washed down the rivers and into the deltas. These mud bricks were then left in the hot sun to dry out. The other rich resource at hand was the thick black bitumen that oozed from the ground.

The local populace exploited this strange resource to the maximum. The bottom of the locally manufactured reed boats were coated with a bitumen and animal fat mixture that was durable, elastic and impermeable to water, thereby maximising the longevity of some of this most basic of building materials. Eventually, bitumen was used as the primary heat source to fire the mud bricks and to further harden them, they are so durable they still survive today. The people weather-proofed buildings and made them watertight. They used the bitumen to bond the newly fired bricks together, to build every increasing size building that could be seen many miles away.

The people brought with them the knowledge how to create pots that would eventually store wines, oil, and preserve the seed for the next set of crops. All created from the local mud and fired them to be durable using the Bitumen as the heat source for firing. Eventually people of the region used a ball of clay and wrote symbols on the clay with a reed, so they could keep a track of different things that maybe forgotten or write calculations down that could aid construction. (We will discuss the development of writing and how these basic symbols became words that once again transformed the world we now live in and aided the rise of the Dynasty of Kings.)

A Brief Overview of the Development of Human Activity

As above, building a home is an essential task. But I want to explain to the reader exactly where we have come from and to stop this notion that people of yesteryear weren't capable of achieving the same results as we do today. The ancient people of Southern Mesopotamia bettered any of today's achievements in the same region and physically changed the landscape beyond all recognition with canals and drainage systems that aided the cultivation of the land and a planting and growing frenzy that has never been surpassed.

The Sumerians seem to have been the only people who successfully tamed the lands of Southern Iraq. I want the reader to appreciate that the world looked physically different with coastlines and rivers situated in different places, that made the landscape look far more different than we see today. The buildings have virtually eroded into the background; now, Tells many metres high or large mounds of earth lay where once large gleaming cities stood and try and help the reader imagine the difference of yesteryear.

The physical topography of Southern Iraq has changed with ancient individual city states seeming to have been built nowhere near any rivers or oceans and explain the reason behind the rise and fall of these once great ancient Cities. I will try to explain what that land once looked like 7,000-8,000 years ago when the ancient people of Sumer decided to build here. But now the land has been transformed to a point when it becomes difficult if not impossible to appreciate how something else could have ever existed in such an inhospitable climate. It's hard for anybody to look beyond what they currently see and believe that this land was so rich in resources. These very same people who changed the direction of human existence and changed the way people lived forever and what we recognise today.

Changing Water Courses

We will also look at how humans have continually manipulated the earth surface for their own gain and realise over time the damage that can occur.[v] A perfect example of this is when populations started to expand in the Mountains that surround the Fertile Crescent, crop sizes started to increase, and new ways of metal working formed. The mountains originally had densely forested areas and were used as a source of heat energy for warmth and also for firing furnaces for an emerging metals industry. These mountains became more barren overtime as populations increased and the first deforestation occurred.

The rains continued to fall in the high mountains and the rich soils previously protected by the previous trees, was quickly washed away. The rich fertile soils now flowed into the tributaries and into the great rivers below. The rivers carried these soil deposits via Tigris and the Euphrates 2,000 kilometres down river to the newly formed settlements of Southern Mesopotamia close to where Shatt Al-Arab River Delta now is.

The first settlements were dependant on being close to the rivers and newly created Persian Gulf Ocean. The embryonic growth of new cities in Sumer was continually hindered by erratic and untimely deluges of the nutrient rich waters of both rivers. Flooding occurred and eventually the delta moved further South due to heavy silting. The cities becoming more distanced and isolated from rivers and further from the sea which was the trading life blood of these early city states. Basra, the second largest city of Modern Iraq sits on top of silt washed down the Tigris and Euphrates rivers. When the cities of Sumer were at their zenith, the location of Basra was actually in the middle of reed marshland.

Some of the first cities of Sumer vanished, some rebuilt and some just didn't re-emerge. Various times throughout history the waters of the major rivers changed their course and further stranded the first cities of civilisation. Without knowing the history of the region, you would ask the same questions as Pietro Della Valle 1625 *why these cities are so far away from any water source, why build them here*? When first built they happened to be in the perfect location (at the time). The Northern end of today's Persian Gulf is now 300 kilometres further south than when these first cities started to appear.

Farming

According to many archaeologists, plants, animal domestication and production of crops started in areas of the Levant and into the Taurus Mountains and other mountainous areas that help form the Fertile Crescent.[vi] Also seems to be true for the Southern region of the Fertile Crescent. Which may have its origins even further South in an area that at one stage was extremely conducive for crop production, the Gulf Oasis which is now the Persian Gulf. During the book, I would like to highlight some historical events that archaeological excavations have discovered, that point to people of the Gulf Oasis having a major role in the development of agriculture in the Northern Region.

This evidence is also supported by paleo climatology and geological records of the time. All of academia doesn't dispute the fact the first truly urban areas and political centres occur in the Southern part of the Fertile Crescent which is now modern-day Southern Iraq. It should be noted that everywhere in the Middle East had varying levels of agricultural development over a prolonged period of time. It is also well established that hunter-gatherers took up the art of agriculture. Therefore, it is correct to assume prior to permanent settlement people continuously migrated following the herds of gazelles in the region taking the ideas of new techniques of farming with them. The development of ideas is bilateral and advancements in agriculture continued to progress over time in the whole region at a steady pace.

Archaeologists do point to a physical step change in the development of agriculture and the domestication of animals in 7000 BC which will be discussed further in the book. But it was the people of Southern Mesopotamia, the Sumerians that catapulted the development in farming to previously unimaginable levels which required advanced organisational skills and a communal belief in the idea. Agriculture had been around for 4-5,000 years, which had started to support larger communities. These larger communities grew to a size that could afford some of the populace to be used for other activities that didn't include farming, such as building projects. But the expansion we talk about in Sumeria went from zero to a hundred in a millisecond.

Archaeological evidence once again points to a time of around 6000 BC when events changed the world again. I will share my hypothesis showing how these events could have turbo boosted the advancement in Sumerian agriculture. True expansion of these vital resources only seems to have come about due to the rapid expansion of a population in an area that couldn't support numerous people for a prolonged time without and the creation of advanced farming techniques and hence the creation of civilisations. This coming together of communities that worked together for common goals, these communities seem to have had a long-term strategy for survival which resulted in the creation of new and previously unknown dynamics that followed these rapidly expanding city states.

Civilisation is known as a place with longevity and growth that breeds thoughts and innovations, but this forward planning doesn't seem to have its rapidly expanding roots from just the local floating communities, floating merrily in the reed delta, but aided from a more advanced and seemingly more stratified, hungry, focused society that aided this rapid development.

The Start of the City States

The ancient Middle East is known as the *Cradle of Civilisation*[5] and for good reason. Mesopotamia, Syria and Anatolia were home to an extraordinarily rich, diverse, and successful cultures. Indeed, it was a time and place of breath-taking changes for humankind on a monumental scale: advanced boat building, beginnings of writing and law, eventually Kingship and bureaucracy, diplomacy, and literature. When civilisation was firstborn it also spawned new problems like state-sponsored warfare. Which then lead to the birth of Empires, not content with their individual area of land that produced more than was required by the local population a more hubris attitude developed.

The need for additional labour in the expanding centres brought about a more industrialised form of slavery, looking towards the *uneducated* people of the mountains. This wasn't the first cases of forced labour, but it was the first time on an industrial scale. Additional people were required to till the fields to feed an ever-increasing population of a city state. The birth of debt as the society became more stratified some become more materialistically wealthy, and some ended with far less.

The original city states of Southern Mesopotamia developed overtime, but the timeline is obscured by mineral deposits from the Tigris, Euphrates, and the Karun. These are not the first Cities of the world, Çatalhöyük predates Southern Mesopotamia by a 1,000 minimum, but Çatalhöyük cannot be called a true City State that we can see in Sumer. This was a time of incredible innovations that seemed to spring from the sands of the surrounding desert. From the invention of the wheel and the plough to early achievements in mathematics. Which aided both astronomy and large building projects. Understanding the movement of the heavens also aided navigation which became the main source of transport for commerce for Southern Mesopotamia. Which brought with it new ideas from faraway lands such as forging and smelting. Techniques that where quickly learnt and new avenues of commerce created.

---

[5]*Charles Rollin's first coined the phrase in (1734 AD) "Egypt that first as the cradle of the Holy Nation."*

As we explore this era, we will overturn many preconceived ideas about the people of this region the popular image of the ancient world as a primitive, violent place. We discover that women had many rights and freedoms: they could own property, run businesses, and represent themselves in court. Diplomats travelled between these immerging new capital cities of major powers ensuring peace and friendship between the kings. Scribes and scholars studied the stars and could predict eclipses and the movements of the planets.

A Word to the Learned:
The Imperfect Historical Record

Before we start our adventure into the past, we must realise a few things. Some primary sources are considered more reliable or trustworthy than others. Hardly any historical evidence can be seen as fully objective since it is always a product of particular individuals, times, and dominant ideas. I am writing this book in full knowledge of this historical path and use the data that is supplied by more science-based methods and not the bias of modern people, and if historical material supports this, then the belief in the evidence would be strengthened.

Historical Bias

The Mediterranean research takes up 80% of all historical and archaeological work. Trying to understand the cultures of Egypt, Greece, Rome, and the movement of people out of Africa through the Levant Valley. It would seem a very Westernised approach that has skewed peoples understanding of how everything started. The majority of the modern-day population believes Egypt as the founder with Greece a very close second and Rome growing from the shadow of Greece (Obviously this opinion differs in China, but we should also be reminded that China has never expanded its interests outside of China until the last few decades, so hasn't impacted Western ideology).

The biases have been part of historical investigation since the ancient beginnings[6] of the discipline. While more recent scholarly practices attempt to remove earlier biases from history, no piece of historical scholarship can be fully free of biases. Two of these former empires have been known about well before

---

[6] *Herodotus: 484-425 BC Wrote the first historical book concerning the Persian Wars with Greece.*

the renaissance in Europe. Nobody in the West had even known of the existence of Southern Mesopotamian high culture until less than 200 years ago. Since that time a constant resistance to change a way of thinking has persisted in the academic world.

Bias in Historical Writing

I would describe bias as *an inclination or outlook to present or hold a partial perspective, often accompanied by a refusal to consider the possible merits of alternative points of view*. I also subscribe to these views at times when I describe the Persian Gulf rather than Arabian Gulf which is the more romantic Westernised description. But we are at a unique point in time when social media is now the driving force and nobody knows where we are heading, so will bias change more readily in the near future? Regardless of whether bias is conscious or learned. History provides an excellent example of how biases change, evolve, but rarely disappear.

History as a modern academic discipline based on empirical methods (in this case, studying primary sources in order to reconstruct the past based on available evidence) rose to prominence during the Age of Enlightenment. Voltaire[7], a French author and thinker, is credited to have developed a fresh outlook on history that shook the foundations of the Catholic strong hold on historical matters. Broke from the tradition of narrating diplomatic and military events and emphasised customs, social history (the history of ordinary people) and achievements in the arts and sciences. His *Essay on Customs* traced the progress of world civilisation in a universal context, thereby rejecting both nationalism and the traditional Christian frame of reference.

Voltaire was also the first scholar to make a serious attempt to write the history of the world, eliminating theological frameworks and emphasising economics, culture, and political history. He was the first to emphasise the debt of medieval culture to Middle Eastern civilisation. Although he repeatedly warned against political bias on the part of the historian, he did not miss many opportunities to expose the intolerance and frauds of the Catholic Church over the ages, a topic that was Voltaire's life-long intellectual interest.

---

[7] *Francois-Marie Arouet, known by his nom de plume, Voltaire the French Enlightenment writer and historian.*

The mountain gets steeper and the challenge harder when trying to replace national, or even nationalist, perspectives with a more inclusive transnational or global view of human history still very present in college-level history curricula. In the United States after World War I, a strong movement emerged at the university level to teach courses in Western Civilisation with the aim to give students a common heritage with Europe.

After 1980, attention increasingly moved toward teaching world history or requiring students to take courses in non-western cultures. Yet, world history courses still struggle to move beyond the Eurocentric perspective, focusing heavily on the history of Europe and the Mediterranean regions that have the common links to all Westerners, so trying to raise the standard for the Middle East, becomes daunting, but the Middle East isn't going anywhere soon.

Preservation of Middle Eastern Culture

The greatest wealth of information concerning the ancient cultures of the Middle East are preserved in Western cities of the world: the British Museum in London; the Le Musee Du Louvre in Paris; the Berlin Museum, Germany; Ashmolean Museum, Oxford, UK; the Smithsonian Institute, Washington; the Metropolitan Museum, New York; University of Chicago; University of Pennsylvania. These are only but a few of the world's museums. The physical sites are in the Middle East, but the best artifacts are now in the West.

At the time these artifacts were taken, they were not being rescued, simply removed for the enhancement of Western Cultures. But during modern conflicts of recent years even I believe it has been a saving grace. to be reminded of the looting of Bagdad's museum when Saddam Hussein was defeated, or the artifacts of Afghanistan destroyed by the Taliban. So, the first world museums have saved a lot of humanity's history, whilst the majority still lays undiscovered.

Our best way for making this area come back to life would be to rebuild using the same methods which isn't really an option as the cost would be astronomical. Or we could use the cheaper alternative by using the techniques and tools we have at our disposal today by using Virtual Reality or 3D Modelling at the original sites when you can bring the original buildings and streets back to life in the natural surroundings. Make the museums of the world that house these precious artifacts to make copies in the same materials using graphic to render the scanned object and make the item *as new* and send back to its original place of origin. This can then give these war-torn countries an opportunity for change, an exit strategy from this perpetual loop of fear and conflict. Therefore, helping the places of antiquity have a chance for the next generation of future historians to enjoy and to be able to bridge the disparity that exists between Western and Eastern cultures[8].

---

[8] A *recent article by Neil Brodie from my Institute of Archaeology in Oxford. https://traffickingculture.org/app/uploads/2020/10/Brodie-2020-Restorative-justice.pdf His theme is the collection of antiquities, specifically the cuneiform tablets, etc. from dubious sources.*

Chapter 1
The Search for Accurate Information

Searching for Sumerian Origins

There is a need to use as many modern techniques as possible to either confirm or deny the movement of people out of Africa between 125,000-30,000 years ago and into the Gulf Oasis via the migration corridor that opened up through the Arabian Peninsula. This was only possible when the Indian Monsoons moved further North due to climatic difference compared to today's weather systems. This weather difference supported vast changes to the Peninsula which allowed new vegetation growth which could support wildlife.

This gives an opportunity for Cognitive Homo Sapiens to breakout from East Africa and into the surrounding lands and the wider world, similar to their Homo ancestors. Eventually, the safe haven of the Gulf Oasis was finally lost to the rising seawaters of the Indian Ocean at the end of the Last Glacial Maximum which ended in 6,200 BC. This body of seawater is now better known as the Modern Persian Gulf that had supported Modern Homo Sapiens for over 118,000 years. The techniques used will either verify or refute that these people really are the Pre-Sumerians, the true indigenous people of the Middle East.

Cognitive Homo Sapiens do not have a herd mentality. They rely on their individual inherent skills to make informed decisions, that will best protect the clan. When Cognitive Homo Sapiens moved out of Africa they dispersed in all directions where possible. This section of the book is dedicated to describing the findings by using various techniques that help build up the story from East Africa to Sumerian rule. At the start of the book, I hadn't even contemplated some of the events which became evident whilst carrying out my research.

The first part of the book will show the reasoning and disprove the old ingrained belief that every Cognitive Homo Sapiens moved through the Levant Valley into the rest of the world and prove this hasn't just been a recent movement, but the people of the Gulf Region are the only true indigenous people 125,000-30,000 years in the making of the Middle East. It is common knowledge that Cognitive Homo Sapiens settling in the Levant, sufficient resources for archaeological digs have proven this. Could I say that I think the Levant is the epicentre of Cognitive Homo Sapiens growth and our climb to civilisation, absolutely not! There is a much more interesting story to tell.

Root Cause Analysis

Part of the reason for writing this book is to discover the root, or *The Start* of the origins of civilisation. I have decided to adopt and stylise the technique used in Engineering as my point of initiation. Root Cause Analysis RCA is carried out to investigate and discover the true source of a problem either a process, material, electrical, mechanical or instrumentation failure or a combination of some, or a failure of all. A chain of events like a *domino effect* or *chain reaction*; something is the initiation and whilst others enable propagation that has a resultant definitive outcome.

I want to take the essence of this system of research and with my background in the area of engineering rather than history, archaeology, linguistics or computational studies. Using this stylised version will be beneficial in being able to investigate what impact one cause of events has on the other and to come to a logical and concise conclusion and to present the facts as seen. I am not a conspiracy theorist and certainly don't adapt anything to fit. Secondly and fortuitously, I have not been influenced by the bias that can seep into historical Westernised learning that can skewer the merits of alternative points of view, I'm coming with a clean slate, and no axe to grind. Thirdly, I'm looking at everything with fresh eyes and my own personal research.

I do have the added benefit of working in many of the countries I am writing about and extremely keen to understand the deep history of the area I am working in. I understood the common regional history, but that history is relatively recent. Until I really started my research, I knew it had a very rich past, as do most of the readers. I understood sufficiently about the Persians and the Babylonians and what the Greeks had said. But once I really started to delve further back in time, I was amazed at my lack of understanding and knowledge and clarity concerning Southern Mesopotamia and its anchor point in World History.

I also found it hard to grasp the magnitude of Sumerian achievements which isn't sufficiently raised in textbooks. It's not just from Westerner's perspective but the people of the Fertile Crescent and Gulf Region who also have a lack of appreciation about Sumerian achievements. We know so much because of the writing left on clay tablet by the Sumerians and Akkadians. The amount of current archaeological digs underway in the Region is embarrassingly low compared to the more affluent Western Nations who trod a well-worn path through the Mediterranean Region.

Apathy in discovering the tangible past seems to have gripped the Middle East, it seems like the clay tablets (in Western cellars) seem to quench the appetite for some unfathomable reason. An added bonus to my learning is being able to live and meet the local people of the Arab speaking world and understanding the various facets each set of people have even though they may share the same beliefs and share the same language as their neighbouring regions but vastly different in other ways. Some areas are more agricultural, some areas pure oil production with some into medical research excellence.

When I meet the local people, you can recognise similar traits commonly shared, and you quickly learn what might inadvertently offend your hosts. Once you have established the basics you look at the differences between you and the local people. If you are lucky you can also observe behavioural patterns and witness how communities work and interact with each other especially within larger groups. I can't help but wonder why the differences seem so ingrained even though the world seems a much smaller place today.

We now share so many similarities via visual communication that you would believe that the regional divide would have melted away, but not so. Tradition is tradition and we all seem to be very proud of our own individual heritage without really understanding or knowing the majority of it; therefore, a cultural identity is buried deep within everyone which stems from our ancient past.

Something Never Comes from Nothing and Changing People's Perceptions

Something never comes from nothing. It's a basic of all science that whatever there is, it must have had some kind of an absolute beginning. Also included in the equation is by the[vii] French philosopher René Descartes[9]: *cogito ergo sum*, translated into English—*I think, therefore I am*. Cogito is a value only to show that humans can never be certain of anything that they believe that they know.

---

[9] *Born 1596, Rene Descartes: French philosopher, mathematician and scientist.*

This is important because it is Descartes' attempt to put an endpoint to scepticism by finding something that must be true. Sometimes when something is in plain sight, it isn't always seen. *You can't see the forest because the tree is in the way.* In the first part of this book, we will look at the movement out of East Africa and the settlement within the Gulf Oasis which is now the modern-day Persian Gulf.

I will also describe the geological evidence taken from the Persian Gulf sediment layers that have been analysed and what the paleo-climatic conditions appertaining to the Gulf Oasis. We need to understand the effects on the indigenous populace during the seawater encroachment on the lands within the Gulf Oasis and the hard choices made by the clan members once critical times approached during the various phases of flooding.

There is no right or wrong, no binary decisions made so a multifaceted approach to resolving matters needs to be taken. If we are discussing one person and tracking an individual's movement then that becomes relatively easy in comparison to thousands of people in multiple areas over thousands of years. If you can appreciate the *domino effect,* then it is easier to understand a reason for a known course of events. There is a reason for everything, and everything has a reason; the reason why Cognitive Homo Sapiens left Africa, the reason a Cognitive Homo Sapiens is writing this book and not Helen Neanderthal.

Why some people speak different from the rest, a reason for the sea levels increasing, the reason certain cultures disappear, the reason agriculture becomes more sustainable, these are domino effect questions. A course of events that have an impact on the final result. The hardest question to ask is why and that's when the Historian takes over, an archaeologist and a scientist can discover evidence of an isolated event. The scientist can give you a probability of why something happened, the archaeological the hypothesis. Not until the written word was first written could we start to corroborate the findings on the ground. This is when a historian looks at the historical fact-based evidence and tells the story, because they may understand other underlying reasons for a decision, they may have a broader knowledge of the subject matter.

The problems arise when there's no written records and then everything becomes circumstantial. That's when pre-history starts relying on the *story of best fit...but with lots of missing pieces, a guesstimation.* I want to rely on the *story of best fit because of the scientific arrows point in a given direction.*[10]

---

[10] *Historical scientists use a method called multiple competing hypothesis in which they seek to infer the best causal explanation of the evidence in question. This requires a*

We live in an age of technology that is allowing people for the first time to understand what has gone on in the past. We use DNA to study *cold cases* to point to the culprit. We take ice samples and count the pollen held within to understand what was happening at a certain time in history. Computer simulations can show what the stars looked like on a certain day 10,000 years ago and where the Earth was in relationship to the sun, to determine what the temperature was. We didn't have these techniques 30 years ago.

Understanding this information and using technology will help determine the origins of the Ancient Sumerians and in understanding how the first custodians of civilisation came to be so advanced, and so quickly. Who the people where and why did they choose such a harsh unforgiving climate to conduct a social experiment that was fraught with failure at every level? This was a climatically severe environment where mistakes couldn't be made.

I have worked in this exact area and fully appreciate; you can't survive if you make a mistake. *Right First Time* must have been the mantra of the day. Failure could easily have meant an entire group of people dispersing into the mountain region already occupied by other clans and disappearing from pre-history forever. We should also remind ourselves of the adage, *Necessity (Desperation) is the Mother of all inventions*.

Still, the majority of historians will find the path of least resistance and follow this well-worn path. What I mean by this statement is, the majority of historians seem to prefer to reiterate and add a slight twist to an old concept, disguised as *new*. Some historians who painstakingly receive very little credit for discoveries that the majority don't want to entertain until the amount of evidence completely outweighs the previous theory. But the collection of information takes time and sometimes critical information is lost when different teams from different countries are involved that may not know of each other's activities and areas of research.

The time when discoveries are openly accepted is when the new discoveries may add to previous wholly accepted concepts. Only if these new discoveries *fit* within or enhance previous theories bolstering a previous historians own modus operandi. I'm waiting to see a new breed of historian instead of the khakis, wide rim big hat, gilet wearing stereo type. Using technology and chasing down the

---

search for all possible causes, then eliminating them until you are left with the best explanation. Charles Lyell 1797-1875 in explaining Principles of Geology phenomena.

sticky awkward problems using science, getting the younger people involved, the ones with a science degree!

It is estimated that only 10% of historical sites have ever been discovered and of those 10% only 10% have been excavated. So only 1% of the Worlds discoveries have so far been discovered. Historians are basing knowledge of a region on 1%, which seems to be ripe for clarity and possible redirection. Leaving the rest untapped and waiting for the next Howard Carter and Lord Carnarvon. What a great time to live in and see if a new scientific based Rosetta Stone[11] can be discovered or physical proof that can caste the gaze of future historians firmly and emphatically in another direction.

To be able, through scientific means, to alter the direction that has been viewed and accepted for over a century can invigorate modern region's economy where these civilisations previously existed. The Sumerian problem, of where do the Sumerian originate from, has for too long been left to best guess and best fit. Now we do know, and we know where the evidence is, and we have the technology to retrieve it. It couldn't be a better time to be involved in history.

Eight Techniques

By using the eight main techniques listed below, we can cross reference one set of material data to the next. We may be able to further solidify or deny if the current hypothesis is a viable option. During my research the circumstantial evidence started to become more conclusive as more data was discovered, but other avenues to the story became apparent. We can start to clearly see a picture materialise that shows how all eight areas of research techniques can merge and substantiate each other's different fields of study. The merging of all data into one main hypothesis.

1. Paleo Climatology and Post Glacial Sea Level Rise

Such a synoptic endeavour is not an easy task, as the data can mirror various phenomena. Paleoclimatology including evidence from the Alluvial Fan records from Southeast Arabia indicates that tropical and subtropical deserts changes in natural environments associated with global climatic oscillations. The research

---

[11] *Rosetta Stone discovered by Pierre-Francois Bouchard in 1799 during Napoleonic Campaign in Egypt.*

indicates nothing about whether humans were really present in such environments but gives a strong indication to Cognitive Homo Sapiens movement and also if the environmental conditions could support life in migration corridor.[viii]

Understanding that the world moves in an elliptical path around the sun and the world axis oscillating whilst over time turning, provides the planet with a multitude of variations over time. With the aid of better computational methods, scientists have a more accurate understanding of climatology that is now substantiated with factual evidence from the planet. The current Persian Gulf is only 40 metres deep and the sea levels at times during Last Glacial Maximum (LMG) were 120 metres lower than current levels we see today, so the area of sustainable freshwater and sufficient livestock that could support human permanent inhabitancy would have been the Gulf Oasis, sustaining life for long periods of time.

2. Migration Patterns

To better infer and perhaps form a more reliable image of Arabian prehistory, Migration Patterns must be taken into consideration as this is the steppingstone between Archaeogenetic and language. Nine probable migration routes (theories) of Cognitive Homo Sapiens must be considered to create the population mix that became the inhabitants of Ancient Sumeria.

a) Migration out of Africa circa 125,000 years ago and into the Gulf Oasis region and beyond, including the hypothesis that people returned back to Africa circa 42,000 years ago then moved back out again. A hypothesis that the Tamil dialect is seen in Sumerian language.

- May have originated in the Gulf Oasis and then moved into South Asia.
- Or brought from South Asia into Gulf Oasis during trade.
- Or brought directly to Sumeria via trade.

b) Migration of Homo Sapiens 125,000 and Cognitive Homo Sapiens into the Levant Region from Africa circa 70,000 years ago.

c) Migration of Homo Sapiens from Northern Mesopotamia into Gulf Oasis circa 60-40,000 years ago. Using both DNA and Paleoclimatic data as a cross reference. This would also include the first migration from Gulf Oasis into the Indian Subcontinent during the same time period.
d) 1st Migration Last Glacial Maximum (LGM). Indian Ocean encroached the Gulf Oasis, cutting off Indian Ocean land bridge 7500 BC.
e) 2nd Migration Last Glacial Maximum (LGM) of indigenous Gulf Oasis into Northern Mesopotamia 7000 BC.
f) 3rd Migration Last Glacial Maximum (LGM) of indigenous Gulf Oasis to Delta of Tigris and Euphrates Rivers 6500 BC.
g) Migration of people from Northern Fertile Crescent and moving through Mesopotamia to the South. Approximately 6000 BC.
h) Migration of people from Northern Fertile Crescent and moving to Egypt. Approximately 6000 BC.
i) Migration of people via Afghanistan and the Caucasus, Approximately 6500 BC.

3. Archaeogenetic Data

This is the youngest discipline in prehistoric research and reveals demographic expansions of past populations by the study of genetic variability in contemporary populations. Cross referencing the archaeogenetic DNA data with the proposed migration routes can confirm or discard a migration theory. If we also cross reference language similarities. A clearer understanding starts to materialise solidifying opinions. Whilst evaluating the DNA results the historical hypothesis has been revised due to cross referencing dates of archaeological events throughout the Fertile Crescent.

4. Language

A computational science data-mining method to analyse the Sumerian and Elam vocabulary.[ix]

5. Biological

Observation: Understanding the deep and its data.

6. Archaeology

Can unambiguously provide direct proof of a human presence, but problems arise when nothing has been discovered or unable to be retrieved. Possible Archaeology sites being under the present Persian Gulf or under vast alluvium layers built-up over thousands of years of yearly flooding of the mouth of both the Tigris, Euphrates and Karun rivers: is it proof of an absence, or the absence of a proof? This is an especially important issue when considering the now submerged Gulf Oasis.

The hard part for most people is when you can't see something. The Persian Gulf is vast expanse of water and it is sometimes hard for people to visualise that this area was once land. When looking at water at sea level, it is also hard to understand the depth and as previously stated, is only 40 metres deep. Today we talk about the sea level rising 0.5 metre and the damage it would cause. So, to understand that the sea level increased 120 metres and would have covered the Statue of Liberty with a further 27 metres above it puts a better perspective on the matter. When you look at the Persian Gulf and vastness, it's a natural assumption to believe *it's always been there*, which it hasn't.

a) Geology can help determine the landscape that previously existed, which can aid and direct archaeologists in their search of human existence and expand our knowledge of the past.
b) The start of Neolithic pottery.
c) Agriculture and its ancient sources and connections to other areas of the world.

7. Social Evolution

This has to be taken into account; social evolution is the glue that ties the paleo climatology, migration patterns, agriculture, understanding the origins of language and myths. Determining if the inhabitants of the Gulf Oasis were surviving or developing. Society takes time to adapt, and archaeologists look through the strata to see how areas developed over time. But the problem occurs when something appears without any previous background; that's when people have to start assuming and hypothesising.

8. Historical Myths, Legends and Religious Material Together

Time and again myths, legends and religious material seem to be discounted by many historians and archaeologists for *good reasons*, until the time that certain *parts* of stories are found to be true via evidence found in writing previously unknown or via archaeological excavations. The problem with using myths, legends, and religious material is that they predominantly pre-date the written language and have been passed down orally or the original writer may have simply fabricated or elongated the truth, knowing nobody in his/her lifetime will discover the truth. My way of thinking is that oral history (story telling) can sometimes be more accurate than first believed; I always believe that strands of truth always lay in an ancient story; it's the ability to disseminate the truth from the fiction.

Two main sources of oral tradition come to mind, *The Iliad*, Homer's epic, only written 350-400 years after the event, and the Quran. The Quran is the best example of this oral tradition, even though it is also written down. Muslims are taught chapter and verse and people of all walks of life continue to recite the Quran daily and have done so for multiple generations for almost 1,400 years. Unfortunately, some people want a certain outcome from these stories and identify small aspects that have been embellished by the storyteller and manipulate these aspects for their own gain. This then becomes a *self-fulfilling prophecy* without using due diligence in their research.

The more information that can be sourced from the eight main specialist areas listed above can either confirm or deny the hypothesis proposed for the origins of Pre-Sumeria and the true start of civilisation as we all know it. In engineering, the basic notion is *if it looks good, it usually is good*, and the same exists with any research.

Reason Behind the Madness

The reason for choosing so many different methods of research to prove a point of reasoning is a basic from my days in the military. I try to cross reference everything I do; therefore, I have basically used the ideas of Map and Compass. If you don't know where you are, you take a bearing with your compass to a fixed object in visible view of yourself that is highlighted on a map; you then take the back bearing (180⁰ opposite direction). That then gives you the true line you are on, on the map.

But at this point in time, you don't know where on the line you are. Therefore, you need to be able to intersect this line with another line that will give you a fixed point (with a margin of error). You take compass readings on several more objects in line of sight, take the back bearing and the intersection will highlight where you are, the more intersections the more accurate you become and you have less margins of error and a definite fixed point is then known, it's the same as satellite navigation systems that have got better over time (more satellites therefore more accurate measurements up to 20 satellites at any one time gives you the accuracy you all use today). Therefore, eight points of reference for the origins of the Pre-Sumerians in this section of the book would seem an adequate number to use.

Understanding the Dates and Terminology of Early History

I, like everyone else, lose track when reading information when my understanding of where places previously existed in ancient times and my perceived understanding of certain times in history that garnish my own confusion. As we set off, we need to understand some of the terminology used as this will be discussed in different parts of the book.

The Holocene is the current geological epoch. It began approximately 9,700 BC years before present, after the last glacial period, which concluded with the Holocene glacial retreat. The Holocene and the preceding Pleistocene together form the Quaternary period. The Holocene has been identified with the current warm period, known by scientists as MIS 1 Marine Isotope Stages.[x] It is considered by some to be an interglacial period within the Pleistocene Epoch, called the Flandrian Interglacial.

The Holocene corresponds with the rapid increase, growth and impacts of the human species worldwide, including all of its written history, technological revolutions, development of major civilisations, and overall significant transition towards urban living in the present which also corresponds with the movement of people en masse from low lying regions of the world during the last glacial thaw eventually raising sea levels 120 metres to its present-day levels.

Human impacts on modern-era Earth and its ecosystems may be considered of global significance for future evolution of living species, we will discuss the evolution of modern man and its impact when first farming and communal living was introduced in the mountainous regions of Anatolia and Syria and the evidence of human impacts far from the original sources.

- Quaternary Period: Covers both the Pleistocene and the Holocene period; 2,580,000 years ago, to present.

    o Pleistocene: is the geological epoch lasted from 2,580,000 years ago to 11,700 years ago. This is the period of time used by archaeologists and Paleo Climatologists. It's the period of time that spans the Earth's last repeated glaciation, the end of Pleistocene concluding with the last glacial period. The Earth has had numerous ice Ages and Pleistocene being the last.
    o Holocene: In July 2018, the International Union of Geological Sciences split the Holocene epoch into three distinct subsections:

- Greenlandian (Early Holocene): 11,700 years ago, to 8,326 years ago. The time when the Last Glacial Maxima (LMG) stopped, and temperatures settled. To, when the ice caps had finally stopped draining into the oceans and sea levels had finally normalised.
- Northgrippian (Mid Holocene) 8,326 years ago, to 4,200 years ago. The normalised sea levels that we would recognise today. To, the 4.2K Climatic Event, a drought of 150-200 years, that also aided the downfall of the Akkad Empire and also brought the death knell to Sumeria, the natural stopping point of this book.
- Meghalayan (Late Holocene) 4,200 years ago, to the present. 4.2K Climatic Event. Let's see if human civilisation brings about the end to Late Holocene, we are due an end to this period.

1. Paleo Climatology and Post Glacial Sea Level Rise

Understanding the Earth's Cycle and Effect on Weather

At the beginning of this book, we described the migration of Cognitive Homo Sapiens out of East Africa around 125-30,000 years ago and the weather conditions experienced. The more scientific name for this phenomenon is called the Milankovitch Cycles, Milutin Milankovic 1879-1958,[xi] it explains the earth's climate changes over hundreds of thousands of years. It is based on two key ideas. First the earth's climate is strongly affected by how much sunlight the Northern latitudes receive during the summer. Second, this amount of sunlight varies based on changes in Earth's orbit and rotation. The Northern latitude retains the ice.

When sunlight hits the ground, most of the energy is absorbed into the Earth as heat. But if the ground is covered in ice then most of the light is reflected away due to ice being white. This creates a positive feedback loop which exacerbates the sequence, making the earth colder which forms more ice, therefore reflecting more sunlight. Both Northern and Southern Hemispheres contain Ice, but ice tends to form on land due to having a lower heat capacity than water.

The Northern Hemisphere simply has more land mass than the South, so the most critical area for ice caps are in the North which dictates the Earth's climate. During winter, ice caps grow in both the North and South, but Southern ice caps don't grow nearly as much as in the North. During the winter, the land above the Arctic Circle is covered in darkness for 24 hours a day this allows ice to form in this extra cold period of time. This is true no matter what's going on with Earth's orbit. The key variable is how much ice melts during the summer. This is dependent upon how much sunlight is received during the summer.

Milankovic proved that over hundreds of thousands of years, the amount of Summer sunlight can shift +/- 15%, which can result in an Ice Age or end an Ice

Age. The distance from the earth to the Sun is changing. Secondly, the Earth's tilt is changing. The Earth's axis is currently tilted at 23.5 degrees but in a state of constant change. Other objects influence the earth gravitational tilt, the Moon aids this stabilisation. Every 41,000 years is one complete cycle. When the Earth is more tilted there's more direct sunlight during the Summer, more sunlight equates to fast ice melt during the Summer. Less ice equals more ground penetrating heat into the Earth and a warmer climate.

The second effect is the distance the Earth is from the Sun. As we are all aware the Earth's orbit is an ellipse. 04th July the Earth is the farthest away from the Sun and 3rd January the closest to the Sun. Now the biggest event that happens during this orbit is that both Jupiter and Saturn's magnetic effect the Earth's orbit slightly, becoming more oval or rounder.[12] This happens over 100,000 years, these subtle changes have massive consequences for the Earth's climate. As a whole the earth receives 6% more sunlight in January than in July.

The seasons change because the North Pole sometimes tilts towards the Sun and sometime away. The change in the distance from the sun, this works against the changes in the seasons. This moderates the seasons in the North since the earth is farthest away in July. But this was not always true. The Earth's axis is a moving circle similar to a spinning top. This is known as precession. What this means is that 13,000 years ago, the tilted earth was reversed.

When the Earth was closest to the sun, it was summer in the North. The distance change didn't oppose the seasons, it exacerbated the seasons. It amplified seasons making them more extreme. Warmer summer means more melting and less reflection and more warming of the Earth. The amount of summer sunlight is affected by 3 long-term cycles, 1st changes the tilt, 2nd makes our orbit more oval or circular around the Sun and the 3rd changes the distance to Sun matches the changing of the seasons. The combination of all three powerfully impacts our climate.

Regional Weather Effects

The Milankovitch Cycles and computer modelling showed large increases in rainfall and vegetation at 125,000, at 105,000, and at 83,000 years ago, with corresponding decreases at 115,000, at 95,000 and at 73,000 years ago. This is when summer monsoons decreased in magnitude and stayed further South.

---

[12] *Jupiter's magnetic field is 20,000 times stronger than Earth's.*

Between roughly 70,000 and 15,000 years ago, this early date of 70,000 years would be when migration of Cognitive Homo Sapiens out of East Africa took place and later became the indigenous inhabitants of the Gulf Oasis during time of regional hyper-aridity.

The Earth was in a glacial period and the model showed that the presence of larger Northern ice sheets and reduced greenhouse gases increased winter Mediterranean storms but limited the Southern retreat of the summer monsoon. The reduced greenhouse gases also caused cooling near the equator, leading to a drier climate their and reduced forest cover.

Sheep grazing, 2021 in Kuwait, highlighting the last remnants of the grassland's DNA from a bygone era; in the summer, the entire area returns to desert with no signs of the land being fertile.

These changing regional patterns of climate and vegetation would have created resource gradients for humans living in Africa. Driving migration and creating a corridor outward to areas with more water and plant life as suggested above. Cognitive Homo Sapiens simply followed the heard and walked straight out of Africa and once any hyper-aridity was felt in the Arabian Savanna that would adversely affect the Savanna wildlife and consequently the hunter-gatherer clan.

Rather than migrating back into Africa, the Gulf Oasis became the sanctum, therefore making these the first indigenous people of Southern Arabian. Unlike the migrating hunter-gatherers who took up residence in the Levant region, moved into North African Sarah Region and also back into East Africa. A study has been made by researchers, including John Kutzbach[xii] of UW-Madison and colleagues Ian Orland and Feng He, along with researchers at Peking University and the University of Arizona, used the Community Climate System Model V3 from the National Centre for Atmospheric Research.

The group ran three types of simulations:

- Simulations that accounted for orbital changes alone.
- Combined orbital and greenhouse gas changes.
- Combined those influences plus the influence of ice sheets.

It was Kutzbach who, in the 1970s and 1980s, confirmed that changes in Earth's orbit can drive the strength of summer monsoons around the globe by influencing how much sunlight. Therefore, how much warming reaches a given part of the planet. Forty years ago, there was evidence for periodic strong monsoons in Africa, but no one knew why, Kutzbach says. The orbital changes on Earth could lead to warmer summers and thus, stronger monsoons. With periods of *greening* in the Arabian Peninsula, *The Saudi Savanna*, which helps explain early human migration into the typically arid Middle East, was made possible.

A Refuge During Hyper-Aridity of Surrounding Arabian Peninsula

Recently discovered archaeological sites in Yemen and Oman have yielded a stone tool style that is distinct from the East African tradition. That raises the possibility that humans were established on the Southern part of the Arabian Peninsula beginning as far back as 100,000 years ago or more, Dr Jeffery Rose an archaeologist and researcher with the University of Birmingham in the U.K says. That is far earlier than the estimates generated by several recent migration models, which place the first successful migration into Arabia between 50,000 and 70,000 years ago. This *Gulf Oasis* would have been available to these early migrants and would have provided.

A sanctuary throughout the ice Ages when much of the region was rendered uninhabitable due to hyper-aridity (having little or no rain, dry parched with heat), Rose said. *The presence of human groups in the oasis fundamentally alters our understanding of human emergence and cultural evolution in the ancient Near East*. It also hints that vital piece of the human evolutionary puzzle may be hidden in the depths at the bottom of the now *Persian Gulf*.

The present Persian Gulf would have been above sea water for approximately 125,000 years ago. And it would have been an ideal refuge from the harsh surrounding, with fresh water supplied by the Tigris, Euphrates, Karun, and Wadi Baton Rivers, as well as subterranean aquifers (Underground Springs) flowing beneath the Arabian subcontinent. Dr Jeffery Rose said[xiii]:

When conditions were at their driest in the surrounding hinterlands, the Oasis would have been at its largest in terms of exposed land area. At its peak, the exposed basin would have been about the size of Great Britain.

Rose's hypothesis introduces a *new and substantial cast of characters* to the human history of the Arabian Peninsula and suggests that humans may have established permanent settlements in the region thousands of years before current migration models suppose. This hypothesis would be the simple link to what is described at the beginning of the book: *Something never comes from nothing.* My quest for facts then started. One very crucial point not taken up by Rose are the two large freshwater lakes within the Gulf Oasis, with large reed beds skirting its banks and thick alluvium plains with forests and lush vegetation which became the key to living within this refugium for both Homo Sapiens and wildlife.

The role of the Gulf Oasis, which, before being submerged beneath the waters of the Indian Ocean for prolonged periods of time had water abundance which was inverse to the amount of annual precipitation falling across the interior. Reduced sea levels periodically exposed large portions of the Persian Gulf, equal at times to the size of Great Britain. Therefore, when the hinterlands were desiccated, populations could have contracted into the Gulf Oasis to exploit its freshwater springs and rivers. This dynamic relationship between environmental amelioration/desiccation and marine transgression/regression is thought to have driven demographic exchange into and out of this area.

One specific time would be 60,000-40,000 years ago when the land bridge that connected the Gulf Oasis to the Indian Subcontinent was exposed due to reduced sea levels. This aided further migration from the Gulf Oasis to South

Asia and beyond into the rest of the Southern Hemisphere. A once fertile landmass now submerged beneath the Persian Gulf due to the end of the Last Glacial Maximum (LGM) this *Gulf Oasis* may have been host to humans for over 118,000 years before finally being swallowed up by the Indian Ocean around 8,500 years ago.

Please note that migration is symbiotic with humans; humans flowed in and out of the Gulf Oasis mixing, learning, and evolving. Migration via the land bridge has been given an arbitrary figure of 60,000-40,000 years yet Cognitive Homo Sapiens will have moved away from the Gulf much earlier due multiple social reasons and a very human trait—*curiosity*. Always wondering *if the grass is greener on the other side*.

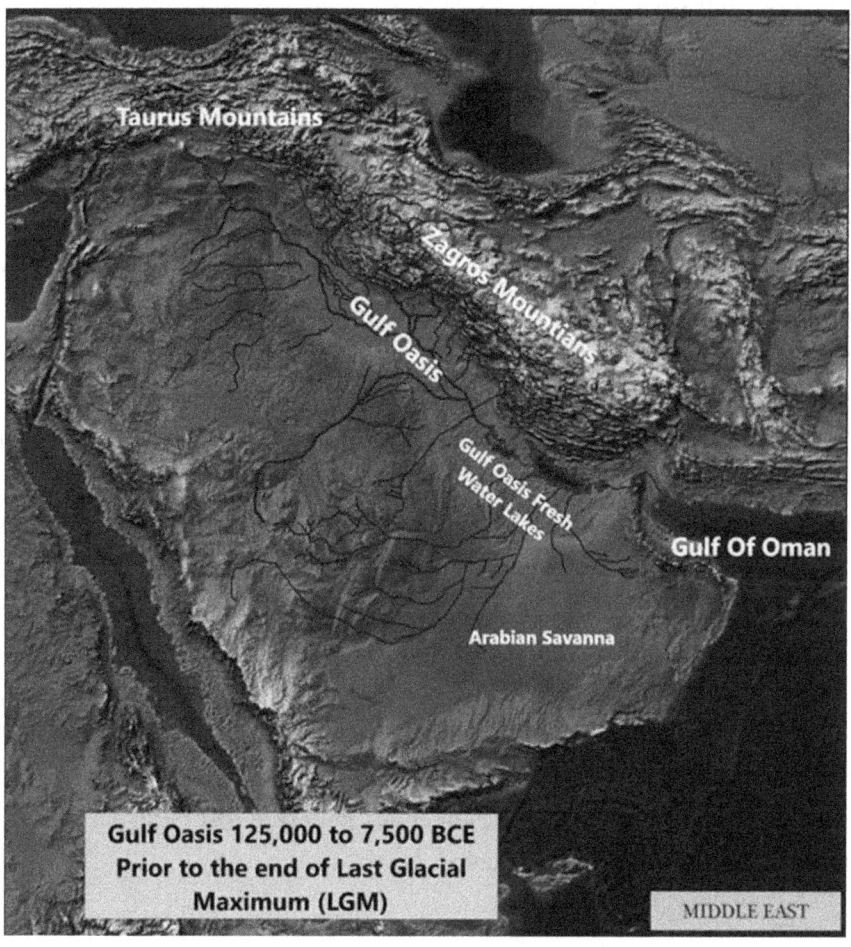

Gulf Oasis 125,000 to 7,500 BC

The Various Dates of Indigenous Habitation of Southern Arabia

Due to the volume of studies on this subject now being released, it is not a case of if the Cognitive Homo Sapiens did decide to turn right out of Africa but a case of when and for what duration 1,000 years or 30,000 years. The discussions now centre on the question of human expansion from Africa into Arabia during the Late Pleistocene 125,000–10,000 BC. Scholars are describing Southern Arabia as a population corridor. Such studies are based on the supposition that Southern Arabia was an important conduit throughout the Pleistocene, facilitating the expansion and contraction of biota to and from East Africa. Hence, the Palaeolithic archaeological record of Arabia can be used to assess the southern route of dispersal for populations expanding out of East Africa.

No Return to Africa

Interest in this topic has now increased exponentially with an increase in fieldwork being conducted throughout the Arabian subcontinent which is indicating that human demography was far more complex than initially considered until now. When we describe a Savanna or Refugia or a Corridor, I feel I must clarify this matter a little more for the reader. These are mere corridors to get from A to B, these areas had become exceptionally diverse areas of woodland, lakes containing all the necessary ingredients to live well off the land. Contrary to expectations of a well-trodden Stone Age highway, new data collected by archaeologists working in Yemen, Oman and the United Arab Emirates UAE[xiv,xv,xvi,xvii,xviii] suggest that parts of the peninsula may have served as population refugia, enabling indigenous hunter-gatherers to survive in localised pockets during periodic climatic downturns.

Now, considering the usual resistance to diverting from the popular thought process, these archaeologists seem to be going against the grain. The amount of information produced in the last decade doesn't just state about the corridor affect, but the longevity that the indigenous populace had been out of Africa, without returning, Jeffery Rose quoted:

Far from finding East African derived lithic technologies spilling over into Arabia, freshly unearthed evidence points to a conspicuous lack of connection with African lithic industries following the last interglacial[xix]. These industries tend to exhibit a distinct Arabian tradition, suggesting minimal demographic input from outside the peninsula. Humans have continuously occupied parts of Arabia for the past 100,000 years, if not longer.

Clarification of timing. I appreciate the earliest known movement out of East Africa of Homo Sapiens is 125,000 years ago yet I constantly mention 70,000 years. This figure is quite arbitrary due to knowing definitively that Cognitive Homo Sapiens had no anatomical or cognitive difference between then and now. The Gulf having a constant habitation of 70,000 years which according to the above statement would seem to be airing on the side of caution and a very conservative estimate. The Arabian subcontinent housed a mosaic of microenvironments. Some of which provided stable, predictable sources of food and freshwater even during the most hyper arid phases of prehistory.

At times when glacial conditions led to increased aridity and widespread environmental degradation. Reduced sea levels exposed large portions of the continental shelf and caused the formation of *Gulf Oasis* fed by upwelling subterranean springs,[xx] taking into account the concentration of freshwater resources in coastal and other low-lying areas, as well as annual rates of precipitation.

Further Climatological Disasters

It should be noted that several other Climatology events occurred at the end of the last glacial ice age. The event may not have affected our overall understanding of what happened in the Persian Gulf, but should be mentioned, yet may have had an impact on future written history. A rapid cooling around 6,200 BC was first identified by Swiss botanist Heinrich Zoller in 1960[xxi]. The strongest evidence for the event comes from the North Atlantic region. The disruption in climate shows clearly in Greenland ice core and sedimentary samples and other records of the temperate and the tropical North Atlantic.

The event may have been caused by a large meltwater pulse from the final collapse of the Laurentide ice Sheet of Northeastern North America, most likely when the glacial lakes Ojibway and Agassiz suddenly drained into the North Atlantic Ocean. Temperature drops between 1 to 5 °C (1.8 to 9.0 °F). In

Greenland the event noticed the cooling was 3.3 °C (decadal average) in less than 20 years. The coldest period lasted for about 60 years, and its total duration was about 150 years.

The end to this *shock* climatic condition also coincides with events at the Eastern end of the Mediterrianian at the Bosphorus when a breach occurred into the Euxin and the creation of the Black Sea occurred. Meanwhile back in the Persian Gulf, this temperature change must have aided the displaced indigeous people of the Gulf Oasis now located at the Delta of the Tigris, Euphrates and Karun Rivers as the weather would have been slightly cooler in Southern Mesopotamia. The initial meltwater pulse caused an artificial rise in the Persian Gulf sea level which later settled back to its set position and where the first cities where built. Archaeologists in the region note these water rises during previous excavations.

The 4.2k Akkad Climatological Disaster

The 4.2K Climatic Disaster in 4,200 BC was a natural event that created a drought thoughout the world which created the largest domino effect during the entire period discussed in the book.[xxii] The beginning of the end of Sumer and the Akkad Empire. During this 200-year drought, many changes and developments occurred affecting societies and ways of life and changing the course of history. The volume of writings and research on this period is so tremendous that it can be summed up here in a very concise and brief manner with the inevitability of not describing many of the details.

It is also necessary to divide this era into periods according to the main actors in the Sumerian theatre. I believe this further climatological event (disaster) would seem to be the perfect *bookend* to my story. The 4.2K Climatic event which lasted for almost 200 years excaserbated the increased salinisation levels in the waters of Mesopotamia and became the main reason behind the downfall of the Akkad Empire. The increase in salinisation in Mesopotamia blighted the much needed wheat crops which to this day have never recovered whereas the barley which is more resilient to salt water incursion continued to prosper and prop-up an aisling crop production.

As previously discussed, the Akkad and the Sumerians are interlinked in all activities and became symbyotic, if one failed, both failed. This 4.2 Kilo Climatic Event changed the course of history in the region and allowed new Empires to assend within Mesopotamia. Whilst in 2,181 BC in Egypt a series of exceptionally low Nile Floods seem to have influenced the collapse of the Old Kingdom after a famine. Modern research have identified the Root Cause to this event which was triggered thousands of miles away in the North Atlantic Ocean, the onset of cooler sea-surface temperatures. As analysis of the modern instrumental record shows that up to 50% inter annual reductions in Mesopotamian water supply resulted when subpolar Northwest Atlantic sea surface temperatures are anomalously cool. A warning for history clearly demonstrates that Mother Earth always has the final say in events and she always recovers...in time!

Post Glacial Sea Level Rise

In recent years, archaeologists have turned up evidence of a wave of human settlements along the shores of the Gulf dating to about 8,200 years ago.

Where before there had been but a handful of scattered hunting camps, suddenly, over 60 new archaeological sites appear virtually overnight, Rose said. *These settlements boast well-built, permanent stone houses, long-distance trade networks, elaborately decorated pottery (please note pottery!), domesticated animals, and even evidence for one of the oldest boats in the world.*

But how could such highly developed settlements pop up so quickly, with no precursor populations to be found in the archaeological record? Rose believes that evidence of those preceding populations is missing because it's under the Persian Gulf. This a very similar scenario to the Sumerian problem, and I wanted to see if they were connected.

Perhaps it is no coincidence that the founding of such remarkably well-developed communities along the shoreline corresponds with the flooding of the Gulf Oasis around 8,000 years ago, Jeffery Rose said. *These new colonists may have come from the heart of the Gulf, displaced by rising water levels that plunged the once fertile landscape beneath the waters of the Indian Ocean.*

It was nice to read such an interesting article, so now I had to work out if this hypothesis of a Gulf Oasis could be true.

Gulf Oasis Becomes the Persian Gulf

The Gulf Oasis should be defined as a wide shallow depression inland flood plain basin that was exposed throughout most of the Late Pleistocene and Early Holocene. It was bounded to the West by the sprawling deserts of the Arabian Peninsula, to the East by the towering peaks of the Zagros Mountain range, and to the North by the Mesopotamian floodplain whilst in the South, the gate way to the Indian Ocean and beyond. Approximately 220 Km wide and over 800 Km long, the Gulf Oasis formed the Southern tip of the *Fertile Crescent*.

This was an extremely lush, very rich fertile soil basin that was well-watered low-lying floodplain beginning at the convergence of both the Tigris and Euphrates Rivers in Mesopotamia and the Karun River draining off the Iranian Plateau. Southwest of the convergence lay the Wadi Batin River flowing across Northern Arabia. These systems joined together into the Ur-Shatt River Valley. Further downstream heading towards the Indian Ocean the Ur-Shatt was fed by additional surface runoff from both Eastern Arabia as well as the Zagros Mountains at multiple points. Its deeply incised channel is still visible in the current bathymetry (measurement of depth of water).

The Ur-Shatt River dropped into several large lakes then drained into the Gulf Oasis's largest lake 11,000 Km² in size which was positioned in the heart of the Gulf Oasis some 100 metres in depth before the flooding occurred. This lake was the epicentre to the development of Cognitive Homo Sapiens into Modern Men and Women. These are the people we would very easily recognise and who, if taught could blend-in or contribute to Modern Society.

Today, the current average depth of the central part of Persian Gulf is 40 metres stepping up to just 25 metres at the surrounding East, West and Northern regions, the shallow areas around the edge of the Persian Gulf. In addition to surface runoff, freshwater within the Gulf Oasis is also supplied by subterranean aquifers which flow beneath the Arabian subcontinent acting as fresh water supplies, known as Khawakb in Bahraini dialect. These are subterranean rivers linked to the Rub Al Khali and Zagros aquifer systems.

Even today, these springs deliver freshwater to the Gulf through fissures in the porous bedrock of the basin. Consequently, this abundant supply was potentially one of the largest and most stable sources of freshwater in Western Asia for the majority of the Late Pleistocene and the Early Holocene. It should be considered that with this abundance of fresh water and plants to consider that the Gulf Oasis was home to a sizable human population.[xxiii]

Prior to the end of the Last Glacial Maximum (LGM) the Gulf Oasis could very easily *home* a wide variety of both human habitation and supporting wildlife. Therefore, we are able to hypothesis the inhabitants of the Gulf Oasis where indigenous to the area rather than descending from migrating populations or colonists' human groups that survived outside of Africa from 125,000 BC onward. The primary population leaving East Africa where able to survive several unfavourable climatic changes throughout this period of time with the Gulf Oasis refugium in Arabia. For the purposes of this hypothesis from 70,000 BC (Cognitive Homo Sapiens) to the final *coup de grace* seawater incursion of the Indian Ocean around 6,200 BC as the last remnants of Last Glacial Maximum (LGM) had finally abated and the world's oceans had finally come to rest.

It may also be considered in the hypothesis that the population settled in the Gulf Oasis region during the Early Holocene, then later partially migrated to South Asia between 60-40,000 BC and beyond whilst a large portion of the population stayed within the protection of the then Gulf Oasis. The Gulf Oasis hypothesis proposes that a highly intelligent, indigenous community not previously known in history was at the vanguard of the ancient world and the cultural revolution. Who were at ground zero of the Agricultural and Urban revolutions? Not only does the proposed scenario introduce a new and substantial cast of characters to Southwest Asia at the critical Pleistocene-Holocene boundary.

It also supplies an ecologically driven mechanism that drove the people into forming a stratified society. It is well documented that every spring the Tigris and Euphrates River continue to burst their banks, depositing large amounts of fertile silt, perfect for growing crops. This same scene was witnessed within the Northern part of the Gulf Oasis. Overtime the banks of the river grew in height and the simplest form of irrigation began to be controlled. The largest difference with the Ur-Shatt and the Tigris and Euphrates is the environmental difference. The Ur Shatt in the Gulf Oasis was surrounded by various types of vegetation whereas Southern Mesopotamia is barren, and sun scorched. The flood plain in the Gulf Oasis only flooded the North part, due to several lakes acting as a form of expansion tank that prevented further flooding in the Southern portion of the Gulf Oasis.

With an ever-fluctuating external landscape, with a cocooned populace predominantly isolated from environmental concerns and cosseted away from external populace of both the Zagros Mountains and Fertile Crescent regions.

These indigenous people of the Gulf played the most important role in human history once they had been forcibly evicted from their homeland due to rising seawater levels. These people also played an important role in shaping cultural evolution throughout the region and the world.

While the bulk of the archaeological record during the Terminal Pleistocene and Early Holocene lies submerged beneath the waters of the Persian Gulf. There are more than 60 archaeological sites that suddenly appear along the newly established shoreline. With evidence a prospering Neolithic population practicing a combination of fishing, date palm cultivation, and animal husbandry. Before the appearance of these sedentary/semi sedentary villages, the few known Early Holocene archaeological sites in the region were characterised by sparse and short-lived hunter-gatherer camp sites scattered along the coast. The wave of settlements derived from an indigenous population displaced by the advancing seawater within the Gulf Oasis.

From that perspective, Terminal Pleistocene and Early Holocene sites around the Gulf represent a more mobile, peripheral elements of a larger core group within the basin, so the 60 sites discovered are only a fragment of the populace that passed by and onwards to pastures new. Just as the 2nd Migration from the Gulf Oasis who by-passed these new *peripheral* settlements and ventured further afield to a land that was ripe for the taking into Northern areas of the Fertile Crescent via the Tigris and Euphrates Rivers all the way to Jericho!

Archaeological remains recovered from these newly founded sites exhibit a suite of characteristics demonstrating a high level of cultural complexity. Including plant and animal domestication, aquatic subsistence, permanent structures, public architecture, pressure flaking, boat construction, a two-tiered settlement hierarchy, and extensive trade networks described as *mature, stable and structured* on their initial appearance in the archaeological record Carter states[xxiv]:

Far from finding East African derived lithic technologies spilling over into Arabia, freshly unearthed evidence points to a conspicuous lack of connection with African lithic industries following the last interglacial. These industries tend to exhibit a distinct Arabian tradition, suggesting minimal demographic input from outside the peninsula.

Taking into account the suite of innovative features appearing around the shoreline of the Gulf. There can be little doubt that the Neolithic demographic  transition had swept across Eastern Arabia by this time. This proposed version of the Oasis Hypothesis predicts that the missing pieces of the archaeological puzzle evidencing the process of Neolithization will be found in the depths beneath the Persian Gulf on the lands of the sunken Gulf Oasis. Abundance of food, water, lithic raw material and its conscripted geographic position.

This sizable inland depression (The Gulf Oasis) is thought to have formed one of the most important Oases in the ancient world. The Persian Gulf is among the shallowest seas in the world, with average depths of just 40 metres. When global sea levels dropped below this mark at the onset of MIS 4, more than 250,000 Km² of land was continuously exposed for the ensuing 125,000-9,200 years. During that period, the basin housed a rich mosaic of freshwater springs, river floodplains, mangrove swamps, and estuaries.

It is very easy today to find high quality deposits of chert (chert is a hard, fine-grained sedimentary rock predominantly from petrified wood) exposed in patches across the landscape. Bahrain, Qatar, and the islands just off the coast of Abu Dhabi. United Arab Emirates are riddled with such outcrops.[xxv] This evidence shines a light on the biodiversity of the Gulf Oasis.

The biodiversity of the Gulf Oasis changed rapidly as the Indian Ocean's salty seawater consumed the freshwater lakes and rivers. At the height of Gulf Oasis human occupation, seawater fishing in the Indian Ocean will have existed, with large freshwater fishing throughout the Gulf Oasis. The fishing combined with the vegetation, fertile lands and wild game could conceivably support a large indigenous populace throughout the Gulf Oasis existence. This is then dramatically changed with the rising sea levels and the incursion of saltwater turning the area into the modern-day Persian Gulf that we know and see today.

The impact on human life would have been dramatic over a prolonged period of time. Fixed habitats would be consumed, and life then became transient forcing the indigenous populace to disperse in all directions. Common foods of the inhabitants would become scarce and indigenous wildlife moved away from the encroaching saltwater and livestock would be continually ushered away from the encroaching ocean. Some of the indigenous people would then be forced onto higher ground and a new way of living would have to be adopted. Only the burning embers using oral traditions would pass on the memories of what had happened to the ancestors of the people who lived in this Eden.

Timeline of the Post Glacial Sea Level Rise Versus the Demise of the Gulf Oasis

It must be noted with the map below the current depths of the Persian Gulf and understand how the sea level effected the Gulf Oasis and when during the Last Glacial Maximum (LGM). At the start of the end of the last ice age 15,000 BC temperatures increased by an average of 4 degrees Celsius. The ice cap reached as far South as Berlin, as the ice caps melted these waters poured back in the oceans.[xxvi]

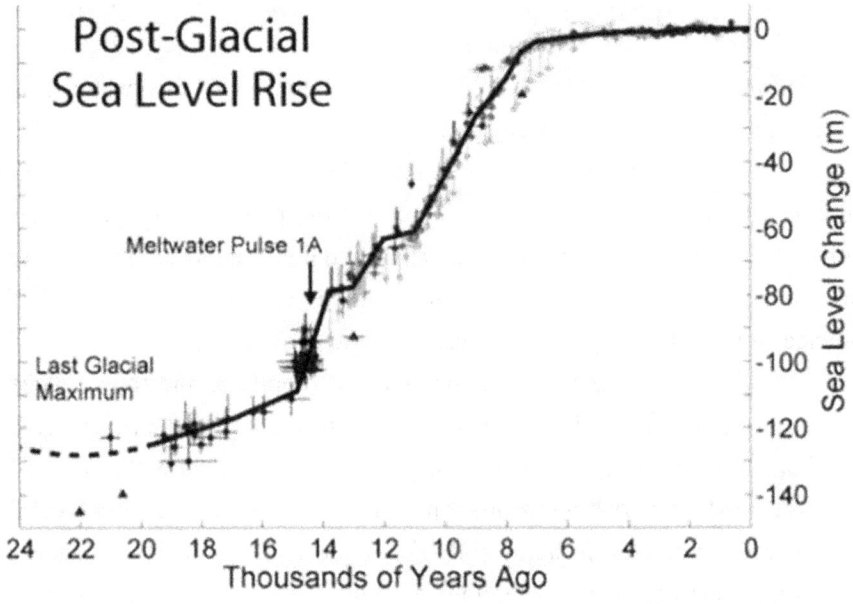

- **15000 BC: The Last Glacial Maximum (LGM)** had just started. The sea levels around the world were 120 metres lower than present day levels, but the climate had changed, and the ice caps slowly but surely started to melt. Therefore, the Gulf Oasis continued unabated as the lowest point of the Gulf Oasis was still 68 metres above the sea.

At the same time, the Indian Monsoons that had been producing grazing lands in the Arabian Savanna started to slowly recede and its eco system started to contract. The weather in the Mediterranean started to improve, in later millennia this warm weather you be aiding the growth of farming.

- **11500 BC:** Archaeologists have confirmed in the Levant Valley the first known farming and the permanent year-round settlements with Stone Based round houses. The Gulf Oasis technologies may pre-date these finds but need under water archaeological digs to confirm or deny this. Or it may provide evidence of rectangular buildings, which gives a strong indication of the 2nd Migration of people left the area in 7,000 BC towards Jericho and the Northern Territories of the Fertile Crescent
- **11000 BC:** The sea levels begin to dramatically increase to 80 metres lower than present day levels. The Gulf Oasis continued unabated as the lowest point of the Gulf Oasis was still 28 metres above the sea.
- **9700 BC:** The end of Pleistocene concluding with the period called Last Glacial Maximum (LGM) an end of the geological epoch. This is the period of time used by Archaeologists and Paleo Climatologists that spans the Earth's last repeated glaciation. The Earth's temperature had stabilised, yet the ice cap melt continued for a further 3,500 years.
- **9000 BC: The sea level continues to rise** at an alarming rate to 65 metres lower than present day levels. The Gulf Oasis continues unabated as the lowest point of the Gulf Oasis is now only 13 metres above the sea.
- **7500 BC: The sea level continues its alarming rise** towards the Gulf Oasis. The sea is now at the edge of the Gulf of Oman, 300 Kilometres South of the Straits of Hormuz. People can actually see the marked difference in height and realise the rise in sea level isn't stopping. The First migration / exodus from the Gulf Oasis has occurred. People had to decide if they would stay in the present location or move to the Indus Valley region along the land bridge before it was totally cut off. The sea eventually closes off the land bridge now submerged to the Indus Valley and no longer able traverse along the continental shelf of the Northern shore of the Indian Ocean. The inhabitants of the coastal region of the Gulf Oasis have 3 options:

- Moved onto higher ground, currently modern Oman.
- Moved further inland, thus encroaching on other inhabitant's land, therefore hunting and farming are starting to be disturbed.
- The 1st Migration. Decide to separate from the main group and move to the Indus Valley Region and be permanently cut off from the rest of the Gulf Oasis, yet sea travel was available and well known therefore the common ties weren't immediately cut…if ever!

- **7200 BC: The sea finally started to consume the first lands** and now for the first time the people of the Gulf Oasis Coastline are starting to pay very close attention to the sea levels and make plans for future evacuation if needed. The indigenous people of the Gulf Oasis seemed to have already had a stratified society in place which means some sort of priest class is assumed to have been present. Whatever this form of religion entailed it would seem that water would have been quite central contributing factor which would have incorporated both freshwater and saltwater. The entire style of living in the Fertile Crescent and Near East including the plains of Turkey began to change, different rituals during death, square buildings, plastered walls, increase in population, the witnessing of a stratified society, better farming techniques, pottery appearing, irrigation farming.
- **7000 BC: The sea level continues its destructive encroachment** into the Gulf Oasis, this becomes the main tipping point for life in the Gulf Oasis. The largest freshwater lake within the Gulf Oasis is now spoilt with seawater from the ever-increasing level of the Indian Ocean. Large swathes of seawater coming to the modern-day shoreline of UAE. The rate of sea encroachment moving inland would have been approximately 1 kilometre per year. The Ur Shatt River fed by the fresh waters of The Tigris, Euphrates, Karun, and the Wadi Batin also supplied the large freshwater lakes of the Gulf Oasis.

At this point, the Ur Shatt River would have started to widen (burst its banks), consuming the fixed stone-built settlements along the banks of the river. This widening of the river extenuated the segregation of the indigenous people. The people continually moving to higher ground as an alternative or moving further North, up the ever-decreasing Gulf

Oasis. The state of flux would have created great anxiety and the oral history of what had once been would be very strong in the mind of the indigenous people. It should also be reminded that the trees and homes would still be visible in the seas for many miles during this transitional episode, which would have looked like an apocalyptic scene.

- o These settlements would have been close to the lakes and rivers that may have already had lowland irrigation channels, locks and dams used for intensive agricultural production. An innovation that some have speculated was the catalyst for the Urban Revolution. The Indian Ocean consumed these villages, the buildings and heavy equipment would have been left behind, the large storage jars, cooking areas, mill stones etc. The wheel at this point had not been invented and everything would have been packed onto animals or carried by hand or sent up the rivers by reed boat.

- **6900 BC:** The sea level would have consumed the second and last remaining lake of the Gulf Oasis and approximately 50% of the previous land mass prevailed as the sea was only 20 metres lower than present day levels. The people once again moved to higher ground with some slight respite as the natural shelf of land remained along modern-day Saudi Arabia and to the North at the head of modern Kuwait and Iraq/Iran boarders.
- **6500 BC:** The 95% of the lands of the Gulf Oasis had been consumed by the sea, with 250,000 Km² of land disappearing under the newly created ocean.
- **6200 BC: The sea levels started to normalise**, and the modern sites of the Ancient Middle East started to appear. It should be noted that the period of Ubaid 0; 6,500–5,400 BC is the sites first discovered and recorded by archaeologists.
- **6000 BC:** The creation of the Black Sea and the final mass migration away from the Euxine catastrophe and the movement of people into both Egypt and into the land of Sumer, the deltas of the both the Tigris and the Euphrates rivers where the Marsh Arabs began to dwell and waiting for the return of the original ingenious Gulf Oasis populous.

Conclusion

Within 1,000 years of the seas first encroachment into the Gulf Oasis, the entire Gulf Oasis had disappeared below the Indian Ocean and creating what is now the modern-day Persian Gulf over 250,000 Km² of land disappeared. The stone-built homes, the tilde land, the mangroves trees, and the date palms all consumed by the unstoppable saltwater sea from the Indian Ocean up the ever-decreasing Gulf Oasis. This was a flood on a monumental scale that has been captured through oral stories and eventually written down and passed down through generations of eyewitnesses.

Therefore, it would be correct to assume that a flood story from Sumerian history may have its origins from these cataclysmic events or even the story of Adapa, a man of vast intelligence who is depicted as an early culture hero from the first city of Eridu, identified with U-an, a half-human half-fish creature from the sea.

Global sea levels rose an average of 2.5 centimetres a year, in the end the sea had risen an incredible 120 metres, around the world the sea engulfed coastal communities, previous land bridges now disappeared under the oceans Russia and Alaska now disconnected, Britain from the Rest of Europe also disconnected, and in the Middle East a similar impact occurred. The Gulf Oasis the Tigris and the Euphrates merged into what is called by historians the Ur Shatt River, the Ur Shatt made its way through the Gulf Oasis and opening on a couple of occasions to large lakes, one such lake was 11,000 Km² in size that could support wildlife and humans in the multitude.

As the glaciers melted, no impact was initial felt in the Gulf Oasis as this land was already 80 metres above the sea levels. Slowly but surely the sea levels continued to rise until the indigenous people of the Gulf Oasis realised the sea level was still increasing. At first nobody would have realised the sea levels increasing as the rise seemed so insignificant as it took several thousand years to eventually reach a critical situation. Once the seawater had encroached onto terra firma the average the coastline would have moved was approximately 120 metres a year. But once the sea reached flat land those effects multiplied exponentially; at times, the land would have been lost at a rate of 1 km per year. Only seeming to pause due to a slight rise in the land both North and South of the Ur Shatt River.

The biggest visual dramatic effect was seen right through the centre area of the Gulf Oasis. Slowly but surely, everything disappeared over time. Some higher ground became islands with dense foliage due to the presence of subterranean aquifers which flowed beneath the Arabian subcontinent acting as fresh water supplies. Whilst headlands poked ominously into the newly created ocean.

Slowly but surely, some small towns and villages which sat atop of Tells will have been swallowed up along with the half sunken forests as a backdrop to the devastation. If this scene couldn't invoke stories of a great flood, surely nothing on earth could. But their where several future tribulations concerning water that would do exactly that which would cement the stories of a *Great Flood*. One of these future events in particular would shake fear into everyone's hearts for thousands of kilometres around.

Before these future events occurred, the people of the Gulf Oasis had started abandoning their homes and became a very regular sight. Was there any tolerance or empathy awarded to the displaced or did everything become fractious and primal? These events happened over many generations, so did the people accept that, at some point they would also have to up-root a move to an unknow place far away. The people of the ever-declining Gulf Oasis somehow adapted to this every changing environment.

The populace was intelligent and the rate of decline in land mass per year would have been well known in advance and the people would have understood that a limited time existed especially in the lowest lying areas towards the Centre of the Gulf Oasis and also a larger reprieve for the populace who happened to be on higher ground, especially when you knew the increase in sea level was 2.5 cm per year. If your home happened to be on ground several metres higher than your surrounding area, this became a real saviour, at least for a few years at least. The original hills would have been veritable heaven-sent bastions against the encroaching water, over a prior of time this high ground would have become well-fortified. Humans are adaptable and people's ingenuity always succeeds when people put their minds to a problem.

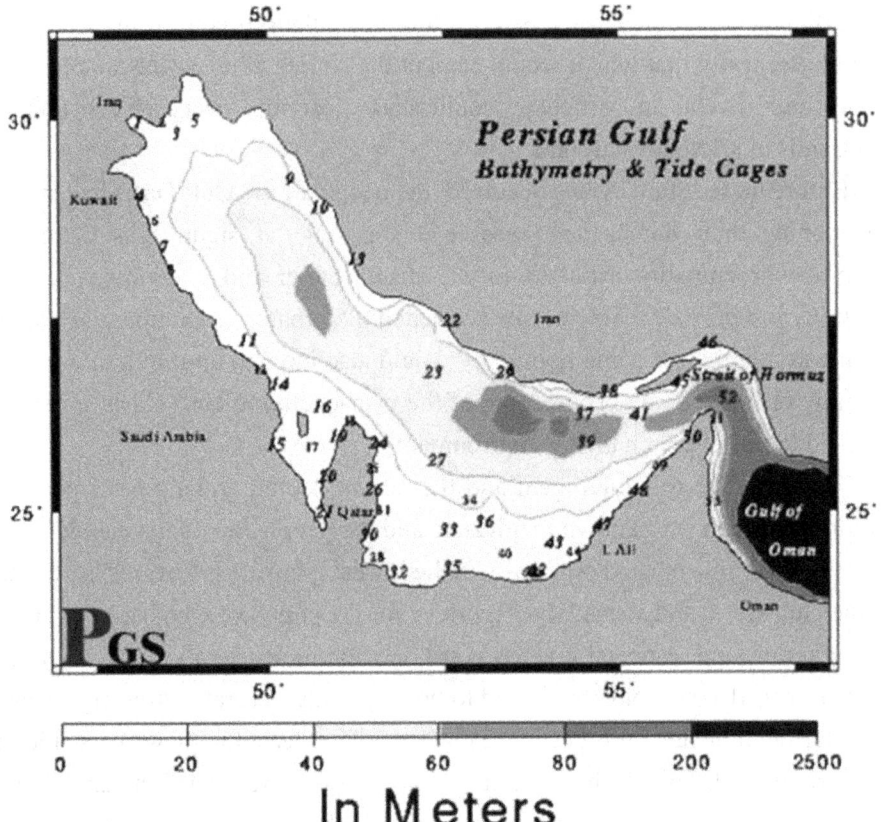

2. Migration Patterns and Archaeogenetic Data

Migration is by far the largest headache. We can very easily speculate what happened to an area once it became dry land and the sea levels lowered allowing easy access to multiple areas previously restricted. We are able to study water tables and temperatures and come to a reasonable hypothesis if an area could sustain life. We can also look at the various climates at different times throughout history. Also looking at archaeological evidence in various locations can also provide a strong hypothesis as to movement. Especially if archaeological evidence can substantiate a specific people of known origin found in a new location.

For example, if one set of people who have specific traits are displaced from a specific region due to a forced natural event and a mirrored society appears instantly somewhere else in a similar time frame. Then it would be reasonable to assume that the people (or parts of) had migrated to the new location. But what the hardest part of the puzzle is, knowing who decided to go where, sometimes it can be obvious but sometimes not knowing the personal dynamics in a group can be speculative at best. Understanding social and human pattern of behaviour can also guide the historian / researcher to a logical conclusion, especially if something similar has previously occurred and been recorded (known).

The reason for continuing with the *Cognitive* Homo Sapiens, because being cognitive they don't follow the rules, they make the rules. Fortunately, we have a scientific trick up the sleeve, Archaeogenetic Data (DNA) Thank you, Sir Alex Jeffreys[13], for pioneering DNA Testing. Now we can look at the migration models and prove or disprove previous theories with accuracy. But Cognitive

---

[13] *Sir Alec John Jeffreys, an English geneticist who developed techniques for genetic fingerprinting and DNA profiling.*

Homo Sapiens do like to throw a curve balls on a regular basis and extrapolating variations can lead to further questions.

Life would be simple if we could say Cognitive Homo Sapiens move from A to B then move from B to C. No no, that would be far too easy, what we see is a strong migration one direction, and everyone can understand the reasoning. But when climatic conditions eventually worsen after 1000's of years, then the group has a tendency to split. Some return back to the place of origin, some stay in the region they now inhabit, and some search for a new place. Therefore, Homo Sapiens at location B, some stay at B, some return to original location A and some go to new location C. Let's call B, The Arabian Peninsula, the Arabian Savanna.

MIS Tracing Archaeogenetic Data

Marine Isotope Stages (MIS): Cesare Emiliani in the 1950's AD pioneered and developed this technique that is now widely used by Archaeologists that are studying the Quaternary Period (2.6 million years to present day) which includes Late Pleistocene and Holocene which captures the necessary data required for this research. MIS are alternating warm and cool periods in the Earth's Paleoclimate; this is calculated from Oxygen Isotope Data (OID) reflecting changes in temperature derived from data from deep sea core samples. It should be noted that further cross referencing/substantiating these cycles is currently been undertaken by testing ice core samples via the study of ancient pollen samples.

Dates of Marine Isotope Stages (MIS):

- MIS 1: 8000 BC to Present (Holocene)
- MIS 2: 23000 BC (Late Pleistocene)
- MIS 3: 50000 BC (Late Pleistocene)
- MIS 4: 70000 BC (Late Pleistocene)
- MIS 5a-d: 110000 BC (Late Pleistocene)
- MIS 5e: 125000 BC (Late Pleistocene)

1st Migration Out of Africa into Southern Arabia and Levant Region

MIS 5a-e, 125000 BC (Late Pleistocene), the climate at this period of time was warm between the interglacial periods and allow the original expansion of Homo Sapiens out of Africa. Those original people didn't travel beyond the Arabian Savanna and Levant until a later period MIS 3 when weather conditions became unsatisfactory in the region and people decided to move further afield.

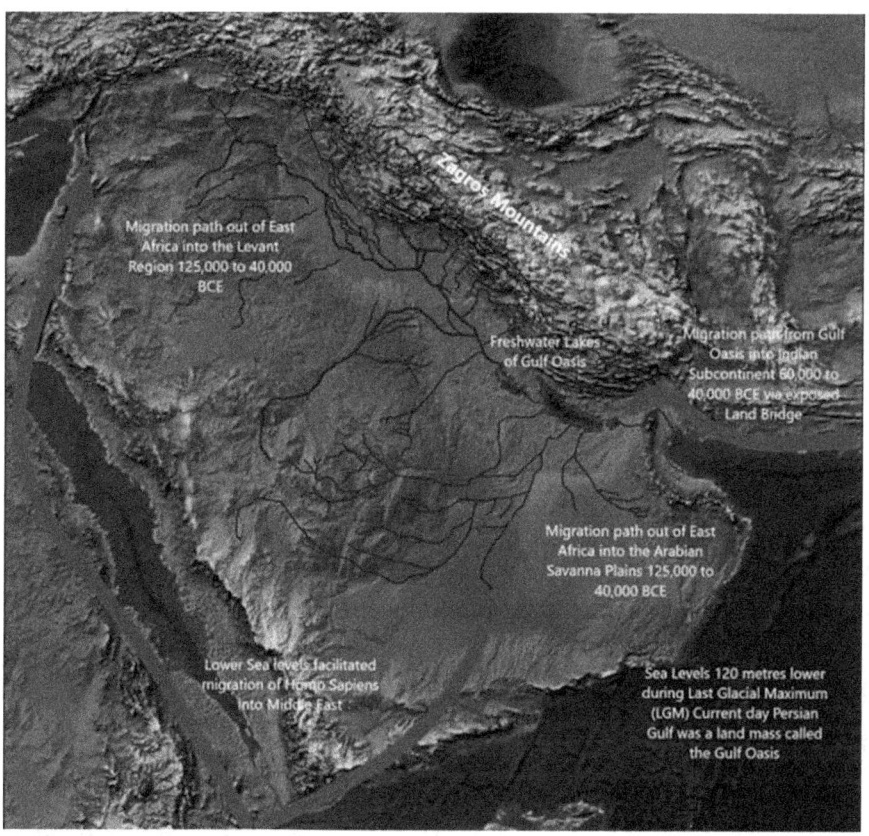

1 X 2nd Migration Out of Africa and into the Southern Arabia and Gulf Oasis Region and Beyond, Including the Return Back to Africa and Back Out Again

MIS 4 70000 BC (Late Pleistocene), second population migrations out of the Horn of (East) Africa and into Asia via the "Arabian Corridor" (i.e., Yemen, Oman, KSA and the UAE). In 43000 BC, due to worsening weather conditions in the region, populace from Saudi Savanna plains then moved from Southern

Arabia and moved back into Africa and also migrating further South via the land bridge corridor connecting the Indian Subcontinent with the Gulf Oasis. The migration starts prior to worsening weather conditions MIS 4-3 60-40000 years but will eventually be exacerbated by deteriorating weather during MIS 3. This witnesses a rapid human colonisation along the rim of the Indian Ocean and ultimately into Australia.

So, what we can consider circa 43000 BC climatic conditions within the region of Southern Arabia, modern hunter-gatherers physically moved in three preferred directions due to the onset of increased aridity on the Arabian Savanna and worsening weather conditions. Therefore, Olivieri, Gonzalez and Rose[xxvii] report the re-introduction of Homo Sapiens originating from Southern Arabia back into Africa. Asiatic origin for this lineage may come partially from Southern Arabian ancestry and not from Africa.

The second parallel migration may have seen a further influx of Homo Sapiens into the Gulf Oasis, this area will have already been inhabited from the first wave up to 125,000 years ago and more recently Cognitive Homo Sapiens 70,000 ago. The hunter-gatherers who had lived in the Arabian Savanna open plains will have had to adapt to new surrounding within the Gulf Oasis as this required living in closer proximity to other clans but with the same amount of resources available. Again, in parallel to these other two migration paths in 43,000 BC, we also see an increase in migration levels into the Indian Subcontinent via the existing land bridge from the mouth of the Gulf Oasis directly into the Indian Subcontinent of modern-day Pakistan and India.

2 X 2nd Migration Out of Africa and into the Levant Region South West Mediterranean

MIS 4 70000 BC (Late Pleistocene), second population migrations (Cognitive Homo Sapiens) out of the Horn of East Africa and into Southwest Asia, the Levant Region is the large area south of the Taurus Mountains and runs between the Mediterranean Sea in the West and the Arabian Desert in the South with Mesopotamia to the East. It stretches 400 miles North to South from the Taurus Mountains to the Sinai desert, and 70 to 100 miles east to west between the Mediterranean Sea and the Arabian Desert.

The term *Levant* refers to the modern Countries of Israel, Jordan, Lebanon, Palestine, and Syria. The archaeological sites throughout the Levant Region have an abundance of archaeological evidence and well documented and it is now quite apparent that the migration out of East Africa didn't just move Eastward through the Levant but dispersed in separate directions and didn't move out of Africa with a herd mentality.

Movement back into African Sahara and East Africa, the original Homo Sapiens hunter-gatherers of the Levant Region but with a slightly earlier date of circa 45,000 BC possibly the onset of the climatic adversity that was felt in the Southern Asian region was also experienced first in Southwest Asia (Levant, Southern Mediterranean) region. Therefore, the hunter-gatherers of the Levant Region, had been unsuccessful in their habitation of the Levant and decided to migrate. Neanderthal groups on the other hand seem to have benefited from the worsening climate and replaced Homo Sapiens. Once again, these Humans, being cognitive, also decided to migrate in several directions.

Similar to their cousins in the South, some of these hunter-gatherers moved back into Africa but not quite from whence they came. DNA testing has suggested that the people migrated into North Saharan Africa and not back to East Africa the original start point, where the weather was more conducive to Homo Sapiens. This is backed-up with analyses within the last decade examining Y chromosome DNA markers, which have produced additional evidence of Late Pleistocene back migrations into Africa. Therefore, there is no reason to presume that the founder M population originated in East Africa rather than Southwest Asia.

In the case of subclade M2,[xxviii] conclude that haplogroup M has in situ origins within Southwest Asia. Parallel to this first group, the next group of hunter-gatherers of the Levant moved onwards. Homo Sapiens are known to have moved earlier into the region around Mount Carmel in modern-day Israel during the Middle Palaeolithic dating from MIS 4/5 90,000 BC eventually onwards to Southern Anatolia and later occupying the area of the Northern Fertile Crescent. During this move in 45,000 BC from the North Region of the Fertile Crescent some of these hunter-gatherers continued their travels and followed the Tigris and Euphrates Rivers until they came to the Northern end of the Gulf Oasis and took up residency.

3rd Migration Back Out of Africa and Back into the Levant

Archaeological evidence has also witnessed migration occurring around MIS 3 52000-50000 BC out of Africa by the Upper Palaeolithic culture with Homo Sapiens at Ksar Akil XXV level. It is interesting to note that discoveries by archaeologists in the Levant region have found that both Neanderthal and modern Homo Sapiens lived in the same area region for over 10,000 years, some groups living within 300 metres of each other's dwellings. It would appear this sets the date by which Homo Sapiens Upper Palaeolithic cultures begin to replace Neanderthal Levalo-Mousterian, and by 40,000 BC Palestine was occupied by the Levanto-Aurignacian Ahmarian culture, lasting from MIS 2/3 39000-24000 BC. This culture was quite successfully spreading once again as far as Southern Anatolia.

After the Late Glacial Maxima (LGM), a new Epipaleolithic (this denotes the transitional period to Stone Age) culture appears in Southern Palestine. The appearance is a significant rupture in the cultural continuity of Levantine Upper Palaeolithic. The Kebaran culture, with its use of microliths (shaped flint used in tools and spears), is associated with the use of the bow and arrow and the domestication of the dog. Extending from MIS 2, 18–10,500 BC, the Kebaran culture[xxix] shows clear connections to the earlier Micro lithic cultures using the bow and arrow, and using grinding stones to harvest wild grains, that developed from the MIS 2, 24000-17000 BC.

Halfan culture of the Upper Nile Region in Egypt came from the earlier Homo Sapiens of the Sahara. Kebaran culture (close to modern Haifa) was quite successful and was ancestral to the later Natufian culture 13,000–9,500 BC, which extended throughout the whole of the Levantine region. These people pioneered the first sedentary settlements and may have supported themselves from fishing and the harvesting of wild grains plentiful in the region at that time.

As of July 2018, the oldest remains of bread were discovered 12,400 BC at the archaeological site Shubayqa, once home of the Natufian hunter-gatherers, roughly 4,000 years before the advent of agriculture.

Natufian culture also demonstrates the early domestication of the dog, and the assistance of this animal in hunting and guarding human settlements may have contributed to the successful spread of this culture. In the Northern Syrian, Eastern Anatolian region of the Levant, Natufian culture at Cayonu and Mureybet developed the first fully agricultural culture with the addition of wild grains, later being supplemented with domesticated sheep and goats, which may have been domesticated first by the Zarzian culture of Northern Iraq and Iran, another person's hypothesis which has to be considered.

Migration Via Afghanistan and the Caucasus into the Middle East and Converging with Local Populace Expansion from the Levant Region

[xxx]Marcel Otto who argues that the point of origin of early modern human expansion into Europe originated between Afghanistan and the Caucasus. In his review of archaeological data from the Middle-Upper Palaeolithic transitions in Europe, Asia, and Africa. Marks (2005) arrives at a similar conclusion: *The immediate origins of the explosion of "modern behaviour" seen in Europe, but not in Africa, might be found at the contact between Eastern Europe and Western Asia*. This is also an important point when studying the language connections between different regions and cultures.

The First LGM Migration Event 9,500 Years Ago, Migration of People Once the Indian Ocean Encroached the Gulf Oasis

This is a fixed date that we have as the last possible migration that was able to use the land bridge that skirted the Indian Ocean from the mouth of the Gulf Oasis. It is very possible that this conduit was a well-travelled bi-directional path. There are several reasons for understanding this connection between the Indus Region and the Gulf Oasis. Once the sea had covered the low-lying Gulf Oasis turning this area into todays the Persian Gulf. It became a highway for trade in the region. A lot of similarities existed with this Indian Subcontinent trading partner and the reason where this trading route came from has not been clearly understood.

The main connection between Ancient Pre-Sumerian and the Indian Subcontinent is language. Lots of ancient Sumerian has strong connections with archaic Tamil or a predecessor to archaic Tamil with Dravidian connections and can still be understood today which will be discussed in further detail. Unfortunately trying to hypothesis that one of the oldest languages in the world could share its roots with Sumeria the birthplace of civilisation has multiple difficulties. If we examine the Marsh Arabs of Southern Iraq, we have to understand where the water buffalo originate from and the rice cultivation. Was this brought to Sumeria later by trade due to the 4.2K climatic event or was this already in the Gulf Oasis, therefore providing more substance to having common ancestry? If this is found to be substantiated, this alone is worthy of its own research.

It should be noted these links would not be between other regions of the Indian Subcontinent, just Tamil and Sumeria. In 1991 AD, Crescent Petroleum ran a feasibility for a gas project named Gulf South Asia (GUSA). A gas pipeline from North Field of Qatar to produce natural gas for export to the Pakistan markets via the now submerged Land Bridge previously used prior to 7500 BC. Survey undertaken by Fugro International for the company.

The Second LGM Migration Event 9,000 Years Ago, Migration of People from the Gulf Oasis into Northern Mesopotamia (Levant Region and Taurus Mountain Region)

The world's seawaters had risen to such a high that the fresh water lakes within the Gulf Oasis had finally been breached and contaminated with the ingress of sea water and overnight changed the entire ecosystem of the dependant wildlife and human inhabitancy of the 11,000 Km^2; the Pre-Pottery Neolithic culture of Jericho was about to come to an abrupt end around 7000 BC when the Tell of Jericho seems to have been abandoned, most of the original walls collapsed/destroyed, burn marks observed at this level and the tower abandoned and eroded away. The original round houses of the indigenous populace replaced with rectangular homes. The population rapidly increased to several thousand and much stronger fortification walls built. Many hypotheses have been suggested, but I strongly believe that the new culture observed throughout the Northern Fertile Crescent, is a true depiction of the people who originated from the Gulf Oasis during the 2nd Migration. These are the people who inhabited the area closest to the fresh water lakes that existed within the Gulf Oasis. All manners of reasons have been explored for the rapid decline, earthquakes, pestilence outside invasion, but this theory stands strongest.

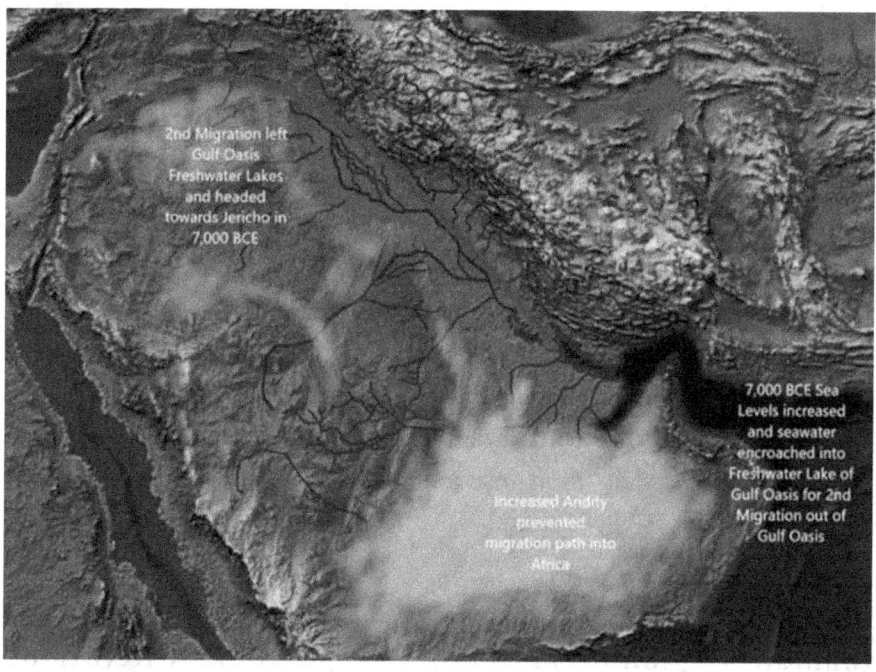

2nd Migration 7000 BC from Gulf Oasis to Jericho and Fertile Crescent

The Third and Final LGM Migration Event 8,200 Years Ago, People from the Gulf Oasis into Southern Mesopotamia

Regarding the ultimate destination of the displaced people of the Gulf Oasis, Rose hints at a key role in populating *the nexus of the ancient world, ground zero of the Agricultural and Urban revolutions*. The people of the Gulf Oasis would have been well adapted to marshy riverine and estuarine conditions, such as were later found in Southern Mesopotamia during the formative Ubaid and Uruk periods and certainly would have followed such environments as they retreated.

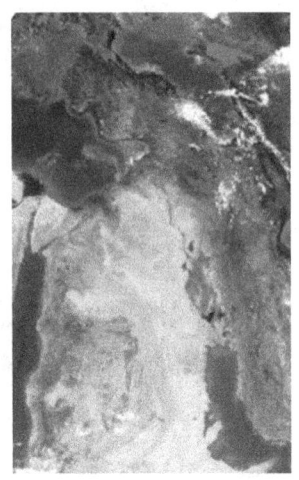

One may therefore propose, a significant population input from the Gulf Oasis into Southern Mesopotamia and Eastern Arabia in the early-mid Holocene, with a later separate phase of Neolithic colonisation of Arabia from the West. In neither area should it be assumed that Neolithization occurred as the result of the demic expansion of Post Pottery Neolithic B (PPNB) groups 11000-9500 BC. Rather, the Southern Mesopotamian chalcothic (early Ubaid) and the Arabian Neolithic (ABT) could have emerged separately from interactions between different local reservoir populations with post-PPNB neighbours.

Migration 8,000 Years Ago from Levant and Taurus Mountain Region to Southern Mesopotamia: A Return of the 2nd LMG Migrants from Gulf Oasis

The culture around the Levant regions lasted just over a thousand years, at the very same time the growth of cities was about to take shape in the South of Mesopotamia in Eridu, Ur and Uruk. At the exact time a great decline in Palestine was just about to take place in 6000 BC. A catastrophe so devastating that the area remained largely depopulated for over 3,500 years. Yet the South was about to experience its boon. Could the people of Northern Fertile Crescent populace who were a mix of both Gulf Oasis Sumerian 7,000 BC refugees and Semitic speaking Northern indigenous people who fled their homes in the North and seeking refuge in the South at the exact place where the last migrant settlers of the Gulf Oasis had come to rest in the Marshes of the Tigris and Euphrates Delta 200 years earlier. Could this migration from the North explain why both Sumerian speaking and Akkad Semitic speaking people lived in close proximity in the land of Sumer in South Mesopotamia?

Migration 8,000 Years Ago from Levant and Taurus Mountain Region to Egypt

When the Euxine had been breached via the Dardanelles from the Mediterranean in 6,000 BC. The people who had come to inhabit the Jericho and surrounding region 1,000 years previously. The people had a very simple choices, when they thought all was lost simply head in the opposite direction of the known catastrophe that was seen and heard in the North, to head towards the mouth of both the Tigris and Euphrates OR move further up the coastline and into the Delta of Egypt. Egyptian history started at this same time.

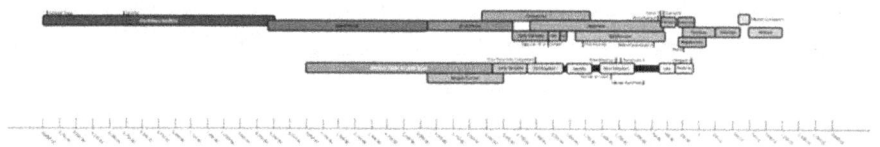

Mesopotamia versus Egyptian Historical Chronology

Conclusion on the Refugees of the 2nd LGM Migration Event 9,000 Years Ago from the Gulf Oasis

By reading the events that occurred in Jericho and its surrounding area and understanding the aggression shown to the indigenous populace of the Northern Fertile Crescent region, archaeologists quickly ascertained certain facts that happened in a very short pace of time in Jericho. Advanced farming techniques that were brought to the area. Advanced domestication of animal compared to previous occupants, confirming domestication of specific animals. The style of the homes introduced in 7000 BC may be a direct replica of their previous home environment in the Gulf Oasis.

The advanced level of engineering compared to the previous inhabitants, the larger much stronger walls that replaced the inadequate defences of the previous inhabitants. The volume of people who settled in the area immediately after Jericho's destruction was far larger than the previous occupancy that was easily overwhelmed. The ferocity of the destruction to the area shows a more brutal aggressive nature to the newcomers. A stratified and very organised society seems to be self-evident due to planning and organisation. Do all these major factors point to an advanced society compared to the previous inhabitants of Jericho and the surrounding area.

Could there have been marked differences within the Gulf Oasis of knowledge and culture compared to everyone else in the region. Could the people of the Gulf Oasis freshwater lakes be far more advanced than the area closest to the Oceans or the area further up the Gulf Oasis, who may be the people of the 3rd Migration out of the Gulf Oasis. Did the people inhabiting the lake area, live closer to other clans and form larger communities or even large towns and created rules and have order and maybe the first laws overseen by a priest class to ensure everyone acted accordingly.

If these people where so advanced and returned back to the area within 1,000 years. Could they have been more advanced and knowledgeable of engineering matters than the people wallowing around in the Delta which may indicate a difference of *class* structure within the inhabitants of the Gulf Oasis prior to any flooding. They may have the same origins but may have been culturally different, similar to city Bankers and Engineering working class communities today living in the same country but on opposite ends of the spectrum.

Fertile Crescent Conduit

MIS 5 a-e, 125,000 BC and beyond, the Fertile Crescent was a perfect conduit for travel from the Northern Regions of the Levant all the way to the Southern part of the Fertile Crescent to the Gulf Oasis and should not be underestimated. The means of transport whilst using the conduit hasn't changed for millions of years, walking. During high antiquity of civilisation in the Middle East travel was unimpeded due to the existence of convenient land bridges and easy river lanes of both the Tigris and the Euphrates River. Also, Cognitive Homo Sapiens had now become the biggest predator on the planet, top of the food chain, so the only thing to be aware of was other Homo Sapiens.

This route was passable in both summer and winter, in both dry and wet seasons. Movement of large numbers of people North of the Caspian Sea was virtually impossible in winter, owing to the severity of the climate; central Eurasia was often too dry in summer. Land passage between Asia and Africa in early times limited to narrow strips of land in the Isthmus of Suez. Large-scale desert travel was limited to special routes in Iran and in North Africa, both East and West of the Nile Valley.

We have to take our lead in this research from other areas of intense archaeological activity in other areas of the Middle East for understanding of how the Gulf Oasis may have looked and what activities will have been common to the area. For this reason, we should look at the Natufian Culture of the Levant, which some archaeologists describe as the instigator of food production of the Levant. This culture was first recognised by the English archaeologist[xxxi] Dorothy Garrod in the 1930s.

It should be noted that the Levant may have *lagged* behind the Gulf Oasis region in terms of farming as mentioned in Sumerian Mythology. But at least the Natufian Culture can give this research a fixed datum of actual dates for Levant archaeological discoveries that would definitely been of the same timeline in the Gulf Oasis. It is suggested that the first people settled in Mesopotamia in the Palaeolithic by 14000 BC. People in the region lived in small settlements with circular houses, the foundations made of undressed stone and retaining walls that supported the circumference of the dwelling. The oval structures form two parallel series of rooms that seem to be a regulated size of 2.5 metres in diameter with a thick perimeter wall one meter thick. The house would have been in close vicinity to other buildings of the same proportions. Each home holding its own reserve of food produce.[xxxii]

During 11000 BC, the Levant Natufian Culture finds evidence of farming culture, sickle blade tools found used for the sole purpose of harvesting various crops and the appearance of cemeteries during this same time period. Due to crops now being cultivated and the stored wheat and barley then it is assumed this was the point at which permanent all year-round settlements began to replace the Hunter Gathering or a combination of both. Very soon after these houses would have formed farming communities following the domestication of animals and the increased development of agriculture, most notably irrigation techniques that took advantage of the proximity of the Tigris and Euphrates rivers.

The Natufian sedentism, farming, and agriculture were in a region between modern South Eastern Anatolia, Iran, Iraq, and Syria, an area traditionally labelled as the Northern Fertile Crescent. Most of the technology and culture associated with farming including domestic sheep, goat, cattle, and pigs have first been discovered here and the first records of rodents, due to the settlements being permanent. The transition from a hunter-gatherer lifestyle to agriculture and sedentism was considered such a radical change in human ecology that the term Neolithic revolution was coined for it.

Some 2,000 years later, the new Neolithic lifestyle appeared in South Eastern Europe and shortly afterwards in Central and Mediterranean Europe. Also, Göbekli Tepe in Southern Turkey has revealed a prehistoric village just 20 miles away where evidence of the world's oldest domesticated strains of wheat which have been recovered. According to radiocarbon dates agriculture developed in the area around 8500 BC, just a few hundred years after the construction of Göbekli Tepe.

3. DNA

DNA Testing

For many years, theories concerning certain historical matters, have been at the sole discretion of the Historian. As laypeople we are not in a position to question the authority of the Historian and to a point correct. We are currently at the starting point of a revolution; with the advent of DNA testing and research we are now in a position to use scientific research to analyse data in the pursuit of the correct answer. It would seem historians change their opinion slower than evolution, some would say, an ingrained institutionalised refusal to change. Now scientists can provide scientific answers with no ambiguity accurately piecing together historical puzzles by using tools never previously available and utilising precious research funds and maximising resources. To try and place this into contents, if we had five initial theories each having a further five potential beginnings.

DNA may be able to conclusively discount four theories, reducing the probability from 25:1 to 5:1 therefore concentrating limited resources into a much smaller area of research increasing the probability of success. It has been quickly realised when using DNA when researching one piece of vital evidence it can actually have a domino effect and help reveal multiple related events which hadn't previously been examined. The example within this book is looking at the origins of Sumerian and starting to decipher fact from fiction. Each set of tests do not always match exactly with another. This is due in part to the test sample size or parameter variables differing. Therefore, you have to weigh-up other contributing factors within the research which may give a leaning to a specific known result. What it has done, is give conclusive proof of the origins of the people in Southern Mesopotamia and also highlighted a possible occurrence 40,000 years ago.

Dates of Marine Isotope Stages (MIS)

- MIS 1: 8000 BC to Present (Holocene)
- MIS 2: 23000 BC (Late Pleistocene)
- MIS 3: 50000 BC (Late Pleistocene)
- MIS 4: 70000 BC (Late Pleistocene)
- MIS 5a-d: 110000 BC (Late Pleistocene)
- MIS 5e: 125000 BC (Late Pleistocene)

DNA Horn of Africa

The discovery of haplogroup M1 Is the human mitochondrial DNA (mtDNA) the genetic marker of humans in the Horn of Africa. Located across the Red Sea and within sight of the Arabian Peninsula. During the Last Glacial Maximum this allowed for an *Arabian Corridor* to be opened up through modern day Yemen, Oman, Saudi (KSA) and the UAE serving as a conduit for the first Cognitive Homo Sapiens moving out of Africa and into Asia. Thereby suggesting the existence of a posited Southern dispersal route during MIS 4 or MIS 3.[xxxiii] More recent studies of subclade M1 in North Africa and the Levant have led to a different explanation for the geographic distribution of this critical genetic marker.

Some researchers now propose that M1 arose in Southwest Asia and moved back into Africa sometime between 45,000 and 40,000 years ago.

[xxxiv]Winters also reports the most ancient M1 lineages in North Africa and the Near East, not East Africa, suggesting an Asiatic origin for this lineage. Other analyses within the last decade examining Y chromosome DNA markers have produced additional evidence of Late Pleistocene back migrations into Africa. There is no reason to presume that the founder M population originated in East Africa rather than South Asia or some other place therein. In the case of subclade M2,[xxxv] conclude that haplogroup M has in situ origins within South Asia.

Thus, it is significant that haplogroup M occurs in low frequencies throughout Arabia Cerny states[xxxvi]:

Among the Yemeni population in Southwestern Arabia, almost every known M marker is derived from an Indian lineage unrelated to M1, leading researchers to conclude that "the available mtDNA data today (in Arabia) show no traces of the initial migration(s) out of Africa".

The Indian lineage within the Yemen maybe from Ancient trading routes with Indian Subcontinent supplying both the Sumerian /Akkadian Empires and the Egyptian Empires with necessary raw goods to feed these new trading centres. Considering the mtDNA phylogenetic structure of populations in and around the Arabian Peninsula,[xxxvii] write that *mitochondrial lineages carried by these colonisers were not yet ripe M and N lineages but their L3 ancestors.*

In their proposed scenario, the post MIS 4 expansion originated in Asia, not Africa, and therefore better explains the rapid human colonisation along the rim of the Indian Ocean and ultimately into Australia between 60-40,000 years ago.

Haplogroup J1 is also well represented in Arabia, with high frequencies in Saudi Arabia (37.5%), Qatar (17.8%), and Yemen (30%). Like R0a, this lineage is characterised by considerable diversity in all its main sub-branches found throughout the subcontinent (J1, J1b, and J1c/J2).

Abu-Amero states[xxxviii]: *Of these sub-branches, J1b is the most common and diverse in Arabia, with a coalescence age estimation of 17,480 to 2,119 BCE. While neither R0a nor J1b reaches back far enough in time to relate directly to the initial modern human expansion out of Africa, they both suggest that some Late Pleistocene groups survived the Last Glacial maximum (LGM) and persist today within the modern Arabian gene pool.*

The archaeological and genetic evidence is not irreconcilable. If we consider that the population bottleneck releases branching from the common ancestral group emanated from Southwest Asia, not Africa, the threads of archaeological, genetic, and fossil evidence agree. The model described in this book proposes that the population movement out of Africa during MIS 5 was not a failed wave of expansion; rather, these carriers of the mtDNA L3 marker were settled and surviving in Southwest and/or Central Asian refugia, such as the Gulf Oasis, until the unsatisfactory conditions that set in during MIS 3 permitted subsequent range expansions.

As such, it is more likely to expect several waves of expansion radiating from multiple population centres at the onset of MIS 3 rather than the single expansion scenario out of Africa. This is in agreement with the archaeological based model put forth by Otte[xxxix], who argues that the locus of early modern human expansion into Europe originated between Afghanistan and the Caucasus. In his review of archaeological data from the Middle-Upper Palaeolithic transitions in Europe, Asia, and Africa, Marks 2005 arrives at a similar conclusion: *The immediate origins of the explosion of "modern behaviour" seen in Europe, but not in Africa, might be found at the contact between Eastern Europe and Western Asia.*

Genetics of Early Farmers: Palaeogenetics

An international research team led by palaeogeneticists of Johannes Gutenberg University Mainz (JGU)[xl] published a study in the journal Science showing that the earliest farmers from the Zagros Mountains in Iran, i.e., the Eastern part of the Fertile Crescent, are neither the main ancestors of Europe's first farmers nor of modern-day Europeans. Dismay to all European Arians, the thousand-year Reich is definitely a nonstarter. *This came as a surprise*, said Farnaz Broushaki, first author of the study and a member of the JGU Palaeogenetics Group.

Our team had only recently shown that early farmers from across Europe have an almost unbroken trail of ancestry leading back to Northwest Anatolia. But now it seems that the chain of migration into Europe breaks somewhere in Eastern Anatolia.

According to the team's previous study, Neolithic settlers from Northern Greece and the Marmara Sea region of Western Turkey reached central Europe via a Balkan route and the Iberian Peninsula via a Mediterranean route. These colonists brought sedentary life, agriculture, and domestic animals and plants to Europe. New research shows that some of the world's earliest farmers from Iran were a genetically distinct group and only very distantly related to the first farmers of Western Anatolia and Europe.

It is interesting that people who are genetically so different, who almost certainly looked different and spoke different languages adopted the agricultural lifestyle almost simultaneously in different parts of Anatolia and the Near East, said Professor Joachim Burger, senior author of the study. *The group of prehistoric inhabitants of the Zagros region separated more than 50,000 years ago from other people of Eurasia and were among the first who invented farming.* Little did Joachim realise at the time that the people of Anatolia (Turkey) and the Near East been congregating together since 10,500 BC at Göbekli Tepe in the Taurus Mountains, sharing ideas on agriculture.

Professor Joachim Burger, his Mainz palaeogeneticists team, and international collaborators have pioneered Paleogenetic research of the Neolithization process in Europe over the last decade. In 2005, they presented the first ancient DNA study on prehistoric European farmers, [xli] and in 2009 and 2013 they analysed their complex interactions with hunter-gatherers. Now they demonstrated that the idea of *ex oriente lux* is true in cultural but not in genetic terms.

Marjan Mashkour, an Iranian archaeozoologist who works at the CNRS in Paris and initiated the study with Burger and Fereidoun Biglari, a prehistoric archaeologist at the National Museum of Iran.

The Neolithic way of life originates in the Fertile Crescent, maybe also some Neolithic pioneers started moving from there. But the majority of ancient Iranians did not move West as some would have thought.

However, they did move east, as the study shows. The research team found that the Iranian genomes represent the main ancestors of modern-day South Asians. Whilst sharing many segments of their genome with Afghani and Pakistani populations, the almost 10,000-year-old genomes from the Iranian Zagros Mountains were found to be most similar to modern-day Zoroastrians from Iran. *This religious group probably mixed less with later waves of people than others in the region and therefore preserved more of that ancient ancestry*, said Broushaki.

It may be said that at the time of the flooding of the Gulf Oasis, there had always been a natural separation of the people in the Gulf Oasis, the lakes, but more significantly the Ur Shatt River that ran central in the basin of the Gulf Oasis. Having similar language, yet distinctly different from people outside the Gulf Oasis.

Could be a main contributing factor why farming never migrated East to West from modern day Iran may have been due to the fact initial farming ideas where more prevalent in the Taurus Mountain region and expanded outwards in all directions from an epicentre at Göbekli Tepe. Therefore, not requiring a backflow from a region deemed to have lesser knowledge or experience. Later a further barrier existed for modern day Iran to be cut-off from the rest of the Northern area of the Fertile Crescent, *the Sumerians, a natural barrier to anybody. Possibly not the best time to come into close proximity when people of lesser standing* could be enslaved and made to work in the fields or on a building project. The best advice would be to look the other way, towards Pakistan and Afghanistan for trade goods and come to Sumeria as a merchant. Trying to teach Sumerians about farming would be similar to trying to sell a handheld catapult to a person holding an M16 assault rifle.

Could the region of the Zagros Mountains of the Eastern Fertile Crescent region have had their own version of Göbekli Tepe, a place for communal gathering to learn the latest farming technology of the day. It seems like at least two highly divergent groups became the world's first farmers: the Zagros people of the Neolithic eastern Fertile Crescent that are ancestral to most modern South Asians and the Aegean's that colonised Europe some 8,000 years ago. *The origin of farming was genetically more complex than we thought and instead of speaking of a single Neolithic centre, we should start adopting the idea of a Federal Neolithic Core Zone*, emphasised Burger.

Researchers have suggested that the successful AMH (Anatomical Human Man) colonists were coastally adapted groups that moved rapidly along the continental shelf rimming the Indian Ocean. This expansion is thought to have occurred during MIS 3-4, 60000 BC, at which time reduced sea levels made habitable vast tracks of fertile land along the exposed coastline[xlii]. Haplogroup R0a has an overall Middle Eastern coalescent age around 19,000 years ago and exhibits a high degree of diversity in Southern Arabia, indicating that it has persisted in the region for this entire span of time. Given the hypothesis proposed in this book, it is noteworthy that the most ancient R0a markers in Arabia are found in the UAE, with a predicted coalescence date of 37800-12100 BC.[xliii]

DNA Marsh Arabs (Madan) Link to the Sumerians

The search for the Genetic footprints of Sumerians[xliv]. (Original Article http://bmcevolbiol.biomedcentral.com) For millennia in Southern Mesopotamia has been a wetland region generated by the Rivers of the Tigris and the Euphrates, joining together to form the Al-Shatt then flowing into the Persian Gulf. This freshwater estuary is believed to have been continuously occupied by one single set of people since ancient times. These people are known as the Marsh Arabs who are considered the population with the strongest link to Ancient Sumerians. The Marsh Arabs have continuously been considered by sections of the Iraq Government as *a foreign group of unknown origin*.

Overtime, many historical and archaeological expeditions have been conducted with the Marsh Arabs of Southern Iraq and consistently reported to have numerous parallels between the modern and ancient lifestyle of the Marsh people. Similarities such as home architecture, particularly the large arched reed buildings, food gathering techniques, grazing, and rearing of water buffaloes, bird trapping, fish spearing, rice cultivation and means of transportation. The slender bitumen covered wooden or reed boats, sometimes up to 13 metres (made for Sheikhs) long called *tarada*.

All these are well documented skills meticulously written down for almost 5,000 years ago and these very same Marsh Arabs continue to follow these skills to the letter and let's be reminded they can't read ancient Sumerian for reference material. These commonly practiced skills by the indigenous population locally named *madan* or better known by the world as the *Marsh Arabs*, these skills are pasted down generation to generation. This village lifestyle seems unchanged for 8,200 years and possibly the most unspoilt indigenous population (barring a few tribes still in the Amazonian Jungles) in the world.

Empires have risen and disappeared many times over, the industrial revolution came and went. Even aviation has simply flew by, many wars have occurred at the very heart of their lands, the greatest leaders in the world Gilgamesh, Sargon, Cyrus, Alexander have ridden or driven past these lands, without even a second glimpse from any invading party. Yet these people who want for nothing and self-sufficient continue to pass on the same traditions, year after year, millennia after millennia. Since this tradition seems unchanged therefore a possible link between the present-day Marsh inhabitants and Ancient Sumerian isn't an impossibility.

In order to shed further light on the origin of the ancient and modern Mesopotamian populations and try and corroborate the hypothesis that they have common ancestry. Genetic variation of a sample of Marsh Arabs has been investigated both for the maternally transmitted mitochondrial DNA and the male specific region of the Y chromosome. The sample relates to samples consisting of 143 healthy unrelated males predominantly from the Al Hawizeh Marshes. For each subject, the Marsh Arabs' ancestry, at least for the last four generations, was ascertained by interview.

The collection of their blood samples was carried out in different villages during a field expedition, for comparison a sample of 154 Iraqi subjects' representative of the general Iraqi population was investigated for mitochondrial DNA and Y chromosome markers and this sample was mainly composed of Arabs living along the Tigris and Euphrates rivers. In addition, the distribution of the Y chromosome haplogroup J-1 Subclades was also investigated in four samples from Kuwait, Palestine, Israeli Druze, and Khuzestan (Southwest Iran) as well. A further 3,700 subjects from 39 populations, mainly from Europe and the Mediterranean area, but also from Africa and Asia.

1. *Analysis of the haplogroups and sub-haplogroups observed in the Marsh Arabs revealed a prevalent autochthonous (indigenous rather than descended) Middle Eastern component for both Male and Female gene pools with weak Southwest Asian and African contributions more evident in mitochondrial DNA. This testing provides a guarantee that the people of the 3rd Migration from the Gulf Oasis who later settled in this region are direct descendants, and more importantly no other region. A higher male than female homogeneity is characteristic of the Marsh Arab gene pool, likely due to a strong male genetic drift determined by socio-cultural factors, patrilocality (social system in which married couples reside), polygamy, unequal male, and female migration rates.*

The alluvial territory of Southern Mesopotamia which emerged progressively by soil sedimentation attracted various small populations from Northern and Eastern Mountain ranges, small settlements hugging the river and coastal regions. Sumerian and Semitic Akkad groups of population arrived in larger numbers and within 3,000 years managed to leave historical records via a writing system they invented. Sumerian civilisation began to flourish around 6000 BC in particular at Eridu, Ur and Uruk, not to say other outlying areas at the estuaries of both the Tigris and Euphrates Rivers. Whereas traces of their culture are present in the territory, as documented by the Ubaid Eridu pottery nothing is available for their identification.

The region of the Fertile Crescent had multiple variations of Semitic speaking people whilst the Sumerians spoke an isolated language not correlated to any linguistic family known in the region. The two groups occupied both the Southern area of Mesopotamia and their Deltas which is one of the oldest continuously occupied inhabited wetland environments in the world. Multiple ethnicities are known to have arrived in the region of Southern Mesopotamia at various times throughout its history helping to blur the lines. This is verified via ancient cuneiform citations of the day and also the Old Testament.

The story of the Temple of Babble or better known as the Eridu Ziggurat, many people from different regions descended open Eridu to build the Ziggurat but failed due to miscommunication due to multiple languages being spoken on the building site. Trade links with the Indian Subcontinent to both Sumer and Akkad are known to have existed 5,000 years ago. Multiple ancient wars and sacking of towns and cities also helps to confuse data being acquired for research. Another set of the Semitic Groups were semi nomadic people and lived predominantly in the Syro-Arabian Desert (Present Day Syria, Jordan, Northern Saudi Arabia, and Western Iraq) breeding small animals, eventually reaching Mesopotamia where they settled among the pre-existing populations. The Semitic people more numerous in the North and in the South the Sumerians where the predominant populace. Semitic speaking city states grew side by side in the region of Sumer eventually melting their cultures and laying the basis for Western Civilisation.

The Mesopotamian Marshes begin at the convergence of both the Tigris and Euphrates Rivers in Mesopotamia and the Karun River draining off the Iranian Plateau. The marshes are amongst the oldest and until 20 years ago the largest wetlands environments in South West Asia, mainly composed of three separate marshes, but adjacent to each other.

- Northern Al Hawizeh
- Southern Al Hammar
- Central Marsh

Rich in both natural resources and biodiversity, the majority of the subjects analysed for this study are from the Al Hawizeh Marshes. The ancient inhabitants of the Marsh Areas were Sumerians.

Two main scenarios have been proposed for the origins of Sumer:

- Scenario 1) The original Sumerians were a group of populations who had migrated from the Southeast India region and took the shoreline route through the Arabian Gulf before settling down in the Southern Marshes of Iraq.
- Scenario 2) That the advancement of the Sumerian Civilisation was the result of Human migrations from the mountainous area of North Eastern Mesopotamia to the southern Marshes of Iraq, ensuing an assimilation of the previous population.

Two main hypotheses have been proposed for the origins of the Marsh Arabs:

- They could be aboriginal inhabitants of Mesopotamia being correlated to the old Sumerians.
- They could be foreign people of unknown origin. Although the origin of Sumerians is yet to be clarified.

The two main scenarios being autochthonous versus foreign ancestry may have produced different genetic outcomes with multiple Marsh Arabs being genetically closer to the Middle Eastern groups or other populations, for example, those of the Indian Subcontinent.

Thus, in order to shed some light on this question, Marsh Arab population was investigated for mitochondrial DNA and Y chromosome markers. Due to their characteristic's uniparental transmission (All the genes in the offspring will originate from only the mother or only the father) and absence of recombination and their wide data sets. They are at present among the best genetic systems for detecting signs of ancient migration events and to evaluate socio-cultural behaviours. Although different western European mitochondrial DNA haplogroups were present in Middle Eastern Paleo Neolithic times they cannot always be interpreted as markers of Middle Eastern origin.

For example, even if the mitochondrial DNA haplogroup H had evolved in the Middle East circa 18,000 to 15,000 years ago, different H subgroups observed in this region, albeit at low a rather low frequency such as H1 rose outside and are most likely the result gene flow from Europe Y-Chromosome variation like that of mitochondrial DNA is highly geographically structured.

2. *However, Middle Eastern Haplogroup which accounts for the great majority of paternal lineages of this region and marks different migration events **towards** Europe, Africa and Asia does not display at present, evidence of back migration (Does not leave the region of Gulf Oasis and back to Africa when climatic conditions worsen!) Haplogroup J with its two branches J1 M267 and J2 M172 is a Y chromosome lineage dating to about 30,000 years ago its place of origin is still under discussion, but it is considered a landmark geographically linked to the Middle Eastern Region where the agricultural revolution and animal domestication appeared for the first time.*

Accordingly, the frequency distribution of HGJ shows radial decreasing clines towards the Levant Area, Central Asia, the Caucasus, North Africa, and Europe from focal points of high frequency in the Middle East. Although both clades involve in situ and participated in the Neolithic Revolution, their different geographic distributions suggest two distinct histories:

3. *While J2-M172 has been linked to the development and expansion of agriculture in the wetter northern zone and also considered the Y chromosome marker for the spread of farming into Southeast Europe.*
4. *J1-M267 has been associated with pastoralism in the semi-arid area of the Arabian Peninsula, despite this purported initial association, no evidence of pastoralism has ever been reported in the marsh area, where one of the J1M267 highest values of 81.1% has been observed.*
5. *Only a small proportion of the Marsh Arabs gene pool derives from gene flow from neighbouring regions, on the paternal side, our Phylogeographic data (geographic distribution of individuals) highlights some Southwest Asia specific contributions, different from the Iraqi control sample. The Marsh Arab gene pool displays a very scarce input from the Northern Middle East (Syria/Jordan/Israel) Could this be the climatic event 40,000 years ago that seen in early migration from the Levant Region down the fertile crescent and into the Gulf Oasis closer*

to the source of the Tigris and Euphrates Rivers. If the J2-M172 is from a distant ancestry, this could account for this reading.

6. *Virtually devoid of Western Eurasian (Afghanistan/Armenia/ Kazakhstan/Mongolia) and Sub-Saharan African (Rwanda/Kenya/ Ethiopia/Eritrea/Somalia) contributions.*

On the other hand, the absence in both the Iraqi groups of North African E M81 Branch, speaks against substantial patrilineage gene (pass through male lineage) flow from this region. On the maternal side (female) a significant East Southwest Asia component is present among Marsh Arabs this observation is likely due to recent gene flow. Worth noting that the ancient silk road passed through the Iraqi region from Basra to Baghdad.

7. *In comparison with the general Iraqi population, the Marsh Arabs are characterised by an important lower Y Chromosome Heterogeneity (Diversity Gene, lack of movement, throughout, no cross pollination with other areas!) the J1-M267 alone characterises more than 80% of the Marsh Y Chromosome gene pool.*

Although patterns of lower male than female Heterogeneity have been reported in many populations and usually ascribed to patrilocal residence (wife moving into husbands' home), such a scenario can only explain part of the large difference observed in the geographically isolated Marsh Population. Among the different factors ergo polygamy, unequal male and female migration rates and selective process that can differently affect the extent of Mitochondrial DNA and Y Chromosome Heterogeneity, non-random mating practices common in the area in association with Cultural beliefs that support polygamy (Partnership chosen to strengthen family ties) may have contributed to cause the difference observed in the Marsh Arabs.

8. *Haplogroup J accounts for 55.1% of Iraqi samples reaching 84.6% in the Marsh Arabs, one of the highest frequencies reported so far. Unlike the Iraqi sample, which displays a roughly equal proportion of J1-M267 (56.4%) and J2-M172 (43.6%) almost ALL Marsh Arabs J Chromosome (96%) belongs to J1-M267 clade and in particular to Sub-Hg. A distinct difference between the people boarding the two rivers in Iraq and the*

Marsh Arabs. The DNA evidence shows the people of the Marsh region are the true descendants of the region, all the way back to the Gulf Oasis.

Conclusion: Evidence of genetic stratification ascribable to the Sumerian development was provided by the Y-Chromosome data where J1-M267 branch reveals a local expansion almost contemporary with the Sumerian city state period. Very interestingly a more ancient background shared with Northern Mesopotamia is revealed by the less represented Y-Chromosome lineage J1-M267. This maybe an indication that hunter-gatherers of the Levant Region in 45,000 BC possibly due to the onset of a climatic adversity moved South using the Gulf Oasis as a refuge. The data shows that the modern Marsh Arabs of Iraq harbour Mitochondrial DNA and Y Chromosome Heterogeneity, that are predominantly of Middle Eastern origin. Therefore, certain cultural features of the area such as:

Water buffalo breeding and rice farming may have been introduced from the Indian Subcontinent via the expansive trade routes that aid the growth of the Sumerian Region. Only marginally affected the gene pool of the autochthonous people of the region.

More importantly, a Middle Eastern origin of the Modern population of the Marsh Arabs of Southern Iraq implies that if the Marsh Arabs are descendants of the ancient Sumerian, also Sumerians were not of Indian or Southern Asian ancestry. Although the Y Chromosome age estimates deserve caution particularly when sample sizes are small and standard errors large, but it is interesting to note that these estimates overlapped the city states period which characterised Southern Mesopotamia and is testified to by numerous ancient Sumerian cities such as Eridu, Lagash, Ur, Uruk and Larsa.

DNA of Bovine

The keeping of livestock began in the Ancient Near East and underpinned the emergence of complex economies and then Cities. Subsequently, it is there that the world's first Empires rose and fell. Now, ancient DNA has revealed how the prehistory of the region's largest domestic animal, the cow, seems to chime with these events. An international team of geneticists, led by members of Trinity College Dublin, have deciphered early bovine prehistory by sequencing 67 ancient genomes from both wild and domestic cattle sampled from across eight millennia.[xlv] Marta said Post-Doctoral Researcher at Trinity author of the article published international journal, *Science*:

This allowed us to look directly into the past and observe genomic changes occurring in time and space, without having to rely on modern cattle genetic variation to infer past population events.

The earliest cattle are Bos Taurus, with no ancestry from Bos indicus, or zebu herds which were from a different origin in the Indus Valley.

However, a dramatic change occurred around 4,000 years ago (4.2K Climate Event) when we detect a widespread, wholesale influx of zebu genetics from the east, added Verdugo.

People from the Indus Valley region seem to have come to the rescue and probably supplied Water Buffalo that could stay within the Reed Deltas along with the Marsh Arabs. The rapid influx that occurred at this point despite Near Eastern Bos Taurus and zebu having coexisted for previous millennia being intrinsically linked to the dramatic 150 years drought experienced across the entire Middle East, the 4.2K climate event. At this time the world's first Empires in Mesopotamia and Egypt collapsed and breeding with arid-adapted zebu bulls may have been a response to changing climate by ancient herders.[xlvi] Professor of Population Genetics at Trinity, Dan Bradley, said:

This was the beginning of the great zebu diaspora that continues to the present-day descendants of ancient Indus Valley cattle are herded in each continental tropics region today.

Sequencing Near Eastern wild cattle, or aurochs, also allowed the team to unpick the domestication of this most formidable of beasts. Whereas their similarity to the early cattle of Anatolia concurs with a primary origin there. It is clear that different local wild populations also made significant additional genetic contributions to herds in Southeast Europe and also in the Southern Levant. Adding to the distinctive make up of both European and African populations today. But what is significant during the 4.2K climate event that eventually brought down the Akkadian Empire. A problem with local domestic cattle was witnessed during this period of time and a positive solution sourced, over 2,500 Km away and acted upon, with positive results.

4. Language

Brief History of the Sumerian Language

Sumerian is a language isolate with no known relatives. It was the dominant language of South Mesopotamia whilst surrounded on all sides by Semitic speaking regions, until it was eventually superseded by Akkad Semitic and stopped being used as the main language around 2,334 BC. Eventually giving way to Babylonian. But it continued to survive as a scholarly and liturgical language, much like mediaeval Latin, until the very end of cuneiform in the late 1st Millennium BCE.

In the absence of related languages, Sumerian has had to be learned through the filter of Babylonian and Assyrian. There are still many disagreements about what words mean, and how the verb behaves, but through all these disagreements our knowledge of it is growing by the year. There is still no full dictionary of Sumerian, though the Sumerian-French lexicon posted online by the Swiss scholar Pascal Attinger would seem to be extremely useful. There is no learner's grammar of Sumerian that can straightforwardly be recommended. Non-specialists may find grammar of 3rd Millennium BC Sumerian by the Dutch scholar Bram Jagersma heavy-going. The open-access publication[xlvii] *Introduction to the Grammar of Sumerian* by Gábor Zólyomi is more accessible or should I say more palatable.

Sumerian language may be a language isolate but it is the oldest written language in existence. I would like to place this into context and use Europe as an example. If the populace of the Fertile Crescent spoke English, German, French, Italian and Spanish then the people of Sumeria spoke Japanese, this is the reason for describing the language as an isolate. People of the Fertile Crescent spoke various languages, but the base connection was that they all spoke a form of Semitic language, unlike Sumer.

First written around 3200 BC in Southern Mesopotamia, it flourished during the 3rd Millennium BC. In 2334 BC, Sumerian was replaced as a spoken language by Semitic Akkadian (Assyro-Babylonian). The *old* but highly regarded language of Sumer was still used extensively attested in legal and administrative texts, as well as in royal inscriptions, which are often bilingual, in Sumerian and Babylonian. It is also believed that the Sumerian language was used for prayers and incantations within the temple complexes of the emerging Kingdoms such as the Assyrians and Babylonians.

The Sumer language continued in written usage almost to the end of the life of the Assyrian language, around the beginning of the Christian era. Sumeria didn't extend much beyond its original boundaries in Southern Mesopotamia apart from Uruk colonies sent out to expand its trading routes. The small number of its native speakers was entirely out of proportion to the tremendous importance and influence Sumerians exercised on the development of Mesopotamian and other ancient civilisations similar to Britain before its Empire and worldwide expansion.

Data Mining the Sumerian Vocabulary

Until these languages could be written down, deciphering the ancient languages would have been impossible. Writing down the history of human accomplishments seems to have been considered a matter of little importance prior to the growth of populations and industries, and as a result the early history of Sumer has been deduced from archaeological and geological records alone. Therefore, the written tradition and a wealth of information is still and will remain unavailable to modern scholars concerning the rise of the first city states that took route within the Sumerian civilisation that was first established in the region by 5500 BC, the end of Ubaid 0 and the start of Ubaid 1: 5400-4700 BC.

By 5500 BC, the Early Mesopotamians had invented the wheel, the sailboat, opened trading routes through the Persian Gulf and beyond, agricultural processes such as irrigation, domestication of farm animals and the embryonic concept of cities had firmly taken root. The first city states in the world generally accepted by scholars in the world rose in Sumer and among the most important were Eridu, Uruk, Lagash, Nippur, Ur, Larsa, Isin, Elam the majority of these first colonies situated close to the newly formed Persian Gulf in 6200 BC.

Proto-Euphratic

Proto-Euphratean is a hypothetical unclassified language or languages which were considered by some Assyriologists, to be the substratum language of the people that introduced intensive farming into Southern Iraq in the Early Ubaid period 5,300-4,700 BC, relating to a precursor of Sumerian Culture. Benno Landsberger and other Assyriologists argued that by examining the structure of Sumerian names of occupations, as well as toponyms and hydronyms. This then lends itself to suggest that there was once an earlier group of people in the region, who spoke an entirely different language. Often referred to as Proto-Euphratean.

Terms for *farmer, smith, carpenter* and *date* (as in the fruit) also do not appear to have a Sumerian or Semitic origin. Sometimes known as a *banana language* based on a characteristic feature of multiple personal names attested in Sumerian texts. Namely reduplication of syllables (like in the word banana): Inanna, Zababa, Chuwawa, Humbaba, Bunene, etc. The same feature was attested in some other unclassified languages, including Minoan. It seems that evidence shows the *borrowing from more than one language*. This theory is now predominant in the field. A related proposal by Gordon Whittaker is that the language of the proto-literary texts from the Late Uruk period (3,350–3,100 BC) is an early Indo-European language which he terms *Euphratic*.

Sumerian Language is Known to Have Had Two Main Dialects

Peter Revesz[xlviii], Department of Computer Science and Engineering University of Nebraska-Lincoln, states: Data mining the Sumerian language is known to have had two main dialects which reveal an incomplete integration of two language families of the Emeĝir and the Emesal dialects of Sumerian language. With the former having mostly Dravidian (Tamil) and the latter mostly Uralic (Siberian) cognates, indicating that Sumerian arose predominantly as a combination of two languages from those language families. That would explain why Sumerian has some word similarities with many languages.

Could this mixing of the languages have originated through the expansion into Jericho in 7,000 BC and the local populace Semitic speaking people. For example, many words have similarities between Emeĝir Sumerian and Dravidian/Tamil and Emesal Sumerian with Uralic/Hungarian. There is also commonality between 3 of the groups or sometimes four.

The chart below presents a brief snapshot of the similar word groups that existed in Sumerian and the relationship between Uralic/Hungarian Dravidian/Tamil. The natural question that arises is which of the two language families existed earlier in Mesopotamia and which came later to the area. What was the original language of Mesopotamia? Whittaker identified an early substrate language within Sumerian that he called Euphratic which would seem to have deeper roots of the Ubaid Culture that had spread throughout the Fertile Crescent to the Gulf Oasis but still having several links with Dravidian/Tamil. Could Dravidian/Tamil have been a language from the Gulf Oasis that was closest to the land bridge that connected the Gulf Oasis and the Indian Subcontinent.

By the time the Gulf Oasis had finally come to its demise, the local populace of the Gulf Oasis had moved into the area of the mouth of the Tigris, Euphrates and Karun Rivers and started to establish the city states and using all the technologies that they had developed in the Gulf Oasis with them.

It should also be noted that Elam also had Dravidian/Tamil (Indian Sub-Continent) cognates which could indicate that the same point of origin prior to finally settling in Sumer and Elam. This indicates that both sets of languages have a common source being the Gulf Oasis. The Ur Shatt River now submerged could have been the dividing point as the sea encroached into the Gulf Oasis, thus widening—*bursting the banks*—of the Ur-Shatt River and thus further dividing the common people of the Gulf Oasis. A basic example is the Angles and Saxon coming to Britain in 450 AD, the British language is similar to the Germanic language but vastly different overtime, merging with surrounding areas and the creation of a new language.

Words with Unknown Origins

At the same time these original studies took place, it was found that several Hungarian words with an unknown origin appeared, that may be cognate with Sumerian words or ancient Greek or Minoan words. These statistics where not gathered on these words because a systematic search would need to consider a huge set of words, that is, much more than the few hundred well-established words that belong to the Uralic, Finno-Ugric and Ugric layers. But it should also be noted that a number of words are also not shared with the Ob-Ugric group of Khanty and Mansi languages suggests that there was a West-Ugric language that was a common origin of Proto-Hungarian, Proto-Minoan and Proto-Sumerian.

There are two scenarios that could have been the reason of the introduction of West-Ugric within the Sumerian language.

1. Could this group be the Homo Sapiens that moved into the Gulf Oasis from the Northern areas of the Fertile Crescent around 45,000 BC after the climate change in the Levant and the introduction of Neanderthal. These Homo Sapiens had successfully inhabited the region up to 80,000 years and gradually spreading throughout the entire Northern Region and Southern Anatolia and possibly beyond. Could this be the origins of West-Ugric?
2. Could this be *part* of the group that re-entered the region of Sumeria 6,000 BC having left Jericho and the Southern Taurus region after *hearing* the flooding of a region north of Anatolia, now known as the Black Sea. The majority of these migrants already descendants of the Gulf Oasis but now bringing indigenous people from the North back into Southern Mesopotamia.

We are already aware of migration patterns and weather conditions using Marine Isotope Stages (MIS) records. Using the DNA information from the Marsh Arabs, *ancient background shared with Northern Mesopotamia is revealed by the less represented Y-Chromosome lineage J1-M267*. DNA and West-Ugric would indicate that a distant relative from the Northern Region be more agreeable to both the Language and DNA evidence and a clearer picture immerging.

Word Samples

English	Uralic/Hungarian	Emesal Sumerian	Emeĝir Sumerian	Dravidian/Tamil
Boil, cook	súl < sút	zil		
Dry up (field)	szik	šeĝ		
Extract	szül	zal		
Bowl	tál	útul		
Bury, hide	zug (nook, hiding place)	zé-èg		
Word	ének (song)	e-ne-èĝ		

What			eṉṉa	ana
Lord	nem	nam	āṉ (man)	Na (man)
Woman	nő	nu-nus		munus
Good	szép	ze-eb		
Lament	sír	a-še-er	kaṇṇīr (tears)	anir
Slave	ara	ere	arad	

The Sumerian Grammar

The Sumerian grammar is already described in several textbooks, for example, by[xlix] Foxvog, Gosztonyi and Thomsen. Among those authors, Gosztonyi gives a detailed comparison between Sumerian and the Hungarian grammars. While Sumerian clearly does not fit neatly into the Uralic family tree, Gosztonyi's list of similarities supports the hypothesis that Sumerian is a mixed Dravidian/Tamil and Uralic language. The Dravidian/Tamil and Sumerian grammatical comparisons also need to develop and listed in a similar manner before being able to decide which language family's grammatical features are present and to what degree.

If you feel you have followed the understanding, so now I'll complicate the picture a bit more, is the fact that Dravidian and Uralic languages are both agglutinative (words consisting of many elements, rather than using isolated elements) and share some other features. For these common features, one cannot decide whether they are inherited from one or the other language family.

Sumerian Tamil Connection

We must also look at language similarities between Sumerian and archaic Tamil (Dravidian).[1] The vowels correspondences between Su (Sumerian) and Ta (Tamil). The spoken language was around thousands of years before the written word was invented, therefore Tamil and Sumerian may have the same source. Please note these are but a very small proportion of vowels and only shown a small example to show the similarities.

Su. a Ta. am = water
Su. aka Ta. Akam = love
Su. ambar Ta. Amparam = sea marsh
Su. amma Ta. amma = mother
Su. Ara Ta. arai = to grind

Su. arali Ta. arali = terrifying
Su. abbal Ta. Aval = curseSu. uname Ta. uLamai = whatever existing
Su. kalam Ta. kalam = boatSu. kar-ra Ta. Karai = quay
Su. kak Ta. Kakam = arrow.
Su. a-. Ta. aa-
Su. ag, ak Ta. aakku = to make do and aaku: become Su. ara Ta. aaraay = investigate
Su. a-ra- Ta. aaRu = course, way
Su. sar Ta. caRRu = to write, relate
Su. sal Ta. caal = to be weary.
Su. a'-: Ta. aa-
Su. a' Ta. aay = wages, toll
Su. aga Ta. aaNai = command
Su. a'm. Ta. aa = to become
Su. a'r Ta. Aar = fullness
Su. m'as Ta. maan = gazelle
Su. g'al, k'al Ta. kaal 'to place'

Furthermore, on the basis of some linguistic and literary evidence, it can be argued that Sumerian could certainly be a close relative of Tamil of the First CaGkam (Archaic Tamil) and that Sumer the cradle of human civilisation is none other than Lemuria, the cradle of Dravidian civilisation. Hypotheses that the Sumerian language is archaic Tamil language or is archaic Tamil a Gulf Oasis language enjoyed by both cultures. Are the Tamil people the *Black-Headed Ones* who served the Righteous Ones? Is Lemuria[14] as described in ancient Tamil and Sanskrit literature once a part of a lost continent (with relatives on two continents) that took thousands of years to disappear below the waves, could it be describing the Gulf Oasis.

Shuruppak's Ne-Ri: Grammatical comparison of Sumerian and Tamil with English translation:

1. **Sumerian:** us si-ga kaskal si-ga-am (A safe foundation is a safe road).
2. **Tamil;** uc.i siGka kasikaal siGka aam (Having a good goal is moving in the good road).

---

[14] *Lemuria is the mysterious "Lost Land (Flooded)" and according to Tamil legend to have been civilised for over 20,000 years.*

3. **Sumerian:** kaskal gi na-du sa-bi sag hul-a (Do not walk on the road at night, its interior is (both) good and bad).
4. **Tamil:** kasikaal mai naa. Udu saaybi saan olla (Do not walk in dark streets, inside there may be evil people).
5. **Sumerian:** anse.edin-na na-ab-sam ugula da-bi-es -e-zal (Do not buy a steppe-ass, constantly the foreman(?) must...at its side.
6. **Tamil:** ansee eetilla naa aab sum.u uukku. Lu idabiceeee cel? (Do not buy a wild horse, rider has to go to its side always?)
7. **Sumerian:** geme-zu-ur gis na-an-du zu-ur su-mu--ri-in-sa (Do not have sexual intercourse with your slave girl, she will call you: Traitor!
8. **Tamil:** kaimmee soora kuc.i naa.an idu soor suu muRaiyin col (Do not have sexual intercourse with an immoral woman, she will announce it to the public).
9. **Sumerian:** as a.zi na-ab-bal-e su-us im-si-nigin (Do not curse with violence, it will turn around your hands).
10. **Tamil:** aasi azi naa avallee suur-usu imsi niiGkin (Do not curse for the destruction of others, it will torture you for a long time).

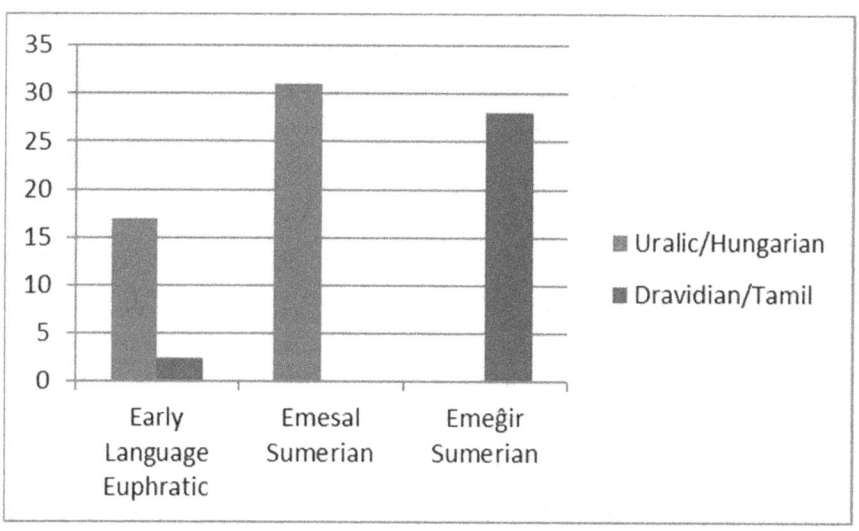

The number of Euphratic, Emesal and Emeĝir cognates with Hungarian/Uralic and Dravidian/Tamil. So, what we might actually be witnessing is the Gulf Oasis consisting of at least two Sumerian languages, in fact we haven't even been looking at Elam (Southern Iran) also another language isolate, or is it a variation? So, if we take the scenario we had earlier. Just as you have several Semitic languages in the Fertile Crescent you will have had several Sumerian languages within the Gulf Oasis.

Therefore, my vocal analogy prior to the Gulf Oasis flooding, you may have had English, German, French, Italian and Spanish as the Semitic Speaking countries of the Fertile Crescent and China, Korea, Vietnam, Thailand, and Japan as the Sumerian speaking nations of Gulf Oasis. Yes, they are totally different, but aren't when compared to their peer group members.

Language Isolate?

It has always looked counterintuitive to have Sumerian be a language isolate given its location in Mesopotamia, which is essentially at the intersection of three continents. It turns out that instead of being a language isolate; Sumerian is actually the combination of at least two major language families. In this book we have identified Dravidian (Indian Sub-Continent) and Uralic and in particular Proto-Tamil and Proto-Hungarian, respectively within those two language families as major contributors to the development of Sumerian. It cannot be excluded currently that a third language to be still identified also contributed to Sumerian.

The use of DNA and understanding the migration paths of the first modern man out of Eastern Africa and then some groups later arriving from the Levant and into the Gulf Oasis could be the point source of the third language. It has to be understood that people overtime didn't know which direction their ancestors had travelled. Whilst climatic changes over time may have forced people back in the direction their ancestors had come from. It seems that the great difficulty in classifying the Sumerian language was not its isolation but its varied interconnections with several other languages.

There still remains much work to be done to fill in the details. In particular, the chronology of the development of Sumerian and its related languages needs to be worked out in more detail over time. It is hoped that the complete settling of the Sumerian language will shed a major light on the origins and prehistory of languages in general.

5. Geology

In and Around the Persian Gulf: Gulf Oasis

The reason for incorporating this small but critical section concerning Geology is to highlight several points, the composition of the seabed in the Persian Gulf with exact dating. It also highlights the richness of the soils below the seabed giving a definitive understanding of the composition of the surroundings during the Last Glacial Maximum (LGM) and thirdly how much subterranean water exists in this region.

Even though this is only limited evidence being provided, it is still extremely important in *putting the pieces of the jigsaw together* and understanding the bigger picture. Before the sea level increased by 120 metres consuming the Gulf Oasis this *valley* virtually oozed water from its geological structure formed over millions of years. It highlights how the Gulf Oasis was amply supplied with fresh water, that helped aid prosperity in the region and support both fauna and life for over 125,000 years. We can now only highlight remaining water sources visible and accounts taken in history.

Currently, much of the subterranean freshwater upwells from beneath the central Gulf through karstic limestone lining the basin, called *khawakb* in local Bahraini dialect. *Coastal Oases* are likely to have formed around these khawakb when reduced sea levels exposed the surrounding landscape and triggered increased pressure on the hydrostatic head of the aquifers.[li] The island of Bahrain, meaning in Arabic *the two seas* is thought to reference the dual saltwater sea surrounding the island and freshwater sea upwelling from the submerged floor of the Gulf.

Portuguese Explorer Pedro Teixeira

Below is the account witnessing the local exploitation of khawakb during his visit in 1603 of the Portuguese explorer Pedro Teixeira[lii] William Sinclair who wrote:

There is water in plenty, rather brackish than sweet. The best is that of Nanya'h, the name of certain very deep wells in the centre of the isle. The next is that got from the bottom of the sea, as follows. The chief town of the isle, Manama, is on the seashore, and near it, in the depth of three or three and a-half fathoms, are several great springs of fresh, clear, and wholesome water. There are some men who make their living by bringing it up from below in water skins, which they do very cleverly and easily, where it bubbles up, and sell it cheap. Certain of the oldest Moors of the isle, with whom I spoke of this, told me that these springs were once far inland; but the sea broke in and overflowed them, as we see at this day.

This just solidifies my belief that oral traditions can last far longer than what is currently believed. As described in the text in 1603 *told me that these springs were once far inland; but the sea broke in and overflowed them, as we see at this day.* An oral account that had lasted for over 8,600 year (You can never beat a good story!). It can't be stressed enough that original texts, be it of the gods or biblical script always contains many strands of truth within. These texts need constantly re-examined as more discoveries are unearthed yearly.

The Facts Outweigh the Theory

For me, this is the Eureka moment when I started to seriously believe that the facts outweighed the theory. This section is a major intersection between Climatology and Geology which accurately and precisely gives an exact time of when Climatology experts stated the rise in sea levels. Backed up by the evidence from core samples taken in the Persian Gulf within the last 20 years, which collaborates those dates. More importantly, these dates fall perfectly in line with events that have been archeologically proven within the Region.

All dates are independent of each other but all correlate to the same date of a specific event that triggered a chain of events that turned the known world on its head. Also add the oral traditions as described by Pedro Teixeira in 1603 about the flooding. Add into the equation soil samples taken in the area reveal the overlying layer, bracketed from 10000 to 4000 BC, is carbonate-rich mud signalling increasingly brackish, marine conditions. This stratum is interpreted as a period of rising sea levels that induced marine conditions within the basin.

The uppermost unit, laid down from 6,000 years ago to present, is composed of carbonate-rich marls characteristic of the current depositional environment. From this, it can be inferred that sea levels have remained relatively stable in the interim.

The lowest unit is made up of silty alluvium attesting to the existence of an ancient river plain before 7,000 BC. BOOM! This is the Eureka Date. The floodplain horizon is capped by a peat layer that formed between approximately 7,000–6500 BC, at which time the rising water table and advancing shoreline transformed the plain into a freshwater marsh and estuarine environment.

By 3500 BC, marine transgression had completely inundated the plain, evidenced by the transition from tidal flat to coastal Shoreline. Reconstructions of marine incursion into the Persian Gulf show that the Indian Ocean ingresses more than 1,000 km between 12,000 and 6,000 years ago. Models of lateral transgression predict a relatively slow, gradual rise in sea level punctuated by a rapid phase of incursion from 10000 to 9000 BC, followed by a second phase from 7000 to 6200 BC, at which times the coastline advanced upward of 1 km per year in some places.

Populations would have expanded from the exposed shelf coastal living when sea levels where extremely low into the hinterland during pluvial episodes from 55,000 to 24,000 years ago and more importantly from 12,000 to 6,000 years ago. Based on this evidence above we can quite accurately surmise that modern techniques start to route themselves at this point. Using various scientific methods to discover what is happening from the very beginning, triangulation points or points of interception continue to show the same data, no matter the scientific method. The Origins of the Sumerians originate from the Gulf Oasis.

The Terminal Pleistocene Early Holocene phase of postglacial flooding coincides with an increase in annual precipitation, which generated both *pulling* mechanisms from amelioration of the interior that drew populations into the hinterlands, as well as *pushing* mechanisms caused by marine inundation of the exposed lowlands. The Holocene incursion was the first time since MIS 5e 125-120,000 Years ago that the Indian Ocean had ingressed so far into the basin.

Consequently, the Gulf Oasis hypothesis predicts an abrupt spike in human settlement after 6,200 BC, at which time displaced communities were forced to retreat upslope as sea levels submerged the floodplain. The presence of archaeological sites around the hinterlands of the basin supports this claim, demonstrating a long tradition of human occupation in the region for more than 100,000 years.

6. Archaeology

Discovering the Past

The lack of resources in Southern Mesopotamia that hindered the First People in settling the region happens to have been a blessing for archaeologists. Wood could easily decay over time. As stone was a scarce commodity, only the first couple of layers of a home would have been stone and the straw mud walls would eventually decay and the house rebuilt. The new mud bricks brought in to build a home on top of existing old property, this happened continuously over millennia, until the entire town is eventually many metres above the surrounding landscape. In this region, this is called a Tell.

Also, the foundations for all the buildings are now like miniature time capsules and archaeologists can glean a wealth of information from the excavation sites. The information contained within these multiple foundation levels has been preserved because they have been totally ignored, apart from the odd local looking for any item of antiquity that they can sell. Going through delicate sites like a bull in a china shop, destroying everything in their wake. Not just homes but government buildings, places of worship, palaces, workshops, foundries all these sites can give the archaeologist and the wider community a good understanding of what was happening at a different time in history.

The stratigraphy of these sites gives the modern archaeologist a clear understanding of what went before. But some of the greater Cities/Tells continued to have been inhabited and modern living continues unabated like the city of Aleppo or Damascus in Syria, or Jericho in the Palestine, also like Alexandria in Egypt, modern living cannot be removed for the vanity of archaeology. In these highly populated areas, the archaeologist can only wait for a moment of opportunity and also government approval to be able to perform any controlled digs.

The wealth of information that can be gleaned from the site can give the archaeologist a better understanding or a new insight in how people previously interacted. Fortunately, the majority of the ancient Sumerian cities in the Southern region of Mesopotamia that previously existed and now consumed by the deserts of modern Iraq have very few modern dwellings situated on the Tells. It may be good for the Archaeologist, but it is also good for the opportunists who scour these sites looking to discover ancient antiquities that can be sold on the black market where there are plenty of eager buyers.

Understanding the Southern region of Mesopotamia is vital to our understanding of world history. Whatever happens in the future there is only ever one beginning. The first laws, the first Cities, the first writing. The first evidence of writing started approximately 3,200 BC on clay tablets. Unlike papyrus that was commonly used in Egypt, papyrus easily degrades in a relatively short span of time so very few records have survived. The majority of saved papyrus scripts have been unearthed and recovered from Tombs which managed to preserve these few scripts. Yet the clay tablets used in Mesopotamia that carry the written word have endured the sands of time and have now been preserved for all eternity in their 100's thousands.

The best-preserved examples of clay tablets discovered by archaeologists are from periods of history when the buildings containing the tablets had been accidentally or deliberately burnt. It is similar to baked bricks; they become harder and far more durable. At the time of the original fire this would have been a tragic time, but for the archaeologist, possibly one of the greatest moments of discovery.

Middle Holocene (8,326 to 4,200 Years Ago) Settlement Activity in Eastern Arabia

The world's seas had abated and finally came to rest marking the start of the Middle Holocene. There seems to be a noticeable spike in settlement activity around the shoreline of the Gulf between 8,500 and 6,000 years ago. In particular, the millennium lasting from 5,500 to 4,500 BC witnessed a dramatic increase in the number of archaeological sites around Persian Gulf. Thus, greater archaeological visibility, and other indications in the material record suggest that the inhabitants of the region underwent a fundamental demographic transformation. Or the rise in settlement may simply be, people moving from large communities or city states and deciding, it simply isn't for them, a movement a conscious decision to have moved away. Afterall, they are human, and nobody is better than going left of field than modern humans.

Middle Holocene sites around the Gulf are distinguished by the appearance of Mesopotamian-style plain and painted pottery called *Ubaid ware* (stylistically). Ceramics from these sites predominantly fall within the Ubaid 3 to Ubaid 5 archaeological phases but earlier examples are found.

Chronology of Pottery Neolithic

People have to eat, and pottery serves as a great way for storage and presenting people with the food of the day.[liii] Pottery has gone through multiple iterations and is an extremely useful way of being able to date, the time and the place that development are first witnessed in an area. (Until the next find turns everything on its head!)

With this in mind, I would like to point to Neolithic Pottery discoveries in various locations in the Middle East that point to something missing and to raise the question why? Where does the Gulf Oasis fit into these results below? We can all appreciate that a cataclysmic event occurred in 7,000 BC within the Gulf Oasis and a migration of people having be forced away from their life and homes and was forced to leave the *once safe haven* for a new land to live in.

We see archaeological evidence of vast changes in the Northern region of the Fertile Crescent at exactly 7,000 BC, everything seems to change. Also, the appearance of pottery in so many areas in and around the same time period of 7,000 BC beggars the question. Could the point of initiation be from one localised event that propagated throughout an entire area that had an accessible conduit as its means of entry into these new regions. We all know the rise of the Muslims and how quickly they advanced into these very same lands. There seems to be a very similar scenario, in a very similar area, but 7,400 years prior to the rise of Muslim. Pottery may not have been invented in 7,000 BC it may have arrived in the region in 7,000 BC. People from a different place could easily have brought pottery with them.

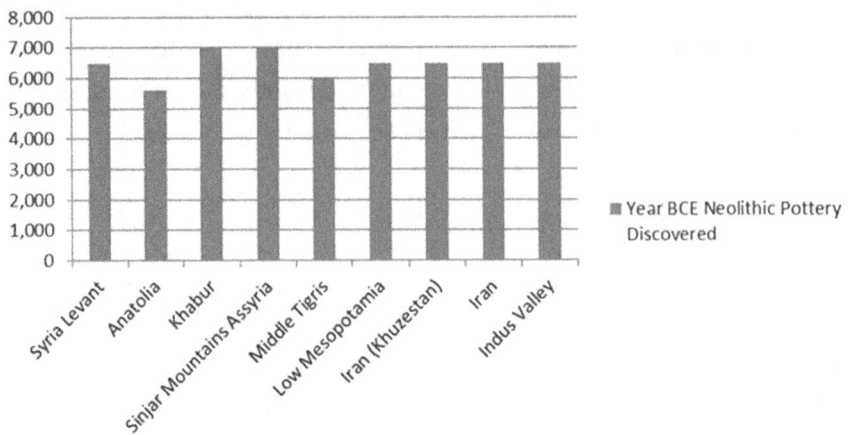

Conclusion to the Dating of Pottery

From archaeological evidence and the hypothesis that connection between different cultures was known prior to or starting around 7000 BC.

- Khabur lays on a fertile estuary off the Euphrates River which is the more navigable of the two main rivers of Mesopotamia to the delta pouring into the Persian Gulf.
- Sinjar Mountains (Assyria) due to its size and location eventually feeds into both the Euphrates River and the Tigris and contact with Khabur would not seem insurmountable. Therefore, contact could also be made South, through Mesopotamia to the delta pouring into the Persian Gulf onwards to the Gulf Oasis. As Neolithic Pottery in the Middle Tigris (currently) dates from 6,000 BC then the route may have been via the Euphrates.
- Lower Mesopotamia, Iran, Khuzestan (Elam), Indus Valley Neolithic pottery all start to be dated from 6,500 BC. All areas at the same time adopted the Neolithic Pottery or did the pottery already exist prior to this period and the knowledge brought from the insatiable flooding Gulf Oasis. Could the people of the Northern part of Mesopotamia already have made regular contact with the people of the Gulf Oasis? Could the pottery of the Indus Valley also have originated from the Gulf Oasis and when the people were forcibly separated due to the incoming salt waters

of the Indian Ocean swelling the Ur Shatt River. Some of the indigenous people headed towards the Indus and others continued to move North up the Gulf, some to the area of Pre-Elam and others to the area of Pre-Sumer, whilst some moved up onto the Iran Plain and directly into Iran.

- Another notable point from the graph above. The Syrian Levant also experienced the Neolithic Pottery advancement in 6,500 BC, could these people have had a direct link to the Gulf Oasis via the Coast of Oman and into the Red Sea or straight up the Rivers flowing in the opposite direction through Mesopotamia, looking for a new place to lay down new roots. Did the people of the Gulf Oasis already know of this area and head directly to the lush green new lands.

- The surprising fact that Neolithic Pottery in Anatolia only starts to flourish in 5,500 BC which seems quite a surprise, when so much early Neolithic buildings have been found in the Region, could this suggest that the people of the area still relied on semi-agriculture and still performed Hunter-Gathering at the same time. Or was this the mass exodus from the region that occurred in 6,000 BC due to the Euxine flooding. I believe archaeological will push this to an earlier time.

Farming Archaeology

Another reason for the early significance of this area in World History is the fact that the water supply and the climate were ideal for the introduction of agriculture. Several species of grain grew wild, and there were marshes and tributary streams that could easily be drained or dammed in order to sow wild wheat and barley. The seed had only to be strewn over a sufficiently moist surface to ensure some kind of crop under normal conditions. It is therefore not surprising that there is evidence of simple agriculture as far back as the 9th-10th Millennium BC, especially in Palestine, where more excavating has been done in early sites than in any other country of the Middle East.

Many bone sickle handles and flint sickle edges dating from between 11,000-9,500 BC have been found in Palestinian sites, predominantly in the Levant Valley where multiple excavation continue to this day. As stated by Joachim Burger[liv]: *we should start adopting the idea of a Federal Neolithic Core Zone.* The excavation sites at the West of the Fertile Crescent help Archaeologist understand how agriculture adapted over time and as explained by DNA (mtDNA) the genetic markers now discovered in the Zagros Mountains.

Gulf Oasis was split into various agricultural areas due to its physical attributes. The central area of the Oasis was supported by the freshwater lakes more reliant on freshwater fishing, pastoral farming supported by hunting. The larger Lake would have acted as an expansion tank which would lessen Spring Flooding beyond the lakes. (this group would be predominantly the largest group). Whilst the Northern region of the Gulf Oasis had the potential for irrigation style farming. The people would have been cultivating Dates, Mangos, Grapes, Garlic, Vegetables due to the alluvium slit deposits every springtime. The farming would not be wheat and barley. The crops would have been more diverse and less intensive compared to future farming techniques used in Southern Mesopotamia.

In Mesopotamia and Iran, remains of this period appear in caves on the lower slopes of the Zagros Mountains between Western Iran and Iraq. The date of the systematic introduction of irrigation on a large scale in Mesopotamia is somewhat obscured due to the early sites of irrigation culture being covered long ago by accumulation of multiple alluvial soil deposits brought down by the spring floods of the Tigris and Euphrates rivers. Irrigation farming might have been more feasible in the Gulf Oasis due to the better surrounding with multiple areas of freshwater displacement and better range of crops.

Archaeologists currently have a difficult time in piecing the early agricultural history of the foothills of Zagros region due to the shear depth of soil deposits 10's of metres deep, that has pushed the shoreline of the Persian Gulf 300 kilometres South where evidence of irrigation and farming of the first true farmers have been consumed by alluvium plains.

Fortunately, recent excavations and surface explorations have proved that irrigation around the upper Tigris and Euphrates, as well as their tributaries, dates from the early 6th Millennium BC (e.g. at Al-Kawm on the Upper Euphrates). Small-scale irrigation was practiced in Palestine (e.g. at Jericho) in the 7th Millennium BC, so this technology was already known process, how expansive farming was in the South and possibly in the Gulf Oasis is yet to be revealed.

In Northern and Eastern regions of Mesopotamia, main streams were soon partly diverted during moderate river floods into canals running more or less parallel to the rivers, which could thus be used to irrigate an extensive area. Such deflector dam irrigation avoided the self-destructive weaknesses of large storage dams, in particular the danger of depositing great masses of refractory mud in the storage basin behind the dam. In the North and East considerable urban installations developed at sites such as Nineveh no later than the 5th Millennium BC when Southern Mesopotamia was still coming to terms with the incremental Gulf Oasis flooding with vast swathes of swampland like the early Egyptian Delta.

The Euphrates had a much more reduced rate of water flow than the nearby Tigris. The Tigris was and still is the swifter of the two rivers, however, so that it was potentially more important for irrigation, even though much harder to tame.

The majority of the understanding of early farming comes from the West of the Fertile Crescent due to the quantity of archaeological digs in and around the Levant and Anatolia regions due to greater financing. The first permanent settlements of the Neolithic period 9,800 BC came after many thousands of years of Hunting and Gathering. Human behaviour changed from a nomadic way of life to living in permanent settlements. From dependence on wild foods to a combination of both agriculture and wild foods and then the total life of agriculture and the domestication of animals. From living as an Egalitarian society (all people are fundamentally equal) into a stratified (grouping people factors like wealth, occupation, and social status) social order, pre-pottery Neolithic.

The first phase of Neolithic period is characterised by small villages of up to 5 acres in size the dwellings were a round or oval structures each containing a cooking area with a half grinding stones. It appears that each building was used by a nuclear family. Artefacts for daily life were made of flint arrowheads, sickle blades, axis limestone and basalt. Items were found including Anatolian obsidian, volcanic glass, seashells, green mineral stones.

Adults were usually buried under the floors of the houses in a flexed position sometimes the sculls were removed and decorated with plaster shells and painted to resemble a living person. A few art objects have been discovered including figurines of women, birds, and limestone artefacts with geometric incisions some. Scholars believe that the female figures represent a great mother goddess who was responsible for the fertility of the land, humans, and animals.

Once again, this deals with the Levant and Anatolia Regions and not the Eastern part of the Fertile Crescent. Pre-pottery Neolithic communities began to live in much larger villages as big as 34 acres between 8600-8000 BC the

Neolithic way of life spread into new areas. During this period of time, sites have been found on Cyprus which clearly indicates maritime transportation was possible. The harness of such skills shows a great understanding of the celestial skies and a collaborate structure in society that can make ships, which require vessels to be watertight.

The use of cordage and sail making skills to build a dwelling is a very basic skill but the manufacture of ships proves the knowledge and skills to harness the seas. These people did not go in a single direction, they returned back to the place of origin. This then opens trade routes by the sea and enhances trading. 8,600 BC colonisation of Cyprus pre-dates all known vessels discovered by archaeologists by 3,000 years, just because they haven't yet found boat building that predates the Reed Boat discoveries in Kuwait 7,500 years.

By 7000 BC, knowledge of wells clearly indicates knowledge of water use and storage. At this same period, the typical architecture in the Levant was rectangular buildings with white plaster walls. The flint industry was characterised by long elegant blades produced from a special type of car, known as Nava form from which arrowheads and sickle blades were made exotic imported items such as obsidian, seashells and beads were also found in the sights and artefacts made from unworked Holyoake in Turkey in the Judean desert. Also discovered are hundreds of items made of perishable material in the Nahal I, a cave with a matt, baskets, liners, textiles a complete circle made of horn wooden beads and wooden tools.

7. Social Evolution in the Gulf Oasis

Shift from Hunter-Gathering

When we describe a revolution, we automatically assume a tidal wave of change similar to a lightbulb being switched on. But a dramatic change can occur similar to the invention of writing. Stepped increments, following the bread crumb trail that has been laid over millennia, ensuring you read the signs correctly. We seem to be in a very fortunate period of time when a lot of the groundwork has already been completed and we now understand the tell-tale signs social evolution/revolution. When specific habits are discovered at a certain time in history in a specific location. We are then able establish with a high degree of certainty if the place in question was ahead, or behind its times, compared to their neighbours.

What becomes even more interesting is the rate of change. When an instantaneous change is witnessed it is usually due to a seismic external event that has brought about that change. War, famine, climatic change are a few trigger points that can force an immediate change in habit. Change affects social understanding and can create its own new caste of pressures.

We are not in a position to excavate the Middle of the Persian Gulf; therefore, we have to look at its periphery and the characteristics of the new settlements appearing along the shorelines of the Persian Gulf. We already understand hunter-gatherers and their habits, and the Northern region of the Fertile Crescent has allowed a wealth of information to be gathered in understanding the transition. We can use the same information and assess and understand the people of Arabia. It has become increasingly clear that pastoralism was a major part of the Arabian Neolithic economy and that the inhabitants of the Arabian Peninsula could no longer be regarded solely as hunter-gatherers.

This is not to say that fishing, hunting, and gathering were not of considerable importance to the herding communities of the Arabian Peninsula.

Yet both means of surviving was adopted which highlights that living is never a simple binary choice, it involves a multifaceted approach, the more diversity the greater the probability of success. Multiple options have been discovered, the shift in food procurement, the domestication of sheep, goat, and cattle first appear in the archaeological record at this time, along with date stones, fish, and shellfish remains and plant processing equipment.

Together, this data signals a fundamental transition from hunting and gathering to fishing, cultivating, and animal husbandry. This is compatible with both the Ubaid economy and that of the Arabian Neolithic. The excavation site H3 in Kuwait also presents additional *craft* production which acts an additional source of income, highlighting commerce now as major activity. At the site the manufacturing of shell jewellery, chiefly simple disc-shaped shell beads. Also including a variety of flat circular, barrel-shaped and violin-shaped mother-of-pearl ornaments, or buttons.

As noted above, the lithic assemblage is oriented towards this industry, and beads and buttons are found in all stages of manufacture. It may be speculated that these items, and perhaps processed fish, animal products and livestock, functioned as items of exchange between the two or more communities. A pierced pearl was also found during a 2001 season. Perhaps supporting the suggestion that Pearls from the Arabian Gulf were traded at this early date subsistence economy of the site is based around fishing. Fish bones are extremely common at the site, and fishing equipment is also found, comprising net-weight sand fish-gorges; fishhooks have not been found. Other faunal remains include hunted prey (gazelle), and also juvenile sheep, goat and cattle are found at the site, providing further evidence that herding was a common practice.

The diversity of the site shows a broad spectrum of activities in one small area including boat building, boat repair, animal farming, cultivation, manufacturing, and fishing and all within a perfect location to trade. This individual site could not state that it was on the cusp of the Urban Revolution, but if multiple sites could provide equal evidence as in H3 then real change is afoot.[lv]

An explosion of settlements around the shoreline of the Gulf has been witnessed, coinciding with the final phase of *Marine Incursion* into the basin. More than just the sheer number of sites that were established within a single millennium. The characteristics of these sites have a profound implication for social evolution in the Gulf Oasis. It was noted that these new emerged communities had already undergone a complete Neolithic demographic transition and were, in fact, on the cusp of the Urban Revolution. Including permanent stone structures, pottery, date palm cultivation and similar activities as H3 Kuwait; animal husbandry, fishing, extensive trade networks and advanced boatbuilding.

It should also be noted that the words for *date and date palm tree* in the earliest written language in Southern Mesopotamia, the land of Sumer. Belong to a linguistic class thought to be carried over from an indigenous, pre-Sumerian language dubbed *Proto-Euphratic*, so the word *date* is older than Southern Iraq settlements of Eridu, Ur and Uruk. While it is unclear whether these were wild or domesticated date palms. An analysis of the earliest date stones in the archaeological record points to an area of initial cultivation around lower Mesopotamia, *in some oases in the Southern fringe of the Near Eastern arc.*[lvi]

As previously discussed in length, the Gulf Oasis served as a demographic refugium, facilitating the indigenous development of a distinctly Arabian Culture group. This is supported by the unique characteristics of lithic industries from both Eastern Arabia and Southern Zagros. Assemblages A and B at the Jebel Faya 1 rock shelter have no known correlates from any surrounding region. Many of the recently discovered *Middle, Upper* and *Epipaleolithic* assemblages in Southern Iran are clearly distinguished from lithic industries in Central and Northern Zagros.

Undoubtedly, the landscape desiccation and low sea levels of MIS 4 72,000-58,000 BC and MIS 2 22,000-10,000 BC would have affected hunter-gatherer ranges and mobility patterns. At that time, the Arabian Peninsula Savanna became desiccated reducing the migration corridor while tens of thousands of square kilometres of fertile land in the Gulf Oasis were exposed. This would have quickened the need for the introduction irrigation farming rather than relying on normal rain fall.

It is possible these shifting environmental dynamics forced hunter-gatherers to increasingly rely on coastal resources and freshwater fishing of the large freshwater lakes of the Gulf Oasis and less reliant on big and medium game hunting in the interior. The transition to aquatic subsistence and *beachcombing* is often invoked to explain the rapid modern human expansion across the Indian Ocean rim.[lvii] In this case, the Gulf Oasis model provides an environmentally driven mechanism that removed Savannah hunting as a viable subsistence strategy during MIS 4. Forcing the adoption of aquatic subsistence and freshwater resources being solely concentrated within the Gulf Oasis.

Fluctuating environmental conditions are likely to have caused populations reliant upon the Gulf Oasis refugium to expand into adjacent areas during periods of growth and expansion. Using the natural land corridor between the Gulf Oasis and the Indian Subcontinent. Subsequently populations constrict back into the core zone during climatic downturns, and as previously alluding to, during harsh climatic conditions Homo Sapien Hunter Gathers from the Middle East also moving into the Gulf Oasis refugium. Inevitably, this continuous flirtation with landscape carrying capacity must have impacted the social evolution.

As groups within the basin living under perpetually oscillating climatic conditions were persistently and consistently thrust into recurring negative feedback loops. This expansion and contraction of population activity may have been the point when social grouping and individual group identification could have occurred. More long-term indigenous peoples depending on location would have had a tendency to *group*.

The people of the Ocean region in the Southern Gulf Oasis would be reliant upon ocean fishing, especially when seawater was rising and coming closer to the Oasis. The central group who was supported by the freshwater lakes more reliant on freshwater fishing, pastoral farming supported by hunting. (this group would be predominantly the largest group). Whilst the Northern region of the Gulf Oasis had the potential for irrigation style farming, these people would have been cultivating Dates, Mangos, Grapes, Vegetables but probably wheat and barley at a lesser level. The crops would have been more diverse and less intensive compared to future farming. All three locations supporting three separate ways of living.

The Ur Shatt River split the entire basin in half so six areas of diversity could easily be supported in the Gulf Oasis. The formation of aquatic habitats along the Northern shorelines and marsh lands of the Persian Gulf at the end of the Last Glacial Maximum looks to have played a critical role in the process of city state formation in Southern Mesopotamia. This hypothesis presents a model in which marine transgression into the Gulf Oasis increased indigenous displacement movement during the climatic optimum created rich coastal zones that promoted the development of future Ubaid communities.

Due to the location of a high-density population within Southern Mesopotamia for various reasons, this forced inhabitants to make use of the high groundwater table and lack of rain, forcing the use of irrigation farming techniques. In turn, the innovation of large-scale agriculture hearkens back to the *hydraulic civilisations* of Wittfogel 1956, who proposed that irrigation had a cascading effect on social evolution and led to annual scheduling/calendars, labour coordination, and the stratification of leadership with increased productivity which amassed wealth for trading.

Similar cultures within the region have emerging clues from the *Epipaleolithic* of Iran[lviii] and Southern Oman suggest that human groups were present in these refugia immediately after the LGM. In the case of Sarab Syah spring, Epipaleolithic artefacts were discovered in conjunction with plant processing equipment. Which suggest intensive plant exploitation in the Southern Zagros during the Terminal Pleistocene. The lithic assemblage from the Al Hatab rock shelter, dating between 11,000 and 9,000 BC suggests that subsequent Early Holocene hunter-gatherer range expansions emanated from within Arabia itself. However, until prehistoric research commences within the depths of the Gulf, most archaeological evidence from the Terminal Pleistocene and Early Holocene will remain hidden.

The earliest state societies in Southern Mesopotamia form during the Uruk Period yet parts of Uruk are dated at the same age as Eridu pre-alluvium deluge. The Ubaid period remains poorly understood yet researches generally agree that this early period of Ubaid 0-1 had witnessed the development of non-egalitarian societies developing in the Tigris-Euphrates alluvial zone. Southern Mesopotamia seems to have formed a Ubaid Socio-Political organisation within a framework based on a *Chiefdom Model*[lix]. This would help clarify the interrelationship of economic organisation, political, leadership and ritual requirements for a pre-existing stratified society that was required to be successful in a newly inhabited heat hostile environment.

The new people of the region did not just survive in the extreme heat of Southern Mesopotamia but prospered. The term Ubaid refers to both a time period and material culture assemblage that lasts over 1,500 years yet the transition to further periods allotted by historians is seamless. The Ubaid period is divided into 5 phases of time 1-4 and an initial period of Ubaid 0 which to date refers to the site close to Eridu of Tell Oueili. This period marks the earliest archaeological documented sedentary occupation discovered in Southern Mesopotamia.

Due to a tremendous degree of alluvium deposits in this region, most of what is known about early Ubaid Period derives from very limited exposure of deep soundings at sites such as Eridu and Oueili. These limited *sampling points* severely limit the amount of available evidence and hence the reliability of interpreting the social and political organisation of these first migrants to the region. This is the same problematic stage of evidence as we have for the Gulf Oasis hypothesis due to the lack of excavation in the area.

Bogucki describes this as a phase of *Trans-Egalitarian* competitive households, in which some fall behind as a result of downward social mobility. Even in our own lifetime we can witness the ever-increasing social disparity within Countries and also between Countries.[ix] Morton Fried and Elman Service have hypothesised that Ubaid culture saw the rise of an elite class of hereditary chieftains *Chiefdom Model*, perhaps heads of kin groups linked in some way to the administration of the temple shrines and their granaries, responsible for mediating intra-group conflict and maintaining social order.

Burial artefacts and architecture (social housing) suggest a slight economic differentiation between wealthier and poorer households. Despite this evidence for emerging social complexity, several aspects of this early period seem at odds with the general model. In many Polynesian and American chiefdoms, political dynamics, and chiefly strategies of control. Often generate an archaeologically recognisable pattern of warfare, long distance exchange of exotic goods as status markers, exaggerated symbolisation of social ranking and an unstable political system which cycles between consolidation and collapse, that is very evident in the latter periods of the region prior to its final collapse.

However, there seems to be no evidence of this behaviour until the very end of the 5th Millennium BC that is over 2,000 years of relative peace in the region, also noted no evidence of warfare with no seals showing any depictions of weapons, prisoners, or combat scenes. No archaeological evidence of fortifications or violent destruction has ever been discovered in these early periods of time. Mortuary data from hundreds of early burials at Eridu and Ur show no signs of chiefly burials or even pronounced elite commoners even after 60 years of excavations there has still been no known striking difference in grave goods no exotic luxury items.

Early Ubaid differs from the generally accepted model of populous, warring theocratic chiefdoms. Instead, should be viewed largely secular, small scale polities ruled by heads of economically dominant local kin groups. It simply means that these polities did not pursue strategies of wealth finance. By contrast, a polity is dependent on staple finance would lack prestige goods or items of wealth, but might still be expected to have:

1. Economic differentiation.
2. Centralised storage facilities for staples.
3. Evidence of rural production of surplus.
4. Evidence of standardisation for ritual offerings.

These four indicators have been witnessed in the archaeological evidence. However, the control of land and water is meaningless unless someone can mobilise the labour necessary for canal maintenance, sowing and harvesting. Therefore, social stratification is seen but in a totally different format to what is generally known. So immediate kin groups and the broader social group who claim association through either marriage or friendship and support. The larger the family group the more chance to witness the emergence of chiefly elite but this seems to have been numerous chiefly elites of large families and numerous families within close proximity to each other. So, no one chief is able to grow to an exurbanite level, therefore keeping stability within the region.

Excavators at Oueili discovered a granary providing evidence for a centralised storage of grain surpluses. Whilst the evidence architectural standardisation of early temples throughout the region shows consistent model of commonality including the use of a standard measurement the cubit (72 centimetres) during the building of temples.

Sometimes the past can be in plain sight. In modern day Southern Iraq, we can still see the past in action and how to acquire the use of surplus labour through the manipulation of community organisations. To give a current example, the Sheikh of the el Shabana tribe reinforces his economic pre-eminence and political legitimacy through his control over the tribal *Mudhif* which is a combination of guesthouse, community centre, administrative and judicial centre. The Sheikh controls a large area of land whose produce is used in the maintenance of the Mudhif, therefore controlled solely by the Sheikh in the local community.

This is direct evidence which shows the ability to mobilise tribal labour to construct and maintain the Mudhif. Along with food surplus animals and grain for periods of tribal feasts, which is essentially a system of staple finance. A cohesive, bonded community with formal institutions whose ideological power crosscuts kin lines to extend over the entire community.

This climatologically deterministic model of social evolution in a fertile yet conscripted oasis is the reiteration of a very old idea. The Oasis Hypothesis, first envisioned by[lxi] Pumpelly in 1908 and later developed by Childe in 1928, 1936 and 1952, was speculated to have occurred within the ancient oases of the Gulf depression that later became the Persian Gulf, around which dense human populations huddled for survival during the LGM, Childe wrote in 1936: *United in an effort to circumvent the terrible power of drought.* The Gulf may very well house Childe's lost oasis, perhaps the most fertile part of the crescent, until it was plunged beneath the waters of the Indian Ocean some 8,200 years ago.

8. Historical Myths, Legends and Religious Material

Historical Hypothesis

The more we look at the Old Testament, the more commonality is seen within the original written works dating thousands of years prior to the Old Testament being written on Mesopotamian Cuneiform tablets discovered in the old ruins of Mesopotamia Cities. More and more of what is being mentioned in the Old Testament is now beginning to show more accuracy as archaeological and historical understanding is better understood. Only a small percentage of these ancient writings have been deciphered and more appreciation of the past will come to light in good time. But the frustration for everyone is that the strands of truth in the Old Testament do not set a clear and specific direction of understanding on what is read.

The Old Testament tells fantastic stories and gives accounts of different events that have or haven't happened in the past. History is not just written by the victor, but by the historian with the best hypothesis, the one that sits well with the general public at a certain point in time. Unfortunately, the historian has to also be aware of their audience and the need to panda to the masses *the vogue of the time*.

If the historian's hypothesis seems interesting with the general public, it will sell and will eventually gain traction and further credence. But we can never dispute the power of oral history, as proven in the story concerning the flooding of the Gulf Oasis oral history 1603 AD Portuguese explorer Pedro Teixeira in Bahrain talked about a flood that wiped everything away.

Dilmun and Its Place in Sumerian Mythology

Apart from being central in the Epic of Gilgamesh, Dilmun is also mentioned in the Myth of Enki and Ninhursag which is presented as an earthly paradise. Dilmun was an ancient Semitic-speaking state in Arabia mentioned in economic text in the late 4th Millennium BC onwards due to trade connections. Dilmun, modern day Bahrain is in the Persian Gulf, on a trade route between Mesopotamia and the Indus Valley Civilisation, close to the sea and to artesian springs. Early trading goods included, Copper, precious stones, pearls, dates, mother of pearl in exchange for agricultural products and textiles.

A number of scholars have suggested that Dilmun *Empire* was originally a set of islands and seems to have spread its regional power to encompassed Bahrain, Kuwait, Qatar and the eastern portion regions of Saudi Arabia notably linked with the major Dilmunite settlements of Umm an-Nussi and Umm Ar-Ramadh in the interior and Tarout on the coast. This area is certainly what is meant by references to *Dilmun* among the lands conquered by King Sargon of Akkad and his descendants.

In the Greek version of the Old Testament called Septuagint, the word *fountain* is used to describe how the Garden of Eden was watered. The phrase *fountains of the deep* was a common saying in Mesopotamia although deep could mean ocean or sea or aquafers which cover the majority of the Persian Gulf region.

For Dilmun, the land of my lady's heart, I will create long waterways, rivers and canals, whereby water will flow to quench the thirst of all beings and bring abundance to all that lives.

The promise of Enki the Lord of Sweet Waters to Ninhursag the Earth Mother, from the Sumerian creation myth *Enki and Ninhursag*;[lxii] Dilmun, sometimes described as *the Land of the Living*, is the scene of some versions of the Sumerian creation myth, and the place where the deified Sumerian hero of the flood, Utnapishtim (Ziusudra), was taken by the gods to live forever. The most celebrated discovered account concerning the garden as a luxuriant place and where gods reside is found in a Sumerian literature called *Enki and Ninhursag*:

The land Dilmun is pure; the land Dilmun is clean.
The land Dilmun is clean; the land Dilmun is most bright...
In Dilmun, the raven utters no cries...
The lion kills not, the wolf snatches not the lamb,
Unknown is the kid-devouring wild-dog...
Its old woman (says) not "I am an old woman."
Its old man (says) not "I am an old man."

Does the flood story of Sumer refer to the rising sea waters of the Indian Ocean that consumed the Gulf Oasis? Dilmun is the original name given to Bahrain by the Sumerians. Dilmun empires, that stretch along the Persian Gulf and was one of the trading posts for goods flowing from the Indus Valley to Sumer which was surrounded by the open lands that the Persian Gulf has now consumed due to the rising sea levels. Dilmun is the Garden of Eden from the biblical text, but was the entire Gulf Oasis the Garden of Eden? It is also called in Genesis the Garden of Yahweh, the God of Israel, and, in Ezekiel, the Garden of God.

The term Eden probably is derived from the Akkadian word Edinnu, borrowed from the Sumerian edin, meaning *plain*. closely related to an Aramaic root word meaning *fruitful, well-watered*. Bahrain is not a plain, but a high point surrounded by a plain. The Gulf Oasis was a protected plain (A walled paradise) with flood plains in the Northern Gulf Oasis and fed by upwelling subterranean springs. The Garden of Eden concept lingers on in Oriental designs. The garlands, vines, flowers, trees, animals, and beasts all strive to create a landscape, picturing hunting scenes or game, lakes with water birds. A symbol of eternal paradise (the English word paradise is ultimately derived from the Persian word meaning *Walled Park* with its flowers, birds, and water, it also symbolised the deliverance from the harsh desert. Could the Gulf Oasis be classified as a walled park, protected on all fronts with the high Zagros Mountains to the East and the harsh deserts to the West?

What also adds some understanding; Genesis 2:10–14 lists four rivers in association with the Garden of Eden: Pishon (Wadi Batin rivers), Gihon (Karun) that is the one that encompasses all the land of Cush (Elam), Chidekel (the Tigris), and Phirat (the Euphrates). The Shatt Al Arab River enters the Gulf in the North along modern-day Iran-Iraq border. The river drains the combined waters of the Euphrates and Tigris Rivers of Iraq and the Karun River of Iran

(Gihon). Genesis also refers to the land of Cush thought by some to equate to Cossaea, a Greek name for the land of the Kassites. These lands lie north of Elam, immediately to the east of ancient Babylon which does lie within the region being described.

Elamite is generally considered a language isolate (Similar to Sumerian) unrelated to the much later arriving Persian and Iranian languages; however, some linguists hypothesise that Elamite and the Dravidian (Once again Sumerian links) languages of India belong to the same language family.

One main feature that is usually overlooked when trying to hypothesis if Dilmun was the original Garden of Eden: was the entire Gulf Oasis or just the island of Bahrain the Garden of Eden? Therefore, the exact size of the Garden of Eden may have been lost through oral traditions and the sunken Gulf Oasis annexed from all knowledge. It maybe the remaining *high points* that remained in the memories of the local population as the islands are still a visual memory of what was. After the encroachment of the seas into the Gulf Oasis and the written language eventually replaced oral tradition describing Dilmun or areas still existing be associated with Dilmun (Bahrain) inclusive of Failaka Island in Kuwait.

One very striking note to be observed is the serpent who lives in Eden. In the seasons of 1957, 1959, and 1961 a Danish expedition discovered snake burials of a Late Dilmun[lxiii]. The building complex at Qalat al-Bahrain excavated thirty-nine deposits described as *sacrificial*, thirty-two of which contained the skeletons of snakes. An even earlier discovery in 1940s around 17,000 of 75,000 burial mounds that are small rock tumuli that are approximately 2,200 BC and older and are a UNESCO World Heritage Site.

The early type mounds which are crudely built and erected before the appearance of monumental buildings, can be seen as evidence for a stratified society. There is hardly any variation in the mounds and in the grave goods, which is a sign for a more egalitarian society, an equal society or of equal rights at the point of burial. Sumerian text describes Dilmun as the Garden of Eden, could it be hypothesised that the population surrounding this area of modern Bahrain looked towards Dilmun as the *ideal* place for burial, basically going back to their roots of origin.

Dilmun Modern Day Name Bahrain

Another legend called *The Myth of Enki and Ninhursag* relates a creation story in which the God Enki creates man in a land called Dilmun. Like the Garden of Eden, Dilmun is an earthly paradise. Arabic name given to Dilmun is Bahrain, an island that is surrounded by that body of water that was once a fertile river valley the Gulf Oasis, could the original Dilmun be the entire Valley and the remaining legacy be those parts that protrude or jut into the Persian Gulf, predominantly speculation but with some very tantalising archaeological discoveries on the islands within the Persian Gulf, the definition of Bahrain is *The two seas*. Could this be the sweet water subsea springs and the salt water of the Persian Gulf, as described by Pedro Teixeira?

1603, Portuguese explorer Pedro Teixeira wrote:

There is water in plenty, rather brackish than sweet. The best is that of Nanya'h, the name of certain very deep wells in the centre of the isle. The next is that got from the bottom of the sea, as follows. The chief town of the isle, Manama, is on the seashore, and near it, in the depth of three or three and a-half fathoms, are several great springs of fresh, clear, and wholesome water.

The Great Flood

Legends and Myths

Some backing may come in the writing of Roman Historian Flavius Josephus who wrote down a Babylonian legend that he heard in the first Century AD, it relates to a half fish called Oannes who walked out of the sea and taught the people of Mesopotamia the secrets of culture. He brought them the knowledge of letters, sciences, all kinds of techniques, he also taught them how too found Cities, build temples, create laws, and measure plots of land. He revealed to them how to work the land and gather fruits. After teaching mankind all these secrets, Oannes leaps back into the sea and swims away.

It would make sense in two different scenarios. Eridu temple is littered with fish offerings, *the first city according to the King List*. Also, could this legend relate to the time before the people came to settle on the lands once the sea levels had abated, the legends could be describing a time at the major lakes that existed in Gulf Oasis before the flooding; remember, people already started to progress and build large monuments in the Taurus Mountains before any flooding occurred. Maybe this *myth* also holds strands of truth, the Gulf Oasis or Pre-

Sumerians eventually landing by reed boat / reed islands identical to the modern Marsh Arabs and bringing with them their advanced urban culture and stratified society that had been honed over previous generations and manipulated by the priest class in the Gulf Oasis.

Some people believe that the Sumerians originate from India, but my hypothesis is that the people of India and Sumer are one of the same and when you compare the DNA of the Marsh Arabs, then I would definitely say the Pre-Sumerians definitely originated from the Gulf Oasis and not India. It's not all Indians, only Tamil, they could be the original blackheads, before the sea levels rose, a land bridge existed between the Gulf Oasis and the Indian Subcontinent which would have already been a well-used route for trade.

They had been migrating from 40-60,000 year previous but the last migration into the Indian Subcontinent was just prior to the Gulf Oasis land bridge being consumed. As the sea levels slowly rose, the people of the region had to make a life-changing decision: *move South into India before the land bridge closes or move further up the Oasis and hope the waters abate soon.* Communities would have split once the seas physically cut off this passageway. But even then, reed boats could hug the coastline and the divided people could still stay connected and shortly afterwards trade would open up between these divided people, the knowledge of each other's existence was known, and trade would flourish and the new cities on these trade routes would prosper and become extremely wealthy.

The linguistic links are well documented, the Sumerians used words for their professions, common jobs that included manual labour used old Pre-Sumerian words, they brought new words to this new land with them to describe more sophisticated and urban occupations, for example scribe and winemaker are both distinctly Sumerian.

The two different speaking sets of people eventually came into close proximity, the language of the Gulf Oasis which had developed independently final met the population scattered throughout the Fertile Crescent a multi-Semitic language speaking people. The first knowledge of any disaster being recited by the displaced Gulf Oasis people.

The Sumerian version of history was dominated with a great flood event, a Sumerian legend passed on eventually to the Babylonian Empire and from there the Hebrew Poets whilst incarcerated in Babylon compiling these legends into the Hebrew Script then forwarded on, into the first books of the Bible as well as the Koran. Every religion that *follows The Book*[15] knows about the flood story. Of all the ancient stories that have been passed down, only a few remain so strong in the mind, the *Gardens of Eden* and *The Flood*. These two examples are so *factual*, yet without the correct due diligence in scientific research, so why do they seem so *cast in stone*.

People of other religious beliefs tell of similar stories around the world and atheists who don't care, do acknowledge some logical belief in these *stories*. Could the reason be that these two stories were not just recited as truth by the priest class but witnessed by a multitude of ordinary folk? Therefore, the multiple sightings that have been recounted even without another person seeing it, becomes evidence enough. A basic example: if a person who had previously belonged to a coastal town moved far away and one day out of the blue, from their old coastal town telephoned to describe a cataclysmic event; A ship had struck the rocks close to the town and the entire coastline was covered in oil and will take years to clean up. Would that person believe them without witnessing the incident?

In 1872, an amateur Assyriologist, George Smith[lxiv], made a discovery that at the time shocked the world. Whilst studying a cuneiform tablet from the ancient Assyrian Capital of Nineveh, he came across a text describing a great flood that closely resembled that paralleled the story of Noah's Ark from the Book of Genesis in the Old Testament. The cuneiform tablet was a copy of a much earlier tablet from the Sumer Region. The Northern shoreline of the Gulf, the region became known as Sumeria and were populated by the world's earliest literate civilisation. It is interesting to note that the oldest known version of the Near Eastern flood myth, the *Eridu Genesis*, was written by the inhabitants of this region.

There are three flood incidents in history that could have been purported to have been the Flood Story in the Eridu Genesis or the Epic of Gilgamesh.

The heavens roared, and the earth roared again, daylight failed, and darkness fell, lightning's flashed, fire blazed out, the clouds lowered, they rained down death. Then the brightness departed, the fire went out, and all was turned to ashes fallen about us and the devastation left in its wake, land was no more!

---

[15] *"The Book" is referring to the Old Testament written by the Jews and followed by Christianity and the Muslim faiths.*

I personally feel that this statement is a first-hand account, the words feel too raw and pain too real, whichever this depiction of the flood it is relating to, comes from a true witness account.

1. The Black Sea Flood of 6000 BC resulting in the Euxine Basin being quickly consumed by a catastrophic breach from the Mediterranean Sea.
2. It could have been the Gulf Oasis being consumed by the rising sea levels and the stories passed down orally from generation to generation.
3. It could very easily be a localised event in Sumer when one looks at the geography. It's more than probable that there was not only one flood in Mesopotamia, but several which over time destroyed several Cities, especially in the plain of Ur where the Tigris and Euphrates overflowed their banks on regular occasions, carrying all that was in their way. Archaeological excavation and examination of the sediments of Kish, Ur, and the city of Shuruppak which was literally stripped from the map around 2,900 BC, have revealed that this was the last significant flood. The rivers Euphrates and Tigris changed their courses, in some places by 30 Km towards the west due to a single flood incident.

Black Sea Flood

During the Last Glacial Maxima LGM (ice age), the Black Sea region was predominantly dry (the Euxine Basin)[16] and up until that time had been separated from the Mediterranean Sea by the Bosporus Strait. Scientists believe that the rises in global sea level due to the LMG starting in 15000 BC. The rising Mediterranean finally spilled over a rocky sill at the Bosporus, caused the Bosporus Strait to catastrophically breach around 6000 BC. The Mediterranean poured large volumes of water into the Euxine Basin rather than the progressive rise in sea level that had been witnessed in the Gulf Oasis.

The Black Sea flooded an area of 100,000 Km² of land mass. What might also add credence to this event has been identified by Swiss botanist Heinrich Zoller in 1960[lxv]. 6200 BC noted climate disruption in the North Atlantic region shows clearly in Greenland ice core samples. Describing an event causing a large

---

[16] *Euxine was an area of land which has now been consumed by seawater that is surrounded by modern day Ukraine and Crimea on the North, Russia on the Northeast, Georgia on the East, Turkey on the South and Bulgaria, Romania on the West.*

meltwater pulse from the final collapse of the Laurentide ice Sheet of Northeastern North America. Most likely when the glacial lakes Ojibway and Agassiz suddenly drained into the North Atlantic Ocean. The coldest period lasted for about 60 years, and its total duration was about 150 years. The end to this *shock* climatic condition also coincides with the creation of the Black Sea.

In the Black Sea, radiocarbon dating of shells from an underwater beach front, as well as the results of core samples taken. Both sets of results point to an abrupt inundation of the Euxine Basin quickly becoming the Black Sea. The deluge would have filled the Euxine Basin with approximately 42 Km^3 of water per day (200 x the water that flows over Niagara Falls). This would have taken about 300 days for the levels within the Mediterranean and the newly form Black Sea to have levelled out.

The noise of the water would have been heard over 1,000 kilometres away and did not replicate the flooding of the Gulf Oasis. It has been estimated that this event would have lowered the world sea levels by as much as 30 centimetres. Nearly nothing is known of the original inhabitants of the Euxine Basin an explanation for the lack of Neolithic sites in Northern Turkey as this event would have been a genuine cataclysmic event with very few survivors to tell the story, but some would have escaped and the story will have been told throughout the region.

Fortunately, the research process is being helped by the fact that the Black Sea has now become the world's largest reservoir of hydrogen sulphide, an extremely deadly substance that has made 90% per cent of the seas volume sterile. It is now considered to be the world's most special deep-water environment because it does not contain microbes or oxygen. As already recently witnessed Shipwrecks in the sea are perfectly preserved. The first 200 metres contains normal marine life and below this level the sea is dead as the day when the flood waters finally settled.

Wherever the survivors moved the story will have been taken and recounted until the flood story could finally be written down. People would have stood on the mountains and witnessed the catastrophe. The volume could be heard across the water over a 1,000 kms away, with a build-up of heavy dark clouds followed by thunder and lighting.

As a final note on this part of research, I must also emphasise that wherever there are large excessive volumes of water vapour, the atmosphere will change. The atmosphere is simply a storage tank and a superhighway. During this breach into the Euxine Basin, storm clouds would have gathered to an excess. The noise of the cascading water pouring into the basin, the physical sight of seeing the land disappear before their very eyes, the storm clouds gathering. What would any god-fearing people, who had grown up with stories of cataclysmic events described by their elders, when water consumed all before them. Who would haven't disappeared, fearing god's wrath!

Gulf Oasis Flood

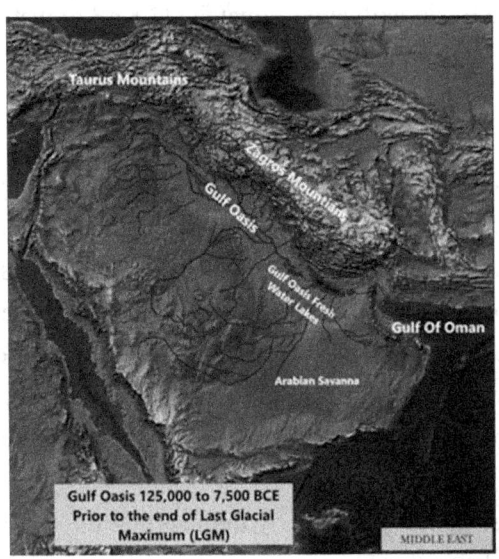

The link between flood mythology and marine incursion into the Gulf Oasis basin has already been thoroughly explored by a number of books or authors, for example the Bible and the Quran[lxvi], which is one source of the universal flood story started around 13,000 BC when Climatology experts have witnessed sea levels starting to rapidly rise around the world with low lying areas succumbing to the oceans quickly.

But it wasn't until approximately 7200 BC when it started to impact the Gulf Oasis and its indigenous population. This flood affected every inhabitant of the Gulf Oasis and would have been told by everyone. Look at the opposite side of the story. It displaced everyone in the Gulf Oasis, could you imagine nobody talking about it and when the opportunity came, writing about it?...no. It's very obvious it was recorded.

The Gilgamesh Flood Epic

After great bitterness over losing his friend Enkidu, Gilgamesh seeks Utnapishtim (the Babylonian equivalent of Noah) to give him the secret of immortality. Utnapishtim tells him of the gods desire to flood the world because they could not sleep for the uproar of mankind. Ea, the god of wisdom, warned Utnapishtim in a dream to convert his reed house to a boat, take in the seed of all living creatures, and tell the people he was building a boat to escape the wrath of the god Enlil. Utnapishtim built the boat in seven days and took in family, kin, creatures both wild and tame, and all the craftsmen.

The great flood came, and even the gods were terrified of it and fled. For six days and nights, the flood overwhelmed the world and on the seventh day grew calm. The boat rested on Mount. Nisir, and Utnapishtim sent out a dove, then a swallow, and then a raven. When the raven didn't return, he made a sacrifice, and the gods gathered like flies over it.

Note: By Ea telling Utnapishtim to convert his reed house into a boat, it shows that the story/myth was constructed/formulated either after the Gulf Oasis had been flooded by the Indian Ocean, as the homes of the first Sumerian settlers, just like present day Iraqi Marsh Arabs, the homes are made of Reeds. Archaeological sites have shown that the homes built after the floods around modern day Saudi Arabia, Oman, Bahrain have stone foundations. Prior to the firing of bricks for structures within Sumeria the locals used Reeds. The memory of the flood would still have been fresh in the oral history of the time. It may have been during the last rises of sea level that finally pushed the Gulf Oasis inhabitants onto new pastures where reed beds would have started to grow that the original myth took root.

Three main stories concerning the flood from various local regions which are identical in essence from Mesopotamian Eridu Genesis but differ in the names and in the forms according to the sources (location and dates) of the tablets but all three originating from Sumer, therefore the same story.

The Five Cities Pre-Flood

What must first be realised is that the Gulf Oasis flooded and then later when the new people settling in Southern Mesopotamia during the Ubaid Period were once again dealt blows from flooding but this time the floods came from the source of the main rivers of the Tigris, the Euphrates and the Karun. This is exemplified by the discovery of a skeleton that is currently in the Pennsylvanian University museum. Therefore, the flood cities that is described in the Kings List maybe from the flooding of the rivers.

- Eridu (the first city according to the Sumerian King List) As described in more detail further in the book, *The Sumerian King List*, a document composed in 2100 BC at Lagash claims the first city, established by the gods, was Eridu and the first King was Alulim who reigned for 28,800

years. The Kings who follow Alulim are mostly all given equally improbable lengths of reign, where the god Nudimmud was in charge. (yet equal in age to the Kings in the Book of Genesis).
- Bad-tibira (the name is on a lost piece of the tablet).
- Larsa; entrusted to the god Endurbilhrsag by AN.
- Sippar; entrusted by AN to the god-hero Utu.
- Shuruppak; whose protective god was the god of the South.

Chapter 2
The Start of the Neolithic Revolution in Northern Mesopotamia

The Development of Agriculture

You can't talk about the Sumerian and Southern Mesopotamia without firstly understanding the Northern part of the Fertile Crescent and its development. The Sumerians were very good at adapting ideas that originated elsewhere using existing techniques used for Northern Mesopotamia had to be adapted for use in the drier climates of Southern Mesopotamia, but the overall concepts of farming started in the North and the surrounding mountains. As we read this section, we will start to unfold a series of events that happened in 7000 BC and the devastating impact that the people of the Gulf Oasis (Pre-Sumerians) had on the entire Northern region of the Fertile Crescent.

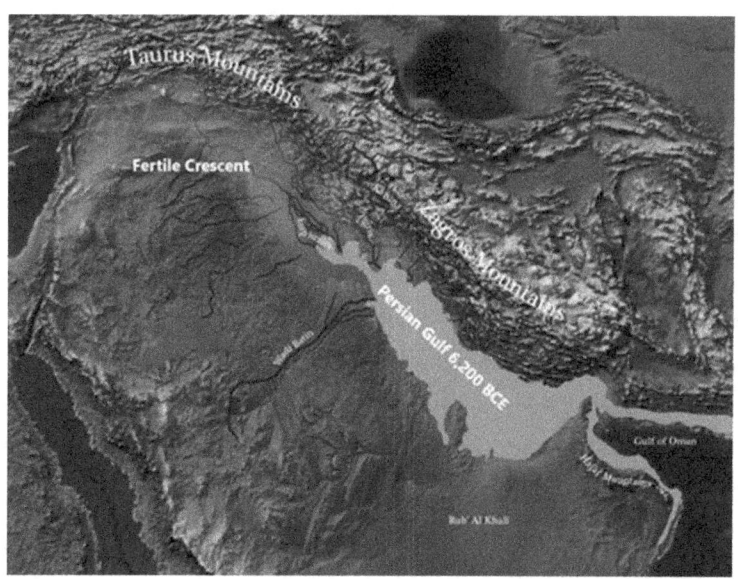

The first Cognitive Homo Sapiens evolved in Africa during the Palaeolithic Era, or Stone Age, which spans the period of history from 2.5 million to about 10000 BC. Palaeolithic Homo Sapiens were nomads, who often moved their settlements as food became scarce, following the herds. Due to the cyclic nature of climates. Humans operated alone but lived in small clans/groups as hunter-gatherers, with clear gender divisions for labour. This was a mobile unit that could operate independently from other clans, a self-contained unit that could cope with all eventualities.

The clan had an area of terrain and understood every aspect of their surroundings, from the flora, fauna, wildlife to weather. It was a compact group and balanced, with everyone sharing the workload. Predominantly, the men hunted animals while the women gathered food, such as fruit, nuts and berries, from the surrounding area. Simple tools made of stone, wood and bone (such as hand axes, flints and spearheads) were used throughout this period of time.

Fire was controlled, which created heat and light, and allowed for cooking. The movement towards agriculture will have been predominantly pursued by the females who main purpose was to carry out the gathering whilst the men hunted. Women who had the curiosity and temperament to nurture food supplies will have noticed subtleties within the wild grain and encourage these embryonic new ideas. The initial crop production would not have originally produced sufficient food to sustain a small group of hunter-gatherers. It did add to the variety of foods already consumed by the groups.

Still semi migratory at first but in time, these *revolutionists* started to cultivate these wild grasses and more edible in time. Dense stands of wild grasses, the antecedents of the oldest grains such as wild wheat, the species known as *Triticum*, and its close relative barley could easily be picked on a seasonal basis to provide food for growing. Stands of wild grasses to spread by deliberately planting seeds to create a more abundant harvest.

Over time, genetic modifications occurred. The stems of the wild wheat and barley became tougher, so that the seed would not be blown away by the wind but remain intact. This allowed for harvesting in greater amounts and began to change the natural growing habits of these plants, ever experimenting like good intelligent humans do and ensuring the best and highest yielding plants are kept. A form of euthanasia in the plant world, but as time went by and ideas shared possibly at areas like Göbekli Tepe. These methods became refined, and the harvest grew which could allow the Hunter Gathers to settle in one area and wait out the months when the herds of wild animals would return. The hunter-gatherers started to complement their new diet during this time when the herds had moved on with other meats that hadn't previously been hunted like birds. These more sedentary hunter-gatherers altered the cause of history of several wild animals.

Wild sheep and goats and animal resources existed in discrete regions, which gave rise to the *herding instinct*, where plants and animals cluster in stands or groups, as did the people who tended them. Similarly, they began to control animals, perhaps starting with young ones captured when their mothers were killed, ensuring a supply of meat on the hoof. Animal behaviour and physical characteristics changed, protected from natural predators by their human caretakers, the herds become more docile and fleshier. Sheep originally were hairy, far less woolly. But when farmers moved South into the warmer alluvium plain South of modern-day Samarra, the sheep adapted by growing a coat of wool, which kept them cool.

Dogs, cattle and pigs were also domesticated whilst other uses for animals produce beyond food evolved: milk, milk products, fibre and eventually yarn and textiles. This domestication of animals aided the survival of families to inhabit a single region. These animals could supply whole families with the necessary substance needed to survive, a necessity for the next phase of humanity. The stockpile of grain grew and couldn't be moved from place to place and permanent homes started to appear along with the experimental keeping of animals.

The early farmers still travelled over considerable distances still supporting their diet with wild animals, but a noticeable change had occurred. Improved techniques of farming and animal husbandry quickly spread from area to area, the best farming techniques adopted within the entire Fertile Crescent and its surrounding mountainous regions. The clan sizes grew larger in various regions but limited by amount of grain that could be harvested with the limited knowledge of cultivation techniques that was available at the time. It has been seen that during this transitional phase that an excess must have been produced to allow other communal activities to have existed, like buildings, towers, and walls. But still these activities were limited by the natural resources that surrounded them and not the norm. If the population expanded to big, some of the people just moved location and settled somewhere else and started again. These displaced *groups* usually stayed in contact with the original place of origin, which is seen around Jericho and its surrounding regional villages. The growth of the Greek and British Empires are very good examples of moving to new locations and setting up colonies and eventually prospering whilst following original traits and traditions from original source.

The perfect example is the colonisation of the US, Canada, Australia, etc., and to see how those new areas originally struggled but then prospered beyond the original *Motherland*. These early humans migrated into Eurasia, via the Gulf Oasis and eventually into the Indian Subcontinent, onwards to Southeast Asia and into Australia. By about 40,000 years ago, they had entered Europe, and by about 15,000 years ago, they had reached North America followed by South America.

Understanding of the Transition from Hunter-Gatherers to Farmers

Until about 13,000 years ago, humans still continued to hunt and gather their food, following the migrations of animals and the seasonal cycles of the crops. These hunter-gatherers established temporary base camps for their activities, and caves continued to serve them for homes and localised meeting-places, but they still didn't establish permanent settlements. But they had not yet begun the systematic practice of agriculture.

Then, about 11000 BC, people began to settle down, constructing the first agricultural villages. Why did they do it? Is food production through agriculture easier than hunting and gathering? Surprisingly, the answer seems to be *no*. Research suggests that with the technology available at that time adult farmers had to work an equivalent of 1,000-1,300 hours a year for their food, while hunter-gatherers needed only 800-1,000 hours. Moreover, agricultural work was more labour intensive and difficult. Homo Sapiens had evolved to perform the task of Hunting and now required to adopt unnaturally long activities the body wasn't *designed* to do. So why change?

An appealing, although unproved, answer is that increasing population pressure, perhaps accompanied by changing climatic conditions which affected the local fauna and migrating cycle of the hunted herds. This could have forced people to take on the more productive methods of agriculture. Scientists estimate that even in a lush tropical environment, 0.4 square miles of land could support only nine persons through Hunting and Gathering. Whereas under-organised, sedentary agricultural techniques the same area could support 200-400 people.

The changing weather conditions brought about by the onset of the end of the Last Glacial Maximum (LGM) in 13,000 BC affect the well-established hunting grounds.

Hunting and gathering became even less productive and couldn't support an expanding population, to survive, sedentary agriculture became a necessity. As previously described, the expansion of population in the Gulf Oasis and this simple calculation can explain a basic need to adapt to cultivation.

The memory of this transition survives in myth from one of the four cultures of the world in modern day China. The myth of Shen Nung, whom the ancient Chinese honoured as the inventor of agriculture and its wooden tools and of poetry, captures the transformation:

The people of old ate the meat of animals and birds. But in the time of Shen Nung, there were so many people that there were no longer enough animals and birds to supply their needs. So it was that Shen Nung taught the people how to cultivate the earth.

In addition to increasing agricultural productivity possibly due to expanded interaction as witnessed at the archaeological site at Göbekli Tepe located in modern day Turkey. Villages facilitated an increase in creativity of all kinds. It may have taken longer to raise food than to hunt and gather it. As a domino effect to this shift the sedentary farmers did not stop work when they had secured their food supply. In their villages they went on to produce textiles, pottery, metallurgy, architecture, tools, and objects of great beauty, especially in sculpture and painting. Did the agriculturists work comparatively harder than the hunter-gatherers simply to survive or because they craved the added rewards of the extra labour? We can never know for sure, but the agricultural village opened new possibilities for economic, social, political, and artistic creativity. Changing forever humanity's concepts of life's necessities.

Time Periods (Levantine, Anatolian and Mesopotamian Broad Dates BCE)

Natufian Culture: 13000-9500 BC
Neolithic Proto-Neolithic (PPNA): 9000-8500 BC Prehistory
Aceramic Neolithic (PPNB-C): 8500-7000 BC
Pottery Neolithic 7000-6500 BC

Amuq B and Hassuna-Samarra 6500-6000 BC Prehistory
Early Halaf and Early Ubaid 6300-5500 BC

Natufian Culture

To be able to better understand the changes that occurred in the Gulf Oasis without any excavation currently being carried out, we can use social development and behaviour patterns that took place in the area of Palestine and modern-day Israel of the indigenous people who are now called Natufian. We can't and will never fully understand the *Big Picture* of Neolithic life, we take *snapshots* of human history as and when they are presented. Sometimes the archaeological digs are planned and sometimes a new discovery is found by accident, which helps build a picture of how this development took place and a better helps our understanding of the past.

The most informative to date has been the Natufian culture which was first identified by Dorothy Garrod[lxvii] during excavation of Shukbah Cave in Samaria and el-Wad at Mount Carmel. Changes that took place in the Levant Valley which provides archaeological evidence for the unique transition from Hunter-Gatherer to agricultural village societies. The Natufian culture 13,000-9,500 BC research has been funded by the Israelis and Western powers to enable teams to carry-out intensive archaeologically digs in the area and is now currently recognised as the harbinger of food-producing cultures in the Levant.

Its importance lies both in the significant cultural changes that have been recorded which can lay witness to the emerging of human settlements becoming more permanent. Setting the stage for the fundamental transformation to agriculturally based societies. Important trajectories of socio-economic change that began in the Natufian include increasingly permanent settlement infrastructure, intensified foraging strategies, heightened symbolic communication and ritual practice, and more concentrated burial of human remains in settlements.

The Natufian has traditionally been divided into Early and Late phases at 11,000 BC based on differences in burial customs (decorated early Natufian burials). The richness of art and ornament assemblages, the size of built structures, and, most importantly, the average greatest length of the lunate (a crescent shaped prehistoric implement). The most historic and important tool introduced by the Natufian is the sickle blade, a hallmark of the Natufian culture used for harvesting. Late Natufian sites are geographically widespread.

The transformation is stepped, even localised. In some areas, the populace became more or less sedentary. Whilst in others, adaptations are more mobile and seasonal, depending on environmental conditions. Late Natufian sites have been recorded as far North as Syria. The distinct features of Natufian sites show the transition to permanent architecture suggested that sedentary settlements, residentially stationary year-round occupation starts to emerge. This new phenomenon of settlement increased the scale of the built environment and had a significant impact on the Natufian landscape.

Architecture included rounded pit houses, with foundations made of local, undressed stones and retaining walls supporting the perimeter of the structure. The strange but all too common feature that is seen in many areas, is the percentage of secondary burials. Combined with skull removal and subsequent reburial in new locations, sometimes with other crania, first emerges in the Late Natufian and continues into the Neolithic Period (I don't think my wife would appreciate being exhumed with my head on her shoulders). By understanding the Mediterranean coastal area of the Levant, Syria, and Lebanon we can start to create a picture of all areas at the time and how we have been able to witness this important transition.

In recent years, other similar settlements have been discovered in the West Bank region, all sharing a similar culture and also described as Natufian. This culture seems to have started approximately 13,000 BC and suddenly disappeared about 7,000 BC. The land seems to have incorporated, areas of Abu Huraya, MuMureybet in the Northern areas (Modern day Syria / Southern Turkey) to Beidha, Wadi Uwainid, Ein Gev, Nahal Oren, Eynan in the central and Southern extremities of the Natufian region. The only difference of these sites to Jericho is the size; Jericho was spread over a ten-acre area, therefore it would seem logical to propose that Jericho seemed to be the central point for these people. Also, its water source seems to have been able to support far greater sized crops produce and subsequentially a much larger populace.

These other sites could easily be satellites of Jericho or may have only been linked by geography but shared economic and cultural links that helped sustain close relationships throughout the region. The extensive archaeological digs in the Levant Region show that Jericho enjoyed widespread trade links throughout the Fertile Crescent and the wider region. One such trade item is obsidian which has been found throughout the region, an especially sharp volcanic rock from

Asia Minor useful in the making of sharp blades and being highly prized material.

It must also be noted that throughout the following 8,000 years the people of the Fertile Crescent continued to prefer to use this same material in statues of future Kings and priests, it seems the lust for obsidian never abated. The timelines maybe different in other areas but the overall stage-by-stage transfer will be the same, no matter the area and into a time period which is seen as the start of humans as we envisage them, the Neolithic!

Göbekli Tepe

Located in modern Turkey, Göbekli Tepe is one of the most important archaeological sites in the world.[lxviii] The discovery of this stunning 13,000-year-old site in the 1990s AD sent shock waves through the archaeological world and beyond. With some researchers even claiming it was the site of the biblical Garden of Eden. (Unfortunately, anything new is always claimed as the Garden of Eden…even if it's on top of a mountain like Göbekli Tepe!)

The many examples of sculptures and megalithic architecture which make up what is perhaps the world's earliest temple at Göbekli Tepe predate pottery, metallurgy, the invention of writing, the wheel, and the beginning of agriculture. The fact that hunter-gatherer peoples could organise the construction of such a complex site as far back as 11,000 BC not only revolutionises our understanding of hunter-gatherer culture. This poses a serious challenge to the conventional view of the rise of civilisation. We have briefly looked at the Natufian development in the Levant region, but we have to realise that there is no epicentre for development but multiple sources of advancement.

The entire area surrounding Mesopotamia and Göbekli Tepe is a prime example of a far different tangential approach in development. Nothing is ever binary and always a multifaceted answer. The very recent discovery will not be the last to be found and the future discoveries and further excavations will alter our understanding of the past that can add a few more missing pieces of the jigsaw of lost knowledge and the history of human development.

Göbekli Tepe (Turkish for the *hill of the navel*) is a 1,000 ft diameter mound located at the highest point of a mountain ridge, around 9 miles Northeast of the town of Sanliurfa (Urfa) in South Eastern Turkey. Since 1994 AD, excavations conducted by Klaus Schmidt[lxix] of the Istanbul branch of the German Archaeological Institute, with the cooperation of the Sanliurfa Museum, have been taking place at the site. Results to date have been astounding; especially bearing in mind the excavators estimate that their work has uncovered a mere 5% of the site.

Göbekli Tepe Megaliths under the night sky

Göbekli Tepe consists of four arrangements of monolithic pillars linked together by segments of coarsely built dry stone walls to form a series of circular or oval structures. There are two large pillars in the centre of each complex which are encircled by slightly smaller stones facing inward. Archaeologists believe that these pillars could have once supported roofs. The structures vary in size between around 33 and 98 feet in diameter and have floors made of terrazzo (burnt lime).

The Megaliths of Göbekli Tepe

So far, 43 Megaliths have been unearthed, are mainly T-shaped pillars of soft limestone up to around 16 feet in height. Excavated and transported from a stone quarry on the lower Southwestern slope of the hill. Geophysical surveys on the hill indicate that there are as many as 250 more megaliths lying buried around the site, suggesting that another 16 complexes once existed at Göbekli Tepe. Although some of the standing stones at Göbekli Tepe are blank, others display extraordinary artwork in the form of elaborately carved foxes, lions, bulls, scorpions, snakes, wild boars, vultures, waterfowl, insects, and arachnids. There are also abstract shapes and one relief of a naked woman, posed frontally in a sitting position.

Prehistoric art of humans is extremely rare at this point and must be extremely symbolic. A number of the T-shaped stones have depictions of what appear to be arms at their sides, which could indicate that the stones represent stylised humans or perhaps gods. Although the pictograms at Göbekli Tepe do not represent a form of writing, they may have functioned as sacred symbols whose meanings were implicitly understood by gathering Hunters.

This site is thought to have been built and used by numerous bands of affluent hunter-gatherers, perhaps sharing a common religion, culture, and a place to share ideas. The strange animal figures all over the pillars also at other neighbouring sites in the region, that stretch deep into the heart of modern-day Turkey. These carvings may even be a form of pictographs a form of primitive hieroglyphics but if this is the case their message is unknown and may stay that way. But if this site was situated in Greece, then we may have quick answers to the questions.

This site can only fuel the idea that religion not agriculture had been the catalyst for the birth of civilisation. It is not hard to surmise that people of Jericho may have had some connection with Göbekli Tepe. Professor Steven Mithen[lxx] (After the Ice) even thinks it possible that after the respective ceremonies undertaken by the various hunter-gatherers would go back to their respective tribes with seeds and the secret how to grow them. Work continues on the site and more is being known every year. Was religion the prime mover in forming the first Cities, perhaps first starting as a ceremonial centre and overtime these gatherings started to settle down and the first communities being created.

Having a large gathering of people will have enhanced the knowledge of how to grow grain successfully and also any implements used to sow or harvest, would have been shared. Therefore, it is not unwise to believe steady growth in the entire region could occur simultaneously. The seeds and knowledge of how to sow could have quickly been taken back to all the various tribal homes. By 9000 BC, new stone tool technology and a whole new way of life came to the Fertile Crescent; this was the Neolithic Revolution when people adopted farming and raising animals and started communal living.

The depictions of vultures at Göbekli Tepe have parallels at other Anatolian and Near Eastern sites. The walls of many of the shrines at the large Neolithic settlement of Çatalhöyük in existence from approximately 7,500-5,700 BC in

South-central Turkey were adorned with large skeletal representations of vultures. One theory put forward to explain the prominence of vultures in the early Anatolian Neolithic is in the context of possible excarnation practices suggesting a funerary cult, some bones have shown cut marks that may have aided the birds eating of the flesh.

After death, bodies would have been deliberately left outside and exposed, perhaps on some kind of wooden frame, where their skeletons were stripped of flesh by vultures and other birds of prey. The skeletons would then be interred somewhere else. Perhaps the ritual of excarnation was the focus of a cult of the dead practiced by the inhabitants of Göbekli Tepe.

It certainly seems to have been elsewhere in Anatolia and the Fertile Crescent in the Pre-Pottery Neolithic but may not necessarily just be a monument for rituals of burial but also as an oracle where people could take advice or settle disputes from the Shaman in residence. We may have to look at the practices of future ancient societies like the Babylonians, Greeks, or Egyptians to be able to realise that the practices known about may have its origins much further back in time.

Curiously, Schmidt and his team have so far found no evidence of settlement at Göbekli Tepe houses, cooking hearths, and refuse pits are all absent. The archaeologists did, however, find over 100,000 animal bone fragments, many of which exhibited cut marks and splintered edges which indicate that animals were being butchered and cooked somewhere in the area. The bones came from wild game such as gazelle (which accounted for over 60% of the bones), boar, sheep and red deer, and different species of birds such as vultures, cranes, ducks, and geese. All of the bones were from wild species; evidence that that the people who inhabited Göbekli Tepe were hunter-gatherers rather than early farmers who kept domesticated animals.

The King is Dead, Long Live the King

The excavations of Göbekli Tepe believe that around 8,000 BC the people at the site deliberately buried the monuments under mountains of soil and the settlement refuge. Could this backfilling of the site be a clear demarcation that Göbekli Tepe had been the principle place of worship of the Hunter and now that agriculture had become the main focus, these old deities had become redundant and an extremely symbolic act. *The King is dead, long live the King*. This backfilling is the main reason why the site has been preserved after so many thousands of years such as flints and animal bones, brought from elsewhere.

Why the inhabitants of Göbekli Tepe abandoned the site is not clearly understood, though the monuments had obviously lost their relevance. Which may have had some connection with the new way of life which accompanied the development of agriculture and animal husbandry which occurred around this time. Göbekli Tepe may have been an area to celebrate the returning herds at various times of the year which was the main food chain for hunter-gatherers with the development of a settled sedentary society with a priest class at the central core then this structure may have been at odds with the new way of thinking so deliberately concealed from the eye of future generations.

We know from typological dating (of stone tools) and radiocarbon dates that the final building phase at Göbekli Tepe dates to 8,000 BC. However, the date of its very earliest occupation is far from clear. Nevertheless, radiocarbon dates (from charcoal) for the most recent part of the earliest layer (stratum III) at the site centre around 9000 BC.

Klaus Schmidt and his team estimate that Göbekli Tepe's stone monuments are about this age, though the structures have not been directly dated themselves. From the available evidence the site's excavators estimate Göbekli Tepe's beginnings at 11,000 BC or earlier, which is incredibly early for such a complex set of monuments. Could the people of late Natufian society been involved at this site, only time and expert analysis will be able to reveal these hidden secrets.

An Organised or Stratified Society?

The planning and building of such a site as Göbekli Tepe would have required a high degree of organisation and resources hitherto unknown in hunter-gatherer societies. Schmidt has made the intriguing suggestion that rather than building temples and other religious structures after they had learned to farm and live in settled communities. The hunter-gatherers of the area first constructed megalithic sites like Göbekli Tepe and thus laid the foundation for the later development of complex societies.

Indeed, investigations of other sites surrounding Göbekli Tepe have left tantalising clues as to the origins of agriculture. The world's oldest known relative to wheat which was a domesticated strain was discovered at a prehistoric village only 20 kilometres from Göbekli Tepe, coincidence ...I don't think so! According to radiocarbon dates, agriculture developed in the area around 8,500

BC, just a few hundred years after the construction of Göbekli Tepe. Other sites in the region show evidence for the domestication of sheep, cattle, and pigs only 1,000 years after Göbekli Tepe's monuments were erected. All this evidence suggests that the area around Göbekli Tepe was at the forefront of the agricultural revolution. This might point to one of the reasons for the expansion of agricultural techniques.

Why did hunter-gatherers construct such elaborate monuments? We know that religion (which ever format) has always been important to earliest Homo Sapien. Also, an indication as to its location. If you aren't bothered looking at the stars, stay in the plains. If you are interested in the stars and want a very clear view, get high on a mountain, and keep away from artificial light. Could Göbekli Tepe have been a place of an original Oracle, looking to the heavens for divine guidance. Also, the place of funeral rites for the entire region? It is too early to fully understand the reasoning behind the building program as only 5% of the area has been excavated. The main understanding that we can take from the site is:

- It shows a high level of organisation and collaboration between hunter-gatherers not previously believed to have happened this early in Homo Sapiens development.
- It may show a level of stratification that had not previously believed this early in human development.
- It also shows that large gatherings took place at the site. Therefore, knowledge of new and improved ideas could easily be shared and spread quickly to further *groups* and regions. So, the development of agriculture could also be shared and could have spread more quickly than previously believed.
- It also shows a more specific date for the start of agriculture 8500 BC whilst domestication of livestock also started to take place at a similar time.
- It also shows that the start of large engineering projects started in 11000 BC and a form of leadership to have decided on such a grand build involving hundreds if not thousands of people in its construction, all who had to be fed and watered.
- A level of engineering not previously believed possible also the craftmanship to carve the stones.

- This was quite an isolated region so people must have known some level of navigation.
- It shows a form of standardisation in Building Techniques comparing to other regions, Burial Rituals (coating of skulls similar to the Natufian culture), symbols and decoration.

All of this before the invention of pottery and writing.

Similar Sites in the Area

Due to the presence of multiple monumental complexes at such an early date, Göbekli Tepe is a somewhat unique site. However, there are some parallels with the site at the early Neolithic settlement of Nevalı Çori, on the middle Euphrates River in Eastern Turkey, which lays only 12.5 kilometres North-West of Göbekli Tepe. The main temple at Nevalı Çori was dated to around 8,000 BC. The cult complexes at the settlement had a number of features in common with Göbekli Tepe, such as a terrazzo-style lime cement floor, monolithic T-shaped pillars built into dry stone walls, and two free-standing pillars in the centre of the complex area. The T-shaped pillars show reliefs of what appear to be human hands. Unfortunately, Nevalı Çori is now lost, submerged beneath a lake created by the Atatürk Dam in 1992 AD. The need for water in the region far outweighs the need of an ancient monument.

Tell Qaramel

In 1999, without even looking for it, a joint Polish Syrian Team found something astonishing Close to the modern city of Aleppo at Tell Qaramel[lxxi] the team found five similar towers to the Tower in Jericho but possibly 2,000 years earlier built in 10,000 BC it would seem the religious centre is a contemporary of Göbekli Tepe. It would seem that the region had a tradition of building these towers. Unfortunately, due to the Civil war in Syria only 2% of the site has been uncovered which may have been a blessing in disguise.

A city will house civic buildings and places of worship as well as homes in close proximity. The wall that surrounds the settlement may have been built to ward off floods. Floods seem to have been extremely common to the region.

The Start of the Neolithic Age 10000 BC-4500 BC

A long line of existing populace of the Middle East, dating back to over 10000 BC, approximately 5,000 years before the founding of Uruk. This region was at the Northern end of the Fertile Crescent and seems to have grown independently of the later Southern *Civilisations* even though common threads between both areas exist. Major changes occurred in the way humans lived as seen in digs in the Levant Region. The style and standard of living would have a cascading effect on every part of human society and culture. That change has been labelled the Neolithic Revolution.

Even though the definitions do vary, the first cities on earth where created and communal living has been witnessed during this period. Communal living during a period of time known to belong to the hunter-gatherer Period. This phenomenon unearthed may well be the transitional point between hunter-gatherer and the time of agriculture societies that we all understand today. This transformation took place over thousands of years and may well stretch back throughout the reign of hunter-gatherers stretching from the Levant Valley and round the entire Fertile Crescent all the way to modern day Iran into the Persian Gulf.

Neolithic Advances in the Northern Powerhouse of Mesopotamia: Jericho and Its Surrounding Area

A new experiment was underway in how to live in a single area helped by the uniqueness of the grasses and seeds in this region. Some which could be cultivated and replanted by human hands rather than simply gathered which enabled a near inexhaustible food source for the future. One such site was Jericho, then a large Oasis in the Jordan Valley. The river flows into the central mountains to the West making life not just possible but incredibly fertile due to the unique low geography of the region making physically closer to the underground water supply.

The idyll may have been one of the earliest places on the planet to try this experiment. Jericho didn't exist in isolation; Jericho lay at the heart of a thriving trading network in the region. More communities are now being discovered throughout the entire Fertile Crescent that casts new light on the region. Jericho may have been one of the largest settlements in the region if not the largest.

The most well-known site due to the heavy investment of archaeological digs compared to similar areas in the region is Jericho due predominantly to the famous biblical story of the great Walls of Jericho. Jericho is an area of firsts, 5,000 years before the Strong Walls of Uruk as depicted in Epic of Gilgamesh, Jericho was also surrounded by Walls, evidence of cooperation between a *group* larger than a clan, living together. (Is this the first "town"?) The first evidence of large-scale communal labour, which then creates more questions on how these *clan* people organised structural work whilst still *Hunting and Gathering*.

People in Jericho lived in round houses about 40 feet in diameter, with sunken mud plaster floors, it would seem that each individual dwelling was virtually identical in size and build. Each home also had a grain storage area incorporated within. Which leads to the theory that each household had control of its own food therefore showing a level of autonomy within the larger group, which also shows a less stratified society. (Once you hold the grain, you hold the power.)

This is extremely different to areas that developed much later in Southern Mesopotamia in the land of Sumer where all produce grown was controlled by the priest class who held a monopoly over food production and distribution. So, the land of Sumerian society would seem to be extremely socially stratified. Back in the Northern Fertile Crescent in Jericho the village seems to be randomly scattered with no fixed layout. The conurbation may have housed distinct family or clan groups/members. Perhaps from tribes who had first come to the *Town* to work together all those centuries ago on the Jericho *Watch Tower*.

Rather than being grouped by profession and class like the Sumerian people, the people in the North seem to have been grouped around tribal houses. This style of grouping showed very little distinction and differentiation between the lowest and highest levels of society. By each clan living in similar sized housing and surrounded by equal sized groups maybe this had the effect of stabilising and subduing any disenfranchised clans within the group. No one individual clan growing faster than the other and exerting power over the rest.

Archaeologists have suggested that Jericho grew with no central organisational structure perhaps being built from the ground up by hunter-gatherer groups. Rather than being deliberately built by priest led societies unlike the future Sumerian Cities.

At the same time of stability that was witnessed in the North, the movers and shakers of the South where only just beginning to stir, a human wave of change. Forcibly being uprooted from their Lake Side dwellings in the Gulf Oasis. These people of the South started to look for new lands to call home, as far away from the encroaching rising water of the newly created seas as possible. It should be remembered that the archaeologists at this point in time had still not discovered any known pottery in the North or South at this time.

The Watch Tower of Jericho[lxxii]

The first city, Jericho's Watch Tower, as it is known is one of the most extraordinary buildings in human history 8300-7800 BC not because of its intricate architecture but simply how old it was. Nothing on its scale or size had been found before. Buildings of this scale would be seen again for thousands of years in Sumeria. At around 30 feet in diameter and 28 feet tall, it's been estimated that it took 11,000 days of labour to build the tower not including the quarrying or planning.

When Kathleen Kenyon first uncovered the tower in 1951, it was thought to be the first example of communal architecture on the planet built at a time when the majority of the world's humans still lived a nomadic hunter-gatherer life. Its wall 5 feet thick incorporated an interior staircase, it would seem that a sudden appearance the Wow factor. It definitely would seem to add more theatrics, more drama on appearance. The visual impacted was thought about, something to impress the onlookers. A significant proportion of labour must have been dedicated to its construction. This implies that a highly organised, motivated and possibly an early form of a stratified society had come into existence.

What was the purpose of the tower? The tower stood in the middle of a settlement we now call Pre-Pottery Neolithic A thrived from around 8,500 to 7,370 BC. It isn't the only settlement in the region also sites in Zaid and Terra, yet with an area of almost 40,000 m² Jericho is by far the largest currently known. The Tower may have been a defensive position against external enemies, but it may also have served as a religious function. The religion of the Pre-Pottery Neolithic people is still unknown was there a common link to a form of animal cult! hunter-gatherers followed the animals throughout the region so not necessarily a massive leap of faith to assume this.

To build such a large structure that is not connected to any other part of the complex around it must have been motivated by religion. The earliest form of yoking the human animal, long before the ox. Maybe it was used in conjunction with observing the night sky, doubling up as an observatory and temple platform. Who was in charge of ceremonies the intermediary between the people and the gods?

The Wall and the Tower of Jericho

What makes Jericho such an interesting site was the discoveries made in the early 20th Century a walled tower with steps leading to the summit. What makes this even more striking is that besides a scattering of mysterious pictographic symbols when writing would not be developed for another 4,500 years. An astonishing point of interest this is a period when even pottery didn't exist, nevertheless these people collectively came together and achieved something astonishing. We know very little about these people, but we do see signs of the domestication of animal and the experimenting of agriculture on a wide scale.

All of this was achieved 11,000 years from the present. Just a few centuries after the end of the last Ice Age, 11700 BC Greenlandian (Early Holocene); a time when woolly mammoth still roamed the world. Jericho is fascinating also due to the fact that unlike other sites such as Uruk where it lay on a very fragile eco system where overnight rivers can change course and leave a city stranded miles from its nearest water source. Jericho has a spring that has never dried up, people still inhabit the region and drink the spring water. Jericho is still considered one of the oldest cities in the world that we know of.

The excavation site of Tell Es Sultan was constantly scrutinised over for 28 years from 1930-1958. In January 1951, work resumed at the excavation site after the long hard attritional war that seen the World set ablaze for six long years. Countries of the Western world looked for solace and a distraction after World War II, so it was decided to continue the search for our past. But this time a new breed of archaeologist was used, people who would bring new ideas to the research.

One of the ground-breaking techniques was the introduction of radiocarbon dating, this helped bring to the fore front a new thirst for knowledge. Radiocarbon dating could accurately date the finding being unearthed in the Middle East thus giving the archaeologist better and more accurate knowledge of the past. This helped archaeologist to be able to determine dates far more accurately than their predecessors.

Unlike the reckless amateur archaeologists like Heinrich Schliemann of Germany who discovered Troy. But at the same time left a wake of destruction in his path, literally bulldozing a path and leaving untold damage. Kenyon was part of a new breed of scholars who could meticulously uncover sites from the top down whilst causing as little damage as possible to the sites and gleaning maximum information in the process. Archaeology was finally a science.

Kathleen Kenyon[lxxiii] was a student of the famous Sir Mortimer Wheeler[17] and daughter of director of the British Museum. She had been drafted into an area close to the Dead Sea to investigate a particular interesting and controversial site. The city had been excavated 20 years previous by fellow British archaeologist John Garstang who had previously taken on a six-year investigation of the same site.

Garstang eventually surmised it to be the site of the famed walls from the Old Testament destroyed by the Israelites Joshua with Trumpets, Garstang's conclusion received heavy criticism. Only when World War II had finally abated was Kenyon sent to investigate the previous claims made by Garstang. This time, she was able to use radiocarbon dating techniques that hadn't been available during the last excavation. She had one very clear instruction, to investigate the site and *to come to her own conclusion.*

Unlike other archaeological sites in the region, often sited out in the desert due to changing river courses or even underwater the geography of Jericho had changed little from when it was first in habited. Sitting comfortably between two mountain ranges and the Dead Sea. It not only rests in a naturally defensible location but as mentioned earlier a never-ending underground water supply that continues to this day. The oasis has been situated their longer than humans have ever lived in the region with its lush, healthy vegetation due to the abundant underground water supply.

This was the first time that true archaeology took place. Kathleen Kenyon's work was to be directed at a solitary mount rising up over the settlement on one edge of Town known today as Tell Es Sultan. A Tell is created overtime by a place of continuous human habitation. Thousands upon thousands of years of collapsed mud brick architecture a mountain of debris of previous cities which have been built one upon the other over millennia. Old buildings collapsed, levelled, and rebuilt, cocooning, and incarcerating the lower level of the previous generation of buildings, waiting for a future when they will be rediscovered.

The Fertile Crescent is quite unique compared to the rest of the world. Tells are not a natural feature of the landscape, but purely manmade. Many thousands of years of habitation, these Tells can be as high as 20 metres and are extremely obvious in the flood plains of Southern Mesopotamia. Kathleen Kenyon

---

[17] *Sir Robert Eric, Mortimer Wheeler British archaeologist, director of both the National Museum of Wales and London Museum, Director General of the Archaeological Survey of India and founder of the Institute of Archaeology in London.*

approached the site and instantly realised the site was extremely old but she and everyone else had no idea what lay before them, only time would tell. The techniques that she and her colleagues used on the site are known as stratigraphic excavation, meticulously recording soil layers as they dug in order to date the various layers of habitation. The level of detail throughout the excavation had never been to such a high standard and ensured set a new benchmark which is still used today.

An accurate understanding of the age of the site with each layer revealing an accurate sequence of events. After brief digging work and a revaluation of Garstang's expedition 20 years previous, Kathleen Kenyon found no evidence to conclusively make a connection with Biblical destruction of the Walls of Jericho as previously stated by Garstang. Further digging was required and a further six years she continued to unearth the site.

After six years of excavation, Jericho had become one of the most famous archaeological sites in history, even without the infamous walls of Jericho. John Garstang had originally dated the earliest settlements in the region as 4th Millennium BC. Kathleen Kenyon turned this date absolutely on its head! Continuous habitation of the site had now been placed from 9,400 BC to 1,580 BC with a potential for even earlier habitation. The end date was later amended to 1,400 BC. Perhaps the most astonishing and iconic buildings discovered turned out not to be the walls of Jericho but a Neolithic Tower which was built 10,000 years ago. At the time, the earliest ever known on earth.

The Fall of Jericho: Death and Destruction
The Status Quo Gone!

If you happen to be near an inexhaustible supply of fresh drinking water that never subsides and which feeds the plants and trees continuously no matter the climatic conditions, be prepared to fend off envious usurpers. Pre-Pottery Neolithic Jericho ended abruptly in 7,000 BC when the Tell of Jericho seems to have been abandoned, most of the wall collapsed and the tower eroded away. All manners of reasons have been looked at for this rapid decline, earthquakes, pestilence, outside invasion.

In an earthquake, the buildings fall down, but can easily be rebuilt, plus the people didn't live in multistorey dwellings, so would seem less feasible. Drought would not necessarily hold up, due to the underwater springs, no main river fearing drying up. If the crops had failed, then the people could fall back on sedentary hunter-gathering techniques that were still semi practiced or had those skills already disappeared. Sufficient wild animals still lived in the region to hunt, even if you are necessarily competent, a little ring rusty, you would soon learn and survive. It could have been a result of over farming therefore the first occurrence of lack of nutrients in the soil from over production.

Remember, these were uncharted waters to the first farmers in the world nobody knew about exhausting the land of its rich nutrient soils. But the strongest and most obvious conclusion seems to fit perfectly in the same timeline of the first marauders in history. The timeline coincides with a major event in the Gulf Oasis which was already in the process of starting to oust the indigenous population of the Gulf Oasis due to the constant onset of the rising ocean levels. At this exact time the largest freshwater lake in the Gulf Oasis which was 11,000 Km² had been breached by the saltwater Indian Ocean.

It is extremely inconvenient to physically move location on a regular basis, but to have your main source of freshwater fish, drinking water, watering hole for all animals and water supply for all agricultural produce immediately spoilt by the ingress of seawater into the eco-system will have caused panic in the populace. Therefore, decisions had to either move along the Oasis basin, upsetting other well-established inhabitants further away from the main lake, or go much further beyond and follow the two main River upstream to higher ground and close to the source.

Had the second wave of the newly displaced people of the spoilt lakes of the Gulf Oasis disappeared without a trace? Or had a significant group, larger in numbers, intelligent, orderly, who worked well in large groups, well equipped, hungry, scared and displaced who are looking for new lands to settle, a land that would no longer be washed away by the relentless, never ending saltwater invasion reappeared on the other side of the Fertile Crescent? If so, when you have the numbers, the balance of power can quickly shift from the haves to the have nots and resistance would have been futile. Maybe a few people first arrived in the region requesting help and then came the deluge, the green-eyed monster of envy appeared, in numbers.

Eventually a new city was erected on top of the old that had little commonality with the previous settlement, this second city lasted from 7,000 BC to 6,000 BC (the Black Sea Deluge Hypothesis). A new culture that seems to have taken over the entire region. Historians have classified this period in very unromantic terminology the Pre-Pottery Neolithic B Culture arose as the results of a possible invasion. Archaeologists know far more about this culture than their predecessors. The skull cult, perhaps one of the earliest known examples of ancestor worship or where they simply advertising their conquering skills similar to the Khmer Rouge which started its genocide in the early 1950's AD.

Kathleen Kenyon[lxxiv], who had just endured World War II, quickly realised that these Pre-Pottery Neolithic B Culture was a hostile conquering people who had drove out their predecessors through fire and bloodshed. It has also been calculated that this new group where far greater in number than their predecessors with a settlement of about 2,000 people which in its day was massive and all defended by a new substantial wall.

This number is extremely intriguing, it is extremely likely that these new people to the region are from the Gulf Oasis and if it was 2,000 people, a couple of questions remain:

- How many of the original group that started from the spoilt lake in the Gulf Oasis separated during their very long journey?
- Did the group manage to stay together from beginning to end?
- If the group did fragment at what point did the group start to splinter off and in which directions did, they go? And how many of the original group separated from the group once they reached Jericho?
- How many people decided to stay at the Gulf Oasis and to try and assimilate into other tribal groups?
- As the initial group left, once gone, was there any chance of recalling members of the separated group back to the newly discovered (taken) lands?

These usurpers fully understood about the vulnerability of weak defences and how to defeat a weaker opposition who weren't prepared for invasion by such a large, organised force. A pivotal point in history of the region had been reached. A place that had been relatively harmonious, now death sang out. Fear and intimidation grew from the ashes of Neolithic A Culture, the region would never be the same again. The round houses of the previous settlement where now replaced by rectangular homes, sometimes two stories in height, suggesting a definitive cultural shift.

Similar to their predecessors, the houses where still made of mud brick, but where organised around rectangular courtyards with gypsum floors and plastered walls often painted red with ochre. We also know that these homes were furnished with reed mats and possibly wall painting for decoration similar too Çatalhöyük. People continued to hunt, and records show that half the bones came from Gazelles. Interestingly, the domestication of animal was much more noticeable with pigs and goats now showing up in significant numbers. So are the new observations described above the observations that would have been seen from people originating from the Gulf Oasis, are these buildings and structures a mirror image of their previous settlement.

With both the ingress of seawater into the large Gulf Oasis lake, forcing the people to move and the destruction of Jericho happening at the same time, with the introduction to a new set of people. Is it too hard to believe they are people of the Gulf Oasis?

During this same period of disturbance, there is also evidence at other sites that round houses where being replaced by the rectangular counterpart with layers of fire destruction in between, particularly in Beidha in modern day Jordan near the Nabatean city of Petra. Could this be part of the original splinter group of the second wave of people to leave the Gulf Oasis. If the group had set off from the Gulf Oasis, the safest route for such a large group would have been up the Tigris and the Euphrates following the Fertile Crescent and into the heart of these embryonic settlements of new farming communities in the surrounding hills and mountains.

Maybe the first people met outside the Gulf Oasis weren't threatening, and little if any friction/resistance was seen. But once the Group moved further North the resistance became greater and eventually force required to *push on past* or simply these refugees settled in small groups throughout the land wherever they could, assimilating into the local groups, but at the same time bringing new ideas and new crafts with them.

Two rooms have been discovered that may have been used for ceremonial purposes along with two small figurines thought to represent fertility deities also throughout the region with animal and human figurines that may have represented ancestors' spirits. The Pre-Pottery Neolithic A Culture was about to end and the dawn a new era was upon them. Pre-Pottery Neolithic B Culture had a very distinctive cult, the practice of plastering skulls a tradition that seems to have been long lasting and widespread. Upon death, the skull is removed from the body more than likely the body is left outside to be picked clean by wild animals and vultures before the ceremony.

Possibly a practice that dates to the time of Göbekli Tepe holding the vulture in high regard, the same vultures that picked the deceased bone clean. The skull removed, filled with clay with external features moulded onto it with plaster and shells used for eyes. The skulls would then be painted to look like the person who has died and then the body interned under the household with the skull left on display. Similar practices have been found at neighbouring sites throughout the region.

We already know the anti-had been upped and the quiet sedate life of the Pre-Pottery Neolithic B Culture was about to end as life would never return. The Gulf Oasis invaders had stepped over the Rubicon and history cannot be undone. Could these heads be proof of manliness and act as a deterrent to possible future antagonists. These practices were not uncommon, could we better label the Pre-Pottery Neolithic B Culture and call them the Headhunters, or is that too much of an injustice. Or could this simply be veneration of the ancestors as seen in many early farming cultures around the world, the passing down of wisdom from one generation to the next.

The Head-hunters make for a better headline, but veneration may seem the most plausible viewpoint. But let's not forget the seismic change in cultural behaviour once these new people of the Gulf Oasis appeared in the Northern Fertile Crescent. They overpowered and destroyed, the Pre-Pottery Neolithic B people and the Gulf Oasis refugees had come for the long-term and nobody was going to move them. Whatever the reason for displaying the heads, good, bad or indifferent, some of the plastered sculls rely looked life like, so we can appreciate they knew and understood art in a macabre weird way.

7300 BC, some of the most life-like depictions of people had started to be seen, some modelers had a true artistic eye. It certainly wouldn't be my *cup of tea* poking around a skull trying to make a true facial likeness of its previous occupant, but it would seem some people had a natural talent. I wonder if these people where in demand, a skill that has disappeared overtime, and one that I don't think will be missed.

The new culture that populated Jericho and the surrounding region of the Northern Fertile Crescent which had introduced Pottery lasted a thousand years. At the end two new civilisation s were about to be born, the development of Eridu/Ubaid/Pre-Sumerians the growth of cities were about to begin in Southern Mesopotamia in Eridu, Ur and Uruk, at the very same time as the Egyptians. In 6,000 BC two powers grew whilst the entire region of the Northern Fertile

Crescent was in terminal decline in Jericho, Palestine, Syria, and the Taurus Mountains of Southern Turkey.

A catastrophe so devastating that the area remained largely depopulated until 5000 BC well over a 1,000 years later, Jericho would never be a regional centre of power again. That decline continued from 6000 to 3100 BC, the lengthy period of 2,900 years up to the Chalcolithic or Copper Age isn't easy to account for. According to Kathleen Kenyon the site was abandoned entirely by around 6,000 BC. Perhaps due to environmental degradation, coupled with over population and poor weather conditions, there are small hints of similar devastating conditions at other sites in the fertile crescent at this time.

This abandonment of such sites also coincided with the ice cap melt concluding, with no further rise in sea levels, yet it was noted by archaeologists that a sudden drop in sea levels occurred at this same time. The event may have been caused by a large meltwater pulse from the final collapse of the Laurentide ice Sheet of North-eastern North America, most likely when the glacial lakes Ojibway and Agassiz suddenly drained into the North Atlantic Ocean. Could this be the cause of the breaching of what we now call the Black Sea from the Mediterranean through the Bosporus with the water pouring into the void, thus accounting for the sudden drop in world ocean levels.

This phenomenon may have been heard across the Mediterranean Ocean, nobody would have known what the sound was, but it certainly wouldn't have sounded like anything previously heard before, the end of all days. Was this the sound of angry gods? Eyewitnesses recounting what had been seen.

The heavens roared, and the earth roared again, daylight failed, and darkness fell, lightning's flashed, fire blazed out, the clouds lowered, they rained down death. Then the brightness departed, the fire went out, and all was turned to ashes fallen about us and the devastation left in its wake, land was no more!

People who knew the area may have witnessed this disaster at first hand, the news would have travelled quickly and fear gripping the population, every man woman and child for themselves, a time to leave with no time to spare. The view of the rich farmland being consumed by a torrent of seawater covering the Euxine from nowhere and almost happening overnight, the sight will have been spectacular and frightening all at the same time. It would have looked like the world had been consumed by seawater, as far as the eye could see. Where had all this water came from? How could this happen? Were the gods angry that so many questions with no earthly answers, this had to be the work of the gods.

This event may have happened after heavy rains, but the rains didn't breach the wall of the Black Sea. Pressure from the Mediterranean with the ever-increasing rise in sea levels created with a shock large meltwater pulse from the final collapse of the Laurentide Ice Sheet compounded the problem. It was going to happen no matter what, but nobody realised it at the time. Locals near the Bosporus will have known the disparity in sea height before the catastrophic breach, but nobody thought to think of the consequences.

Similar to modern people living on the side of an active volcano due to the rich fertile lands that help produce the best crops. The unfolding events in the Euxine soon sent shockwaves around the entire region, the bad news travelled fast engulfing thousands of settlers, who at the time may have already been settled farmers on the rich plentiful plains next to a large freshwater lake that would soon become an ocean. Once the news had reached the people around Jericho and the surrounding region. Maybe they naturally assumed they were next in line, who could guarantee safety when the gods were angry.

A clear line of vision of the ocean you knew you weren't safe; they knew anytime now they could be next. These are the ancestors of the 2nd wave of refugees who had left the Gulf Oasis. So, these ancestors of the Gulf Oasis migrants' memories of past events had it passed down in oral tradition and by the priest upper class. The oral stories would have clearly described the horrors their ancestors had faced at the end of their time in the Gulf Oasis. Unbeknown to the ancestors the land in the Gulf Oasis slowly consumed the land for over 1,000 years, whereas the Black Sea was consumed instantaneously and without warning.

Some people may have decided to stay in the region and not abandon their homes and their cultivated fields and decided not to heed the warnings from the priests and to stay put. But the ones who remained where few in number and nothing as impressive as those that had gone before, nothing significant enough to leave a trace that can be followed today. Some people would move back into a pastoral existence again, taking the domesticated animal with them, that the early settlers had come to rely on. The wandering tribes who had scattered to the four winds during this mysterious epoch brought with it huge changes on the horizon for the rest of the Middle East and surrounding areas.

Pottery was adopted with huge social bonuses which increased the population size of groups, now food could be stored and transported, safely away from mice and rats and stored for leaner times. Some of this excess stock may have even be able to be traded. Around 4,000 BC another huge improvement occurred. Originally brought South from Anatolia, where obsidian had been the choice of tools now came a new material in the form of a metal and soon it would change world forever. The Copper Age or Chalcolithic age from around 4000 BC, places like Jericho which had been abandoned began to slowly be reoccupied.

Çatalhöyük

James Mellaart first discovered the site in 1958 and later led a team back to the area between 1961-1965 AD and by Ian Hodder from 1993-2017 AD. At Çatalhöyük Priest Kings are thought to have controlled city life similar to Eridu and Uruk with extremely prominent sky gods in their religions. Maybe Jericho was at the forefront of a phenomena that continues to have resonance to this day, the religion has changed but the control continues. Çatalhöyük are two separate Tell mounds known as Çatalhöyük East and West.

This is an extremely important and exciting site that may cast further understanding of the development and transience of people starting 9,200 years ago. The wall art alone may help historians understand how this area developed. *The city, a tale of two tells*, also has retained the snapshot of how life looked when part of the area was abandoned 6000 BC, leaving behind a glimpse of how people started to live in close communities and leaving behind impressive wall art that shows certain impressive scenes. Located near the modern city of Konya in South Central Turkey, Mellaart had accurately provided a date of the East Tell occupation of 7100 BC with 26 radiocarbon dates in 1964.

With a population of up to an estimated 8,000 people who lived together in a large town. This alone shows evidence that a stratified society must have existed from the beginning. Çatalhöyük, across its history, witnesses densely packed houses with underfloor burials (West Tell) and a rich symbolic tradition observed over much of its 1,200-year existence when it was finally abandoned. The abandonment of the latest known domestic building (Building 33) is securely dated to 6,015-5,905 BC with a probability of 95% accuracy. By contrast, it also looks like the West mound (Tell) occupancy tentatively dates the West Tell occupancy date of around 5,600 BC so a clear hiatus period between desertion on the Eastern Tell and the occupation of the Western Tell of almost 400 years. Some cross pollination will have occurred during this period.

When the Eastern tell had been abandoned then it would be very realistic for indigenous people of the surrounding area to reoccupy the either or both Tells, not long after desertion. Archaeologists would naturally find remnants confusing and misguiding in trying to piece the history of the mounds and give an exact date at times.

Virtually every home currently excavated was found to have decorations on its wall. What is more impressive is the artwork was renewed on a very regular basis usually between 6 months to a year/season. To-date we can only see the very last of the artwork before the building became abandoned and disused. Future science will help reveal what lays beneath the top set of artworks and help us all to understand what has happened during the different phases of the cities' growth.

Art is everywhere among the remains of Çatalhöyük, geometric designs as well as representations of animals and people. Repeated lozenges and zigzags dance across smooth plaster walls, people are sculpted in clay, pairs of leopards are perched either side of *the seated woman*. Hunting parties are painted baiting a wild boar. The volume and variety of art at Çatalhöyük is immense.

Çatalhöyük was slightly behind the original buildings of Jericho but strikingly in tune with the second phase of Jericho when a new populace forcibly inhabited the area circa 7,200-7,000 BC, on a personal note I don't believe in coincidences and always believe a domino effect of events usually link multiple events that are in close…ish proximity. It is our own failings that inhibit our belief and understanding. We seem to like the idea that ancient peoples lived in isolation from other neighbouring regions when the evidence is contrary to new findings. We moved from roaming hunter-gatherer to a sedentary role overnight which simply isn't the case.

During excavations, visible material changes between East Tell and West tell were considered *rapid* but can't conclude any degree of social differentiation between the Tells. The most striking difference is East Tell had interned burials within the buildings whilst none are evident in the Western tell. So did the Pre-Sumerians carry out burial rituals of internment within the homes and during abandonment indigenous people felt unwilling to inhabit the West (tell) due to these internments.

All areas were well on their way to the domestication of a select few wild animals. Even though it would seem the main meat would have been wild gazelle, bulls and boar due to the abundance of the animals in the area. People where well on the road to domestication of animals but not at a level of sustainability but now a hunter-gatherer lifestyle from a sedentary position. The remains of gazelle, cattle, boar, sheep, and goat have all been found at Jericho and other outlining areas. It would be impossible to say which animals will have become domesticated without trial and error.

Seated Woman of Çatalhöyük

Today, it's easy to know which animals can and can't be domesticated. Our ancestors already done the hard work of trial and elimination, maybe some of these animals were known not to be able to be domesticated but kept for slaughter during the winter months to ensure the sedentary hunter-gatherers didn't have to relocate. Young gazelle could easily have been taken and caged ready for slaughter, no animals need to be domesticated when caged.

Early farming produce included wheat, barley, peas, and beans, all of which were well known to a very sophisticated hunter-gatherers. All this produce had started to be adapted over a prolonged period of time from its wild ancestors to the very growing yield now sown in rows and animals grown up in compounds.

Artwork of Çatalhöyük

The artwork found on the walls in Çatalhöyük raise some serious questions of where these people actually originated from and what some of the artwork physically represents. The Seated Woman of Çatalhöyük is a perfect example of the change in opulence and status. This maybe a true representation of an older female revered, certainly no longer a depiction of hunter-gatherer but a female of fertility of a sedentary opulent nature, only in a stratified society could this be accomplished.

Wall painting in Building 80 Çatalhöyük

The geometric shapes in Building 80 maybe representing a Map of cultivated land allocation to the local populace. If this does represent the proposed theory, it also indicates a system of irrigation canals and a measurement system and again a strong indication of a centrally organised society allotting sections of land for families or individuals.

Most of the animals represented in the art of Çatalhöyük were not domesticated with wild animals dominating the art at the site a remembering of their recent past. The celebrated animals which are part of the memory of the recent cultural past, when hunting was much more important for survival.

A valuable obsidian mirror has also been retrieved from the site which still clearly reflects a true image even after 8,000 years. Therefore, the people could gaze at a reflection of themselves and appreciate what they were looking at.

The photograph above shows the original drawings made by James Mellaart of the unusual wall paintings in Çatalhöyük

There are numerous pictures showing hunting scenes but the original drawing from James Mellaart could be a leading indicator that highlights physical difference within the people hunting. The (pre) Sumerians referred to themselves as Ug Sag GiG Ga, which is translated to the Black Headed People, whilst the eventual close neighbours who occupied large areas of Sumer but had an Akkadian Semitic language called them by the same name but pronounced Tsalmat-Qaqqadi in Akkadian. From many carvings depicting Sumerians, we can see how they wore their hair, curly on top and cut short on the side. Very similar to the paintings of Çatalhöyük.

If we assume the pre-Sumerians heads were black, their bodies will have been a similar colour. The picture represented shows a physical colour difference and I personally don't believe it to be an accident. Could this show two distinct types of people working as a single group assuming the lighter (orca) people are indigenous to the area surrounding Çatalhöyük and the *black* people a representation of *foreigners*, the displaced people of the Gulf Oasis.

Interestingly, several people are depicted two-toned. This may simply be physical painting of the body or showing people who had racially mixed a deliberate point made by the original artist. If it was one picture you couldn't really force this point across, but many pictures show these same differences. Coincidence? as stated throughout the book I don't believe in coincidences.

As I Look at the Dates of Habitation, the Real Standout Dates, they are the Beginning and the End and what drove the change

The appearance of smaller settlements on the plain after 6000 BC would indicate an acceleration of the Late Neolithic of greater mobility and more extensive landscape use, regressing which would reduce the population growth in the region. This flies in the face of continued expansion of cities. A trigger point must have initiated such a rapid change, perhaps a mini *Dark Age* or the *First Dark Age*. It seems people scattered and fled the region in a very short space of time not just Çatalhöyük but other areas around Jericho.

At the very same time Egypt kick-starts into life and Sumerians start to flourish. These two future empires also seem to have very similar traits or is it a case of same origins. The direction of movement is important at this time. All movement is in an arc of South East to South West, this could lead to the assumption something happened more Northerly in 6,000 BC. The rising Mediterranean finally spilled over a rocky sill at the Bosporus, caused the Bosporus Strait to catastrophically breach around 6,000 BC. The Mediterranean poured large volumes of water into the Euxine (the future Black Sea). The displaced people of the Gulf Oasis who had come to settle thousands of kilometres away from the newly created Persian Gulf, now had first-hand experience of a similar event that traditional stories of their ancestors had witnessed a *flooding*.

Fertile land north of Çatalhöyük had been consumed and the large trees had been swallowed up by an ever-rising sea. The people will have a great respect of the sea due the ancient stories pasted from generation to generation. Did they know if this raising sea level would stop, nobody could know for sure? It didn't stop in the Gulf Oasis for over a thousand years. Nobody knew, and the safest option would be to head in the opposite direct to start again. This time the people would be of mixed origin, the Pre-Sumerians and some of the indigenous people of Çatalhöyük. So, these originals of Çatalhöyük may actually be the Semitic speaking Pre-Akkadians who eventually settled next in Sumeria. Wall painting cannot tell you the languages, but if they could we wouldn't need to search so hard for answers.

The Neolithic Revolution:
From hunter-gatherer to Agriculturalist Competing Theories

The beginning of the Neolithic Revolution in different regions of the Middle East including, with some considering the developments of 10-11,000 BC in the Fertile Crescent to be the most important. This transition to a more settled, agrarian-based one, due to the inception of the domestication of various plant and animal species depending on the species locally available, and probably also influenced by local culture. Cultivating plants and domesticating animals is far more labour-intensive. The people may have been aware of the relationship between cultivation of grains and an increase in population. An increase in population is also an added bonus to survival of a large group from external threats. The domestication of animals provided a new source of protein, through meat and milk, along with hides and wool, which allowed for the production of clothing and other objects.

There are several competing (but not mutually exclusive) theories about the factors that drove populations to take up agriculture. The most prominent of these are:

- The Oasis Theory, originally proposed by Raphael Pumpelly in 1908[lxxv], and popularised by V. Gordon Childe in 1928, suggests as the climate got drier due to the Atlantic depressions shifting Northward,

communities contracted to oases where they were forced into close association with animals. These animals were then domesticated together with planting of seeds.
- Raphael Pumpelly seems to have been on the correct track but this book concerning the Gulf Oasis theory has a more scientific based polar opposite theory. Instead of shifting towards the Oasis the Gulf Oasis seems to have been the natural protector of life that could allow Humans to survive outside of Africa during climatic changes. The Gulf Oasis could support a large populace through Hunting and Fishing, especially at the large freshwater lakes.
- I do believe agriculture was common in the Gulf Oasis and the people of that region had developed into a stratified society so the division of labour may have been witnessed before similar regions in Northern Mesopotamia. Prior to the flooding of the Gulf Oasis and forcing the indigenous people to leave. If this is true that the people where organised, then people had various jobs/trades and some of those jobs could very well have been within agriculture some of the words for farming equipment and various works come only from Sumerian words.
- The Hilly Flanks hypothesis, proposed by Robert Braidwood[lxxvi] in 1948, suggests that agriculture began in the hilly flanks of the Taurus and Zagros mountains, where the climate was not drier, as Childe had believed, and that fertile land supported a variety of plants and animals amenable to domestication.
- This theory also has good grounds for validity, as archaeologists have started to realise that not all parts to agriculture started in one area, but the best parts quickly shared throughout the various regions. But it would seem the people of Southern Mesopotamia advanced farming that had never been realised or imagined before. The domestication of animals could very easily be correct, but equally so from the Gulf Oasis.
- The Feasting model by Brian Hayden[lxxvii] suggests that agriculture was driven by ostentatious displays of power, such as giving feasts, to exert dominance. This system required assembling large quantities of food, a demand which drove agricultural technology.
- This only occurs once a stratified society exists and commerce is in full fruition, during this early period of time Kings did not exist in society until much later. Brian Hayden's hypothesis does occur much later in

society but not during these embryonic stages of area settlement. Göbekli Tepe could be used as a yard stick in assuming feasting models and social gathering which occurred at the start of 11,000 BC.

- The Demographic theories proposed by Carl Sauer 1986[lxxviii] and adapted by Lewis Binford and Kent Flannery stated that an increasingly sedentary population outgrew the resources in the local environment and required more food than could be gathered. Various social and economic factors helped drive the need for food.
- The only problem with this theory is during earlier periods of time the population wasn't vast and people did naturally move on to pastures new, perfect examples of this is seen with early expansion of Greece and how the *Mother Country* was always the *Mother Country* until it had reason to go its own separate way. But it could be viewed as accurate if you consider 40-60,000 years ago, the movement out of the Gulf Oasis and into the Indian Subcontinent via the exposed land bridge during the Last Glacial Maximum with oceans 120 metres lower than today.
- The Evolutionary/Intentionality theory, developed by David Rindos[lxxix] and others, views agriculture as an evolutionary adaptation of plants and humans. Starting with domestication by protection of wild plants, it led to specialisation of location and then full-fledged domestication.
- Evolution takes time and had taken time, but my question is, what made this jump in intensive agriculture happen? This is the reason for this book.

Conclusion

All five theories have substance, but something else must be the glue and no one theory from the five listed above seems to be the glue. Also, it is never a binary point for such a large change in attitude. All five theories are individually OK but lack depth or real substance as this is a multifaceted problem when only one theory isn't necessarily the answer to such a complicated riddle, therefore a combination of all five maybe the real answer. I believe the glue is survival, being able to have a larger family group increases the chances of survival if statically located. If other clans are observed to have changed their own habits and seen to prosper with an increase in clan members, then observing clans will quickly follow suit. Therefore, growth of the clan size would seem to be the glue to all the theories above. Regional growth dependent on local environments and then the dispersal of ideas between various communities.

Village Life Begins and a Population Growth

People began to live in permanent settlements, rather than moving around seasonally to follow resources. Population growth was one major consequence. Births among hunter-gatherers tend to be widely spaced, at intervals of 4-5 years, since women can only carry one small child at a time. Village life also meant storage facilities for food, containers of stone, and later clay pottery, and agricultural tools, like sickles and hoes.

Early Agricultural Village Sites

Archaeologists have constructed a chronological sequence of village life, with period names identified by key excavated sites; the pottery from the later ones is used to identify contemporary sites.

- *Natufian,* Eastern Mediterranean into Southern Turkey. First embryonic signs of settlement.
- *Neolithic Proto-Neolithic (PPNA)*, 9,000-8,500 BC Prehistory.
- *Jarmo*, in Iraqi Kurdistan, one of the earliest and best-known sites, excavated by Robert Braidwood of the University of Chicago, with an interdisciplinary team of experts in prehistoric flora and fauna, climatologists and geologists, etc. Pottery appears in the later layers.
- *Hassuna*, near Mosul, provided evidence of decorated pottery.
- *Samarra*, on the right bank of middle Tigris, produced a distinctive pottery with geometric decorations and stylised animals and human figures at sites such as Tell es-Sawwan.
- *Halaf*, on the Habur River (a Euphrates tributary), is known for beautiful painted pottery and evidence of copper implements.

These early settlements were founded by tribes that practiced rain-fed agriculture. Yet populations grew, they moved into the flat silt-laden alluvium, where irrigation created higher crop yields. Supporting ever larger populations and the growth of towns that attracted craft workers, administrators and other specialists who were sustained by these agricultural surpluses. The ancient land of Armenia is situated in the high mountains immediately North of the Great

Plains and rivers of Mesopotamia and shouldn't be forgotten as being an integral part of the *Fertile Crescent.*

Although Mesopotamia, with its ancient civilisations of Sumeria and later Babylon, is usually considered together with the later addition of Egypt as the main source of ancient, civilised life *in the modern sense*. Other areas also have to be considered as they all seem to have early important roles from the Neolithic age in the cultivation of land and the increase in farming which brought to light the Bronze Age. Modern Day, Turkey, Syria, Lebanon, Armenia and Pakistan have an equal role in this development. It was the area of Southern Mesopotamia that has the fortune of foresight and location as this area seems to be at the crossroads of diverse cultures, to the North, East and West and the perfect central point for trade.

Armenia was located between the two rivers, also engaged in agriculture, had numerous thriving areas that quickly became Cities, had exploited metallurgy due to its natural resources, even the discovery of the plough for cultivating the soil aided the shift from Nomadic lifestyle to settled encampments/villages/towns. Later the Kingdom competed with Assyria over supremacy in the highlands of Ararat and the Fertile Crescent.

North Kuwait Agricultural Area (Abdali) 2020

Even today, you can still witness the agricultural area of North Kuwait which is in the Southern part of the Fertile Crescent; this is a sample of proof that farming is capable even when the temperature exceeds 50°C.

Later Agricultural Cities

The key sites that represent the second phase of agriculture and urbanisation are:

- ***Ubaid***, which gives its name to the highly fired painted pottery that was mass produced at this site, and clay artefacts such as sickles, nails, and bricks.
- ***Eridu***, the earliest identifiable site appearing in the Sumerian King's List, where an important sequence of early tri-partite Mesopotamian temples was excavated, typically consisting of a central sanctuary with a raised altar at one end and an offering table, flanked by projecting lateral wings.

Trade was becoming an ever more important factor at this time. When the sheep graze and sheared and the wool spun into yarn, the yarn made into cloth and the cloth used as an export item. Evidence by the abundance of objects made of obsidian, from the Lake Van area, which had been imported since early prehistoric times.

In later periods, metals such as tin, silver and copper were imported South from Anatolia, copper came North from the Gulf and later from Cyprus. Timber came from Lebanon, the famous *Cedars of Lebanon*, are still present today on the modern Lebanese flag. Steatite, a soft stone suitable for carving, came from the Iranian plateau. Precious stones such as lapis lazuli were imported from the Badakhshan mines of Afghanistan. And carnelian travelled the immense distance from India.

Effects of the Neolithic Revolution on Society

The shift to agricultural food production and fundamentally an agrarian society was eventually able to support a denser population. Local isolated farming communities started to combine efforts to enable better resourcing of manpower. Which in turn supported larger agrarian sedentary communities. So immediate kin groups and the broader social group who claim association through either marriage or friendship and support. The larger the family group the more chance to witness the emergence of chiefly elite but this seems to have been numerous chiefly elites of large families and numerous families within close proximity to each other.

So, no one chief is able to grow to an exurbanite level, therefore keeping stability within the region. The accumulation of goods and tools, and specialisation in diverse forms of new labour. This is the point of initiation when a community starts to stratify, and kinship dominates. Overall a population could increase its size more rapidly when resources are pooled together, and people allocated specific tasks. The resulting larger societies led to the development of different means of decision making and eventually the formation of *governmental* organisation, this is when a community starts to move away from agrarian and into a society that we would recognise today.

Food surpluses made possible the development of social elite freed from labour, which dominated their communities and monopolised decision-making. Two main classes came into prominence the Priest Class who had an *understanding* of how everything came to being and later as agriculture increased and the demand of how to export the vital commodity, water, to the fields became more pressing, the Project Manager came to prominence, somebody had to take charge of the growing and ever more complicated engineering tasks, this expansion of engineering also needed to be standardised so people could do repetitive tasks correctly.

Within a short period of time, deep social divisions became apparent and inequality between the sexes expanded, with women's status declining once the knowledge of agriculture was known. Men took on greater roles in the fields ensuring the land was tilde and rocks removed with the land flattened for ease of harvesting the crops, canals and ditches dug.

Later, the males became the leaders and eventually the warriors were created to be able to protect what had been grown in the fields from external people and a social class was determined by occupation, with farmers and craftsmen at the lower end, and priests, engineers and warriors at the higher level, a true stratified society had come into being.

Effects of the Neolithic Revolution on Health

The grass isn't always greener on the other side of the hill. The hunter-gatherers understood what was required to stay fit and mobile and what was good for the individual. If the hunter failed in his tasks then the small clan suffered, everyone had a role to play, and nobody could fall short. The variety of food for hunter-gatherers was exceptionally wide ranging and skeletal remains show that the hunter-gatherer was much taller than the Neolithic populations generally who had a poorer nutrition, shorter life expectancies, and a more labour-intensive lifestyle than hunter-gatherers. Diseases jumped from animals to humans, and agriculturalists suffered from more anaemia, vitamin deficiencies, spinal deformations and dental pathologies than the earlier hunter-gatherer.

Overall Impact of the Neolithic Revolution on Modern Life

The way we live today is directly related to the advances made during the Neolithic Revolution. From the governments we live under, to the specialised work labourers do, to the trade of goods and food, humans were irrevocably changed by the switch to sedentary agriculture and domestication of animals. With this change came the loss of knowledge of how to survive in the outdoors, forgotten by the agrarian society, how to hunt efficiently and the best tactics to be successful and what wild growing berries where medicinally good for a person's health and which plants are edible and which to avoid. All this knowledge that kept a hunter-gather strong and alert predominantly lost forever, a few parts were passed down therefore, the *healers* still had a place in the new society. Human population swelled from five million to seven billion today.

Regional Chronologies

We have briefly discussed several sites that have been excavated and the archaeological evidence that describes changes within each of those areas focusing primarily on sites within Northern Mesopotamia. By understanding the extent of cultural change in the Northern Region we can have a better understanding for the effects on the entire region as a whole and not just the *Ubaid* region which is only a *tagline* not an entire civilisation in itself. We should also give a very brief overview of several other areas as the previous areas mentioned above were not alone, but simply belonged to a much larger network of Northern city states with varying levels of development.

The excavated sequences and multiple radiocarbon dates which will allow us to solidify dates in other towns in the region and the key *Phase Start Date* of existence for this specific area occur at very similar timings; Tell Sabi Abyad 6,300 BC, Fistikli Hoyuk 5,850 BC, Tell Kurdu 5,850 BC and Yarim Tepe 5,850 BC, could 3 of the 4 areas have been settled by other migrants who were moving further South? It is worth emphasising that the spread of painted pottery at the end of the 7th Millennium BC marks a significant development in the way in which ceramics were used and the complexity of symbolism associated with them.

The development is a useful chronological marker, but it is much more significant in terms of social change and where it might have come from. The way in which painted ceramics were incorporated into the wider ceramic assemblage is only completely documented at Tell Sabi Abyad, where it can also be given a fairly precise date. It has been apparent for some time that the emergence of this new painted pottery style happened over a wide area in a very similar way. This generates immediate questions concerning the nature of the phenomenon. Did it develop in one region and then spread through a process of emulation or carried by one culture to all areas of Mesopotamia?

The timing of this rise in painted ceramic ware is very striking and once again an explosion in development at the same time as agriculture and therefore another convergence of dates with the final stage of the Gulf Oasis being consumed by the Indian Ocean and there must be significant social processes underlying the emergence of all these changes.

It has long been argued that the Halaf period in Northern Mesopotamia came to an end when it was replaced by the Ubaid, in an episode in which a cultural tradition from Southern Mesopotamia expanded to dominate. This however was noted by some previous historians as an abrupt change in direction but in more recent radiocarbon dating it would seem a more transitional phase of time occurred therefore the gradual erosion of Halaf Pottery. It is clear from the dates from some of these sites that by 4,900 BC, Ubaid ceramic assemblages were widespread and a few sites even as early as 5,300 BC had finally witnessed Ubaid Pottery in Northern Mesopotamia. So, this may be a result of mere change in taste rather than Ubaid pottery being imposed upon a local populace.

Chapter 3
Pre-Start of Southern Mesopotamia

Rivalry Meaning

It's a state of two groups of people or groups in a lasting competitive relationship trying to gain superiority. The root origin "Rivus" French or "Rivalis" Latin meaning a person who utilises the same brook, stream, river or canal. It entered the English language 1577 AD, over 7,000 years after the realisation of rivalry and the birth of the first hydraulic empires.

Mountains, Plains and Rivers of Mesopotamia

In the highlands of South-eastern Turkey, a range of snow topped limestone peaks rise over 3,000 metres above the plains beneath. These are the Taurus Mountains which is home to some of the most remarkable people, during and after the hunter-gatherer period. In recent years many discoveries have been unearthed in these mountains that have made archaeologists and historians alike reassess previous trains of thought. The mountains of modern-day Turkey rising sharply that rain clouds engross the range. Instead, these clouds pool in their hollows and valleys and give these hills an exceptionally high rate of annual rainfall.

In spring and summer, the warm air means that the clouds are even denser and violent thunderstorms rock the mountains and the thunderous roar of a stampeding bull can be heard echoing down the valleys, an apt name for such awe-inspiring range, Taurus coming from the Latin word Bull. As a result, this is a landscape shaped by water, the steep sides of the Taurus mountains have been eroded to form streams and waterfalls, while underground rivers have cut into the rock and chased out some of the largest cave systems in Asia.

Water is everything to the people of the region and has formed unbreakable bonds with the original people of the Fertile Crescent. The heavy spring rains joined rivers already flowing from the snowy mountain passes of Armenia, soon this multitude of small insignificant rivers join together and flow down from the mountains and into the wide flat plains and creating two of the most famous rivers in the world. The source of this life comes from some of the most lifeless things, the rocks of the mountains, rocks are held together with tiny particles of two different materials called quartz formed from oxygen and silicon and feldspar is a complex mineral derived from silicon.

These rivers have slowly and gently eroded away these rocks since time begun and these small deposits which don't dissolve in water are carried all the way down the river. These two minerals combined are called silt, the miniscule rock debris also has a major impact on agriculture. Soil with a high silt content tends to hold water better whist promoting air circulation and perfect growing material. The delta of both Rivers is exceptionally fertile, these tiny unseen particles where the lifeblood of humanity and the bedrock of civilisation.

As previously explained, the weather is extremely inhospitable and probably the last place on earth you would think of starting to build a new society. And for these exact reasons. The last people to be finally pushed out of the flooded Gulf Oasis lived in the estuaries and deltas of these two great rivers. Slowly but surely the last remaining refugees of the Gulf Oasis hung onto life in an environment totally alien to them, no trees, desert, hot and unforgiving.

But being good intelligent and very desperate modern humans, they adapted and overcame some of the greatest tests any humans have ever endured. *Desperation can be the mother of all inventions*. The people of the Delta's task were as great as any previously known, not for several days, or months but over hundreds of years. Generation after generation, slowly but surely making life slightly better, one basket of soil at a time, one rock at a time. Unfortunately, that wasn't everything these people had to contend with, the two great rivers of the Tigris and Euphrates are not like the Nile River of Egypt that flows directly from the Great Lakes of Africa creating a steady flow.

Whereas the two great rivers of the Tigris and the Euphrates depend on the amount of rain that falls in the Mountains of Turkey, Armenia and Kurdistan, always varying year on year, droughts followed by floods and during winter, the whole plain is covered with a thick layer of mud. hunter-gatherers had no reason to ever wander into Southern Iraq, no woods, no rocky outcrops to find shelter and no animals for hunting and far too hot. Everything a hunter-gatherer needed wasn't there.

Early hunter-gatherers stayed in the mountains and the wetter and more habitable mountain ranges that surrounded Mesopotamia, leaving the early settlers to start eking survival from the pittance that was available. They started in small area and started growing Wheat, Millet and Sesame, and eventually cultivating Date Palms already well known to them. Later they started to grow Pomegranates, grapes, figs as well as chickpeas, lentils, leeks, garlic, cucumbers and watercress in the shade of the palm trees that eventually grew after planting many years before.

The Land of Sumer: The First Hydraulic Civilisation

Before we start advancing in depth with the chronological history and growth of Southern Mesopotamia, it would be mindful to always appreciate the power of water, the power and control that this can have on people, especially when considering the Southern Mesopotamia only has an annual rain fall of 107mm. When you have a plentiful water supply as a country, it is easy to discard the relevance of water and the power it has over its neighbours.

The first civilisations formed close to rivers and were quickly characterized by a stratified social system and a strong government that controlled water access and resources. The waterways helped connect communities and help source supplies and aided the growth in trade which intern created the first civilisation s around the world. Rivers were attractive locations for the first civilisation s because they provided a steady supply of drinking water and game, made the land fertile for growing crops, and allowed for easy transportation.

Key Terms

- **Water Shortage:** Water is less available due to climate, diversion of water source, pollution or overuse.
- **Water Crisis:** There is not enough fresh, clean water to meet local demand.
- **Hydraulic Hierarchies:** Gave rise to the established permanent institution of impersonal government, since changes in ruling were usually in personnel, but not in the structure of government.

- **A Form of Social Stratification:** characterised by endogamy (hereditary transmission of a lifestyle (a king)). This lifestyle often includes an occupation, ritual status in a hierarchy, and customary social interaction and exclusion based on cultural notions of purity and pollution.
- **Hydraulic Civilisation/Empire:** A social or governmental structure that maintains power through exclusive control of water access. A civilisation is created prior to future expansion into becoming an Empire. Early river civilisation s were all hydraulic empires that maintained power and control through exclusive control over access to water. This system of government arose through the need for flood control and irrigation, which requires central coordination and a specialised bureaucracy.
- **Fertile Crescent**: A crescent-shaped region containing the comparatively moist and fertile land of otherwise arid and semi-arid from Southern Mesopotamia, through Iraq and all the way to modern Turkey and Syria called the *Cradle of Civilisation*.
- **Neolithic Revolution**: Also called the Agricultural Revolution, this was the wide-scale transition of human cultures from being hunter-gatherers to being settled agriculturalists.
- **Water Stress**: Difficulty in finding fresh water, or the depletion of available water sources.

Hydraulic Empires

Though each civilisation was uniquely different, we can see common patterns amongst these first civilisation s since they were all based around rivers. Most notably, these early civilisation s all became Hydraulic Empires. A Hydraulic Empire is also known as *Hydraulic Despotism* or *Water Monopoly Empires* and is a social or governmental structure which maintains power through exclusive control over water access. We are able to witness throughout Sumerian history the growth of Hydraulic Empires as first described in Sumerian Cuneiform writing which details the problems between rival city states.

Writing provided information of the world's first known conflict were once cities provided joint building programs that eventually deteriorated to open conflict between the city states of Umma and Lagash. Even though they shared a common language and cultural traditions, the Sumerian city states engaged in near-constant wars that resulted in several different dynasties and Kingships. The first of these conflicts known to history concerns King Eannatum of Lagash, who defeated the rival city state of Umma in a border dispute sometime around 2,450 BC. To commemorate his victory, Eannatum constructed the so-called *Stele of the Vultures*, a grisly limestone monument that depicts birds feasting on the flesh of his fallen enemies.

This system of government rose through the need for flood control and irrigation, which requires central coordination and a specialised bureaucracy. This political structure is commonly characterised by a system of hierarchy and control based around class or caste. Power, both over resources (food, water, energy) and a means of enforcement, such as the military, are vital for the maintenance of control. The majority of Hydraulic Empires exist in arid regions, but Imperial China also had such characteristics, due to the exacting needs of rice cultivation.

The only Hydraulic Empire to exist in Africa was under the Ajuran state near the Jubba and Shebelle Rivers in the 15th Century AD. The Indian Subcontinent state of Harappa who traded heavily with Southern Mesopotamia from in the Indus Valley may fall into category, as the decline came swift when water became a scarce commodity.

Karl August Wittfogel[lxxx], the German scholar who first developed the notion of the Hydraulic Empire, argued in his book, *Oriental Despotism*, that strong government control characterised these civilisation s because a particular resource in the case of Southern Mesopotamia river water. This was both a central part of economic processes and environmental limitations. This fact made controlling supply and demand easier and allowed the establishment of a more complete monopoly. Which also prevented the use of alternative resources to compensate.

However, it is also important to note that complex irrigation projects predated the state in Southern Mesopotamia until the individual states became totally independent. Thus, it cannot be said that a key, limited economic resource necessarily mandates a strong centralised bureaucracy. According to Wittfogel, the typical Hydraulic Empire government has no trace of an independent aristocracy. Hydraulic hierarchies gave rise to the established permanent institution of impersonal government.

Popular revolution in such a state was very difficult; a dynasty might die out or be overthrown by force, but the new regime would differ very little from the old one. Hydraulic Empires were usually destroyed by foreign conquerors as seen with the destruction of the Akkadian Empire by the Mountain people the Gutians who had no prior knowledge of how a state should be maintained with decline rapidly occurring.

Water Scarcity Today and the Same Problems Faced in Southern Mesopotamia

Access to water is still crucial to modern civilisations; water scarcity affects more than 2.8 billion people globally. Water stress is the term used to describe difficulty in finding fresh water or the depletion of available water sources. Water shortage is the term used when water is less available due to water is less available due to climate, diversion of water source, pollution, or overuse. Water crisis is the term used when there is not enough fresh, clean water to meet local demand. Water scarcity may be physical, meaning there are inadequate water resources available in a region, or economic, meaning governments are not managing available resources properly.

This is exemplified by the current situation with Turkey and the ongoing situation in Northern Iraq with the Kurdish population. Turkey wants to control the water in that area, not the large sums of oil and gas that lay just beneath the surface; the water is the main driver for control that will alleviate many problems within modern day Turkey and the oil and gas are simply an added bonus.

North South Divide of Mesopotamia

The Tigris and Euphrates, their tributaries and Mesopotamia have historically embraced all that lay between the foothills of the Iranian mountains to the Northeast, and the great desert of the Arabian Plateau to the Southwest. Less obvious, but no less important culturally, is the North/South dividing line that runs through the modern city of Hit on the Euphrates and Samarra on the Tigris. This line marks the end of the alluvial plain. North of this line, rain-fed irrigation made possible the productive countryside of the Tigris and its tributaries, which constituted the lands of ancient Assyria.

To the South, this same river depositing alluvial sediments for thousands of years built up an immense flat plain that, when irrigated in ancient times, became highly fertile. This was Babylonia, which further divided into the Sumerian South and the Akkadian North along linguistic and cultural grounds (Akkadian being a Semitic language like Arabic and Hebrew; Sumerian being a unique language, not related to any known linguistic group). South of the alluvial plain was the area of marshes and lagoons where the people we call the Marsh Arabs and have lived for a hundred generations in the same Marshes.

Following a traditional lifestyle similar to the ancient Sumerians until the marshes were drained under orders from Saddam Hussein. cities in ancient Sumer were concentrated in areas favourable for irrigation, separated by vast open areas that were more suitable for nomadic herding known as the Edin, perhaps the source of the word Eden that appears in the Bible.

The Need for Irrigation in Southern Mesopotamia

In contrast to Egypt, which has been called the *Gift of the Nile*, Mesopotamia has been the far more contested gift of the Tigris and Euphrates. Unlike Egypt, where the Nile floods in the fall, ideally timed to water newly planted crops, the Tigris and Euphrates flood in the spring, endangering the crops just as they are about to be harvested, and are at their lowest point in the fall, when seedlings are most in need of water.

For this reason, agriculture in Mesopotamia was impossible without irrigation. But with it, farming yields in antiquity rivalled those of modern farming. Yet the gift bestowed by the rivers with one hand was taken away by the other. River water from the Tigris carried dissolved mineral salts that deposited and compromised the once-fertile soil. Over-irrigation caused salts in the soil to rise to the surface. For this reason, wheat and barley cultivation was the norm growing in equal amounts in ancient times. This dramatically changed during the 4.2K Climatic event that exacerbated the salt levels in the alluvium plains.

So, a shift to increased barley production occurred due to barley being more salt-tolerant. Allowing land lie to fallow, lay unplanted in alternating years was one strategy for coping with the mineral deposits. But population growth and economic pressures caused farmers to cultivate three years out of five, leading, over many centuries, to dramatic shrinkage and abandonment of the Fertile Crescent. In the *Epic of Atrahasis*[lxxxi], the Babylonian flood myth written 1800 BC, we are told: *The black field became white, the broad plain was choked with salt*. Environmental degradation was an issue no less present in antiquity than it is today.

Understanding Southern Mesopotamia

Currently, phases of human development within the Fertile Crescent are broken down into specific zones and time frames, Stuart Campbell tries to break down this *pigeon holing*. I can fully appreciate the need for archaeologist to have a common consensus to be able to arrange events and dates to understand the order of their occurrences. Everyone who is carrying-out research in this region needs a common datum point to align with corresponding sites throughout the region to appreciate its place in history.

But an anomaly occurs when the region seems to be at a status quo with nothing really untoward occurring in the region and no power struggle in the formative years of early Mesopotamia. Later history with the use of Cuneiform tablets clearly gives the archaeologist and historian a firm direction of what events were happening at what time and the boundaries to each state or Empire. Stuart Campbell[lxxxii] stated:

Chronologies are also, however, artificial constructs, created by a partial understanding of the past and incorporating a range of assumptions, often unstated and unintended. Even the basic terms with which we use (Hassuna, Samarra, Halaf, Ubaid and so on) shape our view of the past.
Ref: *Rethinking Halaf Chronologies*. In: Paléorient, 2007

The terms Hassuna, Samarra, Halaf and Ubaid are almost entirely based on ceramics which shouldn't be used in the same text as Sumerian, Akkadian, Assyrian, or Babylonian Empires. This would be misleading to people reading the Mesopotamian history timeline as they may believe the ceramic finds are relating to actual developed individual cultures. The pottery may just be a creative use of an individual area, for example Creamware pottery was form Staffordshire, or Denby Pottery, or Lustre types of pottery and all made in the UK and not an individual state or empire.

The First Civilisations

The first civilisations formed on the banks of rivers. The most notable examples are the Ancient Egyptians, who were based on the Nile, the Mesopotamians in the Fertile Crescent on the Tigris and Euphrates Rivers, the Ancient Chinese on the Yellow River, and Ancient India on the Indus. These early embryonic civilisation s began to initially form around the time of the Neolithic Revolution 9000 BC.

Rivers became attractive locations and have always been the case if you look at any major town or city in the world today. The rivers and oceans gave the newly settled Neolithic farmers a sustainable varied food source. This was necessary for the first civilisation s to prosper and grow in numbers because the rivers provided a steady supply of drinking water and made the land fertile for growing crops. Moreover, trading goods and people could be transported easily to more distant areas, and the people in these embryonic civilisation s could fish and hunt the animals that came to drink water.

Additionally, with people moving close to the rivers and seas, people could use these waterways as a navigational aid to return to their newly formed villages and expanding settlements by traveling downstream/upstream. Major centres of populace grew when an area was situated at a natural junction, the merging of two rivers, a shallow area in the river where easy fording of a river was possible or a mountain pass. In the case of Southern Mesopotamia, the new communities where close to two merging rivers, close to the newly formed sea and also close to a mountain region to the North and East.

All these favourable elements existed within Southern Mesopotamia which also enhanced the possibility of trade. The crossroads of differing societies to the West a predominantly Ubaid culture with a Halaf culture further North West but still on the main rivers that feed into the Tigris and the Euphrates rivers. Ubaid culture is characterised by large unwalled village settlements, multi-roomed rectangular mud-brick houses and the appearance of the first temples of public architecture in Mesopotamia, with a growth of a two-tier settlement hierarchy of centralised large sites of more than 10 hectares surrounded by smaller village sites of less than 1 hectare.

Domestic equipment included a distinctive fine quality buff or greenish coloured pottery decorated with geometric designs in brown or black paint; tools such as sickles were often made of hard fired clay in the south. But in the North, stone and sometimes metal were used. Villages thus contained specialised craftspeople, potters, weavers, and metalworkers, although the bulk of the population were agricultural labourers, farmers, and seasonal pastoralists.

The mountains to the North and the East and the sea-born settlements in the South along the Persian Gulf all the way to the Indian Ocean. It should be that chronological testing at Tell Sabi Abyad has collated the dates for Early Pottery

Neolithic for the Pre-Halaf Period and noted that the first levels of this pottery start at 6,300 BC which links extremely well with the dispersal from the Gulf Oasis, is this a mere coincidence or grounds for further research and examination. Could the Pre-Halaf and 0 Ubaid have come from the same origin, the Gulf Oasis; is it a mere coincidence that all these pottery fragments are originating at the same time?

We could also hypothesise that maybe the Gulf Oasis was an area of multicultural living before the flooding and different regions had slightly varying differences. Further levels show that the highly decorated pottery increases in quantity within a relatively short period of time. Could this be the start of mass production and a step up in trading now that the region had a sudden population growth?

The Rise of a New Population During the Pre-Ubaid and Ubaid Period Throughout the Gulf

As described at the beginning of this book, the increasing sea levels that eventually consumed the Gulf Oasis in 6500 BC when 95% eventually finally coming to rest in 6200 BC. The Gulf Oasis had been consumed and had given rise to several mass exoduses. This exodus was the remaining people who tried desperately to stay local to the region. The final ridge of high ground surrounding the newly formed Persian Gulf had started to be consumed by seawater. Therefore, an excessive populace archaeological appeared almost overnight in areas that were not necessarily climatically good for permanent occupation but at least the threat of permanent flooding had stopped.

This has been highlighted at excavation sites throughout the Gulf Region punctuated by a pronounced wave of settlement activity from an original 10 prior to 6,800 BC to 60 Sites after this period of time. But the most striking point with this increase in *new* people, they brought with them a different way of living. The new people had permanent home, livestock, agricultural techniques, and most of all a stratified way of living. The Gulf Oasis dispersed populace forcibly evicted from their old homes onto the higher grounds of the surrounding area.

The Gulf Oasis, prior to flooding, was physically split into Northern and Southern areas within the Gulf Oasis due to the physical location the Ur Shatt River and inland lakes acting as a natural demarcation and of the populace whilst inhabiting the area for 75,000 years or more. The people of the region knew of each other but may have started to form separate cultural identities including religion, language (but the same origin), a different form of stratified society but would still have had some commonality and appreciation between the different sides of the river.

Once the sea started to force its way further into the Gulf Oasis after spoiling the freshwater lakes in 7000 BC, the remaining people would have continued to move North up the remaining Gulf Oasis. Some would have moved East into the Zagros Mountains of today's modern Iran, some of the population dispersed South onto the modern-day Kuwait, Qatar, UAE and Saudi Coastline, some onto close-by higher grounds that became islands for example Bahrain, Kish, Qeshm, Tarout, Dalma and Failaka (to name a few). Others would resist moving into some of these harsher environments and continued to be pushed *upriver* until one half entered the region of Elam in modern day Iran and the other into Southern Mesopotamia (modern day Iraq) which later became the Land of Sumer.

Whichever direction the people of the Gulf Oasis dispersed; they would have encountered a local populace who was already embedded within that region. It would have been a case of either to take over or to assimilate. The local inhabitant may not have been unknown to the new people through old trade routes. It would seem that the people of the Gulf Oasis had already a stratified society therefore the people had specific functions in their previous surroundings. It should also be noted that a larger populace could not necessarily be supported in these harsher environments without being organised from the very start, if they paused to contemplate, they would have vanished within a few years.

This assimilation would have changed the identities of the people leaving the Gulf Oasis, whichever side of the Ur-Shatt River you originated from, and the change would have occurred quickly and a differentiation between the original Gulf Oasis to other previous Gulf Oasis groups would then create their newly formed identities. If there had already been a difference between North and South Gulf Oasis people, then the assimilation with new people would accentuate the differences that already existed.

What should also be noted is that the dispersed people of the Gulf Oasis will have definitely understood that the annexed people of the Gulf Oasis had littered the new coastline with numerous new settlements and will have been in contact with each other during the exodus and long after. So, the links to people throughout this new coastal region will have continued to exit. This opened the door for opportunity and trade or was this continued trade. Now that the area of the Gulf Oasis was covered in seawater, it did give the exiled people an easier opportunity to commute between regions by boat.

Before the engineering feats of road construction and the wheel, rivers and seas were always the highways of the ancient times and the quickest and best way to move from area to area with a large payload. The dispersed people would have quickly adapted to saltwater fishing of the newly formed Persian Gulf supporting a new way of life. Long-distance trade is another primary feature of Ubaid related settlement. The presence of Ubaid pottery exported from Southern Mesopotamia as far as the Strait of Hormuz demonstrates the existence of trade networks operating across more than 1,000 kms.

In exchange for Mesopotamian textiles, grains, bitumen, pottery, a variety of Eastern Arabian exports including pearls, shell beads, chert, livestock and fish this is the starting point of essential trade between newly forming communities. The widespread distribution of Ubaid pottery discovered throughout the Gulf Coast as well as ceramic vessels exported from several manufacturing locations in Southern Mesopotamia, suggests that *this was more than an aggregate of opportunistic exchanges, but was a mature, stable and structured system that persisted for many generations.*[lxxxiii]

Finally Settling on Very Dry Land

The third migration populace from the exiled region of the Gulf Oasis finally gained a foothold on terra firma, the land they called Sumer in Southern Mesopotamia. The land of Sumer was probably already an area of small settlements prior to the last influx that migrated from the flooded Gulf Oasis. Small farming communities would have existed that hugged the rivers sides, digging simple irrigation ditches that would water the small crops close to the rivers. These people may have been local farming populace indigenous to the area before 6,200 BC and may have also had remnants from the second migration in 7,000 BC, where the main body continued further on up the Rivers into Northern region of the Fertile Crescent and all the way to Jericho.

These people would certainly be more amenable to these new migrants who came floating up the newly emerged Persian Gulf. These people where distinctly difference in appearance than the true indigenous people having been the first to leave the sanctuary of the Gulf Oasis and set up in the region of Sumer. This early population known as the Ubaid people (Simply because of the name of the place that the first discoveries where made) already had the makings of a structured society. Most notable for strides in the development of civilisation such as farming and raising cattle, weaving textiles, working with carpentry and pottery, and even enjoying a beer from time to time.

But before all these magnificent achievements could be glorified, the new people had to adapt and overcome the initial shock of settling into this new harsh environment. The land was unforgiving, but this was the hand that had been dealt. Vital to their survival the new people, had to hit the ground running. A larger population needed the basics to survive and the first priority would be preparing the land and planting.

People swimming in the fresh water lagoons next to people cutting the reeds

The people stayed close to the two rivers of the Tigris and the Euphrates with the newly formed Persian Gulf close by with a good source of fishing and the cultivation of reeds. During these early years people had to physically rely on each other. A large new populace could not survive altogether in one place therefore it made common sense for the people to dispersed throughout this new region and create small communities which over a short period of time grew ever larger.

How these groups were organised could be debated but Ubaid Socio-Political organisation within a framework based on a *Chiefdom Model*. This would help clarify the interrelationship of economic organisation, political, leadership and ritual requirements for a pre-existing stratified society that was required to be successful in a newly inhabited heat hostile environment. The previous communities that had been continuously moving up river that had stayed together and creating a Corp D'Esprit which made the group stronger and more durable to their new surroundings, as the old saying states: *what doesn't kill you makes you stronger;* and these new migrants certainly had grit and determination.

The people who had immigrated to the North then back to the South in 6000 BC may have brought other people along with them from the North. Of the first five recorded Cities, some had Semitic speaking populace. At no point did anybody believe the task would be easy, take a look at the first settlers into the US, Canada, or Australia, after the initial adversity these foreigners to a new land hunkered down made everything work overtime.

Marsh Arabs of Southern Iraq 1974 and Modern Floating Home

These are the reed homes in 2020 witnessed in 6200 BC at Eridu

Three types of people first settled in Southern Mesopotamia: The farming community who started to increase the production of crops which in turn helped the second set of people of the city state who created consumer items for trade such as textiles. The third set of people where the equivalent to the Modern Marsh Arabs of Southern Iraq who created floating islands and used the Marsh land as the life source for the community. Reeds for building home, these homes have not altered for over 8,200 years as seen on carvings and pottery from Ancient Mesopotamia and give a true insight of yesteryear.

To this day, you can physically see how our ancestors previously lived and fished the waters of the rivers and deltas. These activities also aid the other members of the local populace when drought may affect crops for prolonged periods. These homes are a 100% direct link to the past, which shows modern historians exactly how 1/3 of the population lived. The reader needs to understand the mindset of the people of this new land and how intrinsic water was in the thought of these people. If the people came from the Gulf Oasis region water had a large part to play in their ideology. It is from the earliest recorded writing that we can get a glance of what the early Sumerians cosmogony which is another way of talking of the theories of the origins of the universe.

If we look at the Sumerian way of life, it is clear that their control of water, especially through the irrigation projects, was absolute usage of water. There would be no successful yield of crops and no way to support the community without fresh water. Water was essentially a giver of life and Sumerians recognise this and respected this spiritually all sources of freshwater were believed to have been supplied to the Sumerians by the gods.

The people of the Gulf Oasis also had to adapt to the scarcity of building materials, no stones to lay the first few courses of brick work or wood for doors and furniture. Reeds where and still are in abundance in the deltas and shorelines of the Tigris and Euphrates rivers. Like all great civilisation s of past history, this civilisation in its rise had also the seeds of decline interwoven in its fabrics, which only could have an effect after it had passed its maturity. Being an agrarian civilisation, it had the two basic elements of land and water resources, which contributed to both its rise and decline.

The Sumerian heartland was a deltaic region built by the sediments of the Tigris and Euphrates Rivers over a very long period. It had the nutrients brought by the floods of these two rivers from the Mountains of modern Turkey and Syria. At the same time, it was low land by nature of its geological origin surrounded by water from three sides: namely the Tigris from the East, the Euphrates from the West and the marshes and lagoons and the Gulf from the South.

It was natural that the water table was very high, and in order to have successful agriculture, the Sumerians had to resort to fallow cultivation to avoid the rise of the water table into the root zone and cause waterlogging. Fallow cultivation refers to land that is ploughed and tilled but left unseeded during growing season. At the site of Eridu according the Kings List which will be described later in the book is classed as the first city, something of this legacy still exists for in the low-lying ground at the foot of the mound the Bedouin can still discover fresh water (even though brackish) at a depth of about 6 feet. below the surface, this freshwater land is known by them as Usaila.

The first settlement to the emergence of the very first city (according to the Sumerian Kings List). All this is captured in the 0 Ubaid period, starting in 6,500 BC. With the final sea levels settling in 6,200 BC and the archaeological evidence in Eridu to fix a date of 5,500 BC, if the King List is deemed to be correct (which it isn't for a lot of other reasons). So, we can accurately scrutinise the birth of a nation and what it entails to come from migrant to industrial farmer that can support a city and have all the necessary mechanisms in place to be classed as the first city. All this within a 700-hundred-year period; from nothing to city in only 700 years!

The Start of the City States

I feel very privileged to be writing this book, history is a very big part of my life and as an engineer. I find myself constantly looking and reading material concerning Mesopotamia, that doesn't have the eye of somebody from an engineering background or a military one. An historian can be told about a feat of engineering or even be lucky enough to have physically seen the remains of breath-taking feats of engineering but can a historian truly appreciate what it takes to not just build a structure but to organise and execute. This task involves multiple facets to each phase of the build.

All these complexities need to be overcome during the build; fortunately, I have been in engineering for 35 years and still counting. I think it is in the interest of all people if somebody of my ilk can cast a critical eye over this period of time and discuss the attributes of these accomplishments. I have read too many descriptions about the start of cultivation and the impressive buildings built for worship and the Mighty Walls of Uruk that are described in the Epic of Gilgamesh and which can still be read today. I have also heard a monumental amount on the pottery shards and the description of various styles of pottery which is an amazing indicator to the extent of trade and how various regions changed over the course of time.

But from an engineering stance, I think the cultivation of the land and canal systems built to support the agricultural revolution have been somewhat airbrushed out of history. This shows a distinct lack of understanding on behalf of the historian whose job is to put the pieces of the *jigsaw* together, not hide some of the pieces. As an engineer, I believe the historian has missed a trick; the entire story of the growth and development of Southern Mesopotamia wasn't because Sumeria had great buildings, that came later. It wasn't because of they had writing skills and divine scripture, that came later. It wasn't because they were brilliant at commerce, that came later. It was solely due to the agriculture and the canals systems that fed the trees and the fields. Once again, the domino effect, water and its control, this direction of thought should then lead to why these emerging city states eventually began to have conflicts which then resulted in the growth of the first Empires.

But before we venture any further, I want to raise an important observation. Basically, you cannot talk about the Sumerians without talking about the Akkadians. Two languages but one culture existed. It leaves some very big questions:

- What were the people of Akkad doing there? Was this due in part to the abandonment of the Northern Region approximately 6,000 BC.
- Could the second migration of 7,000 BC who eventually ended up in Jericho or Çatalhöyük be the same people who eventually returned to the land of Sumer and also onwards to Egypt, but with indigenous people of the North with them.
- If there was so much land in the Fertile Crescent, why move to an area so hot? Did they fear a second flooding in the North?
- Did the second wave of immigration out of the Gulf Oasis, bring an initial mixing of cultures between the Akkadians and the Pre-Sumerians, before the final migrants floated into sight?
- Did the original Semitic speaking people of Akkad, only farm the riverbanks close to the Tigris and the Euphrates or did they understand about irrigation?

- Did these two people already have a level of trust. Did they know of each other's existence prior to the flooding of the Gulf Oasis, so trust could easily be formed?

The Sumerians referred to themselves as Ug Sag GiG Ga, which is translated to the Black Headed People, whilst the eventual close neighbours who occupied large areas of Sumer but had an Akkadian Semitic language called the new arrivals the same name but pronounced Tsalmat-Qaqqadi in Akkadian. From many carvings depicting Sumerians, we can see how they wore their hair, curly on top and cut short on the side. Could these two different sets of people be seen on the wall art of the homes within Çatalhöyük. (The tanned and the black?)

These two great peoples of ancient times, the Akkadians and the Sumerians, formed a deep bond that strengthened overtime, their culture identical and ran in parallel, they developed together and grew together and shared the large engineering projects that benefitted each other. Without each other maybe the people of each culture wouldn't have grown to have been so dominant. Maybe the Semitic speaking Akkadians managed to keep the rest of the Sematic people of the Fertile Crescent at bay and not quash this embryonic experiment of living and farming and the very start of civilisation. The two cultures became so symbiotic that when one succeeded both did and when one failed, they both did.

Growth of the City States

By explaining how all these original embryonic city states heavily relied on each other for their initial survival and then how the growth of the individual city states then over time became self-sufficient to a point in time when prestigious building programs occurred that were superfluous to the needs of the individual city. Then it became very easy to understand the socio-economic impact associated with the rivalry between *competing* city states and the problems woven into the fabric of these new emerging fiefdoms. When the city states were created, the manufactured border between neighbours became necessary, that was not always agreed upon. Then empires created by the amalgamation of several city states which eventually resulted in the birth of nations and the development of what we know today as countries. So, before this period of time people easily migrated from area to area.

The easiest place to witness some of these feats of engineering would be to visit Greece or Rome or even visit Egypt. The sites are remarkable and who hasn't heard of Athens Acropolis or seen the Coliseum in Rome rendered on films to look as new as the day it was built or marvelled at the sheer size of the Great Pyramid of Giza constructed in 2,560 BC at a height of 146.7 Metres with a volume of over 2.5 million cubic metres. But how many people can appreciate that none of this would have been possible without the people of Mesopotamia or do any of the readers know that these three feats of engineering mentioned above are nothing in scale as some of the engineering projects completed up to 4,000 years before some of the others where even considered.

Everyone likes to look up, but how many people are looking down to the ground? The Southern Mesopotamians didn't just build amazing feats of engineering they also invented the complex mathematics that was required to build them and invented the tools to build them and also understood the causes of engineering failure. They fully understood root cause analysis before the words had even been created. The appreciation of what can make a project fail was understood to the nth degree and failure wasn't an option.

What is more remarkable is the sheer size of the building work involved in creating canals and dykes and the engineering it took and the care taken during the design phase of the project. We will discuss why these irrigation systems where needed and what they supported and understand why conflicts occurred during this time and understand that by controlling the water in an arid land, where every drop of water is precious, equals power. We have briefly discussed the ideas of Karl August Wittfogel 1957 Book[lxxxiv], the German scholar who first developed the notion of hydraulic empire oriental despotism, or what could be better termed for Sumeria: *The Hydraulic Civilisation*.

I have worked on numerous engineering projects in the world and pride myself on the quality of the work I have produced, some of the projects run into billions of dollars. But until I started my research into this book, I genuinely didn't realise what was instore for me. The size of projects that were successfully completed could financially paralyse a small country, yet in Southern Mesopotamia individual city states built some of the most complex and structures that modern engineering companies would find difficult to replicate, even with the motorised equipment that is available today.

The people of the region didn't want to *get by*; they wanted to prosper, and they needed to trade with distant lands and the local resources could not be obtained. The main sources of early trade goods where wool, wheat, barley, bitumen, and textiles. But the people realised from the very beginning that they could just produce enough to survive they had to produce a surplus to be able to store in case of weather destruction to crops and make an excess for trade alone.

This period is called the Ubaid Period, historians have named this period even though there is no fixed marker in time. This was a time of massive transformation in the region. The perfect saying to summarise this period is *From small acorns, giant oaks grow.* I will also describe the people of the region before the cultural revolution that occurred and describe what was physically happening in the early 0 Ubaid Period. Prior to stratified society blossoming to full maturity and the problems that it brought.

We cannot ignore some amazing facts about the people who came to the region with a language isolate, who looked different with dark skin and curly hair and who seem to have brought amazing organisational skills with them, there seems to be a coming together of different peoples with different languages, yet they seem to have worked homogenously in perfect unison.

The Urban Revolution: The Ubaid Period, 6500-3800 BC

The alluvium roughly corresponding to the area known as Sumer is often described as resource poor, lacking timber, stone, metal ores and minerals, except for bitumen (a hint of the modern oil wealth of present-day Iraq). Yet the surface of this flat plain, when irrigated, was extremely fertile, which made irrigation and agriculture the defining characteristic of the rise of civilisation in Mesopotamia. Irrigation required collective cooperation in terms of labour and planning, the building of canals, channels, dykes, and reservoirs.

While the frequent and sometimes violent flooding required organised response, frequent repair, desilting and replacement of boundary stones and markers. Gradually, a mosaic of micro-environments took root, each producing tradable commodities: fish and reeds from the marshy lagoons of the South, at the head of the Persian Gulf; date palms and gardens from regions located along the levees; grain crops from the flatlands farther way, irrigated by the canals; and goat and sheep herding, wool, milk and meat production in the open grasslands farther away.

Towns that sprang up in these micro-environments produced and internally traded these commodities as well as value-added products like woollen textiles, dairy foods like cheese, or beer brewed from barley. The volume of trade efficiently transported along the rivers and canals encouraged the growth of larger towns, each with its tutelary god or goddess, and a tripartite temple.

Although gods, like the rich, had multiple residences and were worshipped in several cities. Many inter-related factors explain the development of cities.

Agricultural surpluses led to larger populations, and the ability to support specialised craft workers and social stratification. The need to store and redistribute resources and coordinate agricultural production led to the emergence of professional administrators who worked at the temple and combined religious, economic, and political functions.

Ready Steady Go

The subtitle is not meant to be blasé; everything really had to happen quickly for people to survive. Three things needed to succeed: Location, Location, Location:

- Location near building material to home people, the reeds from the marshes, deltas and waterways that surrounded these early settlements. As seen used by todays Marsh Arabs of Southern Iraq and Iran.
- Location near fertile soil to cultivate, nutrients brought down by the yearly flooding of the Tigris and Euphrates rivers over thousands of years.
- Location near a plentiful water supply to cultivate the land and to fish, therefore not dependant on one sole food supply when times become hard.

As previously stated, the migrants from the Gulf Oasis quickly dispersed throughout the whole of the Mesopotamia. These are the people who were forcibly evicted from the Gulf Oasis decided not to leave the Gulf Oasis to head north into the Zagros Mountains or South onto the newly formed Arabian Coastline or earlier moving to the Indian Subcontinent before the natural land bridge disappeared beneath the Indian Ocean. These people may have been the populace would had originally inhabited the more Northern Region of the now vanished Gulf Oasis being pushed further and further North along the Ur Shatt to the point of the river splitting into both the independently flowing Tigris and the Euphrates Rivers. Some of these people will have continued through the Fertile Crescent until they came to areas of little inhabitants and could finally settle in peace no longer needing to constantly move.

Some of the exiled people decided to stay close to the newly emerged Persian Gulf calculating that sufficient criteria existed to enable a living could be provided from this hostile harsh land for a large gathering of people. Organisation was the main criteria in a situation like this, somebody needed to make very critical decisions very quickly. If we go by the Sumerian King List, it may give an early indication as to where these people decided to locate to. Once a location was decided, cultivating crops was the first IA (Immediate Action), without food there could be no settlements. As excavation sites dating to 6,500 BC within modern Oman and Saudi Arabia have shown evidence of a stratified society already existed, therefore these communities included trades people and the knowledge of farming already in existence.

The rivers, marshlands and deltas of Southern Mesopotamia where capable of providing the nutrient rich soils that could be used for successful agriculture, the hot weather can sustain very good growth of crops, more importantly sometimes up to two crops per year. The main problem was how to get the water to newly cultivated sown fields. Originally, all irrigation would have led directly from the main rivers, settling ponds created, but the rivers constantly flooded when the snow melted in the Anatolian Mountains in the springtime. Fortunately, the Euphrates was far less destructive compared to the Tigris due to the reduced flow and Wadi areas further North of the settled lands that dampened the destructive powers of the rivers.

These embryonic farming techniques where quickly discarded as better techniques where already known, but the toe hold had been established and further growth could commence. It is interesting to note that Eridu, Ur and Uruk seem to be very close to the Euphrates rather than the harder flowing Tigris River and it was also known that the Euphrates river is higher than the Tigris, which is an important fact for the future construction of drainage canals.

Dating of the Ubaid Period

The Ubaid period—6500-3800 BC—is a prehistoric period of Mesopotamia. The name derives from Tell Al-Ubaid where the earliest large excavation of Ubaid period material was conducted initially by Henry Hall and later by Leonard Woolley[lxxxv]. If excavations had been carried out in another town then the name Ubaid wouldn't exist and as Tell Ubaid is in Southern Mesopotamia it fits nicely for all research and the Chronology of history. In South Mesopotamia, the period is the earliest known period on the alluvial plain although it is likely earlier periods exist obscured under the alluvium. In the South it has a very long duration between about 6,500 and 3,800 BC when it finally replaced by the Uruk period.

In North Mesopotamia, the period runs only between about 5,300 and 4,300 BC It is preceded by the Halaf period and the Halaf-Ubaid Transitional period (Even though as stated previously the Pre-Halaf period dates from 6,300 BC, who am I to disagree with Durham University) and succeeded by the Late Chalcolithic period. The term "Ubaid period" was coined at a conference in Baghdad in 1930, where at the same time the Jemdet Nasr and Uruk periods were defined.

- Ubaid 0; 6,500-5,400 BC Sometimes called Oueili, an early Ubaid phase first excavated at Tell el-Oueili. This is an important time as the Sea Levels within the Persian Gulf had finally abated and settlement within the region could begin. Irrigation agriculture, which seems to have developed first at Choga Mami in Eastern Iraq in the Mandali region, which shows evidence of the first canal system in operation in 6,000 BC (is this another coincidence?).
- Ubaid 1; 5,400-4,700 BC Sometimes called Eridu corresponding to the city Eridu, a phase limited to the extreme South of Iraq, on what was then the shores of the Persian Gulf. This phase, showing clear connection to the Samarra culture to the North, saw the establishment of the first permanent settlement South of the 5-inch rainfall isohyet. These people pioneered the growing of grains in the extreme conditions of aridity, thanks to the high-water tables of Southern Iraq.
- Ubaid 2; 4,800-4,500 BC, saw the development of extensive canal networks from major settlements in 4,700-4,600 BC and rapidly spread elsewhere, form the first required collective effort and centralised coordination of labour in Mesopotamia.
- Ubaid 3-4; 4,500-4,000 BC Sometimes called Ubaid I and Ubaid II. In the period from saw a period of intense and rapid urbanisation with the Ubaid culture spread into Northern Mesopotamia and was adopted by the Halaf culture. Ubaid artefacts also spread all along the Arabian littoral, showing the growth of a trading system that stretched from the Mediterranean coast through to Oman.

- Spreading from Eridu, the Ubaid culture extended from the Middle of the Tigris and Euphrates to the shores of the Persian Gulf, and then spread down past Bahrain to the copper deposits at Oman (Magan). The archaeological record shows that Arabian Bifacial/Ubaid period came to an abrupt end in eastern Arabia and the Oman peninsula at 3,800 BC. Just after the phase of lake lowering and onset of dune reactivation. At this time, increased aridity led to an end in semi-desert nomadism, and there is no evidence of human presence in the area for approximately 1,000 years, the so-called *Dark Millennium*.
- That might be due to the 5.9 kiloyear event at the end of the Older Peron when desiccation of the Sahara and other deserts occurred. Also forcing people down from Mountains and into Valleys. Numerous examples of Ubaid pottery have been found along the Persian Gulf, as far as Dilmun, where Indus Valley Civilisation pottery has also been found. Which is evidence of the trade connection that had already been established in the region.

Ubaid Culture

The Ubaid culture spread north across Mesopotamia, gradually replacing the Halaf culture. Baked clay figurines, mainly female, decorated with painted or appliqué ornament and lizard like heads, have been found at a number of Ubaid sites. Ubaid was considered an egalitarian society, due to the roots of this growing population from hunter-gatherer to farmer. In the very beginning of the start of Ubaid Period there seemed no need for a structured society with all the layers of bureaucracy that it entails. The people were producing sufficient food to enable a comfortable if not extravagant lifestyle.

A similar situation appeared in 19th century AD Britain prior to the industrial revolution in the farming regions. People lived a quiet simple lifestyle that hadn't changed in many millennia. Therefore, it is true that social ranking is not very apparent in any Ubaid sites, living a simple basic life with a few small cottage industries that produced goods for locals with some exported further afield. Given the presence of elaborated pottery in the early period, and public architecture in the later. However, that doesn't seem very likely, and archaeologists have recognised subtle cues which appear to support the subdued presence of elites even from Ubaid 0. Although it's possible that elite roles might have been transitory early on. Could these more elite roles be in the form of organising labour to create this early desirable pottery. Taking the people from tilling the fields to produce pottery and ensuring that they received an equal share of produced food.

Scholars are hesitant today to re-define the core area from which the *idea* of Ubaid culture spread out because the regional variation is so extensive. Instead, at a workshop at the University in Durham in 2006, scholars proposed that the cultural similarities seen across the region developed from a *vast inter-regional melting pot of influences.*[lxxxvi] Movement of the material culture is believed to have spread throughout the region primarily by peaceable trade, and various local appropriations of a shared social identity and ceremonial ideology.

While most scholars still suggest a Southern Mesopotamian origin for black-on-buff ceramics, evidence at Turkish sites such as Domuztepe and Kenan Tepe is beginning to question this view. Halaf were thus associated with a spread of painted pottery across the Northern Mesopotamia. It can now be seen that this was indeed a widespread phenomenon extending into Southeast Turkey.

[lxxxvii]Little archaeobotanical evidence has been recovered from Ubaid period sites, except for samples recently reported from a burned tri-partite house at Kenan Tepe in Turkey, occupied between 4,650-4,350 BC, within the Ubaid 3/4 transition. The fire that destroyed the house resulted in the excellent preservation of nearly 70,000 specimens of charred plant material, including a reed basket full of well-preserved charred materials. Plants recovered from Kenan Tepe were dominated by emmer wheat (*Triticum dicoccum*) and two-rowed hulled barley (*Hordeum vulgare* v. *distichum*). Also recovered were smaller amounts of Triticum wheat, flax (*Linum usitassimum*), lentil (*Lens culinaris*) and peas (*Pisum sativum*), which is proof that the dietary needs were well covered in Ubaid 3/4 Period, and who's to say this wasn't the case in much earlier periods.

Elites and Social Stratification

With archaeologists recognising the subtle cues which appeared to support the subdued presence of elites even from Ubaid 0. The Ubaid period remains poorly understood and how elite roles impacted the community. Yet researches generally agree that this early period of Ubaid 0-1 had witnessed the development of non-egalitarian societies developing in the Tigris-Euphrates alluvial zone. Southern Mesopotamia seems to have formed a Ubaid Socio-Political organisation within a framework based on a *Chiefdom Model*.

In Ubaid 2 and 3, there is clearly a shift in labour from decorated single pots to an emphasis on public architecture, such as buttressed temples, which would have benefited the entire community rather than a small group of elites. Scholars suggest that might have been a deliberate action to avoid ostentatious displays of wealth and power by elites and instead highlight community alliances. That suggests that power depended on alliance networks and control of local resources. In terms of settlement patterns, by Ubaid 2-3, Southern Mesopotamia had a two-level hierarchy with a few large sites of 10 hectares or larger, including Eridu, Ur, and Uqair, surrounded by smaller, possibly subordinate group of supporting villages.

Based upon the analysis of grave goods, the Ubaid period in its entirety shows a steady migration of an increasingly polarised social stratification and decreasing egalitarianism. Bogucki: describes this as a phase of *Trans-Egalitarian* competitive households, in which some fall behind as a result of downward social mobility. Even in our own lifetime we can witness the ever-increasing social disparity within Countries and also between Countries. Morton Fried and Elman Service[lxxxviii] have hypothesised that Ubaid culture saw the rise of an elite class of hereditary chieftains *Chiefdom Model*.

Perhaps heads of kin groups linked in some way to the administration of the temple shrines and their granaries, responsible for mediating intra-group conflict and maintaining social order. It would seem that various collective methods, perhaps instances of what Thorkild Jacobsen called primitive democracy, in which disputes were previously resolved through a council of one's peers, were no longer sufficient for the needs of the local community.

Ubaid culture originated in the South, but still has clear connections to earlier cultures in the entire region of Mesopotamia. The Middle East's individual growth resulted from Ubaid expansion, contrasting it to the colonial expansionism of the later Uruk period. Whether this was due to early movement away from the Gulf Oasis to Jericho and eventually back to Southern Mesopotamia in 6,000 BC. But on the whole comparing different regions shows that the Ubaid expansion originally took place largely through the peaceful spread of an ideology, a need to rely upon each other. This invariably led to the formation of numerous new indigenous identities that appropriated and transformed superficial elements of Ubaid material culture into locally distinct expressions.

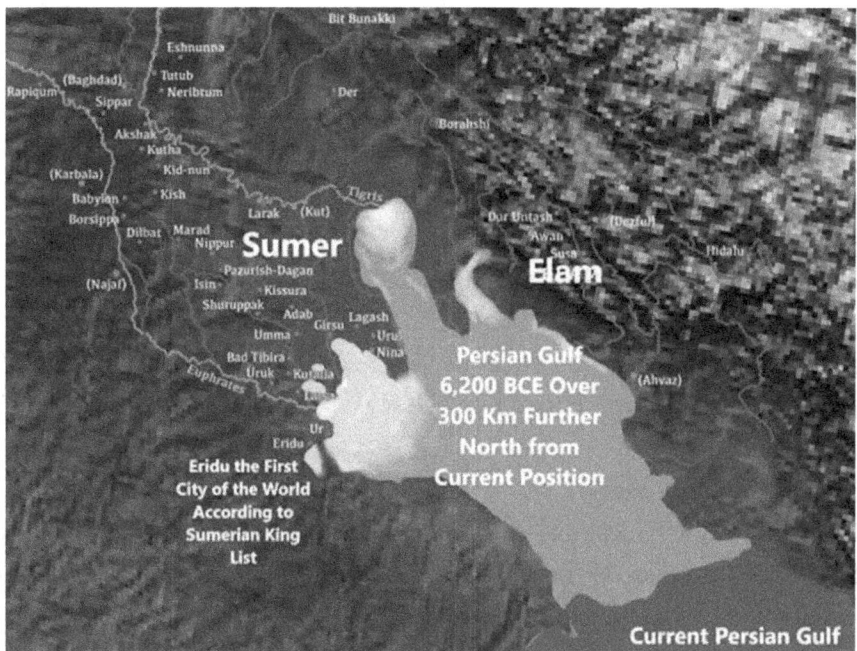

Furthest distance of Persian Gulf prior to silting of northern end of Gulf 6200 BC

Trade by River and Sea

It is very transparent that the importance of shipbuilding and navigation for the people of Southern Mesopotamia as well of its relevant and pioneering role in nautical history permanently and eternally enhanced the Southern Mesopotamian Region and the trading routes. Written sources (principally the cuneiform ones) together with the archaeological material are a precious source for the study of Ancient Middle East ships and shipbuilding, waiting for comprehensive lexical and technical-historical studies.

The oldest texts of mankind show an ideogram for ship and in the inscriptions of the Kings of the first Dynasty of Lagash ships are also mentioned for the first time in maritime trade. A variety of watercrafts are attested to on cylinder seals, wall reliefs, models and in written cuneiform sources, from rafts to freight carrying vessels also various war ships. Boats where intrinsically entwined with the success and development of Southern Mesopotamia.

What has also been shown in cuneiform tablets are examples of haulage of goods, for example, a shipment of 32 tons of cargo could be towed on a boat or barge over water for a distance of 10 km per day. This works out at an efficiency rate of 640,000 kg/km/day compared to a donkey load cargo 1,875-75,000 3,750 kg/km/day. This shows the efficiency of transporting large cargos by water.

Text from Girsu identifies the labour of 10 men towing a boat for 15 days from Lagash to Nippur a distance of 107 km as the crow flies 7.1 km per day travelling upstream. Also, other cuneiform tablets describe the movement of dozens of boats at a time was very common. Coastal societies had the added luxury of being able to traverse and not held to canal systems which could dramatically escalate costs if anything had to be transported over land. With the increased agricultural produce being made then it was essential that the water born traffic had to dock as close to the fields as possible. Less labour for transportation aided larger agriculture field work and larger trading opportunities with more affordable trade goods.

Eridu and Uruk periods would have been able to exploit early trade in the area due to coastal locations and able to exploit the biomass-rich marshes, lagoons, and estuaries. This setting provided the initial impetus for burgeoning trade between city states exploiting various economic resources. Each city state have naturally specialised in the production of a small number of crop commodities which supported by its various locations and surrounding alluvial ecosystem. Goods would have included raw wool, woven and dyed textiles, goat hair products, leather goods, dairy and other pastoral resources.

Some city states would have been on the margins of the better water positioned states and quickly realised the need for connection to all the city states for better commerce. In the Northern trade would have been flax based textiles, garden crops and grain produce, whereas Southern Mesopotamia made irrigation agriculture and horticulture more abundant and more profitable.

The elite would have realised the need to expand trade especially with the increase in technologies being made available. With navigable canals systems entire areas did not need to be micro-regions with specialised expertise but could expand into other markets and creating competition with other city states by creating their own productive capacities creating spurt growths in areas. As each city state started to produce similar comparable product capabilities the need to offer each other goods in terms of exchange then led to further expansion away from the local communities within the Southern Mesopotamian Region and venture further afield to exploit new markets.

All the time the city states at the mouth of the Tigris and Euphrates rivers controlled the passage of goods past its city state. Textiles that were originally for the local market will have been used for external markets then became the principal markets with other Sumerian industries following suit including honey, aromatic oils and ceramic vessels; cross cultural trade would also see further expansion in the region due to the commercial intelligence of the elite class and the local trade compared to other less commercially aware regions.

The Five Cities Prior to the Flood

These five city states listed below are mentioned in the Sumerian King List as the cities which existed before the flood. We should be reminded that the Eridu Flood Epic may originate from actual floods that occurred from the Rivers and not necessarily the flooding of the Gulf Oasis. Even so, the list maybe a good indicator to understanding where the original people of the Gulf Oasis settled and why, also the different cities had specific roles in the newly formed lands, so may be an indicator that these five cities and their surrounding holdings all relied on each other for early survival before growing in strength and becoming self-sufficient and independent.

It should also be noted that the idea of a King (Lugal) was unknown in the early history of this region until 2,900 BC. But of equal note, each city shared the King, once the King had been invented, so the cities transferred the position of power throughout the area (similar to a cycling team, changing the front rider during speed trials). Some common understanding must have been agreed upon before any rivalry set in.

- **Eridu:** Sumerian speaking. As described in the Sumerian King List the First city where the gods Nudimmud was in charge; the city state apparently founded in 5,400 BC. South of the Euphrates and on the bank of the Gulf and only accessible via boat to the other 4 original city states. Sumerian speaking. This concept of the first city existed throughout the entire history of the region for over 4,000 years.
- **Bad-tibira:** Sumerian speaking, was the second city to exercise Kingship (the name is on a lost piece of the tablet) *Wall of the Copper Workers* or *Fortress of the Smiths*, identified as modern Tell Al-Madineh In Sumerian hymns and mythology, Bad Tibira is associated with Dumuzi (Akkadian Tammuz), the god of shepherds and their flocks, and one of the three rulers of the antediluvian dynasty there. As the lover of Inanna (Ishtar), he is also part of a tradition of dying and reborn gods. In

Akkadian times. Tammuz was the name for the lunar month that approximately corresponds with July, and this is still the name for that month in the Jewish calendar.

Does this mean the city state of Bad-tibira could be the area of Copper Smith works surrounded by grazing land for sheep? The wool created an industry of textiles that was known throughout the ancient world and every home of wealth wanted to show these textiles to their neighbours.

- **Larsa:** Sumerian speaking. Modern day Tell Sankarah about entrusted to the god Endurbilhrsag by AN. Larsa grew powerful, but it never accumulated a large territory. At its peak under King Rim-Sin I 1,758 - 1,699 BC, Larsa controlled only about 10-15 other smaller city states, nowhere near the territory controlled by other dynasties in Mesopotamian history. Nevertheless, huge building projects and agricultural undertakings can be detected archaeologically. Interestingly Larsa is thought to be the source of a number of tablets involving Babylonian mathematics, including the Plimpton 322 tablet that contains patterns of Pythagorean triples, pre-dating Greek versions by almost 1,500 years.

- **Sippar:** The only Semitic speaking and most Northernly city state of the original five city states prior to the Flood, according to the King List. Entrusted by AN to the Sun God-Hero Utu and the home of his temple E-Babbara. Sippar has been suggested as the location of the Biblical Sepharvaim in the Old Testament, which alludes to the two parts of the city in its dual form. As was often the case in Mesopotamia, it was part of a pair of Cities, separated by a river. Sippar was on the East side of the Euphrates. While its sister city, Sippar-Amnanum was on the opposite side, the West. Despite the fact that thousands of cuneiform tablets have been recovered at the site, relatively little is known about the history of Sippar.

- **Shuruppak:** Sumerian speaking, whose protective god Ninlil was the god of the South also called Sud, the goddess of grain and the air, the healing place. Modern Tell Fara, was an ancient Sumerian city situated about 55 kilometres (35 miles) South of Nippur on the banks of the Euphrates. Could it be suggested that Shuruppak was the main area of mass production of grain, with a large network of irrigation channels on low lying land and grain storage and distribution city which had more silos than any other Sumerian city. The breadbasket of the region and also known for its healing. Arsenical copper (early form of bronze) was found in Shuruppak dating from the mid-4th to early 3rd Millennium BC.

- o Also associated with a King from the Sumerian King List, the text consists of admonitory sayings of Šuruppak addressed to his son and eventual flood hero Ziusudra (Akkadian: Utnapishtim). Otherwise named as one of the five antediluvian cities in the Sumerian tradition, the name "Šuruppak" appears in one manuscript of the Sumerian King List (written SU.KUR.LAM) where it is interpolated as an additional generation between Ubara-Tutu and Ziusudra, who are in every other instance father and son.
- o Lambert reports that it has been suggested the interpolation may have arisen through an epithet of the father, *Man of Shuruppak*, having been taken wrongly for a proper name. However, this epithet, found in the Gilgamesh XI tablet, is a designation applied to Utnapishtim, not his father.

Conclusion

It would seem that the five pre-flood city states, the originators of Sumer, had built-up a very interesting coalition between all five of the emerging city states that relied on each other's area of expertise. All five would have had control over multiple smaller towns and villages within a close proximity to the individual city state. As the people were forced out of the Gulf Oasis and had to start again from scratch, it would seem that the people had the knowledge and expertise to exist and also worked as a community and not individually which indicates a stratified society.

The new surroundings had potential but wasn't as abundant as the old Gulf Oasis, the people where more exposed and had to work harder to make a success of their new surroundings. Each city state did not have all the practical parts of a city, but segments of the whole. If this is the case, then the forward planning had to be carried out. Which areas where best suited to what form of produce. It takes time to realise which area suits what activity and time to organise the population and segregate them into individual tasks, therefore providing evidence of stratification of society.

Also, the people had to get approval from the gods, where to build these new cities (with a little help of surveys of the land). By having a communal spirit in preparing and clearing the land ready for production showed a determination and resilience that had not previously seen in history. These original embryonic cities must have been extremely well organised as the location during the summer months is extremely unforgiving. The sum of all the actions far outweighed the sum of the individuals involved. All the effort in these first few hundred years took, a monumental undertaking that required perfect organisation to turn the land into a place of abundance, producing wheat, barley, clothe, textiles, infrastructure, irrigation channel, damming, building projects, structured levels of planting of trees that helped mass shading of vast swathes of land. Which also aided the planting that required out of direct sun, sun adverse plants that would not normally survive on their own, but now living in the shades of the vast swathes of date palm trees.

By relying on other neighbouring cities to perform a specific job, it can be surmised that these cities where originally harmonious and lived without fear of its neighbour. These five city states came out of the starting blocks at a fast pace once again proving that the ingenuity of the people already existed and never materialised from nothing, this pace of was relentless for the next 3,000 years. Once again, this highlights that the people of yesteryear are genuinely you and me with no differences, just a gap of time separating us from them. The Sumerian were avid mathematicians. They developed complex systems of measurement, as well as methods for dividing, multiplying and calculating angles. Even writing down the first ever multiplication tables on clay tablets.

I strongly believe that the advent of writing was due to working out intricate mathematical problems. The *Engineer* or *Lugal* couldn't possibly remember the various angles and levels of every calculation needed in a build, so placed them on clay. We are already aware that the people of Göbekli Tepe in the North had accomplished large feats of engineering 3,000 years prior to construction work starting on the lands of Sumer. Engineering certainly wouldn't have stopped outright; it would have continued in some form or other.

Jericho's new walls in 7000 BC were far stronger than they had been before, so we know through archaeological evidence that engineering was far more advanced than originally thought 20 years ago. Then realising the uses, used this system for counting harvests and understanding what proportion the priest class should be allotted. Accounting and mathematical calculations were important in common society, giving no thought to words!

Chapter 4
Sumerian Engineering and Agriculture

Introduction

What we have to appreciate during this transition from discussing the Ubaid Culture and the Sumerians, there is no change. The Sumerians didn't invade the Ubaidian and in turn they didn't invade the Neolithic's. These are simply markers or datum points placed on a region by Historians to allow both Historians and Archaeologists to categorise a specific time and place of origin. Sometimes the place of discovery becomes the name of the culture, very unimaginative but that's how its differentiated. The lines are confusing because some people have decided to dedicate time to research a specific genre, be it The Sumerians or Ubaid Culture.

After the Ur-Amorite wars of 2,025-2,004 BC The Old Assyrian Empire is established, and Southern Mesopotamia had finally lost its hold on any autonomy in the region. The Sumerians gradually lost their cultural identity and ceased to exist as a political force. All knowledge of their history, language, and technology even their name was eventually forgotten. Their secrets remained buried in the deserts of Iraq until the 19th Century, when French and British archaeologists finally discovered evidence of Sumer existence more or less by accident discovering Sumerian artefacts while hunting for evidence of the ancient Assyrians.

Scholars such as Henry Rawlinson, Edward Hincks, Julius Oppert and Paul Haupt later took the lead in deciphering the Sumerian language and cuneiform. Providing historians with their first ever glimpse of the long-lost history and literature of early Mesopotamia. Since then, archaeologists have recovered numerous pieces of Sumerian art, pottery, and sculpture as well as some 500,000 clay tablets, the vast majority of which have still yet to be translated.

Archaeologists and scholars describe being drawn to Mesopotamia in search of biblical correlations, nobody was expecting anything else. The Bible made cities like Babylon and Nineveh infamous, and so the Babylonians and Assyrians were well known to 19th Century scholars. They began their excavations in Mesopotamia in an attempt to confirm the historicity of biblical stories such as The Great Flood or the Tower of Babel. The only reference to Sumer in the Bible is to *the Land of Shinar* in Genesis 10:10 and elsewhere. People naturally assumed Shinar was more than likely an outlining area surrounding Babylon.

Until the Assyriologist Jules Oppert 1825-1905 AD identified the biblical reference with the region of Southern Mesopotamia known as Sumer and, further, asserted that cuneiform writing was Sumerian in origin. This was an astounding feat comparable to someone today asserting that Plato's Atlantis is modern Bermuda and being able to prove it and, even more so, in that there was no comparable *Bermuda* elsewhere. Nobody was looking for Sumer because nobody knew Sumer had ever existed.

Sumerian inventions are used every day, the clock which tells one when to get out of bed, the newspaper or textbook we read from, but nobody attributed this knowledge or inventions to anyone other than our forefathers of the Mediterranean. This phenomenon was very well described by Samuel Noah Kramer:[lxxxix]

One remarkable fact is that only a century ago nothing was known even of the existence of these Sumerians in ancient days. The archaeologists and scholars who, some hundred years ago, began excavating in that part of the Middle East known as Mesopotamia were looking not for Sumerians but for Assyrians and Babylonians. On these peoples and their civilisation s, they had considerable information from Greek and Hebrew sources, but of Sumer and the Sumerians they had no inkling.

There was no recognisable trace either of the land or of its people in the entire literature available to the modern scholar. The very name Sumer had been erased from the mind and memory of man for more than two thousand years. Yet today the Sumerians are one of the best-known peoples of the ancient Near East. We know what they looked like from their own statues and steles scattered throughout several of the more important museums…Moreover, Sumerian clay tablets by the tens of thousands (literally), inscribed with their business, legal, and administrative documents, crown the collections of these same museums, giving us much information about the social structure and administrative organisation of the ancient Sumerians. (History Begins at Sumer, xx)

So, What Did the Sumerians Ever Do for Us?

As a reader, you have to appreciate, before reading this section, that all these inventions or firsts that happened in the land of Sumer didn't materialise overnight. These events happened over many millennia; I'm not detracting from these amazing accomplishments. I'm just trying to allow the reader to further understand how long this culture existed compared to their own. The Land of Sumer equates roughly in size to Britain and as a British Engineer I have been intrigued by some of the marvels of engineering that have developed all around me, in just 200 years the British Revolution changed the world we see today.

But we have been living for Seven Millennia on the backs of all things Sumerian, not Roman, or Greek inventions, but Sumerian. Fortunately, we have the names of the inventors of these great feats of British Engineering. Alan Turin and the first Electronic Computer and the introduction of Artificial Intelligence. George Stevenson the father of Railways. If a name dictates the person you are, you don't get better than Isambard Kingdom Brunel, possibly the greatest engineer ever known.

Charles Babbage and Augusta Ada King, the Countess of Lovelace (you genuinely couldn't make these names up) the birth of the digital programmable computer without this, you wouldn't have known about Alan Turin. Unfortunately, the majority of the inventions listed below, we'll never know the genius behind the idea, and without the inventions listed below, we'll have never had the ones listed above. *The domino effect*!

To imagine something that has never been thought of before. If you hold a book in your hands, and with the technology that you are aware of. It isn't difficult to imagine an e-book, a large-print book, a picture book, a book in brail, and all kinds of books. But how does one imagine a book in a world where even the concept of a *book* does not exist?

It would seem there is an evolution pathway, but to have a stamp seal to the Epic of Gilgamesh in less than 1,000 years is quite impressive. Imagine a day without time. People live in time and time directs the course of people's days. We wake up at a certain hour, go to work or school. We know when it's time to finish work or when its lunchtime. Eating at regular times and going to sleep based upon the revolutions of the clock. Once, however, there existed a time without time. How can you imagine something which does not exist? Again, a process of an evolution pathway.

The cosmos and noticing patterns, noticing the cycles of the moon, and realising everything is cyclic. Both time and writing, and many other aspects of our daily lives, were invented by the Sumerians of ancient Mesopotamia over 7,000 years ago. Before the Sumerians, a day began with the sunrise and ended with the sunset. People went to work from when the sun was positioned at a certain height in the morning sky and returned to their homes when it set. It was the Sumerians who divided the day from the night by time, by increments of sixty-second minutes and sixty-minute hours which made up twelve hours of night and the twelve hours of the day.

Mesopotamian people developed many technologies, among them metalworking, glassmaking, textile weaving, food control, and water storage and irrigation. They were also one of the first Bronze Age people in the world. Early on they used copper, bronze, and gold, and later they used iron. Palaces were decorated with hundreds of kilograms of these very expensive metals. At various stages warfare altered overtime, each revolution bettering the predecessor copper to bronze, and then to iron were used for armour as well as for different weapons such as swords, daggers, spears, and maces.

The Sumerians also seem to have invented the concept of siege warfare and, perhaps, even the *scorched earth* tactic used effectively in military engagements ever since. In the biblical Book of Genesis, Chapter 1, it states that God divided the night from the day and saw that it was good. If you accept God's role in creating day and night then the Sumerians finished the job and if you don't, it was not God who divided night and day, it was obviously the Sumerians.

The Sumerians are responsible for inventing many of the aspects of modern-day life that people so often take for granted. In his work, *History Begins at Sumer*, Samuel Noah Kramer[xc] lists 39 *firsts* in human civilisation and culture that originated at Sumer. His list includes:

The First Schools, The First Case of *Apple Polishing*, The First Case of Juvenile Delinquency, The First *War of Nerves*, The First Bicameral Congress, The First Historian, The First Case of Tax Reduction, The First *Moses*, The First Legal Precedent, The First Pharmacopoeia, The First *Farmer's Almanac*, The First Experiment in Shade-Tree Gardening, Man's First Cosmogony and Cosmology, The First Moral Ideals, The First *Job*, The First Proverbs and Sayings, The First Animal Fables, The First Literary Debates, The First Biblical

Parallels, The First *Noah*, The First Tale of Resurrection, The First *St George*, The First Case of Literary Borrowing, Man's First Heroic Age, The First Love Song, The First Library Catalogue, Man's First Golden Age, The First *Sick Society*, The First Liturgic Laments, The First Messiahs, The First Long-Distance Champion, The First Literary Imagery, The First Sex Symbolism, The First Mater Dolorosa, The First Lullaby, The First Literary Portrait, The First Elegies, Labour's First Victory, The First Aquarium.

In addition to these accomplishments, of course, are the invention of time, a system of numbers, the 360-degree circle, geometry, the first wheeled vehicles, children's toys, writing, writing implements, harnessing the wind, the domestication of animals, agricultural developments such as irrigation, medical advances, dentistry, architectural developments, and urbanisation, not bad for a bunch of people we didn't even know existed less than 200 years ago.

Sumerian Sexagesimal (Also Known as Base 60 or Sexagenary)[xci]

Through many millennia, we have always unwittingly used Sumerian sexagesimal, which continues today for specialised topics such as time, angles, and astronomical coordinate systems, sexagesimal notations have always contained a strong undercurrent of decimal notation, such as in how sexagesimal digits are written. Their use has also always included (and continues to include) inconsistencies in where and how various bases are to represent numbers even within a single text. We still use Sumerian mathematics every day, time divided into 60 seconds to a minute, 60 minutes to an hour.

Sexagesimal is a numeral system with sixty as its base. It originated with the ancient Sumerians in the 6-7,000 BC, then passed down to the ancient Babylonians, and is still used in a modified form for measuring time, angles still use 360 degrees once again a relic of this system, and geographic coordinates. Why 60, it seems that it originated simply because of the hand. It is possible for people to count on their fingers to 12 using one hand only, with the thumb pointing to each finger bone on the four fingers in turn. A traditional counting system still in use in many regions of Asia, still works in this way.

This could help explain the occurrence of numeral systems based on 12 and 60 besides those based on 10, 20 and 5. In this system, one hand counts repeatedly to 12, displaying the number of iterations on the other, until five dozens, i.e. the 60, are full. The number 60, a superior highly composite number, has twelve factors, namely 1, 2, 3, 4, 5, 6, 10, 12, 15, 20, 30, and 60, of which 2, 3, and 5 are prime numbers. With so many factors, many fractions involving sexagesimal numbers are simplified. For example, one hour can be divided evenly into sections of 30 minutes, 20 minutes, 15 minutes, 12 minutes, 10 minutes, 6 minutes, 5 minutes, 4 minutes, 3 minutes, 2 minutes, and 1 minute. 60 is the smallest number that is divisible by every number from 1 to 6; that is, it is the lowest common multiple of 1, 2, 3, 4, 5 and 6.

Trigonometry and the Need in Ancient Building Projects

As we will see in this chapter, the breath-taking size of the Canals, Reservoirs and Levies needed far more than a strong will to build they needed mathematics. The only way to ensure that these, very time-consuming projects which could generate massive wealth for each city state if successful was to ensure the build was with MATHS! as its guarantor. One main necessity for the success of these large structures was the use of trigonometry. Trigonometry simply means calculations with triangles that where the tri comes from. It is a study of relationships in mathematics involving lengths, heights, and angles of different triangles.

As will be described, the Southern Mesopotamians already had extreme projects being created. city walls started to appear, massive canal systems being created, and temple structures and trade routes opened in all directions predominantly by open seas all the way to the Indus Region. All these mentioned needed a form of mathematics to be successful.

Until recently, a lot of historians hadn't appreciated the requirement for trigonometry in ancient time and may have felt it was predominantly trial and error in construction. But once we start to look at the complexities of the Canal, Reservoirs and Levies systems created and over time just increased in size we have to believe that very advanced mathematics was required for this to become successful. The Plimpton 322 tablet which is the size of a post card but extremely detailed uses a totally different form of trigonometry which is extremely accurate, discovered in Babylon and dated 1,800 BC. Yet this form of trigonometry must have been understood long before this time which will predate the writing system from 3,200 BC.

Plimpton 322

Daniel Mansfield describes the Plimpton 322. [xcii] The field of trigonometry had to have emerged during the 6th and 5th Millennia BE at the start of building canal systems for irrigation agriculture, which seems to have developed first at Choga Mami in Eastern Iraq in the Mandali region, which shows evidence of the first canal system in operation in 6,000 BC. The trigonometry tablet is believed to have originated from the city state of Larsa in Sumer, one of the original five founding Cities. From applications of geometry to astronomical studies, it is now coming to light, how well the stars and orbits where understood.

Trigonometry spreads its applications into various fields such as architects, surveyors, physicists, and engineering. The immediate answer expected would be mathematics, but it doesn't stop there even physics uses a lot of concepts of trigonometry. Trigonometry was first developed in connection with astronomy, with applications to navigation and construction of calendars. Geometry is much older, and trigonometry is built upon geometry. However, the origins of trigonometry can be traced to the civilisation s of ancient Mesopotamia and India.

Plimpton 322 (P322) tablet

Plimpton 322 is one of the most sophisticated scientific artefacts of the ancient world, containing 15 rows of arithmetically complicated Pythagorean triples. But the purpose of this tablet has mostly eluded scholars, despite intense investigation until recent. The numerical complexity of P322 proves that it is not a scribal school text, as many previously believed. Instead, P322 is a trigonometric table of a completely unfamiliar kind and was ahead of its time by thousands of years.

First, we abandon the notion of angle and instead describe a right triangle in terms of the short side, long side, and diagonal of a rectangle. Second, we must adopt the OB number system and its emphasis on precision. The OB scribes used a richer sexagesimal (base 60) system which is more suitable for exact computation than our decimal system, and while they were not shy of approximation, they had a preference for exact calculation. A modern trigonometric table is a list of right triangles with hypotenuse 1and approximations to the side lengths sinθ and cosθ, along with the ratio tanθ=sinθ/cosθ.

It is proposed that P322 is a different kind of trigonometric table which lists right triangles with long side 1, exact short side βand exact diagonal δ- in place of the approximations sinθ and cosθ. The ratios β/δor δ/β (equivalent to tanθ) are not given because they cannot be calculated exactly on account of the divisions involved. Instead P322 separates this information into three exact numbers: a related squared ratio which can be used as an index, and simplified values band d for βand δ which allow the user to make their own approximation to these ratios.

If this interpretation is correct, then P322 replaces Hipparchus' *table of chords* as the world's oldest trigonometric table but it is additionally unique because of its exact nature, which would make it the world's only completely accurate trigonometric table. These insights expose an entirely new level of sophistication for Old Babylonian (Sumerian) mathematics.

Understanding the Forces in Trigonometry

Understanding the forces at work on objects is a critical part of statics, which is an essential area of engineering. The study of statics and the related calculations are used by engineers to ensure that large structures do not collapse due to forces acting on them. In the design of large structures, engineers must ensure that forces acting on the structure will balance so that they remain stationary. Engineers use trigonometry to account for vertical and horizontal components of the different forces that act on structures. Determining that the structure will be able to stand without collapsing before it is even constructed.

These strategies, based on mathematical knowledge, enable engineers to design solutions to problems that might otherwise be unsolvable. If you know the distance from where you observe the building, temple or canal system and the angle of elevation you can easily find the height of the structure or the slope required to allow the flow of a body of water at a given rate to irrigate the crops. Similarly, if you have the value of one side and the angle of depression from the top of the structure you can find and another side in the triangle, all you need to know is one side and angle of the triangle.

Reasons for Trigonometry in Construction

- Measuring fields, lots and areas.
- Making walls parallel and perpendicular.
- Canal wall angles, levy walls, and reservoirs.
- Understanding which river is higher than the other, and understanding what gradient is required for drainage canal to be successful.
- Roof inclination.
- It is used in cartography (creation of maps).
- The height of the building, the width length etc. and the many other such things where it becomes necessary to use trigonometry.
- Trigonometry is used in finding the distance between celestial bodies.
- Also can be used to measure the distance from underground water systems.

Architects use trigonometry to calculate structural load, roof slopes, ground surfaces and many other aspects, including sun shading and light angles which was also important in the Ziggurat and temple walls using 28-inch standard cubic Sumerian/Ubaid measurement which was adopted throughout the entire area of both Northern and Southern Mesopotamia before writing had been invented. In marine engineering trigonometry is used to build and navigate marine vessels over long distances.

Trigonometry Used in Navigation

The only reason the region of Sumer/Ubaid/Southern Mesopotamia expanded was because of trade, so it was vital that the people who navigated the various types of vessels knew how to get from A to B. Trigonometry is used to set directions such as the north south east west, it tells you what direction to take with the compass to get on a straight direction. It is used in navigation in order to pinpoint a location. It is also used to find the distance of the shore from a point in the sea. It is also used to see the horizon.

The Need to Supply Fields with Large Amounts of Water for Cultivation

In general terms, irrigation can be defined as the artificial supply of water to supplement natural precipitation or substitute for it for the purpose of agricultural production. In Southern Mesopotamia, irrigation has been the life blood of the region which has allowed history to be created. The early developments evolved gradually over time and provided the foundations for today's water technologies that have spread throughout the world. Irrigation agriculture, which seems to have developed first at Choga Mami[xciii] in Eastern Iraq in the Mandali region, shows evidence of the first canal system in operation in 6,000 BC.

Now that trigonometry has been explained then understanding the engineering helps tie the mathematical knowledge that was required by the Sumerian/Ubaid culture into context. It was impossible to build the structures that can still be seen today without the high level of maths required. Understanding the shock loading from a volume of water entering a settling area, velocity of drain-off, irrigation capacity (what can I grow with X-Volume of water), Calculating the evaporation of a given volume of water at a given temperature.

I think that it is now necessary to appreciate the Engineering prowess of the Ubaid and Sumerian people as there is no real distinction between both during this period of time in Southern Mesopotamia. We have described that it was this region that didn't necessarily invent agriculture, but they were the people who *lit the blue touch paper* on advancement of agriculture. The reader is also now aware of the importance of water and the decision of the early inhabitants of the area to settle in the harsh environment. We also understand what the basics requirements are to successfully grow crops.

So, we will jump ahead of the timeline and see exactly what was required when agriculture became intensive, and we will discuss how the land was transformed beyond all recognition and then back again to what we see today.

Adamo, Nasrat and Nadhir Al-Ansari have written an excellent paper on this topic in *Journal of Earth Sciences and Geotechnical Engineering, Vol.10, No.3, 2020, 17-39. Scientific Press International Limited* which will help the reader understand how influential the Sumerians where in everything we know today.[xciv]

Irrigation by the Sumerians, Akkadians and Regions Throughout Mesopotamia: 2900-2004 BC

It was quickly realised that the new expansion of crop growing due to irrigation that it had to be controlled by the word of *Law*. Power can be abused and ill will practiced upon neighbours. Eventually when writing was fully developed then these Laws where finally set down and standardised. The first recording of *Water Laws* was from Hammurabi 1,792 to 1,750 BC; the regulations of water usage followed the initial irrigation development in the region. The first known written rules related to irrigation.

3 key concepts were:

1. Proportional distribution, whereby the grower, receives water proportion to the amount of farmed land
2. Definition of an individual farmers responsibility towards the community, by safeguarding the canal sections on his property, accepting community-shared rules such as water rotations and liability for damage caused to neighbours owing to negligence or malice
3. Water apportionment and policy of irrigation arrangements being the collective responsibility of beneficiary farmers

Today we now see a desert. 7,000 years ago, this would have been a normal sight to a Sumerian

The Sumerian power transfer to the Akkadians seems to be on the whole a smooth transition compared to the city state rivalry that plagued the Land of Sumer for several centuries, these rivalries where later mirrored by the Greek city states. Once the lands of Akkad and Sumer were under a single control the time of Sargon was seen as a time of building large canal systems including his new capital city. This is why both *Nations* don't describe any abrupt changes occurring whilst building these monumental canal systems.

Sumerians were the first people in history to invent the cuneiform script so we can only describe what happened once the written language was known from 3,200 BC onwards. Which has made the reporting of their achievements, possible. We fully understand how organised the people of this region where, the bookkeeping is extremely detailed and explains how organised and structured the society had become. This is a fixed point in time when we are considering engineering achievements that predate writing by 2,800 years. These systems and techniques will have been adapted overtime but cannot be verified due to the lack of written evidence prior to 3,200 BC marking the beginning of written history and the limited archaeological research carried out in the region as a whole.

This land could easily have been called *The Land of the Canals* as the Sumerians and Akkadians are the original pioneers in practicing large-scale irrigation with intricate canal networks systems woven throughout the land. Sumerians and Akkadians jointly continued to construct these immense feats of engineering connecting every city state together. The land is flat, and the two rivers had built themselves to higher levels than the surrounding lands by the continuous silting process from the Tigris and Euphrates Rivers. Therefore, gravity irrigation became possible and the people took the opportunity to construct these networks once the displaced populace of the Gulf Oasis had established their communities in the unforgiving landscape.

Description of the political and social developments, which led to the establishment of the city states has already been described but we are going to *jump* to post flood cities which later became the most prominent ones in the region, and their locations are shown on a map indicating the heartland of Sumeria in Southern Mesopotamia; close to the Persian Gulf.

We should be reminded that all these systems still existed for over 4,000 years, all the remnants of the canal systems and intricate water systems where actually destroyed by the Mongolians in 1219-1221 AD. It had still managed to stand the test of time until it was deliberately sabotaged by the Mongolians. They couldn't just marvel at what was in front of them, they had to destroy the past. As history continues to repeat itself, the modern-day Mongolians have recently been quashed in recent events in the Middle East.

In many parts of the region, ruins and historical remnants of ancient water structures and irrigation schemes, dating back to 6,000 BC can still be found in Choga Mami in Eastern Iraq. The people of this civilisation were the first to learn that, among the tasks needed for growing crops and ensuring food production, the provision of water was a vital one. This constituted the first steps of harnessing water resources for irrigation which became later a technology underlying the success of the greatest. This technique of understanding and controlling of water may have been harnessed during the Gulf Oasis flooding.

As the water encroached at a steady 2.5 cm (1 inch) per year, then the pre-Sumerians needed to understand how to control and manipulate the advancing sea water incursion for periods of time. Valuable respite from the constant onslaught of rising water levels was needed. Many of these engineering crafts will have been engrained within the people who stayed in the region praying for an end, these people stayed to fight the impossible fight. But in doing so, a wealth of knowledge will have been garnished which would aid the coming future developments in the Land of Sumer and would clearly mark a significant difference between the first people to leave the Gulf Oasis travelling to the Indian Subcontinent and the people who stayed to the bitter end.

Civilisation of the Region

As we go through the various stages of building and organisation of irrigation systems, we have to consider the mirrored increase in the development of the bureaucratic system. Prior to this peak in power the first settlements were situated very close to the rivers and estuaries and the fear of flooding was a constant bed fellow during these early stages. The transition from those humble beginnings to the height of the irrigation canal build program and the supporting hydraulic structures are genuinely admirable.

Only when wealth and power became excessive for each city state have, we witnessed the *wheels falling off* this social experiment. The biggest difference from early farming to its height, was the need for more land and that's when problems intensified. Maybe at the time, the land was so fertile that nobody could envisage a desert. Maybe it was impossible to envisage a breakdown of social order and the Great Walls crumbling back into the desert. The people of Sumer didn't realise that well-structured order was the only thing preventing city states form disappearing into the sands. The blindingly obvious wasn't seen; *They couldn't see the forest because the tree was in the way.*

Canals were required to be built to supply the region with the excess required for Trade the Sumerians were versed in hydraulic principles. One of the best mapped canal systems in the Middle Euphrates region of Mari in modern day Syria. This gives a particularly good indicator that trade by River or Canal system was the most important for of connection throughout Mesopotamia. As stated, we can only rely on the cuneiform writing of once everything was documented. The majority of these canal systems had already been built or in the process of being built prior to the invention of writing.

Could it be hypothesised that writing may have become necessary not just because of accounting purposes for agricultural produce controlled by the priest class, but also due to the large building programmes that had already began and a form of aid required to aid builders to help plan may have been needed to help the engineer.

A common sight within Sumeria

What Southern Mesopotamia currently looks like is nothing like what the area looked like in ancient times. You have to go beyond the imagination to even start to realise the reality of the area. The area of ancient Southern Mesopotamia even had more people living on the land than in the present day. The systems put in place and the organisation it took, transformed what we see as a desert today. An absolute breathe-taking sight of crops of all descriptions in all directions, as far as the eye could see, a hive of activity with boats being towed on canal systems through these large, irrigated fields.

Physical land preparation will not have changed from the very on-set of farming. The methods of land preparation, seeding, irrigation and harvesting indicates they were highly skilful intensive farmers with diverse crops. Eventual as agriculture intensified the tools and implements invented for field operations changed. Millions of Date Palm Trees row upon row also lining walkway to allow shade of the workers and also protecting the more sun adverse plants. The date palm was a real *tree of life* because it was used to produce about 360 different products. Artificial pollination was used to increase its yield 4,000 years ago.

Although smaller, they also grew apple trees and pomegranate trees, and grapes. Bulls pulling ploughs in the fields, 100's of thousands of sheep grazing in meadows with reed marshes in the lowest area below the grazing sheep. People could be seen transporting the produce from the fields whilst labourers and some slaves worked on maintenance of the canals ensuring they wouldn't become silted over. Whilst people working on the canal walls and opening sluice gates for different crops while some fields lay fallow. People working in the warehouses unloading carts whilst others are taking records of produce stored and examining the quality of produce.

Whilst accounts worked out how it should be segregated into temple offerings, workers allowance of produce and the remainder for export. Ships tied up at a quay on the side of the canals at the wharfs waiting to be loaded to take to more needy areas. You could see people collecting wool and dyeing the wool into a myriad of colours. Spinning the wool ready for the mass production factories that churned out the highest quality textiles that where the envy of all the people of the region and beyond. In the distance the kiln works firing millions of bricks, gushing thick black smoke into the clear blue sky with the iron works close by. Everyone had a job to do to support the state and the temple and if they worked hard the gods would surely reward their city as they had always done.

A constant procession of festivals and the celebration of the gods were a frequent occurrence and a welcome respite from the hard labour in the fields.

This isn't the description of a utopian society but what would have been seen if you cast your gaze over one small area of Southern Mesopotamia in one of the many city states at this point in time.

These amazing feats were hard-won, they did not materialise overnight but took hundreds of years before they could even begin to prosper. The vast sites described above could not be simply completed with the local populace as the physical manual labour this would have been mathematically impossible, especially when you consider the building programs within the city walls and the support of the temple class. People must have been brought in at some point, either through a natural magnetism drawn to these cities due to the increasing appeal or the forced labour of the mountain people.

If you consider the Old Testament and the reason the Tower of Babel had stopped being built, was due to the multi languages of the building site. If this was the case for the Tower of Babel, then it must also be considered for any large building program. A perfect modern example is in the 19th Century AD in Britain when the railway system started to be laid and the main people to dig the tunnels and cut through Ravines came from Ireland. If this labour force used throughout the Fertile Crescent was forced, then discontent was sown in the hill tribes that surrounded the Fertile Crescent.

During the earlier stages of cultivation, all people would have been involved in the natural survival of the people of the new embryonic civilisation. People could not afford to stand back and admire what was going on, the back was arched, and the work was difficult.

The person in charge of the organisation and division of labour before writing was invented must have been the *main man* or the *big man*, the decision maker on all things to deal with construction. Many people would have been technically superior within their own personal field of expertise, but someone was definitely in charge of construction. Could the word Lugal which means Big Man, stem from the person in charge of the building and construction works taking place in each city state?

Lugal became the name of King, and the majority of statues of Kings or depictions on friezes show the King with a bucket of earth similar to the picture of King Shulgi of Ur which was Foundation Figure found during excavations of the site. Yes, the King would like to be known and praised for his/her exploits in battle but also be renowned as a builder. Could these depictions of Kings stem from the original Lugal as the Project Manager rather than stem from the common thought as the man stemming from the warrior class that controlled people through warfare. The gods had Kings and the people eventually had Kings, but Kings haven't always been renowned for their skills in battle.

The outside trading partners grew in number and overtime the diversity of different goods grew and the rarer the better. It may be more expensive but that meant less people had it consumerism had finally taken a grip on society. So new commercial relations were developed in all corners of the globe. The economic aspects of this civilisation such as wages and loans for farmers, work specialisation and the appearance of new professions to meet cultivation requirements.

Flood protection works needed for better safety from the Tigris and Euphrates rivers recurrent floods were routine practices of the Sumerians to protect themselves and their lands from the grave dangers of these regular constant threats to floods. Therefore, they excelled in preventative maintenance, while canal maintenance by constant dredging of the silt brought down by the two rivers every year was a constant and real concern. The indigenous people of these lands had two different languages spoken in the Region of Sumer, Sumerian and Semitic Akkadian so a lot of the population would have been bilingual even though the predominant language was Sumerian once again showing that a state of peace must have existed before the city states expanded, and friction reared its head.

The Akkadians to the North who intermingled with them, lived in their Cities, and even mixed with them in marriages. This later explains how a smooth transition of power had resulted in the rise of the Akkadians King Sargon, after he had started as a high-ranking official at the court of Ur-Zababa the last Sumerian King and replaced him, marking the start of the Semitic speaking Akkadian domination, which lasted almost 200 years to 2,150 BC. Sargon managed to unite all the independent city states under one banner and establish the first Empire in the world extending well beyond Sumeria, so it was said that his influence was felt from Egypt in the West to India in the East.

Choga Mami Irrigation System

In ancient myths, a great conflict among the gods led to the creation of humanity. There were ranks of gods, and the lesser gods, the Igigi, who were assigned laborious tasks by Enlil such as digging canals, of which they grew tired leading to a rebellion against him. If ancient myth describes the gods building canals before men were created, helps shows how long canals had been worked on.

These cities and towns became possible because they developed in close harmony with the natural waterworks of the region, these societies also developed irrigation works and other water features. Settlements were built along levees if you see the image below it shows a of Southern Iraq showing a vast array of ancient sites and channels along with major ancient Cities.[xcv] During the time 6,000 BC in the Samarran settlement in Diyala province in Southern Iraq in the Mandali region. It shows the first canal irrigation in operation.

The site, about 70 miles Northeast of Baghdad, has been dated to the late 6th Millennium BC. It was occupied in several phases from the Samarran culture to the Ubaid. Buildings were rectangular and built of mud brick, including a guard tower at the settlement's entrance. Irrigation supported livestock including cattle, sheep and goats also arable agriculture including wheat, barley, and flax. Artefacts found at Choga Mami include Samarran painted pottery and elaborate clay female figurines.

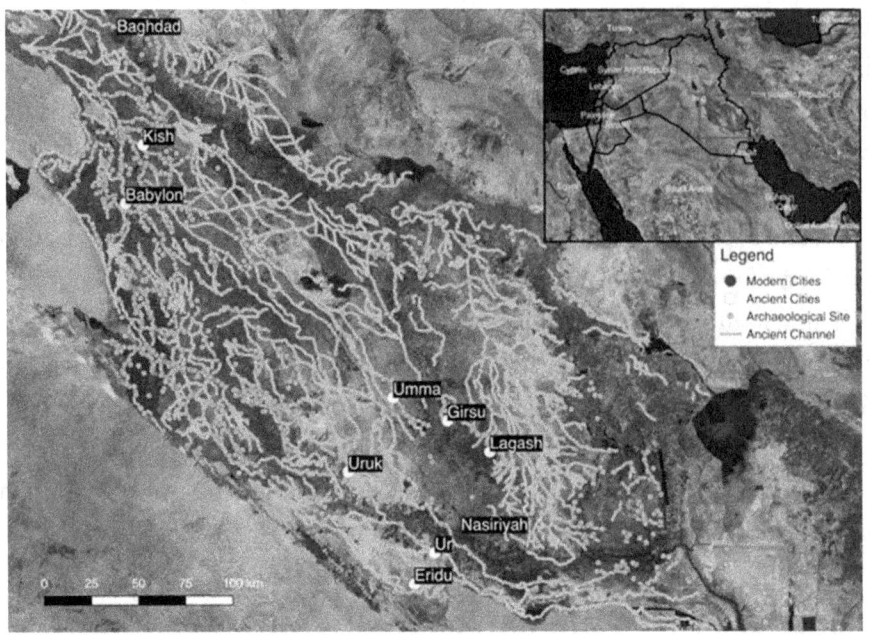

Within the next decade, archaeological evidence that is currently underway in modern Iraq will change our way of perceiving the Ancient Mesopotamians, the examples listed below are singular in their description, but as seen above these activities where everywhere throughout the region. The example above highlights the effort and resources placed on the land and attention to detail in expansion of the water systems. We also need to remember the people of this area continued to expand for 4,000 years before the 4.2K Climatic Disaster. These original canal systems expanded over time to ensure maximum yield was obtained from the crops.

Mari Canal System

During the time period between 2,900-1,700 BC, in the area of the ancient city of Mari centrally located in the Euphrates valley, in today's Syria.[xcvi] On the right bank of the river there was two successive and independent irrigation systems, each one depending upon such a canal as long as 20 to 30 km. The map of this area is shown on figure below. In the ancient texts from Mari, such canals are called *rakibum*, a name which means *the one which rides* (over the land).

The next figure shows a typical cross-section of present remains, showing how large the dikes used to be. These *rakibum* were not in use all the yearlong, but only during the irrigation season, and there were no villages along their course. Considerable maintenance work was necessary every year prior to the opening and use of these canals. On the left bank of the Euphrates, there was another canal, 120 km in length. This navigation canal may have been dug when the city of Mari was founded by 2,900 BC. It is known from the texts that in later times it was also used for irrigation. Mari was destroyed in 1,761 BC by Hammurabi, King of Babylon.

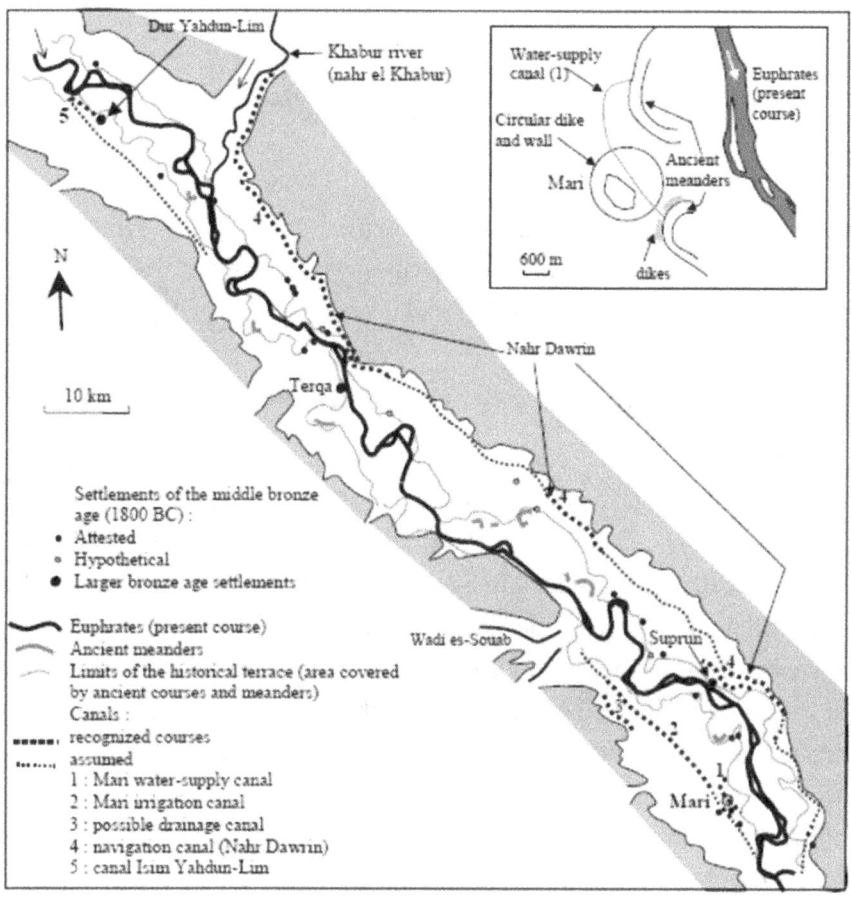

Two canals used to be directly associated with the city of Mari: a water-supply canal (1) and irrigation canal (2). Both canals are contemporary to the foundation of Mari, by 2,900 BC. The long navigation canal Nahr Dawrin (4) was also probably built at the same period. North, a city called Dur Yahdun Lim, associated to a water-supply and irrigation canal, it is unknown if there was one single or two different canals? It may have been founded by King Yahdun-Lim of Mari by 1,850 BC. From the texts dated 1,800-1,760 BC, it is known that the Isim Yahdun Lim irrigation canal extended as far as towards Terqa, and that the Nahr Dawrin was at that time also used for irrigation of the left bank of the Euphrates- drawn by the author using the results of the field surveys Geyer and Monchambert, 2003 and Margueron, 2004 and additional sources Viollet, 2000 AD.

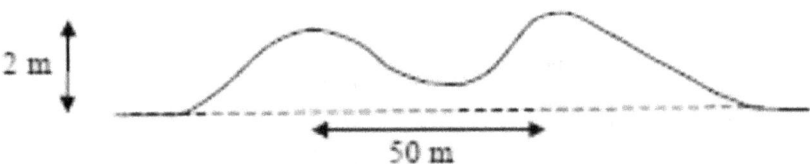

A typical cross-section of the present remains of the Mari irrigation canal (*rakibum*) the canal N°2, Figure above; present state of conservation[xcvii]. Horizontal and vertical scales are different.

Sumerians, Akkadians and People of the Fertile Crescent

It is an established fact that the first successful efforts to control the flow of water on a very large scale were made in Mesopotamia. The Sumerians in Southern Mesopotamia eventually built city walls and temples and dug long, wide, and deep canals, which may be counted as the world's first large engineering works of their kind. It is also of interest to note that these people from the beginning of recorded history fought over water rights and agricultural land, and irrigation were extremely vital to them. These city states had formed boundary markers to protect the rights of each individual city state which became controversial marks that ended in long drawn-out disputes.

A city state could only up to the boundary marker, so land became the biggest issue along with water rights. Flooding problems were more serious in Southern Mesopotamia than in Egypt because the Tigris and Euphrates were much swifter than the Nile and carried several times more silt per unit volume of water than the Nile did. This resulted in rivers rising faster and changing their courses more often in Mesopotamia, later to the detriment of some cities and eventually all cities that disappeared and reclaimed by the sands of the desert.

Your average dictionary will define irrigation as *the artificial application of water to land to assist in the production of crops*. That is exactly how the

Mesopotamians used it 8,000 years ago in Choga Mami. Today, it's still used in most of the world, in a similar fashion. People didn't really need to improve on the methods, because the irrigation system was efficient and simple from the start. Irrigation was basically required for large-scale agriculture, especially in the middle of the desert. Its only downside was that it had to be used close to a water source, at least when the Mesopotamians used it. You could move the river or simply add a tributary or canal to stretch deep into the land.

In fact, irrigation was the first spectacle of engineering that the Mesopotamians due to the need to survive in the Southern Region. At first, it seemed almost impossible to grow crops. Thankfully, someone had the good idea to make levees between the two rivers surrounding the area, so that water would flow from the higher one to the lower one. It worked for the farmers upstream. Unfortunately, the people downstream often had to deal with dirty water filled with silt or sometimes, during dry seasons, no water at all. It was simple; without a levee or a canal, you couldn't grow anything on the scale that was required. The Sumerians were the first to make canals between the two rivers that enclosed Mesopotamia the Tigris and Euphrates.

The canals took water out of one river, and distributed it among many agricultural fields, and then led to the other river. These canals were made by digging a trench, then piling up dirt on both sides, creating breaks in it when needed to water plants. Later on, the Sumerians made further adjustments to their levees, basically a larger canal that could handle much more water. all the time the two rivers often spilt their flood waters over the banks into the surrounding plains. Their heavy loads of silt were deposited on these lands. But the coarser parts were deposited on the banks close to the rivers themselves and by so building higher grounds in the form of berms.

As more silt was deposited on the bottom, the water level became increasingly higher than the adjacent land. The berms then arc backwards to land. The Sumerians replicated natural affect by making small walls by fire-hardening reeds, tying them together, and then packing mud around them. They would then stack clay bricks around the exterior. Afterwards, they built canals leading deep inland and to neighbouring city states. All these innovations helped the settlers along the rivers to use gravity irrigation and flood their fields to grow their needed food.

And this is how Sumerians, Akkadians and later on the Babylonian civilisations constructed canals to carry the water further and extend the irrigated areas which helped these civilisations to flourish. Water lifting devices may have been in use throughout this period of time for lifting water into the Cities, but no archaeological evidence has been retrieved to date. They are perpendicular to the water's surface,

The Sumerians and the people of the Fertile Crescent had to solve much bigger hydraulic problems than the Egyptians whose civilisation had not even started to develop at the start of this problem-solving exercise in Southern Mesopotamia. The processes leading to the Sumerian Civilisation cannot be understood except as creative adaptation to the priceless resources of the Tigris and Euphrates waters. Which led to the birth of civilisation and the creation of the city states starting with Eridu in 5,400 BC.

As the water levels in the Persian Gulf had finally abated, all eyes were drawn to the land and how to get the best from it. No mistakes but lots of problems would have been encountered and the path to success was neither straight nor smooth, but success was gained, and riches flooded into individual city states. The vigorous later traditions continued to build on assured food supply ensured by the two rivers. To study the full role of the two rivers in history one cannot but consider the whole geographic unit comprising their watershed area and their whole valley.

Archaeological findings from Tell Bark on the Khabour tributary and from Ancient Mari on the Euphrates in Syria, which belonged to the third millennia and second millennia. Show the strong relationship between these parts of Northern Mesopotamia in modern Syria and Southern Mesopotamia in modern Iraq. There were to be sure some periods when deep socio-political divisions extended across the two rivers during Parthians, Sasanian, the Umayyad, and Abbasid empires. But trade is trade, and nothing comes between it for any sustained length of time, trade never picks a side. The valley of the two rivers, however, remained in other extended periods open for inter-regional contacts, and the banks of the Tigris and Euphrates were vital for heavily travelled routes between Mesopotamia and the world around the Mediterranean and the Indus Trade Routes through the Persian Gulf.

Fertile Crescent and Persian Gulf Trade Routes

The initial embryonic growth of the region when it is easily susceptible to invasion also relied on the natural protection granted to it, the protective barrier of both the Tigris and the Euphrates River, early protection against potential provocateurs. The Persian Gulf also acted as a natural defence until the silt laden rivers finally started to *clog* the delta and made the land between Elam its constant nemesis and Southern Mesopotamia accessible to invaders.

Resources Required for Starting a Project

To successfully accomplish a project on the sizes that have been witnessed in Mesopotamia, certain criteria is required. First the survey of the land and to calculate how much effort will be required to accomplish this engineering task. One or two modifications to a plan can drastically reduce the time and effort in completing a project. So, an accurate and detailed survey needs to be completed before anything else can be planned. The survey team need to understand what material obstructions are going to be encountered during the build. The surveyors need to understand the topography so excessive effort is not required to create high wall ravines and the possibility of wall collapse.

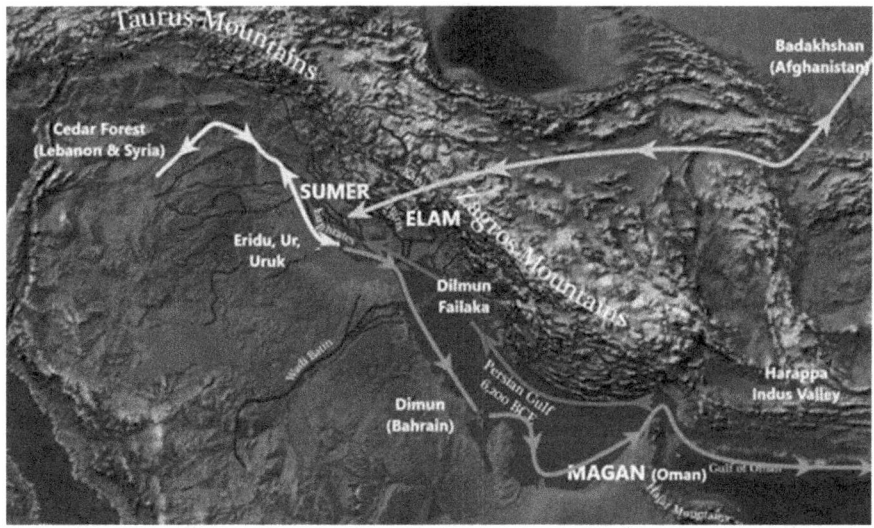

Understanding the strata permeability and formation which needs to be known to see if the earth is to porous and the precious canal water simply soaks into the ground with insufficient water reaching the necessary point of farmland. A form of engineering consultant will be required to oversee the multiple surveys that are required and give his/her best judged opinion on the best course of action required.

Required Teams

- These come in multiple forms, the team to make and fire the bricks which has to be in an area with good clay, a water source, and a fuel source. The closer you are to all three then less effort is required for moving the build material multiple times.
- Third party labour; the hard work, the physical digging of the canals, the back-breaking work which might be done by external work force or a slave force possibly taken from the mountain people and forced to work for an individual city state. This scenario would have fuelled resentment from the surrounding hill tribes. These various tribes waiting their time. A mood of vengeance will have been festering for a very long time, waiting for an opportunity to *strike back* at their oppressors, which eventually happened curtesy of the 4.2K Climatic Event and the geological composite of the source waters transported from the mountain ranges that created the Tigris and Euphrates Rivers.
- Artisan trades for making lock gates, laying the bricks, foundry work making the necessary tools required for making the equipment and the hinges and bolts for the lock gates.
- Transportation: how these newly made fired bricks and bitumen are brought to site for construction. Also, the transportation of food and water for camp support. The use of boats had a large bearing on how items had been moved. Wood and masonry that is not locally available and needs transporting long distances.
- Camp support: The team required to support the onsite work force, the making of bread and food also the movable accommodation the making of clay bowls for cooking and eating from. Drinking water/beer required with the vessels for moving the liquids. The larger the group the bigger the logistical nightmare.
- Architects required to mathematically ensure the work will be fit for purpose with no rework, rework means delays.
- Project management and cost manager: even if no money had been invented, the project still had costs in time, feeding and project support, everything has a cost.

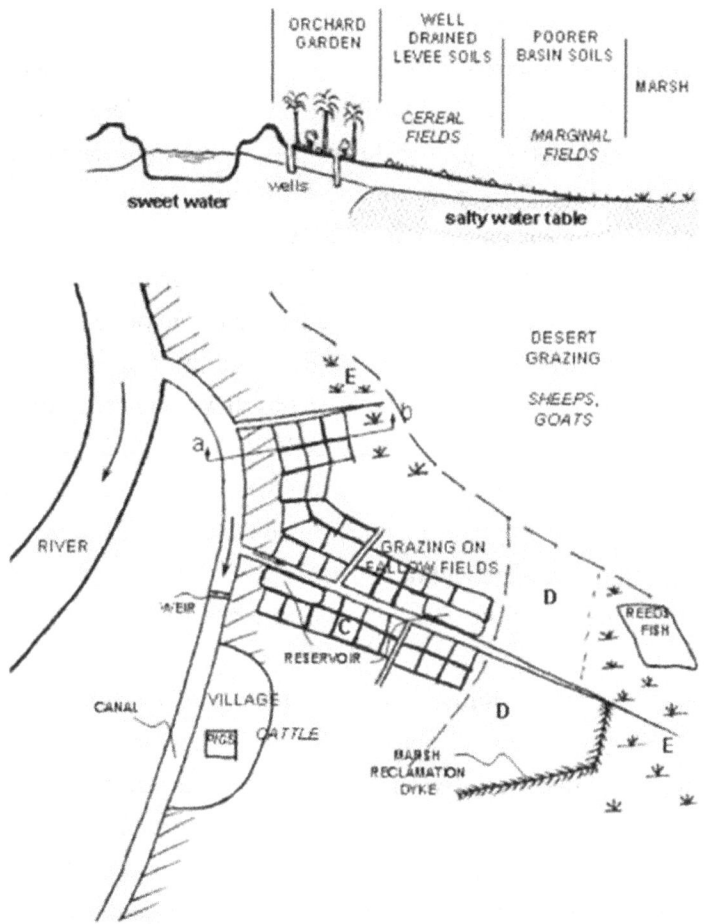

Layout of an Agricultural Cell in Southern Mesopotamia[xcviii]

The two rivers, however, remained a source of constant danger to the people living along them as destructive floods were also frequent, which caused destruction and the loss of human life. Such catastrophic floods together with wars obliterated some of these civilisations and opened the way for others. During all these times, the inhabitants had also to invent ways to protect themselves and their lands from flooding by means of building dykes and learn how to close breaches in these dykes. High floods didn't only threaten the safety and the cultivations of the inhabitants but also caused from time to time the shifting of the two rivers away from their original courses as characterised by fluvial rivers.

The consequences were of such large magnitude that people had to abandon some of their flourishing cities since canals, and their intakes became obsolete. This meant building new cities, and new canal systems and new intakes to follow the new courses of these rivers. Also, during the long drought period that started in 2,200 BC for over 200 years an influx of people moved to the South from the North of Mesopotamia, the existing canal systems will have had to be re-engineered to account for the drop in river level.

The long history of Mesopotamia is full of such occurrences as discovered from archaeological excavations and the remnants of the old courses of the two rivers. As evidence for these changes, we may cite the fact that the Tigris and Euphrates at the Sumerian times did not meet as they do today to form Shatt-Al Arab, but they emptied separately in the Gulf as shown in the figure below, a fact which underscores the changing nature of their watercourses. The Euphrates bed, being higher than that of the Tigris, provided a natural gradient for irrigation and drainage schemes: the Euphrates water was used as supply, whereas the Tigris River provided a drain and the flooded lands in between were used for growing crops.

The locations of the Sumerian settlements and city states: More than often, these cities were established closer to the Euphrates River than to the Tigris, although the distance between the two rivers was not great in this delta as seen clearly from the map below. The obvious reasons can be summarised. First, the general grade of land was in the direction from the Euphrates towards the Tigris which resulted in the irrigation networks slope being in this direction toward the fertile lands below. Second, is the milder slope of the Euphrates River itself, which resulted in calmer flow and slower water level rise and fall, making the construction of diversion works and canals off takes much easier.

Finally, the Euphrates was characterised by much smaller flood volumes than the Tigris due to curtailment of the very high flood peaks by flooding upstream natural depressions such as Al-Habaniyah and Abu Dibs depressions whose excess water could replenish the Euphrates flow later on in the season.

In any study, which aims at the understanding of agricultural society of the Sumerians, it is especially important to understand the social background of such societies. Social and governance system in Sumeria was based on the city state system; whereby every city state was sovereign and had its Deity, King (Engineer), Temple, Priests, the Noblemen and the majority of the ordinary people who depended mostly on cultivating the agricultural land of the state; but there were also the Tradesmen, the Scribes and Artisans in addition to Slaves. The Mesopotamians depended on their irrigation to provide all of their water, and without it, there most likely would have been no Southern Mesopotamia at all.

The irrigation also played a large role in the opposite respect. They would redirect water from the river during the flood season, saving countless crops in the process. Since the rivers carried enormous amounts of silt, which could have been harmful to the crops, people helped every year to change the arrangement of the canals and clean up the silt from the previous ones. It was an efficient system, but it was also open to manipulation.

Prior to the start of large engineering projects, each community will have built independent small canal systems of their own until the communities became larger and more independent. Once this phase appeared it would seem that each community had a strong working relationship with its neighbour. The reason for such a statement is that the new large canal systems envisaged to increase production levels to greater heights physically went through neighbouring communities and then onwards to other areas. Therefore, a level of combined and mutual cooperation was required and obviously didn't anticipate any conflict with their neighbours, or the project would never have succeeded.

In most cases, irrigation water was carried to the cultivated lands by main canals, which were often shared between city states. This eventually gave rise to constant tensions and a city state at the higher end of the canal system could distribute water as they saw fit. This often led to hoarding which resulted in conflicts and eventually all out wars between these emerging city states over water rights. At the same time encouraged some of the Kings of these states to construct new canals and diversion works, which means that instead of *areas* combining labour efforts each city state became so large that even large engineering project where undertaken by individual states once the funding for such feats of engineering could be secured.

The list of important city states of Sumeria is long, and they belong to different periods, but each individual city state had major engineering projects completed individually until an Empire was created and the controlling state dictated what building project where most important. The most important of these city states are Ur, Eridu (the first city), Uruk, Girsu, Umm, Lagash and Kish, and history recorded to us some of the fierce wars between some of them.

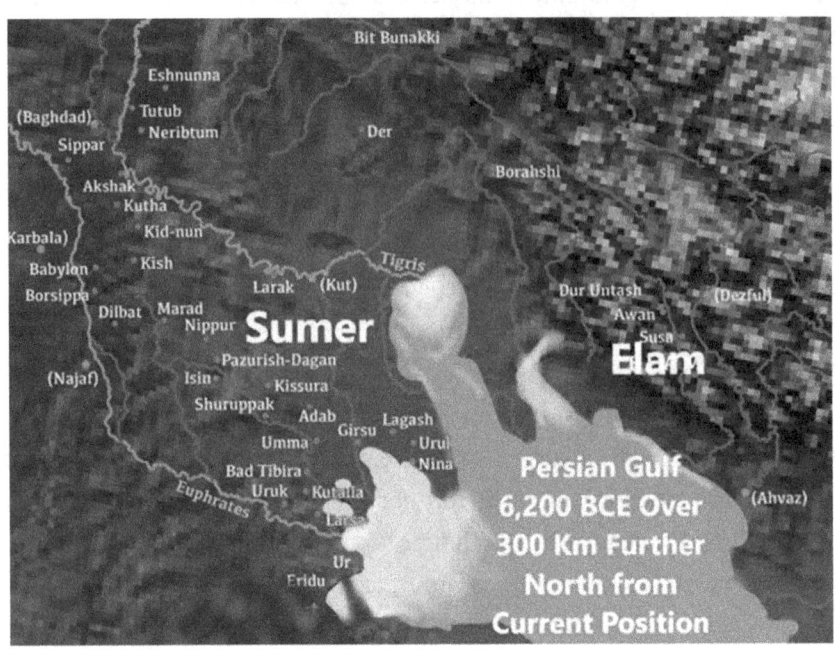

Map showing the Sumerian heartland and Tigris and Euphrates estuaries

In Sumeria, and generally in Lower Mesopotamia, the alluvial plains agriculture depended completely on irrigation in contrast to the upper Mesopotamia where dry farming (no need for canal systems as the cooler wetter climate conditions which could support crop growth) was possible. For the inhabitants of Lower Mesopotamia irrigation had a prime importance for survival, and the control of water was decisive to ensure perpetual prosperity. Therefore, complex systems of canals, reservoirs, dykes and control structures had to be planned and constructed to meet this end.

Such works necessitated knowledge of hydraulic principles, which the Sumerians had developed and mastered in their applications. They dug canals, which followed the grade of the land to ensure the water had a smooth flow and the incoming water didn't erode or damage/scour the bottoms or side walls of the canals; some of these canals reached a width of 120 metres or large enough to permit navigation, and frequently such canals had levees or dykes. Sumerian texts described many of their canals and gave very precise details of their lengths and dimensions. One of these described was 198 metres long canal, 1 meter wide and 0.25 m deep. In their irrigation networks, principal canals feed the smaller ones as clearly shown in previous illustration.

As shown with the Middle Mesopotamian region of Mari, research has shown the several different kinds of Canal where built, Navigation Canals to reduce time from point A to point B, Irrigation Canals for the various crops and drainage canals, a plethora of variations that points to an ever increasing command and knowledge of water hydraulics.

A levee with its remaining water being divided into multiple irrigation canals

Irrigation Canals

Just as a side note, as I haven't been able to find in any literature on this subject, the area is subject to frequent earthquakes predominantly emanating from the Zagros Mountains, but still sizable and during the construction of these canal systems this was another physical element that had to be taken into consideration during the construction phase. Not just the water turbulence and the dampening in settling pools. The people of this region used bitumen between the brick which helps absorb shocks and underneath the settling pools a layer of Bitumen wrapped in palm leaves also allowed for absorbing shock loads and dampening the vibrations creating when the weirs where first opened. These intricate points point to a level of sophistication unheard of before this point in time.

The description of an irrigation system which belonged to Umma[xcix] mentioned one branch canal with depth of 0.5-1 metre, and another having 6 metres width with length reaching up to 1,710 metres which equates to 7,785m³ of earth removed. Secondary canals could be as wide as 1.00-1.25 metre and 0.5-2.25 metre in depth. The material from the excavation was probably used to raise the levees, increasing the canals depth.

Although most of the received mathematical texts dealt with rectangular shaped canals, probably this was simplified of trapezoidal shape in order to facilitate quick computations for recording the daily progress during excavation as implied by these cuneiform texts. On one tablet, two trapezoidal channels were presented, where the concept of side slopes was introduced, measured as the horizontal distance per 1 unit of length in the vertical. Side inclination in both canals was V: H = 1:0.5.

In the intricate systems of irrigation, the Sumerians constructed control structures in the form of weirs across main streams to divert part of the flow into large lateral canal intakes, Figure below. Such a weir consisted of two gates that can turn, blocking the river or the entrance to the canal depending on their positions. Probably they were made of reeds and bitumen or, also wood. In more advanced works such as weirs were built with fire-baked clay bricks and earth.

Under the reign of the Akkadian ruler Sargon, the first conscripted army was organised to provide labour for flood-control projects. Under his rule, canals and channels were built to control the onslaught of the seasonal floods by diverting the water and gradualising the flow.

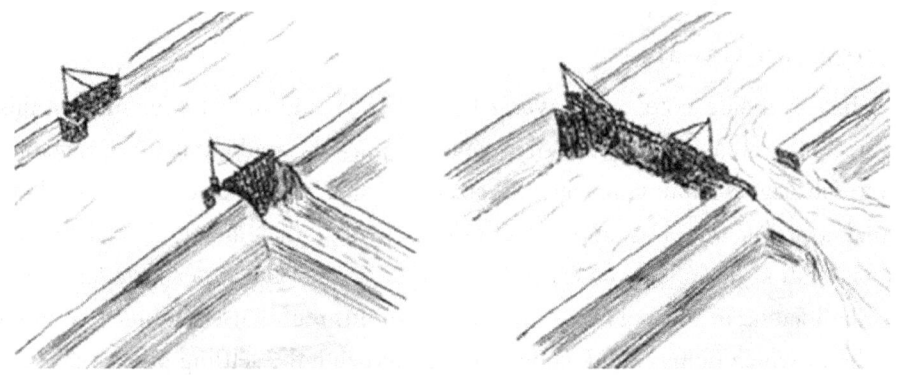

Sluice gate of a large stream, Lambert (2007)

Sluice Gate

Another arrangement of feeder canals intakes may have looked like where a sluice gate was placed at the head reach of feeder canals to regulate the flow entering the canal or shut it off completely. This arrangement was documented by Buccellati from excavations in Terqa in Middle Euphrates in Syria, but it can very well represent similar situations in Lower Mesopotamia. Other arrangements were also used as indicated by many tablets left by the Sumerians.

More elaborate works were constructed to fulfil multipurpose objectives, such as, slowing down the flow to avoid scouring of the canals, settling basins to reduce the silt load and provide clear water, in addition to acting as water storage for later uses; one example is given in the figure below.[c]

The inscriptions recorded different designs with different dimensions for reservoirs, and examples were given of dimensions, which varied between 12 metres to 72 metres long and widths ranging between 6 metres to 12 metres, and heights between 3 metres to 5 metres. Conceived from Ur III text, which was reconstructed by Shin T. Kang and quoted by Tamburrino. The nomenclature shown on this figure gives the Sumerian names and their equivalent in English as translated by Kang.

The Sumerians did not fail to control the flow in their canals by constructing regulators similar in many respects to regulators of modern times. Genouillac and Parrot[ci] uncovered one example of such structures during excavation from 1929 AD to 1932 AD in a site at Tello, the ancient town of Girsu.

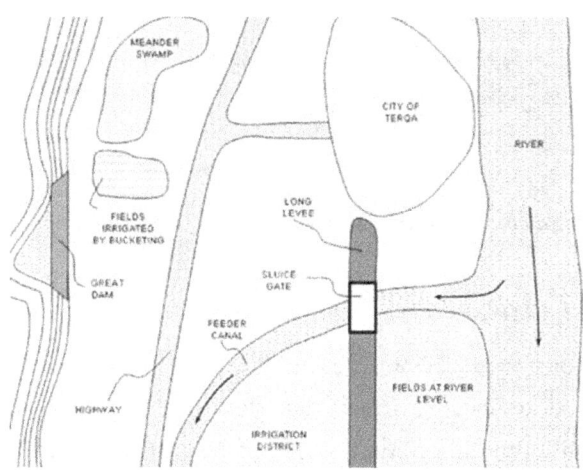

Schematic layout of an agricultural complex in middle Mesopotamia. From Buccellati

Ancient Reservoir[cii]

A recent dig in Iraq by Licia Romano and Franco D'Agostino of Rome's Sapienza University 2017 discovered the remains of an ancient reservoir in Abu Tbeirah, a desert site about 7 kilometres (4.3 miles) south of the town of Nasiriyah. The reservoirs basin, measuring 130 metres (142 yards) in length and 40 metres (44 yards) wide, with a capacity equal to nine Olympics-sized pools, may have also served as a giant reservoir and as a tank to contain river flooding and useful as a port for loading grain produced from the nearby fields as water was always the main mode of transport.

Its discovery suggests that Sumerian city states remained connected to the Delta of the Tigris and Euphrates rivers until much later than previously thought. It could also help archaeologists shed light on the great climate change that shocked the area around 2,270 BC that is presumed to have caused a huge drought in Mesopotamia, bringing about the end of the Sumerian civilisation.

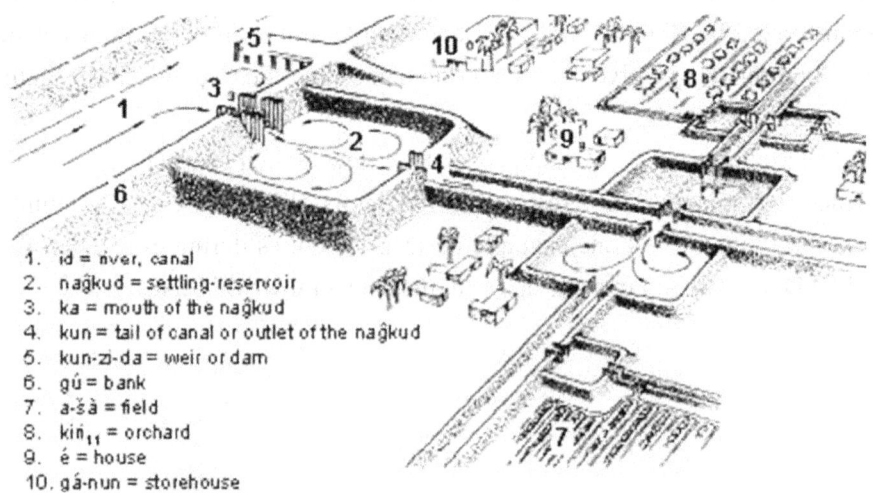

An example of a settling reservoir and complementary waterworks

Regulator of Nina-Gena Canal

This regulator was placed at the eastern levee of an affluent of the Euphrates, which was called Nina-Gena Canal that flowed from North to South.[ciii] The original plan and full description were given by Parrot, in addition to his visualisation shown in the figure below. The structure was made entirely of baked bricks bonded with bitumen. Sounding done in the site during excavation discovered a bitumen impregnated reed mat under the brickwork of the foundation. Bricks of various sizes were used in different parts of the structure, but this had no significance to its length or mode of action.

The brickwork walls (A-B) and (C-D) were protecting the clayey silty banks from erosion and were set at an angle forming the funnel shaped entrance and were supported by the external brickwork projections (a, b, c) and (d, e, f, g) which added extra support to these walls. The walls (B-E) and (C-F) which formed the rectangular section of the main structure were supported by the buttresses (h, l, j), and (k, i, m) respectively that took the impact loading from the river water.

Moreover, the thick sluice floor was made of six courses of bricks laid on a bed of reeds and bitumen, and the sluice measured 11.4m x 3m. The downstream part was formed from the wing walls (E-G-H) and (F-I-J) which were supported by buttresses and formed a fan that directed the flow into the 16 m wide canal. From the excavation, the sidewalls were about 5 m high, but bricks may have been pillaged from the top of the structure, so it is possible that the structure could have been higher enabling it to cope with most flood conditions and provide water from April to June. Throughout the excavation works, it was revealed that the soil filling adjoining the structure was of compacted clay while loose materials that had concealed it during all those years buried the structure itself.

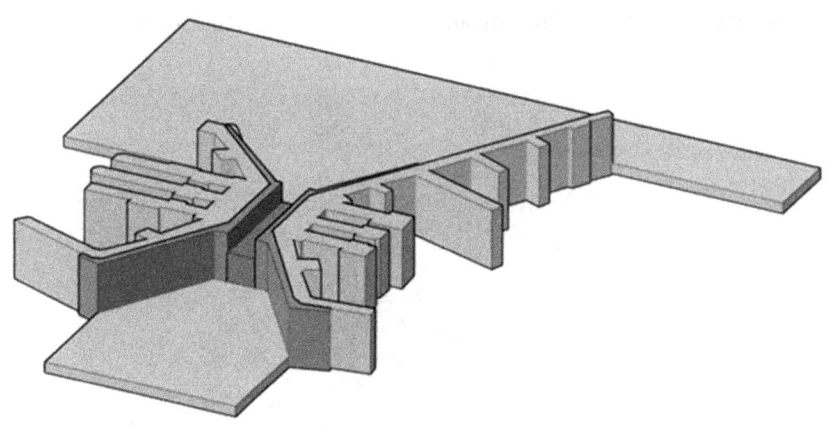

Head regulator of Nina-Gena Canal

Plan and cross-section with a perspective view image modified from Parrot by Steven Convery; The longitudinal and transverse buttresses that prevent the structure from collapse are of a monumental scale. The calculations made, in ensuring these structures required minimum maintenance is quite breath-taking and shows the level of mathematics shown, to be exceptional. Control of the flow through the regulator was done by using horizontal wooden beams, which may have been similar to the stop logs we use today in such hydraulic structure.

But there were, however, no side grooves in the walls to install the beams and it is assumed that these beams were held in position using wooden supports. The number of beams could be increased or decreased following the fluctuations of water level in the river, and the discharge required in the canal. Evidence of the use of such beams was revealed in the *Epic of Gilgamesh*, the great Sumerian version of the Great Flood. In one text, which belonged to Pre-Sargonic Lagash, description is found of one irrigation system on three tablets, which described the length of a canal that was under construction or repair, and the description of a regulator, which fed another canal.

From information given by Stienkeller, the dimensions of this regulator were 18 x 3 metres as visualised in the sketch of Figure below. In addition, it had upstream wing walls 27 and 24 metres long to protect the structure which itself cut through the levee on the riverbank and fed a canal 6m wide. Other details are similar to the regulator in Tello Girsu which indicated that such structures were very common, and that there was an accumulated wealth of experience in such works at the disposal of the planners and constructors of these networks.

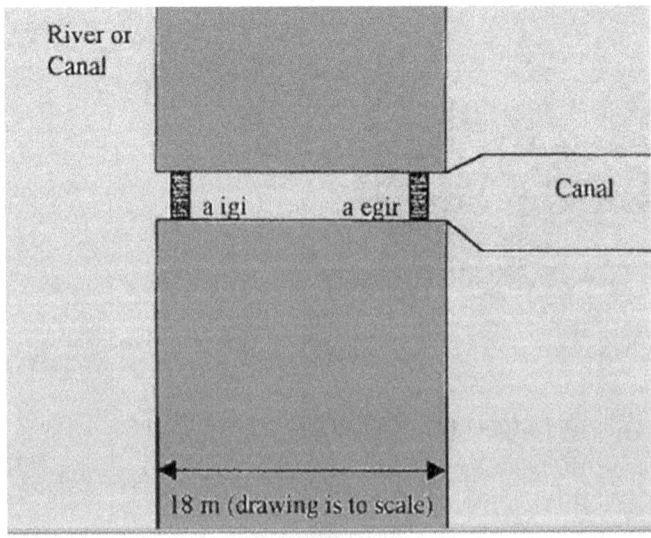

The Sumerian Irrigation Canal System

It was very extensive, and the number of excavated archaeological sites was so large that the remnants of many major canals could be pinpointed and traced as shown in the map in Figure below which was originally produced by Jacobson[civ]. In this map, the old Euphrates river course is shown from which all the major canals were branching. Locations of major regulators are also shown on this map and indicated by red colour rectangles. The sites of some of the most important Sumerian cities are shown also, where it is clear that these cities were located close to these headwords in order to control the water flow to the territories along these canals. Modern cites of Iraq are also shown in addition to so many locations of excavation sites, which were dug during the period from the end of the 19th century to well into the 20th century.

It must be emphasised here that there are probably thousands of such sites waiting to be investigated. The area irrigated from two of these canals, namely Girsu canal and Kimah canal, were estimated by Dight, based on their dimensions of 16 m width and 6 m width respectively assuming a four-month irrigation period during winter and growing cereal crop with a water requirement of 600 l/m2 per year and 40% of water losses due to evaporation and seepage in the distribution network. The conclusion was that the Girsu canal and Kimah canal irrigated 10,000 ha and 2,000 ha respectively. Considering that the cultivation system was based on the fallow system it follows then that the total areas served by the two canals can be doubled to 20,000 ha (200 Km²) and 4,000 ha (40 Km²).

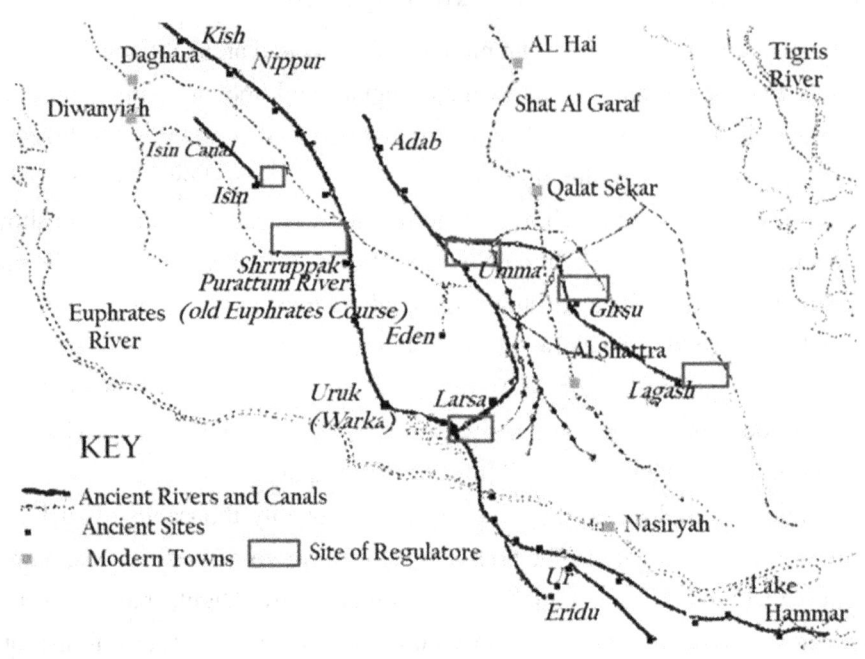

Map of the remains of major irrigation canals and regulators produced by Jacobson.

Water Disputes[cv]

As the social system changed over time that supported agriculture and land cultivation and the independent city states grew in size ended up being closer to a feudal system. As one city state started to have issues with its neighbours owing to water rights. Fighting erupted and then the advent of conquering one another's city state then the land ownership of the conquered city state is turned to the king and the temple of the victorious city state. There were also the other lands which are under the collective ownership of groups of farmers, in addition to many other holdings, which belonged to landlords from noble families who had acquired written documents verifying their ownership.

Maintenance of the canals was a continuous task, and major canals were supervised by high officials who reported directly to the King. Large gangs of workers were necessary to free the canals of silt, which demanded the removal of enormous amounts of mud. This was clearly documented on clay slabs of the types used at the time for writing and found during archaeological excavations reported by Tamburrino.

The secondary irrigation canals, however, were solely owned and controlled by the farmers and owners of the served plots of land, and on their shoulders rested the duty of clearing them from sediments and maintain the continued discharge. In a similar parallel in modern Iraq up to the middle of the 20th century, large groups of peasantries called *Hushoor* used to get together to remove the silt depositions from irrigation canals and keep the free flow going in them.

The list below sheds light on the hierarchy in the Sumerian society in which obviously the last rank in this hierarchy, consisting of slaves and criminals, were an important source of free labour in all the heavy tasks of farming and canals maintenance works. Most slaves were prisoners of war once warfare came into being, but the original slave labour to carry out the original works would have come from external sources like the Zagros Mountain region as they were deemed substandard, but a free man could also become a slave in case of failing the payment of a debt or committing a grave offence.

The distribution of water between users followed a fixed system agreed upon and followed by all those users, but this did not prevent conflicts and skirmishes over water rights. In the exploitation of their lands often, landlords of the larger holdings used hired hands to cultivate their land and paid their wages after harvest either in barley, sheep wool, and live animals or even in silver. Some of the poorer owners were forced to mortgage their land to buy seeds, tools and other cultivation requirements and pay back after the harvest, in which cases they were protected from the exploitation of greedy money lenders by the law. If the harvest failed, however, for reasons beyond the control of the farmers, the law also exempted them from the payment of the interests.

Class hierarchy in the Sumerian society:

- King/priests/project managers
- Elders and the noble counsellors
- Landowners, government officials (scribes), wealthy merchants
- Farmers and artisans
- Salves and criminals

Conflicts over water rights and agricultural lands between city states became quite common. These conflicts were settled either by, arbitration or even by one of the two states digging a new canal and building new control and distribution structures to avoid sharing. If all means of settling the matter failed through arbitration it then ended in the eruption of full-scale war between these states. Such wars may end by conquering of one of the two city states and taking over its lands or, by signing a new reconciliation treaty with new conditions and payments of large penalties.

In this respect, many examples are given in the Sumerian history. One such example is found in the long feud between the city state Lagash and the other Sumerian city state Umma. The conflict focused over the irrigation of the lands around the present-day town called Al-Shatra very close to the southern part of the present-day river Shatt-Al-Garaf. Lagash was located on the left side of this river, 20 kilometres Northwest of Al-Shatra, while Umma was situated near the present-day mound called Tel Khoja on the right side of Shatt-Al-Garaf river at a time when this artificial river did not exist.

The lands of Lagash were irrigated from the watercourse branching from the old course of the Euphrates River and passed through Umma's territory, which had also water rights to the same water course. There were many instances when Umma had taken more than its share of water, and other times when it diverted the flow on purpose to damage the Lagash cultivations which heightened the animosity between these neighbouring states. In addition to the ambitions perpetuated by Umma to take over one of the larger and more fertile estates of Lagash called Gu'edina and annex it to its own lands. This estate, however, had been the subject of a claim by Umma, especially as it was irrigated from the same canal supplying both Lagash and Umma. This led to a series of skirmishes and bitter disputes between the two city states.

An old inscription, however, states that the dispute was solved at least temporarily by arbitration. Both parties had accepted that Mesilim, the King of Kish, who seemed to have patronage over both of the conflicting Cities, should act as an arbitrator. Mesilim in his turn proceeded to arbitrate the controversy by measuring the boundary line between the two city states and reached his decision, which was in favour of Lagash. He then installed landmarks of stone to mark the border and settle the case.

Later on, the new King of Umma called Ur-Nanshi who removed those landmarks, crossed the border, and then seized the land again violated this decision. Fighting erupted many times until this was settled in a fierce battle between the armies of the two states in which victory was the share of Eanna-Atum, King of Lagash and the killing of Ayna-Kala King of Umma and son of

Ur-Nanshi at about 2,470 BC. The victorious King took further steps to remove all reasons for such fights with Umma and he accomplished this by digging a new large canal off taking this time from the Tigris River and not from the Euphrates.

The new large canal he called Lumna-Gimdug which is the present-day Shatt-Al Garaf, mentioned previously, and which extended for 130 kilometres to reach Lagash territory. This work remained an example of very highly sophisticated engineering achievements for a very long time, in which technical methods and surveying works were utilised. It was lined with baked clay bricks and plastered with bitumen, and bunds were constructed along its banks.

In the passage of time, however, the dimensions and depth of this large canal increased steadily due to its steep slope, and it became the main branch of the Tigris River the Shatt-Al-Garaf itself. From Sumerian inscriptions, it is known also that Eanna-Atum accomplished more of such engineering achievements. Among these, he had built a small reservoir and a new canal connected to it and called Khoma-Dimsha, and a submerged weir on a canal called *Jarso* at about 2,430 BC to raise the water level and have a higher command of the land. Another inscription also indicates that the successor King Enti-Mena had also constructed such a weir at about 2,400 BC. The quantity of bitumen used in both weirs was about 270, 000 litres and the number of burnt bricks were more than eight million bricks.

This first Sumerian dynasty continued from 2,900 BC. It ended in 2,334 BC at the hand of Sargon I, who had started as a high ranking official at the court of Ur-Zababa the last King of this dynasty and had probably killed him and replaced him to mark the start of the Semitic Akkadian domination which lasted 180 years to 2,154 BC. Sargon was a powerful man and a military genius and administrator who probably consciously or not began to change the Sumerian culture to the Semitic one but failed to stamp out the Sumerian culture, which continued even after the fall of *Agade*, his capital some 200 years later. One thing, which may be said on Sargon's credit, is his unification of all Sumerian city states under his rule and extending his Empire, so it was said that his influence was felt from Egypt in the west to India in the east.

During this period of Akkadian control, the Sumerian-Akkadian culture was dominant in every day's life and practices and irrigation, and agriculture continued to flourish until the Akkadian empire collapsed in the destruction of its capital *Agade* at the hand of the barbaric and nomadic people, the Gutians.

These tribes had descended from the mountainous region of Elam in the east and ruled for a very short period, but this did not prevent the rise of a second Sumerian dynasty (Ur III) which continued to rule from 2,047 BC until 1,750 BC, and so the Sumerian- Akkadian temple culture was kept alive during all this long period.

The Sumerians and Akkadians of ancient Iraq were indeed *The Peoples* who had laid the foundation of civilisation as we know of today. To describe this civilisation, it was an agrarian civilisation based on irrigated agriculture; so, it may be worthwhile here to describe some of the methods, equipment and far-reaching technologies and achievements developed by the Sumerians and Akkadians in the fields of irrigation and agriculture.

Each of these innovations represented at that time a real breakthrough, which was used in so many countries of the world for thousands of years, afterwards without much change or improvement and even being used nowadays in some communities. These achievements can be clearly seen in the construction of an intricate system of canals, weirs, dykes, and reservoirs, which demanded considerable engineering skills and knowledge. Surveys and plans had to be prepared, which involved the use of levelling instruments and rods, in addition to drawings and mapping. The need for calculating areas and volumes enhanced trigonometric and geometric methods.

Improvements in Farming and Irrigation[cvi]

Efficiency of farming improved with the invention of the plough, no longer did the farmers have to poke holes in the ground and seed each individual holes. The blade on a plough turned the soil and seeding machines used to sow the seeds. The growing of crops and farming operations had to follow strict time schedules and instructions which the farmer had to adhere to in order to fulfil the tasks in the best possible way and get the full reward for his work. Sumerians, therefore had to follow the change of seasons and the sun movement, which gave fruit in the developing astronomy. An account of some of the farming operations, rules and instruction was inscribed on a clay tablet uncovered during excavations in the city state Ur and described by Kramer.

On this tablet, there were inscriptions of such detailed instructions that give clear insight into all farming operations followed at that time. At the start, the dry soil is wetted by flooding the farm with water; as water recedes then lose shod oxen are let loose to crumble the wet ground, thus stamping out the weeds and levelling the surface which must be dressed with small light axes until it is even. Since the hoofs of oxen have left their mark on the still wet ground, men with pickaxes must go around the field to smooth it out. While the field is drying, the farmer is advised to prepare his tools, equipment, beasts, and seeds that are necessary for the next stage which involves such operations as harrowing and raking the ground to break the clods and removing the weeds.

The actual ploughing and seeding can now take place by ploughing the field twice using two different deep soil ploughs. Seeding will be done simultaneously with the second ploughing operation by means of a seeder; that is an attachment to the plough which carries the seeds from a container through a narrow funnel down to the furrow as shown in Figure below. Seed sowing machine could plant seeds quickly with an even distribution compared to hand sowing.

A plough and seeder of the type used by Sumerians

The farmer was advised to plough eight furrows in each strip, which was about six to seven metres wide. Following all this the field had to be cleared of clods and ground elevations and depressions and levelled off so that sprouting of barley would not be restricted in any way. When the plants had grown sufficiently to fill the narrow furrows, it was time to water it; and when it stood a little higher than the furrow's top, it was time to water a second time. The third irrigation would then take place when it reached its full height.

If the barley or wheat was doing well then fourth irrigation could be done to obtain an extra yield of about ten per cent. As the time of harvest arrived, the farmer was informed not to wait until the barley bends under its own weight but to harvest it while it is still erect. Teams each of three men were to reap, bind and arrange the yield in the sheaves.

The threshing, which followed harvesting, was done in two stages. First, the mounds of crop were trampled down by wagons drawn back and forth over them for five consecutive days. Then threshing sled, consisting of beams with iron teeth fastened with leather strips and held secure by bitumen, was used to *open the barley*. Next step in this sequence of work was winnowing, which was done by two men who used large wooden forks or shovels to lift the mixture of barley or wheat and chaff it in the air thus freeing the grains from the straw and husk.

The Sumerians and Akkadians in developing these procedures had to invent and manufacture all the equipment and tools required to fulfil the intended tasks and to use available recourses such as wood, bitumen, leather, and iron which they had already mastered its production. Photographs illustrate many of the tools and equipment they used in this work.

Tools and equipment used in Sumeria

On the irrigation side (Adamo, 2020) Sumerians used gravity irrigation helped by the extensive network of canals and the many weirs they had built on rivers and large canals to get the required command. On the field level, they practised such methods like basin flooding, check flooding, border strip irrigation and furrow irrigation. These methods are still used in a great many countries of the Middle East and the world now. When water levels are low in the main feeders, they devised ingenious ways to practice lift irrigations.

Among such devices was the *Dalia* which is still in use in Basra in Iraq. Other devices were used such as the *Charid* or *Kared*, water wheels driven by oxen or mules, in addition to the huge water wheels driven by river's flow. Many examples of such water wheels can still be seen on the upper Euphrates in Iraq and Syria. Full description of these devices is given by Sousa.

Many of the mentioned implements have proven their efficiency and usefulness till very recent times and some are still in use, even today in many places in Iraq. In fact, the southern district of Baghdad called *Karrada* has taken its name from the *Kareds* used to irrigate its extensive palm trees and mandarin orchards until the early days in the 20th century.

The Sumerians had excelled in hydraulics; apart from designing and constructing irrigation system they had to device ways and means for flood control as they were constantly threatened by the floods of the two rivers, so they had to learn ways to protect themselves and their lands from such floods, which came periodically every spring. In this way, they constructed levees along the banks of the Tigris and Euphrates and kept them maintained. They even devised methods of protecting the levees side slopes in contact with water from the erosive power of the strong flood currents. This was done by laying mats of woven date palm fronds on these slopes and pins them down by long slender wooden poles.

These mats and poles were still in use in Iraq until only few years ago, whereby the mats were called *Bawari* for the plural and *Baria* for the singular, and the wooden rods were tagged as *Hawalesh* for the plural or *Halosh* for the singular. The most recent use of these *Hawalesh* and *Bawari* in Iraq was during the Euphrates floods in the sixties of the last century, and in the floods of the Diyala River in 1973 and 1974, which had threatened the capital Baghdad.

If any breach developed in these levees during one of these floods, the Sumerians could use ways to close the breach quickly before it enlarged to threaten the collapse of the whole levee. This was done by use of *Batkha* which again remained in use until a few years ago in the lower Euphrates area. The *Batkha* itself consisted of a long role of brushwood and reeds bound together by ropes made out of the fronds of date palms. A completed *Batkha* would be laid in the stream against the breach and loaded with layers of palm tree fronds, dry branches of trees, dry thorn, thistle and earth to sink it to the bottom and to be followed by the next one which should be ready by now. The process would continue until the breach was closed. Sussa again describes the process in full.

The Sumerian ecosystem may be described as being very fragile. The nature of alluvial delta, its geography, topography and its bordering marshes and lagoons imposed strict organisation and operation procedures to keep the fertility of the land to produce enough yield. The shallow depth of groundwater and the danger of salinisation required that the fallow system of cultivation be adopted, whereby a plot of land could not be cultivated in two consecutive years but left one year to rest to keep the groundwater level below the root zone.

The second matter, which had its bearing, was the arid climate with precipitation below 250 mm/ year, which forced artificial irrigation on the communities of the lower Mesopotamian region. The intensive canalisation dictated communal work to keep irrigation canals free from sediments and to maintain constant full discharge.

Natural levees are embankments created by deposited river sediments as a river floods. They are asymmetrical structures with almost vertical walls adjacent to the river while tapering landwards along a gentle slope. Levee widths during the Sumerian period were commonly over 1 kilometre (.62 mile). River levels could vary between 4 and 6 metres (13 to 19.7 feet) during flooding. The levee crest could rise up to 10 metres (32.8 feet) above surrounding plains. Sumerians built up the levees by making foundations of reeds impregnated with bitumen, sun-baked surface seepage of crude oil common in the region.

Baked mud bricks, also bonded with bitumen, were placed on top of the foundations. This not only increased the height of riverbanks, it also protected them from erosion by water currents. During dry periods, Sumerians made a simple drainage system by hoisting water in buckets over the levees and watered cultivated land. They also poked holes into the hard and dry levee walls, allowing the water to flow and irrigate crops in adjacent fields. Initially, Sumerians depended on a network of natural, anastomosing river channels for their water supply. They began to dig artificial feeder channels and canals between the Fourth and Third Millennia BCE, making use of the rivers' avulsions. These are the shifts of water courses created by natural breaks in levee walls, or a weakened part of a levee wall caused by man-made drainage holes. This process caused the water course to split in two. The new river branch either carved an entirely new course or meandered and re-joined the original channel.

Sumerians excavated canals along these new water courses and dug smaller feeder channels. They used the excavated soil and debris to construct further levees. The canals could be up to 16 metres (52.5 feet) wide. Water flow was controlled by regulators dams and sluice gates erected at points between specially strengthened levee walls. Sumerian farmers faced a constant battle in dredging the canals free from deposited silt.

This communal work also reflected on the organisation and administration aspects of the irrigation and agriculture procedures. The land or farms were mostly divided into plots of elongated and rectangular strips to allow the irrigation of each of them from a single outlet. The area of each farm had to be limited to a manageable size between 90 and 135 Sumerian iku which would approximately equal 32 to 49 hectares. Texts retrieved from Ur III revealed that in provincial land, *cultivators* were organised in groups of fives under the direction of an *inspector*, who in turn answered to an *overseer* (Uggula) and one *cultivator* was usually to be in charge of one field or a parcel of fields.

Some of the agricultural workers on the provincial fields had even full rights to plots of the land and such holders would receive fixed annual grain ration based on the plot size according to the predetermined production rate irrespective of the inevitable regional and annual yield fluctuations.

Historians agree that the Sumerians were successful in establishing the first great civilisation in the history of mankind, where it had all the characteristics for any civilisation to be worthy of the name. In its fabric, all the elements for such civilisations were present, including socio-politico-economic features, centralisation, the domestication of animals, specialisation of labour, monumental architecture, and taxation. It was organised in densely populated settlements divided into hierarchical social classes with ruling elite and subordinate urban and rural populations, which engage in intensive agriculture, mining, small-scale manufacturing and trade.

The Sumerian civilisation was agrarian as one would expect to have in such a long past. One great danger facing the Sumerians; was the salinisation of the land. The semiarid climate of southern Mesopotamia and the general low permeability of the soils exposed it to the dangerous accumulation of salts, which are harmful to crops and could cause the abandonment of the land. The source of these salts was the irrigation water from the two rivers that had been dissolved from the sedimentary rocks forming their catchments in South Eastern Anatolia.

Even though the concentrations were low, the accumulation of these salts in the soils over hundreds of years resulted in generally inferior soils that had to be managed with care. Citations of salinity problems from ancient records indicate that a serious problem of salinisation of the land appeared from 2,400 BC on ward after a time when agriculture had just flourished to an extremely high level. Apparently, this problem had its roots in over irrigation of the land. The long and bitter conflict between the two city states Girsu (Lagash) over one of the largest canals taking off from the Euphrates had lasted for many generations. The matter was not settled until the King of Lagash had dug a large canal, which was already described, to transfer large quantities of water from the Tigris.

Finally, this had contributed to the rise of the groundwater table to unmanageable levels. To this fact, Jacobsen[cvii] attests that the abundant source of water had simply resulted in over irrigation and led to the salinisation of the soil. The presence of patches of saline ground was mentioned in records of ancient temples' surveyors. In a few cases, individual fields, which at that time were recorded as salt free, were shown in an archive from 2,100 BC to have developed conditions of sporadic salinity during the 300 intervening years of cultivation. The choice of the crop that was grown in the region showed another indication of these deteriorating land conditions.

Counts of grain impressions in excavated pottery from sites of about 3,500 BC suggested that at that time the proportions of wheat and barley were nearly equal. A little more than 1,000 years later at Girsu, the less salt tolerant wheat accounted for only one-sixth of the crop. By about 2,100 BC wheat had slipped still further down, and it accounted for less than two per cent of the crop in Girsu area. By 1,700 BC the cultivation of wheat was abandoned completely in the southern part of Mesopotamia. The shift to barley cultivation was due to serious decline in fertility, which for the most part, can be attributed to salinisation.

In 2400 BC at Girsu, a number of field records gave an average yield of 2,537 litres per hectare. This is a very good figure even in advanced courtiers today. This figure had declined to 1,460 litres per hectare by 2,100 BC, and by about 1700 BC, the yield recorded by Larsa had shrunk to an average of only 897 litre per hectare. This general decline in the yields had its adverse impacts on the wealth and livelihood of the region, which was not abandoned completely but had caused the cultural and political leadership to pass permanently out of it with the rise of Babylon in 2004 BCE. This is how the story of this great civilisation ended. Other civilisations which followed will remain indebted, however, to the Sumerians for all what they have contributed.

Chapter 5
Eridu: The First City in the World

Introduction

Until 200 years ago, nobody knew of the existence of Ubaid/Sumerian Culture, therefore no facts had to be discovered. The British and the French felt nothing more was needed to be done in the region. Historical events well known and the only thing to do was to place the final pieces of the jigsaw into place and the road map for these endeavours was the Bible. The only requirement was a few surveys of the area and some atmospheric water colours would seal the deal.

In the colonial's opinion the world had almost been mapped with a few remnants in South East Asia and deepest darkest Africa remaining. This was the time of the industrial revolution a time of wonder and amazement. Hieroglyphics had finally been decoded by Jean Francois Champollion and now the Western Powers were very interested in reading everything that they could lay their hands on, a civilisation that pre-dated even the Holy Roman Empire.

At this point in time Southern Mesopotamia simply wasn't on the radar of the Western Colonial powers. All eyes were firmly fixed on Egypt and more importantly anything relating to Biblical events. This was Christian based research and learning which revolved around the Old Testament and Christian *values*. Western cultures wanted to not just spread Christianity but find anything involving the fables.

Babylon and the Egyptian had featured heavily in cultural learning of its day with descriptions of the early stories of Adam and Eve in the Gardens of Eden, the Temple of Babel, Noah, and the Great Flood. Jens Jacob Asmussen Worsaae Archaeologist 1821-1885 AD had noted the lack of British interest in the Middle East and its perceived place in history as he noted in a letter to fellow Assyriologists:

The British Museum is an utter shambles! Only the Egyptian and Roman antiquities are beginning to be improved, but there is no prospect of this for their national antiquities. I demonstrated at length to Hawkins, about the importance of paying them more regard than has previously been the case. They promised they would, but the situation is awkward.

Quoted by Peter uRowley-Conwy page 796.

Nothing seemed to relate to anything in Southern Mesopotamia of any real value. The place was simply full of hot scorching deserts, so surely nothing of any significance could possibly originate from the barren wasteland. But things started to change when with the explorations of Austen Henry Layard at Nimrud and Nineveh in the 1840s AD[cviii], continuing through the 1920s-1950s AD with the research of Sir Max Mallowan at Nimrud, Arpachiyah, Tell Brak and Chagar Bazar, Sir Leonard Woolley[cix] at Ur, and Seton Lloyd at Tell Uqair, Eridu and Tell Hassuna.

In Iraq during the 1960s-1980s AD, archaeological teams excavated at Tell al-Rimah, Abu Salabikh, Umm Dabaghiyah and at Choga Mam. This pandoras jar of history had finally been reopened by the pantheon of Assyriologists and new understanding of our previous history should have consumed Western interest for understanding. Each excavation caste new light on a time that really wasn't known to people of the mid-19th century. Any build-up of interest in Southern Mesopotamia soon evaporated in the early 20th century, to be precise, November 1922 AD.

As one of the final digs was coming to an end in the Valley of the Kings in Egypt, a staircase was discovered. Excitement began to build, could this be access to a new discovery, they discovered the Royal Seal unbroken. Nothing could prepare the world for what was found by Howard Carter and Lord Carnarvon, discovering an intact tomb of the Pharaoh Tutankhamun. The worlds press was diverted to Egypt and Egypt alone. The world went crazy for Egypt, the visual wonderment left nothing to the imagination, which in turn left Southern Mesopotamian discoveries being unearthed in the land of Sumer a little bit of a damp squib.

Egypt joined the elite, a very exclusive group that only had Rome and Greece in its ranks. The three have honed and maximised their worth and played admirably to the masses, leaving all others in their wake. It has always been hard for Mesopotamia to break from the shadows of mighty Rome, Greece and now Egypt.

There has always been a difference in Mesopotamia, a feeling of divide. To the South and West, the vast desert of Arabia exists, a rolling sea of sand dunes where nothing seems to grow. Home to fierce nomadic tribes, who could well be part of the indigenous clans of Southern Arabia who first came to the area up to 125,000 years ago after leaving Africa. Close relatives of the original Gulf Oasis left to roam and forage in the hot desert sun. To the North, the Rocky Taurus Mountains and the Mountain Range of Armenia, the original Semitic speaking tribes who may have been quickly consumed in 7000 BC by the 2nd Migration of people forced to leave the Gulf Oasis when the freshwater lakes first became spoilt by the encroaching Indian Ocean.

Some of these migrant people quickly assimilated into the local tribes in the Taurus Mountains of modern-day Turkey, Kurdistan and Armenia hemmed these blood relations in, previous common links forgotten over the course of hundreds of years. Last but certainly not least the hardiest of all the mountain people the tribesmen of the Zagros Mountains of Iran. Sea, Mountains and Desert constituted the boarders of Mesopotamia in modern Lebanon, Syria, Turkey, Iraq, Iran, and Kuwait is this land between the rivers is simply called Al Jazeera *the island*, which gives a distinct feeling of *us and them*.

The Ubaid material culture in Southern Mesopotamia is best exemplified by the material from Eridu. Nowhere else has such a complete architectural and ceramic sequence been recovered for this period anywhere else. Ubaid 0; 6,500-5,400 BC sometimes called Oueili is the earliest known Ubaid phase at present. The Sumerian city state of Eridu and Ubaid Phase 1: 5,400-4,700 BC (Tell Abu Shahrain) in Iraq is basically one of the same.

When you talk of the start of Eridu, you are simply talking about Ubaid Phase 1. Its earliest phase was distinguished by a type of painted pottery otherwise unknown except for some unstratified shards from Ur and Usaila near Eridu. Once again could these painted vessels design originate from the now lost region of the Gulf Oasis. Archaeologists have found the remnants of living in the area as early as 8,000 BC but the large alluvium deposits that run many metres deep prevent any accurate picture to be formed in the previous existing delta region that have now pushed the Persian Gulf 300 Kilometres further South of its original site at Eridu and Uruk over 8,200 years ago.

According to the King List, two of the cities of the Pre-Flood, also according to the Sumerian King List, when the gods first gave human beings the gifts necessary for cultivating society, they did so by establishing the city of Eridu in the region of Sumer while the Sumerian city of a Uruk is held to be the oldest city in the world the ancient Mesopotamians believed that it was Eridu that it was here, that order was established, and civilisations began.

The land in the South differs drastically from the Northern region, the small villages were built around Ubaid farming communities close to rivers. Whilst other people inhabited the floating reed islands that formed in the deltas. Life wasn't so much difficult, but it was unpredictable at times, but life simply ticked on with expansion growing gently overtime. But only once the people drifting around on the reed islands had a major foothold on the land and became accustom to their new surroundings.

From 6000 BC, the region began to rapidly improve, everything became more organised, a little more structured. This sudden increase may possibly be due to the rapid growth in population quickly dispersing throughout the entire region. A major contributing factor may simply be a rapid influx of people from the Northern region of the Fertile Crescent moving to the South. It should also be noted no form of writing had developed at this time and nothing can fix an exact time for reference apart from archaeological digs and carbon dating the discoveries. The classification as previously mentioned of Ubaid and Sumerian will continue in the next part of the book so we can further develop a more meaningful historical timeline of this region.

We can witness uncanny similar traits in Greek city states and the city states of Sumer. The fierce rivalry that manifests itself over a short period of time. Just when these city states have worked so hard to finally start enjoying the fruits of their labour the people launch into competition. Competition in itself, isn't a bad thing but this rivalry quickly escapes any positive focus and becomes a danger to itself, risking all when nothing needs risking.

The best analogy would be a gambler; a little bet here and there is enjoyable, a horse race is nice, but if you have money on one of the horses in the race, it's so much more exciting. But some gamblers continue to increase the stakes, looking for the bigger win, to the point of bankruptcy. This is exactly the same as decisions eventually made by city states: *The bigger the risk, the bigger the prize*, but the flipside to this would be: *The bigger the risk, the bigger the loss.*

Divine intervention doesn't always manage to save you, but it does give the ruler a *get out clause*, insisting the Gods are unhappy with the temple offerings and better attention in the future will help the cause. The alpha male that presides in all of us is possibly the most detrimental of all traits, if not channelled correctly.

Eridu Period 5400-4700 BC: The First City in the World

It should be noted that in the depiction of the boat leaving the harbour front of Eridu into the lagoon, the boat is made from local reeds but would have been coated in bitumen to prevent the material rotting quickly; both reeds and bitumen are in plentiful supply in this region. Since the rise of sea levels post ice age, the trade routes were already known to the first civilisation of Eridu and their surrounding neighbours.

Eridu and Its Significance

Today, little remains of Eridu. To be honest, you could quite easily drive past and not realise you had seen anything of any interest. There is nothing that could catch your attention and make you look at the area in a different light. No reason to believe that this seemingly random place was once of such great importance in the ancient world. A place where *true* man was created, the birthplace that divided a cultured person from the others. By examining Sumerian mythology, architecture, The Book of Genesis and Texts, you quickly start to understand what a rich and intriguing place the first city of civilisation must once have been.

In my own personal opinion, this is the place is more intriguing than any other city in the World. Every other city of the world, you have *roads and signposts* leading you to the next part of the storyline. But Eridu is the very start of all stories concerning cities and Culture. While many ancient Mesopotamian cities have unique aspects Eridu is respected, never feared, simply respected amongst its peers. Eridu's purported definition of *guidance place*, a spiritual home for the people of all of Sumer, Akkad, Assyria and most importantly Babylon for the next 4,800 years.

I think the best analogy for the reader to understand what this place felt like would be thanks to JRR Tolkien's *Lord of the Rings*. Eridu would be in a very similar vein to the Kingdom of the Elves. It was the oldest, it had respect throughout the region, it didn't compete for power and it had an air of mystery surrounding it. Many aspects of Sumerian civilisation were quickly absorbed by future Empires and the memories of their beginning forgotten apart from a faint distant rumble that never disappeared.

Eridu was the place of the Gods and associated with spiritual and rural life, a mystical place which helped enable the language of Sumer to continue for a further 6,200 years. Its longevity is hard for any normal person to fathom and therefore places mental limitations on our own thinking and our association with the past. Today we usually talk in 100's of years not 1,000's of years. These people of yesteryear are you and me in every single way, the humour, the sarcasm, the music, the communal spirit, the thinking, the problem-solving abilities, and the sociability.

Several differences existed which gave them a much stronger identity, the need to survive and grow as a people which we take for granted. These people knew that they had turned a desert into lush green farmland with beautiful gardens, the pride and bonding of a community must have been immense, the feeling of worth. This belief in themselves must have spawned a strong self-belief and a form of inner calm. As modern people we look at the Maslow Hierarchy of Needs as individuals. The main criteria in early Southern Mesopotamian must have been survival and the understanding that the only way to succeed was to ensure the whole was far greater than the sum of the individuals.

Only when the people pulled in the same direction could they achieve a positive outcome as a unit in a place so climatically challenging. Towns and cities today don't have that common strong bond that Eridu possessed. It wasn't a total Utopia, levels of stratification had started to appear and required somebody to initially organise the work groups to be successful as a whole and not necessarily anything to do with self-actualisation as stated with Maslow. Even as hunter-gatherers somebody in the group had to *make a plan* so the family group could be successful.

The early people of Southern Mesopotamia, the direct relative of Cognitive Homo Sapien that walked out of Africa, could discuss everything in detail and could form very intricate detailed plans. The people of Sumer didn't have a herd mentality they realised that doing a specific job was a contributing factor to the entire group, everyone relied on each other for survival. Modern Projects fail very regularly because a feeling of elitism takes over, Eridu couldn't afford to fail, the plan to succeed would have needed everyone onboard, everyone working together as a single unit.

Surviving on Terra Firma

Birth of irrigation will have existed at the very beginning of farming. People came into a region that wasn't wanted by anyone else, it was simply too hard to farm, in the North and in the Mountains, you could guarantee the yield year in year out, no need to roll the dice of fortune. Given the sustained periods without rainfall in Southern Mesopotamia the first farmers simply diverted water to the dry lands when they had an opportunity.

In Sumer's arid climate, irrigation is needed to sustain agriculture production because of insufficient rainfall during the crop growing season and therefore requiring additional requirements, such as water storage facilities had to be constructed to buffer water demand and supply the required irrigation periods.

The simplest technique is to divert the water source by hand to a nearby crop. Physical remnants of such practices are not likely to remain beyond a couple of decades. Once a community started to increase in size, early farmers had to maximise the available land usage, water had to then be transported further from its original source. So new techniques had to be developed such as the use of earthen ridges and the digging of canals to convey the water over much greater distances became necessary. As agricultural expansion intensified, new techniques started to appear. The hydraulic and reclamation works such as flood protection, land levelling and drainage, apart from the building of dikes, weirs and settling ponds.

It would have been impossible for a large group of people to survive and prosper in Southern Mesopotamia with traditional Northern Fertile Crescent farming techniques. The area lies beyond the rain-belt which made dry farming essential and certainly beyond the capacity of simple irrigation techniques farmers of the Fertile Crescent had been using. The early techniques quickly improved around 6,000 BC possibly when new inhabitants from the North arrived en masse to take up home in the South. Ideas in farming had to dramatically change in Southern Mesopotamia if this new influx of people had even a remote possibility to survive and eke out a living off the land.

Fortunately, these new inhabitants to the area seemed to be organised which leads to the conclusion they already belonged to a stratified society that is the forerunner of any true civilisation. These stratified people also brought with them key skills to survive such as, communal living, improved irrigation techniques which enabled the future opportunity of intensive farming. These new inhabitants of Sumer who had finally settled (imposed themselves) on the local indigenous inhabitants of the Rivers and Marsh Deltas who had just recently staked their claim to the area once the sea levels stopped increasing and the boundaries between land and sea had become fixed…ish.

We know it was a coming together of different people due to the different languages spoken, with Sumerian having several versions and also several versions of the Semitic language. It seems that all people within this newly formed region seemed to live in relative peace due to the acceptance of each other. These new people to the land of Sumer will have brought new ideas never previously seen before, but if the hypothesis is true, these people from the North weren't uncommon to the ancestors of the Marsh Arabs.

They had both originated from the Gulf Oasis but forced to separate 1,000 years previously, so the social diversification over 1,000 years will have been quite prominent but to what extent is unknown. The people from the North may have brough the Semitic speaking tribes with them, or after a thousand years of living side by side in the North the lines may have become slightly blurred. The people who hadn't relocated from the Gulf Oasis, but simply pushed to its farthest point, to the end of the Persian Gulf also looked difference as depicted on early pottery.

The word 'Sumer' comes from the Akkadian word and means *The Land of the Kings (Noble Lords)*; this must be relating to Priest Kings as Kings weren't invented until 2,900 BC. The Sumerians called themselves *The Black-Headed People* and their land in cuneiform script was *The Land of the Black-Headed People*. Therefore, the people, who came to inhabit the region from the Gulf Oasis, spoke a different language, may have also had the means to develop the area via advanced methods of cultivation that was not previously known to the area. They also brought pottery techniques never seen before and more importantly looked very different in their appearance.

Two Cultures Colliding

One from the North and one that had never moved from the South, both told great stories of flooding. The people of the South talking about the rising of the waters and consuming all before it. Many generations had witnessed the slow methodical destruction on a monumental scale of their previous homes and talked about the old lands they had come from. The land had been flat lush plains with an abundance of animals, fruits, crops, and large freshwater lakes with magical spring with freshwater gushing from the ground. Whilst the people of the North had known about the events in the South, the people of the North described entire lands that disappeared, everything before it simply washed away. They will have spoken about the deafening roar.

At dawn a black cloud came from the horizon; it thundered within where Adad (Iskur), lord of the storm was riding. In front over hill and plain Shullat and Hanish (Protectors of Adad), heralds of the storm, led on. Then the gods of the abyss rose up; Nergal (Irra, the god of scorched earth and war) pulled out the dams of the nether waters, Ninurta (Ningirsu) the warlord threw down the dykes, and the seven judges of hell, the Anunnaki (group of Deities), raised their torches, lighting the land with their livid flame. A stupor of despair went up to heaven when the god of the storm turned daylight to darkness, when he smashed the land like a cup. One whole day the tempest raged, gathering fury as it went, it poured over the people like the tides of battle. If that event couldn't conjure a story to last an eternity, then nothing could.

When these people decided in stay in *The Land of the Kings* (Sumer), they used the natural resources at hand with sun-dried bricks and making ovens for cooking. Archaeologists have found no signs of warfare among this pre and 0 Ubaid culture, it seems to be a concentrated focus on *carving out* an existence from the surrounding arid landscape and building a life literally from the dust on the floor and nothing much else. This tranquil but hardworking lifestyle seems to have existed for over a 1,000 years before the world became more commercialised.

A community spirit and a sense of accomplishment must have been felt throughout the population of the area, how they conquered adversity and turned this barren heartless land into a place of beauty with lush green gardens which continued to improve year on year. The task must have seemed daunting if not impossible, yet every embryonic city state had similar hardships to deal with. It must be realised that Eridu is stated as the first city, but it belonged to a conglomerate of towns and villages, all starting together, but acting as one.

The majority of the communities would have expanded at a similar the same rate in the same manner, with similar building, sharing the best ideas. There wasn't any envy because nobody had anything to be envious of. Only later was another advantage realised, the proximity to the ocean, once the city states had managed to over produce and new skills learnt, commerce appeared. If you controlled the water, you could control the trade of Sumer to the rest of the world.

The Land of Firsts

Everything that we take for granted started in Eridu, communities started to appear close to the temple complexes though the purposes of the temples would have been vastly different in later years than when it first started. The first shops and trading networks will have emerged in the courtyards of these first temple complexes. The first secular jobs were also created at this time. The embryonic farming had already started to take root, but even some of these early farms spotted an opportunity to come into the towns and become *professional trades*: leather workers, seamstresses, artists, bakers, beer makers, cloth makers, weavers. If you made the 36 types of beer that became available, you might have considered building an area to drink the beer and to socialise with friends after a long hard day's work, so the first taverns and landlords appeared. The domino effect of life and new opportunities were being created.

Walking with the Gods

In Sumerian mythology, the *Legend of Creation* was originally discovered on a clay tablet at Sippar. It stated that Eridu was the *First city* to be created when all the land was sea, it was said to be one of the five cities built before the *Deluge* occurred (The Great Flood). Dates do become confusing as archaeological evidence does show multiple *flooding* events and especially one in 2,800 BC that has a layer of mud and clay deposit 2.5 metres deep throughout the region, but this is definitely localised. To the local inhabitants of the time, it certainly wouldn't have felt localised.

The local inhabitants always felt disaster was around the corner waiting to spoil all the hard work already accomplished, therefore an air of sarcasm became part of their *new culture*. Modern scholars reading ancient texts, was awash with paradoxical proverbs and satire. The comical effect of any given statement appears only if contains a contradiction in itself. *A thief who is too clumsy to be able to escape. The fox with the side of a crab! A manicurist dressed in dirty clothes. A hero who hesitates whilst twiddling his thumbs. A nose protector that does not keep back the dust and a sunshade which does not afford shade at noon are abominations!* If the people were sarcastic, surely the gods were also sarcastic?

For a Mesopotamian in ancient times to actually be able to walk in the very streets that the gods had created must have been intoxicating, full of mystery and awe. The centre of the beginning of life, to go to another city state and announce, *I'm from Eridu!* must have felt extremely special and satisfying, one of the founding fathers. Understanding Eridu in the eyes of all Mesopotamians, was the equivalent of the Holy city of Jerusalem or Mecca to the Muslims. Both Jerusalem and Mecca grew to prominence overtime and built by man, whereas Eridu was created by the gods. It symbolised the higher planes of the beginnings of the region the place chosen by the gods to create a civilisation by entering through the city Gates, the city of sweet water of life itself.

Passing through the gates was as close to the start of creation as a mortal could possibly get. Eridu was thought by the people of Mesopotamia to have been created by the gods and was home to the great god Enki (also known as Ea by the Akkadians) who would later develop from a local god of fresh water into the god of wisdom and magic, among other attributes. Enki would stand equal with other deities such as Anu, Enlil and Inanna as the most important in the Mesopotamian Pantheon.

But before the awe of wonder that was witnessed in Eridu at its height, a lot of hard work was required. The sweat of the brow needed to toil for food, the people had to find a way to irrigate the land, first starting close to the fresh water supplies and sowing and cultivating the land and eradicating all the weeds and thistles that strangled the crops. The stones removed and the land levelled to allow for ploughing the land. Eventually, trees were planted which were much easier to maintain but took time to develop. You planted the trees, not for you, but for future generations to enjoy, this was a long-term plan.

Due to the natural resource of fresh water, these first settlers of Eridu could realistically get a foot hold on this arid land, aided by the lagoons and the copious amounts of reeds that could be made into housing. What is evident is that everyone was expected to own their own land and be self-sufficient. Many people lived in exactly the same manner as the Marsh Arabs that still exist today in the deltas and who seem to share the same DNA.

It may be feasible that the first people who came to the area stayed on the individual floating Islands and used reed boats ferrying them onto the land to farm it before thinking about permanently moving onto dry land. These floating islands may have developed whilst the sea levels continued to increase and slowly eradicated all existence of the Gulf Oasis. Inching their flotilla of islands wherever the reed beds grew further up the coast to the newly formed deltas of the Karun, Tigris and Euphrates rivers. Once the sea levels had finally settled then a genuine belief that a life on land could restart whilst some preferring to stay on the floating islands that has now lasted over 8,200 years, with no change in routine.

Living Together, Religion and Laws

What should be realised that religion is the fabric of all life interwoven with the people of Sumer and exponentially greater in Eridu. The *myths* weren't seen as myths, these were facts. But once again how much of these myths really were fact, elements of truth, an enigma wrapped in a mystery, surrounded by a conundrum with all lines blurred. The first part of the Eridu origin myth describes how the mother goddess Nintur called to her nomadic children and recommended they stop wandering, build cities and temples, and live under the rule of Kings. The second part lists Eridu origin myth as the very first city, where the Kings Alulim and Alagar ruled for nearly 50,000 years. (Well, it is a myth, after all, but the city is real, and the ages are intriguing.)

The King List gave particularly long reigns to the Kings who ruled before a great flood occurred. Adapa, a man of vast intelligence but not necessarily that intelligent since he unwittingly refused the gift of immortality. Adapa of Eridu, is depicted as an early culture hero, identified with U-an, a half-human half-fish creature from the sea (Abgallu, from ab=water, gal=big, lu=man therefore a King (Lugal equates to Big Man) of the Water. Was Abgallu the Big Man who controlled the water, in-charge of water work construction? Or was he the man who led his people from the flooding of the Gulf Oasis onto dry land?

He may have been the person who the rest of the people relied on in their hour of need. He may have made some important decisions which they simply followed and prospered from. Abgallu was considered to have brought civilisation to the city, a bit of a chicken and egg scenario, during the time of King Alulim. As we have already discussed, the only way you created civilisation was from producing extra crops to sell. But in order to grow more crop you need the infrastructure to be in place to carry the water to crops that are further from the original water source.

So is King Alulim the *Chief* who was part of the original inhabitant of the area. Is the word King (Lugal) simply being confused with organiser/engineer? Could he simply be a descendent of the Marsh Arabs Sumerian speaking local people of small individual farmsteads, living predominantly on floating reed islands who were the wandering displaced people of the Gulf Oasis. Could the story of U-an just be a distant memory of people leaving the Northern Fertile Crescent once they had witnessed the tragedy of the Euxine being consumed by seawater approximately 6,000 BC North of Anatolia, the modern-day Black Sea. These displaced people of the North moving into Southern Mesopotamia en masse and witnessed these strange events by the local inhabitants. There is always an element of truth within all stories.

If not the first city, Eridu was certainly amongst the oldest. Excavations at Eridu have revealed a sequence of construction dating back to the Ubaid Period 6,500-3,800 BC and continuing on from there to reach its height during the Ur III Period 2,047-1,750 BC under rulers such as Ur-Nammu 2,047-2,030 BC who was the first ruler to have laid down laws in writing that were later added to by Hammurabi, and Shulgi of Ur 2,029-1,982 BCE. To live closely with other people, some basic rules have to be adhered to, these rules become *The Law*, different societies adapt these rules overtime. Eridu seems to have had no political significance and was never a seat of a ruling dynasty except for the first two (George, 2011)legendary Kings before the Deluge and quickly relinquished its Kingship to Bad-Tibira.

After the Kingship descended from heaven the Kingship was in Eridug. In Eridug Alulim became King; he ruled for 28,800 years. Alaljar ruled for 36,000 years. 2 Kings; they ruled for 64,800 years. Then Eridug fell and the Kingship was taken to Bad-Tibira.

This was according to the Sumerian King List, a list which was designed by the Kings to *prove* their legitimacy and order in the grand scheme of their surroundings. Eridu didn't need to be a seat of a dynasty, it ran much deeper than that. It looked at the spiritual side of a person, remember Kings didn't exist in the beginning (Only if you believe the Sumerian King List). But religion always has been part of the people, Eridu was the powerhouse of religion rather than political. Politics became dark and murky and relied on the masses, whilst religion was aloof and was deliberately kept away from the masses.

Religion kept its distance and became ever more mysterious, constantly mixing truth with myth a real game of *Smoke and Mirrors*. Maybe the very beginning of a civilisation was more harmonious due to the fact original city states had no Kings to sow discord and self-elevate themselves, the people seemed to have a more equal status. Maybe all these early communities required was guidance from the gods and a natural harmony grew looking at the night skies that rotated above their heads.

With subtle changes observed, believing something external was guiding them, an unseen force that only the priests could decipher. But even though these people had survived the rising waters of the Gulf Oasis new unforeseen dangers lay ahead. The rivers flooded, as expected on a yearly basis, but sometimes monumental flooding occurred as nature does from time to time clearing all before it and making the people start all over again, no wonder the people where sarcastic. Picking the remnants from the newly wasted land and again rebuilding a life, but a life that could withstand even the harshest floods. The temple complexes grew higher with sturdy bases and large thick walls and the people in time of need could quickly move to the newly built high ground in case of another cataclysmic deluge occurred, but this time the gods will have protected them.

Discovering Eridu, Its Location and Size

Before we start to describe Eridu's features, we must realise that when we talk about an individual city state, these places where unlike anything we know today. Each place was totally self-sufficient, unlike our towns and villages we live in. When we purchase an item it predominantly comes from China, USA, fruit from New Zealand, beef from Australia. We take these goods for granted, but 8,000 years ago, everything was produced and manufactured in their own community. When the size of Eridu is described, we must consider the size of the building and the size of the city.

The city controlled its surroundings, this wasn't a place of mass population, this housed the people of Eridu who directly supported the city. Eridu didn't house the farmers, or the traders. The city didn't house the weavers or the shoemakers, the city didn't house people who fired bricks or dug canals or even maintained the canals. All these people mentioned lived on site, they lived close to their place of work. The barley or wheat didn't need to come into the centre of the city, or the sheep for shearing, it was a place of administration.

All these tasks are done externally away from the city walls. People will have thronged the streets during festivals and times of celebration. Many more multiples of people lived outside the physical city boundaries but where still the life and sole of the city state. The steady development of the city state is demonstrated by the repeated rebuilding of temples in the same place throughout the prehistoric period. Excavation has shown the city was founded on a virgin sand dune and the sequence of plans recovered from the Temple Sounding starting as a simple shrine in Level XVII and ending as a huge and elaborate temple of the proto literate period in Level I, providing a vivid illustration of the evolution of religious architecture in Mesopotamia.

A sequence of sanctuaries underlies the large later sacred precinct of 2,100-2,000 BC, providing further evidence of continuity of temple building in the same spot from Ubaid 1 right through into the historical period to its final demise. This Ubaid 1 phase, showing clear connection to the Samarra Culture 5,500-4,800 BC from Northern Mesopotamia, could these people have come with the people from Jericho in 6,000 BC and pre-date Samarra Culture. The reader should be made aware, that wherever a new discovery is made, that then becomes the point of origin, even though it may have originated somewhere completely different. Tell Abu Shahrain was first excavated in 1854 by J.G Taylor, the British Vice-Consul at Basra.

British archaeologist Reginald Campbell Thompson[cx] excavated there at the end of World War I in 1918 and H.R. Hall followed up Campbell Thompson's research in 1919. The most extensive excavations were completed in two seasons between 1946-1948 by Iraqi archaeologist Fuad Safar[cxi] and his British colleague Seton Lloyd. Minor excavations and testing have occurred several times there since then, but nothing on the scale of excavations allotted to the chosen few of Greece, Rome, and Egypt. Sumer can simply eclipse all three, yet alas, the powers to be are simply not interested.

Today Eridu is a Tell, located in the Ahmad (or Sealand) wetland of the ancient Euphrates River which has moved its course many miles from its original location when the city was first inhabited. The site of Eridu in Southern Iraq, seven mounds of Eridu lie about 24 km South-West of Ur and by the Early Dynastic Period probably had an area of 8-10 hectares. Today an immense mound made up of the ruins of thousands of years of occupation. As the temple rested on previous temples, it physically became more distant from the people at its base and continued to compound the class difference that had eventually materialised.

The Tell is now a large oval, the weather over time has taken all the clean lines away and created a *blob*. A light brown blob measuring 1,900 x 1,700 feet (580 x 540 metres) in diameter and rising to an elevation of 23 ft. (7 m). Archaeological evidence shows that in 4,000 BC, Eridu covered an area of 100 acres (40 hectares/0.4 Km2), with 50 acres (20 ha) residential section and a 30 ac (12 ha) acropolis. Most of its height is made up of the ruins of the Ubaid period town (6,500-3,800 BC), including houses, temples, and cemeteries built over on top of one another for nearly 3,000 years.

Eridu is surrounded by a drainage canal an early form of *moat* which would have allowed all homes and building within Eridu ample water. Also, a relic watercourse abuts the site on the West and South exhibiting many other channels. The ancient main channel of the Euphrates spreads to the West and Northwest of the Tell and a crevasse splay where the natural levee broke in ancient times is visible in the old channel. The earliest occupation hitherto discovered was at Eridu XIX-XV and is now known as the Eridu phase of the Ubaid culture.

The reader should also be reminded that the discovery of the Reed Boat at M3 in Kuwait was 5,570 BC, a reed boat that was conveying trade throughout the Persian Gulf into Sumeria, so sufficient surplus was made to allow for trade. Therefore, no buildings have yet to be discovered of sufficient magnitude, but finding those buildings, is an extremely difficult task. No building remains are known from the lowest level (XIX) and these may have been of a temporary nature, this maybe the point of transition from Reed Islands to solid Terra-Firma.

A total of 18 occupation levels have been identified within the site, each containing mud brick architecture built between the Early Ubaid to Late Uruk periods.

This would be similar to Britain and its various changes with Elizabethan, then Tudors, the Stuarts, the Georgian, the Victorian, Edwardian and the *Modern* periods. At the top are the most recent levels, the remainders of the Sumerian sacred precinct, consisting of a ziggurat tower and temple and a complex of other structures on a 1,000 ft. (300 metres) square platform. Surrounding the precinct is a stone retaining wall. That complex of buildings, including the ziggurat tower and temple, was built during the Third Dynasty of Ur 2,112-2,004 BC.

This is important evidence for cultural continuity despite the technological and political changes that occurred over 4,000 years. Eridu is best known for its temples, called ziggurats. The first layer prior to the construction of the ziggurats consisted of a small room with what scholars have termed a cult niche and an offering table. After a break, there were several ever-larger temples built and rebuilt on this temple site throughout its history.

From the earliest temple to the very last temple built, all of the complexes were situated at the same spot. Built directly over each other and never moving location the original sacred spot continued to be the sacred spot. This provides evidence that the priest class existed in 6,200 BC chose this sacred ground.

Each of these later temples was built following the classical, early standardised Mesopotamian format of a tripartite plan, with a buttressed façade and a long central room with an altar. The Ziggurat of Enki, the one modern visitor can see at Eridu was built 3,000 years after the city's founding. But what is more remarkable is the standardisation of building ziggurats in the whole of Mesopotamia followed the same style and similar footprint, with the same standard measurements. These ever-increasing sized buildings used the same design, same standard measurements, therefore evidence that the people's religious beliefs, architectural design and weights and measurements throughout 2,000 kms of Mesopotamian land had become standardised.

It shows that even at this early stage in time, the people seem to have been in harmony with no evidence of warfare and this is before the advent of writing. Having the same weights and measurements make trade very uncomplicated. Therefore, it is self-evident that commerce and architectural mathematics seems to have been the main driving force behind the advent of writing, not to learn the lyrics to a song or tell a good story.

Water and Religion

The city's importance was always more religious than political but more importantly religion revolved around the presence of fresh water. The primary economic foundation of the earliest settlement at Eridu was associated with spiritual and rural life and fishing. Fishing nets and weights and whole bales of dried fish have been found at the site: models of reed boats, the earliest physical evidence we have for constructed boats anywhere, are also known from Eridu. The oldest remnants of a boat are 7,500 years old in Kuwait on the trading route from the land of Sumer.

But it is evident that in prehistoric times there must have been an abundance of fresh water the gift of Enki who dwelt in the apsû (water table) below the city reputedly founded by Enki the god of exceptional wisdom and strength who become the god of the *subterranean sweet waters*. Something of this legacy still exists for in the low-lying ground at the foot of the mound the Bedouin can still discover fresh water (even though brackish) at a depth of about 6 feet below the surface; this freshwater land is known by them as Usaila. These people in the South pioneered the growing of grains in the extreme conditions of aridity thanks to the high-water tables of modern-day Southern Iraq.

In this first phase, commonly designated the Ubaid I or Eridu Period 5,400-4,700 BC, copious marsh resources were exploited in a sophisticated manner. Part of a *broad-spectrum economy* that employed for instance canoes and nets for fishing. Ubaid origins on the Southern alluvium were thus almost certainly around the Marshes and watercourses. Eridu, in spite of being located in a low-lying depression Southwest of Ur has an eight-meter scarp of the Upper flat's formation running well to the North and South of it, possibly blocking any marine infilling into the depression also could be acting as a settling pond for further irrigation of crops when required.

A survey of the Ubaid period in the region reveals that only four sites were occupied during the Ubaid 1 period including Ur and Eridu, whilst a marsh/riverine environment was exploited at Usaila and the place that gave this period in time its name Tell Ubaid.

In 1945, during the first expeditions by the Iraq Government, freshwater mussel shells were found in great quantity in different strata. When taken into consideration with the very few finds of marine shells leads us to the assumption that the freshwater lake led into the Persian Gulf water and strongly suggests Eridu was not actually on the seashore. The brackish (fresh) water that is collected by modern day Bedouins may attest to the reasoning that brackish water is usually found at a tidal estuary where sea water and freshwater mixes.

Although Eridu now lies nearly 300 kilometres from the Persian Gulf, at the time of its foundation and for many centuries thereafter it was probably directly connected with the seashore through a number of vast tidal lakes. Indeed, the Sumerians themselves in their legends referred to the city in this way: *all the lands were sea, then Eridu was made.*

In later Ubaid times, Ubaid 3-4 it is clear that Ur lies on a major Euphrates channel and a series of sites Northwest of Eridu could be interpreted as forming a possible Southern channel or Canal System. Eridu itself may have had access to the sea, but not on the shoreline. Since fish deposited in temples VIII-VI and the sounding datable to the late Ubaid period have been defined as marine or as sea-perch from brackish tidal waters. An actual Southern channel of the Euphrates running through or by Eridu in fact was not known about until much later.

But the sea in its climatic optimum approximately 6,200 BC of three metres higher than at present the spike in temperature before settling. The contraction means the water levels dropped due to the water been recaptured into ice in either pole. Could probably just enter the depression by an opening at the Ridge of Al Hazm to the West of Ur which is at present only about 3 metres above sea level. But more probably the water which filled the depression forming the great lagoons (Apsû) was fresh from the Euphrates ever existing at the head of Persian Gulf. How long that rise of the three metres continued is not known but at Eridu the settlement which appeared for the first time outside Tell Abu Shahrein in the plain (in the Palace Sounding at the North Mound) in the middle of the Uruk Period in about 3,300 BC may indicate that there was no more the threat of high water to the nearby plain.

In his memoirs, Seton Lloyd[cxii] wrote of *the almost total lack of building material* for *setting up base* at Eridu: *To solve this, we felt justified in looting the ruins of Woolley's old expedition-house at Ur ten miles away and bringing in lorry-loads of baked bricks many of them stamped with royal names but beautifully intact.*

Eighteen successive levels of mud brick temple architecture dating from the Early Ubaid to the Late Uruk periods were exposed during the 1940's excavations on Mound 1; the painted pottery recovered provided the basis for the fourfold division of the Ubaid period. An extensive Ubaid period cemetery was also excavated. The remains of a ziggurat of the Ur III period dominate the centre of the mound. Early dynastic palaces were excavated on mound 2.

Based on the evidence that Eridu was a navigable port some five thousand years ago. It should also be noted through calculations that about 7,000 BC the Babylonian plain was just beginning to form and the site of later Babylon didn't even exist, similar to modern day Basra, when Eridu was at its height, Basra was located in the middle of the Marshes. In the Sumerian literature Eridu was on the shore at least in the time of Shulgi 2,033-1,988 BC King of Ur according to the following cuneiform chronicle: *Shulgi the son of Ur-Nammu cared greatly for the city of Eridu, which was on the shore of the sea.* Eridu actually on the shore of a freshwater sea, a great marsh (or lagoon) formed by the floods of the Euphrates? Was the sea of Shulgi a mass of water regardless whether marine or fresh water?

Campbell Thompson's following statement has a bearing on these raised questions: *I think that the freshwater mussel shells which I found in great quantity in different strata when taken into consideration with the very few finds of marine shells will definitely compel us to give up the idea that Eridu was in ancient times actually on the seashore.*

The conclusion of Thompson is confirmed by the fact that the main temple at Eridu was called E-Apsû, i.e. the temple of apsû or nearby apsû which is the primeval freshwater ocean. Eridu was formed around three separate ecosystems, supporting three distinct lifestyles. The lagoon water gave the people of Eridu access to fresh water in a desert environment. The oldest agrarian settlement seems to have been based upon intensive subsistence irrigation agriculture derived Pre-Sumerian who may have inhabited the region once the Gulf Oasis flooded. Characterised by the building of canals, and mud-brick buildings.

The earliest occupation hitherto discovered was at Eridu XIX-XV and is now known as the Eridu (phase of the Ubaid) culture. No building remains are known from the lowest level (XIX) and these may have been of a temporary nature. Reed homes which are still built by todays Marsh Arabs. The fisher-hunter cultures of the indigenous folk who lined the shores of both the Euphrates and the Persian Gulf and fished the tidal lagoons close to Eridu were responsible for the extensive fish offering seen at the Temple of Eridu and may have been the original Sumerians.

The finding of extensive deposits of fishbones associated with the earliest levels also shows a continuity of the Abzu cult associated later with Enki and Ea.

The local people seem to have lived in reed huts and fished in boats made from the same the natural occurring reeds in every format the same as todays Marsh Arabs. The third culture that contributed to the building of Eridu was an amalgamation of Semitic-speaking migrants descending from the Northern Regions along with the ancestors of the 2nd Migration out of the Gulf Oasis. This early migrator who had travelled North in 7,000-7,200 BC now both reappearing in the South after the latest *Great Flood*. The filling of the Euxine.

Picking up on the way, the nomadic herders of sheep and goats living in tents in semi-desert areas. All descending en masse into Southern Mesopotamia. All three cultures seem implicated in the earliest levels of the city and the irrigation of the land. The urban settlement was centred on a large temple complex built of mudbrick, within a small depression that allowed water to accumulate. Enki's temple was called E-Abzu, as Enki was believed to live in Abzu, an aquifer from which all life was believed to stem. His Kingdom was the sweet waters that lay below earth these are the same fresh waters that the Bedouin can still retrieve at a depth of about 6 feet.

Producing Surplus and the Starting of Trade

The only reason we know anything about Eridu is because of its size and prominence within ancient times. The only reason it became prominent was because of trade. The only transport available at the time for trade were reed boats. Fortunately for us, parts of boats and models of boats have been discovered and carbon dated which helps give a true understanding of what and when trading occurred. Instead of surmising that trade only occurred once, the city states had grown in size goes against logic. The city can't grow without trade. As previously stated in the book, trade had been on-going from the start of the flooding of the Gulf Oasis and hadn't stopped. The Gulf Oasis took over 1,000 years to submerge and during this entire time, boats kept using this natural highway.

Boat Model and Actual Boats

In the 1980s AD, a Kuwaiti archaeologist[cxiii] named Dr Fahadal-Wohaibi, who was the Director of the National Museum of Kuwait, discovered remains of a *model boat* but more importantly, the remains of a reed boat. Although there is indirect evidence for maritime exchange networks as early as 12,000 years ago in the Aegean.[cxiv] The bitumen fragments at H3 represent the oldest physical remains from a seafaring vessel currently discovered. Moreover, the masts shown on the painted clay disc are the earliest indication for the use of sails. The site is in an area on the North Side of Kuwait Bay called As-Sabiyah and was named H3 by Dr Fahadal-Wohaibi, not necessarily the most exciting name in the world, but that's what we have.

The site excavated in Kuwait resembles the larger ones of the Central Gulf region, although certain Mesopotamian style artefacts occur there that are absent from the Central Gulf sites. This may indicate that the site could be on the very cusp between the eventual Dilmun Empire and its trading network throughout the Persian Gulf and the Region of Sumeria.

At the time of its Neolithic occupation, it was on a narrow peninsula or long island that enclosed a shallow bay which was ideal for boat repair. Since then, thick deposits of mud have partly filled the bay and extended the coastline several kilometres to the South but in Neolithic times the site was in an area of diverse plants with reed beds covering the region which were idea for boat repairs and sheltered anchorage. The fieldwork carried out between 1998 and 2002 AD, has shown that H3 began as a campsite with many fire pits which grew and developed over a period of time.

Bitumen was often reused and very common in Mesopotamia, but less common as you enter the Persian Gulf. Bitumen from H3 was identified as having an origin at Burgan Hill in Kuwait, therefore locally sourced. The site was close to the shoreline and in this respect, it is typical of other Arabian Neolithic sites. Ubaid pottery is rare but present in this earliest fire-pit phase, which has been dated by radiocarbon to approximately 5,570 BC years ago. So, we can accurately state with conviction that known trade was occurring almost immediately the Sea Levels had settled and the people of the old Gulf Oasis had finally settled on terra firma.

Similar areas would have existed earlier, but the ocean has risen and consumed them at the very end of the Last Glacial Maximus (LGM). Later in the Neolithic period, a remarkable change occurred. Stone structures were built, in the form of cellular buildings divided into chambers. Some of the chambers were used for living and eating, but the function of others remains unknown, but quite easily these other chambers could have been workshops for manufacturing tackle. Many of them were subsequently added to or subdivided.

This highlights that trade was expanding when the stone structures appear in the archaeological record of the site. Ubaid pottery becomes common, and personal ornaments typical of Ubaid Mesopotamia begin to occur. However, the stone-tool technology and shell jewellery found at the site remain typical of the Arabian Neolithic. The bitumen fragments from boats are associated with this occupation phase, as is the boat model.

Reed Boats

Interestingly, reed boats are an important part of Near Eastern mythologies. In the Mesopotamian Gilgamesh myth and also Sargon the Great of Akkad is described as having floated as an infant in a bitumen-coated reed basket down the Euphrates River. This must be the original form of the legend found in the Old Testament book of Exodus where the infant Moses floated down the Nile in a reed basket daubed with bitumen and pitch. A Norwegian called Heyerdahl in 1977 AD led the Tigris expedition, in which he navigated a Reed Boat, down the Tigris River to the Persian Gulf, across the Indian Ocean to Pakistan and finally to the Red Sea.

The goal of this expedition was to verify that the great cultures of both Mesopotamia and the Indus Valley could be conveniently navigated, which was successfully proven. Mesopotamian reed boats constitute the earliest known evidence for deliberately constructed sailing ships, dated to the early Neolithic Ubaid culture of Mesopotamia. The masted Mesopotamian boats are believed to have facilitated significant long-distance trade between the emerging villages of the Fertile Crescent and the Arabian Neolithic communities of the Persian Gulf. Boatmen followed the Tigris and Euphrates rivers down into the Persian Gulf and along the coasts of Saudi Arabia, Bahrain and Qatar.

The first evidence of Ubaidian boat traffic into the Persian Gulf was recognised in the mid-20th Century when examples of Ubaidian pottery were found in scores of coastal Persian Gulf sites. However, it is best to keep in mind that the history of seafaring is quite ancient. Archaeologists are convinced that both the human settlement of Australia (about 50,000 years ago) and the Americas (about 20,000 years ago) must have been assisted by some sort of watercraft to assist moving people along the coastlines and across large bodies of water. It is quite likely that we will find older ships than those of Mesopotamia. Scholars are not even necessarily certain that Ubaid boat-making originated there. But at present, the Mesopotamian boats are the oldest known.

Thor Heyerdahl VIRACOCHA II is a similar representation of early long-distance trade boats of Persian Gulf

The VIRACOCHA II length 55ft (16.5m) breadth 16ft (4.9) reed-made hull, successfully completed a journey in 2,000 AD of 2,850 miles. Proving long-distance travel in reed-made boats was more than capable.

While these changes took place[cxv], subsistence activities continued, including herding, hunting, and especially fishing and shell gathering. A few date stones recovered during the excavation imply that food was also brought from elsewhere, possibly as a trade good, a system of bartering with a stricken merchant who needed urgent repairs to their vessel.

This part of Kuwait does have a farming community in Abdali but at the time it is unknown if the area could have supported wild or cultivated date palms. Other activities at the site included the large-scale manufacture of shell jewellery, principally small, simple disc-shape beads, therefore multiple trade options came from this small community. But it would look to be, local Persian Gulf trade only and not future foreign trade.

Archaeologists have assembled quite a bit of evidence about the ships themselves. Ceramic boat models have been found at numerous Ubaid sites, including Ubaid, Eridu, Oueili, Uruk, Uqair and Mashnaqa, as well as at the

Arabian Neolithic sites of H3 located in Kuwait and Dalma in Abu Dhabi. Based on the boat models, the boats were similar in form to bellums (spelt bellams in some texts) used today on the Persian Gulf. Small, canoe-shaped boats with upturned and sometimes elaborately decorated bow tips.

Lost knowledge, it is purported by the current Marsh Arabs, that if the reeds are gathered in August. Then they are more resistant to water damage and will last up to 1 year without any bitumen protection. So much more knowledge has been lost and will never be known about.

Unlike wooden-planked bellams, Ubaid ships were predominantly made from bundles of reeds roped and pegged together then covered with a thick layer of bituminous material for waterproofing. An impression of string on one of several bitumen slabs found at H3 suggests that the boats may have had a lattice of ropes stretched across the hull, similar to that used in later Bronze Age ships from the region. In addition, bellams are usually pushed along by poles, which would be ideal manoeuvring up and down the Tigress and Euphrates.

This would also aid manoeuvring through the vast reed beds that developed around the delta and also during the encroaching sea into the last remnants of the Gulf Oasis. At least some of the Ubaid boats were apparently masted. Enabling them to hoist sails to catch the wind, the winds and currents operating in an anticlockwise direction. An image of a boat on a reworked Ubaid 3 sherd (a ceramic fragment) at the H3 site in coastal Kuwait had two masts. The flat bottom of the model may represent the true shape of the vessel. The Mashnaqa example also displays a flat bottom, though the Eridu and Al-Ubaid models have curved bottoms. The flat bottom of the H3 model may simply be to ensure that it sat flat on a surface.

It may alternatively represent the appearance of such a vessel when in the water. Many variations of the same theme will have been built and with ever increasing sizes as trade expanded to ever more distant locations. Flat bottomed boats tend to have stability issues in open water; therefore, the M3 model boat may just represent the lower curved part of the craft being submerged. Such finds are reasonably frequent in Ubaid Mesopotamia, though very few have been illustrated or published in any detail. Three whole or partial examples are found at Eridu, another are known from Al-Ubaid, and two fragments were found at Mashnaqa in North Eastern Syria.

The Eridu again is quite different from the H3 model and the Ubaid-period boat models published from Mashnaqa and Al-Ubaid, the chief dissimilarity lying in the breadth of the Eridu model's beam and the presence of a *mast socket*. No mast socket is evident on the H3 example; this however doesn't prove that it does not represent a masted sailing ship, as bipod masts may have been used which do not require a socket. Bipod masts are suitable for reed vessels, where no part is strong enough to support a pole mast therefore allows the possibility of a pole mast being used on Bronze Age reed vessels.

By the H3 model was a sailing craft, or whether it relied on another means of propulsion such as rowing or punting. Considerably later model boats from the Ur cemeteries are associated either with oars or punt poles[cxvi] though these may represent only river or marsh-boats rather than sea going vessels. There is no evidence to indicate the size of the vessel represented by the H3 model. A cylinder seal from Uruk shows that cattle could be transported in reed vessels at least by the late 4th millennium[cxvii]. On the other hand, modern reed canoes resembling the models from H3 and al-Ubaid were sometimes very small in size, perhaps able to carry not more than two or three individuals.

Some of the most exciting finds from H3 consist of reed-impressed bitumen slabs and fragments, many of which bear barnacles on one side. These are interpreted as their mains of bitumen-coated reed-bundled seafaring boats or ships. The presence of barnacles on artefacts sometimes indicates an episode of post-depositional submersion. For example, at certain coastal Ubaid-period sites in Eastern Saudi Arabia[cxviii]. At H3, the complete absence of barnacles on associated stones and pottery suggests the bitumen pieces could not have been submerged in situ during a high sea-level stand. Further-more, some were found with their impressed surface up-wards, and barnacle covered surface facing downwards. These pieces of bitumen had been taken from the previous and was about to be reused.

Similar techniques were used until the last century in the Marshes of Southern Iraq, as previously discussed many ancient techniques have been continuously conducted by the modern-day descendants of the Gulf Oasis—*the Marsh Arabs*! Who coated their boats with bitumen from Hit, near Baghdad in the case of wooden *canoes*.[cxix] The old coating was chipped off and new melted bitumen was applied over the upturned boat with a roller? The coating was said not to last over a year, and to be a quarter of an inch thick. Even today, you can see bitumen-coated reed boats known as tarada being used in the marshes, though now predominantly appear to be made with wood.

Also, a much smaller vessel made of reed bundles called a zaima. These were coated externally with bitumen. It has been noted that such craft could only be used for one year, as the bitumen coating could not be renewed. If this is also true of larger vessels, it raises the possibility that reed-bundle boats were being built from scratch at H3 and then being coated with bitumen removed from unusable vessels. Rather than existing vessels being stripped and recoated at a great use of labour for very little gain to the merchant.

At present, we can only speculate on the timing and routes taken by Ubaid-period sea-going vessels. The prevailing winds of the Arabian Gulf are from the north-west, implying that the journey back up the Gulf to Southern Mesopotamia could be problematic, they may have crossed the Gulf to the Iranian side, to use the counter clockwise current of the Arabian Gulf to carry them home, therefore archaeological sites found on the Iranian side of the Arabian Gulf become more important.

Conclusion

Ubaid pottery entered the Gulf on bitumen-coated reed-bundle vessels. The model boat and bitumen slabs from H3 represent the first hard archaeological evidence that this was indeed the case. Comparisons with contemporary Ubaid-period models and later Mesopotamian iconography imply that the vessels were Mesopotamian in concept, though the possibility exists that the vessels were manufactured in Kuwait, or elsewhere in the Gulf. The extent of modification is not yet discernible, but it is likely that Mesopotamian riverboats were being or had been adapted to maritime conditions at the time of the Ubaid phenomenon in the Persian Gulf.

This proves that in 5,570 BC sufficient surplus of foods had been accumulated long before Historians like to state. This increase in surplus can only come from early irrigation systems between the two Rivers of the Tigris and the Euphrates. The city states where on the verge of being born as early as 5,570 BC. Early evidence of secondary trading items being manufactured at M3 such as shells shows that the evolving stratified society of Eridu and surrounding regions had started to want one of Cognitive Homo Sapiens basic desirable items—*Jewellery*. From surviving on barren earth, to requesting jewellery within a few hundred years is quite a quantum leap and a thirst that couldn't be quenched for over 4,400 years finally stopping at the start of the Bronze Age Collapse.

Ubaid and Sumerian Trade

Since the Sumerian homeland was largely devoid of timber, stone and minerals, the Sumerians were forced to create one of history's earliest trade networks over both land and sea. Their most important commercial partner may have been the island of Dilmun (present day Bahrain), which held a monopoly on the copper trade. But their merchants also undertook months-long journeys to Anatolia and Lebanon to gather cedar wood and to Oman for copper and the Indus Valley for gold and gemstones.

The Sumerians were particularly fond of lapis lazuli a blue coloured precious stone used in art and jewellery and there is evidence that they may have roamed as far as Afghanistan to get it. Historians have also suggested that Sumerian references to two ancient trading lands known as *Magan* and *Meluhha* are referring to Oman and Indus Valley. Oman became extremely vital during the Bronze Age due to its abundance of copper in the region.

The geographic Armenian Highlands bounded by the Mediterranean and the Black Seas and the Caucasus, then known as the highlands of Ararat (Assyrian: Urartu). Originally inhabited by Proto-Armenian tribes which did not yet constitute as a unitary state or nation. The highlands were first united by tribes in the vicinity of Lake Van into the Kingdom of Van (Urartian: Biainili).

Only later when the Assyrians of Mesopotamia came to power where the riches of Anatolia finally extracted on a more enterprising level. For Mesopotamian expansion and hunger for raw minerals and resources that could be later transformed in the homeland of Sumer, Armenia's abundant wealth in the less inhospitable regions trade grew for these raw products also aided the strengthening and later expansion of trade routes.

Increasing in Early Trade Throughout the Gulf

Long-distance trade[cxx] is another primary feature of Ubaid related settlement. The presence of Ubaid pottery exported from Southern Mesopotamia as far as the Strait of Hormuz demonstrates the existence of trade networks operating across more than 1,000 km. Using the Reed Boats of M3 in exchange for Mesopotamian pottery and quality textiles manufactured in Sumer. A variety of eastern Arabian exports including pearls, shell beads, chert, livestock, and fish.

Widespread distribution of Ubaid pottery at both, larger settlements, and more peripheral encampments, as well as ceramic vessels exported from several manufacturing locations in Southern Mesopotamia, suggests that:

This was more than an aggregate of opportunistic exchanges, but was a mature, stable and structured system that persisted for many generations.

The Gulf Oasis hypothesis supplies an explanation for the introduction of an already developed trade network in the Middle Holocene 8,326 years ago to 4,200 years ago. Allowing for an incipient interaction sphere that had begun to form around Terminal Pleistocene Early Holocene waterways within the basin.

A shared culture may have existed between the two trading areas which may have been previously highlighted via the linguistic data mining previously discussed that trade with the Northern larger Ubaid Euphratic/Emesal Sumerian speaking area of Mesopotamia have previously been forged with the more dispersed old Gulf Oasis Emeĝir indigenous people, now scattered thinly around the newly formed coast line of the now present Persian Gulf. The main market early trade from region of Southern Mesopotamia may have also been the highly desirable bitumen for the use on reed boat.

The bitumen may have been at early premium bartering product. Bitumen chunks, black-on-buff pottery and boat effigies are fairly rare but as discussed above, not uncommon. Also, the trade items might have been perishables, perhaps textiles or grain. The trade efforts were likely to be small to medium boats once the Gulf Oasis had flooded and the remaining exposed higher ground that had become islands as trading post and ship repair yards dropping in at Arabian coastal towns. Hugging the Arabian Coastline on the outward-bound journey and then traversing pass modern Iranian coastline on the inward bound journey back to the Northern Part of the Persian Gulf, due to the trade Winds associated with the area.

It was a fairly long distance between the Ubaid communities and the Arabian coastline, approximately 450 kilometres (280 miles) between Ur and Failaka Island in modern Kuwait. It should also not be discounted that trade routes may have been kept open during the flooding of the Gulf Oasis between the Indus Region who may have shared the same origins as the Sumerians described early. As the land bridge disappeared between the two regions, the routes may not have been prolific but may have still been open allowing for future expansion.

Creation of Persian Gulf Trading Partners, Dilmun

The great commercial and trading connections between Mesopotamia and Dilmun were strong and profound to the point where Dilmun was a central figure to the Sumerian creation myth. Dilmun was described in the saga of Enki and Ninhursag as pre-existing in paradisiacal state, where predators don't kill, pain and diseases are absent, and people do not get old. Therefore, Dilmun became/was an important trading centre. At the height of Dilmun's power, it controlled the Persian Gulf trading routes. According to some modern theories, the Sumerians regarded Dilmun as a sacred place, but that is never stated in any known ancient text. Dilmun was mentioned by the Mesopotamians as a trade partner, a source of copper and a trade entrepôt.

Also, the island of Failaka is known to have been an ideal location for human settlements, known for its wealth in natural resources such as harbours, fresh water, fertilised soil, lush vegetation as well as being a strategic maritime commercial route. Which links the civilisations of Mesopotamia from the Northern side and the Gulf from the Southern side. Studies indicate traces of human settlement can be found on Failaka dating to a minimum of the 3rd Millennium BC, it should also be noted that the Shipyard at M3 is actually within sight of Failaka Island.

Failaka was first known as Agarum, the land of Enzak, the great god of Dilmun civilisation according to Sumerian cuneiform texts found on the island. So Agarum could be the spiritual home for Dilmun just as Eridu was for Sumer.

As part of Dilmun, Failaka became a hub for the civilisation which radiated around Bahrain from the end of the 3rd Millennium BC. Dilmun was a necessary interlocutor for its powerful neighbours in their need to exchange processed goods against raw materials. Sailing the Persian Gulf was by far the most convenient way of trade at a time when transportation by land meant a much longer and hazardous journey.

Later Expansion of Mesopotamia Trade and Its Outposts

As Mesopotamian trade developed, merchants even set up trade emporiums in other regions and other emerging cities where opportunity beckoned. Trade was no longer restricted to the Persian Gulf but to the Far Northern extremes of the Fertile Crescent and beyond the Taurus Mountains into the heart of Anatolia and also as far as Egypt. By around 1,700 BC, the Assyrian had the majority of Trade, they had set-up a trading outpost in Kanesh, Anatolia.

The traders travelled over 1,000 miles to this city in today's Turkey. There the merchants paid a tax to the city's ruler to live in their own quarter of Kanesh and trade with the city dwellers and other merchants who came from afar to trade for their Mesopotamian goods. The Assyrian traders came with a caravan of donkeys loaded with fine textiles their womenfolk wove enroute, and tin forwarded on, for an increase in profit that originally came from farther east. They traded the textiles and tin for silver and other goods. The Assyrian merchants were part of a family business that traded all over Mesopotamia and beyond.

An archaeological excavation of 20,000 clay tablets in present-day Kultepe, Turkey, brought these detailed merchant records to light. By the time of the Assyrian Empire, Mesopotamia was trading exporting grains, cooking oil, pottery, leather goods, baskets, textiles and jewellery and importing precious commodities such as Egyptian gold, Indian ivory and pearls, Anatolian silver, Arabian copper and Persian tin, to lavish within the temples and palaces that sat high above the people of the city, an ever-increasing gap between the elites and the workers. Trade was always vital to feed the hegemony of the elite Mesopotamians.

Eridu's Temples and Ziggurat, Berossus the Tower of Babel?

An immense effort was made to harness the unwieldy rivers of Mesopotamia into dikes, canals and lay out irrigation systems for the agricultural fields which helped to consolidate the survival of the Sumerian embryonic cities such as Eridu. Agricultural towns grew and prospered on the slower-moving and more manageable Euphrates, such as Eridu, Uruk, Nippur, Lagash, Ur and Kish, growing and developing into sizeable city states with an average of 10,000-20,000 inhabitants.

Each city built a set of double walls and at least one towering temple as the centre of its surrounding agricultural estates. Sumerian architects designed sacred enclosures, temenos, and ziggurats, temples that rose on one or more platforms to create a stepped profile. It was extremely easy to have visual contact with neighbours in the area, if you could have visual contact, was there any chance of having any form of visual communication, just like the black and white movies with the cowboys and Indians sending smoke signal but understanding the Sumerians they will have had a very good way of communicating which is currently unavailable to our present understanding.

Axis mundi is a sacred marker indicating a local culture's centre of the world. Eridu's temple to Enki used external buttresses, spur walls. By the end of the third millennium the worshippers at the Enki Temple had incorporated many previous versions into a colossal, stepped mound that took the form of a proper ziggurat.

The temples in Sumerian city states functioned primarily as economic institutions, central authorities which collected and distributed surpluses, agricultural goods, and products of the specialised industries, such as metal working and weaving, which they supervised. Temples played a role with religious, economic, and social dimensions that we still do not fully understand. The very terms *religious*, *economic* and *social* are modern constructs that we use to describe behaviours and structures for which there was no true counterpart in ancient times.

Modern people have set modern parameters on descriptions on what constitutes as a civilisation, but these parameters didn't exist 4,5,6 or even 7,000 years ago. The Mesopotamian ziggurat crowned the city, flaunting a tangible axis mundus, the vertical link to the supernatural. Eridu was an important centre for trade as well as religion and, at its height, was a great *melting pot* of cultures and diversity, as evidenced in the various forms of artistry found among the ruins. Under the reigns of Ur-Nammu and Shulgi, the city prospered.

The citizens of ancient Eridu were justly proud of another structure besides Enki's temple the mighty ziggurat erected around 2,100 BC by Ur-Nammu, King of Ur, and his son. Though its eroded platform stands only about 30 feet today. Its base of oven-baked brick measures over 150 by 200 feet and once supported a far more imposing structure.

A sounding excavated underneath the current ziggurat, these grand structures had the form of a terrace-step pyramid, with successively receding levels. Each ziggurat was part of a larger temple complex, which included other buildings. Inside, they often consisted of a small room and offering table. Because Eridu's ziggurat ruins are older and larger than any others, some believe these ziggurats are those mentioned in the Bible when referencing the Tower of Babel.

The Tower of Babel was said to have been created not for the worship and praise of a God, but to glorify the builders of the temple itself. This is an interesting statement because, competition on building new structures has always been a symbol of the power of a region apart from the Spartans in Greece. The settlement at Eridu can also be regarded as proto-urban from the beginning; it grew into a substantial city by the Early Dynastic Period and two royal palaces of this period have been excavated.

Outside the temple precinct, a large cemetery of the late Ubaid Period was found; this contained perhaps 1,000 graves of which 200 were excavated. Grave goods include painted pottery vessels, terracotta figurines and baked clay tools such as sickles and shaft-hole axes. The results of excavation on the main mound and the soundings made at the smaller mounds in the neighbourhood indicate that the area was inhabited continuously from the earliest known cultural period in Southern Mesopotamia.

Many people and historians alike have always associated the Book of Genesis description of the Tower of Babel *a city in Shinar* (Sumer) being in Babylon, yet Babylon had always been symbiotic with Eridu. So, an easy mistake to believe that Babel was in Babylon and not in its *Mother city*, Eridu Sumer (Shinar) as the true site of Babel. In the Book of Genesis, it also states: *the Tower (Ziggurat) was halted by the confusion of tongues.*

Archaeological evidence also shows that the expansion of Eridu's last Ziggurat of Amar-Sin 2,047-2,039 BC was unfinished. The great Ziggurat of Amar-Sin in the centre of the city association which springs from archaeological discoveries which also support the claim that the Ziggurat of Amar-Sin more closely resembles the description of the Biblical Tower than any description of the ziggurat at Babylon. Additionally, the Babylonian historian Berossus 200 BC[cxxi] who was a major source for later Greek historians seems to be clearly referring to Eridu when he writes of *Babel* as *Babylon*.

His *Babylon* is in the Southern Marshes of the Euphrates and is patronised by the god of wisdom and fresh water. This association strongly suggests that Eridu is the original biblical Babel as the story of the great Ziggurat of Amar-Sin was most likely passed down orally before Berossus set the legendary structure down in writing. Each city state was under the special protection of its own god, and although multiple gods were worshipped, the total identification of each city with its god was both the defining and unifying feature of Sumerian civilisation.

The cuneiform names for some of the earliest cities incorporate a sign representing the raised mound of the main temple platform, which (then as now) was clearly visible across the flat alluvium plain. Evidence suggests that at the end of the Uruk Period and the beginning of the Early Dynastic Period, some city states were united into leagues of some sort. Perhaps for purposes of trade, for sharing manpower on large-scale projects, or perhaps for mutual protection. But these affiliations were informal, possibly fickle at best and did not persist. We can take our understanding from the later Greek states on this matter, as we seen with both the Athenians and the Spartans during the Peloponnesian War of 431-404 BC.

One of the striking characteristics of the classic Mesopotamian city state is its individualism and resistance to centralised control (a useful fact to consider in today's political context). And while the individual city states were united by force into states and empires after the inevitable collapse of older regimes. These new alliances would just as inevitably decompose into the more enduring city state political units.

Another striking feature to keep in mind is just how small the original area of Sumer actually was prior to its expansion. It was about the size of Northern Ireland, with few natural boundaries between the various city states. Sippar which was one of the original cities prior to the flooding was the only one detached from this original group, and also Semitic speaking. Eridu, Ur, Uruk and Larsa were actually within sight of one other, competing for resources and dominance with about a dozen other city states, such as Lagash, Umma, Kish, Adab and Shuruppak. The only exception was Nippur (Semitic-speaking), which housed the temple of Enlil, the paramount god of the pantheon, and thus was treated as a kind of national shrine.

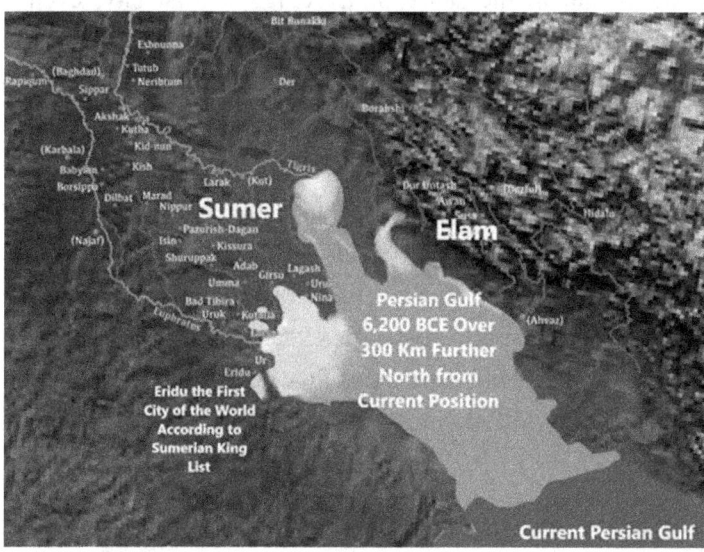

Magic and Myths of Eridu

Eridu[cxxii] is the oldest religious centre of the Sumerians, they divided water into two types, that of the rain and rivers, sweet waters and that of the sea, bitter water. Sumerians called their homeland Ki-En-Gi(-r) which means *the Land of the Noble Lords*; both Akkadians and Sumerians used the word to describe the lands as *Kalam*, meaning civilised, whilst using the word *Kur* to describe the mountain zones the surrounded the eastern plains / frontiers / boundaries of Sumeria, but those words over time became to mean rebellious, barbarous and wild.

The people became so distinctly different to all other area that the Akkadians and Sumerian must have viewed all others as *Kur*. Eridu is described in the ancient Babylonian records as the city of the deep. The special god of this city was Ea, god of the sea and of wisdom, and the prominence given to this god in the incantation literature of Babylonia and Assyria suggests not only that many of our magical texts are to be traced ultimately to the temple of Ea at Eridu. Despite the thickness of the deposit, it appears like the other Mesopotamian floods to have been a purely local.

Other texts linked to Eridu connect it more closely to Sumerian magic and myths as Eridu was still the *Mother city* of Babylon the city, whose name became interchangeable with Babylon and the holy city in which Hammurabi King of Babylon was crowned. Babylon seems to have been an original colony of Eridu and Ur and the reason for the close ties to each other, especially when Babylon was in the ascendancy and Eridu was definitely on the wane. Eridu was politically significant in the sense of it being the first city, even late in its occupancy, during the Neo-Babylonian period 625-539 BC.

Located in Sealand, the large marshland home to the Chaldean Bit Yakin tribe, Eridu was supposed to be the home of the Neo-Babylonian ruling family. Its strategic location on the Persian Gulf and its power trade and commercial connections maintained Eridu's power until the consolidation of the Neo-Babylonian elite in Uruk, in the 6th Century BC. The association of Eridu's fruit-tree garden with the Garden of Eden is further strengthened by additional motifs found in myths regarding Enki who dwelt at Eridu. Enki's human servant, Adapa, is a baker of bread and fisherman of the nearby marshlands, who prepares these items as offerings to Enki in his shrine.

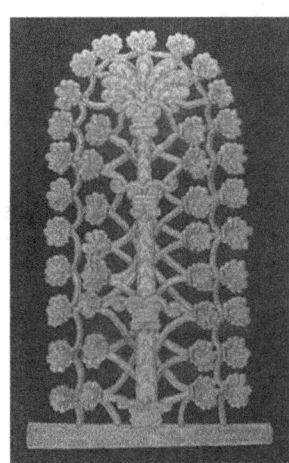

A representation of the holy tree in the Holy Grove of Eridu

These writings,[cxxiii] in particular, the Incantation of Eridu, were believed to compel the gods in the name of Marduk (Babylonian), a significant deity of Mesopotamian religion, which began a larger system of magical hierarchies. This incantation has been credited with the source of power for Mardukite magic. Some of what is known about such magic has been gained from these *spiritual* or *magical* cuneiform tablets/texts.

According to studies of Mesopotamian magic, priests learned prayers such as the Incantation of Eridu to compel the gods in the name of Marduk and recited the hymns in "Old Sumerian" and not in the Semitic language that reigned, Sumerian became a forgotten language which was only recited by the priest class, similar to Latin used in Churches today. Through such structures used by those practicing Mesopotamian magic, it is said magical hierarchies were created.

Certain such powers were said to have been sealed in Eridu, such as petitions to assume god-form, wherein the individual would continue a ceremony or proceeding, acting as a divine representation of the God *invoked*. This practice has similarities with other religious practices, such as in a Catholic priest taking on a Christ form in imitating and re-enacting the *Last Supper*.

Magic and Myths Passed on Through Time

Westerners still use Lucky Seven. Seven is the main number in Sumerian myths as these represent the seven planets and the seven main gods of the heavens, seven levels on a Ziggurat, just read Gilgamesh, seven is everywhere! The Sumerians must have used cosmology and understood the planetary movement of the heaven and noticed the main planets. Mesopotamian religion was polytheistic, with followers worshipping several main gods and thousands of minor gods. The three main gods were Ea (Sumerian: Enki), the god of wisdom and magic, Anu (Sumerian: An), the sky god, and Enlil (Ellil), the god of earth, storms and agriculture and the controller of fates.

Ea is the creator and protector of humanity in both the Epic of Gilgamesh and the story of the Great Flood. In the latter story, Ea made humans out of clay, but the God Enlil sought to destroy humanity by creating a flood. Ea had the humans build an ark and mankind was spared. If this story sounds familiar, it should; foundational Mesopotamian religious stories about the Garden of Eden (Dilmun, modern day Bahrain or Failaka a principality of Dilmun), the Great Flood, and the Creation of the Tower of Babel found their way into the Bible, and the Mesopotamian religion influenced both Christianity and Islam.

Each Mesopotamian city had its own patron god or goddess, and most of what we know of them has been passed down through clay tablets describing Mesopotamian religious beliefs and practices.

Ishtar and Easter

Sacred stories or myths are sometimes passed from culture to culture (The Domino Effect) and have an impact on today's readings, even if not realised. A myth isn't necessarily a false tale, rather a message that has a powerful spirituality containing a message within, just like the Epic of Gilgamesh. The majority of all religions and cultures deal with these issues on a daily basis. The story of death and resurrection is one such story from Sumerian tradition that has passed the sands of time, for example: *From the Great above to the Great below* or *The Descent of Inanna* and Babylonian text—*The Descent of Ishtar*.

The Sumerian goddess Inanna is the personification of the planet Venus who is the Queen of Heaven, also known as the Goddess of the store house, which was essentially a harvest festival. Inanna's husband Dumuzi is the shepherd god who represents the harvest season (Dumuzi is presented in the in writings of the Bible. In Ezekiel 8:14, the prophet sees women of Israel weeping for Tammuz (Dumuzi) during a drought.

Inanna and the Resurrection Story

Before humans are created, Inanna makes a journey to the underworld, ruled by her sister Ereshkigal. Before entering the underworld, she gives instructions to her assistant about rescuing her if she is in danger. In the underworld, she enters through seven gates, and her worldly attire is removed. *Naked and bowed low*, she is judged, killed and hung on display. The resulting death of Inanna bears witness to the earth becoming sterile. Plants start to die, and animals stop reproducing. Unless something is done all life on earth will end. After Inanna has been missing three days her assistant goes to the remaining gods for help. Enki creates two creatures that carry the plant of life and water of life down to the underworld and sprinkling them on Inanna and resurrecting her and she returns to the upper realm.

Inanna becomes known outside of Mesopotamia by her Babylonian name, *Ishtar the Holiday of Easter* was traditionally called *Pascha*, and still is in many languages, named after the Jewish festival of *Pesach* or Passover. In the Germanic and Anglo-Saxon world, we have, however, come to name the holiday *Easter*. This name is almost surely a reflex of the goddess Ishtar. In the pagan spiritual traditions of Germany and England in the medieval period Ishtar, who came to be called the goddess Easter, and who as a deity of resurrection and rebirth became strongly associated with the season of springtime and ultimately gave her name to Christianity's main holy day.

The story of Inanna (Ishtar) descent returning from the underworld and her husband Dumuzi (The celebration in March-April, that marked his death was also a major ancient Sumerian festival) for her rash choices predates the Classical Period Greek myth of Hades and Persephone descent which also tells a similar story of death and resurrection, with the Greek God Demeter causing the Earth to stop flourishing until her daughter Persephone's return.

Pre-Flood King List

The list of pre-flood Sumerian Kings has some curious similarities to the list of patriarchs in Genesis. For example, Genesis and the Sumerian list both refer to the Flood. Both refer to men of great ages, and when the differing numeric systems are considered, they provide similar totals. The lists, however, have three significant differences.

1. At first glance, the ages and lengths of reigns of the Sumerian Kings are much longer than that of the biblical patriarchs. Some of the Sumerian Kings supposedly reigned for more than 30,000 years. Once it was realised that the Sumerians used a sexagesimal system rather than a decimal system of counting, the number where revaluated. The longer life spans in the Sumerian list are converted to a very similar number with the life spans of eight correlating patriarchs in the biblical account.
2. The Sumerian Kings List has only eight in the list while the Bible gives 10 patriarchs before the Flood (including Noah). Although a close correlation exists between these lists, it seems the Sumerian list has omitted the first man and the man who survived the Flood (Adam and

Noah). The similarities between the other eight men make this a reasonable consideration.

3. The Bible has a clear difference in the quality of information, the spiritual and moral superiority of the patriarchs, and the completeness of the list. The Genesis account explains in great detail the struggle of mankind with sin and the effects of the Curse. It highlights those who walked with God and also provides details about humanity apart from the patriarchs. Such detail is not found in the Sumerian Kings List. (Not yet anyway, a lot of this information is sitting on a clay tablet in a Western Museum waiting to be deciphered.)

Early Dynastic Eridu

Eridu was associated with spiritual and rural life and had grown into a substantial city of mudbrick and reed houses by 2,900 BC and during the Ubaid period Eridu became an unusually large city with a population of not less than 4,000 people but with an even larger number in very close proximity to the main city. This may not seem a substantial amount of people but for Neolithic times was an amazing size.

What is also not described is the amount of people who actually lived outside the *town* in very close proximity to Eridu, people working in the fields or on canal structures. During the many days of various celebrations, everyone will have come into the town to celebrate the festivals, so the atmosphere would have been one of great noise and excitement. Yet Eridu was for all practical purposes abandoned after the Ubaid period as the sands of the desert encroached and the agriculture declined and unable to support the current population.

Although it did recover by Early Dynastic II as there was a massive Early Dynastic II palace approximately 100 metres square and has been partially excavated. Ruth Whitehouse called it *a Major Early Dynastic city*. By 2,050 BC the city had declined; there is little evidence of occupation after that date. Eridu's unfinished Ziggurat of Amar-Sin 2,047-2,039 BC underlies the eighteen superimposed mudbrick temples below it. Eridu was abandoned for long periods of time, intermittently, before it was finally deserted and allowed to fall into ruin in the 6th century BC. The encroachment of neighbouring sand dunes and the rise of a saline water table set early limits to its agricultural base so in its later Neo-Babylonian development Eridu was rebuilt as a purely temple site in honour of its earliest history.

Hence, the temple platform was being used during the Jemdet Nasr Period 3,100-2,900 BC even though the old abandoned city near the Eridu temple was buried under sand dunes. There was a settlement about a kilometre North of the temple mound. This may have been where the Enki priests lived after the old Eridu city became uninhabitable. There were also nearby coastal towns on the shore of the Persian Gulf that were occupied during the Jemdet Nasr Period 3,100-2,900 BC.

The Ubaid material culture complex in Southern Mesopotamia is best exemplified by the material from Eridu. Nowhere else has such a complete architectural and ceramic sequence been recovered for this period. Eridu was one of the first centres of civilisation in southern Mesopotamia and in its earliest phase was distinguished by a type of painted pottery otherwise unknown except for some un-stratified sherds from Ur and Usaila near Eridu. These people pioneered the growing of grains in the extreme conditions of aridity thanks to the high-water tables of Southern Iraq.

Enki, Local God of Eridu [cxxiv]

As the site of the main sanctuary of Enki, the god of wisdom, featured prominently in many Mesopotamian texts and especially in the tale of the Great Flood as told in the Atrahasis Epic and the Eridu Genesis. Eridu was the home of Enki and the centre of his cult. Bertman comments on the ruins of Enki's temple, *The God's Temple*, has been found and shows that it was rebuilt over the course of thousands of years.

In its earliest structure of the temple dating back to about 5,500 BC, it measured about 12 by 15 feet, was made of mud brick, and featured a simple podium or altar for sacrifices and a niche meant to hold a statue of the god. Evidence later found in a niche of fish bones and ashes scattered on the floor around the altar the god's favourite meal was freshwater fish. The temple's antiquity makes it the oldest temple in Sumer to date.

Eridu First Temple Level XVI (Safar 1981)

This temple of Enki in Eridu also contained a holy tree in a holy grove, which was the central point for the King to perform various rites, as he was known as a *master gardener*. Many ancient Mesopotamian cities have intriguing aspects about them, and Eridu is certainly no exception. Thanks to its ties to Sumerian mythology and magic, remnants of what the complex city might have been in the past suggest it was indeed, a mighty place. Its old age alone sets it apart from similar Mesopotamian Cities. In addition, the Temple of Eridu, Eridu Genesis, and Incantation of Eridu are all remnants of this city's history that seems to invite more research and interest, as they connect the Sumerian faith with other religions still practiced today.

As we discussed throughout the earlier part of the book, water is the main driving force that moulded the people and everything related to water, the first Hydraulic Empire! The most famous part of the Eridu myth describes a great flood, which was caused by the god Enlil. Enlil became annoyed at the clamour of human cities and decided to quiet down the planet by wiping the cities out. Nintur warned the King of Shuruppak (the last king before the Great Flood), Ziusudra, and recommended he build a boat and save himself and a pair of each living being in order to save the planet.

This myth has clear connections to other regional myths such as Noah and his ark in the Old Testament and the Nuh story in the Koran, and the origin myth of Eridu is the likely basis for both of these stories. Archaeological evidence actually described a *local deluge* in 2,800 BC occurring 3-400 years after the advent of writing and about 100 years before the story of Gilgamesh supposed to have occurred.

The Chief God of Eridu is Enki, the god of wisdom and strength, who became the god of subterranean sweet waters. He saved the lives of the young gods by slaying the father of all gods, Apsû, and established on his slain body his spacious abode which he names Apsû, which is the name of the temple at Eridu. The House of the Aquifer (E-Abzu). Archaeological evidence at the temple has shown the actual temple location never changed or moved from its original position.

Was there a confrontation during the transitional years of local inhabitants and newly arrived migrants, and to justify their presence, history was slightly distorted as means of justification? The major structural work grew in size around the original temple structure. 18 levels of temple construction have been noted and recorded. The last level of the temple complex is around 3,200 BC therefore for over 2,000 years this building had great important not just to the local inhabitants but to the entire region of Mesopotamia. The earliest building was a simple mud-brick shrine resting on virgin sand.

By the time of its tenth rebuilding, it had acquired the standard form of the Sumerian temple with tripartite plan consisting of a long central room flanked by symmetrically grouped side chambers and was built on a substantial platform, it would seem that a standardised temple complex was used in all the surrounding city states, possibly not to upset the other gods of other cities. The settlement at Eridu can also be regarded as proto-urban from the beginning; it grew into a substantial city by the Early Dynastic Period and two royal palaces of this period have been excavated.

The Eridu Genesis

The Genesis Myth of Eridu[cxxv] is an ancient Sumerian text written around 1,600 BC which states the gods created mankind to farm, herd, and worship them. According to its account, Ziusudra was instructed by Enki to build a boat to survive the Deluge or Great Flood, a version of the flood story used in Gilgamesh and later the Old Testament of the Bible. Sources for the Eridu myth include a Sumerian inscription on a clay tablet from Nippur (also dated about 1,600 BC), another Sumerian fragment from Ur (about the same date) and a bilingual fragment in Sumerian and Akkadian from Ashurbanipal's library in Nineveh, about 600 BC.

The Eridu Genesis may have been the first written record of a long oral tradition of a time around 2,900 BC when the Euphrates raised high above her banks and flooded the region. Excavations at Ur by Leonard Woolley[cxxvi] revealed an eight-foot (2.5 metres) layer of silt and clay, consistent with the sediment of the Euphrates, which seemed to support the claim of a catastrophic flood in the area around 2,900 BC. Notes of the excavation taken by Woolley's assistant, Max Mallowan, however, showed the event was clearly a local, not a global, event. A proto-Genesis tale of the Garden has been found at Eridu in which Tagtug the Weaver (or gardener) is cursed by Enki for eating of the fruit of the forbidden tree in the garden after being told not to.

Eridu is further associated with the tale of the great sage Adapa (son of Enki), who was initiated into the meaning of life and all understanding by the god of wisdom. But was ultimately tricked by him and denied the one thing he most wanted: knowledge of life without death, to live forever, not such a clever man. Eridu's initial importance was later eclipsed by the rise of Uruk.

This transference of power and prestige has been seen by some scholars (the historians Samuel Noah Kramer and Paul Kriwaczek among them) as the beginnings of urbanisation in Mesopotamia and a significant shift from the rural model of agrarian life to an urban-centred model. Civilisation had come to Sumeria, but not necessarily as we would know it, whereas urbanisation of Uruk would definitely be recognised.

The Eridu Genesis is written on a Sumerian cuneiform tablet of which about two thirds are now lost and extremely fragmentary. The majority of the text comes from a single tablet found in Nippur by an expedition from the University of Pennsylvania 1893-1896 AD[cxxvii]. The tablet has a date of Old Babylonian 1,600 BC but the text is in Sumerian which is the historical text and a time of the Gods and the creation of man. The missing parts can be reconstructed from texts like the Sumerian King List and Berossus: the first part of the Eridu Genesis, *Their Miserable Condition*; the original myth describes how the mother goddess

Nintur called to her nomadic children and recommended they stop wandering, build cities and temples, and live under the rule of Kings.

It is extremely relevant that Nintur in the Eridu Genesis called to her nomadic (wandering/lost?) children, this seems to point to a change from either hunter-gatherer society to the creation of a settled agricultural society or as the god says: *let me lead the people back from their trails* or is she describing something totally different. Is this back to a normal way of living that had previously existed in the Gulf Oasis. Basically, *you can't come back from somewhere, if you have never been there before*, the trials and tribulations of being forcibly removed from the Gulf Oasis, from a once settled state to a time of convulsion and displacement back to a settled way of life?

Personally, I believe the wandering, lost, coming back scenario is the closest to the truth. As first described in the book, we must always look for strands of truth even in ancient stories as there always seems to be more than a few grains of truth lying in the texts.

1. The creation of men (now lost).
2. Their miserable condition.
3. Creation of Kingship; the first city to hold Kingship (taken with a little pinch of salt!); kings didn't exist until 2,700-2,600 BC Me-Baragesi is called the first ruler of Mesopotamia First Dynasty of Kish (evidence from an inscription found on a vase).

    a) *and let me have him advise*; advise on building programmes?
    b) *let me have him oversee their labour*; overseeing building work, canal systems?
    c) *and let him teach the nation to follow unerringly like cattle*; you have no autonomy when you are part of a large group of workers. Ensure the work is regulated, organised and standardised.
    d) *laid the bricks of those cities in pure spots*; definitely in charge of building work.
    e) *They were named by name and allotted half-bushel baskets*; it would seem the work carried out produced canal systems to be able to produce the half-bushel baskets as a form of payment of work carried out.

f) Kingship sounds more like a project manager, was a king originally a project manager?

4. The First Cities:

   a) *These Cities, which had been named by names, and had been allotted half-bushel baskets, dredged the canals, which were blocked with purplish wind-borne clay, and they carried water. Their cleaning of the canals established abundant growth.* So, it would seem that all the original cities prior to the flooding had been successful in agriculture, with canal systems. It also states they dredged the canals, which means the canal systems already existed, maybe from the original works that had gone into disrepair and needed someone to organise groups into resurrecting these original systems and eventually as the population expands then the canals reworked and expanded.

5. The Kings who ruled before the Great Flood (lost).
6. The supreme god Enlil's decision to destroy sinful humankind (lost).
7. Ziusudra learns of the approaching calamity.
8. Building of the Ark (lost).
9. The Great Flood.
10. Ziusudra's sacrifice.
11. An offer of eternal life to Ziusudra.

At some point soon, these lost pieces will be found, and all current unknowns will be known. The story of the Creation and the Flood has been extremely influential throughout the history of humankind because we have always wondered where we come from, how are we here. The Eridu Genesis points us all in a direction which we are familiar with and has resonance with our understanding, but it also helps (slightly) how these cities came to be into being.

The translation of the Eridu Genesis offered here is adapted from a translation by Thorkild Jacobson. It starts after a long lacuna, in which the creation of man must have been described.

The Creator Goddess Thinks About Humankind (1)

Ninturnote was paying attention:

*Let me bethink myself of my humankind, all forgotten as they are; and mindful of mine, Nintur's, creatures let me bring them back, let me lead the people back from their trails. Let they come and build cities and cult places, that I may cool myself in their shade; may they lay the bricks for the cult cities in pure spots (*as described above via archaeological evidence the original temple complex resting on virgin sands*), and may they found places for divination in pure spots*!

She gave directions for purification, and cries for clemency, the things that cool divine wrath, perfected the divine service and the august offices, said to the surrounding regions: *Let me institute peace there!* You wouldn't mention peace if peace didn't already exist.

When An, Enlil, Enki and Ninhursaga fashioned the dark-headed people (obviously a people uncommon to the area, but the people who came from the Gulf Oasis, this is prior to the current time scale of the word Sumerians and belong with the Ubaid Culture, so these people are originally foreign to the region), they had made the small animals that came up from out of the earth come from the earth in abundance and had let there be, as befits it, gazelles, wild donkeys, and four-footed beasts in the desert. large parts lost. Perhaps a story of a failed attempt to build a city.

One day the rest of this text will be discovered, and further knowledge of the time lost to modern people will once again be revealed and our understanding of this time strengthened even more, perhaps this tablet is already in a basement of a University or a great museum in the US, UK, France or Germany, forgotten about and waiting to be *rediscovered.*

Creation of Kingship (3)

...and let me have him advise; let me have him oversee their labour and let him teach the nation to follow unerringly like cattle! This is very interesting, to make an inhospitable area of land thrive and to work correctly the people had to be organised and stratified, people had to work efficiently to enable others to create goods to increase the wealth of a city state.

When the royal sceptre was coming down from heaven, the august crown and the royal throne being already down from heaven, the King regularly performed to perfection the august divine services and offices and laid the bricks of those cities in pure spots. They were named by name and allotted half-bushel baskets. The King seems to be the builder, how interesting when modern day royalty breaks ground on a new construction site.

The Sumerian King List cites Eridu as the city *of the First Kings*, stating, *After the Kingship descended from heaven, the Kingship was in Eridu*, and the city was looked back upon by the various city states of Mesopotamia as a metropolis of a *golden age* in the same way the writers of the biblical narrative of Genesis created a *Garden of Eden* as their mythical paradise, most likely modelled on Eridu or the Gulf Oasis. This is similar to talking of the Flood, several events all relate to great floods but for different reasons and the Garden of Eden should also fall into this same bracket.

Eridu will have had beautiful, lush fields and an abundance of greenery with the deserts as a backdrop reminding anybody who visited that this was certainly a *miracle to behold* and the hot burning sun high in the sky, yet the original story that may have passed down in oral tradition may have been from the wealth of natural beauty which the original people of the Gulf Oasis had previously inhabited.

Enki's temple was called E-Abzu, as Enki was believed to live in Abzu, an aquifer from which all life was believed to stem. His Kingdom was the sweet waters that lay below earth (Sumerian ab=water; zu=far). Eridu was the southernmost of a conglomeration of Sumerian city states that grew around temples, almost in sight of one another. Once again, the great flood story is all important to the Eridu.

The First cities Before the Flood (4)

The firstling of the cities, Eridu, she gave to the leader Nudimmud, the second, Bad-Tibira, she gave to the Prince and the Sacred One, the third, Larak, she gave to Pahilsag, the fourth, Sippar, she gave to the gallant Utu, the fifth, Šuruppak, she gave to Ansud. These Cities, which had been named by names, and had been allotted half-bushel baskets, dredged the canals, which were blocked with purplish wind-borne clay, and they carried water, their cleaning of the canals established abundant growth. (Large part lost, in which the antediluvian Kings must have been mentioned.) Working in the canals and on the fields, they produced so much noise, that the supreme god Enlil persuaded the other gods to destroy humankind.

That day, Nintur wept over her creatures and holy Inanna was fill of grief over her people; but Enki took counsel with his own heart. An, Enlil, Enki, and Ninhursag had the gods of heaven and earth swear by the names of An and Enlil.

Ziusudra's Vision (7)

At that time Ziusudra was King and lustration priest. He fashioned, being a seer, the god of giddiness and stood in awe beside it, wording his wishes humbly. As he stood there regularly day after day something that was not a dream was appearing: conversation, a swearing of oaths by heaven and earth, a touching of throats, note and the gods bringing their thwarts up to Kiur.

Enki's Advice

Enki had been instrumental in the creation of humanity and when Enlil, King of the Gods, grew tired of humanity's noise and decided to destroy them, it was Enki who preserved life on earth by saving as Ziusudra (Utnapishtim) and all the animals in the world.

And as Ziusudra stood there beside it, he went on hearing: *Step up to the wall to my left and listen*! (The whispering wall?) Let me speak a word to you at the wall and may you grasp what I say, may you heed my advice! By our hand, a flood will sweep over the cities of the half-bushel baskets, and the country; the decision, that mankind is to be destroyed, has been made. A verdict, a command of the assembly, cannot be revoked.

No order of An and Enlil is known to have been countermanded, their Kingship, their term, has been uprooted; they must bethink themselves... Now...What I have to say to you. Enki orders Ziusudra to build the ark and load it with pairs of animals. The assembly of the gods having decided to destroy mankind, the god Utu informed Ziusudra (a King and a priest), that a terrible flood was going to cover the country and that he was to build a gigantic boat. The flood lasted seven days and seven nights, when it had left, Utu came out, he who gives light to the sky and on the ground.

Utu the immortal hero sent his rays into the gigantic boat. Ziusudra prostrated himself before Utu and immolated an ox and a sheep. Later AN and Enlil would receive the homage of Ziusudra, who received the life-giving breath of immortality, and lived in the Paradise of Dilmun, where the sun rises.

The Flood (9)

All the evil winds, all stormy winds gathered into one and with them, them, the Flood was sweeping over the cities of the half-bushel baskets, for seven days and seven nights. After the flood had swept over the country, after the evil wind had tossed the big boat about on the great waters, the sun came out spreading light over heaven and earth.

Ziusudra's Sacrifice (10)

Ziusudra then drilled an opening in the big boat and the gallant Utu sent his light into the interior of the big boat. Ziusudra, being the King, stepped up before Utu kissing the ground before him. The King was butchering oxen, was being lavish with the sheep, barley cakes, crescents together with…he was crumbling for him …juniper, the pure plant of the mountains he filled on the fire and with a …clasped to the breast he…

[Lacuna; Enlil is angry at finding survivors, but Enki explains himself]
End of Enki's speech:

You here have sworn by the life's breath of heaven, the life's breath of earth that he verily is allied with you yourself; you there, An and Enlil, have sworn by the life's breath of heaven, the life's breath of earth, that he is allies with all of you. He will disembark the small animals that come up from the earth!

Reward of Ziusudra (11)

Ziusudra, being King, stepped up before An and Enlil, kissing the ground, and An and Enlil after honouring him were granting life like a god's, were making lasting breath of life, like a god's, descend into him. That day they made Ziusudra, preserver, as King, of the small animals and the seed of mankind, live toward the east over the mountains of Dilmun.

The Demise of Eridu

As a popular religious and trade centre, Eridu no doubt attracted many people as pilgrims and merchants, not to mention its citizens, and so the drain on the surrounding regions resources could have been quite significant and, finally, simply too much to endure. It is possible, even likely, that the city was periodically abandoned to allow the land to recover. Whatever the reason for its final abandonment, the ruins of Eridu today are largely wind-swept sand dunes. Unfortunately, very little now remains of Eridu to remind any visitor to this very hot inhospitable desert of the once mighty city of Eridu, which was founded and loved by the gods but now forgotten.

Eridu was abandoned for long periods of time, intermittently before it was finally deserted and allowed to fall into ruin in the 600 BC when it would not be discovered again for another 2,400 years. The encroachment of neighbouring sand dunes and the rise of a saline water table set early limits to its agricultural base so in its later Neo-Babylonian development Eridu was rebuilt as a purely temple site in honour of its earliest history.

Hence, the temple platform was being used during the Jemdet Nasr Period 3,100-2,900 BC even though the old, abandoned city near the Eridu temple was buried under sand dunes. There was a settlement about a kilometre north of the temple mound; this may have been where the Enki priests lived after the old Eridu city became uninhabitable. There were also nearby coastal towns on the shore of the Persian Gulf that were occupied during the Jemdet Nasr Period. Eridu seems to have had no political significance and was never a seat of a ruling dynasty except for the first two legendary Kings before the Deluge.

Over millennia, several contributing factors continued to compound Eridu's demise such as the overuse cultivation of the land, saline water, drought, the Euphrates moving further away from the city, the regular flooding of the major rivers and the Delta moving further South and away from the city so an invasion by both the desert and external cities and also the loss of the *Sister city*, Babylon, was the final coup de grace. Studies of the phenomenon of the city both ancient and modern can point to a cities decline when it is no longer in a symbiotic relationship with its surrounding land. This is no doubt what brought down many, if not most of the great cities of Mesopotamia that were not destroyed in conquest.

Passing the Baton to Uruk

The city of Eridu features prominently in Sumerian mythology, not only as the first city and home of the gods, but as the locale to which the goddess Inanna travelled in order to receive the gifts of civilisation which she then bestowed upon humanity from her home city of Uruk. Uruk vies with Eridu among modern scholars for the honour of the oldest city in Mesopotamia or even the oldest in the world. The stories of Inanna, goddess of Uruk, describe how she had to go to Eridu in order to receive the gifts of civilisation.

At first Enki, the God of Eridu, attempted to retrieve these sources of his power but later willingly accepted that Uruk now was the centre of the land. The story of Inanna and the God of Wisdom, in which the goddess of Uruk takes away the sacred meh (gifts of civilisation) from Enki, the God of Eridu, can be seen as an ancient story symbolising this shift in the paradigm of Sumerian culture. The prosperous commercial centre of Uruk superseded the rural Eridu. Inanna successfully tricked her father and made Uruk, not Eridu, the seat of power in Sumeria.

The moral to this story, particularly in relation to how Sumerians viewed the Goddess Inanna, would be that Eridu was associated with spiritual and rural life, whereas Uruk was the embodiment of the new way of life which was the city. This seems to be a mythical reference to the transfer of power northward and a power share in the region. Also interesting is in the court of Assyria, special physicians trained in the ancient lore (special knowledge) of Eridu, far to the south, foretold the course of sickness from signs and portents on the patient's body and offered the appropriate incantations and magical resources as cures.

The first site to reach the proportions that can truly be described as urban was Uruk, which gives its name to the period during which cities in Mesopotamia emerged. Uruk occupied an area of about 200 hectares, about one-third of this covered with elaborately decorated temples and public buildings, reconstructed in a continuous sequence. The largest area is the Eanna precinct, a complex of temples dedicated to Inanna, the Sumerian goddess, queen of heaven, primarily responsible for fertility and later identified with the Akkadian Ishtar, goddess of love and war.

Uruk's status as the world's first city may yet be challenged by future excavations in northern and North-Eastern Syria, or in other parts of the world. But none so far can surpass Uruk's antiquity or five millennia of continuous occupation. Uruk's cultural influence extended as far as Syria Anatolia and Iran.

Chapter 6
Strong-Walled Uruk:
"The Venice of the Desert"

Introduction

Uruk seems to have embraced the adjustment to city living quite quickly and accepted new norms that this entailed. This adapted behaviour quickly made the people of Uruk much more aware of its natural surroundings and people wondered how they could exploit the natural resources that lay beyond its boundary stones. Aid that would have a positive and direct impact on Uruk's prosperity. Therefore, it was inevitable that the people of this bulging new city state seemed to be very much interested in the world beyond its current limits and what it had to offer. By 3,500 BC it was the biggest city in the world and the city required resources, more than it already had, if it was to continue its upward trajectory.

Uruk was definitely mighty and needed to supersede Eridu as the main city state in Sumer, as previously described. If Eridu was JRR Tolkien's *Kingdom of the Elves*, then Uruk was Ridley Scott's *Blade Runner* of its day. Nothing had ever been seen on this scale. It really was like having the two best football teams in the world in just one city, Inanna FC and Anu United, both had the largest and most beautiful temple complexes in Sumer to support the prestige of the city. You had the visual impact beyond all comprehension and Uruk certainly had the WOW factor.

Nobody had ever seen this many people in just one city. Uruk predates Rome by almost 4,300 years and had a very similar presence to Rome. It had the architecture, the grand temples, the administrative buildings, a place of commerce. But it was never a Rome, the reason is, Uruk at its time of conception already had equals in the area, this was never a standalone city like Rome. The other city states had their own area of expertise and Uruk during its initial growth traded equally with all other city states. Whereas Rome had no equals, you were with Roman, or you were against Rome.

Uruk was never in that controlling position. What Uruk was best at, was commerce, trading was its strength and all future *Empires* realised that trading was the root to all Empires and Uruk gave them the blueprint to success. Uruk was urban, it was the first urbanised city in the World. An urban city can last for a while, but to ensure its stability everyone had to follow the rules of Civilisation, which Uruk performed to perfection. It was the first Capitalist *Mini Empire*, Uruk seen potential areas of growth outside its own territorial boundaries since it had no previous competition. Expansion was quick to capitalise on these new areas of resource sending out colonies right across Syria, Iraq and Turkey.

Archaeologists have noted a definitive change at sites in these new areas of influence with Uruk style architecture and pottery as well as cylinder seals and tools. The change is unlike the typical interaction during the Ubaid Period when people where merely influenced by one another. The people of Uruk seemed to have physically moved to these new evolving locations in the new colonies, but not at the level of building an Empire. These early colonies were used to facilitate trade back to Uruk who could then use these incoming raw products and turn them into desirable and useful artifacts by utilising the newly invented crafts within Uruk. These refined completed products along with manufactured goods already made within Uruk could be forwarded on to further sites in and around the Persian Gulf and also sent back to the newly established colonies thus strengthening commerce.

The colonies started supplying Uruk with Obsidian, Copper, Wood, Lapis Lazily, Stone back to Southern Mesopotamia where the centre of trade was utilising the more expansive marketplace compared to the rest of the region. Three different types of colonies existed. Some Sumerians built homes in unoccupied areas, other *conquered* existing settlements whilst the third type lived peacefully side by side with local inhabitants of the new colonists. Hamoukar in modern day Syria was one of these places where oppressive power seems to have been the bargaining tool of choice. Evidence of buildings burnt down, and walls pulled down. Clemens Reichel described the excavation discovery as:

The attack must have been swift and intense. Buildings collapsed, burning out of control, burying everything in them under vast piles of rubble.

This highlights the second recorded evidence of some sort of warfare, Jericho being the first in 7,000 BC. The evidence shows that buildings where quickly erected on top of the devastation in the Uruk style. The Uruk period culture exported by Sumerian traders and colonists had an effect on all surrounding regions of the Fertile Crescents. These regions gradually evolved their own comparable, competing economies and cultures and the appearance of Kingship starting in 2,900 BC started to rear its head thus changing the political landscape to a much greater extent. Ultimately, Uruk could not maintain long-distance control over colonies such as Tell Brak by military force, but other regions took note and learnt from Uruk's failings. It was at this same time that the people of Uruk seem to have been in contact with Egypt.

Archaeological Levels of Uruk

In Sumerian, the word uru means *City, town, village or district.* In addition to being one of the first cities, Uruk was the first city state of true urbanisation and governmental bureaucracy during the Uruk period, or *Uruk expansion*. The Arabic name of Babylonia which eventually became the name of the present-day country, al-Iraq is thought to have derived from the name Uruk via Aramaic (Erech) and possibly via Middle Persian (Erāq).

According to the Sumerian King List, it was founded by King Enmerkar sometime around 4,500 BC. On both accounts, this is untrue; first the city is at least 5,000 BC and secondly the first archaeological evidence of Kings start around 2,900 BC. Located in the Southern Region of Sumer modern day Warka, Iraqi archaeologists have discovered multiple cities of Uruk built atop each other in chronological order. For ease of understanding this extensive period of time, historians have segregated the Uruk Period, which has been subdivided into 8 phases from the oldest, through its prominence and into its decline. Based upon the levels of the ruins excavated and the history which the artefacts have been discovered.

The city was most influential between 4,100-2,900 BC when Uruk was the largest urban centre and the hub of trade and administration. This period of 1,200 years was the golden years which saw a shift from small established embryonic city state with surrounding agricultural villages to a larger urban centre with a full-time bureaucracy, military, and a stratified society.

1. Uruk XVIII Eridu period 5,000 BC; the founding of Uruk.
2. Uruk XVIII-XVI Late Ubaid period 4,800-4,200 BC.
3. Uruk XVI-X Early Uruk period 4,200-3800 BC.
4. Uruk IX-VI Middle Uruk period 3,800-3,400 BC.
5. Uruk V-IV Late Uruk period 3,400-3,100 BC; The earliest monumental temples of Eanna District are built.
6. Uruk III Jemdet Nasr period 3,100-2,900 BC; The 9 km city wall is built.
7. Uruk II 2,900 BC the appearance of the first Kings.
8. Uruk I.

Discovering Uruk, Its Location and Size

Uruk is an ancient city of Sumer (and later of Babylonia) situated east of the present bend of the Euphrates River on the dried-up ancient channel of the Euphrates 30 km (19 mi) east of modern Samawah, Al-Muthannā, Iraq. Uruk is the is the forerunner in what archaeological evidence indicates that the Sumerians established roughly a dozen city states by the 4th Millennium BC. These usually consisted of a walled metropolis dominated by a ziggurat the tiered, pyramid like temples associated with the Sumerian religion.

Homes were constructed from bundled marsh reeds or mud bricks, and complex irrigation canals were dug to harness the silt-laden waters of the Tigris and Euphrates for farming. Uruk was one of the oldest and most sprawling was Uruk, a thriving trading hub. Uruk played a leading role in the early urbanisation of Sumer at this point in time. At its height 2,900 BC, Uruk 80,000 residents living inside 6 km^2 (2.32 sq. mi) of land surrounded by a defensive walled area, making it the largest city in the world at the time. The Legendary King Gilgamesh, according to the chronology presented in the Sumerian King List, ruled Uruk in the 27th century BC.

The city lost its prime importance around 2,004 BC in the context of the struggle of Babylonia against Elam, but it remained inhabited throughout the Seleucid 312-63 BC and Parthian 227 BC to 224 AD periods until it was finally abandoned shortly before or after the Islamic conquest of 633-638 AD.

William Kennett Loftus[cxxviii] visited the site of Uruk in 1849 AD, identifying it as *Erech*, known as *the second city of Nimrod*, and led the first excavations from 1850 to 1854 AD. Uruk played a very important part in the political history of Sumer. Starting from the Early Uruk period, the city exercised hegemony over nearby settlements. At this time 3,800 BC there were two centres of 20 hectares, Uruk in the South and Nippur in the North surrounded by much smaller 10-hectare settlements.

Later, in the Late Uruk period, its sphere of influence extended over all Sumer and beyond to external colonies in upper Mesopotamia and Syria, it could be stated that Uruk was the First Empire. Or was Uruk just a very strong influencer of all areas in Mesopotamia. Uruk was prominent in the national struggles of the Sumerians against the Elamites up to 2,004 BC, in which it suffered severely; recollections of some of these conflicts are embodied in the Gilgamesh Epic, in the literary and courtly form.

The recorded chronology of rulers over Uruk includes both mythological and historic figures in five dynasties. As in the rest of Sumer, power moved progressively from the temple to the palace. Rulers from the Early Dynastic period exercised control over Uruk and at times over all Sumer. Hopefully, time will tell, but the physical location of Uruk compared to Ur, places Uruk at a bit of a disadvantage, yet you would never guess. Whatever the grand plan of Uruk was, it worked. Should we place more of the laurels of success associated with Sumer as a whole at the strong walls of Uruk? Did Uruk drive the majority of inventions and the rest of the city states of Sumer, simply follow?

In myth, Kingship was lowered from heaven to Eridu then passed successively through five cities until the deluge which ended the Uruk period. Afterwards, Kingship passed to Kish (Semitic) at the beginning of the Early Dynastic period, which corresponds to the beginning of the Early Bronze Age in Sumer. In the Early Dynastic I period 2,900-2,800 BC, Uruk was in theory under the control of Kish. It should be worth noting that a devasting flood occurred around 2,800 BC and the transfer of power from one city state to the next maybe due to this natural *manmade* disaster.

This period is sometimes called the Golden Age. During the Early Dynastic II period 2,800-2,600 BC, Uruk was again the dominant city exercising control of Sumer. This period is the time of the First Dynasty of Uruk sometimes called the Heroic Age. However, by the Early Dynastic IIIa period 2,600-2,500 BC Uruk had lost sovereignty, this time to Ur. This period, corresponding to the Early Bronze Age III, is the end of the First Dynasty of Uruk and this is when location plays a leading role. All Copper and Tin would have to be routed past

Ur prior to heading further upriver to Uruk. In the Early Dynastic IIIb period 2,500-2,334 BC, also called the Pre-Sargonic period referring to Sargon of Akkad, Uruk continued to be ruled by Ur.

The Start of Inventions

Uruk seems have been a catalyst for inventions, if it didn't actually invent a specific item it certainly maximised its potential far beyond its original intension. From bronze production, wheeled pottery, the wheeled transport, the cylinder seals and a writing system. They also created an effective centralised government system at which point the people of Uruk still don't seem to have been ruled by Kings. Some of these inventions may not seem too important to the reader yet the impact on society was immense.

Early bronzes weren't made from the classical mixture of Copper and Tin, but with copper and arsenic which made the bronze more durable for the use in tools and weapons. Bronze weathers to a green patina and shines brightly if polished therefore these attributes made the material very versatile in its use. The additional bonus of bronze was that it never rusts, and old bronze objects could be melted down and recast into something else. A material that can be reconstituted in an area devoid of natural resources made this the new wonder material of its day.

Uruk found a way of casting bronze into moulds, so the metal could just about take any shape. Sculptures, bowls, cups, shields, daggers, razors, knives many things. Imports of copper from the Southern tip of the Arabian Peninsula, Magan, which is present day Oman and from Turkey must have increase dramatically to meet the new demand. People didn't stop using stone tools which was still required by many in society, but bronze became the material of choice, but only to the people who could afford it.

Due to the bronze revolution, pottery lost a lot of its prestige. Why would you eat off pottery when you could impress the neighbours with your bronze plates when serving lunch? This is one small aspect of consumerism which has been noted, no longer did the people require essential items, they now possessed items of envy. At the same time clay pots became less interesting during this period of time. Yet one type of clay bowl dramatically increased in production and is found at all excavation sites throughout the Middle East. This is called the *Bevelled Rim Bowl*[cxxix], made in moulds by tens of thousands. Coarse and undecorated, as if they needed to be discarded once they had been used once, just like today's tin foil trays.

It is now considered that they were used to measure out rations to workers, a *standardised* amount. Jars, dishes, cups, etc. started to be made in far greater numbers than previous, not by moulds like the bevelled rim bowls or coiled by hand. Potters started to use the pottery wheel; a mass production replaced the finely handmade pieces previously witnessed. The potter's wheel may have preceded the actual wheel. Wheels seem so obvious that we tend to think they were invented very early. It's not an obvious development at all, whole civilisation s in other regions of the world still managed to prosper without ever having invented the wheel.

The invention of the wagon was a marvel, but it also vastly improved production quotas in the fields. Less people to move the produce from the fields and therefore more people managing production. The wheel had to turn, be sturdy for the journey, turn on an axle and the axle had to turn to enable the cart to move in a different direction. Tripart wheels, the carts could carry far more than a donkey or an ass. It became a land boat, to help with loads that had to be moved beyond the banks of a canal or river.

The limitation of smaller unnavigable canal systems limited how far the field could be extended. A scribe will have carried out a simple time and motion study and quickly realised the additional manpower required to physically move the grown produce to an area where it could be transport by boat simply wasn't viable. Not the cart changed this calculation. This allowed farmers to building further inland away from the main watercourses and increase product levels and have more tradeable products gained in taxes which aided the large temple building programmes. *The Domino Effect!*

The Two Most Important Inventions in the Uruk Period

The formation of a government capable of forming and administrating a state, and the invention of writing. The new Government used writing extensively to keep records. No painting or statues of kings, no secular palaces dominating cities, they are small sculptures of men wearing hats with belts, they aren't depictions of gods because gods always wore pointy hats or horned helmets so they may be priests.

Powerful men may have been in each of the powerful cities that was growing at this period of time. But they may have ruled as representatives of the gods rather than as Kings. Each city state had a particular god who was meant to look after the people. Maybe the rulers had a close tie to the city God.

Uruk Period (Largest Urban Area)

The Uruk period 4,100-2,900 BC saw several transitions. First, pottery began to be mass-produced. Second, trade goods began to flow down waterways in Southern Mesopotamia, and large, temple-centred cities most likely theocratic and run by Priests-Kings rose up to facilitate this trade. Slave labour was also strongly utilised and encouraged during such expansion that was seen. Other major advances of this period, besides urbanisation, was the development of monumental architecture between 3,500-3,300 BC.

All of these advances became more highly developed during the Early Dynastic Period. In precisely what manner Uruk ruled the region, why and how it became the first/largest city in the world, and in what manner it exercised its authority is not fully known. The historian Gwendolyn Leick (pages 183-184) writes[cxxx]:

The Uruk phenomenon is still much debated, as to what extent Uruk exercised political control over the large area covered by the Uruk artefacts, whether this relied on the use of force, and which institutions were in charge. Too little of the site has been excavated to provide any firm answers to these questions. However, it is clear that, at this time, the urbanisation process was set in motion, concentrated at Uruk itself.

Since the city of Ur had a more advantageous placement for trade, further South toward the Persian Gulf, it would seem to make sense that the city state of Ur rather than Uruk, would have wielded more influence but this is not the case. Artefacts from Uruk appear at virtually every excavated site throughout Mesopotamia. The historian Julian Reade[cxxxi] notes:

Perhaps the most striking example of the wide spread of some features of the Uruk culture consists in the distribution of what must be one of the crudest forms ever made, the so-called bevelled-rim bowl. This kind of bowl, mould-made and mass-produced, is found in large numbers throughout Mesopotamia and beyond.

We talked about many items being standardised, but the most significant would seem to be a Bowl! This bowl was the means by which workers seem to have been paid. A standardised Bowl gave a certain amount of grain ladled into a standard "sized" bowl. The remains of these bowls, throughout all of Mesopotamia, suggest that they *were frequently discarded immediately after use, like the aluminium foil containing a modern take-away meal.*[cxxxii] This suggests it was a form of payment, because nobody was carrying their own bowl, the bowl was *given*. So popular was the bevelled-rim bowl that manufacturing centres sprang up throughout Mesopotamia extending as far away from Uruk as the city of Mari in the far north.

Because of this, it is unclear if the bowl originated at Uruk or elsewhere (though Uruk is generally held as the bowl's origin). If not at Uruk, then the bevelled-rim bowl must be counted among the many of the city's accomplishments as it is the first known example of a mass production.

At this same time, the people of Uruk seem to have been in contact with Egypt. During this period, the Egyptian tombs where built in the Niche and Buttress style of architecture and Egyptians also started to use cylinder seals and Mesopotamian boats started to appear in Egyptian art. Egypt was rich in gold and may have been a lucrative source for trade. It doesn't look like Mesopotamians tried to set up home in Egypt and it's not beyond reason to believe that Egyptians would have travelled to Mesopotamia but for reasons not yet known to historians, this brief flurry of interaction ended abruptly maybe one day clay tablets buried in the vaults of academic institutes in the West will be able to give the reason for this sudden end of trading.

After this short period of trade, no more signs exist of each other's existence. Both setting their own individual courses on expansion and development. Uruk in 3,200 BC would have been an exciting time for development in many new areas, living in the most advanced civilisation the world had ever seen, paling all other areas into insignificance, it really was the only place to be at the time.

The Greatest Gift to Humanity

Jean Chardin (1643-1713 AD) explored the region and wrote about his discoveries in his book, *Travels in Persia*, published in 1686 AD. Chardin was the first European to claim that the strange marks found on clay tablets and architectural ornamentation were not mere decoration but, in fact, an advanced writing system. It was not until the mid-19th century AD; however, that scholars and archaeologists such as William Kennet Loftus 1820-1858 AD, George Smith 1840-1876 AD, Robert Koldewey 1855-1925 AD, and Henry Rawlinson 1810-1895 AD began to bring to light the civilisation of ancient Sumer and the many accomplishments of the Sumerian people.

Unbeknownst to Jean at the time of writing about his discoveries when analysing these strange wedge-shaped markings seen in stone and clay. He was actually looking at the very origins of writing itself.

The Written Word

All historians agree writing was invented in Uruk, at no time or place anywhere else in the World has a clear system of written communication been present before its true inception in 3,500 BC. It should be noted that *Bullae* and the *Stamp Seals* predate any forms of early writing and both developed in Northern Mesopotamia. But this development has to be included due to the fact that the seal started to share information of the persons origin or activity.

Many historians argue over the exact time of invention, but the caveat to this exact dating becomes slightly blurred. Writing developed in known stages. So, from initial concept of using markings on clay tablets for accounting purposes to actual written communication between city states, this process took 1,000 years. But the vast impact at each stage of development bore great benefits and improvements within all aspects of society who used the system. This is also attested to by the people of the time, with its gradual spread and standardisation throughout the Middle East.

- Bullae: 7,500-8,000 BC, three dimensional tokens.
- Stamp Seals: 7,600-6,000 BC in Syria Northern Mesopotamia.
- Cylinder Seals: 3,600 BC, although the basic paradigm of the seal was already known.
- Pictographs 1: Around 5,000 BC first witnessed in Southern Mesopotamia.
- Pictographs 2: 3,600-3,500 BC two-dimensional representation, solely used by officials in the Temple administration and accounting department. These are the embryonic first signs of the beginning of writing.
- Proto-Cuneiform: 3,200 to 2,900 BC. First sign of phonetic signs being introduced. Wedge shapes that simplified the time-consuming pictures.

With the volume of words expanding. In 3,200 BC which is exemplified in lexical lists essentially scribal dictionaries of cuneiform signs and their meaning in Sumerian and Akkadian for governmental bureaucracy.
- Logogram and Rebus: 3,000 BC the year the written language matured.
- The written word: Cuneiform 2,600 BC reduced its complexity and introduced syntax.
- Cuneiform: 2,500 BC syllabic script adapted by the majority of Middle East regions.

More than five thousand years ago in Early Dynastic Uruk, the world's first literate and urban society arose in the region of Sumer. Mesopotamia was diverse and constantly changing with the city states vying for supremacy using any means as an advantage. After the early historical cultures of Sumer and Akkad, the region was later dominated by the great empires of Assyria and Babylonia and was in constant interaction with the contemporary cultures of Anatolia (modern Turkey), Northwest Syria, the Levant, Egypt, Iran and the Gulf. The development of writing system is arguably the most defining feature of the Uruk period and possibly anything else that was developed in Southern Mesopotamia.

Bullae

7,500-8,000 BC, A bulla(e), Latin for *Round Seal* is an inscribed clay ball used in a commercial transaction, usually with an intricate seal motif on the outer part to prevent tampering once hardened. The bullae, hollow, rounded balls of clay which held tokens representing a financial transaction, for example, four white pebbles to represent four sheep. The advent of writing was purely developed for accounting purposes and initially the verbal word was deemed unnecessary to record.

It started during the prehistoric periods, several kinds of clay counting devices were invented representing commodities such as the sheep. The creation of writing is extremely multi-faceted. The bullae's a contributing factor, which some scholars see as one of several precursors to writing. With the development of the bullae, a seal which could be rolled onto rounded clay was required, and so eventually the seal was developed to identify who the bullae actually belonged to.

The Stamp Seal

First appeared in Northern Mesopotamia in Syria they originated in the Late Neolithic Period 7,600-6,000 BC. Simple clay tokens may have been used for the symbolic representation of commodities, and pendants and stamp seals may have had a similar symbolism, if not function. During this period, the repertory of seal designs expanded to include snakes, birds, and animals with humans. There was much continuity between the Ubaid culture and the succeeding Uruk period, when many of the earlier traditions were elaborated, particularly in architecture. Contemporaneous with cylinder seals were stamp seals which were smaller and less ornate in design.

Stamp seals started off quite large in size but over a period of time the stamp seals ended up less than an inch (2 cm) in size and more closely resembled the later signet rings. With some scholars claiming the stamp seal preceded the cylinder seal by many millennia. The claim that the stamp seal came first would seem to make sense as it is a less refined means of sealing a document. Logically assuming that the more refined and ornate cylinder seal developed from the more primitive stamp seal. While that may be, evidence suggests that stamp seals were popular throughout Mesopotamia at the same time as cylinder seals, and especially in the regions known today as Syria and Turkey.

Some scholars argue that cylinder seals developed from stamp seals owing to the need to seal the predominantly round bullae. While stamp seals were used to secure flat clay envelopes which would be broken open upon receipt. The flat envelopes, the theory goes, were used before the development of the bullae, and so the stamp was an efficient means of securing a message or transaction. The problem with this theory is that the broken envelopes discovered in the present day are clearly stamped by cylinder seals and bullae which were marked by stamp seals. So, we can accurately summarise by saying whatever seal was available was used for either envelopes or bullae.

While the stamp seal preceded the cylinder seal, the stamp continued in used perhaps owing simply to personal attachment. Stephen Bertman[cxxxiii] notes that cylinder seals *sometimes became heirlooms and as such were passed on from one generation to the next*. Cylinder seals are very costly item whereas the Stamp Seal will have been relatively in expensive. Using a Parker pen compared to a very high-end Montblanc would be the best analogy. The archaeological evidence makes clear that both kinds of seals were used by the people of Mesopotamia pre-dating the invention of cuneiform writing.

Scholar Clemens Reichel in Joshua Engelhardt's work *Agency in Ancient Writing*, notes:

Unlike the Northern sealing tradition of using stamp seals, Southern Mesopotamians used cylinder seals, consisting of stone cylinders into which seal designs were engraved. The difference between stamp seal and cylinder seal is much more than a technical one and, in fact, tells us about the very nature of scribal agency behind the seal. The limited space on the reverse side of a stamp seal also limited the potential variability in the iconographic repertoire of seal designs.

Accordingly, the number of easily discernible variations on a theme is limited. The surface of a cylinder seal, by comparison, provides the "canvas" for a long rectangular image, making it a perfect place to apply an elaborate design with "narrative" depictions. Sufficient room meant that the same theme easily could be varied without confusion or mix-up. This medium, therefore, suited the requirements of an increasingly complex bureaucratic entity which required subtle details to identify individual agents within its system.

As the bureaucracy of Uruk and the rest of Southern Mesopotamia was far more complex and widespread than that of the North regions and their colonies. Coupled with Uruk's panache for the desirable rather than just the useful. It would make sense that Uruk would have favoured the cylinder seal and all its glamour whilst the robust, dependable stamp seal remained popular in the North.

The Cylinder Seals

3,600 BC, prior to the invention of writing people sealed the contents from the person who had sent the item, the Cylinder Seals where a personal

identification from the sender. Among the most interesting and revealing artefacts discovered from ancient Mesopotamia are the objects known as cylinder seals. These fairly small items may be seen today in museum exhibits around the world but, perhaps owing to their size, they are not given the kind of consideration by the general public which larger and more commanding artefacts, such as reliefs or statuary enjoy.

Cylinder seals began to be used in the Uruk Period to identify people who were responsible for the production of goods and their movement. In the Ubaid era that preceded the Uruk period, stamp seals were already been used in the North, but once cylinder seals became available, they became a fixture of Mesopotamian society for everyday use for the next 3,000 years.

Today, we use signatures to attest transactions, we sign for credit cards, contracts, letters. A signature is a commitment, a guarantee. In the Uruk period, people had just started to write but hadn't used it to write names and nobody had a signature. Signing your name was never used in Mesopotamian history. You could buy a seal or be given one as a family heirloom and use the seal to identify things as yours, or that you had been somewhere or approved something. The seal provided evidence of your involvement. This is an intellectual development which is similar to writing which developed at the same period.

People assume cylinder seals where large, due to the detail incorporated on them. But these items where usually around 2.5 to 3.0 cm in height. Great craftsmanship was used in the manufacture of these items. Each one was a cylindrical bead carved out of a hard stone, with the seal engraved in a negative relief. When the scene was rolled on clay it seemed one continuous scene that could cover as much of a surface as needed. In later times the cylinder seal became formulae, but in the Uruk period everyone one had one. The leather maker, the weaver (usually a web (to weave a web)). Artist were still experimenting with this new medium.

The cylinder seal, however, was an integral part of daily life in ancient Mesopotamia and tells the story of the people more completely than royal reliefs or towering statues ever could. They were known as kishib in Sumerian and kunukku in Akkadian and were used by everyone. Since they were an easy item to use, without any training everyone used a cylinder seal from royals to slaves, in the transaction of business and later sending correspondence. Originating in Uruk in the land of Sumer these intricate objects were made from semiprecious stone such as marble, obsidian, amethyst, lapis lazuli or metal such as gold or silver.

These seals were worn by their owners on strings of leather or other material around the neck or wrist or pinned to a garment. Their purpose was to serve as a personal signature on a document or package to guarantee authenticity or legitimise a business deal as one would sign a letter or form in the present day. The seal was rolled onto the moist clay of the document as an official, binding signature.

Intricacy of the Seals

The rise in bureaucracy during this period necessitated the kind of guarantee of authenticity which these seals provided and, in time they became increasingly intricate in design and scope. Unlike the smaller stamp seals, cylinder seals provided an artist with the room to explore a certain motif. These motifs not only make clear the identity of the individual who bore the seal but give significant details about their jobs and way of life. Leick writes:

The pictorial scenes that refer to activities such as weaving, attending domestic animals, hunting, and apparently ritual actions may indicate spheres of administrative competence within the Uruk economy.

Manufacture

This *administrative competence* was demonstrated through the sophisticated work of the artists who created the seals. Cylinder seals were made by a seal-cutter known as a *burgul* in Sumerian and as a *purkullu* in the Akkadian language. A person would have apprenticed with a master seal-cutter for four years minimum before setting up their own shop as a professional. Stephen Bertman writes of a seal cutter's toolkit found in the ruins of the ancient city of Ugarit, Syria:

In a clay jar were found a small copper chisel, two-pointed copper gravers (for detail), a whetstone, a borer (for drilling holes), and some seals that had not yet been completed.

The seal cutter also used bronze and flint engraving tools as well as drills and blades to work the stone into a seal. Bertman claims that *rather than cutting rough cylinders from stone, the seal cutters may have bought blanks from dealers, adding the finishing touches in their workshops.* If so, this would mean there were two types of artisans at work on the seals: those who crafted the blank cylinders from quarried stone and those who did the intricate engraving to personalise the cylinder for a customer.

At some point in the process, either when the blank was created or after it was engraved, holes were drilled into the cylinder so that the owner could wear it on a string or pinned to a garment, as Bertman notes, *just such a pinned seal was found resting on the skeletal chest of Queen Puabi in her grave at Ur*. The seal of a queen like Puabi had a gold cap at one end fastened on with bitumen while those of less noble status would have their seals capped with less expensive metal.

The seals were carved in intaglio, a process of carving beneath the surface of the stone so an impression of that carving creates an image in relief. The easiest way to think of this is as a photographic negative. In order to achieve this effect, the artist would have had to reverse the image he wanted in his mind and carve accordingly. This required enormous skill and seal cutters were highly paid and greatly respected for their craft. There was no shortage of demand for cylinder seals by the people of Mesopotamia.

Bertman notes how *2,000 cylinder seals have been recovered* in Mesopotamian digs thus far and that *based on the theory that for every archaeological object in a museum at least a hundred still lie buried, some 200,000 such seals from the Uruk period alone still await excavation*. The seal cutter, therefore, was very much in demand and a highly skilled cutter would have lived very comfortably.

Use of Cylinder Seals

The seals were used by people in every strata of Mesopotamian society from the ruling class to the merchant and even to the slave. Lewis and Feldman identify the four uses of cylinder seals:

1. Authenticating or legitimating a transaction (in a similar way to the modern-day signature).
2. Preventing/restricting access to containers, rooms or houses.
3. Amuletic.
4. Sign of personal identity or professional affiliation.

The uses of the seals were both practical and spiritual. The Lewis and Feldman list above addresses the practical use of signing the name, restricting access only to those allowed to break the seal, and as a means of personal identification, or a kind of badge of authority or specialised occupation. The third use listed, *amuletic*, refers to the Mesopotamian belief in the seal as an amulet, a kind of charm, which could ward off evil spirits and protect one from harm.

The seal could also work as well to bring one luck and prosperity depending on the stone used. A seal may have been engraved with a certain scene from a story or legend about the gods or perhaps with an image of a demon, which would have meant 'powerful spirit' and did not have the universal negative connotation it has today. The demon Pazuzu, for example, was a frightening looking creature but protected pregnant women and their unborn children from harm if they were wearing an amulet with his face carved on it.

Whatever the use of the seal it was a prized possession and its loss was taken as seriously as you would today if you lost an American Express Platinum credit card with your pin number taped to the front! Bertman writes what happened after an individual realised their personal seal was lost: *the former owner would record the date and time of loss with an official to ensure that transactions made after the loss would be invalid.*

As noted above, some seals depicted the persons occupation, sometimes more intimate whilst revealing a personal identity, very rarely a person's name. It is no wonder, then, that people were so worried over the loss of their seal. The personal identity was made clear either by the likeness engraved on the seal or by symbols surrounding an image. In the case of such seals, then, the loss would have been as serious to an ancient Mesopotamian as the loss of one's personal identification is today and the threat of *identity theft* just as great then as it is now.

The seals are deeply personal identification of an individual, the seal is an expression of the person who owned it. Their style, their quality their beliefs, a multitude of personal details. These people are me and you of yesteryear, so these little subtleties weren't overlooked in their day by envious onlookers. It not always the big bling items that impress people. It's the underrated quality and style that is the most fascinating aspects about them. Not just to archaeologists and scholars in the present day, but also designers of then and now. Dr Senta Green, writing on the interest seals hold for the modern-day researchers notes how historians are interested in these artifacts because:

...the images carved on seals accurately reflect the pervading artistic styles of the day and the particular region of their use. In other words, each seal is a small-time capsule of what sorts of motifs and styles were popular during the lifetime of the owner.

She also notes, however, that the identity of the owner is of equal interest in that a modern-day historian has the chance to meet someone *in person* who lived more than 2,000 years ago. Regarding the iconography of the seals, Dr Senta Green also writes:

...each character, gesture and decorative element can be read and reflected back on the owner of the seal, revealing his or her social rank and even sometimes the name of the owner. Although the same iconography found on seals can be found on carved stelae, terra cotta plaques, wall reliefs, and paintings, its most complete compendium exists on the thousands of seals which have survived from antiquity.

Lewis and Feldman note that the meaning of the seals' imagery related to three areas:

1. Specific families, administrative department, or specific events related to the administration.
2. Different stages of the administrative hierarchy, the object or persons involved in the transaction.
3. The owner or the user of the seal, or details of the transaction—the commodity in question, its source or destination, or a specific event relating to its use.

Even after the invention of cuneiform writing 3,200 BC, the seals remained in popular use. Mesopotamian legal documents translated by the scholar Theophile J. Meek always note how, after the details of the case or transaction are recorded in writing on the clay tablet, the names of the persons involved are signed *each preceded by 'The seal of...'*[cxxxiv]

The cylinder seal, then, remained as significant to its owner after the advent of writing as it had been previously. The symbols which once indicated the name of the owner were now replaced by cuneiform script and, as Bertman writes, additional data might include the name of the owner's father, the owner's title and/or occupation, and the ruler or god he served. So, although the style and details of the seals changed after the invention of writing, the significance of the seals did not. Bertman offers an interesting explanation for this:

The ancients were intimate with something that more and more has come to characterise our lives today: impermanence. In a land where a raging flood could wash away an entire city, the ancient Mesopotamian understood that few things including life itself are guaranteed and secure. Gilgamesh, we remember, held the fragile secret of eternal life in his hand only to see it snatched away. For the people of Mesopotamia then, the stone cylinder seal was the ultimate symbol of permanence in an impermanent world. Perhaps that is why it occupied such an important position in their lives and was worn as a badge of honour.

Pictographs

Pictographs have been seen in many regions and the actual longevity of its use is very debatable. But around 3,500 BC, a fairly extensive pictographic system of signs and numbers appears rather suddenly symbols impressed on clay tablets with a reed stylus, which we know as cuneiform. Originally the early Pictograms were written in small square boxes found in the context of temples. These numerous written tablets were developed initially to record economic transactions: sheep delivered, grain dispersed, workers mobilised. Writing was used as a memory aid. Just as a cylinder seal could give evidence of who was accountable.

A picture of a cow and a bushel of wheat might be used to record what was in the accountable assignment. Two marks next to a cow could indicate two cows were sent. For several hundred years this was the type of writing done. By having a pictograph, the picture transcended all languages. A cow is a cow, in any language…unless it looks like a horse, then your newly appointed scribe better *write* quickly. This new way of tracking numbers and commodities, the administration could now control taxes or contributions to the temple.

Continued to be used primarily as a means of recording and storing economic information. Pictographs became more abstract and no longer easily identifiable as a pure representation of what was described. The markings started to be used became straight lines with wedges at the ends and set at differing angles which could be written far more quickly.

The clay tablet to the side shows the typical mix witnessed in Proto-Cuneiform, the sexagesimal numerical value seen by round holes. The typical compartmentalising of each part of the tablet.

Lexical lists are a long list of words that are placed together to aid the new scribes in teaching. These lexical lists, archaeological sites have found these lists all over Mesopotamia wrote out in exactly the same order so prove that teaching had also been standardised.

The lexical lists also give us a view into the perception of knowledge, the words define the world, the society, and the understanding of the universe. Writing wasn't organised alphabetically or standard order for cuneiform signs. Another advancement towards creating writing as we know today where organised based on sound, words that sounded the same in Sumerian, but had different means but grouped together. Other signs that looked similar were placed together. The third type of list had a conceptual framework, grouping words in categories. Once grouped, this list is almost 10,000 lines long and covers several clay tablets and covered words that would have been frequently used by scribes on a daily basis.

The list included legal and administrative terms, tree, wooden objects, objects made of reeds, clay, items made of clay, types of leather, objects made from these various leathers, metals, domestic animals, wild animals, cuts of meat, stones, plants and vegetables, birds and fish, textiles, geographic terms, food and beverage. The words in the list were Sumerian but the list also gave a translation into another local language, Akkadian.

Akkadian was the main area directly to the North of Sumer, a region called Akkad close to modern Bagdad at the closest point between the Tigris and Euphrates. Akkadian is a Semitic language which is related to Modern day Arabic and Hebrew. Both Sumerian and Akkadian were spoken at the very beginning of writing.

Pictographs showing the wheat. The start of stylised motifs representing other items of commodities using straight lines. But the best part is at the bottom. A cylinder seal mark from the owner, showing a god in a hunt with is dog in the reed beds. This stylised version of pictographs became extremely complicated but did provide additional information concerning a multitude of evidence for a diverse variety of professions. Both productive and administrative, these tablets reveal a society of considerable complexity.

Early Cuneiform, or Proto-Cuneiform also started in individual boxes including early sexagesimal numbering system used. A tablet which contained a phase or a coherent this contained hundreds of signs, and exponential number of values dependent on its context and was extremely complicated.

This new form of writing was not called Cuneiform in Sumeria, the Latin word for a wedge is cuneus meaning wedge and only given the name we all know from Western Civilisation. The wedge was pressed into clay at a prescribed angle in the clay to create the new format of accounting, both materials readily available throughout the entire region.

To compound the complexity of Proto-Cuneiform, the earliest texts lacked grammatical elements, making it impossible to identify the language they represented and often difficult to interpret. The only reason for writing was its ability to track commerce, a form of accounting that didn't require any formality. The format of the actual piece of clay allowed the reader of the text to understand the concept of its contents simply by the shape of the tablet. The type of transaction, just as in modern business, where the form of a document like a memo or receipt or travel voucher identifies its purpose before it is filled in.

The earliest tablets tend to be oval or round rather than rectangular, which is the common shape in later tablets. Most of these tablets can be easily held in the hand and range in size from matchbox to the size of a small blotter. The majority of the people of Mesopotamia, never knew how to write. It was left to the scribes, a new class of people, a further layer of stratification within Uruk's bureaucracy.

Unlike the stamp or cylinder seal which allowed laypeople to use them, scribes were employed to keep accurate records for the people of the city state. This also placed the scribe in a position of power, this is why, very early records also show signs of coding information therefore making the original writer indispensable. By extending the vocabulary during the Proto-Cuneiform phase, it now introduced a multitude of descriptions that weren't previously captured in pictographs.

Logogram

Centuries continued to pass with no requirement for a literary purpose to writing by 3,000 BC the shift from visual to aural occurred. Signs representing the sound of speech. This is the monumental step change in world evolution. For the first time a system that doesn't just involve physical depictions concerning material. The use of speech now expands the use of symbolisation for traded commodities to the description of everything; how you feel, the names of people or cities or the name of a foreign land. Sumerian was mostly a monosyllabic language the logograms lent themselves perfectly for their use.

A syllable is a unit of spoken language consisting of one or more vowel sounds. Signs now represented a word in a particular tongue and no longer looking like a representation of the commodity. Writing was a real breakthrough; it may not have seemed so initially. These first written signs that now represented sound weren't an attempt to write a love song or write to a close friend. All items being moved could be accounted for on lumps of clay the same material used for the cylinder seals.

This wasn't just a memory aid but now you could physically sound out a word that had no pictorial or abbreviated/stylised representation of an object this system introduced a new= way to gather all information rather than just an aid to accounting. The restrictions to the written word had been just been lifted. Using the syllabic Sumerian language people started to use word association method for recording names or places that weren't just fixed commodities. When a name required several phonetic units, they were assembled in a system called Rebus.

Rebus

An ingenious method of solving this problem was using the *Rebus Principle*. An illusional device, somebodies name could be broken up into syllables, each syllable represented by a picture of a *thing* that had that name. So, if your name in English was Barbie, you could draw a picture of a Bar and a Bee. Sumerian language was extremely well suited to write this way, all the words were one syllable in length. For example, an arrow was the word Ti, so if your name had the word Ti in it, you could draw an arrow; Ti also meant Life, so if your name had the word Ti and Life in it, you could draw two arrows.

This principle made it about possible to write every word in Sumerian. So now words had actual sounds as well as signs for whole words. Now writing could be used for writing a list of commodities and who sent them and what was still owed. All transactions could now be fully recorded which helped the urban society of Uruk run even more efficiently. We always seem to revert back to trade for descriptions, but trade really was the lifeblood of Uruk. One of the finest examples of a Rebus style system comes from the Kuwait Gold Disc discovered on Failaka Island.

The Island became extremely strategic due to its location within the Persian Gulf and was also admired by the Sumerians. Failaka was on the trade route through the Arabian Gulf that stretched all the way to the Indus Valley in modern day Pakistan. The example of a Rebus describes a puzzle which words are presented by a combination of pictures as shown in the Kuwait Gold Disc. The gold disc origin is apparently from the Indus Valley region and depicts a *mirrored* scene that includes various domesticated animals, trees, birds, crops, fish, people and even combs. What is even more striking is the representation of the symbols have a double intension.

Using rebus, we can individually verbalise the depicted figures within the Gold Disk and then the merchants can produce their wears of that similar sound and shown to the potential client. By using Data Mining techniques, the meaning of the symbols denotes another meaning due to the word association involved. The most obvious element of the Kuwait Disc is everything are shown in pairs: dula *pair* (Kashmiri); rebus = dul = *cast metal* (Mu.).

Thus, all the depictions on the Gold Disc can be read as Indus writing related to one Bronze-Age artefact category. The Kuwait Gold Disc is from the 3rd Millennium BC. The real purpose of the merchant disc denotes the trade in blacksmithing, copper casting, smithing, alloys, various cast metals, braziers, fireplaces, fire alters, kilns, stone ores and metal iron. The merchant's *gold calling card* showed the desirability that these precious far away products had, and the high value placed on each of the items. The merchant seems to be a one-stop shop for all these products including the transferral of skills which included blacksmithing and also the importing of kilns.

By the merchant willing to sell/transfer these skills to Southern Mesopotamia then new products could be manufactured with Sumer and only then required the cheaper imported raw products. A larger profit margin could be seen by the local merchant if they invested in these imported technologies (and more than likely improved, because that's what the people of Uruk did). A new niche market and a competitive edge over rival local tradesmen could be gained. This was similar to the bead trades that preluded the Bronze Age.

Paper: Maritime Trade of Meluhha (Indus Valley) with Dilmun Kuwait (Failaka Island) Gold Disc with Indus Script[cxxxv]

Al-Sabah collection of Kuwait National Museum. Gold disc of 9.6 cm diameter believed to be from the Indus Valley period in India. Typical of that period, it depicts zebu, bulls, human attendants, ibex, fish, partridges, bees, an animal-headed standard and, best of all, a Pipal tree also known as the Bodhi Tree, as Gautama Siddhartha attained enlightenment under such a tree.

Kuwait Gold Disc (Al-Sabah Collection) with Indus Script Hieroglyphs Data Mining 3rd Millennium BC

1. A pair of tabernae montana flowers tagara *tabernae montana* flower; rebus = tagara *tin*
2. A pair of rams tagara *ram*; rebus = damgar = *merchant* (Akkadian)

    - Next to one ram: kuTi *tree* Rebus = kuThi = *smelter*
    - Alternative: kolmo *rice plant* Rebus = kolimi = *smithy, forge.*

3. Ficus religiosa leaves on a tree branch *loa* ficus leaf; rebus = loh = *metal*. kol in Tamil means pancaloha *alloy of five metals.*

    - Also, a flanking pair of lotus flowers: tAmarasa *lotus*; Rebus = tAmra = *copper.*
    - *dula* pair; Rebus = dul = *cast metal*; therefore denoting copper castings.

4. A pair of bulls tethered to the tree branch: barad, barat *ox*; Rebus = bharata *alloy of copper, pewter, tin* (Marathi)

    - *kola* man Rebus = kolhe *smelter*, *kur.i* woman; Rebus = kol = *working in iron.*
    - *ḍhangar* bull; Rebus = *ḍhangar* = *blacksmith*
    - Two persons touch the two bulls: *med* body (Mu.) Rebus = med = *iron* (Ho.) Therefore, the hieroglyph composition denotes ironsmiths.

5. A pair of antelopes looking back: *krammara* look back; Rebus = kamar = *smith*.
6. A pair of antelopes *mḗḍh* antelope, ram; Rebus: *mḗḍ 'iron' (Mu.)*
7. A pair of combs *kāṅga* comb; Rebus = kanga = *brazier, fireplace*
8. A pair of fishes *ayo* fish (Mu.); Rebus = ayo = *metal, iron* (Gujarati); ayas *metal* (Sanskrit)
9. A pair of buffaloes tethered to a post-standard *kāṛā* buffalo கண்டி kanṭi buffalo bull (Tamil); Rebus = kaṇḍ = *stone ore*; kāṇḍa = *tools, pots and pans and metal-ware*; kaṇḍ = *furnace, fire-altar, consecrated fire.*
10. A pair of birds

- Rebus 1 = kōḍi. [Tel.] = *A fowl, a bird.* (Telugu) Rebus = khōṭ = *alloyed ingots.*
- Rebus 2 = kol = *the name of a bird, the Indian cuckoo* (Santali) kol 'iron, smithy, forge'. Rebus 3 = baṭa = *quail* (Santali) Rebus = baṭa = *furnace, kiln* (Santali) bhrāṣṭra = *furnace* (Skt.) baṭa = *a kind of iron* (G.) bhaṭa = *furnace* (Gujarati)

11. The buffaloes, birds flank a post-standard with curved horns on top of a stylised 'eye' PLUS 'eyebrows' with one horn on either side of two faces.

Standardising Cuneiform

By 2,600 BC Sumerian script was becoming increasing complex and difficult to master. It quickly became self-evident that the early forms of writing needed to be consistent to enable this new invention to be used more accurately adopted, Sumerian script mixed Logograms and Phonetic signs which aided writing into a spoken language. The vocabulary needed to be *standardised* and reduced to prevent miss communication. Who better to maximise the potential of writing far beyond its original intensions, the people of Uruk were ready to *Standardise*?

At some point, a person unknown to modern day scholars realised that writing had to become more consistent. Each scholar could not depict a cow in several different formats. It's in Sumerians DNA to make everything more efficient and the same was for writing. At a specific point in time a conscious effort was made to streamline the writing system. Removing many signs and standardising the remaining and over just a couple of generations writing did become consistent.

The best analogy would be the early video recorder, many versions entered the marketplace, looking a gaining dominance. Many versions fell by the wayside quickly, leaving Betamax and VHS to slog it out. With VHS becoming the victors—*the people had voted with their money*—Cuneiform could be read as a syllable or an entire word called a Logogram, using syntax and an abbreviated and standardised set of phonetic signs.

Cuneiform Script 2,500 BC

The world becomes written history with kingship poised to take full advantage the script that originated with humble accounting beginnings within Uruk. But now advanced and durable it could be transferred to other civilisations throughout the world. It became the building block for a number of languages, including Akkadian in Mesopotamia and the Indo-European language known as Hittite in Turkey. Akkadian cuneiform became the diplomatic lingua franca in the mid-second Millennium BC where it was used as far away as Egypt.

It would seem that a lot of forethought went into the creation of writing, if something is robust it stands the test of time and the format created early on, does exactly that. The first written laws, the first written poetry, the written jokes, the first letter to a neighbouring King sent by a messenger, the first written treaty all originally written in Sumerian and Akkadian language all in the newly adopted style of cuneiform writing. At the time nobody could have envisaged the impact the language would have had on the entire world.

As Uruk was the world's first fully urban society. Mesopotamia was open on all sides to its neighbours and traded far and wide and its influence can be traced from India to Greece. The Pharaoh's scribes used cuneiform script to correspond with the Great Kings of the Hittites in Turkey, at Ugarit on the Syrian coast the forerunners of the Phoenicians kept their legal and commercial records on cuneiform tablets. In Babylonian, and later the Biblical and Classical worlds grew up in the shadow of these ancient cultures to the east (and sometimes under their direct political domination).

The scribe will have had to memorize the signs, but also the spelling of words to accurately record the information. This will have included administrative, temple or even engineering terminology used and needed to be good at mathematics to do the necessary accounting correct for any of the specialized *white collar* newly created offices. Dividing up estates, the area of land allocated to a specific person, quota of canal water to be used for crops, how much labour required for canal repairs, or new construction work.

The writing material became an art form, ensuring the writing clay didn't have any impurities that could disturb the fine accurate writing required, ensuring that the reeds have a sufficient sharp edge. Also deciding how big the clay tablet should be to complete the necessary work required. A form of apprenticeship was created to teach these potential scribes, so schools where created but extremely strict in its training with regular beatings for not following instructions correctly, but a lot better than working the fields or digging canals. This also started to become a generational occupation that started to be passed down through families.

Archaeologists have discovered that a shared curriculum in schools stretched from today's Modern Syria to the Persian Gulf, over 2,500 Km, all the wedge-shaped characters in writing or calculations being standardised. So, we now have at this point in time, Standard Measurements, Standard Weights, Standard Payments and now Standard Writing throughout the entire Fertile Crescent. This meant that all people could now communicate via cuneiform tablet messenger without the need for a messenger to recite information in person.

The Sumerians first developed cuneiform for the mundane purposes of keeping accounts and records of business transactions. But over time it blossomed into a full-fledged writing system used for everything from poetry and history to law codes and literature. Since the script could be adapted to multiple languages, it was transformed from its original format over the course of several millennia by more than a dozen different cultures. Archaeologists have found evidence that Near East astronomical texts were still being written in cuneiform as recently as the first century A.D.

The Sumerian language is the oldest linguistic record but was mostly replaced by Akkadian around 2,004 BC but held on as a written language in cuneiform for another 2,000 years. Writing remains one of the most important cultural achievements of the Sumerians, allowing for meticulous record keeping from rulers down to farmers and ranchers. The oldest written laws date back to 2,400 BC. in the city of Ebla, where the Code of Er-Nammu was written on tablets. The Sumerians were considered to have a rich body of literary works, though only fragments of these documents exist. As with the wheel, cities and law codes, the earliest examples of written literature appear to have aided developments that we, today, take for granted.

Sumerian scribes were also copying down essays, hymns, poetry and myths. Two of their oldest known literary works are the *Kesh Temple Hymn* and the *Instructions of Shuruppak*, both of which exist in written versions dating to around 2,500 BC, right at the very dawn of writing as we know it. The former is an ancient ode to the Kesh temple and the deities that inhabited it, while the latter is a piece of *wisdom literature* that takes the form of sagely advice supposedly handed down from the Sumerian King Shuruppak to his son, Ziusudra.

One of Shuruppak's proverbs warns the boy *not to pass judgment when you drink beer*. Another counsels that *a loving heart maintains a family; a hateful heart destroys a family*. Shuruppak's fatherly wisdom is one of the most ancient examples of written literature. At no point in history at that time had the people been able to successfully control the land and build such vast structure, creating new types of work away from just farming and to grow wealthy at the same time. Led by priest rulers and organised by scribes using writing to keep the administration running smoothly.

Assyrian and Babylonian are Members of the Semitic Language Family

Like Arabic and Hebrew. Because Babylonian and Assyrian are so similar at least in writing, they are often regarded as varieties of a single language, today known as Akkadian. How far they were mutually intelligible in ancient times is uncertain. During the 2nd Millennium BC Babylonian was adopted all over the Middle East as the language of scholarship, administration, commerce, and diplomacy. Later in the 1st Millennium BC it was gradually replaced by Aramaic, which is still spoken in some parts of the Middle East today.

Babylonian was deciphered in the mid nineteenth century. As there was controversy over whether the decipherment had been achieved or not. In 1857 AD the Royal Asiatic Society sent drawings of the same inscription to four different scholars, who were to translate without consulting one another. A committee (including no less than the Dean of St Paul's Cathedral) was set up to compare the translations. The committee's report is still fascinating read even after over 160 years.

Deciphering the Lost Writing of Cuneiform

Prior to the discovery and decipherment of cuneiform script, human beings understood the origins of certain aspects of life in quite a different way. Writing was thought to have originated in Phoenicia, time-telling in China, schools in Greece, and the first love song in the biblical book of The Song of Solomon. The Old Testament of the Bible was considered the oldest book in the world until this was disproven by the German Assyriologist Friedrich Delitzsch 1850-1922 AD, building upon the work of men like George Smith.

The subject which studies Mesopotamian languages and the sources written in them are called Assyriology. Friedrich showed that the Sumerians had written stories concerning a fall of man and a great flood before the narratives of Genesis were ever set down. The scholar Paul Kriwaczek writes:

Thus, it was established that long before Genesis was committed to writing, the ancient Mesopotamians had themselves told the story of a universal flood sent by divine decree to destroy humanity. Soon other texts were discovered that gave similar accounts in several different languages Sumerian, Old Akkadian, Babylonian and in several different versions. In the oldest, found on a tablet from the city of Nippur, dated to around 1800 BC and written in Sumerian, Noah's role is taken by a King of Shuruppak called Ziusudra or Ziusudra, meaning "the Saw Life", because he was awarded immortality by the gods. In another, written in the 1600s BCE in the Akkadian language, the protagonist is called Atrahasis, meaning Extremely Wise.

Finally deciphered by Henry Rawlinson and other scholars in the 1850s. Being incredibly durable, clay tablets have been recovered in 10's of thousands at archaeological sites from the Mediterranean to Bahrain to Iran. More are found by the year. As well as records of daily life and administration, they include religious, mathematical, musical, and astronomical texts, the earliest known laws, and a rich literature that includes the Epic of Gilgamesh and the oldest versions of the Flood Story also known from the Bible.

History Revealed Due to Cuneiform

Once Cuneiform had eventually been deciphered, further treasures were unveiled to Western Societies. The most fortunate result for people today is that the ancient people of the Middle East loved to write. Therefore, a plethora of cuneiform clay tablets have survived the ravages of time and allowed historians to gaze with full insight into various matters of state. The bare bones of political history can be fleshed out with deep insights into the social, economic, and religious conditions including the scientific and literary traditions.

We can also see what common people of the day thought of the King, not all descriptions were subservient echoing today's sentiments. From the wealth of cuneiform documents which survive from public and private libraries and archives. We have the personal correspondence received or dictated by figures such as Hammurabi of Babylon or Sargon of Assyria. Every day legal and commercial transactions which allow us to approach the reality behind the propaganda the Kings have left us and see into the lives of farmers and merchants and what the people thought of their Kings and officials.

The scribal classes have left us the original record of their astronomical and mathematical expertise, and the handbooks of diviners and exorcists give us an insight into those branches of contemporary science. In a very real sense, ancient Mesopotamia is a long first chapter in the history of the Western World.

Conclusion

The Sumerians, therefore, can also be credited with the earliest form of one of the most potent myths of western civilisation: The Great Flood. In attempting to prove the historical truth of the Bible, the archaeologists and scholars of the 19th Century AD revealed that the biblical narratives held as absolute divine truths were later interpretations of the literature of the Sumerians.

As noted, however, it is not simply in the field of religious studies that the discovery of Sumer changed the way people understand the world in the present. In their many inventions and innovations, the Sumerians laid the groundwork for so many advancements in the daily lives of human beings that, today, it is impossible to imagine life without these things. Somehow, the people of Sumer were able to imagine things which had never existed on earth before and, in expressing their imaginations, invented the future.

Uruk Art and Architecture

As previously discussed, some of the very first buildings had been standardised, the look, the size, the measurements all following the same criteria. Where the main difference lay, was the physical temples of the gods. The gods lived in the city, so the people paid special attention and gave special praise to their local gods. If they looked after their gods, surely their gods would aware them special attention. Uruk architecture on a grand scale is generally credited to have begun with religious structures dating back to 3,400 BC, although it appears that the basics of the structures began in the Ubaid period as far back as 5,200 BC and were improved upon through the centuries. Homes were made from mud bricks or bundled marsh reeds. The buildings are noted for their arched doorways and flat roofs.

Elaborate construction, such as terra cotta ornamentation with bronze accents, complicated mosaics, imposing brick columns and sophisticated mural paintings all reveal the society's technical sophistication. Sculpture was used mainly to adorn temples and offer some of the earliest examples of human artists seeking to achieve some form of naturalism in their figures. Facing a scarcity of stone, Sumerians made leaps in metal-casting for their sculpture work, though relief carving in stone was a popular art form.

One of the biggest failing of the Sumerians was their love of precious metals and expensive stones. They decorated the status with items, made the status out of bronze, coated relief work in thick lapis lazuli. When these city states finally deteriorated and overran, invariably this is what happens to all cities throughout the world, the victors would cart away anything of any value and reconstitute the metal and stones into some other item. The very lack of statues and items is testament to this. The only thing that does survive is *Stone*, large and awkward to move stone statues.

A perfect example is Hammurabi's Stele concerning his laws. If his code were caste onto bronze, nobody today would be any the wiser to what had been wrote. So unfortunately, archaeologists now have to *strike it lucky* to find anything of any worth. Fortunately, archaeologists know where to go to first, for any prize possessions we have become modern day grave robbers, the best artefacts are those that are buried with an individual and they can reveal so much about the status of a person.

Under the Akkadian dynasty, sculpture reached new heights, as evidenced by intricate and stylized work in diorite dated to 2,100 BC. Ziggurats began to appear around 2,200 BC. These impressive pyramid-like, stepped temples, which were either square or rectangular. The Ziggurats featured no inner chambers, these really were solid earth filled platforms and stood about 170 feet high. Ziggurats often featured sloping sides and terraces with gardens. Once the people had moved away and the weather invariably worked its magic, the earth overtime simply oozed out, creating the blob we see today. The Hanging Gardens of Babylon was one of these. When the Kings finally came to prominence Palaces also reach a new level of grandiosity. In Mari around 1,779 BC, an ambitious 200-room palace was constructed.

Sumerian Science

Sumerians had a system of medicine that was based in magic and herbalism, but they were also familiar with processes of removing chemical parts from natural substances. Gold plating, arsenic bronzing the people of Uruk understood the art of alchemy. They are considered to have had an advanced knowledge of anatomy, and surgical instruments have been found in archaeological sites.

One of the Sumerians greatest advances was in the area of hydraulic engineering, the full extent is still not known today, but eventually we will know. Early in their history they created a system of ditches to control flooding, and were also the inventors of irrigation, harnessing the power of the Tigris and Euphrates for farming. Canals and settling ponds were consistently maintained from dynasty to dynasty. Their skill at engineering and architecture both point to the sophistication of their understanding of math.

At some point, more of the Sumerians knowledge will be unlocked to modern society that will allow us a further, deeper understanding of the Sumerians. The origins of the sixty-second minute and sixty-minute hour can be traced all the way back to ancient Sumerians. In the same way that modern mathematics is a decimal system based on the number ten, the Sumerians mainly used a sexagesimal structure that was based around groupings of 60.

It is believed that the origin of 60 came the counting of the 3 divisions on each finger with the thumb as the counter, once twelve (12) had been counted one finger was raised on the opposite hand, thus the maximum number counted was 60. This easily divisible number system was later adopted by the ancient Babylonians, who used it make astronomical calculations on the lengths of the months and the year. Base-60 eventually fell out of use, but its legacy still lives on in the measurements of both hour and the minute. Other remnants of the Sumerian sexagesimal system have survived in the form of spatial measurements such as the 360 degrees in a circle and the 12 inches in a foot. The structure of modern time keeping, with sixty seconds in a minute and sixty minutes in an hour, is attributed to the Sumerians.

Sumerian Culture

Schools were common in Sumerian culture, marking the world's first mass effort to pass along knowledge in order to keep a society running and building on itself.

Sumerians left behind scores of written records, but they are more renowned for their epic poetry, which influenced later works in Greece and Rome and sections of the Bible. Most notably the story of the Great Flood, the Garden of Eden, and the Tower of Babel. Stories laced with a heavy truth and it's up to historians and archaeologists to unpick the fact from fiction. Are the people of the Persian Gulf siting at the site of Eden, just a few shallow metres under the sea, could the discovery of people be living harmoniously before the land of Sumer change people's opinions.

The Sumerians were musically inclined and a Sumerian hymn, *Hurrian Hymn No. 6,* is considered the world's oldest musically notated song. Along with inventing writing, the wheel, the plough, law codes and literature. The Sumerians are also remembered as some of history's original brewers. Archaeologists have found evidence of Mesopotamian beer-making dating back at least to 4th Millennium BC. The brewing techniques they used are still a mystery, but their preferred ale seems to have been a barley-based concoction so thick that it was sipped through a special kind of filtration straw.

The Sumerians prized their beer for its nutrient-rich ingredients and hailed it as the key to a *joyful heart and a contented liver*. There was even a Sumerian goddess of brewing called *Ninkasi* who is celebrated in a famous hymn as the *one who waters the malt set on the ground.*

Uruk City, Districts and Gods [cxxxvi]

Uruk had two major temple precincts with a temple at each with surrounding courtyards and buildings. One was dedicated to the Goddess Inanna, goddess of love; the other was dedicated to Anu, the God of the Heavens. The amount of people called upon to build these temples must have been enormous, some people have suggested that the temples must have took 100 years to build and immediately rebuilt to ensure the population was kept in gainful employment. The buildings were designed to impress, similar to cathedrals in the middle ages. The temple was constructed of stone and extremely rare in this barren land. The other temple had an eye dazzling mosaic of coloured geometrical patterns, these were made of clay cones pressed into the side, then highly polished.

The city was divided into two sections, the Eanna District, and the older Anu District, named for, and dedicated to, the goddess Inanna and her Grandfather-God Anu, respectively. The famous Mask of Warka (also known as *The Lady of Uruk*) a sculpted marble female face found at Uruk, is considered a likeness of

Inanna and was most likely part of a larger work from one of the temples in her district.

The Eanna District was walled off from the rest of the city, but it is unclear if this was for ceremonial purposes or if, in building the newer Eanna District, the builders required a wall for some reason. The historian Samuel Noah Kramer suggests that Anu, the male god, presided over the early city until the rise in popularity of his daughter Inanna and, at this time, she was given a private dwelling, complete with a wall, in the Eanna District.

Since temples were considered the literal dwelling place of deities on earth, and since Inanna is regularly depicted as a goddess who very much preferred things her own way. Perhaps the walled district was simply to provide her with some privacy. Kramer also notes that, even though Inanna continued to be a popular deity throughout Mesopotamia (eventually merging into Ishtar) goddesses declined in power and prestige at the same time, and at the same rate, as women's rights deteriorated.

This being the case, perhaps the Eanna district was walled off to restrict access to a male priestly class. As with much concerning Uruk's history, however, this theory remains largely speculation. Inanna played a pivotal role in the mythological history of Uruk as it was, she who stole the sacred meh from her father-god Enki at the sacred city of Eridu and brought them to Uruk. The Meh were, in the words of Kramer[cxxxvii] (who first translated the cuneiform) *divine decrees which are the basis of the culture pattern of Sumerian civilisation.* As Eridu was considered, by the Sumerians, the first city created by the gods and a place holy to them, the removal of the meh to Uruk signified a transference of power and prestige from one city to the other.

In the tale of Inanna and The God of Wisdom, Enki god goes to great lengths, once he finds the meh are stolen, to have them brought back to Eridu but in vain. Inanna has tricked her father and now Uruk, not Eridu, would be the seat of power. Eridu was associated with rural life and the primordial sea from which life sprang; Uruk was the embodiment of the new way of life the city. The story would have provided an ancient Mesopotamian with the reason why Eridu declined in importance and Uruk rose to the heights it did: it was the work of the gods.

Uruk could also be credited as the city which first recognised the importance of the individual in the collective community. The city was continuously inhabited from its founding until the rise of the Muslim Empire when, owing to both natural and man-made influences, people began to desert the area. It lay abandoned, buried and forgotten until excavated in 1853 AD by William Loftus for the British Museum.

Uruk: Facade of Inanna's Temple

Anu District[cxxxviii]

The great Anu district is older than the Eanna district; however, few remains of writing have been found here. Unlike the Eanna district, the Anu district consists of a single massive terrace, the Anu Ziggurat, dedicated to the Sumerian sky god An. Sometime in the Uruk III period the massive White Temple was built atop of the ziggurat. Under the northwest edge of the ziggurat an Uruk VI period structure, the Stone Temple, has been discovered.

The Stone Temple was built of limestone and bitumen on a podium of rammed earth and plastered with lime mortar. The podium itself was built over a woven reed mat called *giparu*, a word which originally referred a reed mat used ritually as a nuptial bed but took on the meaning as the source of abundance which radiated upward into the structure. The structure of the Stone Temple further develops some mythological concepts from Enuma Elish, perhaps involving libation rites as indicated from the channels, tanks, and vessels found there.

The structure was ritually destroyed, covered with alternating layers of clay and stone, then excavated and filled with mortar sometime later. A bathing pond was located at the front, capturing the *sweet* heaven water and some sort of ritual perform with that. Similar to modern day baptism. Could the ritual have it roots back through the ages to Sumeria?

The Anu Ziggurat began with a massive mound topped by a cellar during the Uruk period 4,000 BC and was expanded through 14 phases of construction. These phases have been labelled **L** to **A₃** (**L** is sometimes called **X**). The earliest phase used architectural features similar to PPNA cultures in Anatolia: a single chamber cellar with a terrazzo (bonded with quartz chippings, and polished to a high finish) floor beneath which classical ox head carvings were found. In phase E, corresponding to the Uruk III period 3,000 BC, the White Temple was built.

The White Temple could be seen from a great distance across the plain of Sumer, as it was elevated 21m and covered in gypsum plaster which seems to be a very Gulf Oasis by product, that was later seen in Jericho and the Taurus Mountains which reflected sunlight like a mirror. For this reason, it is believed the White Temple is a symbol of Uruk's political power at the time. In addition to this temple the Anu Ziggurat had a monumental limestone-paved staircase, which was used in religious processions. A trough running parallel to the staircase was used to drain the ziggurat.

Eanna District[cxxxix]

The Eanna district is historically significant as both writing and monumental public architecture emerged here during Uruk periods VI-IV. The combination of these two developments places Eanna as arguably the first true city and civilisation in human history. Eanna during period IVa contains the earliest examples of cuneiform writing and possibly the earliest writing in history. Although some of these cuneiform tablets have been deciphered, difficulty with site excavations has obscured the purpose and sometimes even the structure of many buildings. The first building of Eanna, Stone-Cone Temple (Mosaic Temple), was built in period VI over a pre-existing Ubaid temple and is enclosed by a limestone wall.

This would have been imported from the Zagros Mountains at great cost to the Temple. With an elaborate system of standardised buttresses. The Stone-Cone Temple, named for the mosaic of coloured stone cones driven into the adobe brick (mud Brick) façade, may be the earliest water cult in Mesopotamia. It was ritually demolished in Uruk IVb period and its contents interred in the Riemchen Building. In the following period, Uruk V, about 100 m east of the Stone-Cone Temple the Limestone Temple was built on a 2 m high rammed-earth podium over a pre-existing Ubaid temple. Similarly, the Stone-Cone Temple represents a continuation of Ubaid culture.

However, the Limestone Temple was unprecedented for its size and use of stone, a clear departure from traditional Ubaid architecture. The stone was quarried from an outcrop at Umayyad about 60 km east of Uruk. It is unclear if the entire temple or just the foundation was built of this limestone. The Limestone temple is probably the first Inanna temple, but it is impossible to know with certainty. Like the Stone-Cone temple the Limestone temple was also covered in cone mosaics. Both of these temples were rectangles with their corners aligned to the cardinal directions, a central hall flanked along the long axis flanked by two smaller halls, and buttressed façades: the prototype of all future Mesopotamian temple architectural typology.

Between these two monumental structures, a complex of buildings (called A-C, E-K, Riemchen, Cone-Mosaic), courts and walls was built during Eanna IVb. These buildings were built during a time of great expansion in Uruk as the city grew to 250 hectares and established long-distance trade and are a continuation of architecture from the previous period. The Riemchen Building, named for the 16×16 cm brick shape called Riemchen by the Germans, is a memorial with a ritual fire kept burning in the centre for the Stone-Cone Temple after it was destroyed for this reason, Uruk IV period represents a reorientation of belief and culture.

The facade of this memorial may have been covered in geometric and figural murals. The Riemchen bricks first used in this temple were used to construct all buildings of Uruk IV period Eanna. The use of coloured cones as a façade treatment was greatly developed as well, perhaps used to greatest effect in the Cone-Mosaic Temple.

When the cone was highly polished, the distinctive red cone mosaic would have been seen for many miles. The Temple composed of three parts: Temple N, the Round Pillar Hall, and the Cone-Mosaic Courtyard, this temple was the most monumental structure of Eanna at the time. They were all ritually destroyed, and the entire Eanna district was rebuilt in period IVa at an even grander scale.

During Eanna IVa, the Limestone Temple was demolished, and the Red Temple built on its foundations. The accumulated debris of the Uruk IVb buildings was formed into a terrace, the L-Shaped Terrace, on which Buildings C, D, M, Great Hall, and Pillar Hall were built. Building E was initially thought to be a palace, but later proven to be a communal building. Also, in period IV, the Great Court, a sunken courtyard surrounded by two tiers of benches covered in cone mosaic, was built.

A small aqueduct drains into the Great Courtyard, which may have irrigated a garden at one time. The impressive buildings of this period were built as Uruk reached its zenith and expanded to 600 hectares. All the buildings of Eanna IVa were destroyed sometime in Uruk III, for unknown reasons. The architecture of Eanna in period III was very different from what had preceded it. The complex of monumental temples was replaced with baths around the Great Courtyard and the labyrinthine Rammed-Earth Building.

This period corresponds to Early Dynastic Sumer 2,900 BC. A time of great social upheaval when the dominance of Uruk was eclipsed by competing city states. The fortress like architecture of this time reflects that turmoil. The temple of Inanna continued functioning during this time in a new form and under a new name, *The House of Inanna in Uruk* The location of this structure is currently unknown.

Uruk's Importance and Long Decline

Mesopotamian history is the first chapter in the history of the Western World. Uruk went through several phases of growth, from the Early Uruk period 4,000-3,500 BC to the Late Uruk period 3,500-3,100 BC. The city was formed when two smaller Ubaid settlements merged. This isn't as strange as first thought, quite a regular sight witnessing a single Sumerian city state being either side of a River or Estuary. The temple complexes at their cores became the Eanna District and the Anu District dedicated to Inanna and Anu, respectively.

The Anu District was originally called *Kullaba* (Kulab or Unug-Kulaba) prior to merging with the Eanna District. Archaeologist have been able to date the Kullaba to the Eridu period when it was one of the oldest and most important cities of Sumer. The rest of the city was composed of typical courtyard houses, grouped by profession of the occupants, in districts around Eanna and Anu. Uruk was extremely well penetrated by a Canal system that has been described as the *Venice of the Desert*.

This canal system flowed throughout the city connecting it with the maritime trade on the ancient Euphrates River as well as the surrounding agricultural belt. After the first flourishing of urban culture, associated particularly with the spectacular temple architecture and the earliest written archives excavated at Uruk. It is obvious to the reader, no other place in the world could possibly compete with Uruk and its surrounding city states in Sumer.

Sumer could only be hurt from within, and Sumer seemed to be very good at hurting herself. On a very regular basis, for a very long time. Early Dynastic period saw rival city states vying for control of the irrigated land of South Mesopotamia and extending their economic and cultural influences to neighbouring lands. The dynasty founded by Sargon of Akkad and the Third Dynasty of Ur each united the region under one ruler for a Century or more, and later all the South fell under the control of Hammurabi of Babylon, an achievement he celebrated by promulgating his laws and inscribing them on his famous Stele (now in the Louvre).

Even after turmoil and unrest, the wilting Uruk during the Early Dynastic Period 2,900-2,334 BC, which followed the Uruk Period. Was still the seat of power in the region, though in a much-diminished state, and the major dynasties of the time ruled from the city. People knew of its great power and still carried respect for the city, even though its heyday had long passed. The Great Wall of Uruk, which was said to have been built by King Gilgamesh himself. The Wall rose as an awesome memory of defiance around the city when King Eannatum forged his First Dynasty of Lagash in 2,500 BC and established the first empire in the region.

The later King of that empire, Lugal-Zage (also known as Lugalzagesi) so admired the city that he chose Uruk as his capital and seat of power. Who wouldn't want to have the seat of an Empire in strong-walled Uruk? When Sumer was brought under the rule of the Akkadian Empire in 2,334 BC, Sargon of Akkad continued to pay special reverence to Uruk and the sacred districts of Inanna and Anu continued in use and, in fact, were renovated and improved upon. Although it had been a thriving city in Early Dynastic Sumer, especially Early Dynastic II, Uruk was ultimately annexed to the Akkadian and went into decline, its slide had started, but the Great city of Uruk doesn't fade away that quickly.

Even though the city lost the position of pre-eminence it had enjoyed during the Uruk Period, it continued to play an important position down through the Ur III Period 2,047-1,750 BC. The Third Dynasty of Ur governed in such a way as to give birth to a Sumerian Renaissance and Uruk benefited from this as much as the rest of the region. Later, in the Neo-Sumerian period, Uruk enjoyed revival as a major economic and cultural centre under the sovereignty of Ur. The Eanna District was restored as part of an ambitious building program, which included a new temple for Inanna.

This temple included a Ziggurat, the *House of the Universe* to the Northeast of the Uruk period Eanna ruins. The ziggurat is also cited as Ur-Nammu Ziggurat for its builder Ur-Nammu. With the fall of the city of Ur in 1,750 BC and the invasion of Sumer by Elamites, along with the incursions of the Amorites, Following the collapse of Ur 2,004 BCE, Uruk went into a steep decline along with the rest of Sumer.

In 850 BC, when the Neo-Assyrian Empire annexed Uruk as a provincial capital under the Neo-Assyrians and Neo-Babylonians, Uruk regained much of its former glory. By 250 BC, a new temple complexes the *Head Temple* (Akkadian: *Bīt Reš*) was added to northeast of the Uruk period Anu district. The *Bīt Reš* along with the Esagila was one of the two main centres of Neo-Babylonian astronomy. All of the temples and canals were restored again under Nabopolassar.

During this era, Uruk was divided into five main districts: the Adad Temple, Royal Orchard, Ištar Gate, Lugalirra Temple, and Samas Gate districts. Uruk, continued to thrive under the Seleucid Empire. During this period, Uruk was a city of 300 hectares and perhaps 40,000 inhabitants. In 200 BC, the *Great Sanctuary* of Ishtar was added between the Anu and Eanna districts. The Ziggurat of the temple of Anu, which was rebuilt in this period, was the largest ever built in Mesopotamia.

The city continued to play a significant role. When the Seleucids lost Mesopotamia to the Parthians in 141 BC. Uruk again entered a period of decline from which it never recovered. Throughout the Seleucid and Parthian periods of Sumer's late history other Sumerian cities fared far less well at this same time. The sacred districts continued to be maintained, though to lesser degrees, into the 7th Century AD, long past the time when many other Mesopotamian cities had been abandoned. The decline of Uruk may have been in part caused by a shift in the Euphrates River. By 300 AD, Uruk was mostly abandoned, and by 700 AD it had become completely abandoned. The historian Bertman writes:

Uruk had a life-span of 5,000 years. Its oldest layers lie virtually unexplored, submerged deep in the mud of the alluvial plain from which its life once sprouted.

Perhaps buried in the ancient ruins is the answer to why the first city in the world rose as it did, where it did, and remained so important to the people of Mesopotamia for so long. Unlike other cities throughout the region, it was not abandoned until the Muslim Conquest of Mesopotamia in 630 AD.

The answer to the mystery of Uruk's prominence, however, may be simpler than it appears. The historian Paul Kriwaczek has noted that any important change in a society spring from:

...the everlasting conflict between progressives and conservatives, between the forward and backward looking, between those who propose let's do something new and those who think "the old ways are best". No great shift in culture ever took place without such a contest.

Perhaps the story of Inanna and Enki and the shift of power from Eridu to Uruk told of this very contest and showed how the old ways of rural life. Exemplified in the ancient site of Eridu, gave way to the rise of the city and a new kind of community. It had to happen somewhere, once the process of urbanisation began, and the place where it happened was at Uruk.

The Rise of the King, Smoke and Mirrors: The Sumerian King List

As a reader, we have completed most of the book but only now are we discussing the birth of Kingship. From the Gulf Oasis starting to flood right up to 2,900 BC, no Kings existed, but now the creation of Kings changes the dynamics of regional power forever. One of the greatest sources of information on ancient Mesopotamia is the so-called *King List* a clay tablet that documents the names of most of the ancient rulers of Sumer as well as the lengths of their reigns. This list was composed at a time when writing had finally become the information highway of its day.

If you could write history, you could distort history and unfortunately, the *King List* does exactly that. More than anyone else of the day the new ruling class fully understood the importance of writing. By rewriting the history of the Kings, then it was a form of legitimising their rule. To add a layer of stratification to Sumerian bureaucracy, is understandable, but to add a level equal to the Priest Class, is extremely strange, was the priest class overworked and needed help? It would seem strange for the priests to allow this senior level to come into being. Did the people push for a Lugal, a big man, a King?

The list is a strange blend of historical fact and myth one early King is said to have lived for 43,200 years. Utu-Hegal it is thought was trying to link himself to such earlier hero Kings through the creation of the King List. Since the Mesopotamians believed that the gods had set everything in motion and that human beings created as co-labourers with the gods to maintain order and hold back chaos the earlier writers of history in the region concentrated more on links between the rulers and their gods.

The first King on the list, ruler of Sumer whose deeds are recorded if only in the briefest kind of statement is a King by the name of Etana of Kish who may have come to the throne quite early in the 3rd Millennium BC in the King list he is described as he who stabilised all the lands. He is considered historical and best known from The Myth of Etana, a work belonging to the genre of Mesopotamian Naru Literature in which Etana flies to heaven on the back of an eagle to win what he desires most from the gods. We now have a *historical* list of Kings, we have stories that connect the gods with the earliest Kings and the Kings usually have some sort of superhuman power.

It would seem that the early Kings seem to have been in overdrive in creating a *legitimate* lineage to prove to the people their worth to the city states. Our own destinies are not known from birth unless you are born into Kingship, once born into that environment the eyes of the population are always upon the future ruler. Kings of Mesopotamia had within their power to be able to do anything that they wanted without retribution.

The perfect example would be in the early part of the Epic of Gilgamesh when he terrorised the people of Uruk. The need for an heir to a throne provided a city state continuity and hope that the future ruler may serve the people well, even if their previous ruler may have been a tyrant. This was true ever since Kingship was invented. It seems quite difficult to understand how one person was allowed to rule over 10's of thousands of people and to decide their future, be it good or bad and to allow their son to be given automatic rights over the people without proving themselves.

The Sumerians King List is a Cuneiform document written by a scribe of the city state of Lagash sometime around 2,100 BC. It lists all the Kings of the region and their accomplishments in an attempt to show continuity of order in society dating back to the beginning of civilisation. Mesopotamians generally, and the Sumerians specifically believed that civilisation was the result of the gods triumph of order over chaos the King list is thought to been created to legitimise the reign of a King named Utu-Hegal of Uruk 2,100 BC by showing him as the most famous from the myth of the man who ascends to heaven on the back of an Eagle. Like other Kings mentioned in the list Gilgamesh among them was known for superhuman feats of heroism.

The list of Sumerian rulers includes one woman. In 2,500 BC, the only woman to rule the Sumerians, Kubaba, took the throne. She is the only female listed on the Sumerian King List, which names all rulers of Sumer and their accomplishments. Sumer's lone female monarch Kubaba a *woman tavern-keeper*, who supposedly took the throne in the city state of Kish sometime around 2500 BC.

Very little is known about Kubaba's reign or how she came to power. But the list credits her with making *firm the foundations of Kish* and forging a dynasty that lasted 100 years. Kubaba's son, Puzur-Suen, eventually reigned, bringing in the fourth dynasty of Kish, following a brief ascendency of Unzi, the first in the Akshak Dynasty.

The Sumerian King List notes that the Kingship passed from Eridu to other cities and the list was composed to create an unbroken line between the present Kingship and the illustrious past going all the way back to Eridu. The dates of most of these Kings are doubtful and their length of reign is impossible, but it is clear that the cities of Mesopotamia developed steadily from the foundation of Eridu 5,400 BC throughout Early Dynastic I. To be able to recite the Kings that belonged to a given city state and a very specific time, something of the History of the Region must have been known.

The Instructions of Shuruppak are attributed to the ruler of Shuruppak, the last King of Sumer to have reigned before the time of the Great Flood. (the Flood of 2,800 BC was localised and not the entire region) The father of this King was Ubara-Tutu, whose name is recorded in most copies of the Sumerian King List and is reputed to have lived for 18,500 years before Mesopotamia was struck by the Great Flood. Ziusudra is perhaps best known for being a character in the Epic of Gilgamesh. The name of this King means 'found long life', and, according to the records, he reigned as both King and priest for 36000 years. In one recension of the Sumerian King List, Ziusudra, instead of Shuruppak, is recorded as being the last King before the flood.

Without relying on the Sumerian King List, we are able find out via written records, who the first King was. The first King of a united Sumer is recorded as Etana of Kish. It's unknown whether Etana really existed, as he and many of the rulers listed in the Sumerian King List that was developed around 2,100 BC. Are all featured in Sumerian mythology as well. Etana was followed by Meskiaggasher, the King of the city state Uruk. Uruk is always going to be at the forefront of any dynastic movement. A warrior named Lugalbanda took control around 2,750 BC.

The first Kings ruled in Mesopotamia or Egypt, it's difficult to decide as both areas which were totally independent of each other decided on a course of a new level of stratification at the same time. But it is interesting that both regions were in contact with each other at this time between 3,800 to at least 3,100 BC. Up to this point in time the Priests had always been at the top of the stratification as they understood what the gods required and could relay their messages to the people. Obviously, they had a good track record as could be witnessed, so why change something if it wasn't broken? How did this new version of rule come about?

One theory is that at first an individual person could be granted power for a limited amount of time when something had occurred. A flood, somebody had to be in charge to enable a rescue plan to be able to right the disaster. It could be a large, complicated building works that required expert planning and sole control of all resources. It could be organising people in protecting against an external invasion or simply to heavily control a neighbour and make them commit to their own rule thus resolving issues of who owns what land, a common theme later in the history of the area.

But eventually, the limited time of control was extended and maybe to that person's son who showed equal or comparable abilities to which ever task. Maybe when a dispute had been resolved the people felt the need for the individual to stay in that position to negotiate a treaty.

By 2,900 BC, Kings do seem to have appeared in Mesopotamia and once the position of Lugal (King) had been formalised, it would seem that the position was inherited, and to this day has never went away! Very quickly the position of a King was expected, as if it had always been there, and the people conformed, maybe the priests gave their blessing to this new position and helped take some of the strain from just one individual. The person who had the most rights to the throne would be the son of the King and the oldest son would have the best opportunity to take the roll. It wouldn't take long to create something permanently.

The earliest period of Kings is known as Early Dynastic Period 2,900-2,300 BC. The position really wasn't of strength for about 400 years as scribes failed to record anything of any real interest concerning Kings. This may have been because writing wasn't really used to record events, but to record accounts until about 2,500 BC. Only when the King started to write royal inscriptions was it noted that the institute of Kingship was so well established that nobody would have known what went before, it had stealthily grown in power and by 2,500 BC had become part of the fabric of the institution.

A much later document called the Sumerian King List recites that the Kingship had descended from Heaven and that the Gods had wanted Humans to have Kings. By purporting this, Kingship had blurred the lines between Priests who had always been the hegemony of an individual city state and started usurping power. By using the newfound writing techniques Kingship gained the upper hand in stating *facts* concerning the longevity of Kingship even though it is totally unfounded in modern research. It would seem that Historian have a better understanding on one small aspect of cultural events than the people of the time. The scribes were used to immortalise Kings.

Ur-Nanshe King 2,500 BC founded a dynasty in the city state of Lagash it had grown rich through its crops and animals, but also had a direct trade route with Susa in the East. Through images we know that he shaved off his hair and his beard, which was an unusual feature of its day, and more of the priest class. Is image showed that he was a builder, with a basket of bricks perched on his head, could this be in respect that the common ancestry of all Kings was from being the Big man (Lugal) of building works. The inscription on the relief states *Ur-Nanshe, King of Lagash, built the temple of Ningirsu, he built the temple of Nanshe*. It also described that boats from distant Dilmun brought the wood for him to build the temple.

Ur-Nanshe also has a long list of other building projects, including nine temples, a wall around Lagash and two canals. His reign wasn't always peaceful, he fought and defeated two other neighbouring city states of both Ur and Umma. He states that he took the Kings and a number of commanders captive and heaped up a burial mound. These battles where the start of a long series of battles that carried on long after Ur-Nanshe's death, especially with the land of Umma.

His successors-controlled Lagash for almost 200 years. Nine descendants ruled the Kingdom one after the other in an extremely stable dynasty. Virtually all of them fighting against Umma. The reason for such a long feud was due to some disputed land that lay between the two city states called Gu-Edena. Most of the description of events come from excavations belonging to Lagash so are extremely one sided. One of the successors of Lagash. King Eannatum of 2,450 BC immortalised his victory over Umma with a stone inscription called *The Stele of the Vulture* It clearly shows the troops being led into battle in a very distinctive phalanx all equally equipped with shield protection, this shows an extremely well organised and equipped army.

The second depiction show a form of victory parade and the third stone shows a pile of dead soldiers and a bull (possibly for sacrifice). The back of the Stele shows a religious interpretation of the battle with the God Ningirsu with a net of dead enemies from Umma. King Eannatum giving praise for Ningisu's victory over their enemy. The boarder between the two states was re-established between the two states into the more favourable position of the victorious people of Lagash. King Eannatum didn't kill the King of Umma, he forced him to swear an oath. It was sworn in front of the Battle Net of Enlil who was a greater god than either of the cities Gods which both Kings would have acknowledged.

The Kings' inscriptions; the Kings wanted to be seen in the best possible light by not discussing any failures and by embellishing the successes. But the information gleaned from these inscriptions gave an insight into the activities of what a King had to deal with.

- Planning and leading military campaigns.
- Levying taxes, the previous task of the priest.
- Choosing officials to serve the state.
- Performing rituals to appease the gods, another task removed from the priest class.
- Inspiring and controlling subordinates, ask any good engineer today, the work isn't a problem it's only the people doing the work.
- Planning and implementing the building programmes and organising repairs to canals and waterways, the job of a project manager.
- Forging alliances with neighbouring states to strengthen your boundaries or enlarging your own area through marriage.

Keeping the alliance with the population of the city state was a fine balance as fear doesn't always work as a tool for longevity. The ruling King had to discourage any form of rebellion and ensure any external prospect looked less favourable than themselves. The King had to be seen to be providing more than what the populace already had. Festivals were a good enticement, ensuring the people were given free food, music, entertainment, beer and wine, a day of rest from the toils of the field work. A day to be with family and rejoice in what they had.

In return the people had to pay taxes, turn up for Corvee Labour Duty, a form of national service work completed by free men and women, cleaning and repair canals, new canal systems dug or new buildings to be erected. The strongest way of influence over the highly religious people was to inform them that the gods had chosen the King to rule over the people, who would be brave enough to disagree with the gods! Even after a short time of Kingship they actually believed their own propaganda. The divide between the monarchy and the people grew to a point when the monarchy believed that the gods must have chosen them for this important role.

Each King in the early dynastic period ruled an individual city state, all the cities where within sight of each other and all developed either on the River or the Sea, or a major tributary. All cities could prosper only when water was available. As these cities expanded the need for more water was required, canals were dug, usually with the help from neighbouring city states. There was no way to survive away from the rivers. The King lived in the city along with the Priests and all the mechanisms of state, the ruled over several towns and villages outside the walls of the city.

These city all had their own protectorates various gods' deities used within the cities. Kings praised the gods for the cities prosperity and their victory over their neighbours, they also believed that all gods were powerful, but the King of the Gods Enlil lived in the city of Nippur.

Chapter 7
The Epic of Gilgamesh

History's oldest known *fictional* story is probably the *Epic of Gilgamesh*, a mythic poem that first appeared as early as the 3rd Millennium BC. The adventure filled tale, centres on a Sumerian King named Gilgamesh who is described as being *one-third man and two-thirds god* (which doesn't equate unless incest was involved). Over the course of twelve clay tablets worth of text, he goes on the first classic hero's journey. He is seen slaying a forest monsters, rubbing elbows with the gods and searching for the key to immortality after his friend and fellow warrior Enkidu is slain *Life, which you look for, you will never find. For when the gods created man, they let death be his share, and life withheld in their own hands*, all with predictably tragic results.

It would be inappropriate not to place the entire *Epic of Gilgamesh* within the book as this book unequivocally shows how relevant it is to the entire history of Mesopotamia. but more importantly I believe the Epic of Gilgamesh had a much greater bearing on the lives of the Mesopotamians as a whole for thousands of years and future people of Western and Middle East societies. Rather than recite the 3,000-line poem, in my opinion it is best exemplified as a story. This version is based on N. K. Sanders[cxl] Assyrian International News Agency Books Online www.aina.org

Source of Gilgamesh Information

The Epic of Gilgamesh started out as a series of Sumerian poems and tales dating back to 2,100 BC, but the most complete version was written around the 12th century BCE by the Babylonians. The story was later lost to history after 600 BC, and it wasn't until the mid-19th century that archaeologists finally unearthed a copy near the Iraqi city of Mosul. Since then, scholars have hailed the 4,000-year-old epic as a foundational text in world literature.

The Sumerian ruler, Gilgamesh, Lugalbanda's son, King of Uruk, is still remembered to this day for his fictional yet laced with historical facts Epic. The first epic poem in history and inspiration for several Biblical stories, Roman and Greek myths thought by some to have been the original idea for Homer's *Iliad*. *The Iliad* had a direct bearing on how Alexander the Great conducted himself whilst on campaign and kept a copy under his pillow throughout his short life. So many similarities with the *Iliad* and if the name had been omitted then it certainly has very Homeric tendencies. A 3,000-line poem which is one of the crowning achievements of Mesopotamian literature, the *Epic of Gilgamesh* that follows the adventures of a Sumerian King as he battles a forest monster.

Most scholars believe he is based on an actual King who served as the fifth ruler of the city of Uruk. The historical Gilgamesh appears on the Sumerian *King List* and is thought to have lived sometime around 2,700 BC. That is actually 100 years after a great localised flood recorded by archaeological digs in the area. Few contemporary accounts of his reign have survived today. But archaeologists have found inscriptions that credit him with building Uruk's massive defensive walls and restoring a temple to the goddess Ninlil. Which could suggest he may have been a real ruler whose deeds were later repurposed as a myth. Once again truth has been shrouded in a myth.

The Bible, another ancient near Eastern text, has been extremely influential on the modern world more so than Gilgamesh yet the Bible is a scripture, whereas the epic of Gilgamesh isn't and can be viewed as an epic along with the Iliad and the fall of Troy by Homer, wrote some 1,200 years after Gilgamesh's exploits had been recounted by Utu-Hegal. A devastating flood in the region was used as a pivotal point in the epic poem and later reused in the Old Testament story of Noah.

Gilgamesh King in Uruk

I will proclaim to the world the deeds of Gilgamesh. This was the man to whom all things were known; this was the King who knew the countries of the world. He was wise, he saw mysteries and knew secret things, he brought us a tale of the days before the flood. He went on a long journey, was weary, worn-out with labour, returning he rested, he engraved on a stone the whole story.

When the gods created Gilgamesh, they gave him a perfect body. Shamash (Utu) the glorious sun endowed him with beauty, Adad the god of the storm endowed him with courage, the great gods made his beauty perfect, surpassing all others, terrifying like a great wild bull. Two thirds they made him god and one third man.

In Uruk, he built walls, a great rampart and the temple of blessed Eanna for the god of the firmament Anu, and for Ishtar (Inanna) the goddess of love. Look at it still today: the outer wall where the cornice runs, it shines with the brilliance of copper; and the inner wall, it has no equal. Touch the threshold, it is ancient. Approach Eanna the dwelling of Ishtar (Inanna), our lady of love and war, the like of which no latter-day King, no man alive can equal. Climb upon the wall of Uruk; walk along it, I say; regard the foundation terrace and examine the masonry. Is it not burnt brick, and good (fired bricks for better solidity)? The seven sages laid the foundations.

The Coming of Enkidu

Gilgamesh went abroad in the world, but he met with none who could withstand his arms till be came to Uruk. But the men of Uruk muttered in their houses, *Gilgamesh sounds the tocsin (alarm bells) for his amusement, his arrogance has no bounds by day or night. No son is left with his father, for Gilgamesh takes them all, even the children; yet the King should be a shepherd to his people. His lust leaves no virgin to her lover, neither the warrior's daughter nor the wife of the noble; yet this is the shepherd of the city, wise, comely, and resolute.*

The gods heard their lament, the gods of heaven cried to the Lord of Uruk, to Anu the God of Uruk: *A goddess made him, strong as a savage bull, none can withstand his arms. No son is left with his father, for Gilgamesh takes them all; and is this the King, the shepherd of his people? His lust leaves no virgin to her lover, neither the warrior's daughter nor the wife of the noble.* When Anu had heard their lamentation, the Gods cried to Aruru, the goddess of creation, *You made him, O Aruru; now create his equal; let it be as like him as his own reflection, his second self; stormy heart for stormy heart. Let them contend together and leave Uruk in quiet.*

So, the goddess conceived an image in her mind, and it was of the stuff of Anu of the firmament. She dipped her hands in water and pinched off clay, she let it fall in the wilderness, and noble Enkidu was created. There was virtue in him of the god of war, of Ninurta (God of War) himself. His body was rough, he had long hair like a woman's; it waved like the hair of Nisaba, the goddess of corn (later writing and learning). His body was covered with matted hair like Lahar, the god of cattle.

He was innocent of mankind; he knew nothing of the cultivated land. Enkidu ate grass in the hills with the gazelle and lurked with wild beasts at the waterholes. He had joy of the water with the herds of wild game. But there was a trapper who met him one day face to face at the drinking-hole, for the wild game had entered his territory. On three days he met him face to face, and the trapper was frozen with fear. He went back to his house with the game that he had caught, and he was dumb, benumbed with terror. His face was altered like that of one who has made a long journey.

With awe in his heart, he spoke to his father: *Father, there is a man, unlike any other, who comes down from the hills. He is the strongest in the world; he is like an immortal from heaven. He ranges over the hills with wild beasts and eats grass; the ranges through your land and comes down to the wells. I am afraid and dare not go near him. He fills in the pits which I dig and tears up my traps set for the game; he helps the beasts to escape and now they slip through my fingers.*

His father opened his mouth and said to the trapper, *My son, in Uruk lives Gilgamesh; no one has ever pre-vailed against him, he is strong as a star from heaven. Go to Uruk, find Gilgamesh, and extol the strength of this wild man. Ask him to give you a harlot, a wanton from the temple of love; return with her and let her woman's power overpower this man. When next he comes down to drink at the wells she will be there, stripped naked; and when he sees her beckoning, he will embrace her, and then the wild beasts will reject him.*

So, the trapper set out on his journey to Uruk and addressed himself to Gilgamesh saying, *A man unlike any other is roaming now in the pastures; he is as strong as a star from heaven and I am afraid to approach him. He helps the wild game to escape; he fills in my pits and pulls up my traps.'* Gilgamesh said, 'Trapper, go back, take with you a harlot, a child of pleasure. At the drinking hole she will strip, and when, he sees her beckoning he will embrace her, and the game of the wilderness will. Surely reject him.

Now the trapper returned, taking the harlot with him. After a three days' journey they came to the drinking hole, and there they sat down; the harlot and the trapper sat. Facing one another and waited for the game to come. For the first day and for the second day the two sat waiting, but on the third day the herds came; they came down to drink and Enkidu was with them. The small wild creatures of the plains were glad of the water and Enkidu with them, who ate grass with the gazelle and was born in the hills; and she saw him, the savage man, come from far-off in the hills.

The trapper spoke to her: *There he is. Now, woman, make your breasts bare, have no shame, do not delay but welcome his love. Let him see you naked; let him possess your body. When he comes near uncover yourself and lie with him; teach him, the savage man, your woman's art, for when he murmurs love to you the wild beasts that shared his life in the hills will reject him.*

She was not ashamed to take him, she made herself naked and welcomed his eagerness; as he lay on her murmuring love, she taught him the woman's art. For six days and seven nights they lay together, for Enkidu had forgotten his home in the hills; but when he was satisfied, he went back to the wild beasts. Then, when the gazelle saw him, they bolted away; when the wild creatures saw him, they fled. Enkidu would have followed, but his body was bound as though with a cord, his knees gave way when he started to run, his swiftness was gone. And now the wild creatures had all fled away; Enkidu was grown weak, for wisdom was in him, and the thoughts of a man were in his heart.

So, he returned and sat down at the woman's feet, and listened intently to what she said. (From hunter-gatherer, a civilised man cannot compete.) *You are wise, Enkidu, and now you have become like a god. Why do you want to run wild with the beasts in the hills? Come with me. I will take you to strong-walled Uruk, to the blessed temple of Ishtar and of Anu, of love and of heaven there Gilgamesh lives, who is very strong, and like a wild bull he lords it over men.*

When she had spoken, Enkidu was pleased; he longed for a comrade, for one who would understand his heart. "Come, woman, and take me to that holy temple, to the house of Anu (An) and of Ishtar (Inanna), and to the place where Gilgamesh lords it over the people. I will challenge him boldly, I will cry out aloud in Uruk, *I am the strongest here, I have come to change the old order, I am he who was born in the hills, I am he who is strongest of all.*"

She said, *Let us go, and let him see your face. I know very well where Gilgamesh is in great Uruk. O Enkidu, there all the people are dressed in their gorgeous robes, every day is holiday, the young men and the girls are wonderful to see. How sweet they smell! All the great ones are roused from their beds. O Enkidu, you who love life, I will show you Gilgamesh, a man of many moods; you shall look at him well in his radiant manhood. His body is perfect in strength and maturity; he never rests by night or day.*

He is stronger than you, so leave your boasting. Shamash (Utu) the glorious sun has given favours to Gilgamesh, and Anu of the heavens, and Enlil (The god who granted Kingship), and Ea (Enki) the wise has given him deep understanding. if I tell you, even before you have left the wilderness, Gilgamesh will know in his dreams that you are coming.

Now Gilgamesh got up to tell his dream to his mother; Ninsun, one of the wise gods. *Mother, last night I had a dream. I was full of joy, the young heroes were round me and I walked through the night under the stars of the firmament, and one, a meteor of the stuff of Anu (An, The Sky God), fell down from heaven. I tried to lift it, but it proved too heavy. All the people of Uruk came round to see it, the common people jostled, and the nobles thronged to kiss its feet; and to me its attraction was like the love of woman. They helped me, I braced my forehead and I raised it with thongs and brought it to you, and you yourself pronounced it my brother.*

Then Ninsun, who is well-beloved and wise, said to Gilgamesh, *This star of heaven which descended like a meteor from the sky; which you tried to lift, but found too heavy, when you tried to move it, it would not budge, and so you brought it to my feet; I made it for you, a goad and spur, and you were drawn as though to a woman. This is the strong comrade, the one who brings help to his friend in his need. He is the strongest of wild creatures, the stuff of Anu (An); born in the grasslands and the wild hills reared him; when you see him you will be glad; you will love him as a woman and he will never forsake you. This is the meaning of the dream.*

Gilgamesh said, *Mother, I dreamed a second dream. In the streets of strong-walled Uruk there lay an axe; the shape of it was strange and the people thronged round. I saw it and was glad. I bent down, deeply drawn towards it; I loved it like a woman and wore it at my side.*

Ninsun answered, *That axe, which you saw, which drew you so powerfully like love of a woman, that is the comrade whom I give you, and he will come in his strength like one of the hosts of heaven. He is the brave companion who rescues his friend in necessity.*

Gilgamesh said to his mother, *A friend, a counsellor has come to me from Enlil, and now I shall befriend and counsel him.* So, Gilgamesh told his dreams; and the harlot retold them to Enkidu.

And now she said to Enkidu, *When I look at you, you have become like a god. Why do you yearn to run wild again with the beasts in the hills? Get up from the ground, the bed of a shepherd.* He listened to her words with care. It was good advice that she gave. She divided her clothing in two and with the one half she clothed him and with the other herself and holding his hand she led him like a child to the sheepfolds, into the shepherds' tents. There all the shepherds crowded round to see him, they put down bread in front of him, but Enkidu could only suck the milk of wild animals. He fumbled and gaped, at a loss what to do or how he should eat the bread and drink the strong wine.

Then the woman said, *Enkidu, eat bread, it is the staff of life; drink the wine, it is the custom of the land.* So, he ate till he was full and drank strong wine, seven goblets. He became merry, his heart exulted, and his face shone. He rubbed down the matted hair of his body and anointed himself with oil. Enkidu had become a man; but when he had put on man's clothing he appeared like a bridegroom. He took arms to hunt the lion so that the shepherds could rest at night. He caught wolves and lions and the herdsmen lay down in peace; for Enkidu was their watchman, that strong man who had no rival.

He was merry living with the shepherds, till one day lifting his eyes he saw a man approaching. He said to the harlot, *Woman, fetch that man here. Why has he come? I wish to know his name.*

She went and called the man saying, *Sir, where are you going on this weary journey?*

The man answered, saying to Enkidu, *Gilgamesh has gone into the marriage-house and shut out the people. He does strange things in Uruk, the city of great streets. At the roll of the drum work begins for the men, and work for the women. Gilgamesh the King is about to celebrate marriage with the Queen of Love, and he still demands to be first with the bride, the King to be first and the husband to follow, for that was ordained by the gods from his birth, from the time the umbilical cord was cut. But now the drums roll for the choice of the bride and the city groans.*

At these words Enkidu turned white in the face. *I will go to the place where Gilgamesh lords it over the people, I will challenge him boldly, and I will cry aloud in Uruk, "I have come to change the old order, for I am the strongest here."*

Now Enkidu strode in front and the woman followed behind. He entered Uruk, that great market, and all the folk thronged round him where he stood in the street in strong-walled Uruk. The people jostled; speaking of him they said, *He is the spit of Gilgamesh. He is shorter. He is bigger of bone.* This is the one who was reared on the milk of wild beasts. His is the greatest strength. The men rejoiced: *Now Gilgamesh has met his match. This great one, this hero whose beauty is like a god, he is a match even for Gilgamesh.*

In Uruk, the bridal bed was made, fit for the goddess of love. The bride waited for the bridegroom, but in the night, Gilgamesh got up and came to the house. Then Enkidu stepped out, he stood in the street and blocked the way. Mighty Gilgamesh came on and Enkidu met him at the gate. He put out his foot and prevented Gilgamesh from entering the house, so they grappled, holding each other like bulls. They broke the doorposts, and the walls shook, they snorted like bulls locked together. Gilgamesh bent his knee with his foot planted on the ground and with a turn Enkidu was thrown. Then immediately his fury died.

When Enkidu was thrown, he said to Gilgamesh, *There is not another like you in the world. Ninsun, who is as strong as a wild ox in the byre, she was the mother who bore you, and now you are raised above all men, and Enlil has given you the Kingship, for your strength surpasses the strength of men.* So, Enkidu and Gilgamesh embraced, and their friendship was sealed.

The Forest Journey

Enlil of the mountain, the father of the gods, had decreed the destiny of Gilgamesh. So, Gilgamesh dreamed, and Enkidu said, *The meaning of the dream is this. The father of the gods has given you Kingship, such is your destiny, and everlasting life is not your destiny. Because of this do not be sad at heart, do not be grieved or oppressed. He has given you power to bind and to loose, to be the darkness and the light of mankind. He has given you unexampled supremacy over the people, victory in battle from which no fugitive returns, in forays and assaults from which there is no going back. But do not abuse this power; deal justly with your servants in the palace, deal justly before Shamash (Utu).*

The eyes of Enkidu were full of tears and his heart was sick. He sighed bitterly and Gilgamesh met his eye and said, *My friend, why do you sigh so bitterly?*

But Enkidu opened his mouth and said, *I am weak, my arms have lost their strength, the cry of sorrow sticks in my throat, I am oppressed by idleness.* It was then that the lord Gilgamesh turned his thoughts to the Country of the Living; on the Land of Cedars the lord Gilgamesh reflected.

He said to his servant Enkidu, *I have not established my name stamped on bricks as my destiny decreed; therefore, I will go to the country where the cedar is felled. I will set up my name in the place where the names of famous men are written, and where no man's name is written yet I will wise a monument to the gods. Because of the evil that is in the land, we will go to the forest and destroy the evil; for in the forest lives Humbaba whose name is "Hugeness", a ferocious giant.*

But Enkidu sighed bitterly and said, *When I went with the wild beasts ranging through the wilderness, I discovered the forest; its length is ten thousand leagues in every direction. Enlil has appointed Humbaba to guard it and armed him sevenfold terrors, terrible to all flesh is Humbaba. When he roars it is like the torrent of the storm, his breath is like fire, and his jaws are death itself. He guards the cedars so well that when the wild heifer stirs in the forest, though she is sixty leagues distant, he hears her. What man would willingly walk into that country and explore its depths? I tell you; weakness overpowers whoever goes near it: it is not an equal struggle when one fights with Humbaba; he is a great warrior, a battering-ram. Gilgamesh, the watchman of the forest never sleeps.*

Gilgamesh replied: *Where is the man who can clamber to heaven? Only the gods live for ever with glorious Shamash (Utu), but as for us men, our days are numbered, our occupations are a breath of wind. How is this, already you are afraid! I will go first although I am your lord, and you may safely call out, "Forward, there is nothing to fear!" Then if I fall, I leave behind me a name that endures; men will say of me, "Gilgamesh has fallen in fight with ferocious Humbaba." Long after the child has been born in my house, they will say it, and remember.*

Enkidu spoke again to Gilgamesh, *O my lord, if you will enter that country, go first to the hero Shamash (Utu), tell the Sun God, for the land is his. The country where the cedar is cut belongs to Shamash (Utu).*

Gilgamesh took up a kid, white without spot, and a brown one with it; he held them against his breast, and he carried them into the presence of the sun. He took in his hand his silver sceptre and he said to glorious Shamash (Utu), *I am going to that country, O Shamash (Utu), I am going; my hands supplicate, so let it be well with my soul and bring me back to the quay of Uruk. Grant, I beseech, your protection, and let the omen be good.*

Glorious Shamash (Utu) answered, *Gilgamesh, you are strong, but what is the Country of the Living to you?*

O Shamash (Utu), hear me, hear me, Shamash (Utu), let my voice be heard. Here in the city man dies oppressed at heart, man perishes with despair in his heart. I have looked over the wall and I see the bodies floating on the river, and that will be my lot also. Indeed, I know it is so, for whoever is tallest among men cannot reach the heavens, and the greatest cannot encompass the earth. Therefore, I would enter that country: because I have not established my name stamped on brick as my destiny decreed, I will go to the country where the cedar is cut. I will set up my name where the names of famous men are written; and where no man's name is written I will raise a monument to the gods.

The tears ran down his face and he said, *Alas, it is a long journey that I must take to the Land of Humbaba. If this enterprise is not to be accomplished, why did you move me, Shamash (Utu), with the restless desire to perform it? How can I succeed if you will not succour me? If I die in that country I will die without rancour, but if I return, I will make a glorious offering of gifts and of praise to Shamash Utu).*

So, Shamash (Utu) accepted the sacrifice of his tears; like the compassionate man he showed him mercy. He appointed strong allies for Gilgamesh, sons of one mother, and stationed them in the mountain caves. The great winds he appointed: the north wind, the whirlwind, the stone and the icy wind, the tempest and the scorching wind. Like vipers, like dragons, like a scorching fire, like a serpent that freezes the heart, a destroying flood and the lightning's fork, such were they and Gilgamesh rejoiced.

He went to the forge and said, *I will give orders to the armourers; they shall cast us our weapons while we watch them.* So, they gave orders to the armourers and the craftsmen sat down in conference. They went into the groves of the plain and cut willow and boxwood; they cast for them axes of nine score pounds, and great swords they cast with blades of six score pounds each one, with pommels and hilts of thirty pounds. They cast for Gilgamesh the axe *Might of Heroes* and the bow of Anshan (Anzan); and Gilgamesh was armed and Enkidu; and the weight of the arms they carried was thirty score pounds.

The people collected and the counsellors in the streets and in the marketplace of Uruk; they came through the gate of seven bolts and Gilgamesh spoke to them in the marketplace: *I, Gilgamesh, go to see that creature of which such things are spoken, the rumour of whose name fills the world. I will conquer him in his cedar wood and show the strength of the sons of Uruk, the entire world shall* know of it. I am committed to this enterprise: to climb the mountain, to cut down the cedar, and leave behind me an enduring name.

The counsellors of Uruk; the great market, answered him, *Gilgamesh, you are young, your courage carries you too far, you cannot know what this enterprise means which you plan. We have heard that Humbaba is not like men who die, his weapons are such that none can stand against them; the forest stretches for ten thousand leagues in every direction; who would willingly go down to explore its depths? As for Humbaba, when he roars it is like the torrent of the storm, his breath is like fire and his jaws are death itself. Why do you crave to do this thing, Gilgamesh? It is no equal struggle when one fights with Humbaba, that battering-ram.*

When he heard these words of the counsellors, Gilgamesh looked at his friend and laughed, *How shall I answer them; shall I say I am afraid of Humbaba, I will sit at home all the rest of my days?* Then Gilgamesh opened his mouth again and said to Enkidu, *My friend, let us go to the Great Palace, to Egalmah (The Exalted Palace in Uruk), and stand before Ninsun the queen. Ninsun is wise with deep knowledge; she will give us counsel for the road we must go.*

They took each other by the hand as they went to Egalmah, and they went to Ninsun the great queen. Gilgamesh approached, he entered the palace and spoke to Ninsun, *Ninsun, will you listen to me; I have a long journey to go, to the Land of Humbaba, I must travel an unknown road and fight a strange battle. From the day I go until I return, till I reach the cedar forest and destroy the evil which Shamash (Utu) abhors, pray for me to Shamash (Utu).*

Ninsun went into her room, she put on a dress becoming to her body, she put on jewels to make her breast beautiful, she placed a tiara on her head and her skirts swept the ground. Then she went up to the altar of the Sun, standing upon the roof of the palace; she burnt incense and lifted her arms to Shamash (Utu) as the smoke ascended: *O Shamash (Utu), why did you give this restless heart to Gilgamesh, my son; why did you give it? You have moved him and now he sets out on a long journey to the Land of Humbaba, to travel an unknown road and fight a strange battle. Therefore, from the day that he goes till the day he returns, until he reaches the cedar forest, until he kills Humbaba and destroys the evil thing which you, Shamash (Utu), abhor, do not forget him; but let the dawn, Aya (Sheridan consort of Utu), your dear bride, remind you always, and when day is done give him to the watchman of the night to keep him from harm.*

Then Ninsun the mother of Gilgamesh extinguished the incense, and she called to Enkidu with this exhortation: *Strong Enkidu, you are not the child of my body, but I will receive you as my adopted son; you are my other child like the foundlings they bring to the temple. Serve Gilgamesh as a foundling serves the temple and the priestess who reared him. In the presence of my women, any votaries and hierophants, I declare it.* Then she placed the amulet for a pledge round his neck, and she said to him, *I entrust my son to you; bring him back to me safely.*

And now they brought to them the weapons, they put in their hands the great swords in their golden scabbards, and the bow and the quiver. Gilgamesh took the axe, he slung the quiver from his shoulder, and the bow of Anshan (Anzan) and buckled the sword to his belt; and so, they were armed and ready for the journey. Now all the people came and pressed on them and said, *When will you return to the city?*

The counsellors blessed Gilgamesh and warned him, *Do not trust too much in your own strength, be watchful, and restrain your blows at first. The one who goes in front protects his companion; the good guide who knows the way guards his friend. Let Enkidu lead the way, he knows the road to the forest, he has seen Humbaba and is experienced in battles; let him press first into the passes, let him be watchful and look to himself. Let Enkidu protect his friend, and guard his companion, and bring him safe through the pitfalls of the road. We, the counsellors of Uruk entrust our King to you, O Enkidu; bring him back safely to us.*

Again, to Gilgamesh, they said, *May Shamash (Utu) give you your heart's desire, may he let you see with your eyes the thing accomplished which your lips have spoken; may he open a path for you where it is blocked, and a road for your feet to tread. May he open the mountains for your crossing, and may the night-time bring you the blessings of night, and Lugalbanda (possibly 2nd King of Uruk), your guardian god, stand beside you for victory. May you have victory in the battle as though you fought with a child. Wash your feet in the river of Humbaba to which you are journeying; in the evening dig a well and let there always be pure water in your water-skin. Offer cold water to Shamash (Utu) and do not forget Lugalbanda.*

Then Enkidu opened his mouth and said, *Forward, there is nothing to fear. Follow me, for I know the place where Humbaba lives and the paths where he walks. Let the counsellors go back. Here is no cause for fear.*

When the counsellors heard this, they sped the hero on his way. *Go, Gilgamesh, may your guardian god protect you on the road and bring you safely back to the quay of Uruk.*

After twenty leagues (72 miles-115 kms), they broke their fast; after another thirty leagues they stopped for the night. Fifty leagues they walked in one day; in three days they had walked as much as a journey of a month and two weeks. They crossed seven mountains before they came to the gate of the forest. Then Enkidu called out to Gilgamesh, *Do not go down into the forest; when I opened the gate, my hand lost its strength.*

Gilgamesh answered him, *Dear friend, do not speak like a coward. Have we got the better of so many dangers and travelled so far, to turn back at last? You, who are tried in wars and battles, hold close to me now and you will feel no fear of death; keep beside me and your weakness will pass, the trembling will leave your hand. Would my friend rather stay behind? No, we will, go down together into the heart of the forest. Let your courage be roused by the battle to come; forget death and follow me, a man resolute in action, but one who is not foolhardy. When two go together each will protect himself and shield his companion, and if they fall, they leave an enduring name.*

Together they went down into the forest and they came to the green mountain. There they stood still, they were struck dumb; they stood still and gazed at the forest. They saw the height of the cedar; they saw the way into the forest and the track where Humbaba was used to walk. The way was broad, and the going was good. They gazed at the mountain of cedars, the dwelling-place of the gods and the throne of Ishtar (Inanna). The hugeness of the cedar rose in front of the mountain, its shade was beautiful, full of comfort; mountain and glade were green with brushwood

There Gilgamesh dug a well before the setting sun. He went up the mountain and poured out fine meal on the ground and said, *O mountain, dwelling of the gods, bring me a favourable dream.*

Then they took each other by the hand and lay down to sleep; and sleep that flows from the night lapped over them. Gilgamesh dreamed, and at midnight sleep left him, and he told his dream to his friend. *Enkidu, what was it that woke me if you did not? My friend, I have dreamed a dream. Get up, look at the mountain precipice. The sleep that the gods sent me is broken. Ah, my friend, what a dream I have had! Terror and confusion; I seized hold of a wild bull in the wilderness. It bellowed and beat up the dust till the whole sky was dark, my* arm was seized, and my tongue bitten. I fell back on my knee; then someone refreshed me with water from his water-skin.

Enkidu said, *Dear friend, the god to whom we are travelling is no wild bull, though his form is mysterious. That wild bull which you saw is Shamash (Utu) the Protector; in our moment of peril, he will take our hands. The one who gave water from his water skin that is your own god who cares for your good name, your Lugalbanda. United with him, together we will accomplish a work the fame of which will never die.*

Gilgamesh said, *I dreamed again. We stood in a deep gorge of the mountain, and beside it we two were like the smallest of swamp flies; and suddenly the mountain fell, it struck me and caught my feet from under me. Then came an intolerable light blazing out, and in it was one whose grace and whose beauty were greater than the beauty of this world. He pulled me out from under the mountain, he gave me water to drink and my heart was comforted, and he set my feet on the ground.*

Then Enkidu the child of the plains said, *Let us go down from the mountain and talk this thing over together.* He said to Gilgamesh the young god, *Your dream is good; your dream is excellent, the mountain which you saw is Humbaba. Now, surely, we will seize and kill him, and throw his body down as the mountain fell on the plain.*

The next day after twenty leagues they broke their fast, and after another thirty they stopped for the night. They dug a well before the sun had set and Gilgamesh ascended the mountain. He poured out fine meal on the ground and said, *O mountain, dwelling of the gods, send a dream for Enkidu, make him a favourable dream.*

The mountain fashioned a dream for Enkidu; it came, an ominous dream; a cold shower passed over him, it caused him to cower like the mountain barley under a storm of rain. But Gilgamesh sat with his chin on his knees till the sleep which flows over all mankind lapped over him. Then, at midnight, sleep left him; he got up and said to his friend, *Did you call me, or why did I wake? Did you touch me, or why am I terrified? Did not some god pass by, for my limbs are numb with fear? My friend, I saw a third dream and this dream was altogether frightful. The heavens roared and the earth roared again, daylight failed, and darkness fell, lightning's flashed, fire blazed out, the clouds lowered, they rained down death. Then the brightness departed, the fire went out, and all was turned* to ashes fallen about us. Let us go down from the mountain and talk this over and consider what we should do.

When they had come down from the mountain, Gilgamesh seized the axe in his hand: he felled the cedar. When Humbaba heard the noise far off, he was enraged; he cried out, *Who is this that has violated my woods and cut down my cedar?*

But Glorious Shamash (Utu) called to them out of heaven, *Go forward, and do not be afraid.* But now Gilgamesh was overcome by weakness, for sleep had seized him suddenly, a profound sleep held him; he lay on the ground, stretched out speechless, as though in a dream.

When Enkidu touched him, he did not raise; when he spoke to him, he did not reply. *O Gilgamesh, Lord of the plain of Kullab, the world grows dark, the shadows have spread over it, now is the glimmer of dusk. Shamash (Utu) has departed; his bright head is quenched in the bosom of his mother Ningal (Goddess of the Reeds). O Gilgamesh, how long will you lie like this, asleep? Never let the mother who gave you birth be forced in mourning into the city square.*

At length Gilgamesh heard him; he put on his breastplate, *The Voice of Heroes*, of thirty shekels' weight; he put it on as though it had been a light garment that he carried, and it covered him altogether. He straddled the earth like a bull that snuffs the ground and his teeth were clenched. *By the life of my mother Ninsun who gave me birth, and by the life of my father, divine Lugalbanda, let me live to be the wonder of my mother as when she nursed me on her lap.*

A second time, he said to him, *By the life of Ninsun my mother who gave me birth, and by the life of my father, divine Lugalbanda, until we have fought thus man, if man he is, this god, if god he is, the way that I took to the Country of the Living will not turn back to the city.*

Then Enkidu, the faithful companion, pleaded, answering him, *O my lord, you do not know this monster and that is the reason you are not afraid. I who know him, I am terrified. His teeth are dragon's fangs, his countenance is like a lion, his charge is the rushing of the flood, with his look he crushes alike the trees of the forest and reeds in the swamp. O my Lord, you may go on if you choose into thus land, but I will go back to the city. I will tell the lady your mother all your glorious deeds till she shouts for joy and then I will tell the death that followed till she weeps for bitterness.*

But Gilgamesh said, *Immolation and sacrifice are not yet for me, the boat of the dead shall not go down, nor the three-ply cloth be cut for my shrouding. Not yet will my people be desolate, nor the pyre be lit in my house and my dwelling burnt on the fire. Today, give me your aid and you shall have mine: what then can go amiss with us two? All living creatures born of the flesh shall sit at last in the boat of the West, and when it sinks, when the boat of Magilum (The boat of the underworld) sinks, they are gone; but we shall go forward and fix our eyes on this monster. If your heart is fearful throw away fear; if there is terror in it throw away terror. Take your axe in your hand and attack. He who leaves the fight unfinished is not at peace.*

Humbaba came out from his strong house of cedar. Then Enkidu called out, *O Gilgamesh, remember now your boasts in Uruk. Forward, attack, son of Uruk, there is nothing to fear.*

When he heard these words, his courage rallied; he answered, *Make haste, close in, if the watchman is there do not let him escape to the woods where he will vanish. He has put on the first of his seven splendours but not yet the other six, let us trap him before he is armed.* Like a raging wild bull, he snuffed the ground; the watchman of the woods turned full of threatening, he cried out. Humbaba came from his strong house of cedar. He nodded his head and shook it, menacing Gilgamesh; and on him he fastened his eye, the eye of death.

Then Gilgamesh called to Shamash (Utu) and his tears were flowing, *O glorious Shamash (Utu), I have followed the road you commanded but now if you send no succour how shall I escape?* Glorious Shamash (Utu) heard his prayer, and he summoned the great wind, the north wind, the whirlwind, the storm and the icy wind, the tempest and the scorching wind; they came like dragons, like a scorching fire, like a serpent that freezes the heart, a destroying flood and the lightning's fork. The eight winds rose up against Humbaba, they beat against his eyes; he was gripped, unable to go forward or back.

Gilgamesh shouted, *By the life of Ninsun my mother and divine Lugalbanda my father, in the Country of the Living, in this Land I have discovered your dwelling; my weak arms and my small weapons I have brought to this Land against you, and now I will enter your house.*

So, he felled the first cedar and they cut the branches and laid them at the foot of the mountain. At the first stroke Humbaba blazed out, but still they advanced. They felled seven cedars and cut and bound the branches and laid them at the foot of the mountain, and seven times Humbaba loosed his glory on them. As the seventh blaze died out, they reached his lair. He slapped his thigh in scorn. He approached like a noble wild bull roped on the mountain, a warrior whose elbows are bound together.

The tears started to his eyes and he was pale. *Gilgamesh, let me speak. I have never known a mother, no, nor a father who reared me. I was born of the mountain, he reared me, and Enlil made me the keeper of this forest. Let me go free, Gilgamesh, and I will be your servant, you shall be my lord; all the trees of the forest that I tended on the mountain shall be yours. I will cut them down and build you a palace.*

He took him by the hand and led him to his house, so that the heart of Gilgamesh was moved with compassion. He swore by the heavenly life, by the earthly life, by the underworld itself: *O Enkidu, should not the snared, bird return to its nest and the captive man return to his mother's arms?*

Enkidu answered, *The strongest of men will fall to fate if he has no judgement. Namtar (God of Death, Son of Enlil), the evil fate that knows no distinction between men, will devour him. If the snared bird returns to its nest, if the captive man returns to his mother's arms, then you my friend will never return to the city where the mother is waiting who gave you birth. He will bar the mountain road against you and make the pathways impassable.*

Humbaba said, *Enkidu, what you have spoken is evil: you, a hireling, and dependent for your bread! In envy and for fear of a rival you have spoken evil words.*

Enkidu said, *Do not listen, Gilgamesh: this Humbaba must die. Kill Humbaba first and his servants after.*

But Gilgamesh said, *If we touch him the blaze and the glory of light will be put out in confusion, the glory and glamour will vanish, its rays will be quenched.*

Enkidu said to Gilgamesh, *Not so, my friend. First entrap the bird, and where shall the chicks run then? Afterwards we can search out the glory and the glamour, when the chicks run distracted through the grass.*

Gilgamesh listened to the word of his companion, he took the axe in his hand, he drew the sword from his belt, and he struck Humbaba with a thrust of the sword to the neck, and Enkidu his comrade struck the second blow. At the third blow Humbaba fell. Then there followed confusion for this was the guardian of the forest whom they had felled to the ground. For as far as two leagues the cedars shivered when Enkidu felled the watcher of the forest, he at whose voice Hermon and Lebanon used to tremble.

Now the mountains were moved and all the hills, for the guardian of the forest was killed. They attacked the cedars; the seven splendours of Humbaba were extinguished. So, they pressed on into the forest bearing the sword of eight talents. They uncovered the sacred dwellings of the Anunnaki (Descendants of An (God of Heaven) and Ki (God of Earth)) and while Gilgamesh felled the first of the trees of the forest Enkidu cleared their roots as far as the banks of Euphrates. They set Humbaba before the gods, before Enlil; they kissed the ground and dropped the shroud and set the head before him.

When he saw the head of Humbaba, Enlil raged at them, *Why did you do this thing? From henceforth may the fire be on your faces, may it eat the bread that you eat, may it drink where you drink.* Then Enlil took again the blaze and the seven splendours that had been Humbaba's: he gave the first to the river, and he gave to the lion, to the stone of execration, to the mountain and to the dreaded daughter of the Queen of Hell.

O Gilgamesh, King and conqueror of the dreadful blaze; wild bull who plunders the mountain, who crosses the sea, glory to him, and from the brave the greater glory is Enki's (Ea)!

Ishtar and Gilgamesh, and the Death of Enkidu

Gilgamesh washed out his long locks and cleaned his weapons; he flung back his hair from his shoulders; he threw off his stained clothes and changed them for new. He put on his royal robes and made them fast. When Gilgamesh had put on the crown, glorious Ishtar (Inanna) lifted her eyes, seeing the beauty of Gilgamesh.

She said, *Come to me Gilgamesh, and be my bridegroom; grant me seed of your body, let me be your bride and you shall be my husband. I will harness for you a chariot of lapis lazuli and of gold, with wheels of gold and horns of copper; and you shall have mighty demons of the storm for draft mules. When you enter our house in the fragrance of cedar-wood, threshold and throne will kiss your feet. Kings, rulers, and princes will bow down before you; they shall bring you tribute from the mountains and the plain. Your ewes shall drop twins and your goat's triplets; your pack-ass shall outrun mules; your oxen shall have no rivals, and your chariot horses shall be famous far-off for their swiftness.*

Gilgamesh opened his mouth and answered glorious Ishtar (Inanna), *If I take you in marriage, what gifts can I give in return? What ointments and clothing for your body? I would gladly give you bread and all sorts of food fit for a god.*

I would give you wine to drink fit for a queen. I would pour out barley to stuff your granary; but as for making you my wife that I will not. How would it go with me? Your lovers have found you like a brazier which smoulders in the cold, a backdoor which keeps out neither squall of wind nor storm, a castle which crushes the garrison, pitch that blackens the bearer, a water-skin that chafes the carrier, a stone which falls from the parapet, a battering-ram turned back from the enemy, a sandal that trips the wearer.

Which of your lovers did you ever love for ever? What shepherd of yours has pleased you for all time? Listen to me while I tell the tale of your lovers. There was Tammuz, the lover of your youth, for him you decreed wailing, year after year. You loved the many coloured roller, but still you struck and broke his wing; now in the grove he sits and cries, "kappi, kappi, my wing, my wing." You have loved the lion tremendous in strength: seven pits you dug for him. You have loved the stallion magnificent in battle, and for him you decreed whip and spur and a thong, to gallop seven leagues by force and to muddy the water before he drinks: and for his mother Silili (Divine Mare Mother of the Stallion) lamentations.

You have loved the shepherd of the flock; he made meal-cake for you day after day, he killed kids for your sake. You struck and turned him into a wolf, now his own herd-boys chase him away, his own hounds worry his flanks. And did you not love Ishullanu, the gardener of your father's palm grove? He brought you baskets filled with dates without end; every day he loaded your table.

Then you turned your eyes on him and said, "Dearest Ishullanu, come here to me, let us enjoy your manhood, come forward and take me, I am yours." Ishullanu answered, "What are you asking from me? My mother has baked, and I have eaten; why should I come to such as you for food that is tainted and rotten? For when was a screen of rushes sufficient protection from frosts?" But when you had beard his answer you struck him. He was changed to a blind mole deep in the earth, one whose desire is always beyond his reach. And if you and I should be lovers, should not I be served in the same fashion as all these others whom you loved once?

When Ishtar (Inanna) heard this, she fell into a bitter rage, she went up to high heaven. Her tears poured down in front of her father Anu (An), and Antum (Antu) her mother. She said, *My father, Gilgamesh has heaped insults on me, he has told over all my abominable behaviour, my foul and hideous acts.*

Anu (An) opened his mouth and said, *Are you a father of gods? Did not you quarrel with Gilgamesh the King, so now he has related your abominable behaviour, your foul and hideous acts.*

Ishtar (Inanna) opened her mouth and said again, *My father, give me the Bull of Heaven to destroy Gilgamesh. Fill Gilgamesh, I say, with arrogance to his destruction; but if you refuse to give me the Bull of Heaven I will break in the doors of hell and smash the bolts; there will be confusion of people, those above with those from the lower depths. I shall bring up the dead to eat food like the living; and the hosts of dead will outnumber the living.*

Anu (An) said to great Ishtar (Inanna), *If I do what you desire there will be seven years of drought throughout Uruk when corn will be seedless husks. Have you saved grain enough for the people and grass for the cattle?*

Ishtar replied. *I have saved grain for the people, grass for the cattle; for seven years of seedless husks, there is grain and there is grass enough.*

When Anu (An) heard what Ishtar (Inanna) had said, he gave her the Bull of Heaven to lead by the halter down to Uruk: When they reached the gates of Uruk the Bull went to the river; with his first snort cracks opened in the earth and, a hundred young men fell down to death. With his second snort cracks opened and two hundred fell down to death. With his third snort cracks opened, Enkidu doubled over but instantly recovered, he dodged aside and leapt on the Bull and seized it by the horns. The Bull of Heaven foamed in his face, it brushed him with the thick of its tail.

Enkidu cried to Gilgamesh, *My friend, we boasted that we would leave enduring names behind us. Now thrust in your sword between the nape and the horns.* So, Gilgamesh followed the Bull, he seized the thick of its tail; he thrust the sword between the nape and the horns and slew the Bull. When they had killed the Bull of Heaven, they cut out its heart and gave it to Shamash (Utu), and the brothers rested.

But Ishtar (Inanna) rose up and mounted the great wall of Uruk; she sprang on to the tower and uttered a curse: *Woe to Gilgamesh, for he has scorned me in killing the Bull of Heaven.*

When Enkidu heard these words, he tore out the Bull's right thigh and tossed it in her face saying, *If I could lay my hands on you, it is this I should do to you, and lash the entrails to your side.*

Then Ishtar (Inanna) called together her people, the dancing and singing girls, the prostitutes of the temple, the courtesans. Over the thigh of the Bull of Heaven she set up lamentation.

But Gilgamesh called the smiths and the armourers, all of them together. They admired the immensity of the horns. They were plated with lapis lazuli two fingers thick. They were thirty pounds each in weight, and their capacity in oil was six measures, which he gave to his guardian god, Lugalbanda. But he carried the horns into the palace and hung them on the wall. Then they washed their hands in Euphrates, they embraced each other and went away. They drove through the streets of Uruk where the heroes were gathered to see them, and Gilgamesh called to the singing girls, *Who is most glorious of the heroes, who is most eminent among men?*

Gilgamesh is the most glorious of heroes; Gilgamesh is most eminent among men. And now there was feasting, and celebrations and joy in the palace, till the heroes lay down saying, *Now we will rest for the night.*

When the daylight came, Enkidu got up and cried to Gilgamesh, *O my brother, such a dream I had last night. Anu (An), Enlil, Ea (Enki) and heavenly Shamash (Utu) took counsel together, and Anu (An) said to Enlil, "Because they have killed the Bull of Heaven, and because they have killed Humbaba who guarded the Cedar Mountain one of the two must, die."*

Then Glorious Shamash (Utu) answered the hero Enlil, *It was by your command they killed the Bull of Heaven, and killed Humbaba, and must Enkidu die although innocent?*

Enlil flung around in rage at Glorious Shamash (Utu), *You dare to say this, you who went about with them every day like one of themselves!*

So, Enkidu lay stretched out before Gilgamesh; his tears ran down in streams and he said to Gilgamesh, *O my brother, so dear as you are to me, brother, yet they will take me from you.* Again, he said, *I must sit down on the threshold of the dead and never again will I see my dear brother with my eyes.*

While Enkidu lay alone in his sickness, he cursed the gate as though it was living flesh, *You there, wood of the gate, dull and insensible, witless, I searched for you over twenty leagues until I saw the towering cedar. There is no wood like you in our land. Seventy-two cubits high (32 metres) and twenty-four wide (12 metres wide), the pivot and the ferrule and the jambs are perfect. A master craftsman from Nippur has made you; but O, if I had known the conclusion! If I had known that this was all the good that would come of it, I would have raised the axe and split you into little pieces and set up here a gate of wattle instead. Ah, if only some future King had brought you here or some god had fashioned you. Let him obliterate my name and write his own, and the curse fall on him instead of on Enkidu.*

With the first brightening of dawn, Enkidu raised his head and wept before the Sun God, in the brilliance of the sunlight his tears streamed down. *Sun God, I beseech you, about that vile Trapper, that Trapper of nothing because of whom I was to catch less than my comrade; let him catch least, make his game scarce, make him feeble, taking the smaller of every share, let his quarry escape from his nets.*

When he had cursed the Trapper to his heart's content, he turned on the harlot. He was roused to curse her also. *As for you, woman, with a great curse I curse you! I will promise you a destiny to all eternity. My curse shall come on you soon and sudden. You shall be without a roof for your commerce, for you shall not keep house with other girls in the tavern but do your business in places fouled by the vomit of the drunkard. Your hire will be potter's earth, your thieving's will be flung into the hovel, you will sit at the cross-roads in the dust of the potter's quarter, and you will make your bed on the dunghill at night, and by day take your stand in the wall's shadow. Brambles and thorns will tear your feet, the drunk and the dry will strike your cheek and your mouth will ache. Let you be stripped of your purple dyes, for I too once in the wilderness with my wife had all the treasure I wished.*

When Shamash (Utu) heard the words of Enkidu, he called to him from heaven: *Enkidu, why are you cursing the woman, the mistress who taught you to eat bread fit for gods and drink wine of Kings? She who put upon you a magnificent garment, did she not give you glorious Gilgamesh for your companion, and has not Gilgamesh, your own brother, made you rest on a royal bed and recline on a couch at his left hand? He has made the princes of the earth kiss your feet, and now all the people of Uruk lament and wail over you. When you are dead, he will let his hair grow long for your sake, he will wear a lion's pelt and wander through the desert.*

When Enkidu heard glorious Shamash (Utu), his angry heart grew quiet, he called back the curse and said, *Woman, I promise you another destiny. The mouth which cursed you shall bless you! Kings, princes and nobles shall adore you. On your account a man though twelve miles off will clap his hand to his thigh and his hair will twitch. For you he will undo his belt and open his treasure and you* shall have your desire, lapis lazuli, gold and carnelian from the heap in the treasury. A ring for your hand and a robe shall be yours. The priest will lead you into the presence of the gods. On your account a wife, a mother of seven, was forsaken.

As Enkidu slept alone in his sickness, in bitterness of spirit, he poured out his heart to his friend. *It was I who cut down the cedar, I who levelled the forest, I who slew Humbaba and now see what has become of me. Listen, my friend, this is the dream I dreamed last night. The heavens roared, and earth rumbled back an answer; between them stood I before an awful being, the sombre-faced manbird; he had directed on me his purpose. His was a vampire face, his foot was a lion's foot, and his hand was an eagle's talon.*

He fell on me and his claws were in my hair, he held me fast and I smothered; then he transformed me so that my arms became wings covered with feathers. He turned his stare towards me, and he led me away to the Palace of Irkalla (Also Ereshkigal), the Queen of Darkness, to the house from which none who enters ever returns, down the road from which there is no coming back. There is the house whose people sit in darkness; dust is their food and clay their meat. They are clothed like birds with wings for covering, they see no light, they sit in darkness.

I entered the house of dust and I saw the Kings of the earth, their crowns put away for ever; rulers and princes, all those who once wore Kingly crowns and ruled the world in the days of old. They who had stood in the place of the gods like Ann (An) and Enlil stood now like servants to fetch baked meats in the house of dust, to carry cooked meat and cold water from the water-skin. In the house of dust which I entered were high priests and acolytes, priests of the incantation and of ecstasy; there were servers of the temple, and there was Etana, that King of Kish whom the eagle carried to heaven in the days of old.

I saw also Samuqan, god of cattle, and there was Ereshkigal the Queen of the Underworld and Goddess of Kur; and Befit-Sheri (Keeps the book of the dead) squatted in front of her, she who is recorder of the gods and keeps the book of death. She held a tablet from which she read. She raised her head; she saw me and spoke: "Who has brought this one here?" Then I awoke like a man drained of blood who wanders alone in a waste of rashes; like one whom the bailiff has seized and his heart pounds with terror.

Gilgamesh had peeled off his clothes, he listened to his words and wept quick tears, Gilgamesh listened, and his tears flowed. He opened his mouth and spoke to Enkidu: *Who is there in strong-walled Uruk who has wisdom like this? Strange things have been spoken, why does your heart speak strangely? The dream was marvellous, but the terror was great; we must treasure the dream whatever the terror; for the dream has shown that misery comes at last to the healthy man, the end of life is sorrow.* And Gilgamesh lamented, *Now I will pray to the great gods, for my friend had an ominous dream.*

This day on which Enkidu dreamed came to an end and he lay stricken with sickness. One whole day he lay on his bed and his suffering increased. He said to Gilgamesh, the friend on whose account he had left the wilderness, *Once I ran for you, for the water of life, and I now have nothing:* A second day he lay on his bed and Gilgamesh watched over him but the sickness increased. A third day he lay on his bed; he called out to Gilgamesh, rousing him up. Now he was weak, and his eyes were blind with weeping.

Ten days he lay, and his suffering increased eleven and twelve days he lay on his bed of pain. Then he called to Gilgamesh, *My friend, the great goddess cursed me, and I must die in shame. I shall not die like a man fallen in battle; I feared to fall, but happy is the man who falls in the battle, for I must die in shame.* And Gilgamesh wept over Enkidu. With the first light of dawn, he raised his voice and said to the counsellors of Uruk:

Hear me, great ones of Uruk, I weep for Enkidu, my friend, bitterly moaning like a woman mourning I weep for my brother.

O Enkidu, my brother, you were the axe at my side, my hand's strength, the sword in my belt, the shield before me, a glorious robe, my fairest ornament; an evil fate has robbed me.

The wild ass and the gazelle that were father and mother, all long-tailed creatures that nourished you Weep for you, all the wild things of the plain and pastures.

The paths that you loved in the forest of cedars night and day murmur.

Let the great ones of strong-walled Uruk weep for you.

Let the finger of blessing be stretched out in mourning.

Enkidu, young brother. Hark, there is an echo through all the country like a mother mourning.

Weep all the paths where we walked together; and the beasts we hunted, the bear and hyena, tiger and panther, leopard and lion, the stag and the ibex, the bull, and the doe.

The river along whose banks we used to walk, weeps for you,

Ula of Elam and dear Euphrates where once we drew water for the waterskins.

The mountain we climbed where we slew the Watchman, weeps for you.

The warriors of strong-walled Uruk where the Bull of Heaven was killed, weep for you.

All the people of Eridu weep for you Enkidu.

Those who brought grain for your eating mourn for you now; who rubbed oil on your back mourn for you now; who poured beer for your drinking mourn for you now.

The harlot who anointed you with fragrant ointment laments for you now; the women of the palace, who brought you a wife, a chosen ring of good advice, lament for you now.

And the young men your brothers as though they were women go long-haired in mourning.

What is this sleep which holds you now? You are lost in the dark and cannot hear me.

He touched his heart, but it did not beat, nor did he lift his eyes again. When Gilgamesh touched his heart, it did not beat. So, Gilgamesh laid a veil, as one veils the bride, over his friend. He began to rage like a lion, like a lioness robbed of her whelps. This way and that he paced round the bed, he tore out his hair and strewed it around. He dragged of his splendid robes and flung them down as though they were abominations.

In the first light of dawn, Gilgamesh cried out, *I made you rest on a royal bed, you reclined on a couch at my left hand, and the princes of the earth kissed your feet. I will cause all the people of Uruk to weep over you and raise the dirge of the dead. The joyful people will stoop with sorrow; and when you have gone to the earth, I will let my hair grow long for your sake, I will wander through the wilderness in the skin of a lion.* The next day also, in the first light, Gilgamesh lamented; seven days and seven nights he wept for Enkidu, until the worm fastened on him. Only then he gave him up to the earth, for the Anunnaki (group of Deities), the judges, had seized him.

Then Gilgamesh issued a proclamation through the land, he summoned them all, the coppersmiths, the goldsmiths, the stoneworkers and commanded them, *Make a statue of my friend*. The statue was fashioned with a great weight of lapis lazuli for the breast and of gold for the body. A table of hard wood was set out, and on it a bowl of carnelian filled with honey, and a bowl of lapis lazuli filled with butter. These he exposed and offered to the Sun; and weeping he went away.

The Search for Everlasting Life

Bitterly, Gilgamesh wept for his friend Enkidu; he wandered over the wilderness as a hunter, he roamed over the plains; in his bitterness he cried, *How can I rest, how can I be at peace? Despair is in my heart. What my brother is now, that shall I be when I am dead. Because I am afraid of death I will go as best I can to find Utnapishtim (He who saw life! Ziusudra of Shuruppak Noah of Sumer) whom they call the Faraway, for he has entered the assembly of the gods.* So Gilgamesh travelled over the wilderness, he wandered over the grasslands, a long journey, in search of Utnapishtim (*Ziusudra*), whom the gods took after the deluge; and they set him to live in the land of Dilmun, in the garden of the sun; and to him alone of men they gave everlasting life.

At night when he came to the mountain passes Gilgamesh prayed: *In these mountain passes long ago I saw lions, I was afraid and I lifted my eyes to the moon; I prayed and my prayers went up to the gods, so now, O moon god Sin, protect me.* When he had prayed, he lay down to sleep, until he was woken from out of a dream. He saw the lions round him glorying in life; then he took his axe in his hand, he drew his sword from his belt, and he fell upon them like an arrow from the string and struck and destroyed and scattered them.

So, at length Gilgamesh came to Mashu, the great mountains about which he had heard many things, which guard the rising and the setting sun. Its twin peaks are as high as the wall of heaven and its paps (hanging breasts) reach down to the underworld. At its gate the Scorpions stand guard, half man and half dragon; their glory is terrifying, their stare strikes death into men, their shimmering halo sweeps the mountains that guard the rising sun. When Gilgamesh saw them, he shielded his eyes for the length of a moment only; then he took courage and approached.

When they saw him so undismayed, the Man-Scorpion called to his mate, *This one who comes to us now is flesh of the gods.*

The mate of the Man-Scorpion answered, *Two thirds is god but one third is man.*

Then he called to the man Gilgamesh, he called to the child of the gods: *Why have you come so great a journey; for what have you travelled so far, crossing the dangerous waters; tell me the reason for your coming?*

Gilgamesh answered, *For Enkidu; I loved him dearly, together we endured all kinds of hardships; on his account I have come, for the common lot of man has taken him. I have wept for him day and night, I would not give up his body for burial, I thought my friend would come back because of my weeping. Since he went, my life is nothing; that is why I have travelled here in search of Utnapishtim (Ziusudra) my father; for men say he has entered the assembly of the gods and has found everlasting life: I have a desire to question him, concerning the living and the dead.*

The Man-Scorpion opened his mouth and said, speaking to Gilgamesh, *No man born of woman has done what you have asked, no mortal man has gone into the mountain; the length of it is twelve leagues (17 miles) of darkness; in it there is no light, but the heart is oppressed with darkness. From the rising of the sun to the setting of the sun there is no light.*

Gilgamesh said, *Although I should go in sorrow and in pain, with sighing and with weeping, still I must go. Open the gate of the mountain.*

And the Man-Scorpion said, *Go, Gilgamesh, I permit you to pass through the mountain of Mashu and through the high ranges; may your feet carry you safely home. The gate of the mountain is open.*

When Gilgamesh heard this, he did as the Man-Scorpion had said, he followed the sun's road to his rising, through the mountain. When he had gone one league the darkness became thick around him, for there was no light, he could see nothing ahead and nothing behind him. After two leagues the darkness was thick and there was no light, he could see nothing ahead and nothing behind him. After three leagues the darkness was thick, and there was no light, he could see nothing ahead and nothing behind him.

After four leagues, the darkness was thick and there was no light, he could see nothing ahead and nothing behind him. At the end of five leagues the darkness was thick and there was no light, he could see nothing ahead and nothing behind him. At the end of six leagues the darkness was thick and there was no light, he could see nothing ahead and nothing behind him. When he had gone seven leagues, the darkness was thick and there was no light, he could see nothing ahead and nothing behind him.

When he had gone eight leagues, Gilgamesh gave a great cry, for the darkness was thick and he could see nothing ahead and nothing behind him. After nine leagues he felt the north-wind on his face, but the darkness was thick and there was no light, he could see nothing ahead and nothing behind him. After ten leagues the end was near: After eleven leagues, the dawn light appeared. At the end of twelve leagues, the sun streamed out.

There was the garden of the gods; all around him stood bushes bearing gems. Seeing it he went down at once, for there was fruit of carnelian with the vine hanging from it, beautiful to look at; lapis lazuli leaves hung thick with fruit, sweet to see. For thorns and thistles there were haematite and rare stones, agate, and pearls from out of the sea. While Gilgamesh walked in the garden by the edge of the sea, Shamash (Utu) saw him, and he saw that he was dressed in the skins of animals and ate their flesh. He was distressed, and he spoke and said, *No mortal man has gone this way before, or will, as long as the winds drive over the sea.*

And to Gilgamesh, he said, Y*ou will never find the life for which you are searching.*

Gilgamesh said to glorious Shamash (Utu), *Now that I have toiled and strayed so far over the wilderness, am I to sleep, and let the earth cover my head for ever? Let my eyes see the sun until they are dazzled with looking. Although I am no better than a dead man, still let me see the light of the sun.*

Beside the sea she lives, the woman of the vine, the maker, of wine; Siduri (Female Fermentation Divinity) sits in the garden at the edge of the sea, with the golden bowl and the golden vats that the gods gave her. She is covered with a veil; and where she sits, she sees Gilgamesh coming towards her, wearing skins, the flesh of the gods in his body, but despair in his heart, and his face like the face of one who has made a long journey. She looked, and as she scanned the distance, she said in her own heart, *Surely this is some felon; where is he going now?*

And she barred her gate against him with the crossbar and shot home the bolt. But Gilgamesh, hearing the sound of the bolt, threw up his head and lodged his foot in the gate; he called to her, *Young woman, maker of wine, why do you bolt your door; what did you see that made you bar your gate? I will break in your door and burst in your gate, for I am Gilgamesh who seized and killed the Bull* of Heaven, I killed the watchman of the cedar forest, I overthrew Humbaba who lived in the forest, and I killed the lions in the passes of the mountain.

Then Siduri said to him, *If you are that Gilgamesh who seized and killed the Bull of Heaven, who killed the watchman of the cedar forest, who overthrew Humbaba that lived in the forest, and killed the lions in the passes of the mountain, why are your cheeks so starved and why is your face so drawn? Why is despair in your heart and your face like the face of one who has made a long journey? Yes, why is your face burned from heat and cold, and why do you come here wandering over the pastures in search of the wind?*

Gilgamesh answered her, *And why should not my cheeks be starved, and my face drawn? Despair is in my heart and my face is the face of one who has made a long journey, it was burned with heat and with cold. Why should I not wander over the pastures in search of the wind? My friend, my younger brother, he who hunted the wild ass of the wilderness and the panther of the plains, nay friend, my younger brother who seized and killed the Bull of Heaven and overthrew Humbaba in the cedar forest, my friend who was very dear to me and who endured dangers beside me, Enkidu my brother, whom I laved, the end of mortality has overtaken him. I wept for him seven days and nights till the worm fastened on him.*

Because of my brother, I am afraid of death, because of my brother I stray through the wilderness and cannot rest. But now, young woman, maker of wine, since I have seen your face does not let me see the face of death which I dread so much.

She answered, *Gilgamesh, where are you hurrying to? You will never find that life for which you are looking. When the gods created man, they allotted to him death, but life they retained in their own keeping. As for you, Gilgamesh, fill your belly with good things; day and night, night and day, dance and be merry, feast and rejoice. Let your clothes be fresh, bathe yourself in water, cherish the little child that holds your hand, and make your wife happy in your embrace; for this too is the lot of man.*

But Gilgamesh said to Siduri, the young woman, *How can I be silent, how can I rest, when Enkidu whom I love is dust, and I too shall die and be laid in the earth. You live by the seashore and look into the heart of it; young woman, tell me now, which is the way to Utnapishtim (Ziusudra), the son of Ubara-Tutu (Last pre-deluge King of Shuruppak)? What directions are there for the passage;*

give me, oh, give me directions. I will cross the Ocean if it is possible; if it is not, I will wander still farther in the wilderness.

The wine-maker said to him, *Gilgamesh, there is no crossing the Ocean; whoever has come, since the days of old, has not been able to pass that sea. The Sun in his glory crosses the Ocean, but who beside Shamash (Utu) has ever crossed it? The place and the passage are difficult, and the waters of death are deep which flow between. Gilgamesh, how will you cross the Ocean? When you come to the waters of death what will you do? But Gilgamesh, down in the woods you will find Urshanabi (Who overseen the building of the Arc, at the time named Puzur-Kurgal, then became the Ferryman after the Great Flood Sur-Sunabu, the protector of eternity), the ferryman of Utnapishtim (Ziusudra); with him are the holy things, the things of stone. He is fashioning the serpent prow of the boat. Look at him well, and if it is possible, perhaps you will cross the waters with him; but if it is not possible, then you must go back.*

When Gilgamesh heard this, he was seized with anger. He took his axe in his hand and his dagger from his belt. He crept forward and he fell on them like a javelin. Then he went into the forest and sat down. Urshanabi (Sur-Sunabu) saw the dagger flash and heard the axe, and he beat his head, for Gilgamesh had shattered the tackle of the boat in his rage.

Urshanabi (Sur-Sunabu) said to him, *Tell me, what your name is? I am Urshanabi (Sur-Sunabu), the ferryman of Utnapishtim (Ziusudra) the Faraway.*

He replied to him, *Gilgamesh is my name; I am from Uruk, from the house of Anu (An).*

Then Urshanabi (Sur-Sunabu) said to him, *Why are your cheeks so starved and your face drawn? Why is despair in your heart and your face like the face of one who has made a long journey; yes, why is your face burned with heat and with cold, and why do you come here wandering over the pastures in search of the wind?*

Gilgamesh said to him, *Why should not my cheeks be starved, and my face drawn? Despair is in my heart, and my face is the face of one who has made a long journey. I was burned with heat and with cold. Why should I not wander over the pastures? My friend, my younger brother who seized and killed the Bull of Heaven, and overthrew Humbaba in the cedar forest, my friend who was very dear to me, and who endured dangers beside me, Enkidu my brother whom I loved, the end of mortality has overtaken him. I wept for him seven days and nights till the worm fastened on him. Because of my brother I am afraid of death, because of my brother I stray through the wilderness. His fate lies heavy upon me. How can I be silent, how can I rest? He is dust and I too shall die and be laid in the earth for ever. I am afraid of death, therefore, Urshanabi (Sur-Sunabu), tell me which is the road to Utnapishtim? If it is possible, I will cross the waters of death; if not I will wander still farther through the wilderness.*

Urshanabi (Sur-Sunabu) said to him, *Gilgamesh, your own hands have prevented you from crossing the Ocean; when you destroyed the tackle of the boat you destroyed its safety.*

Then the two of them talked it over and Gilgamesh said, *Why are you so angry with me, Urshanabi (Sur-Sunabu), for you yourself cross the sea by day and night, at all seasons you cross it.*

Gilgamesh, those things you destroyed, their property is to carry me over the water, to prevent the waters of death from touching me. It was for this reason that I preserved them, but you have destroyed them, and the urnu snakes (possibly sailing ropes) with them. But now, go into the forest, Gilgamesh; with your axe cut poles, one hundred and twenty, cut them sixty cubits long, paint them with bitumen, set on them ferrules and bring them back.

When Gilgamesh heard this, he went into the forest, he cut poles one hundred and twenty; he cut them sixty cubits long, he painted them with bitumen, he set on them ferrules, and he brought them to Urshanabi (Sur-Sunabu). Then they boarded the boat, Gilgamesh and Urshanabi (Sur-Sunabu) together, launching it out on the waves of Ocean. For three days they ran on as it were a journey of a month and fifteen days, and at last Urshanabi (Sur-Sunabu) brought the boat to the waters of death.

Then Urshanabi (Sur-Sunabu) said to Gilgamesh, *Press on, take a pole and thrust it in, but do not let your hands touch the waters. Gilgamesh, take a second pole, take a third, take a fourth pole. Now, Gilgamesh, take a fifth, take a sixth and seventh pole. Gilgamesh take an eighth, and ninth, a tenth pole. Gilgamesh, take an eleventh, take a twelfth pole.* After one hundred and twenty thrusts Gilgamesh had used the last pole. Then he stripped himself, he held up his arms for a mast and his covering for a sail. So Urshanabi (Sur-Sunabu) the ferryman brought Gilgamesh to Utnapishtim *(Ziusudra)*, whom they call the Faraway, who lives in Dilmun at the place of the sun's transit, eastward of the mountain. To him alone of men, the gods had given everlasting life.

Now Utnapishtim *(Ziusudra)*, where he lay at ease, looked into the distance and he said in his heart, musing to himself, *Why does the boat sail here without tackle and mast; why are the sacred stones destroyed, and why does the master not sail the boat? That man who comes is none of mine; where I look, I see a man whose body is covered with skins of beasts. Who is this who walks up the shore behind Urshanabi (Sur-Sunabu), for surely, he is no man of mine?*

So Utnapishtim *(Ziusudra)* looked at him and said, *What is your name, you who come here wearing the skins of beasts, with your cheeks starved and your face drawn? Where are you hurrying to now? For what reasons have you made this great journey, crossing "the seas whose passage is difficult"? Tell me the reason for your coming.*

He replied, *Gilgamesh is my name. I am from Uruk, from the house of Anu (An).*

Then Utnapishtim *(Ziusudra)* said to him, *If you are Gilgamesh, why are your cheeks so starved and your face drawn? Why is despair in your heart and your face like the face of one who has made a long journey? Yes, why is your face burned with heat and cold; and why do you come here, wandering over the wilderness in search of the wind?*

Gilgamesh said to him, *Why should not my cheeks be starved, and my face drawn? Despair is in my heart and my face is the face of one who has made a long journey. It was burned with heat and with cold. Why should I not wander over the pastures? My friend, my younger brother who seized and killed the Bull of Heaven and overthrew Humbaba in the cedar forest, my friend who was very dear to me and endured dangers beside me, Enkidu, my brother whom I loved, the end of mortality has overtaken him. I wept for him seven days and nights till the worm fastened on him.*

Because of my brother, I am afraid of death; because of my brother I stray through the wilderness. His fate lies heavy upon me. How can I be silent, how can I rest? He is dust and I shall die also and be laid in the earth for ever.

Again, Gilgamesh said, speaking to Utnapishtim *(Ziusudra)*, *It is to see Utnapishtim (Ziusudra) whom we call the Faraway that I have come this journey. For this I have wandered over the world, I have crossed many difficult ranges, I have crossed the seas, I have wearied myself with travelling; my joints are aching, and I have lost acquaintance with sleep which is sweet. My clothes were worn out before I came to the house of Siduri. I have killed the bear and hyena,* the lion and panther, the tiger, the stag and the ibex, all sorts of wild game and the small creatures of the pastures.

I ate their flesh, and I wore their skins; and that was how I came to the gate of the young woman, the maker of wine, who barred her gate of pitch and bitumen against me. But from her I had news of the journey; so, then I came to Urshanabi (Sur-Sunabu) the ferryman, and with him I crossed over the waters of death. Oh, father Utnapishtim, you who have entered the assembly of the gods, I wish to question you concerning the living and the dead, how shall I find the life for which I am searching?

Utnapishtim *(Ziusudra)* said, *There is no permanence. Do we build a house to stand forever; do we seal a contract to hold for all time? Do brothers divide an inheritance to keep forever; does the flood-time of rivers endure? It is only the nymph of the dragonfly who sheds her larva and sees the sun in his glory. From the days of old there is no permanence. The sleeping and the dead, how alike they are, they are like a painted death (Skull culture?). What is there between the master and the servant when both have fulfilled their doom? When the Anunnaki, the judges, come together, and Mammetun (Mamitu Goddess of Fate) the mother of destinies, together they decree the fates of men. Life and death, they allot but the day of death they do not disclose.*

Then Gilgamesh said to Utnapishtim *(Ziusudra)* the Faraway, *I look at you now, Utnapishtim (Ziusudra), and your appearance is no different from mine; there is nothing strange in your features. I thought I should find, you like a hero prepared for battle, but you he here taking your ease on your back. Tell me truly, how was it that you came to enter the company of the gods and to possess everlasting life?*

Utnapishtim *(Ziusudra)* said to Gilgamesh, *I will reveal to you a mystery; I will tell you a secret of the gods.*

The Story of the Flood

You know the city Shuruppak; it stands on the banks of Euphrates? That city grew old and the gods that were in it were old. There was Anu (An), lord of the firmament, their father, and warrior Enlil their counsellor, Ninurta (Ningirsu) the helper, and Ennugi watcher over canals; and with them also was Ea. In those days the world teemed, the people multiplied, the world bellowed like a wild bull, and the great god was aroused by the clamour. Enlil heard the clamour and he said to the gods in council, *The uproar of mankind is intolerable, and sleep is no longer possible by reason of the babel.*

So, the gods agreed to exterminate mankind. Enlil did this, but Ea because of his oath warned me in a dream. He whispered their words to my house of reeds, *Reed-house, reed-house! Wall, O wall, hearken reed-house, wall reflect; O man of Shuruppak, son of Ubara-Tutu; tear down your house and build a boat, abandon possessions, and look for life, despise worldly goods and save your soul alive. Tear down your house, I say, and build a boat. These are the measurements of the barque as you shall build her: let hex beam equal her length, let her deck be roofed like the vault that covers the abyss; then take up into the boat the seed of all living creatures.*

When I had understood I said to my lord, "Behold, what you have commanded I will honour and perform, but how shall I answer the people, the city, the elders?" Then Ea opened his mouth and said to me, his servant, "Tell them this: I have learnt that Enlil is wrathful against me, I dare no longer walk in his land nor live in his city; I will go down to the Gulf to dwell with Ea my lord. But on you he will rain down abundance, rare fish and shy wild-fowl, a rich harvest-tide. In the evening, the rider of the storm will bring you wheat in torrents."

In the first light of dawn, all my household gathered around me, the children brought pitch and the men whatever was necessary. On the fifth day I laid the keel and the ribs, then I made fast the planking. The ground-space was one acre, each side of the deck measured one hundred and twenty cubits, making a square. I built six decks below, seven in all, I divided them into nine sections with bulkheads between. I drove in wedges where needed, I saw to the punt poles, and laid in supplies.

The carriers brought oil in baskets, I poured pitch into the furnace and asphalt and oil; more oil was consumed in caulking, and more again the master of the boat took into his stores. I slaughtered bullocks for the people and every day I killed sheep. I gave the shipwrights wine to drink as though it were river water, raw wine and red wine and oil and white wine. There was feasting then as there is at the time of the New Year's festival; I myself anointed my head. On the seventh day the boat was complete.

Then was the launching full of difficulty; there was shifting of ballast above and below till two thirds was submerged. I loaded into her all that had of gold and of living things, my family, my kin, the beast of the field both wild and tame, and all the craftsmen. I sent them on board, for the time that Shamash (Utu) had ordained was already fulfilled when he said, *In the evening, when the rider of the storm sends down the destroying rain, enter the boat and batten her down.*

The time was fulfilled, the evening came, the rider of the storm sent down the rain. I looked out at the weather and it was terrible, so I too boarded the boat and battened her down. All was now complete, the battening and the caulking so, I handed the tiller to Puzur-Amurri (later the Ferryman of the underworld) the steersman, with the navigation and the care of the whole boat.

With the first light of dawn a black cloud came from the horizon; it thundered within where Adad (Iskur), lord of the storm was riding. In front over hill and plain Shullat and Hanish (Protectors of Adad), heralds of the storm, led on. Then the gods of the abyss rose up; Nergal (Irra, the god of scorched earth and war) pulled out the dams of the nether waters, Ninurta (Ningirsu) the warlord threw down the dykes, and the seven judges of hell, the Anunnaki (group of Deities), raised their torches, lighting the land with their livid flame. A stupor of despair went up to heaven when the god of the storm turned daylight to darkness, when he smashed the land like a cup.

One whole day the tempest raged, gathering fury as it went, it poured over the people like the tides of battle; a imam could not see his brother, nor the people be seen from heaven. Even the gods were terrified at the flood, they fled to the highest heaven, the firmament of Ann; they crouched against the walls, cowering like curs.

Then Ishtar (Inanna) the sweet-voiced Queen of Heaven cried out like a woman in travail: *Alas the days of old are turned to dust because I commanded evil; why did I command thus evil in the council of all the gods? I commanded wars to destroy the people, but are they not my people, for I brought them forth? Now like the spawn of fish they float in the ocean.* The great gods of heaven and of hell wept, they covered their mouths.

For six days and six nights, the winds blew, torrent and tempest and flood overwhelmed the world, tempest and flood raged together like warring hosts. When the seventh day dawned the storm from the south subsided, the sea grew calm, the, flood was stilled; I looked at the face of the world and there was silence, all mankind was turned to clay. The surface of the sea stretched as flat as a roof-top; I opened a hatch and the light fell on my face.

Then I bowed low, I sat down, and I wept, the tears streamed down my face, for on every side was the waste of water. I looked for land in vain, but fourteen leagues distant there appeared a mountain, and there the boat grounded; on the mountain of Nisir (Pir Omar Gudrun *The Mount of Salvation*) the boat held fast, she held fast and did not budge. One day she held, and a second day on the mountain of Nisir she held fast and did not budge. A third day, and a fourth day she held fast on the mountain and did not budge; a fifth day and a sixth day she held fast on the mountain.

When the seventh day dawned, I loosed a dove and let her go. She flew away but finding no resting-place she returned. Then I loosed a swallow, and she flew away but finding no resting-place she returned. I loosed a raven, she saw that the waters had retreated, she ate, she flew around, she cawed, and she did not come back. Then I threw everything open to the four winds, I made a sacrifice and poured out a libation on the mountain top.

Seven and again seven cauldrons I set up on their stands, I heaped up wood and cane and cedar and myrtle. When the gods smelled the sweet savour, they gathered like flies over the sacrifice. Then, at last, Ishtar (Inanna) also came, she lifted her necklace with the jewels of heaven that once Anu (An) had made to please her. *O you gods here present, by the lapis lazuli round my neck I shall remember these days as I remember the jewels of my throat; these last days I shall not forget. Let all the gods gather round the sacrifice, except Enlil. He shall not approach this offering, for without reflection he brought the flood; he consigned my people to destruction.*

When Enlil had come, when he saw the boat, he was wrath and swelled with anger at the gods, the host of heaven, *Has any of these mortals escaped? Not one was to have survived the destruction.*

Then the god of the wells and canals Ninurta (Ningirsu) opened his mouth and said to the warrior Enlil, *Who is there of the gods that can devise without Ea? It is Ea alone who knows all things.*

Then Ea opened his mouth and spoke to warrior Enlil, *Wisest of gods, hero Enlil, how could you so senselessly bring down the flood?*

Lay upon the sinner his sin,
Lay upon the transgressor his transgression,
Punish him a little when he breaks loose,
Do not drive him too hard or he perishes,

Would that a lion had ravaged mankind, Rather than the flood,
Would that a wolf had ravaged mankind, Rather than the flood,
Would that famine had wasted the world, Rather than the flood,
Would that pestilence had wasted mankind, Rather than the flood.
It was not I that revealed the secret of the gods; the wise man learned it in a dream. Now take your counsel what shall be done with him.

Then Enlil went up into the boat, he took me by the hand and my wife and made us enter the boat and kneel down on either side, he is standing between us. He touched our foreheads to bless us saying, *In time past Utnapishtim (Ziusudra) was a mortal man; henceforth he and his wife shall live in the distance at the mouth of the rivers.* Thus, it was that the gods took me and placed me here to live in the distance, at the mouth of the rivers.'

The Return

Utnapishtim *(Ziusudra)* said, *As for you, Gilgamesh, who will assemble the gods for your sake, so that you may find that life for which you are searching? But if you wish, come and put into the test: only prevail against sleep for six days and seven nights.*

But while Gilgamesh sat there resting on his haunches, a mist of sleep like soft wool teased from the fleece drifted over him, and Utnapishtim *(Ziusudra)* said to his wife, *Look at him now, the strong man who would have everlasting life, even now the mists of sleep are drifting over him.*

His wife replied, *Touch the man to wake him, so that he may return to his own land in peace, going back through the gate by which he came.*

Utnapishtim *(Ziusudra)* said to his wife, *All men are deceivers, even you he will attempt to deceive; therefore, bake loaves of bread, each day one loaf, and put it beside his head; and make a mark on the wall to number the days he has slept.*

So she baked loaves of bread, each day one loaf, and put it beside his head, and she marked on the wall the days that he slept; and there came a day when the first loaf was hard, the second loaf was like leather, the third was soggy, the crust of the fourth had mould, the fifth was mildewed, the sixth was fresh, and the seventh was still on the embers. Then Utnapishtim *(Ziusudra)* touched him and he woke. Gilgamesh said to Utnapishtim *(Ziusudra)* the Faraway, *I hardly slept when you touched and roused me.*

But Utnapishtim *(Ziusudra)* said, *Count these loaves and learn how many days you slept, for your first is hard, your second like leather, your third is soggy, the crust of your fourth has mould, your fifth is mildewed, your sixth is fresh and your seventh was still over the glowing embers when I touched and woke you.*

Gilgamesh said, *What shall I do, O Utnapishtim (Ziusudra), where shall I go? Already the thief in the night has hold of my limbs, death inhabits my room; wherever my footrests, there I find death.*

Then Utnapishtim *(Ziusudra)* spoke to Urshanabi (Sur-Sunabu) the ferryman: *Woe to you Urshanabi (Sur-Sunabu), now and for ever more you have become hateful to this harbourage; it is not for you, nor for you are the crossings of this sea. Go now, banished from the shore. But this man before whom you walked, bringing him here, whose body is covered with foulness and the grace of whose limbs has been spoiled by wild skins, take him to the washing-place. There he shall wash his long hair clean as snow in the water, he shall throw off his skins and let the sea carry them away, and the beauty of his body shall be shown, the fillet on his forehead shall be renewed, and he shall be given clothes to cover his nakedness. Till he reaches his own city, and his journey is accomplished, these clothes will show no sign of age, they will wear like a new garment.*

So Urshanabi (Sur-Sunabu) took Gilgamesh and led him to the washing-place, he washed his long hair as clean as snow in the water, he threw off his skins, which the sea carried away, and showed the beauty of his body. He renewed the fillet on his forehead, and to cover his nakedness gave him clothes which would show no sign of age but would war like a new garment till he reached his own city, and his journey was accomplished.

Then Gilgamesh and Urshanabi (Sur-Sunabu) launched the boat on to the water and boarded it, and they made ready to sail away; but the wife of Utnapishtim *(Ziusudra)* the Faraway said to him, *Gilgamesh came here wearied out, he is worn out; what will you give him to carry him back to his own country?*

So Utnapishtim *(Ziusudra)* spoke, and Gilgamesh took a pole and brought the boat in to the bank. *Gilgamesh, you came here a man wearied out, you have worn yourself out; what shall I give you to carry you back to your own country? Gilgamesh, I shall reveal a secret thing, it is a mystery of the gods that I am telling you. There is a plant that grows under the water, it has a prickle like a thorn, like a rose; it will wound your hands, but if you succeed in taking it, then your hands will hold that which restores his lost youth to a man.*

When Gilgamesh heard this, he opened the sluices so that a sweet water current might carry him out to the deepest channel; he tied heavy stones to his feet, and they dragged him down to the waterbed. There he saw the plant growing, although it pricked him, he took it in his hands; then he cut the heavy stones from his feet, and the sea carried him and threw him on to the shore. Gilgamesh said to Urshanabi (Sur-Sunabu) the ferryman, *Come here, and see this marvellous plant. By its virtue a man may win back all his former strength. I will take it to Uruk of the strong walls; there I will give it to the old men to eat. Its name shall be "The Old Men Are Young Again"; and at last I shall eat it myself and have back all my lost youth.*

So, Gilgamesh returned by the gate through which he had come, Gilgamesh and Urshanabi (Sur-Sunabu) went together. They travelled their twenty leagues and then they broke their fast; after thirty leagues they stopped for the night.

Gilgamesh saw a well of cool water and he went down and bathed; but deep in the pool there was lying a serpent, and the serpent sensed the sweetness of the flower. It rose out of the water and snatched it away, and immediately it sloughed its skin and returned to the well. Then Gilgamesh sat down and wept, the tears ran down his face, and he took the hand of Urshanabi (Sur-Sunabu).

O Urshanabi (Sur-Sunabu), was it for this that I toiled with my hands, is it for this I have wrung out my heart's blood? For myself I have gained nothing; not I, but the beast of the earth has joy of it now. Already the stream has carried it twenty leagues back to the channels where I found it. I found a sign and now I have lost it. Let us leave the boat on the bank and go.

After twenty leagues, they broke their fast, after thirty leagues they stopped for the night; in three days they had walked as much as a journey of a month and fifteen days. When the journey was accomplished, they arrived at Uruk, the strong-walled city. Gilgamesh spoke to him, to Urshanabi (Sur-Sunabu) the ferryman, *Urshanabi (Sur-Sunabu), climb up on to the wall of Uruk, inspect its foundation terrace, and examine well the brickwork; see if it is not of burnt bricks; and did not the seven wise men lay these foundations? One third of the whole is city, one third is garden, and one third is field, with the precinct of the goddess Ishtar (Inanna). These parts and the precinct are all Uruk.*

This too was the work of Gilgamesh, the King, who knew the countries of the world. He was wise he saw mysteries and knew secret things, he brought us a tale of the days before the flood. He went a long journey, was weary, worn out with labour, and returning engraved on a stone the whole story.

The Death of Gilgamesh

The destiny was fulfilled which the father of the gods, Enlil of the mountain, had decreed for Gilgamesh: *In nether-earth the darkness will show him a light: of mankind, all that are known, none will leave a monument for generations to come to compare with his. The heroes, the wise men, like the new moon have their waxing and waning. Men will say, "Who has ever ruled with might and with power like him?" As in the dark month, the month of shadows, so without him there is no light. O Gilgamesh, this was the meaning of your dream.*

You were given the Kingship, such was your destiny, everlasting life was not your destiny. Because of this do not be sad at heart, do not be grieved or oppressed; he has given you power to bind and to loose, to be the darkness and the light of mankind. He has given unexampled supremacy over the people, victory in battle from which no fugitive returns, in forays and assaults from which there is no going back. But do not abuse this power, deal justly with your servants in the palace, deal justly before the face of the Sun.

The King has laid himself down and will not rise again,
The Lord of Kullab will not rise again.
He overcame evil, he will not come again.
Though he was strong of arm he will not rise again.
He had wisdom and a comely face; he will not come again.
He is gone into the mountain; he will not come again.
On the bed of fate, he lies, he will not rise again,
Front the couch of many colours he will not come again.

The people of the city, great and small, are not silent; they lift up, the lament, all men of flesh and blood lift up the lament. Fate has spoken; like a hooked fish he lays stretched on the bed, like a gazelle that is caught in a noose. Inhuman Namtar (the god of Death!) is heavy upon him, Namtar that has neither hand nor foot, that drinks no water and eats no meat.

For Gilgamesh, son of Ninsun, they weighed out their offerings; his dear wife, his son, his concubine, his musicians, his jester, and all his household; his servants, his stewards, all who lived in the palace weighed out their offerings for

Gilgamesh the son of Ninsun, the heart of Uruk. They weighed out their offerings to Ereshkigal, the Queen of Death, and to all the gods of the dead. To Namtar, who is fate, they weighed out the offering.

Bread for Ned the Keeper of the Gate, bread for Ningizzida (Ningishzida, the god of medicine) the god of the serpent, the lord of the Tree of Life; for Dumuzi (Tammuz) also, the young shepherd, for Enki (Ea) and Ninki (Ninsar (Lady Green)), for Endukugga and Nindukugga (Parents of Enlil), for Enmul and Nimnul, all the ancestral gods, forbears of Enlil, a feast for Shulpae the god of feasting. For Samuqan, god of the herds, for die mother Ninhursag, and the gods of creation in the place of creation, for the host of heaven, priest and priestess weighed out the offering of the dead.

Gilgamesh, the son of Ninsun, lies in the tomb. At the place of offerings, he weighed the bread-offering, at the place of libation he poured out the wine. In those days the lord Gilgamesh departed, the son of Ninsun, the kung, peerless, without an equal among men, who did not neglect Enlil his master. O Gilgamesh, lord of Kullab, great is thy praise.

Gilgamesh Conclusion

We need to understand why the *Epic of Gilgamesh* has received such longevity and how the piece of work has been passed from each dominant Middle Eastern Kingdom to the next. But it has very similar undertones as the Iliad and an exhausting, mystical filled journey similar to the Odyssey. Both the Epic of Gilgamesh and the Iliad have followed a similar trajectory and captured the imagination of modern society.[18] Gilgamesh has really entered the artistic consciousness of the West, from Iraq to Europe and to North America.

In 1912, the first translation appeared into a modern language; the Gilgamesh epic is at least 4,000 years old which has had a profound influence on modern Western Culture. It gives great *snapshot* of what was actually happening at the time. Not the main story, but how people interacted with each other and what their role was in society. Even the weapons taken to slay Humbaba and noticing the Bow made in the Zagros Mountains. The names of the gods give a clear indication as to the importance to certain professions.

---

[18] *Tzvi Abusch in Journal of American Oriental Society Vol 121 No4 (Dec 2001) The Development and Meaning of the Epic of Gilgamesh. The essay traces several versions of the same story.*

Engineering was extremely important to them. Arazu the God of completions and Ennugi the Canal Inspector. Again, you can see the importance of seven throughout the entire story. An important understanding since there is no archaeological remains of the tops of any buildings, that Ishtar (Inanna) made offering on the top of the palace and not just in the temple. So many similarities with the Iliad, that Gilgamesh must have been a very well-known *story* to all the people of the Middle East.

Due to archaeology, we know when the last localised deluges occurred, and scholars have a good understanding when the Epic of Gilgamesh was originally written, and the era that appertains to the story line. The regionalised flooding had a profound impact on the Sumerian people, so to have a story that skirts on this very topic is extremely helpful to researches and students alike. It would be hard to recite a full-blown synopsis of Gilgamesh when such illustrious and learned people know so much more on the subject such as Andrew George, his knowledge of Gilgamesh is breath taking.[19]

The main story has not been overtly corrupted and altered for the sake of change. I believe the multiple messages that Gilgamesh has within the Epic shows the fallibility of humans and therefore resonates at an individual level to all readers. The poem is divided up into several simple sections; the first part introduces Gilgamesh King in Uruk the Ancient city to the South of Babylon in the Ancient Area of Sumer. Uruk was one of the original imposing *City State* that has had several incarnations before its demise and according to *The Sumerian King List*, Gilgamesh was apparently the residing King of Uruk around 2,600 BC.

The Epic shows all of Gilgamesh's imperfections and let's not beat around the bush, he was a narcissistic bastard and ruled terribly over his people with no repercussions, so the Epic reveals the level of divide between the commoners and the King and a whole lot in-between. The Epic does not seek to turn this Greatest of Kings and most glorious of heroes into a one directional arrow, not like every other King in History. Instead it turns him instead into a human being, he is a tyrant, a bully, and an abuser of power. Gilgamesh has been given power and he used it absolutely as a King of the time could. But in doing so he upsets the Gods and they listened to the complaints of the town. So, the Gods sent a

---

[19] *Andrew R George, a British Academic best known for his Epic of Gilgamesh, a Professor of Babylonian, Department of Languages and Cultures of Near and Middle East at the School of Oriental and African Studies, University of London.*

Wild Man (Enkidu) down who is in every respect the image of Gilgamesh. It is also very interesting that the writer can appreciate that the lifestyle isn't as healthy for an individual as a hunter-gatherer. Weakness due to idleness is soon realised, therefore physical problems are disguised with alcohol. except that Gilgamesh is a man of the city and can do anything he wants. This is done through a sequence of events involving the seduction Shamkat the sacred prostitute who is the main protagonist in the emergence of Enkidu. Bringing Enkidu to the city to halt Gilgamesh's wrong doings and to divert his superhuman energies. It gives tantalising geographical glimpses into Dilmun, could this be the Island of Failaka off the coast of modern-day Kuwait city.

Chapter 8
Trade Routes of Southern Mesopotamia

Trade

Commercial instincts are inherent to all of mankind, and to deny the ingenious inter-clan exchange between hunter-gatherers in Neolithic society is to disclaim any contacts with strangers. The earliest evidence of trade in Mesopotamia can be seen in the earliest parts of the Ubaid Period. Sedentary communities conducted barter deals with the neighbouring nomadic groups. These trans-cultural contacts were individual, sporadic, spontaneous, and fragile. But as Eridu and the surrounding villages grew, a clear and distinct trade a multifaceted and complex network began to emerge.

According to Sing C. Chew[cxli] and Daniel Sarabia, trade seems to emanate due to climatic events. Chew and Daniel wrote an interesting article which describes the relations between globalisation, trade, economic processes, nature, and the rhythms of the climate. For the latter, an awareness of the natural rhythms of the climate as well as human induced changes or climate events which triggered system-wide level collapses. Chew states:

In trying to explain globalization there are basically two narratives. The first argues that globalization is the stage reached with the process of accumulation starting at the nation-state level followed with the export of capital in the form of imperialism and overtime the accumulation of capital covers the globe. The other states that globalisation is a process that has occurred through world history, and that it is not a stage reached but one that started at different time periods. With the process starting at least 5000 years ago.

By appreciating that the process of trading / globalisation has its roots in history pre-dating 5,000 years ago, we can confidently link the discovery of the

H3 Site in Kuwait which acted as a mini trade centre. So, we can say with a high degree of certainty that trade was buoyant in 5,570 BC. With sufficient surplus of foods to be able for other members of the group to concentrate on marketing items. From either end of the trade network being accumulated much earlier than current historical findings have suggested. A chicken and two egg scenario.

Can't build a boat if you don't have the trade, can't trade until producing enough and also need at least two points of contact who are willing to trade with each other. Recognising a commercial opportunity helps protect the clan group but may also allow the community to thrive as a whole. Both sides are prospering from the exchange process, increasing the clan's chances of success (survival).

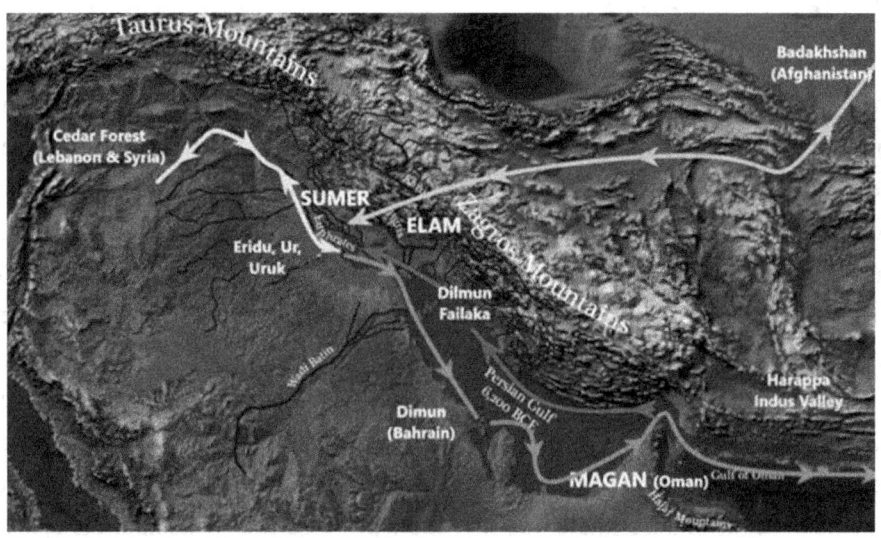

Before describing the trade between the trading partners of the Sumer region of the Fertile Crescent, it would be useful for the reader to understand some of the distances from point-to-point so the reader can visualise the trade distances and to appreciate these distances where not insurmountable. Ur to Bahrain (Dilmun) is approximately 650 Kilometres, Dilmun Bahrain to Muscat, Magan /Oman 1200 Kilometres, Muscat to Karachi the start of Indus Valley 870 Kilometres. As modern humans we have become self-absorbed within national boundaries. Because a Country is classified as being in a different geographical location on a map.

It was easier to go from the Arabian Peninsula to the Indian Subcontinent by boat than Mid-point Persian Gulf to Arabian Peninsula. What became apparent throughout the research for this book, is that commerce always seems to be the driving force that binds all nations together. Conflicts occur between different city states especially within Southern Mesopotamian and its neighbouring regions. But the desire for the aesthetically pleasing items either for the individual or the local temples are a trait of natural human behaviour. Starting with seashells in early trading and leading to intricate cylinder seals at the height of its Commerce.

Therefore, foreign trade is a voluntary transfusion of commodities that another community may not be able to acquire locally but may be rich in other resources that a neighbouring area is lacking *from the land of plenty to the island of deficiency*. It is part of human nature which gained momentum with the arrival of the Neolithic era, bonded by an unbreakable chain of supply and demand. Some people settled on the fertile plains whilst others continued to wander with their livestock. Whilst others took control of mineral resources and some even risked their lives seawater pearl diving, to maintain a source of additional income, and providing a commodity only afforded by the wealthy elite.

Each trading group possessed a unique commodity which could be shared with others. The transition to sedentary life led to the accumulation of food surplus, the basic commodity whose value diminishes with time. Irrigation farming of Southern Mesopotamia allowed a massive surplus stock to be harvested. In turn this surplus could be exchanged for what the towns and villagers lacked, namely vital raw materials and attractive items or metals or stones not commonly available to the local inhabitancy.

The next stage occurred when advanced village communities discovered the potential of the waterborne trade along rivers and coastlines the first glimpses of the Hydraulic Empires. Boats could carry much more weight, grain one direction and building material the opposite direction. Desperately needed commodities could be delivered in bulk directly to the point of request on the banks or shores. Some merchant became the *go between*, buying from one trader and forwarding the goods on to the end user. This only becomes possible if unloading boats can restock with freshwater and make running repairs to vessels before returning homeward such as the Kingdom of Dilmun.

The so-called *Sumerian expansion* created a class of merchants, full-time traders who functioned as part-time government agents. They played the crucial role in establishing diplomatic ties between ambitious governments. The lifelong journey between the lesser of two evils the Scylla of high risk and Charybdis of extreme profit opened the window of business opportunities whilst messengers gradually transformed into self-employed entrepreneurs. The government acted not only as the major customer but also as the protector of lucrative trade. The emergence of the Sumerian trade assumes the existence of firm diplomatic relations between the Sumerian elite and the elite societies of emerging city states. The cities that had grown from the colonies of Uruk and the elderly states in the North of the Fertile Crescent which were surrounded by plenty of natural raw products, primed for exploiting.

If agriculture can be showcased as the driver of the Sumerian economy, its steering wheel was the cross-cultural trade. Over time trade links had become ever more sophisticated, that had tied together the economies of distant lands, and the major factors that shaped the earliest complex societies. In the course of the 6th and 5th Millennium BC, the whole Ancient Middle East was embraced by a web of long-distance trade. This web could channel raw materials such as copper from Magan, obsidian from beyond the Taurus Mountains, ornamental items such as lapis lazuli from Badakhshan, and manufactured products like chlorite bowls from the Elamite Region.

Over hundreds and sometimes thousands of miles and months of travel days. These and other commodities were passed down the line by numerous intermediaries from Anatolian highlands to the Indus Valley through Mesopotamia and the Gulf Region. As well as between the shores of Levant and the deserts of the Central Asia via Mesopotamia, Elam, the Iranian Plateau, and Afghanistan via the Indus Valley. The world trade network had never stopped transforming. Although it would be an exaggeration to claim that all these far-off territories had bilateral relations.

The exchange of commodities took place on a regular basis throughout the entire route, this is when the rise of the Dilmun *Empire* came into existence after previously watching the trade, float by. Contraction and expansion of trading partners was multifaceted affair and very fluid which depended on range of constantly moving variables such as alliances, political, weather, invasion etc. Each territory that formed the ancient trade route possessed unique trading resources, social structure of population, and means of transportation to add to the vast array of shifting political alliances being formed for increased stakeholder share and an increased profit margin.

This wide web of foreign trade was controlled by local rulers who were placed at different stages of power accumulation. The elite groups needed an external mechanism for channelling or acquiring of prestige commodities and raw materials to and from emerging empires that grew or collapsed over time. The economic bridge of inter-regional trade was built by entrepreneurs who took high risks setting off on long hazardous journeys. Through unknown and mostly uncontrolled areas of land via mountain passes or dense woodland or by sea to distant unknown lands.

These journeys were high risk, but extremely profitable, once a secure route was known this could be strengthened and exploited. From 2,900 BC onwards, Kings appeared. The Kings of the different regions called each other brother and classed as an equal and when a King of one area requested particular gifts then that King, would never be denied his request. But the requesting King could also receive an equally challenging demand back, this tested the relationships and sometimes strengthened the bonds between regions.

This is why a large section of the populace sole purpose was to garnish elite consumption with crafted goods that could be used as a form of bartering King-to-King which helped strengthen the unity between Kingdoms, especially in a time of need. Local governments throughout the route promoted the cross-cultural trade. By following their own vested interests, they participated in the broadest contacts throughout the Fertile Crescent and way beyond. The magnets of these contacts were the complex societies of Egypt, Sumer and the Indus Valley that offered an ever-growing market for all sorts of ideas, items and services.

Each one of the complex societies, also had a vast web of trade that stretched far beyond what we realise today. The key position in the external commerce was occupied by mediators whose welfare depended on the development of friendly relations. Merchants often acted both as emissaries of their rulers and the self-employed entrepreneurs. Outside the jurisdiction of the central agency, merchants could pursue their own luck making personal profit or suffering private loss.

The Socioeconomic Control of Surplus

As the control of each community's surplus was in the hands of the elite parts of society, the bulk of foreign import served for the elite consumption bridging the gap between concrete economic environment which included skilled workforce, effective management, raw materials, means of transportation, potential market, and ardent aspirations of the decision makers for a luxurious lifestyle. The idea of urbanisation became possible with the growth of a stratified ruling class in society. This class promoted long-distance trade as a chance of procuring exotic materials to be used as distinct status markers. First used in temple gifts to the gods, but quickly expanding into larger temple complexes and more ornate goods spread throughout the inner temple precinct and then to the King's temple complex.

Larger and better status markers than neighbouring city state's complexes. Inter-cultural trade fed the elite's insatiable appetite for power. The role of the middlemen both in overland delivery and waterborne transportation became decisive. The geographical location was crucial. Susa in Elam happened to stay on the crossroads of caravan routes and was exposed to Sumerian influence since both had originated from the Gulf Oasis. Bahrain was an island that could supply freshwater due to the subterranean aquafers, ever since the flooding of the Gulf. With anchorage facilities for partners engaged in maritime commerce across the Gulf.

The earliest mention of Dilmun was at the start of writing in 3,300 BC. So, it would be safe to assume that trade pasted through Dilmun (Bahrain) from the earliest beginnings. The trade had become a multi-functional activity; it refers to both utilitarian and elite consumption. Utilitarian can be single staged e.g., cereals consumed as bread or beer or multi-staged e.g., partially smelted copper ingots to be transformed into refined copper. Copper alloyed with tin to be fashioned into bronze items thus giving a massive advantage to an army bearing bronze weapons on the field of battle.

Bronze also had another unique quality, able to be recycled as scrap metal and reproduced as another consumer desirable artefact. The elite consumption luxury objects which can remain in the family line for several generations and serve as a status marker such as weapons, shields. Or precious jewellery which is sometimes reconstituted into more *modern* pieces. Or these items where simply buried as grave goods accompanying the owner in his/her eternal journey.

Mesopotamia trade grew organically from the crossroads nature of the civilisation s that dwelt between the rivers and the fertility of the land. Because of irrigation, Southern Mesopotamia was rich in agricultural products, including a variety of fruits and vegetables, nuts, dairy, fish, wool for textiles, 360 items exclusively from date palm and meat from animals both wild and domestic. Other than these items, Mesopotamia was rich in mud, clay, and reeds out of which they built their Cities.

Intra-city state commerce continued up to the time when each city state had grown sufficiently to be able to produce the same goods as a neighbouring city states. Once this tipping point had been reached then external trade was required, for most other essential goods, such as metal ores and timber. Mesopotamia required external because local trade only brought food and animals into the city and took tools, ploughs and harnesses out to the countryside. Long-distance trade was needed for resources like copper and tin and for luxury items for the nobility or the expanding elite classes.

Merchants and traders in early Mesopotamian cities began to form caravans for long-distance trading. With the development of the wheel and sail, transportation of goods became easier. Heavy bulk goods could travel by ox cart or be loaded onto riverboats. Most long-distance trade, however, was carried out by caravans using donkeys as pack animals. Donkeys could carry about 150 pounds and travel on the plains and into the mountains, places were wheeled carts couldn't go.

Over time, Mesopotamian craftsmen had expanded the variety of trade goods from fine textiles to sturdy, nearly mass-produced pottery made in temple workshops to leather goods, jewellery, basketry, devotional figurines, and ivory carvings, among others. Agricultural products such as grains and cooking oils were also exported as were dates and flax. Mesopotamian cities established trade all up and down the Tigris and Euphrates rivers and into Anatolia, today's Turkey. Other overland trade routes went east over the Zagros Mountains into present-day Iran and Afghanistan. A busy sea route went through the Persian Gulf across the Arabian Sea to the Indus Valley in what is today's Northern India and Pakistan. By the 4th Millennium BC, Mesopotamia trade went in every conceivable direction.

Feeding the Elite Consumption with Gemstones and Precious Metals

Gemstone and precious metals do not originate in the Southern Mesopotamian Region, the main local resources are, reeds, mud, bitumen, and an abundance of wheat and barley from agriculture. Plus, the use of wool products from the grazing sheep. Excessive/surplus: textiles, wheat, barley and bitumen are very useable commodities that can be exchanged for luxury items that are later sort after by the stratified society of the growing city states of

Southern Mesopotamia in the Sumer Region. The surplus textiles and grain were used to purchase items that weren't readily available within the area of Sumer.

Precious gems and stones used predominantly in the making of beads, stamps and cylinder seals. Most of the precious stones and gems did not originate in Mesopotamia and had to be transported over great distances; therefore, trade routes had to be continuing with people of various locations. These gems were required for items such as pearls, mother of pearl, amethyst, quartz which was used in the manufacture of cylinder seals, sapphires, peridotite mainly used in the use for amulets, pendants, seals and vessels, agate, onyx, cornelian only second to lapis lazuli in Mesopotamia.

Lapis lazuli was the stone that was sort after by the early Mesopotamians, there are isolated reports of lapis lazuli beads at Yarim Tepe (level 8: Early Hassuna Period) in Northern Mesopotamia in 6th Millennium BC with production sites close to Badakhshan in the 7th Millennium BC.

Lapis lazuli was always favoured by both the Mesopotamians and the Egyptians which was thought to be key to spiritual attainment and facilitating personal and spiritual power bringing deep inner self-knowledge, this was the *Royal Stone* which contained the soul of the gods, so no wonder it was so well sort. Old World Lapis Lazuli mines, on the upper reaches of the Kokcha River which runs into the Oxus in Badakhstan in modern day Afghanistan.

Evidence of bead manufacturing at Shortugai has been discovered which is located on the Oxus River which is described as part of the Harappan civilisation. [cxlii] A literary text T*he Hymn to Ninurta* refers to the *Cornelian and Lapis Lazuli in the land of Meluhha* current Indus Valley. Gudea of Lagash 2,150 BC also describes his procurement of *Blocks of Lapis Lazuli and bright cornelian from Meluhha*. Commonly thought to have been transported by Ship up the Persian Gulf. Unbeknown to Sumerians, Meluhha was only the *middleman* as was the land of Dilmun during the export of this highly prized stone.[cxliii]

Scientific chemical finger printing of lapis lazuli has been difficult to determine sources apart from reports that thin section microscopy and sulphur-isotope analysis allowed attribution of archaeological samples of Lapis from sites in Ur and Hissar to the mines of Badakhstan.

Importance of Trade Links with Bitumen

Bitumen is a naturally occurring material and has some amazing attributes that are not fully realised in today's society, due to the use of so many different modern materials. But many millennia ago, the vast array of materials we see today simply didn't exist, so the wonder material of its day was Bitumen. It was black in colour, flexible, bonded other items together, water resistant and could be used as a source of heat and if you added reeds into the fire, sufficient heat was produced to be able to smelt metals. So versatile bitumen was a high-end trading commodity. Bitumen tested from Early Ubaid Chogha Mish, Tell El Oueili and Tell Sabi Abyad all came from a wide variety of different sources. Some come from North-Western Iran, Northern Iraq and Southern Turkey.

Bitumen from H3 was identified as having an origin from Burgan Hill in Kuwait. Some of the other Arabian Neolithic sites in the Persian Gulf imported their bitumen from the Mosul area of Iraq which would indicate that this trade existed for many years prior to the archaeological evidence provided in Kuwait. Bitumen coated reed boats were involved in the expansion of such trade. Lapis lazuli, turquoise, and copper were exotics in the Mesopotamian Ubaid sites that potentially could have been imported, in small amounts, using the bitumen covered reed boat traffic. Indirect evidence for seafaring was discovered at the site of Marawah 11 off the coast of Abu Dhabi.

Domesticated faunal remains were discovered on the island that could only have been transported there via boat.[cxliv] This unique development of advanced nautical technology around the Gulf is yet further evidence as to the level of complexity Ubaid related groups had already achieved before becoming archaeologically visible along the newly configured shoreline.

Bitumen caulking of the reed boats was made by applying a heated mixture of bitumen, vegetable matter, and mineral additives and allowing it to dry and cool to toughen. The boat then had a water-resistant elastic covering. Unfortunately, the reeds had to be replaced frequently. Hundreds of slabs of reed-impressed bitumen have been recovered from several sites in the Persian Gulf. It may be that the H3 site in Kuwait represents a place where boats were repaired. The present state of knowledge concerning bitumen trade in the Middle East is limited.

During the Palaeolithic period, approximately 70,000 BC and into the Early Neolithic period, bitumen utilisation was mostly concentrated in settlements close to oil seeps. From the Ubaid period 6,500 BC, bitumen from the Mosul area became more important and was traded as far as the Southern Persian Gulf. The Uruk period is a turning point for Mesopotamian history as settlements evolved into city states. These cities had a great need for raw materials, and this marks the beginning of large-scale exploitation of Hit bitumen. This bitumen was traded at settlements along the Euphrates, where a large trade network had continued to prosper throughout multiple climatological events that affected Middle East history.

Explosion of the Bronze Age and the Search for Tin

Trade for the raw materials that make up bronze saw a boost in overseas trade, similar to the Klondike Gold Rush 1896, but this was far more important. The race was on! It wasn't anything to do with nice decorative objects for the dining table. It was everything to do with weaponry, arming and protecting the fighting men with the best equipment of the day. This made all the difference to winning campaigns, it changed the tactic on the Field of Battle and gained critical advantages.

What helped Sumer in its quest to seek out these ores, Sumer already a thriving trade and was *Cash Rich with a strong line of credit* when it came to purchasing power. Sumer had built-up a plethora of trade goods such as fine textiles, pottery, leather goods, fine jewellery and ivory carvings, all goods wanted by traders willing to sell Tin and Copper.

Metal working in the Ancient Mesopotamian region is well understood and the original use of arsenic as an alloying element with the easily sourced Copper (Modern day Cyprus, Turkey, Palestine, Oman, and Iran) was the first discovery made in the production of Bronze. This may have been accidental as trace elements of tin and arsenic can be discovered in copper ores such as tennantite. The addition of a second metal to copper increases its hardness, lowers the melting temperature, and improves the casting process by producing a more fluid melt that cools to a denser, less spongy metal.

Necessity is the mother of all inventions, the production of weapons of war, stronger sharper and if bronze was worn as protection then less men killed on the field of battle, giving a further advantage against your foe. The Bronze Age is a set period of time from 3,000 BC, but the knowledge of bronze manufacture pre-dates this time period. Arsenic has its own inherent dangers, so other elements were tested and using 10% tin with 90% copper produced the necessary results. This gave a city state a massive advantage over its rival when the two sides were equally matched.

But the sourcing of tin had its own inherent difficulties. Multiple areas in Europe could produce tin, but at this point in time, Europe wasn't even an option due to its lack of sophistication. The general barbaric nature of Europe left it as an untapped and unknown resource to the culturally civilised Harappa, Egyptians, and Sumerians. The trade routes and maritime links that already existed exploded into life on the realisation that this new source of trading income had a massive potential of wealth for traders. The Bronze age was a game changer, therefore it was imperative to ensure that whichever city state you belonged to had sufficient tin, to aid the manufacture of bronze, the copper was amply available, the only caveat was where to get the tin.

The major tin sources in the world that could be accessed by Mesopotamia via intermediators were Malaya, Indonesia, Thailand, and China. As we described earlier the understanding of writing and the step changes that occurred to make a system of writing viable. Yet China developed a system of writing were no precursor ever existed, so it would be logical to believe some form of contact with Tin supplying countries of the Far East already existed. The strongest link is currently Thailand, but the other areas should not be discounted. We should remind ourselves that traders from the Indus Valley looked West to the Sumerian trade but will have equally looked in the opposite direction to feed the trade in the West, using its web of trade links.

Recent excavations in Thailand at Non Nok Tha and Ban Chiang have shown a flourishing bronze working tradition which highly likely predates the mid-4th Millennium BC. The earliest analysed find from Ban Chiang is a dagger which dates to about 3,600 BC which contains approximately 2.5% tin, a figure which indicates a deliberate alloy. By 3,000 BC the start of the Bronze Age, ancient metalsmiths in Thailand were producing good bronze with about a 10% tin content and were competently handling casting, cold working, and annealing.

The early production of bronze in Thailand may eventually be found to have some relationship with the development of alloying techniques in Mesopotamia. It would be quite difficult to find original sources, as bronze was constantly melted down to produce multiple *modern* artefacts.

Meluhhan trade did not just go between the Indus Valley and Sumer, the trade routes of the Indus Valley also stretched to the East of India, which also followed the original migration paths of Cognitive Homo Sapiens around 45-60,000 years ago out of Africa along the land bridge between the Indian Subcontinent and the Gulf Oasis and into Malaya, Indonesia, Thailand and beyond. A maritime tin route from Hanoi to Haifa has been posited to transport tin which was a critical to the Bronze Age revolution.

On this route, which predates the Silk Road by 2,000 years, the Persian Gulf, together with the Straits of Malacca, was the critical maritime link the Tin Belt of the world in Ancient Far East. It is an archaeon-metallurgical challenge to trace the Maritime Tin Route from the tin belt of the world on Mekong River Delta (Vietnam) in the Far East and trace the contributions made by seafaring merchants of Meluhha in reaching the tin mineral resource to sustain the Tin/Copper/Bronze revolution. The Kuwait Gold Disc provide pictorial evidence that the trade routes for tin stretch much farther than people first thought.

The Rise of Sumer's Ancient Indus Trading Partner

The Indus Valley was integral to the rise and development of Sumeria. Without Harappa's unique set of trading goods and the Elite consumerism of Sumer technological advancements may never have reached the heights prior to 4.2K Climatic Event. The fall of Harappa didn't affect the hunt for tin in the Bronze Age as areas of the supply chain from Thailand via Tamil region enroute to Southern Mesopotamia wasn't affected by Harappa's sudden demise. It also gives the reader a brief understanding that other civilisations existed at exactly the same time as both Egypt and Sumer were starting to advance and become regional powers.

In 6,200 BC, similar time period to the start of Ubaid Period 0 and the end of the Gulf Oasis being consumed. Intensive agriculture emerged in Baluchistan, on the margins of the Indus alluvium. Could this be related to the DNA testing of the Iran Farmers who did not migrate West towards Europe, but went East into Baluchistan and its surrounding region, long before the arrival of the Arians. In the following millennia, settled life made inroads into the Indus plains, setting the stage for the growth of rural and urban human settlements.

The more organised sedentary life in turn led to a net increase in the birth rate and the greater the population grew. The ruins of Harappa were first described in 1842 AD by Charles Masson in his book, *Narrative of Various Journeys in Baluchistan, Afghanistan, the Panjab, and Kalât*.[cxlv] The Greater Indus Region which contains the Indus Valley Civilisation is also known as the Harappan Civilisation, after the city of Harappa.

In 1856 AD, British engineers John and William Brunton were laying the East Indian Railway Company line connecting the cities of Karachi and Lahore, when their crew discovered hard, well-burnt bricks in the area. At no point where they led to believe that these well-built walls were the remnants of a lost civilisation that predated the two British engineers by 5,000 years. Ignorance is bliss and the two engineers used the bricks for ballast for the railroad track and completed their task. Unwittingly destroying the ruins of the ancient city of Brahminabad.

Villages quickly became towns and towns quickly became cities eventually this conglomeration of city states would be later classed as the Indus Valley Civilisation, the Indus River Valley Civilisation contained urban centres with well-conceived and organised infrastructure, architecture, and systems of governance. By 2,600 BC, the small Early Harappan communities had become large urban centres. These city states included Harappa, Ganeriwala, and Mohenjo-Daro in modern-day Pakistan, and Dholavira, Kalibangan, Rakhigarhi, Rupar and Lothal in modern-day India.

In total, more than 1,052 cities and settlements have been found, mainly in the general region of the Indus River and its tributaries. The population of the Indus Valley Civilisation has been conservatively estimated to have held over five million people. Apart from Indus Valley Civilisation cities being well organised there had an extremely efficient wastewater drainage system and trash collection systems with public granaries and baths. This conglomeration of cities was predominantly were artisans and merchants grouped together in distinct neighbourhoods. The quality of urban planning suggests efficient municipal governments that placed a high priority on hygiene or religious ritual.

The civilisation's economy appears to have depended significantly on trade and all trade was required to go from A to B, so trade was facilitated by major advances in transport technology. The Harappan Civilisation may have been the first to use wheeled transport, in the form of bullock carts that are identical to those seen throughout South Asia today. It also appears they built boats and watercraft a claim supported by archaeological discoveries of a massive, dredged canals with large docking facilities at the coastal city of Lothal.

Trade focused on importing raw materials to be used in Harappan city workshops, including minerals from Iran and Afghanistan, lead, and copper from other parts of India, jade from China, and cedar wood floated down rivers from the Himalayas and Kashmir. Other trade goods included terracotta pots, gold, silver, metals, beads, flints for making tools, seashells, pearls, and coloured gemstones, such as lapis lazuli and turquoise. There was an extensive maritime trade network operating between the Harappan and Mesopotamian civilisations. Harappan seals and jewellery have been found at archaeological sites in regions of Mesopotamia, which includes most of Modern-day Iraq, Kuwait and parts of Syria.

Long-distance sea trade over bodies of water, such as the Arabian Sea, Red Sea, and the Persian Gulf, may have become feasible with the development of plank watercraft that was equipped with a single central mast supporting a sail of woven rushes or cloth. During 4,300-3,200 BC of the Chalcolithic period, also known as the Copper Age, the Indus Valley Civilisation area shows ceramic similarities with southern Turkmenistan and Northern Iran. During the Early Harappan period about 3,200-2,600 BC, cultural similarities in pottery, seals, figurines, and ornaments document caravan trade with Central Asia and the Iranian plateau.

The city of Harappa[cxlvi] was not discovered until the start of excavations in the 1920's. In what was then the Punjab Province of British India which is todays Pakistan. The discoveries in Harappa, and the site of its fellow Indus city Mohenjo-Daro, were the culmination of work beginning in 1861 with the founding of the Archaeological Survey of India in the British Raj. The common name for British colonial rule over the Indian subcontinent from 1858 through 1947 AD. Harappa Civilisation was home to the largest of the four-ancient urban civilisation s of Egypt, Mesopotamia, South Asia and China who had become integral trading partners with all the known civilisations of the time.

Most of Harappa's ruins, even its major cities have still not been excavated, waiting to reveal further secrets of its history. The ancient Indus Civilisation script has not been deciphered. Harappa was a Bronze Age civilisation in the North Western regions of South Asia a city in the Indus Valley that has been permanently inhabited for several thousand years prior to its rise in 3,300 BC and to prominence around 2,600 to 1,700 BC. in the western part of South Asia continued until 1,300 BC.

This period of prior inhabitancy is referred to as *The Ancient Indus Civilisation*. The most widespread Civilisation, its sites spanning an area stretching from Northeast Afghanistan, through much of Pakistan, and into Western and North Western India covering an area as large as Western Europe living in peace and social harmony. It flourished in the basins of the Indus River, which flows through the length of Pakistan, and along a system of perennial, mostly monsoon-fed rivers. These rivers once coursed in the vicinity of the seasonal Ghaggar-Hakra River in Northwest India and Eastern Pakistan.

Until the writing is finally deciphered, we can only rely on the archaeological evidence and so far, everything points a kingless state living in peace and all things being equal the polar opposite to both Sumeria and Egypt. It is not evident of any discord between trading partners due to these opposite ways of living, but there is no indication that the people of Sumer had ever settled in the Harappa Civilisation unlike the evidence found in Sumer. Commercial, religious, and artistic connections have been recorded in Sumerian documents, where the Indus valley people are referred to as Meluhhaites and the Indus valley is called Meluhha.

The Curse of Agade[cxlvii], the following account has been dated to about 2,000 BC: *The Meluhhaites, the men of the black land, bring to Naram-Sin of Agade all kind of exotic wares.*

Two cities, in particular, have been excavated at the sites of Mohenjo-Daro on the lower Indus, and at Harappa, further upstream. The evidence suggests they had a highly developed city life. There was a lot of similarity between the two civilisations of Sumeria and the Ancient Indus. But striking difference occurred due to the physical location, the land of Sumer with very little rainfall and Harappa with an abundance of water from the skies and the rivers.

Many homes in Harappa had both wells and bathrooms as well as an elaborate underground drainage system. The social conditions of the citizens were comparable to those in Sumeria and superior to the contemporary Babylonians and Egyptians. These cities display a well-planned urbanisation system. We are already aware of the long-term level of contact between the Indus Valley Civilisation and the Middle East. Harappa was a walled city in modern-day Pakistan with residents living in sculpted houses with flat roofs made of red sand and clay. The city spread over 150 hectares (370 acres). The modern village of Harappa, used as a railway station during the Raj, is six kilometres (3.7 miles) from the ancient city state, which suffered heavy damage during the British period of rule.

The joint Pakistani American Harappa Archaeological Research Project HARP (Harappa.com) carrying out major excavations at the site and has revealed that Harappa was far larger than once thought. The large cities of Mohenjo-Daro and Harappa very likely grew to containing between 30,000 and 60,000 individuals. This would have made Harappa a contender with Uruk and later Ur. A mound has risen (Tell) on this site, which is 12 metres higher from its surrounding area, due to the continued habitation of Harappa for many millennia.

These continuing excavations are rewriting assumptions about the Indus Civilisation, including recent work by archaeologists in neighbouring India.

New facts, objects and examples of writing are being discovered every year in India and Pakistan. Including Harappa's own advanced technology, economy, and culture. The Indus Valley Civilisation is the earliest known culture of the Indian subcontinent of the kind, which can now be called *urban* or centred on large municipalities similar to Uruk.

Mohenjo-Daro is thought to have been built around 2,600 BC Located west of the Indus River in the Larkana District, Mohenjo-Daro was one of the most sophisticated cities of the period, with sophisticated engineering and urban planning. Cockfighting was thought to have religious and ritual significance, with domesticated chickens bred for religion rather than food (although the city may have been a point of origin for the worldwide domestication of chickens). Mohenjo-Daro was abandoned around 1,900 BC when the Indus Civilisation went into sudden decline.

The writing system of Indus Civilisation to this day still remains a mystery and all attempts to decipher it have failed. This is one of the reasons why the Indus Valley Civilisation is one of the least known of the important early civilisations of antiquity. Examples of this writing system have been found in pottery, amulets, carved stamp seals, and even in weights and copper tablets. Another very similar trait to the Sumerians was standardisation which was the key to the Harappan culture. Using the same size bricks and standardised weights and measurements were used in other Indus cities such as Mohenjo Daro and Dholavira therefore providing evidence of close commercial ties.

These cities were well planned with wide streets, public and private wells, drains, bathing platforms and reservoirs. There were other highly developed cultures in adjacent regions of Baluchistan, Central Asia, and Peninsular India. Material culture and the skeletons from the Harappa cemetery and other sites testify to a continual intermingling of communities from both the West and the East with no direct evidence of a stratified society or Kingship.

The people of this region seemed to have a less personal requirement for consumerism, as noted that very few grave artefacts interned with the skeletal remains unearthed. Very sparse amount grave goods with the exception of several beads and bangles. It may be presumed that people buried within the walls of the city may have had a higher importance within the city and others buried outside the Walls of the city. Harappa had city walls but used for totally opposite conventional reasons. Walls were built to keep people in and not out. Used to control commerce and the taxes associated with these activities. These massive walls where never used as defence but also protection from the Monsson floods.

The Harappan religion remains a topic of speculation. It has been widely suggested that the Harappans worshipped a mother goddess who symbolised fertility. In contrast to Egyptian and Mesopotamian civilisations, the Indus Valley Civilisation seems to have lacked any temples or palaces that would give clear evidence of religious rites or specific deities. Some Indus Valley seals show a swastika symbol, which was included in later Indian religions including Hinduism, Buddhism, and Jainism. Many Indus Valley seals also include the forms of animals, with some depicting them being carried in processions.

While others show chimeric creations, leading scholars to speculate about the role of animals in Indus Valley religions. One seal from Mohenjo-Daro shows a half-human, half-buffalo monster attacking a tiger. This may be a reference to the Sumerian myth of a monster created by Aruru, the Sumerian earth and fertility goddess Inanna (Ishtar), to fight Gilgamesh, the hero of an ancient Mesopotamian epic poem. This is a further suggestion of international trade in Harappan culture.

Indian Communities that Settled in the Land of Sumer 3rd Millennium BC

As with any large trading nation in the world, Sumer became the very first melting pot of many diverse cultures. As the identification of the land of Meluhha with the coastal areas controlled by the Indus Civilisation is almost universally accepted. The textual evidence dealing with individuals qualified as *men* or *sons* of Meluhha or called with the ethnonym Meluhha, living in a separate rural settlement in Mesopotamia and of a *Meluhha village* established at Lagash.

It shows a community maintaining its original ethnic affiliation but successfully integrated with the Sumerian society, particularly in contexts suggesting economic and ideological interaction with temples and local cults. Meluhhans bear Sumerian names or are identified by their ethnical or professional identity. The community owns or rents its cultivated land and manages a central granary that delivers rations or payments in barley to craft specialists. They appear variously involved with the management of temples and other religious institutions. This unescapably points to the existence of enclaves settled by Indian immigrants.

This may have been another business opportunity seen by a Harappan businessman, why not bring the cheaper raw goods directly to the consumer market and produce bespoke items on demand within the Sumerian city states with Harappan craftsmen. Many of the Carnelian beads found in the graves within the main Sumerian cities also at Susa in the second half of the 3rd Millennium BC are presently *interpreted* as made locally by Indus craft persons or artisans trained in an Indus technical tradition but producing shapes and decorations after the specific local demand.

Another important point is description in Sumerian Cuneiform describes offerings to a goddess from the sacred *Meluhha Garden*, possibly a precinct where fruits and flowers imported from India are cultivated. The presence of individuals or groups emigrating from the Indo-Pakistani Subcontinent to Mesopotamia in the 3rd Millennium BC has been a well-established fact since the 1920's AD. Excavations within Mesopotamia discovered Indus Civilisation artefacts and inscriptions throughout the 3rd and 2nd Millennium BC. Harappa and Mohenjo-Daro Indus-like seals have been discovered in stratified contexts in some of the most important Sumerian cities showing trade was well established.

To the same period is ascribed a famous cylinder seal owned by a certain Su-ilisu, *Meluhha interpreter* Another Akkadian text records that Lu-Sunzida *a man of Meluhha* paid to the servant Urur, son of Amarlu-KU 10 shekels of silver as a payment for a tooth broken in a clash. The name Lu-Sunzida literally means *Man of the just buffalo cow* a name that, although rendered in Sumerian, according to the authors does not make sense in the Mesopotamian cultural sphere and must be a translation of an Indian name.

By Ur III times, this intense trade had definitely promoted the formation of local enclaves of Indus origin. The ethnic name points to a settlement originally founded as a trade enclave by foreign merchants. The texts indicate that Meluhhans were perceived as distinct ethnic group. Living in a separate settlement but largely integrated in the contemporary Sumerian society. Owning or renting land and accumulating and variously distributing their agricultural products. The absence of reference to craft production in the Ur III times could indicate that the Indus communities in Mesopotamia had been largely integrated in Sumerian society and had fully adopted a subsistence based upon agriculture, while a state of crisis in the motherland had disconnected the traditional long distance trade routes and craft organisations.

The Indus Valley: the Land of the Socialist, Peaceful, Clean Harappa [cxlviii]

Since the beginning of excavational work in the 1920s AD, the Harappa cities have been noted for their extraordinary level of Urban planning and demonstrated advanced architecture with dockyards, granaries, warehouses, brick platforms with large retaining walls, baked brick houses, elaborate drainage systems, water supply systems, clusters of large non-residential buildings. New techniques in handicraft have been discovered, used on precious stones ready for export to The Land of Sumer. Proficient in seal carving, achieved many notable advances in technology, including great accuracy in their systems and tools for measuring length and mass.

Harappans were among the first to develop a system of uniform weights and measures that conformed to a successive scale. The smallest division, approximately 1.6 mm, was marked on an ivory scale found in Lothal, a prominent Indus Valley city in the modern Indian state of Gujarat. It stands as the smallest division ever recorded on a Bronze Age scale. The cutting of patterns into the bottom face of a seal and used distinctive seals for the identification of property and to stamp clay on trade goods.

Seals have been one of the most commonly discovered artifacts in Indus Valley cities, decorated with animal figures, such as elephants, tigers, and water buffalos. Carnelian products used in cylinder seal carvings, and metallurgy including copper, bronze, lead and tin.

Unlike Mesopotamia and Ancient Egypt, the inhabitants of the Indus Valley Civilisation did not build large, monumental structures. There is no conclusive evidence of palaces or temples or even of Kings, armies, or priests, and the largest structures Harappa are the granaries. Another point of debate is the nature of the relationship between the cities of the Indus Valley. Whether they were independent city states similar to Sumeria or part of a larger Kingdom is not entirely clear. Because the writing of the Indus people remains un-deciphered and neither sculptures of rulers nor depictions of battles and military campaigns have been found.

Maybe these destructive battles had been averted due to the reason for not having a King or Priest Class. Or where all the 1,052 cities and Settlements currently known about of the Harappa Civilisation under one single rule and maybe the very first *Great Empire*.

Several remarkable features during archaeological excavations have shown no evidence of a standing army, no heavy armour, swords, maces, shields of any note and none of the cities in the region have any archaeological evidence of being set ablaze at any time during their long history. From the evidence seen, the region seems to have been a pure trading and agricultural centre.

The city of Mohenjo-Daro contains the *Great Bath*, which may have been a large, public bathing and social area. By focusing building projects within the cities on to the common populace which are used by all. A place of equality which can calmed even the most discontent within the populace. It may also be a reason for the Sumerian not seen in the Indus Valley. Maybe the consumerist Land of Sumer didn't like the idea of mixing with the Socialist Harappans, or they had discourse with Harappans other potential trading partners the Egyptians. Harappa[cxlix], Mohenjo-Daro and the recently, partially excavated Rakhigarhi demonstrate the world's first known urban sanitation systems.

The ancient Indus systems of sewerage and drainage developed and used in cities throughout the Indus region were far more advanced than any found in contemporary urban sites in the Middle East, and even more efficient than those in many areas of Pakistan and India today. Individual homes drew water from wells, while wastewater was directed to covered drains on the main streets. Houses opened only to inner courtyards and smaller lanes, and even the smallest homes on the city outskirts were believed to have been connected to the system, further supporting the conclusion that cleanliness was a matter of great importance.

Archaeological records provide no immediate answers regarding a centre of authority, or depictions of people in power in Harappan society. The extraordinary uniformity of Harappan artifacts is evident in pottery, seals, weights, and bricks with standardised sizes and weights, suggesting some form of authority and governance. Over time, three major theories have developed concerning Harappan governance or system of rule:

1. The first is that there was a single state encompassing all the communities of the civilisation, given the similarity in artifacts, the evidence of planned settlements, the standardised ratio of brick size and the apparent establishment of settlements near sources of raw material.
2. The second theory posits that there was no single ruler, but a number of them representing each of the urban centres, including Mohenjo-Daro, Harappa and other communities.
3. Finally, experts have theorised that the Indus Valley Civilisation had no rulers as we understand them, with everyone enjoying equal status.

On the other hand, it soon became clear that no Mesopotamian article, for example, not a single Sumerian cylinder seal has been recovered at Mohenjo-Daro nor have been found in later excavations at other Indus sites. As the elevated compound of Mohenjo-Daro has been excavated for about 350 houses and buildings, accounting for about 10% of the total built mounded surface. It is hardly possible that such absence is casual. On the basis of the present evidence, it is more likely that, although we have ascertained that Indian groups travelled, traded, and settled in the West. Sumerians don't seem to have travelled en masse directly to the coasts and plains of the Indus, nor do they seem to have settled, at least in substantial groups in the Indus cities from current archaeological excavations to-date.

We must realise that trade is and always has been bilateral. Indus Valley provided the essential raw materials required by the Sumerians and due to no artefacts of any real meaning found within the Indus Valley area may indicate that the Sumerian textiles would have been the main trade from Mesopotamia to the Indus Region. Both regions had advanced agricultural prowess that had advanced at exactly the same time in both regions, so no trade was required in barley or wheat.

Meluhha and Meluhhans have been featured on 9 texts dating to Ur III times, but also included references to Sargonic texts. The maximum archaeological evidence of Indian imports and Indus related artefacts in Mesopotamia may be dated to latest phases of ER III (at the Royal Cemetery of Ur) and immediately later to the Akkadian period. When Sargon claimed with pride that under his power Meluhhan ships docked at his capital, and at least one tablet mentions a person with an Akkadian name qualified as a *The holder of a Meluhha Ship*.

According to the literary sources, between the end of the 3rd and the beginning of the 2nd Millennium BC Meluhhan ships exported to Mesopotamia precious goods among which exotic animals, such as dogs, perhaps peacocks, cocks, bovid and the possibility of elephants, precious woods and royal furniture, precious stones such as carnelian, agate and lapis lazuli, and metals like gold, silver and tin. In his famous inscriptions, Gudea, in 2,150 BC, states that *Meluhhans came with wood and other raw materials for the construction of the main temple in Lagash.*

The most evident raw materials imported from India are marine shell, used for costly containers and lamps, inlay works and cylinder seals; agate, carnelian and quite possibly ivory (elephant or hippopotamus teeth). Hard green stones, including garnets and abrasives might also have been imported from the Subcontinent and Eastern Iran. Carnelian could have been imported in form of raw nodules of large size to be transformed into long beads, or as finished products. It may be suggested that the Indus families in Mesopotamia imported raw materials rather than finished beads.

Writing might be able to present an outlook as to how we view Harappa compared to Sumeria and what could maybe a plausible reason for the final disappearance of the Harappa Civilisation. While in Mesopotamia writing was cared for and taught in professional schools maintained in palaces and temples for control purposes with all details accurately record in detail. Nothing similar was observed in the Indus valley. This may be due to the fact temples and palaces have not been identified or simply didn't exist within the Indus Region, so no centralised government with written tablets difficult to trace.

It is always good to be reminded that the people of Sumer had a very structured way of life and the whole was always greater than the sum of the individuals, discipline was drilled into the Sumerian. The people of Sumer relied on organisation and structure. Scribes of the Indus Region seems to be a widespread function, possibly performed by consistent groups of urban scribes.

The production of this key administrative tool, in fact, does not appear to have been centralised by a state or urban authority. This may be due to the fact that the fertile lands supplied by the rivers with palatable weather all year round did not require the extreme organisational requirements of Sumer. Writing in the Indus city states seems to have been performed at different places and houses at the same time which may present the absolute lack of standardisation in the written form.

The roots of failure within the Harappa Socialist civilisation may have been sewn into the cultural fabric of its people via its total lack of control of the populace within the region. Whichever form of Harappan governance or system of rule was true, it didn't work when the chips were down. Can an Empire be a true Empire when it was knocked out with a single blow? Or is that a massive injustice against such a cultured populace. Was the event so catastrophic that no Empire could survive?

We know they had managed to survive the power shift from Sumerians to the Akkadians and the 4.2K Climatic Event 200-year drought, also the usurping of trade from Dilmun. So, something significant happened and it is now believed that due to one single event the Rivers totally changes their course and all life stopped functioning as a single unit. An immediate life-changing event with no recovery plan.

High Quality and High Skill Levels

In some Sumerian cities, such as Ur, so far excavation brought to light only such round seals with Indus inscriptions, while at Kish and Umma circulated standard square Indus seals. There is little wonder that Carnelian, a form of Agate mined for over 5,000 years in Gujarat. Quoted by ancient texts as an important article of Indo-Mesopotamian trade of the 3rd and early 2nd Millennium BCE.

To give an estimated understanding of the possible cost of an Indus necklace or belt made of long barrel-cylinder carnelian beads, on the basis of experimental replications it's calculated that the production of one of these ornaments roughly amounts to 480 days of work by a highly skilled artisan.

The prime example of this type of work lays 3,000 kilometres to the West in

the ancient Mycenaean site in Pylos, called the *Pylos Combat Agate*. An intricately carved seal stone that researchers are calling *one of the finest works of prehistoric Greek art ever discovered*. A victorious warrior, one defeated opponent, beneath his feet and the second in the process of defeat at the tip of his sword. And all this was carved in meticulous detail on a piece of stone just over 1.4 inches long.

This unique shaped agate has also been seen in Failaka Island part of the trading route of Dilmun *Empire*. Such work has never been seen before in art from the Aegean Bronze Age. What is fascinating is that the representation of the human body is at a level of detail and musculature which isn't witnessed again until the classical period of Greek art 1,000 years later. It's a spectacular find. The reason for presenting *The Griffin Warrior* agate is to provide evidence to the reader, the high level of sophistication in such an early period of time.

The people of yesteryear had the ability to perform extraordinary masterpieces just like us today and hopefully change our perception on viewing History. The Griffin Warrior who was buried in the tomb and gets his name from an adorned ivory plaque buried with him, probably died around the time when the militaristic and austere Mycenaean culture, based in mainland Greece, conquered the culturally sophisticated Minoans, based on the large island of Crete, just south of Pylos. It should also be noted that the Island of Crete was first inhabited in 6,000 BC. A date that resonates as one of the critical dates in History, the emptying of the Mediterranean Sea into the Euxine which created the Black Sea.

Trade Disruption Between Indus Valley and Mesopotamia

Long-distance[cl] trade by navigation between the two poles of the Gulf was already established by late-Neolithic and early Chalcolithic times. It was the beads and shell trade that, in Mesopotamia, in the Gulf, most probably at Susa and possibly even in Bactria. Gradually promoted the local settlement of families of specialised merchants and crafts persons from the Indus valley, who channelled along their tracks the supply of raw materials and, in general, the complex know-how of the Indus crafts.

Archaeological evidence pushes back the beginning of this process at least to the end of the 4th Millennium BC, when late Uruk Sumerian engravers frequently employed the columella of the Indian shank shell for their cylinder seals. While these early imports might have been due to indirect or occasional trade. By Early Dynastic II-III times, Indian traders and crafts persons were asked to provide more and more substantial amounts of highly prestigious and costly products such as shell ornaments and lamps, inlay pieces, and high-quality carnelian strictly reserved to the courts of the lords of the Sumerian city states.

If we have to believe to the cuneiform texts that insistently ascribe to Meluhha the lapis lazuli trade. Meluhhan traders would also have been promoted the flowing, in a relatively short time, of incredible amounts of the blue stone at the courts of Ur. About 95% of the entire inventory of the lapis lazuli ever found in the Middle East and South Asia comes from the graves excavated by Leonard Woolley in the Royal Cemetery. The precise role of the Indus valley civilisation in the lapis lazuli long-distance trade is still a major open question in the proto history of South Asia and the ancient Near East.

What should also be noted is that trade is a multifaceted entity, with trade comes opportunity and wealth and with wealth comes control and opportunity. Meluhhan trade actually took a few blows before its final demise. The first blow to production of Meluhhan trade, comes from the Akkad invasion and the overthrow of the Sumerian lords in 2,334 BC. As Sumerian aristocratic families had such a high demand that suddenly collapsed with the invasion of Sargon. This had an immediate and far-reaching impact on the Indus traders. This shouldn't have been devastating of its own accord, as trade is trade.

But it would seem that Meluhhan traders had part of their fortune and projects upon alliances and close personal relationships with the defeated and deposed elites of Sumer, directly impacting the craft groups. The sudden, unexpected fall of the Sumerian demand might have caused in the specialised manufacturing settlements of the Indus valley a ruinous collapse of bead production, followed by a general crisis of the local craft organisation. The collapse might be evident in the crisis of the carnelian bead *workshops* of Chanhu-Daro (Sindh, Pakistan).

During excavations, a single stratigraphic horizon were hundreds of semi-finished long-barrel carnelian beads were suddenly abandoned and dumped for a mysterious reason. Whatever the cause, this evidence should have depended, besides the fall of the demand, upon a major, sudden disruption of the contextual relationships of production. At this same high point in trade is also the moment of the maximum diffusion of Indus ceramics along the coasts of the Gulf. Matching with the times of the occupation phase of the settlement of Ras Al-Jinz in Oman, showing the most intensive interaction of the local communities with the Indus Traders?

But trade is trade and soon the Meluhhan traders soon forged links with the new powers of the area. The Akkadian rulers after the conquest had no direct political ties with the Indian traders. Sargon's famous statement resounds[cli] of the pride of having re-established a fruitful economic and political relationship with the eastern prestigious partner. The Meluhhan trading communities could not have asked for a more favourable solution. The prompt mass production of etched carnelian beads after the conquest is a perfect example of the intelligent, creative, and highly opportunistic behaviour exhibited by Indian craft communities.

The production of beads etched with the symbol of Shamash archaeologically shows the same attitude revealed by the later Ur III texts: Indian bead makers and traders immediately adapted to the changing ideological environment and soon came terms with new cults, tastes and ritual habits, inventing new, ad hoc types of ornaments.

The majority of trade at this point in time came from the seas and waterways. To control the sea was to control the trade. By 2,100 BC the descendants of the original immigrant Meluhhans living and working in Mesopotamia had little direct connections with the motherland. During the 4.2 Kilo Climatic Event the invasion of the starving Zagros Mountain people the Gutians on the Akkadian Capital marked by decentralised time of chaos and neglect and considered a time of disorder within Southern Mesopotamia that caused a severe downturn in the Akkadian Empire's prospects.

It was during Gutian reign and the disruption to the long-distance trade, was now seized upon, and monopolised by the Dilmun sailors and traders. The Dilmun civilisation of the late 3rd Millennium BC, with its emphasis based on long-distance trade and navigation, whilst managing of intercultural diversity from various trading partners. Dilmun was overall a non-farming subsistence which reacted at an opportunistic event that represents a rapid successful adaptation of social, ecological, and geopolitical setting of the Arabian Peninsula. This was a fortuitus time for Dilmun usurping the Meluhhan trade route.

Dilmun's powers could now exact *The Middleman Tariffs* from the end user. The competition with the Dilmun traders at Failaka, Tarout and Bahrain must have been hard at first for the end users. The presence of Dilmun seals both from the cities of Sumer up to the Diyala Valley (Close to modern day Baghdad), as well as in the Iranian Plateau, Susa and Tepe Yahya which is 100Km from the Straits of Hormuz and in the Indus Valley centres points to a very active role for these New Dilmun merchants. (Pirates?)

In time, they attempted to establish their own trade outposts at both poles of the Gulf Trade. Perhaps trying to intercept the flow of exchanged commodities before their ultimate loading and maximising trade profits. If this was their strategy, in the long run they should have been very successful, given the disappearance of Meluhha as a trading partner from the cuneiform records in the first two centuries of the 2nd Millennium BC and the correspondent rise in its place of Magan for copper, and later of Dilmun alone.

The Decline of the Indus Valley Civilisation

Gradual drying of the region's soil during the 3rd Millennium BC may have been the initial spur for the urbanisation associated with the civilisation, but eventually also reduced the water supply enough to cause the civilisation's demise, and to scatter its population eastward. By 1,800 BC seemed to be quite swift and it seems the people of the region didn't have the necessary organisational skills to be able to survive any changes to the way of life. But once again just like its trading partner the Sumer Region a change in rivers conditions had a devastating effect on the Indus Region.

The Indus Valley Civilisation saw the beginning of their decline. Writing started to disappear, standardised weights and measures used for trade and taxation purposes fell out of use, the connection with the Near East was interrupted, and some cities dwindled and then eventually abandoned and forgotten until their rediscovery in the 20th century AD almost 4,000 years later. The reasons for this decline are not entirely clear, but it is believed that the drying up of the Saraswati River, a process which had begun around 1,900 BC, was the main cause.

The Indus Valley Civilisation declined around 1,800 BC due to climate change and migration. The great Indus Valley Civilisation, located in modern-day India and Pakistan, began to decline around 1800 BC. The civilisation eventually disappeared along with its two great Cities, Mohenjo-Daro, and Harappa. Archaeological evidence indicates that trade with Mesopotamia, located largely in modern Iraq, seemed to have ended. The advanced drainage system and baths of the great cities were built over or blocked. Writing began to disappear, and the standardised weights and measures used for trade and taxation fell out of use.

Other experts speak of a great flood in the area. Either event would have had catastrophic effects on agricultural activity, making the economy no longer sustainable and breaking the civic order of the Cities. Around 1,500 BC, a large group of nomadic cattle-herders, the Aryans, migrated into the region from Central Asia. The Aryans crossed the Hindu Kush Mountains and came in contact with the Indus Valley Civilisation. This was a large migration and used to be seen as an invasion, which was thought to be the reason for the collapse of the Indus Valley Civilisation, but this hypothesis is not unanimously accepted today.

Thus, the Indus Valley Civilisation came to an end. Over the course of several centuries, the Aryans gradually settled down and took up agriculture. The language brought by the Aryans gained supremacy over the local languages: the origin of the most widely spoken languages today in South Asia goes back to the Aryans, who introduced the Indo-European languages into the Indian subcontinent. Other features of modern Indian society, such as religious practices and caste division, can also be traced back to the times of the Aryan migrations.

Many Pre-Aryan customs still survive in India today. Evidence supporting this claim includes: the continuity of pre-Aryan traditions; practices by many sectors of Indian society; and also, the possibility that some major gods of the Hindu pantheon actually originated during the time of the Indus Valley Civilisation and were kept *alive* by the original inhabitants through the centuries.

The flourishing cities of Sumer in Mesopotamia, the sophisticated Harappan people from the Indus Valley (Meluhha in Sumerian texts), the industrious inhabitants of Magan (The Oman Peninsula during the Bronze age period) and of the Iranian hinterland have left many archaeological traces of their encounters on the island. From a less tangible point of view, it is still debated among academics whether Failaka might be the mythical Eden, the place where Sumerian hero Gilgamesh almost unravelled the secret of immortality, the paradise later described in the Bible.

As a result of changes in the balance of political powers in the region towards the end of the 2nd Millennium BC and beginning of 1st Millennium BC, the prominence of Failaka began to deteriorate.

In the end of the 4th century BC, Failaka appears to be the island which saved the Greek traveller Sotelos[20] and his companions from sinking (as described by Sotelos stone which was found on the island). Studies indicated that Alexander

---

[20] *It is reputed to have been the refuge of 4th Century BC Greek Traveller Sotelos and his Companions who were saved from Sinking and left an engraved Stela dedicated to Zeus and Artemis.*

the Great received reports about two islands from the missions sent to discover the Arabian shoreline of the Gulf, one of which located around 120 Stadia (one stadia is roughly equivalent to 185 metres) from the estuary, where the second island located a complete day and night sailing journey with proper climate conditions.

As the historian *Aryan* stated[21] that Alexander the Great ordered to name the nearer island *Ikaros*, which is known as Failaka now and the distant island as *Tylos* which is now known as the Kingdom of Bahrain. Ikaros was described by the explorers as an island covered with rich vegetation and a shelter for numerous wild animals, considered sacred by the inhabitants who dedicate them to their local goddess. After Alexander's death, the island became an important harbour for the Seleucid Kingdom. *The Sumerian tale of the garden paradise of Dilmun may have been an inspiration for the Garden of Eden story.*

Failaka, a Kuwaiti Island in the Persian Gulf, once an outpost of Alexander the Great, the Greek for Outpost is thought to be the origins of the name Failaka which was an ideal location due to its position for trade and the presence of ground water. The first modern maps in 1596 named in Portuguese as the water Island. Also, Bahrain, the ancient Dilmun, first mentioned in Sumerian Cuneiform clay tablets in 3,300 BC. Describing trade listing wool issued to people connected with the Island. Dilmun is a very unique and important subject matter that is a key area for early Gulf Oasis agriculture and the start of trade during the Pre-Ubaid period.

I believe that further research will show the entire island to be a major *Cultural Centre* for the people of Sumeria. It is somewhat frustrating that insufficient attention has been placed on the Island of Failaka due to its physical appearance. Even when the Greek inhabited the island, it was described as Lush with lots of vegetation, so what happened? why would the land die-off straight after Greek occupation? I understand that everything changed once Kuwait city started to excessively use the same water table as Failaka Island, but it had deteriorated long before Kuwait city existed. Maybe I have a better understanding of a military mind compared to most historians.

I truly believe the Aquafers water supply on Failaka was spiked by the Greeks. To prevent hostiles using the lush landscape to survive on and using the island as a vantage point in the Persian Gulf. Make the area barren and

---

[21] *This is Arrian of Nicodemia, who wrote the Anabasis of Alexander. He is our best source on Alexander's life.*

inhospitable by preventing the water to soak the land. Could this be reversed, yes. Find the original source and unblock. I believe the entire island could be turned back into its former *Paradise*.

The Climate Change Theory 1,800-1,500 BC

Other scholarship suggests the collapse of Harappan society resulted from climate change. Some experts believe the drying of the Saraswati River, which began around 1,900 BC, was the main cause for climate change, while others conclude that a great flood struck the area. Any major environmental change, such as deforestation, flooding, or droughts due to a river changing course, could have had disastrous effects on Harappan society, such as crop failures, starvation, and disease.

Skeletal evidence suggests many people died from malaria, which is most often spread by mosquitoes. This also would have caused a breakdown in the economy and civic order within the urban areas. Another disastrous change in the Harappan climate might have been eastward-moving monsoons, or winds that bring heavy rains. Monsoons can be both helpful and detrimental to a climate, depending on whether they support or destroy vegetation and agriculture. The monsoons that came to the Indus River Valley aided the growth of agricultural surpluses, which supported the development of cities, such as Harappa.

The population came to rely on seasonal monsoons rather than irrigation, and as the monsoons shifted eastward, the water supply would have dried up. By 1,800 BC, the Indus Valley climate grew cooler and drier, and a tectonic event may have diverted the Ghaggar-Hakra river system toward the Ganges Plain. The Harappans may have migrated toward the Ganges basin in the east, where they established villages and isolated farms.

These small communities could not produce the same agricultural surpluses to support large cities. With the reduced production of goods, there was a decline in trade with Egypt and Mesopotamia. By around 1,700 BC, most of the Indus Valley Civilisation cities had been abandoned and forgotten.

Chapter 9
A Time for Change and the Shift in Power

Early Dynastic Period of Mesopotamia Inclusive of Sumer

The Early Dynastic Period of Mesopotamia is the modern-day archaeological term for the era in Mesopotamian history 2,900-2,334 BCE during which some of the most significant cultural advances were made including the rise of the Cities, the development of writing, and the establishment of governments. This era was preceded by the Uruk Period 4,100-2,900 BC when the first cities were established in the region of Sumer (southern Mesopotamia) and succeeded by the Akkadian Period 2,334-2,154 BC when Mesopotamia was conquered by Sargon of Akkad 2,334-2,279 BC and ruled by him and his successors as the Akkadian Empire.

The term was coined by Orientalist Henri Frankfort 1897-1954 AD[clii] to mirror the Early Dynastic Period in Egypt, a similar period of development. It should be noted, however, that the advances of Mesopotamia's Early Dynastic Period differed from Egypt's in significant ways, notably in that Mesopotamia even under the rule of Sargon or later Empires was never the cohesive ethnic or political entity Egypt was and the kinds of cultural development cited for this era were not as uniform as they were in Egypt.

The city states of Sumer were, for much of their history, each independently governed not united under the reign of a single King as in the case of Egyptian government and so a city like Uruk or Ur might have developed some important cultural advance which was not shared at least not readily known with others.

The era is divided by archaeologists into three sub-periods:

- Uruk Period 4,100-2,900 BC
- Dynastic I - 2,900-2,800 BC
- Dynastic II - 2,800-2,600 BC

- Dynastic III - 2,600-2,334 BCE
- Akkadian Empire 2,334-2,154 BCE
- Gutian - 2,154-2,055 BCE (defeated by Utu-Hegel King of Uruk)
- Third Dynasty of Ur - 2,047-1,750 BC (founded by Ur-Nammu)

These are considered arbitrary divisions by some scholars and historians as there is no clear demarcation line separating one from the next. Even so, there is enough of a subtle difference that division is considered somewhat justified.

Between the Uruk Period and the Early Dynastic Period, the rivers around the region of the city of Shuruppak overflowed, causing severe flooding from the Southern plains up through the North. This event, which severely disrupted the society, is considered the origin of the Great Flood story as reimagined as the gods wrath in the Eridu Genesis and the Atrahasis. The Mesopotamian works now recognised as the inspiration for the famous tale of Noah and his ark from the Bible.

The exact date of the flood is unknown but archaeological evidence shows that the flood occurred 2,900 BC and left a silt level 2.5 metres deep. The flooding was localised from the rivers of Mesopotamia destroying Shuruppak and not the flooding of the entire region. Most scholars set this date at of the destruction of Shuruppak at around 2,900 BC approximate 3,300 years since the main event in the Gulf Oasis, but still managing to invoke memories of the original flood. The flooding wasn't catastrophic because the city was rebuilt and continued it place in Sumerian history.

Shuruppak

At the end of the Jemdet Nasr period, there was an archaeologically attested river flood in Shuruppak. Polychrome pottery from a destruction level below the flood deposit has been dated to the Jemdet Nasr period that immediately preceded the Early Dynastic I period. Shuruppak, Sumerian: ŠuruppagKI, *the healing place*, modern Tell Fara, was an ancient Sumerian city situated about 55 kilometres South of Nippur on the banks of the Euphrates in Iraq's Al-Qādisiyyah Governorate. Shuruppak was dedicated to Ninlil, also called Sud, the goddess of Grain and the Air.

Shuruppak became a grain storage and distribution city and had more silos than any other Sumerian city, so known for its abundance in grain production. The earliest excavated levels at Shuruppak date to the Jemdet Nasr period about

3,000 BC; it was abandoned shortly after 2,000 BC. Erich Schmidt found one Isin-Larsa cylinder seal and several pottery plaques which may date to early in the 2nd Millennium BC. Surface finds are predominantly Early Dynastic. Several objects made of arsenical copper were found in Shuruppak/Fara dating from the mid-4th to early 3rd Millennium BC (approximately Jemdet Nasr period), which is quite early for Mesopotamia. The city expanded to its greatest extent at the end of the Early Dynastic III period 2,600 to 2,334 BC when it covered about 100 hectares. At this stage, it was destroyed by a fire which baked the clay tablets and mudbrick walls, which then survived for many Millennia.

The Instructions of Shuruppak (or Instructions of Šuruppak son of Ubara-tutu) are a significant example of Sumerian wisdom literature. Wisdom literature, intended to teach proper piety, inculcate virtue, and preserve community standards, was common throughout the ancient Near East. The text is set in great antiquity by its incipit: *In those days, in those far remote times, in those nights, in those faraway nights, in those years, in those far remote years.* The precepts are placed in the mouth of a King Šuruppak (SU.KUR.RUki), son of Ubara-Tutu.

Ubara-Tutu is recorded in most extant copies of the Sumerian King List as being the final King of Sumer prior to the deluge. Ubara-tutu is briefly mentioned in tablet XI of the Epic of Gilgamesh. He is identified as the father of Utnapishtim, a character who is instructed by the God Ea to build a boat in order to survive the coming flood. Grouped with the other cuneiform tablets from Abu Salabikh, the Instructions date to the early 3rd Millennium BC, being among the oldest surviving literature.

The text consists of admonitory sayings of Šuruppak addressed to his son and eventual flood hero Ziusudra (*Akkadian: Utnapishtim*). Otherwise named as one of the five antediluvian cities in the Sumerian tradition, the name "Šuruppak" appears in one manuscript of the Sumerian King List. Where it is interpolated as an additional generation between Ubara-Tutu and Ziusudra, who are in every other instance father and son. Lambert reports that it has been suggested the interpolation may have arisen through an epithet of the father *Man of Shuruppak* having been taken wrongly for a proper name.

However, this epithet, found in the Gilgamesh XI tablet, is a designation applied to Utnapishtim (Ziusudra), not his father. The Abu Salabikh tablet, dated to the 3-4th Millennium BC, is the oldest extant copy, and the numerous surviving copies attest to its continued popularity within the Sumerian and Akkadian literary canons.

Counsels in the three conjoined lists are pithy, occupying one to three lines of cuneiform. Some counsel is purely practical: *You should not locate a field on a road...You should not make a well in your field, people will cause damage on it for you*. Moral precepts are followed by the negative practical results of transgression. *You should not play around with a married young woman: the slander could be serious*. Community opinion and the possibility of slander play a major role, whether the valued opinion of *the courtyard* or the less valued opinion of the marketplace, where insults and stupid speaking receive the attention.

Early Dynastic Period, 2,900-2,334 BC

This period witnessed the birth of writing, in contrast to pictograms, become commonplace and decipherable. The Epic of Gilgamesh mentions several leaders, including Gilgamesh himself, who were likely historical Kings. The first dynastic King was Etana, the 13th King of the first dynasty of Kish. War was on the increase, and cities erected walls for self-preservation and Sumerian culture began to spread from Southern Mesopotamia into surrounding areas.

A brief account must be given to the history of the next period, which witnessed some of the most important changes in Mesopotamian history. A beginning is made here with what we may call the Early Dynastic and preceded by the Uruk and-Jemdet Nasr periods. It saw the invention of the cuneiform text and the formation of the first city state. This development ultimately led to the unification of much of Mesopotamia under the rule of Sargon, the first monarch of the Akkadian Empire. Despite this, the early dynasties city states continued to share a relatively homogeneous material culture even though separated by language. Yet in the Temples of Akkadia, Sumerian was still the ritual language and continued even into the Babylonian times.

During the Early Dynastic Period, the Sumerian cities such as Uruk, Ur, Lagash, Umma and Nippur located in Lower Mesopotamia, were extremely powerful and influential. To the North and West stretched states centred on Semitic speaking cities such as Kish, Mari, Nagar and Ebla. It would seem that unrest occurred immediately after the flood of 2,900 BC. The Sumerian King List describes as having the First King following the deluge, Ishtar (Inanna) Etana *The Shepherd who ascended to Heaven and made firm all the lands*.

This may be alluding to chaos in the region and the leaders of Kish bringing everything back under control. Semitic speaking Kish eventually became the city state that tried to resolve Sumerian issues, which may have been the early prelude to eventual Semitic dominance. It tried to mediate problems throughout the region, especially the problems surrounding Lagash and Umma and both city states which may have already been a vassal to Kish during this time. Kish continued to be a place of symbolic significance of strong political connections that tied Northern Mesopotamia to the South.

The population of Ur, which was one of Sumer's largest Cities, has been estimated to have had 64,000 inhabitants at its peak. Given the other city states in Sumer and their large agricultural population some historians place the estimated population of Sumer somewhere between 200,000 and 260,000. But as an engineer and understanding what was required to make these canal systems, not in one city state but all city states, I can't see this estimate being correct. I believe the population had to be a lot greater and as previously stated, the use of slave labour must have contributed to the size of populace.

Agriculture in all this time continued to be the most important source of living for these city states. The Early Dynastic Period ended by the accession of King Sargon to the throne of Sumer and Akkad and the unification of the Sumerian city states into the Akkadian Empire and the inauguration of the Akkadians period 2,334-2,154 BC. The transition is purported as being very smooth, and the mixture of the Sumerian and Akkadian cultures continued to flourish and then passed to the Neo- Dynasties of Ur, known as the Ur or Ur III.

The period between the Akkad Dynasty and Ur III is not well documented. Most scholars believe that there was a short period of power struggle between the most powerful city states after which the city of Ur rose to prominence during the period 2,047-1,750 BC, and so Ur III controlled the cities of Isin, Larsa and Eshnunna and extended as far north as Jazira. This glory ended at last at the hands of the Gutian invaders from the Zagros Mountains, whose Kings ruled in Mesopotamia for an indeterminate period until the rise of Babylonia. These people were illiterate and nomadic, and their rule was not conducive to agriculture or developments in other fields.

Early Dynastic I, 2,900-2,800 BC

These Cities, as noted, grew from small villages but the core of those villages as evidenced by administrative records was a social organisation known as a *household* or Chiefdoms. Scholar Marc van de Mieroop explains:

Households were social units larger than nuclear families whose members reside together. An important aspect of the household is the fact that it acted as a single unit of production and consumption: most goods needed for its survival were produced in the household itself. Households may have originated in economically autonomous kinship groups and eventually coalesced into institutions centred around a god or the King.

Each household followed the same hierarchy with the King at the top, then the queen (who sometimes had her own household) Gods of the city always represented by the temple, the priests of the city's God, the military, administration and bureaucracy, merchant and artisan class (skilled workers), and the unskilled workers such as labourers at the bottom. Labourers were paid through rations distributed by the administrator of the King, queen, or temple and usually consisted of barley, wool and oil in the bevelled rim bowl standardised size. The King, the queen or someone of substantial wealth and power.

People also fished and cultivated private gardens to supplement their income. Eventually the garden which had been a necessity to support the nutritional requirements of a family eventually became a luxury item which started to grow items that had a visual impact, rather than needed. Marc van de Mieroop comments on the rations provided:

It is clear that these rations constituted the support given to the household's dependents, whether productive or not. The amounts were provided according to the sex and status of the worker: a male worker regularly received double the amount of grain given to a female worker, supervisors received more than their subordinates, specialised craftsmen more than unskilled labourers, and so on.

Although Sumerian women had nearly equal rights, this paradigm did not extend to the lowest classes who had few rights overall. The policy and practices of the household would remain a constant as the early cities of Dynastic I developed and became the powerful city states of Dynastic II.

Early Dynastic II, 2,800-2,600 BC

The Dynastic II Period saw the development of these earlier advances as the individual cities expanded. Technology was improved and the household paradigm maintained a cohesive structure for the developing culture. Scholar Wolfram von Soden comments:

The culture was based on the formation of a society based on a division of labour which freed large groups of the population such as artisans, merchants, and cultic and administrative personnel from the production of food. As well as on an advanced technology for the production of clay vessels using the potter's wheel, metallurgy, and the mass production of heavily used objects.

This model worked well for the upper class, and the mass-produced items, bread, and woven cloth were also lucrative trade items. Powerful city states started to grow throughout the Middle East and Egypt in North Africa. With the advent of Cuneiform correspondence quickly picked up pace between *Brothers*[22]. Kings' description of a King of equal status in another region. But this wealth never trickled down to the lower-class labourers who produced the merchandise. Marc van de Mieroop explains:

The majority of workers provided repetitive manual labour. Women were especially used as millers and weavers. Milling at this time was a backbreaking task which required that grain be rubbed back and forth over a stone slab with a smaller hand-held stone. The women were supposed to produce set quotas on a daily basis...[later] weaving quotas could easily be as high as 2 square metres a day. Those were heavy tasks, that could lead to physical injuries, as is shown by the skeletons of women.

As the wealth and power of the cities grew, they attracted more and more people from rural areas. Taxation hit a refined level that allowed commerce

---

[22] *Brother describes the relationship between Kings of equal status, correspondence between both parties always described each other as brother.*

between *Brothers*. Sending large amounts prized localised manufactured goods to different regions. A request from one brother to another could not be refused, but an equal request was expected in return. cities afforded protection from raiders, slavers, and the elements in addition to providing opportunities for work and taxation. Those who remained in rural communities were left with the burden of providing at least the same amount of grain to the cities and then increasingly more than they had before. Scholar Gwendolyn Leick notes[cliii]:

> As the city grew larger and more populous, attracting more and more people eager to escape the drudgery of subsistence farming, and perhaps also the narrow horizons of traditional communities. The demands on the remaining rural population increased. Tension and unrest seem to have been met with violent repression; pictorial scenes on seals and other objects show groups of prisoners, their hands bound behind their backs.

These scenes clearly depict fellow citizens, not foreign prisoners held as slaves, but nothing was done to stop this practice because of the very same model of the household which held society together. The upper-class heads *Chiefdoms* of the households maintained large estates and the workers on those lands were expected to produce to the household's expectations. This placed a tremendous burden on the workers to the extent that they seem to have seen the mundane work in the city as preferable. As an outsider, everything seemed to be going according to plan. Each city state seemed to be prospering, trade was now universal and opportunities becoming greater.

The social divide grew and internally pressures grew, this then created internal friction and the start of descent. Expansion of land between the Rivers of Mesopotamia was impossible due to boundary markers set-up in an era long forgotten. Friction between neighbouring city states intensified which started to sow the seeds of Sumerian implosion with suitors waiting in the wings and in the mountains. Each city rivalled the next in population growth, as cities became wealthier and their greed was even greater, the start of hubristic tendencies first started to appear.

Around 2,700 BC, Enmebaragesi of Kish led the Sumerian cities in a distracting war against Elam the Sumerian neighbours, from domestic problems. This was the first war in recorded history and defeated the Elamites, carrying back the spoils to Sumer. Elamite revenge would be total, and they sat on the side-lines biding their time and waiting for an opportunity for revenge. This is one example of the city states working together for a common goal and using a collective war as a distraction from internal fighting and the Elamites also had natural resources that the Sumerian craved. If a war was won, the writes over the Elamites rich resources didn't require any form bartering as they were the spoils of victory.

Samuel Noah Kramer points out, they had needed to find a way to do that individually and collectively long before the war and it was this need for cooperation, in fact, which had given rise to the city states to begin with.

While the Sumerians set a high value on the individual and his achievement, there was one overriding factor which fostered a strong spirit of cooperation among individuals and communities alike: the complete dependence of Sumer on irrigation for its well-being indeed, for its very existence. Irrigation is a complicated process requiring communal effort and organisation. Canals had to be dug and kept in constant repair. The water had to be divided equitably among all concerned. To ensure this, a power stronger than the individual landowner or even the single community was mandatory: hence, the growth of governmental institutions and the rise of the Sumerian state.

When they had to, the city states cooperated and were able to accomplish their goals. Apart from necessary cooperation for survival, however, and this would include trade agreements the cities pursued their own self-interest, often to the detriment of others. This was the period when commerce and greed started to raise its ugly head.

Early Dynastic III Growth of the First Empire 2,600-2,334 BC

The Early Dynastic III Period witnessed the rise of Kish in the North and Uruk in the South as the two dominant political powers. This is the era in which the Kings are both historically and archaeologically attested. The Dynasties of

some Cities, like Lagash, are not included in the Sumerian King List and the dates of that list for other Kings often do not correspond to dates in other documents or the archaeological record.

The Great Kings of Uruk, for example, such as Meskiaggasher, Enmerkar who was said to have first founded Uruk, Lugalbanda, Dumuzi, and the great hero-King Gilgamesh are all listed toward the beginning of the Early Dynastic III Period 2,600 BC but are also associated with earlier rulers such as Enmebaragesi and later Kings like Eannatum 2,450-2,400 BC. There seems to be no reconciling these differences in chronology as each version of the Kings List has variations and none state the same names, the first depiction of propaganda and disinformation. Raising some Kings and ignoring others that best suite a particular Empires interests or it could simply be a lack of Historical Knowledge.

The first King of the First Dynasty of Lagash, Ur-Nanshe, established Lagash as a strong political presence and his son Eannatum expanded on his policies and conquer all of Sumer. Eannatum, calling upon Enlil patron God of Lagash and Ninurta God of War led his armies against all the other city states of Sumer. Eannatum's most famous monument celebrates a victory over their neighbours Umma which is called the *Stele of the Vulture*. The Stele is extremely vivid in its depiction and highlights the barbaric nature of its warfare.

It also highlights the organisation of its troops. This was no ordinary city state army but a well-equipped and well-organised army, marching in a tight phalanx with their enemies being trampled underfoot, with severed heads in the beaks of the vultures. We can safely say, that *War was Total* and left nothing to ambiguity. Eannatum continued his conquest of Sumer including Uruk and Kish and then moved against the Elamites and took large portions of their territory.

Again, focussing all city states in the direction of an external foe therefore distracting from internal fragilities and now a much transparent show of Hubris. By the time his campaigns were over, he had created the *First Empire in Mesopotamia*, largely comprised of the city states of his former-fellow-monarchs. His Empire was challenged shortly after his death, however, and his successors could not maintain it.

The City of Ur, 5,000-500 BC

Ur was a city in the region of Sumer, Southern Mesopotamia, in what is modern-day Iraq. The Second Dynasty is known to have had four Kings but about them, their accomplishments, or the history during this time, nothing is known. The early Mesopotamian writers did not consider it worthwhile to record the deeds of mortals and preferred to link human achievements to the work and will of the gods. Ancient hero-Kings such as Gilgamesh or those who performed amazing feats such as Etana were worthy of record, but mortal Kings were not afforded that same level of concern.

According to biblical tradition, the city is named after the man who founded the first settlement there, Ur, though this has been disputed. The city's other biblical link is to the patriarch Abraham who left Ur to settle in the land of Canaan. The Old Testament tells us that Abram lived his childhood in Ur. It is plausible that the Terach family who bred herds and would have lived outside the city Walls knew Ur at the height of its splendour. Prior to any invasion and destruction by the Gutians descending from the Northern Zagros Mountains and predominantly the Elamites from the land of Elam descending from the mountains around 2,135 BC which witnessed the collapse of the Akkadians in 2,115 BC.

This was in revenge for previous attacks on the Elamites first in 2,700 BC by Enmebaragesi of Kish and then Eannatum of Lagash in 2,450 BC. His father was called Terach, and he had three sons: Haran, Nachor and Abram. We know that the town of Ur was destroyed between during the Gutian reign 2,154 and 2,055 BC. A great famine preceded its total destruction by the Elamites. *Those in the city who had not been felled by weapons died of hunger, Hunger filled the city like water, it would not cease.* So, it is more than plausible that the refugees of the Abram family emigrated Northward to Syria past the marauding Amorites who also attacked the Akkadians before the destruction of the royal city of Ur as very few escaped the wrath of the Elamites.

Is this because of the famine or a divine warning? The patriarch Terach left for Syria with all his family, including Abram and his wife Sarah, Nachor and his wife Milca the daughter of the late Haran and thus also the niece of Nachor, as well as Loth and Jisca the brother and sister of Milca. Whatever its biblical connections may have been, Ur was a significant Port city on the Persian Gulf. From the beginning, Ur began as a small village in the Ubaid Period of Mesopotamian history 5,000-4,100 BC. As with other great urban complexes in the region, the city began as a small village which was most likely led by a priest or priest-king.

The King of the First Dynasty, Mesannepadda, is only known through the Sumerian King List and from inscriptions on artefacts found in the graves of Ur. Ur as with Eridu was extremely important, well positioned for commercial expansion and control of all trade centre pivotal point where the Tigris and Euphrates run into the Persian Gulf and trade into the heartland of Sumer and beyond with countries as far away as India as trading partners. Ur was established as a city by 3,800 BC of enormous size at its maximum between 2,030-1,750 BC an occupancy of up to 65,000 people within its city Walls. This is not including the surrounding towns and villages its opulence which drew its vast wealth and continually inhabited until 450 BC.

Archaeological excavations have substantiated that, early on, Ur possessed great wealth and the citizens enjoyed a level of comfort unknown in other Mesopotamian cities. Ur's biblical associations have made it famous in the modern-day, but it was a significant urban and trading centre long before the biblical narratives were written and highly respected in its time.

Ubaid Cemetery at Ur

Cuneiform tablets show that Ur was, during the 3rd Millennium BC, a highly centralised, wealthy, bureaucratic state. The discovery of the Royal Tombs, dating from about the 2,500 BC. The Royal Tombs showed that Ur had luxury items made out of precious metals and semi-precious stones, which would have required importation. The definitive excavation of the ruins of Ur was conducted between 1922-1934 AD by Sir Leonard Woolley[cliv]. Working on behalf of the British Museum and the University of Pennsylvania excavated the ruins and discovered what he called The Great Death Pit an elaborate grave complex.

The famous Tomb of Tutankhamun had been discovered by Howard Carter in 1922 AD and Woolley was hoping for an equally impressive find. At Ur he uncovered the graves of sixteen Kings and Queens, including that of the Queen Puabi (also known as Shub-ad) and her treasures. More significantly to Sir Leonard Woolley claiming to have found evidence of the Great Flood described in the Book of Genesis. The present site of the ruins of Ur are much further inland than they were at the time when the city flourished owing to silting of the Tigris and Euphrates rivers.

The Great Death Pit, as Woolley named it, was the largest of those uncovered and, in it:

Woolley found six armed guards and 68 serving women. They wore ribbons of gold and silver in their hair, except one woman who still held in her hand the coiled-up silver ribbon she was unable to fasten before the sleeping potion took hold that painlessly carried her away to the after world with her master[clv].

The Front and rear of the royal standard of Ur

Woolley also uncovered the Royal Standard of Ur which celebrated the city's triumph over her enemies in war and the festivities which the people enjoyed in peace. In an effort to out-do Carter's triumph in the discovery of Tutankhamun's tomb, Woolley claimed that he had found evidence at Ur of the biblical Flood. But notes taken by his assistant, Max Mallowan[23], later showed that the flood record at the site in no way supported a world-wide deluge. The flooding was more in keeping with the regular flooding or a localised deluge caused by the Tigris and Euphrates Rivers.

Further excavations at Ur since Woolley's time have corroborated Mallowan's notes and, in spite of persistent beliefs to the contrary, no evidence

---

[23] *Max Mallowan, famous to most people as the husband of Agatha Christie, who followed him on many archaeological digs.*

supporting the Great Flood story from the Bible has been found at Ur nor anywhere else in Mesopotamia. Still, as Bertman notes:

Even if stripped of its biblical claims to fame, Woolley's Ur is still a glittering example of Sumerian golden age. Though its original lyres no longer sound, with our inner ear we can still hear their melodies.

After excavating the Royal Cemetery at Ur, Woolley sought the earliest levels of the tell by excavating an enormous trench. At the bottom of the trench, he discovered a thick layer of water-laid silt, in places as much as 10 feet thick. The Ubaid-period burials had been excavated into the silt, and beneath the cemetery was yet another cultural layer. Woolley determined that in its earliest days, Ur was located on an island in a marsh: the silt layer was the result of a great flood. The people buried in the cemetery had lived after that flood and were interred within the flood deposits.

In 2012 AD, scientists at the Pennsylvania Museum in Philadelphia and the British Museum began joint work on a new project, to digitize C. Leonard Woolley's records at Ur. Members of the Ur of Chaldees: A Virtual Vision of Woolley's Excavation project recently rediscovered skeletal material from Ur's Ubaid levels, which had been lost from the record database. The skeletal material, found in an unmarked box within Pennsylvania's collections, represented an adult male, one of 48 interments found buried in what Woolley called the *flood layer*, a silt layer some 40 feet deep within Tell al-Muqayyar.

The ruins of Ur today are a significant archaeological site which continues to yield important artefacts when the troubles of the region allow. The great Ziggurat of Ur rises from the plains above the mud-brick ruins of the once-great city and, as Bertman suggests, in walking among them one relives the past when Ur was a centre of commerce and trade, protected by the gods and flourishing amidst fertile fields.

The Ziggurat of Ur

The word *ziggurat* is from an extinct Semitic language and derives from a verb that means *to build on a flat space*. This temple was built in the 21st Century BC, during the reign of Ur-Nammu, and was reconstructed in the 6th Century BC by Nabonidus, the last King of Babylon. The ruins, which cover an area of 3,900 feet by 2,600 feet, were uncovered in the 1930s AD. It was part of a temple complex that served as an administrative centre for the city of Ur, and was dedicated to Nanna, the moon god.

A ziggurat is a very ancient and massive building structure of a particular shape that served as part of a temple complex in the various local religions of Mesopotamia and the flat highlands of what is now Western Iran. Sumer, Babylonia, and Assyria are known to have about 25 ziggurats, evenly divided among them. The shape of a ziggurat it clearly identifiable, the original foundation of the ziggurat will have accumulated over millennia, and the rebuilding phase of simply encases the debris of the previous structure.

As the wall become higher, then it becomes more obvious to place a *different structure* on top of the new base. But at some point, the *lucky number seven* comes back into play and all ziggurats end-up with seven distinctive level. Fortunately for the building team the sixes of these new levels are ever decreasing. Roughly square platform base with sides that recede inward as the structure rises, and a flat top presumed to have supported some form of a shrine. Sun-baked bricks and previous incarnations of the building form the core of a ziggurat, with fire-baked bricks forming the outer faces. Unlike the Egyptian pyramids, a ziggurat was a solid structure with no internal chambers. An external staircase or spiral ramp provided access to the top platform.

Sumerian Power Struggles and Chaos

Each city state of Sumer was surrounded by a wall, with villages settled just outside and distinguished by the worship of local deities who would protect them in times of need. Somewhere around 2,600 BC, a power struggle erupted between the leaders of Kish, Erech and Ur, which set off a *musical-chairs* scenario of rulers for the region for the next 270 years. Even though the Sumerians shared a common language and cultural traditions, the Sumerian city states engaged in near-constant wars that resulted in several different dynasties and Kingships and short-lived Empires.

The first of these conflicts known to history concerns King, Eannatum of Lagash, who defeated the rival city state of Umma in a border dispute in 2,450 BC. To commemorate his victory, Eannatum constructed the so-called *Stele of the Vultures*, a grisly limestone monument that depicts vultures feasting on the flesh of his fallen enemies. Under Eannatum, Lagash went on to conquer the whole of Sumer, but it was just one of several city states that held sway over Mesopotamia during its history. The infighting led to several military advancements the Sumerians seem to have invented the phalanx formation and siege warfare, but it also left them vulnerable to invasions by outside forces.

One conflict resulted in the Kingdom of Awan seizing control and shifting the ruling body outside of Sumer until the Kingship was returned to the Kish. Kish kept control briefly until the rise of Uruk King Enshakushanna, whose brief dynasty was followed by Adabian Empire conquering King Lugalannemundu, who held power for 90 years and is said to have expanded his Kingdom up to the Mediterranean. Lugalannemundu also conquered the Gutian people, who lived in the Eastern Iraqi Mountains and who would later come to rule Sumer.

Following Lugalannemundu, the King List indicates that Kingship fell to a several concurrently competing regions all gaining independence. During this unrest the entire region became easy pickings and the King of Umma Lugal-Zage-Si eventually went on to seize his own Empire throughout the Fertile Crescent.

Rise of Kish

One of the most interesting and mysterious of the monarchs who are said to have freed their cities from the Empire of Lagash is the only female ruler on the Sumerian King List: Kubaba (also given as Kug-Bau), who founded the Third Dynasty of Kish. The Sumerian King List describes her briefly as *the woman tavern-keeper who made firm the foundations of Kish*, who she was, where she came from, and how she came to power is unknown. Her son, Puzur-Suen, and grandson, Ur-Zababa, were both successful Kings and Kubaba herself was deified after her death. Her cult, in fact, would inform the later goddess of the Hurrians (Hepat) and, famously, the Phrygian mother goddess Matar Kubileya *Mother Cybele* who was worshipped by the Ionian Greeks of Anatolia/Cilicia as Cybele.

Checkmate: The Rise of Sargon

Sargon was an Akkadian whose past is shrouded in legends that some claims were ignited by Sargon himself. Sargon of Akkad's *biography* which scholars consider a highly mythologised version of events claims that he was born in the North. The illegitimate son of a *changeling*, who gave birth to him in secret and

then set him afloat on the river in a basket of reeds which brought him to the city of Kish where he was found by the royal gardener Akki.

The claim is that he was the secret child of a high priestess who placed him in a bitumen coated reed basket and cast him off into a river, a story that was later utilised for Moses in the Old Testament. Little is known of Sargon's background, but legends give him a similar origin to the Biblical story of Moses.

Ur-Zababa 2nd King of 4th Dynasty of Kish and Grandson of Queen Kubaba had appointed somebody of total trust within his ranks as Cupbearer. Whatever the royal accomplishments of Queen Kubaba grandson Ur-Zababa were, they were eclipsed by the legends which came to define the reign of the man who enters history as Ur-Zababa's court aid. Sargon grew up in the palace. Sumerian tradition says that he was the son of a gardener who rose to the position of cupbearer for Ur-Zababa, King of Kish, which was not a servant position but a high official a prestigious position and a position of total trust.

Sargon was favoured until the King had a disturbing dream suggesting Sargon would depose him. At the same time, the King of the Third Dynasty of Uruk, Lugal-Zage-Si who had ruled for 25 years, embarked on a campaign of conquest to reunite the whole of Sumer under a single ruler. Just as Eannatum had done earlier in 2,450 BC. Ur-Zababa sent Sargon as an emissary to Lugal-Zage-Si, who was on the march toward Kish, possibly with terms, but according to legend, with the request that the King of Umma kill the messenger.

Sargon so impressed Lugal-Zage-Si the last King of Sumer, King of Umma. However, the King of Umma Lugal-Zage-Si ignored the request and asked Sargon to join him. They marched on Ur, Umma, Lagash and its fertile plains of

Gu-Edin and the city state Uruk taking the title King of Uruk, following this success he then united Sumer very briefly as a single Kingdom extending his dominion from the Lower Sea (Persian Gulf) to the Upper Sea the coast of the Mediterranean. He already had a previous agreement with the King of Kish never to invade Kish, but once Uruk had been taken and became King of Uruk quickly reneged on the previous agreement.

Together, Lugal-Zage-Si and Sargon led the army and defeated Ur-Zababa King of Kish with Ur-Zababa going into hiding and never heard of again. For reasons unknown (possibly fell in love with Lugal-Zage-Si wife) Sargon and Lugal-Zage-Si became enemies with Sargon and met for battle at Uruk. Sargon had turned on his benefactor and defeated him, dragging him in chains, with a rope around his neck, to the city of Nippur where he was publicly humiliated in being marched through the sacred gate of the god Enlil who was Lugal-Zage-Si patron god who was entrusted for victory. After this humiliation, Lugal-Zage-Si was presumably, executed.

His militaristic reign reached to the Persian Gulf. Sargon built the city of Agade as his base, South of Kish, which became an important centre in the ancient world and a prominent port. Agade was also home to Sargon's army, which vastly improved warfare techniques and is considered the first organised standing army in history and the earliest to use chariots in warfare. Sargon expanded his empire proclaiming himself King and went on to conquer all of Mesopotamia including Sumer and founded the Akkadian Empire, the first multi-national political entity in history.

Moving into what is now Syria, under King Sargon's rule, trade beyond Mesopotamian borders grew, and architecture became more sophisticated, notably the appearance of ziggurats. The Akkadian Empire brings the Early Dynastic Period to a close but, contrary to Sargon's later boasts and the legends that grew up around him, he could not have established his empire without the foundation laid by his predecessors. Sargon's greatest strength, in fact, was learning from the mistakes of the earlier conquerors and placing people he could trust in positions of authority throughout his empire including his daughter Enhedu-Anna 2,285-2,250 BC.

Sargon took control of the religious cultures of the Akkadians and the Sumerians, making his daughter Enhedu-Anna was appointed high priestess of the temple of Inanna at the city of Ur. In doing so Sargon enamoured himself to the powerful city of Ur and brought peace to the whole of Sumer. Enhedu-Anna is best remembered for her transcriptions of temple hymns, which she wrote and are preserved to this day on cuneiform clay tablet and the first author in history known by name. Sargon also routinely sending trusted officials throughout his realm to maintain order.

Sargon's example would be followed by the later Assyrian Empire and the Roman Empire in terms of cohesive government. The model of that government, however, was set down by the Sumerian Kings of the Early Dynastic Period. These monarchs established a society which, in spite of its weaknesses and rivalries, allowed for the development of many of the most fundamental aspects of civilisation so often taken for granted in the present day.

The Akkadian Period

The Akkadian Empire briefly existed from 2,334 BC under the leadership of the now-titled Sargon the Great. It was considered the world's first multicultural empire with a central government and the First United Empire in Mesopotamia which thrived with the development of irrigation. The Akkadian Empire existed from 2,334-2,154 BC. The Empire of Akkad collapsed in 2,154 BC, within 180 years of its founding. The collapse ushered in a Dark Age period of regional decline that lasted until the rise of the Third Dynasty of Ur in 2,047 BC. Sargon ruled with Queen Tashlultum for 55 years.

After his death, his son Rimush 2,279-2,270 BC replaced him, but the city states throughout Mesopotamia soon saw an opportunity to try and revolt and regain regional city state powers. The widespread revolts led to Rimush reconquering the cities of Ur, Umma, Adab and Lagash from rebellious Ensis (originators also *fool's gold*) and was killed. Rimush's brother Manishtushu 2,270-2,255 BC who led a fleet into the Persian Gulf conquering and looting on the way. This will probably be the time when Persian Gulf started to speak Semitic and also brought the war back to Elam in the city of Shirasum assassinated met by member of his own court.

- During the Akkadian Empire period 2,334-2,154 BC, many in the region became bilingual in both Sumerian and Akkadian. Toward the end of the empire, though, Sumerian became increasingly a literary language.
- The Gutian period 2,154 until 2,055 BC was marked by a period of chaos and decline, as the Guti barbarians defeated the Akkadian military but were unable to support the civilisations already set in place.

- The Sumerian Renaissance and Third Dynasty of Ur 2,047-1,750 BC saw the rulers Ur-Nammu and Shulgi, whose power extended into Southern Assyria. However. The region was becoming more Semitic, and the Sumerian language became a religious language.
- The Sumerian Renaissance ended with invasion by the Ur-Amorites wars 2,025-2,004 BC, whose dynasty of Isin continued until 1,700 BC, at which point Mesopotamia came under Babylonian rule.

The Propaganda Hero-Kings of Akkad and Birth of Legends

The Akkadian Empire ruled over diverse regions of Mesopotamia between 2,334-2,154 BC. Sargon the Great later claimed to have been born of a priestess and a god, floated down the river in a bitumen covered reed basket to be found by the servant of the King of the city of Kish rising from obscurity. Through the will of the goddess Inanna was destined to rule all of Mesopotamia. The inscriptions he left dare those who follow him to do the deeds he did if they hope to call themselves a King and his life was worthy of the efforts of the scribes of the region for centuries after his death.

Sending military expeditions as far South as Dilmun and Magan (modern day Bahrain and Oman). His grandson, Naram-Sin 2,254-2,218 BC, learning well the lessons of the importance of personal propaganda, claimed he had gone further than his grandfather and had himself deified during his reign. In doing so, he provided a model for those Kings who would follow him. Under Naram-Sin the Akkadian Empire reached its zenith, he took the throne considering himself divine and was levelled with charges of sacrilege. The next King of the Akkadian Empire was the son of Naram-Sin Shar-Kali-Sharri 2,217-2,193 BC, was unable to prevent the Empire collapsing outright from the invasion of barbarian peoples.

The Gutians, from the Zagros Mountains, the Amorites of modern-day Syria invading from the North and their regular foes the Elamites of Elam and the Akkadian Empire had been significantly weakened to a point of collapse. There was a period of anarchy between 2,192-2,168 BC. Some centralised authority may have been restored under Shu-Durul 2,168-2,154 BC. In 2,154 BC the Gutians starving and hostile to everyone in the basin of Mesopotamia looked for an opportunity and also revenge from the Adabian King Lugalannemundu and attacked with vengeance.

The invasion marked by decentralised chaos and neglect considered a disorderly that caused a severe downturn in the Empire's prospects. It was during Gutian reign that the grand capital of the Akkadians the city of Agade decayed into wreckage and disappeared from history to this day never found.

Sargon the Great and Naram-Sin were the most powerful rulers of the Akkadian Empire and, once it fell, their names became legend and their deeds worth emulating. At Ur, the heroes of Akkad were closely emulated by the rulers of the Third Dynasty. This period in the history of Sumer is known as the Ur III Period 2,047-1,750 BC and was the age in which the city of Ur reached its height. The great ziggurat of Ur, which can still be visited in modern times, dates from this period as do most of the ruins of the city and the cuneiform tablets discovered there.

The two greatest Kings of the Third Dynasty were Ur-Nammu 2,047-2,030 BC and his son Shulgi of Ur 2,029-1,982 BC who created an urban community devoted to cultural progress and excellence and, in doing so, gave birth to what is known as the Sumerian Renaissance.

End of the World's First Empire Due to Climate Change

All the great changes that occurred in the history of Cognitive Homo Sapiens always had the backdrop of some climatic effect. We tend to assume that these events occurred in the dim and distant past, but unfortunately, we continue to see these changes on a very regular basis creeping closer and closer to Modern Humans. We have to understand the *Cause and Effect* of the latest Climatic Event during the reign of the Akkadians and what triggered it, what exacerbated it, and what effect it had on region and the people, that resulted in a shift of power which changed our entire history.

The climatic change hasn't been at the forefront of the historical narrative of this time. The lines became blurred due to the rise of such an enigmatic figure as Sargon and his *First Real Empire the Akkadians* and the gaze of history was solely focused upon King who took control of the Land of Sumeria in 2,334 BC. Only 64 years after the Sargon and the Akkadians took power did the world start to feel the effects of the latest climatic events.

Looking at several scientific researches and through archaeological trolling of the Cuneiform archives, it has been possible to understand what had happened during this time and to put together a clear a concise picture of events.

If we are to believe the records, no external force of its day could possibly beat the extremely organised Akkadian Army, the first professional army in the world, especially a bunch of mountain tribesmen. Fortunately, we are aware of concurrent historical events of the Fertile Crescent and its neighbours throughout the Middle East, North Africa, and the Indus Valley due to cuneiform writing, hieroglyphics, scientific and archaeological evidence. We also fully understand the backdrop to these historical events.

Another climatic event that pushed entire Empires and regions to the point of total collapse. It would seem that our history has always be dictated to, by climatic events; the Milankovitch Cycles described the Earth Cycle that allowed large increases in rainfall and vegetation in 125,000 BC that allowed Homo Sapien to migrate out of East Africa. The end of the Last Glacial Maximum (LGM) that caused 120 metre increase in seawater levels in just a few thousand years which resulted in Gulf Oasis flooding creating todays Persian Gulf.

The breaching of the Bosporus channel which in-turn flooded of the Euxine, North of Anatolia which created the Black Sea. Entire cities engulfed by massive deposits of silt at the mouth of the Tigris and Euphrates rivers (several times) as described in the Eridu Genesis and subsequent Holy Scriptures, and the decline of the Akkad Empire of Southern Mesopotamia attributed to a long-term drought that began in 2,270 BC. This latest event is known as the Rapid Climatic Changes (RCC) 4.2K Climatic Event associated with widespread changes.

This event was triggered thousands of miles away in the North Atlantic Ocean, the onset of cooler sea-surface temperatures. As analysis of the modern instrumental record shows that up to 50% inter annual reductions in Mesopotamian water supply resulted when subpolar Northwest Atlantic sea surface temperatures are anomalously cool. The headwaters of the Tigris and Euphrates Rivers are fed by elevation-induced capture of winter Mediterranean rainfall.

The second back drop that exacerbated Akkadian and Sumerian decline was a geological phenomenon. Because of their origin as snowmelt, the Tigris and Euphrates River waters have always contained high concentrations of dissolved salts. Over millennia, these salts accumulate in the groundwater and are whipped up to the surface through capillary action in plant roots. Marine transgressions during geological times also left smaller salt accumulations in rocks underlying the soil.

Further, salt was blown into the Sumerian plains by winds from the Persian Gulf. Also, the natural high-water table in Southern Mesopotamia the Sumerians had to resort to fallow cultivation to avoid the rise of the water table into the root zone and cause waterlogging and crop failure. Unfortunately, rainfall was, and remains, insufficient to flush the groundwater while increased irrigation exacerbates the salinisation. Evaporated salt forms a white crust on the surface of fields and levee walls and still witnessed to this day. For centuries, the wheat crop managed to survive, but the strain of mass production started to take its toll and slowly but surely deceased.

Unbeknown to the Sumerians, the land was always balancing on the edge of a precipice. Due to the 4.2K Climatic Event that lasted 200 years from 2,270 BC triggering a chain of events that spelt disaster for the local populace who could never fully recover with the balance of power shifting further North over the coming Centuries to areas that didn't rely solely on irrigation and also virgin land not previously used for intensive crop production.

The reduced rainfall in the mountains with 50% inter annual reductions in Mesopotamian water which was required for crop production started to have an impact on the masses. First the people of Northern areas of Mesopotamia that relied on regular rainfall for agrarian crops. These people who had strong trade links and similar cultural ties to Southern Mesopotamia descended upon the Sumerians for help. The population swelled and the first strains on production were felt, prices increased whilst the government took a greater control on water management and distribution.

A further compounding negative was the failure of the crops in the mountainous areas that flanked Mesopotamia from the Persian Gulf all the way to the Taurus Mountains who contained tribes that weren't associated or didn't have fixed trade links with Akkad and Sumer. The mountains contained multiple different tribes who weren't classed as civilised and didn't follow the rule of law (Akkadian and Sumerian Law) with an increase in raiding the plains for food. The worsening climatic conditions didn't just affect the mountain regions but also the desert. These increased arid conditions made the deserts less hospitable so the herdsmen and desert tribes who also started to migrate into the fertile plains of Mesopotamia from the Southern flanks.

As soon as the rain failed to materialise, the population in Southern Mesopotamia grew exponentially therefore increasing the strain on the already failing crops due to salinisation. An increase in engineering works was required on the existing canal systems. River levels had decreased, and the systems required deeper systems to not just feed the fields but to allow the boats to transport the crops.

Neuman and Parpola (1987)[clvi] found documentary proof of a reduction of water levels of both the Tigris and Euphrates and an increase in the salinity of the soils from 2,270 BC. The deterioration of the climate had caused the geo-political crisis in Mesopotamia. Clay tablets discovered have clearly shown the changes in crops during the climatic change. Originally, both barley and wheat had been grown to equal quantities during this period of change whilst the wheat crops diminished the barley being more tolerant of soil salinity therefore continued unabated whilst the wheat production barely limped along.

The collapse of rain-fed agriculture in the Upper Country due to drought meant the loss of the agrarian subsidies which had kept the Akkadian Empire solvent in Southern Mesopotamia. Rivalries between pastoralists and farmers increased. Attempts to control access to water led to increased political instability. Eventually culminating into a severe depopulation, famine, pestilence, a movement away from many of the cities of Middle and Southern Mesopotamia and the start of a new dark age.

The South had lost all cohesion and opportunity rested elsewhere within Mesopotamia. Now paleo-climatologists propose that a similar fate at the same time, occurred to the enigmatic Indus Valley Civilisation the trading partners of Sumerians. Based on isotope data from the sediment of an ancient lake. The researchers suggest that the monsoon cycle, which is vital to the livelihood of all of South Asia, essentially stopped there for as long as two centuries. It has been hypothesised to have also collapsed the Old Kingdom in Egypt as well as the Liangzhu culture in the lower Yangtze River area.

The drought looks to have also initiated the collapse of the Indus Valley Civilisation, with some of its population moving South-Eastward to follow the movement of their desired habitat, as well as the migration of Indo-European speaking people into India.

The Indus Valley[clvii] in present Pakistan and Northwest India, was home to the Harappan civilisation who traded very heavily with the Sumerian city states along with the cities of the Persian Gulf. The entire Harappan Civilisation disappeared and was not known of until being rediscovered in the 19th century. But the Harappans seemed to slowly lose their urban cohesion, and their cities were gradually abandoned. The link between this gradual decline and climate had been tenuous because of a dearth of climate records from the region. So, Yama Dixit, a paleo-climatologist at the University of Cambridge, UK examined sediments from Kotla Dahar.

An ancient lake near the North Eastern edge of the Indus Valley area in Haryana, India, that still seasonally floods. The team assigned ages to sediment layers using radiocarbon dating of organic matter. In various layers, they collected the preserved shells of tiny lake snails (Melanoides Tuberculata), which are made of a form of calcium carbonate (CaCO3) called aragonite. The team also looked at the oxygen in the aragonite molecules, counting the ratio of the rare oxygen-18 isotope to the more prevalent oxygen-16.

Kotla Dahar is a closed basin, filled only by rain and runoff and without outlets. The precipitation and evaporation alone determine its water volume. During drought, oxygen-16, which is lighter than oxygen-18, evaporates faster, so that the remaining water in the lake and, consequently, the snail's shells, become enriched with oxygen-18. The team's reconstruction showed a spike in the relative amount of oxygen-18 between 4,200 and 4,000 years ago.

This suggests that precipitation dramatically decreased during that time. Moreover, their data suggests that the regular summer monsoons stopped for some 200 years. The result supports the idea that monsoon failure led to the civilisation's decline.

Archaeological evidence documents widespread abandonment of the agricultural plains of Northern Mesopotamia and dramatic influxes of refugees into Southern Mesopotamia, around 2,170 BC which had seen massive prosperity in the region due to the canal building that had taken place. The 200-year long drought totally and utterly destabilised the region with more building programs undertaken to take up the influx of people into the region from the North.

The decreased river levels due to the 50% reduction in water feed from the Mountains at the heads of the rivers created a strain on the economies of the region. Fortunately, the South did not rely on rainfall, but it would have definitely had to rethink its engineering to enable the region to survive the long drought period. The water levels in both rivers would have been drastically reduced and all the locks, weirs and canal systems would have had to have been altered to accommodate this change in river levels. So, a large canal re-engineering works had to be completed in the South during all the chaos.

The Sudden Collapse of the Akkadian Empire

Some centralised authority may have been restored under Shu-Durul 2,168-2,154 BC. But he was unable to prevent the Akkadian Empire collapsing outright from the invasion of barbarian peoples, known as the Gutians, from the Zagros Mountains and their regular foes the Elamites of Elam. cities and settlements appear to have been suddenly abandoned over 4,150 years ago, causing its collapse. The area would also not experience resettlement until about 300 years later. Scientific research has shown several dramatic changes to the climate at this time this is known as the 4.2K Climate Event.

This led to a transition of a new culture. Not a better culture but a different one during the Middle Bronze age and brought with it a period of massive collapse of the urban centres and a move to a general transition to pastoral and nomadic way of life born through necessity to survive. The cities could no longer support the large communities due the consistent failure of crops due to increased salt.

Past studies have shown that the Akkadian Empire likely collapsed due to abrupt drought and civil turmoil. The fossil evidence shows that there was a prolonged winter shamal season accompanied by frequent shamal days. The impact of the dust storms and the lack of rainfall would have caused major agricultural problems possibly leading to social instability and famine, both factors which have been previously associated with the collapse of the Empire.

At the same time, the canal engineering works had to be completed in the South. A 180 km long wall had to be hastily built, the *Repeller of the Amorites*, was built across central Mesopotamia to stem nomadic incursions to the South that stretched from the Tigris to the Euphrates. Alas, this wall did not stop the incursion of the Amorites into the South, the Gutian hordes attacking from the Zagros Mountains or the Elamites attacking Ur.

But it was the catalyst for a new period of prosperity for one particular region the Babylonians. Building the wall was one thing but to keep it permanently manned seemed and was an impossibility. Although the official historical mark of the collapse of the Akkadian Empire is the invasion of Mesopotamia by the Gutians of the Zagros Mountains, it was climatic conditions that brought the real downfall.

The Gutians

They were described as part of the horde that toppled the Kingdom of Akkad (or Agade) known for their light skin and blond hair with a platted braid hanging down the chest with a pointed beard. It was a conglomeration of tribes that descended from the Zagros Mountains and known for their hit-and-run warfare tactics. The Gutians defeated the demoralised Akkadian army, took Akkad, and destroyed it around 2,115 BC. Possibly drawn to the plains for its prosperity or seen an opportunity due to the continuing drought wreaking havoc on the people of Mesopotamia.

The ancient Mesopotamians had previously treated the Gutian as subnormal beings for their unwillingness to conform to customs and laws of civilisation and used as slave labour, fettered, and given nose rings as a means of control. You reap what you sow, and the seeds of discontent grew strong amongst the Gutian hordes. I maybe said that the reason the Sumerians are called the "Black-Headed People" may also lay with the marked contrast of the people from the surrounding mountains. The King List tells us, the Gutians horde also subdued Uruk for hegemony of Sumer, in 2,154 until 2,055 BC. However, it seems that autonomous rulers soon arose again in a number of city-States, notably Gudea of Lagash.

Enlil then sent down Gutium from the mountains. Their advance was as the flood of Enlil that cannot be withstood. The teeming plain of Sumer was destroyed. No one moved about there. The snake of the mountain made his lair there, it became a rebellious land. The Gutians bred there, issued their seed (raping the local people). Enlil brought down the Elamites the enemy from the Highlands. Fire approached Nimar in the shrine Guabba. Large Boats were carrying off its precious metal and stones (Plunder back to Elam) (Eventually destroying Ur). To the South, the Elamites stepped In, slaughtering. To the North the Amorite Vandals. The Amorite Tidnumites daily strapped the mace to their loins ready for battle.

Ultimately, Akkad bore the brunt of this as the centre of the Empire was so thoroughly destroyed that its site is still not known. The Guti then established their own centre in place of the destroyed Akkad. Unfortunately for the people of Sumer and Akkad the Guti proved to be extremely poor rulers. Prosperity declined and showed little concern for maintaining agriculture, written records, or public safety, and they released all farm animals to roam about Mesopotamia freely, bringing about famine and rocketing grain prices.

They were too unaccustomed to the complexities of civilisation to organise matters properly, particularly in connection with the canal network. This was allowed to sink into disrepair, with famine and death resulting. Thus, a short *dark age* swept over Mesopotamia. Gutians did not conquer the rest of Sumer, and they were not accustomed to civilisation. Some of the Sumerian cities in the South took advantage of the distance and lack of total rule and purchased a certain amount of self-government by paying tribute to the new rulers.

In 2,055 BC, King Ur-Nammu expelled the Gutians from Mesopotamia and back into the Zagros Mountains, and they came to inhabit Media. Widespread agricultural changed in the Middle East is visible at the end of the 3rd Millennium BC.

The description of the suffering of the people of Ur, The Elamites, the enemy from Elam attack on Ur:

Those in the city who had not been felled by weapons died of hunger,
Hunger filled the city like water, it would not cease.
Its people dropped their weapons, their weapons hit the ground.
Ur, inside it there is only death, outside it there is only death,
Inside it, we are being finished off by famine,
Outside it we are being finished off by the Elamite weapons
Elam, like a swelling flood wave, left only the spirit of the dead,
Ur's refugees were unable to flee, they were trapped inside the walls,
In Ur no one went to fetch food, no one went to fetch drink.
Its people rush around like water churning in a well.
Their strength has ebbed away, they cannot even go on their way.
Enlil afflicted the city with an inimical famine,
He afflicted the city with something that destroys Cities, that destroys temples,
He afflicted the city with something that cannot be withstood with weapons,
He afflicted the city with dissatisfaction and treachery.

Resettlement of the Northern plains by smaller sedentary populations occurred near 1,900 BC, 150 years after the collapse of the Akkadian Empire. The anthropogenic climate changed the landscape of the region for good with new seats of power appearing and the slow decline of the most Southernly city states irreparably damaged whilst the North began to grow in stature and influence until the first comprehensive dark age in 1,187 BCE *The Bronze Age Collapse.*

Third Dynasty of Ur 2,047-1,750 BC: Ur-Nammu and Shulgi

The Sumerian Renaissance In 2,047 BC the city of Ur attempted to establish a dynasty for a new empire. The ruler of Ur-Namma, the King of the city of Ur, brought Sumerians back into control after Utu-Hengal, the leader of the city of Uruk, defeated the Gutians. Under Ur-Namma, the first code of law in recorded history, The Code of Ur-Nammu, appeared. Ur-Namma was attacked by both the Elamites and the Amorites and defeated in 2,004 BC. The final gasp of Sumer leadership came in 2,055 BC. When Utu-Hengal, King of Ur, overthrew the Gutians. Utuhegal's reign was brief, with Ur-Nammu, the former governor of Ur, taking the throne, starting a dynasty that would rule for about a century.

Ur-Nammu was known as a builder. Figurines from the time depict him carrying building materials. During his reign, he started massive projects to build walls around his capital city, to create more irrigation canals, construct new temples and rebuild old ones. Ur-Nammu also did the considerable work of constructing an organised and complicated legal code that is considered the first in history. Its purpose was to ensure that everyone in the Kingdom, no matter what city they lived in, received the same justice and punishments, rather than rely on the whims of individual governors.

Ur-Nammu also created an organised school system for state administrators. Called the Edubba, it kept an archive of clay tablets for learning. Ur-Nammu wrote down the first codified law system of the land, some three hundred years before Hammurabi of Babylon would write his and governed his realm in accordance with a patriarchal hierarchy in which he was the father guiding his children to prosperity and continued health. Under Ur-Nammu the great ziggurat was built, and trade flourished. The arts and technology for which the Sumerians are most famous were all encouraged in Ur during this time.

The scholar Paul Kriwaczek observes that, in order for such a patriarchal system of government to succeed, the people must believe that their ruler is greater, more powerful, than they are in the same way that children regard their father. To this end, it seems, Ur-Nammu presented himself to his subjects in line with the hero-Kings Sargon and Naram-Sin in order to encourage the populace to follow him in the pursuit of excellence. His son Shulgi, in an effort to surpass the achievements of his father, went even further.

One example of this is his famous run when, to impress his people and distinguish himself from his father, Shulgi ran 100 miles (160.9 kilometres) between the religious centre of Nippur and the capital city of Ur and back again in one day in order to officiate at the festivals in both Cities. Shulgi continued his father's policies, bettering them when he saw fit, and is considered the greatest King of the Third Dynasty of Ur for the heights civilisation reached under his reign.

Among his many building projects was a wall which ran 155 miles (250 kilometres) along the border of the region of Sumer to keep out the barbarian tribes known as the Martu (also as the Tidnum) who are most recognisable to modern readers from their biblical designation as Amorites. Shulgi's wall was maintained by his son, grandson, and great grandson but could not hold back the tribes on the borders. The wall was too long to be properly manned and, since it was not anchored at either end, invaders could by-pass the obstacle simply by marching around it.

In 1,750 BC, the neighbouring Kingdom of Elam breached the walls again, sacked Ur and carried away the last King as a prisoner. The Amorites, who had already found their way around the wall, merged with the Sumerian populace and, in this way, Sumerian culture came to an end with the fall of Ur.

The Disappearance and Rediscovery of Ur

In the Old Babylonian Period 2,004-1,600 BC, Ur remained a city of importance and was considered a centre of learning and culture. According to the historian Gwendolyn Leick, *The heirs of Ur, the Kings of Isin and Larsa, were keen to show their respect to the gods of Ur by repairing the devastated temples*, and the Kassite Kings, who later conquered the region, did the same as would the Assyrian rulers who followed them. The city continued to be inhabited through the early part of the Achaemenid Period 550-330 BC but, due to climate change and an overuse of the land, more and more people migrated to the northern regions of Mesopotamia or south towards the land of Canaan (the patriarch Abraham, some claim, among them, as previously noted).

Ur slowly dwindled in importance as the Persian Gulf receded further and further south from the city and eventually fell into ruin around 450 BC. Between 2,334-2,154 BC, Ur was controlled by Sargon's Akkadian Empire. Ur was sacked by the Elamites and ruled by the barbarian Gutians. The Gutians were eventually overthrown by Utu-Hegel King of Uruk Father-In-Law of King Ur-Nammu who came to power 2,047-2,030 BC (the Third Dynasty of Ur) taking a leading role when Utu-Hegel died and Ur-Nammu took the leading role, yet still only ousted the Gutian from Sumerian Cities. Shulgi, the son of Ur-Nammu, succeeded defeating the Gutians. Ur-Nammu was able to increase Ur's power by creating a highly centralised bureaucratic state. Shulgi, who eventually declared himself a god, ruled from 2,029-1,982 BC, and was well-known for at least two thousand years after.

Advances during this time included the building of temples, like the Ziggurat, better agricultural irrigation, and a code of laws, called the Code of Ur-Nammu, which preceded the Code of Hammurabi by 300 years.

Three more Kings, Amar-Sin, Shu0Sin and Ibbi-Sin, ruled Ur before it fell to the Elamites in 1,940 BC. Although Ur lost its political power, it remained economically important. It was ruled by the first dynasty of Babylonia, then part of the Sealand Dynasty, then by the Kassites before falling to the Assyrian Empire from the 10th-7th Century BC. After the 7th Century BC, it was ruled by the Chaldean Dynasty of Babylon. It began its final decline around 550 BC and was uninhabited by 500 BC. The final decline was likely due to drought, changing river patterns and the silting of the Persian Gulf.

The area was buried under the sands until it was visited by Pietro Della Valle in 1625 AD who noted strange inscriptions on bricks (later identified as cuneiform script) and images on artefacts which were later recognised as cylinder seals used to identify property or sign letters. In 1853 -1854 AD the first excavation of the site was made by John George Taylor in the interests of the British Museum who noted multiple grave complexes and concluded the site may have been a Babylonian necropolis.

Chapter 10
Akkadian and Sumerian Legacy

The Assyrians

Centred on the Upper Tigris River, in Northern Mesopotamia todays Northern Iraq, Northeast Syria, and Southeastern Turkey. The Assyrians came to rule powerful Empires at several times, the last of which grew to be the largest and most powerful Empire the world had yet seen. The Assyrians were a major Semitic Empire of the Ancient Middle East, who existed as an independent state for approximately nineteen centuries between 2,500-605 BC which incorporated the Early Bronze Age through to the late Iron Age and enjoying widespread military success in its heyday.

It was one of the very few Empires that survived the Bronze Age Collapse 1,187 BC. It substantially reduced in size but did regain its strength much later. The civilisation had already existed but with the collapse of Akkadian Empire the Assyrians reaped their neighbours misfortunes and learnt by their mistakes. The Assyrian Empire became the preeminent powerhouse of the Mesopotamia Semitic speaking Kingdom, and predominant Empire, of the Ancient Middle East. From 605 BCE to the mid-7th century AD, it survived as a geo-political entity ruled, for the most part, by foreign powers. Although a number of small Neo-Assyrian states arose at different times throughout this period.

As a substantial part of the greater Mesopotamian *Cradle of Civilisation*, Assyria was at the height of technological, scientific, and cultural achievements for its time. At its peak, the Assyrian Empire stretched from Cyprus in the Mediterranean Sea to Persia (Iran), and from the Caucasus Mountains (Armenia, Georgia, Azerbaijan) to the Arabian Peninsula and Egypt. Assyria is named for its original capital, the ancient city of Ašur (aka Ashur) and first built by Adad Nirari I. It originally occupied in 2,500 BC and was located in what is now the Saladin Province of Northern Iraq.

Ashur was originally one of a number of Akkadian city states in Mesopotamia and protected by encircling walls 4 Km long. On the Eastern side the Tigris flowed. On the North side an arm of the river and a high escarpment gave a natural defence which also encompassed by system of buttressed walls. In the late 24th Century BC, Assyrian Kings were regional leaders under Sargon of Akkad, who united all the Akkadian Semites and Sumerian speaking peoples of Mesopotamia under the Akkadian Empire 2,334-2,154 BC. Following the fall of the Akkadian Empire, 2,154 BC, and the short-lived succeeding Sumerian Third Dynasty of Ur, which ruled Southern Assyria, Assyria regained full independence.

The history of Assyria is roughly divided into three periods. These periods roughly correspond to the Middle Bronze Age, Late Bronze Age and Early Iron Age, respectively:

- Old Assyrian late 21st-18th century BC. In the Old Assyrian period, Assyria established colonies in Asia Minor and the Levant. Under King Ilushuma, it asserted itself over southern Mesopotamia. From the late 19th century BC, Assyria came into conflict with the newly created state of Babylonia, which eventually eclipsed the older Sumero-Akkadian states in the south, such as Ur, Isin, Larsa and Kish. Assyria had a period of empire under Shamshi-Adad I and Ishme-Dagan in the 19th and 18th centuries BC. Following the reigns of these two Kings, it found itself under Babylonian and Mitanni-Hurrian domination for short periods in the 18th and 15th centuries BC, respectively.
- Middle Assyrian 1,365-1,056 BC. However, a shift in the Assyrian's dominance occurred with the rise of the Middle Assyrian Empire 1,365-1,056 BC. This period saw the reigns of great Kings, such as Ashur-uballit I, Arik-den-ili, Tukulti-Ninurta I, and Tiglath-Pileser I. Additionally, during this period, Assyria overthrew Mitanni and eclipsed both the Hittite Empire and Egyptian Empire in the Near East. Long wars helped build Assyria into a warrior society, supported by landed nobility, which supplied horses to the military. All free male citizens were required to serve in the military, and women had very low status.
- The Assyrian Empire under the leadership of Ashur-Uballit I, rose around 1,365 BC, in the areas between the lands controlled by the Hittites and the Kassites. Around 1,220 BC, King Tukulti-Ninurta I

aspired to rule all of Mesopotamia and seized Babylon. The Assyrian Empire continued to expand over the next two centuries, moving into modern-day Palestine and Syria.

- Neo-Assyrian 911- 612 BC. Under the rule of Ashurnasirpal II in 884 BC, the empire created a new capital, Nimrud, built from the spoils of conquest and brutality that made Ashurnasirpal II a hated figure. His son Shalmaneser spent the majority of his reign fighting off an alliance between Syria, Babylon and Egypt, and conquering Israel. One of his sons rebelled against him, and Shalmaneser sent another son, Shamshi-Adad, to fight for him. Three years later, Shamshi-Adad ruled. Everything came crushing down in 614 BC when everything was destroyed by the Babylonians.

Homes were spacious, with vaults beneath the floors. The irregular planning of the town indicates a strict respect for property right and land tenure. Also known for their law, particularly relating to women.

The Rise of the First Babylonian Dynasty

Babylonia was a state in ancient Mesopotamia. The city of Babylon, whose ruins are located in present-day Iraq, was founded more than 4,000 years ago as a small port town on the Euphrates River. It grew into one of the largest cities of the Ancient World. Following the disintegration of the Akkadian Empire. The Sumerians rose up with the Third Dynasty of Ur in the late 2,054 BC and ejected the barbarian Gutians from Southern Mesopotamia. The Sumerian *Ur-III* dynasty eventually collapsed at the hands of both the Elamites and the Amorites and defeated in the Ur-Amorites wars 2,025-2,004 BC, another Semitic people.

In 2,002 BC, conflicts between the Amorites (Western Semitic nomads) and the Assyrians continued until Sargon I 1,920-1,881 BC succeeded as King in Assyria and withdrew Assyria from the region, leaving the Amorites in control, the Amorite period. One of these Amorite dynasties founded the city state of Babylon 1,894 BC, which would ultimately take over the others and form the short-lived first Babylonian Empire, also called the Old Babylonian Period. A chieftain named Sumuabum appropriated the then relatively small city of Babylon from the neighbouring Mesopotamian city state of Kazallu, turning it into a state in its own right. Sumuabum appears never to have been given the title of King, however.

The Babylonians remained a minor territory for a Century after it was founded, until the reign of its sixth Amorite ruler, Hammurabi 1,792-1,750 BC. His family was descended from the Amorites, a semi-nomadic tribe in western Syria, and his name reflects a mix of cultures: Hammu, which means *family* in Amorite, combined with rapi, meaning *great* in Akkadian, the everyday language of Babylon. He was an efficient ruler, establishing a centralised bureaucracy with taxation. In the 30th year of his reign, Hammurabi began to expand his Kingdom up and down the Tigris and Euphrates river valley, overthrowing the Kingdoms of Assyria, Larsa and Eshnunna until all of Mesopotamia was under his sway.

Hammurabi combined his military and political advances with irrigation projects and the construction of fortifications and temples celebrating Babylon's patron deity, Marduk. The Babylon of Hammurabi's era is now buried below the area's groundwater table, and whatever archives he kept are long dissolved, but clay tablets discovered at other ancient sites reveal glimpses of the King's personality and statecraft. One letter records his complaint of being forced to provide dinner attire for ambassadors from Mari just because he'd done the same for some other delegates: *Do you imagine you can control my palace in the matter of formal wear?*

Hammurabi freed Babylon from Elamite dominance, and then conquered the whole of Southern Mesopotamia, bringing stability and the name of Babylonia to the region. The armies of Babylonia under Hammurabi were well-disciplined, and he was able to invade modern-day Iran to the East and conquer the pre-Iranic Elamites, Gutians and Kassites. To the West, Hammurabi enjoyed military success against the Semitic states of the Levant (modern Syria), including the powerful Kingdom of Mari. Hammurabi also entered into a protracted war with the Old Assyrian Empire for control of Mesopotamia and the Middle East.

Assyria had extended control over parts of Asia Minor from the 2,100 BC, and from the latter part of the 19th Century BC had asserted itself over Northeast Syria and Central Mesopotamia as well. After a protracted, unresolved struggle over decades with the Assyrian King Ishme-Dagan, Hammurabi forced his successor, Mut-Ashkur, to pay tribute to Babylon 1,751 BC, thus giving Babylonia control over Assyria's centuries-old Hattian and Hurrian colonies in Asia Minor.

In addition to developing an extensive code of law and establishing Babylon as a *Holy city* of Southern Mesopotamia. These people founded the first dynasty of Babylon 1,895-1,595 BC. In the 17th century BC new ethnic groups appeared in both Babylonia and Syria-Palestine: Kassite's from the Zagros Mountains, Hurrians from what is now Armenia and Indo-Europeans from Central Asia. This period marked the end of the formative phase of Mesopotamian civilisation. Choosing Babylon as the capital, the Amorites took control and established Babylonia. Kings were considered deities and the most famous of these was Hammurabi, who ruled 1,792-1,750 BC. Hammurabi worked to expand the empire, and the Babylonians were almost continually at war.

From before 3,000 BC until the reign of Hammurabi, the major cultural and religious centre of Southern Mesopotamia had been the ancient city of Nippur, where the god Enlil reigned supreme. However, with the rise of Hammurabi, this honour was transferred to Babylon, and the god Marduk rose to supremacy (with the god Ashur remaining the dominant deity in Assyria). The city of Babylon became known as a *Holy city*, where any legitimate ruler of Southern Mesopotamia had to be crowned.

Hammurabi turned what had previously been a minor administrative town into a major city. With a population in excess of 200,000 people, monumental architectural achievements including the Ishtar Gate and the Hanging Gardens of Babylon increased it.

Stele of Hammurabi Rediscovered

In 1901, archaeologists[clviii] including Jacques de Morgan, a French mining engineer who led an archaeological expedition to Persia to excavate the Elamite capital of Susa in Khuzestan, more than 250 miles from the centre of Hammurabi's Kingdom. Here they uncovered the stele of Hammurabi broken into three pieces that had been brought to Susa as spoils of war, likely by the Elamite King Shutruk-Nahhunte in the mid-12th Century BC. The stele was packed up and shipped to Paris. A basalt stele containing the code in cuneiform script inscribed in the Akkadian language is currently on display in the Louvre, in Paris, France.

Replicas are located at other museums throughout the world. A translation was published in 1902 by Jean-Vincent Scheil and widely publicised as the earliest example of a written legal code one that predated but bore striking parallels to the laws outlined in the Hebrew Old Testament.

The US Supreme Court building features Hammurabi on the marble carvings of historic lawgivers that lines the south wall of the courtroom. Although other subsequently discovered written Mesopotamian laws, including the Sumerian

Lipit-Ishtar and *Ur-Nammu*, predate Hammurabi's by hundreds of years, Hammurabi's reputation remains as a pioneering lawgiver who worked in the words of his monument to *prevent the strong from oppressing the weak and to see that justice is done to widows and orphans.*

Hammurabi's Code of Laws

One of the most important works of this First Dynasty of Babylon was the compilation in about 1,754 BC of a code of laws, called the Code of Hammurabi, which echoed and improved upon the earlier written laws of Sumer, Akkad and Assyria. The Code consists of 282 laws, nearly one-half of the Code deals with matters of contract. A third of the code addresses issues concerning household and family relationships. The Code of Hammurabi written in Babylon by the sixth King of Babylon, Hammurabi. The Code was written on stone stele and clay tablets. It consisted of punishments that varied based on social status including slaves, free men and property owners. Also focused on contracts and family relationships, featuring a presumption of innocence and the presentation of evidence.

It is most famous for the *an eye for an eye, a tooth for a tooth* (*lex talionis*) form of punishment. Other forms of codes of law had been in existence in the region around this time, including the Code of Ur-Nammu, King of Ur 2,050 BC, the Laws of Eshnunna 1,930 BC, and the codex of Lipit-Ishtar of Isin 1,870 BC. The laws were arranged in groups, so that citizens could easily read what was required of them. Some have seen the Code as an early form of constitutional government. Intent was often recognised and affected punishment, with neglect severely punished.

Some of the provisions may have been codification of Hammurabi's decisions, for the purpose of self-glorification. Nevertheless, the Code was studied, copied, and used as a model for legal reasoning for at least 1,500 years after. The prologue of the Code features Hammurabi stating that he wants *to make justice visible in the land, to destroy the wicked person and the evil-doer, that the strong might not injure the weak.*

Major laws covered in the Code include slander, trade, slavery, the duties of workers, theft, liability and divorce. Nearly half of the code focused on contracts, such as wages to be paid, terms of transactions, and liability in case of property damage. A third of the code focused on household and family issues, including inheritance, divorce, paternity and sexual behaviour. One section establishes that a judge who incorrectly decides an issue may be removed from his position permanently. A doctor's fee for curing a severe wound would be 10 silver shekels for a gentleman, five shekels for a freedman and two shekels for a slave.

Penalties for malpractice followed the same scheme: a doctor who killed a rich patient would have his hands cut off, while only financial restitution was required if the victim was a slave. Capital crimes, meanwhile, were often met with their own unique and grisly death penalties. If a son and mother were caught committing incest, they were burned to death; if a pair of scheming lovers conspired to murder their spouses, both were impaled. Even a relatively minor crime could earn the offender a horrific fate. For example, if a son hit his father, the Code demanded the boy's hands be *hewn off*.

The Code of Hammurabi includes many harsh punishments, sometimes demanding the removal of the guilty party's tongue, hands, breasts, eye, or ear. If a man steals an ox, then he must pay back 30 times its value. The Code also includes a modern take on judicial procedures. For example, when two parties had a dispute, legal protocol allowed them to bring their case before a judge and provide evidence and witnesses to back up their claims. A few sections address military service.

One of the most well-known sections of the Code was law #196: *If a man destroys the eye of another man, they shall destroy his eye. If one break a man's bone, they shall break his bone. If one destroys the eye of a freeman or break the bone of a freeman, he shall pay one gold mina. If one destroys the eye of a man's slave or break a bone of a man's slave, he shall pay one-half his price.*

Hammurabi's Code

The Code of Hammurabi is often cited as the oldest written laws on record, but they were predated by at least two other ancient codes of conduct from the Middle East. The earliest, created by the Sumerian ruler Ur-Nammu of the city of Ur, dates all the way back to the 21st Century BCE, and evidence also shows that the Sumerian Code of Lipit-Ishtar of Isin was drawn up nearly two centuries before Hammurabi came to power.

These earlier codes both bear a striking resemblance to Hammurabi's commands in their style and content, suggesting they may have influenced one another or perhaps even derived from a similar source. The black stone stele containing the Code of Hammurabi was carved from a single, four-ton slab of diorite, a durable but incredibly difficult stone for carving. At its top is a two-

and-a-half-foot relief carving of a standing Hammurabi receiving the law symbolised by a measuring rod and tape from the seated Shamash, the Babylonian god of justice. The rest of the seven-foot-five-inch monument is covered with columns of chiselled cuneiform script.

Trial by Ordeal

For crimes that could not be proven or disproven with hard evidence (such as claims of sorcery), the Code allowed for a *trial by ordeal* an unusual practice where the accused was placed in a potentially deadly situation as a way of determining innocence. The Code notes that if an accused man jumps into the river and drowns; His accuser *shall take possession of his house*. However, if the gods spared the man and allowed him to escape unhurt, the accuser would be executed, and the man who jumped in the river would receive his house. Hammurabi's Code took a brutal approach to justice, but the severity of criminal penalties often depended on the identity of both the lawbreaker and the victim.

While one law commanded, *If a man knock out the teeth of his equal, his teeth shall be knocked ou*t, committing the same crime against a member of a lower class was punished with only a fine. Other rank-based penalties were even more significant. If a man killed a pregnant *maidservant*, he was punished with a monetary fine, but if he killed a *free-born* pregnant woman, his own daughter would be killed as retribution.

The Code also listed different punishments for men and women with regard to marital infidelity. Men were allowed to have extramarital relationships with maidservants and slaves, but philandering women were to be bound and tossed into the Euphrates along with their lovers.

Minimum Wage

Hammurabi's Code was surprisingly ahead of its time when it came to laws addressing subjects like divorce, property rights and the prohibition of incest, but perhaps most progressive of all was a stipulation mandating an ancient form of minimum wage. Several edicts in the Code referenced specific occupations and dictated how much the workers were to be paid. Field labourers and herdsmen were guaranteed a wage of *eight gur of corn per year*, and ox drivers and sailors received six gur. Doctors, meanwhile, were entitled to 5 shekels for healing a freeborn man of a broken bone or other injury, but only three shekels for a freed slave and two shekels for a slave.

The Social Classes

Under Hammurabi's reign, there were three social classes. The *amelu* was originally an elite person with full civil rights, whose birth, marriage, and death were recorded. Although he had certain privileges, he also was liable for harsher punishment and higher fines. The King and his court, high officials, professionals, and craftsmen belonged to this group. The *mushkenu* was a free man who may have been landless. He was required to accept monetary compensation, paid smaller fines, and lived in a separate section of the city. The *ardu* was a slave whose master paid for his upkeep, but also took his compensation. *Ardu* could own property and other slaves and could purchase his own freedom.

Women's Rights

Women entered into marriage through a contract arranged by her family. She came with a dowry, and the gifts given by the groom to the bride also came with her. Divorce was up to the husband, but after divorce he then had to restore the dowry and provide her with an income, and any children came under the woman's custody. However, if the woman was considered a *bad wife* she might be sent away or made a slave in the husband's house. If a wife brought action against her husband for cruelty and neglect, she could have a legal separation if the case was proved. Otherwise, she might be drowned as punishment. Adultery was punished with drowning of both parties unless a husband was willing to pardon his wife.

Babylonian Culture

Hallmarks of Babylonian culture include mudbrick architecture, extensive astronomical records and logs, diagnostic medical handbooks, and translations of Sumerian literature.

Art and Architecture

In Babylonia, an abundance of clay and lack of stone led to greater use of mudbrick. Babylonian temples were thus massive structures of crude brick, supported by buttresses. The use of brick led to the early development of the pilaster and column, and of frescoes and enamelled tiles. The walls were brilliantly coloured, and sometimes plated with zinc or gold, as well as with tiles. Painted terracotta cones for torches were also embedded in the plaster.

In Babylonia, in place of the bas-relief, there was a preponderance of three-dimensional figures the earliest examples being the Statues of Gudea that were realistic, if also somewhat clumsy. The paucity of stone in Babylonia made every pebble a commodity and led to a high perfection in the art of gem cutting just like the Sumerian forefathers.

Astronomy

During the 8th and 7th Centuries BC, Babylonian astronomers developed a new empirical approach to astronomy. They began studying philosophy dealing with the ideal nature of the universe and began employing an internal logic within their predictive planetary systems. This was an important contribution to astronomy and the philosophy of science, and some scholars have thus referred to this new approach as the first scientific revolution. Tablets dating back to the Old Babylonian period document the application of mathematics to variations in the length of daylight over a solar year.

Centuries of Babylonian observations of celestial phenomena are recorded in a series of cuneiform tablets known as the *Enūma Anu Enlil*. In fact, the oldest significant astronomical text known to mankind is Tablet 63 of the Enūma Anu Enlil, the Venus tablet of Ammi-saduqa, which lists the first and last visible risings of Venus over a period of about 21 years. This record is the earliest evidence that planets were recognised as periodic phenomena.

The oldest rectangular astrolabe dates back to Babylonia 1,100 BC. The MUL.APIN contains catalogues of stars and constellations as well as schemes for predicting heliacal risings and the settings of the planets. As well as lengths of daylight measured by a water-clock, gnomon, shadows, and intercalations. The Babylonian GU text arranges stars in *strings* that lie along declination circles (thus measuring right-ascensions or time-intervals), and also employs the stars of the zenith, which are also separated by given right-ascensional differences.

Medicine

The oldest Babylonian texts on medicine date back to the First Babylonian Dynasty in the first half of the 2nd Millennium BC. The most extensive Babylonian medical text, however, is the Diagnostic Handbook written by the ummânū, or chief scholar, Esagil-kin-apli of Borsippa. The Babylonians introduced the concepts of diagnosis, prognosis, physical examination, and prescriptions. The Diagnostic Handbook additionally introduced the methods of therapy and aetiology outlining the use of empiricism, logic, and rationality in diagnosis, prognosis, and treatment.

For example, the text contains a list of medical symptoms and often detailed empirical observations along with logical rules used in combining observed symptoms on the body of a patient with its diagnosis and prognosis. In particular, Esagil-kin-apli discovered a variety of illnesses and diseases and described their symptoms in his diagnostic handbook, including those of many varieties of epilepsy and related ailments.

Literature

Libraries existed in most towns and temples. Women as well as men learned to read and write, and had knowledge of the extinct Sumerian language, along with a complicated and extensive syllabary. A considerable amount of Babylonian literature was translated from Sumerian originals, and the language of religion and law long continued to be written in the old agglutinative language of Sumer. Vocabularies, grammars, and interlinear translations were compiled for the use of students, as well as commentaries on the older texts and explanations of obscure words and phrases. The characters of the syllabary were organised and named, and elaborate lists of them were drawn up.

There are many Babylonian literary works whose titles have come down to us. One of the most famous of these was the Epic of Gilgamesh, in twelve books, translated from the original Sumerian by a certain Sin-Liqi-Unninni, and arranged upon an astronomical principle. Each division contains the story of a single adventure in the career of King Gilgamesh. The whole story is a composite product, and it is probable that some of the stories are artificially attached to the central figure, but once again strands of truth lay within the text.

Philosophy

The origins of Babylonian philosophy can be traced back to early Mesopotamian wisdom literature, which embodied certain philosophies of life, particularly ethics, in the forms of dialectic, dialogs, epic poetry, folklore, hymns, lyrics, prose, and proverbs. Babylonian reasoning and rationality developed beyond empirical observation. It is possible that Babylonian philosophy had an influence on Greek philosophy, particularly Hellenistic philosophy. The Babylonian text Dialogue of Pessimism contains similarities to the agonistic thought of the sophists. The Heraclitan doctrine of contrasts, and the dialogs of Plato, as well as a precursor to the maieutic Socratic method of Socrates.

Would any of these achievements been made possible without the advances made in Southern Mesopotamia. Would the local inhabitants of Southern Mesopotamia have advanced without the intervention of the migrants from the Gulf Oasis, or would the local inhabitants eke a living from the banks of the Tigris and Euphrates just fizzled away into obscurity? Would growth been far less dramatic in the rest of Mesopotamia, would the Assyrians and the Babylonians have even existed. Would agrarian lifestyle have ticked along with far less hostilities or is that wishful thinking on my behalf.

Warning

Climatic change was the reason for migration of Homo Sapiens out of Africa and into the Middle East and the rest of the world. It was also instrumental in the eviction of the Gulf Oasis indigenous population. It also brought about the end of Akkadian and Sumerian reign of Southern Mesopotamia and later in 1,1187 BC the Bronze Age collapse of multiple Empires and the introduction of the first real dark age in history.

Consumerism expanded city states, but also aided their collapse in Southern Mesopotamia with continued city state rivalry and the advent of wars. Greece also mirrored the Sumerian expansion 5,000 years later, which also witnessed the same expansion and collapse through city state rivalry. European history also bears witnessed national expansionism and rivalry. Hope is used to try and tip the balance of probability in your favour.

Can modern nations withstand another climatic event of the type witnessed in Sumer for 200 years of drought whilst continuing on its path of consumerism and destruction? Or will future historians talk about the cyclic nature of Homo Sapiens rise and fall without heeding the lessons of history and the warnings of Mother Earth's unpredictability? We cannot live in hope and expect change without drastic measures to repair the manmade effect on the planet or do we wait for the inevitability that will affect all living creatures?

THE END

End Notes

[i] Huxley, J. (2003). *Charles Darwin; The Origin of Species: 150th Anniversary Edition*. Mass Market Paperback.

[ii] Rose, Jeffrey. I. (2010). *New Light on Human Prehistory in the. Current Anthropology* Volume 51, Number 6, December 2010.

[iii] Sissakian, Varoujan K. (2020). *Sea Level Changes in the Mesopotamian Plain and Limits of the Arabian Gulf. Journal of Earth Sciences and Geotechnical Engineering*, Vol.10, No.4, 2020, 87-110.

[iv] Jerry X. Mitrovica (2003). *On post-glacial sea level: I. General Theory. Geophysics Journal International* (2003), 253–267 2.1.3 Page 260.

[v] Sissakian, Varoujan K. (2020). *Sea Level Changes in the Mesopotamian Plain and Limits of the Arabian Gulf. Journal of Earth Sciences and Geotechnical Engineering*, Vol.10, No.4, 2020, 101.

[vi] Munro, L. G. (2017). *The Natufian Culture: The Harbinger of Food-Producing Societies*. Publisher: Cambridge University Press, 266-707.

Chapter 1

[vii] Watson, R. (2007). *Cogito Ergo Sum*. David R. Godine Publisher.

[viii] Cronin, T.M. (2007). *Rapid Sea Level Rise and Ice Sheet Response to 8,200-year Climate Event*. Copyright 2007 by the American Geophysical Union.

[ix] Sahala, A. (2013). *Sumero Indo European Language Contact*. Helsinki: University of Helsinki.

[x] Lang, N. (2011). *Interglacial and glacial variability from the last 800 ka in marine*. Wellington: Climate of the Past.

[xi] Campisano, C. J. (2012). *Milankovitch Cycles, Paleoclimatic Change, and Hominin Evolution*. Nature Education Knowledge 4(3):5.

[xii] Kutzbach, John. E (2019). *Resolving seasonal rainfall changes in the Middle East during the Last Interglacial Period.* Madison: Department of Geoscience, University of Wisconsin–Madison.

[xiii] Rose, Jeffery. I. (2010). *New Light on Human Prehistory in the.* Current Anthropology Volume 51, Number 6, December 2010.

[xiv] Petraglia, Michael D. (2010). *Out of Africa: New Hypotheses and Evidence for the Dispersal of Homo Sapiens along the Indian Ocean Rim.* Annals of Human Biology, 288-311.

[xv] Crassard, R. (2009). *Modalities and characteristics of human occupations in Yemen during the.* Comptes Rendus Géoscience, 713-725.

[xvi] Delagnes, A. (2008). *New paleo-anthropological research in the Plio-Pleistocene Omo Group, Lower Omo Valley, SNNPR (Southern Nations, Nationalities and People Regions), Ethiopia.* © 2008 Académie des science, 429-439.

[xvii] Rose, Jeffery. I. (2010). *New Light on Human Prehistory in the.* Current Anthropology Volume 51, Number 6, December 2010. *(Also referencing Jagher 2009; Usik 2009).*

[xviii] Hans-Peter Uerpmann, D. P. (2009). *Holocene (re-)Occupation of Eastern Arabia.* In M. P. Rose, The Evolution of Human Populations in Arabia (pp. 205-214). Springer Science + Business Media.

[xix] Petraglia, Michael D. (2010). *The "Upper Palaeolithic" of South Arabia.* In The Evolution of Human Populations in Arabia: Paleoenvironments, Prehistory and Genetics (pp. 169-185). Springer.

[xx] Subterranean springs *(Also referencing Faure, Walter, and Grant 2002),*

[xxi] Zoller, Heinrich (1960). *Pollenanalytische Untersuchungen zur Vegetationsgeschichte der insubrischen Schweiz.* Germany: Denkschriften der Schweizerischen Naturforschenden Gesellschaft.

[xxii] M. Staubwasser, F. S. (2003). *Climate change at the 4.2 ka BP termination of the Indus valley civilisation and Holocene south Asian monsoon variability.* American Geophysical Union.

[xxiii] Rose, Jeffrey. I. (2010). *New Light on Human Prehistory in the.* Current Anthropology Volume 51, Number 6, December 2010. *(Also referencing Church 1996; Shiraz and Munster 1992 Sultan 2008).*

[xxiv] Carter, R. (2019). *The Mesopotamian frontier of the Arabian Neolithic: A cultural borderland of the Sixth–fifth millennia BC.* Arabian Archaeology and Epigraphy.

[xxv] *Rose, Jeffrey. I. (2010). New Light on Human Prehistory in the. Current Anthropology Volume 51, Number 6, December 2010. (Also referencing Beech, Elders, and Shepherd 2000; Cavelier 1970; Edgell 1992; Kapel 1967).*

[xxvi] *Post Glacial Sea Levels Rise; Sea Level Rise (antarcticglaciers.org).*

[xxvii] *Rose, Jeffrey. I. (2010). New Light on Human Prehistory in the. Current Anthropology Volume 51, Number 6, December 2010 (Also referencing Olivieri, Gonzalez)*

[xxviii] *Thangaraj, K. (2006). In situ origin of deep rooting lineages of Mitochondrial Macrohaplogroup 'M' in India. Tartu, Estonia: BMC Genomics.*

[xxix] *Prausnits, M. W. (1966). A Study in Terminology: The Kebaran, the Natufian and the Tahunian. Israel Exploration Journal, 220-230.*

[xxx] *Otte, M. (2007). The Origins of Language: Material Sources. SAGE Journals Research Article.*

[xxxi] *Smith, P. J. (2015). Dorothy Garrod, first woman Professor at Cambridge. Cambridge: Cambridge University Press.*

[xxxii] *Bar-Yosef, O. (2011). Climatic Fluctuations and Early Farming in West and East Asia. Current Anthropology 52.*

[xxxiii] *Petraglia, Michael D. V. Hannah, A. James (2005). Modern Human Origins and the Evolution of Behaviour in the Later Pleistocene Record of South Asia. Current Anthropology Volume 46, Supplement, 3-27. (Also referencing Field and Lahr 2007; Lahr and Foley 1994, 1998; Mellars 2006; Stringer 2000).*

[xxxiv] *Clyde Ahmad Winters, Olivieri, Gonzalez. (2010). The African Origin of mtDNA Haplogroup M1. Research Journal of Biological Sciences.*

[xxxv] *Thangaraj, K. (2006). In situ origin of deep rooting lineages of Mitochondrial Macrohaplogroup 'M' in India. Tartu, Estonia: BMC Genomics.*

[xxxvi] *Cerny, V. R. (2010). Out of Arabia—The Settlement of Island Soqotra as Revealed by Mitochondrial and Y Chromosome Genetic Diversity. American Journal of Physical Anthropology, 71-78.*

[xxxvii] *Cabrera, Vicente M and Khaled K. Abu-Amero (2010). The Arabian Peninsula: Gate for Human Migrations Out of Africa or Cul-de-Sac? A Mitochondrial DNA Phylogeographic Perspective Pages 79-87. Springer.*

[xxxviii] *Abu-Amero (2010). The Arabian Peninsula: Gate for Human Migrations Out of Africa or Cul-de-Sac? A Mitochondrial DNA Phylogeographic Perspective Pages 79-87. Springer.*

[xxxix] *Otte, M. (2007). The Origins of Language: Material Sources. SAGE Journals Research Article.*

[xl] Broushaki, Farnaz. Mark G. Thomas, Vivian Link, Saioa López, Lucy van Dorp, Karola Kirsanow, Zuzana Hofmanová (2016). *Early Neolithic genomes from the eastern Fertile Crescent*. Johannes Gutenberg Universität Mainz, 499-503.

[xli] Burger, Joachim. (2009). *Genetic discontinuity between local hunter-gatherers and central Europe's first farmers*. American Association for the Advancement of Science.

[xlii] Petraglia, Michael D. V. Hannah, A. James (2005). *Modern Human Origins and the Evolution of Behaviour in the Later Pleistocene Record of South Asia*. Current Anthropology Volume 46, Supplement, 3-27. (Also referencing Field and Lahr 2007; Lahr and Foley 1994, 1998; Mellars 2006; Stringer 2000).

[xliii] Rowold, D. J. (2007). *Mitochondrial DNA geneflow indicates preferred usage of the Levant Corridor over the Horn of Africa passageway*. National Library of Medicine.

[xliv] Al-Zahery, Nadia. Maria Pala, Vincenza Battaglia, Viola Grugni, Mohammed A Hamod, Baharak Hooshiar Kashani, Anna Olivieri, Antonio Torroni, Augusta S Santachiara-Benerecetti and Ornella Semino. (2011). *In search of the genetic footprints of Sumerians: a survey of Y-chromosome and mtDNA variation in the Marsh Arabs of Iraq*. BMC Evolutionary Biology.

[xlv] Verdugo, Marta and Dan Bradley (2019). *Ancient Genomics Pinpoint Origin and Rapid Turnover of Cattle in the Fertile Crescent*. The International Journal Science.

[xlvi] Verdugo, Marta and Dan Bradley (2019). *Ancient Genomics Pinpoint Origin and Rapid Turnover of Cattle in the Fertile Crescent*. The International Journal Science

[xlvii] Zólyomi, Gábor (2017). *An Introduction to the Grammar of Sumerian*. Eötvös University Press Eötvös Lorand University, 1-271.

[xlviii] Revesz, Peter Z. (2019). *Sumerian Contains Dravidian and Uralic Substrates Associated with the Emeĝir and Emesal Dialects*. Nebraska: WSEAS Transactions on Information Science and Applications.

[xlix] Revesz, Peter Z. (2019). *Sumerian Contains Dravidian and Uralic Substrates Associated with the Emeĝir and Emesal Dialects*. Nebraska: WSEAS Transactions on Information Science and Applications.

[l] Loganathan, Dr K. (2004). *Sumerian as Archaic Tamil*. Tamil: Arutkural Tripod.

[li] Hugues Faure, Robert C. Walter, Douglas R. Grant (2002). *The Coastal Oasis: Ice Age Springs on Emerged Continental Shelves*. Elsevier Science B.V.

[lii] Irvine, W. Donald Ferguson, Sinclair, William F (1903). *The Travels of Pedro Teixeira with his Kings of Harmuz and extracts from Kings of Persia 1802*. London: The Hakluyt Society.

[liii] Pritchard, Anne Valerie (1974). *The Origin of Neolithic Pottery Forms*. Wilfrid Laurier University.

[liv] Burger, Joachim (2009). *Genetic discontinuity between local hunter-gatherers and central Europe's first farmers*. American Association for the Advancement of Science.

[lv] Carter, Robert. (2008). *Excavations and Ubaid-Period Boat Remains at H3, As-Sabiyah (Kuwait) page 92-102*. BAR International Series 1, 92-102. (Also referencing Uerpmann and Uerpmann 1996; Contra Cleuziou and Tosi 1998).

[lvi] Beech, Mark, Joseph Elders and Elizabeth Shepherd (2001). *Reconsidering the 'Ubaid of the Southern Gulf: new results from excavations on Dalma Island, U.A.E.* Archaeopress, 41-47

[lvii] Michael D. Petraglia, Michael Haslam, Dorian Q. Fuller, Nicole Boivin, Chris Clarkson (2010). *Out of Africa: New Hypotheses and Evidence for the Dispersal of Homo Sapiens along the Indian Ocean Rim*. Annals of Human Biology, 288-311.

[lviii] Rose, Jeffrey. I. (2010). *New Light on Human Prehistory in the*. Current Anthropology Volume 51, Number 6, December 2010 (Also referencing Conard 2005, 2006, 2007).

[lix] Lawrence, Seth Abrutyn and Kirk (2010). *From Chiefdom to State: Toward an Integrative Theory of the Evolution of Polity*. Sage Publications, Inc., 419-442.

[lx] Service, Elam and Morton Fried (2001). *From Leaders to Rulers*. New York: Springer.

[lxi] Pumpelly, Raphael (1908) *Journal of Near Eastern Studies*. The American Journal of Semitic Languages and Literatures.

[lxii] Kramer, Samuel Noah (1945). *Enki and Ninhursag*. American Schools of Oriental Research, 1-40.

[lxiii] Kramer, Samuel Noah (2015). *Dilmun: Quest for Paradise*. Cambridge University Press.

[lxiv] Smith, George (2014). *Assyrian Discoveries*. Cambridge: Cambridge University Press.

[lxv] Zoller, Heinrich (1960). *Pollenanalytische Untersuchungen zur Vegetationsgeschichte der insubrischen Schweiz*. Germany: Denkschriften der Schweizerischen Naturforschenden Gesellschaft.

[lxvi] Kennett, Douglas J. (2006). *Early state Formation in Southern Mesopotamia Sea Levels, Shorelines and Climate Change*. Journal of Island and Coastal Archaeology, 67-99. (Also referencing Cooke 1987; Hamblin 1987; Lambeck 1996; Sanford 2006; Teller 2000).

Chapter 2

[lxvii] Garrod, Dorothy (1907-1965). *The Journal of the Royal Anthropological Institute of Great Britain and Ireland*. The Journal of the Royal Anthropological Institute of Great Britain and Ireland.

[lxviii] Curry, Andrew (2008) November. *Gobekli Tepe: The World's First Temple?* Smithsonian Magazine.

[lxix] Schmidt, Klaus (2010). *Göbekli Tepe – the Stone Age Sanctuaries*. Berlin: Deutsches Archäologisches Institut, Orient-Abteilung, Berlin.

[lxx] Mithen, Steven (2006). *After the Ice: A Global Human History, 20,000-5,000 BC*. Harvard: Cambridge: Harvard University Press.

[lxxi] Kanjou, Yousef (2018). *Archaeological Excavations at Tell Qaramel 1999-2011*. Oxford: Archaeopress Publishing Ltd.

[lxxii] Davis, Miriam C (2008). *Dame Kathleen Kenyon: Digging Up the Holy Land (UCL Institute of Archaeology Publications) 1st Edition*. Routledge.

[lxxiii] Kenyon, Kathleen M. (1954). *Excavations at Jericho*. The Journal of the Royal Anthropological Institute of Great Britain and Ireland, 103-110.

[lxxiv] Kenyon, Kathleen M. (1954). *Excavations at Jericho*. The Journal of the Royal Anthropological Institute of Great Britain and Ireland, 103-110.

Chapter 3

[lxxv] Pumpelly, Raphael (1908). *Prehistoric Civilisations of Anau*. Washington: Carnegie Institution of Washington.

[lxxvi] Braidwood, Robert John (2006). *ROBERT JOHN BRAIDWOOD*. Washington: National Academy of Sciences.

[lxxvii] Hayden, Brian (2009). *The Proof Is in the Pudding*. he University of Chicago Press, 597-601.

[lxxviii] Solot, Michael (1986). *Carl Sauer and Cultural Evolution*. Annals of the Association of American Geographers, 508-520.

[lxxix] Rindos, David (2013). *The Origins of Agriculture*. Elsevier Science.

[lxxx] Wittfogel, Karl (1981). *Oriental Despotism: A Comparative Study of Total Power*. Vintage.

[lxxxi] Millard, Alan Ralph (1966). *The Atrahasis Epic*. ProQuest LLC (2018).

[lxxxii] Campbell, Stuart (2007). *Rethinking Halaf Chronologies*. Parcourir Les Collections, 103-136.

[lxxxiii] McMahon, Augusta (2019). *Early Urbanism in Northern Mesopotamia*. Journal of Archaeological Research (2020), 289-337. (Also referencing Carter 2006).

[lxxxiv] Wittfogel, Karl (1981). *Oriental Despotism: A Comparative Study of Total Power*. Vintage.

[lxxxv] Woolley, Leonard C. L. (1934). *Ur Excavation. Vol. II: The Royal Cemetery. A report on the Predynastic and Sargonid Graves excavated between 1926 and 1931*. Journal of the Royal Asiatic Society.

[lxxxvi] Carter, Robert (2019). *The Mesopotamian frontier of the Arabian Neolithic: A cultural borderland of the Sixth–fifth millennia BC*. Arabian Archaeology and Epigraphy. (Also referencing Carter and Philip 2010).

[lxxxvii] Graham, Philip Joseph (2011). *Ubaid Period Agriculture at Kenan Tepe, South-eastern Turkey*. Uconn Library.

[lxxxviii] Service, Elman and Morton Fried (2001). *From Leaders to Rulers*. New York: Springer.

Chapter 4

[lxxxix] Kramer, Samuel Noah (2015). *Dilmun: Quest for Paradise*. Cambridge University Press.

[xc] Kramer, Samuel Noah (1988). *History Begins at Sumer Thirty-Nine Firsts in Recorded History 416 pages*: Capitable.

[xci] Powell, Marvin A. (1972). *The origin of the sexagesimal system: The interaction of language and writing*. Cleveland: Visible La11guage.

[xcii] Mansfield, Daniel F and Wildberger, N. J. (2017). *Plimpton 322 is Babylonian exact Sexagesimal Trigonometry*. Sydney: Elsevier.

[xciii] Helbaek, Hans (1972). *Samarran Irrigation Agriculture at Choga Mami in Iraq*. British Institute for the Study of Iraq, 35-48.

[xciv] Adamo, Nasrat and Nadhir Al-Ansari (2020). *Man's First Strides, The Prehistoric Era. Journal of Earth Sciences and Geotechnical Engineering.*

[xcv] Helbaek, Hans (1972). *Samarran Irrigation Agriculture at Choga Mami in Iraq. British Institute for the Study of Iraq, 35-48.*

[xcvi] Geyer, Bernard and Jean-Yves Monchambert (2015). *Canals and water supply in the lower Euphrates valley. Springer.*

[xcvii] Geyer, Bernard and Jean-Yves Monchambert (2015). *Canals and water supply in the lower Euphrates valley. Springer. (Also referencing Margueron, 2004 and additional sources Viollet, 2000).*

[xcviii] Adamo, Nasrat and Nadhir Al-Ansari (2020). *Man's First Strides, The Prehistoric Era. Journal of Earth Sciences and Geotechnical Engineering.*

[xcix] Adamo, Nasrat and Nadhir Al-Ansari (2020). *Man's First Strides, The Prehistoric Era. Journal of Earth Sciences and Geotechnical Engineering.*

[c] Adamo, Nasrat and Nadhir Al-Ansari (2020). *Man's First Strides, The Prehistoric Era. Journal of Earth Sciences and Geotechnical Engineering. (Also referencing Shin T. Kang and quoted by Tamburrino).*

[ci] Berking, Jonas (2018). *Water Management in Ancient Civilisations. Berlin: Berlin Studies of the Ancient World. (Also referencing Genouillac and Parrot).*

[cii] Adamo, Nasrat and Nadhir Al-Ansari (2020). *Man's First Strides, The Prehistoric Era. Journal of Earth Sciences and Geotechnical Engineering.*

[ciii] Adamo, Nasrat and Nadhir Al-Ansari (2020). *Man's First Strides, The Prehistoric Era. Journal of Earth Sciences and Geotechnical Engineering.*

[civ] Adamo, Nasrat and Nadhir Al-Ansari (2020). *Man's First Strides, The Prehistoric Era. Journal of Earth Sciences and Geotechnical Engineering.*

[cv] Adamo, Nasrat and Nadhir Al-Ansari (2020). *Man's First Strides, The Prehistoric Era. Journal of Earth Sciences and Geotechnical Engineering.*

[cvi] Adamo, Nasrat and Nadhir Al-Ansari (2020). *Man's First Strides, The Prehistoric Era. Journal of Earth Sciences and Geotechnical Engineering.*

Chapter 5

[cvii] Valipour, Mohammad Valipour, M. (2020). *The Evolution of Agricultural Drainage from the Earliest Times to the Present. MDPI, 1-30.*

[cviii] Brusius, Mirjam (2012). *Misfit Objects: Layard's Excavations in Ancient Mesopotamia and the Biblical Imagination in mid-nineteenth Century Britain. Journal of Literature and Science, 38-52.*

[cix] Crawford, Harriet (2015). *Ur The city of the Moon God.* London: Bloomsbury.

[cx] Thompson, Reginald Campbell (2011). *IV.—The British Museum Excavations at Abu Shahrain in Mesopotamia in 1918.* Cambridge: Cambridge University Press.

[cxi] Safar, Fuad (1954). *Archaeological Finds of 1952 on Exhibition in the Iraq Museum, Baghdad.* Museum International Volume 7 1954 Issue 1, 33-36.

[cxii] Lloyd, Seton (2014). *Ur—Al 'Ubaid, 'Uqair and Eridu: An Interpretation of Some Evidence from The Flood-Pit.* Cambridge: Cambridge University Press.

[cxiii] Olijdam, Eric and Richard H. Spoor (2008). *Intercultural Relations between South and Southwest Asia.* Oxford: Archaeopress.

[cxiv] Broodbank, Cyprian (2006). *The Origins and Early Development of Mediterranean Maritime Activity.* Journal of Mediterranean Archaeology.

[cxv] Carter, R. (2008). *Excavations and Ubaid-Period Boat Remains at H3, As-Sabiyah (Kuwait) page 92-102.* BAR International Series 1, 92-102.

[cxvi] Woolley, Leonard C. L. (1934). *Ur Excavation. Vol. II: pages 71-145 The Royal Cemetery. A report on the Predynastic and Sargonid Graves excavated between 1926 and 1931.* Journal of the Royal Asiatic Society.

[cxvii] Miroschedji, Pierre de (2011). *THE Origin of Canaanite Cult and Religion: The early Bronze Age Fertility Ritual in Palestine:* Israel Exploration Society, Pages 74-103 (Also referencing Johnstone 1980).

[cxviii] McClure H. A., Al-Shaikh N. Y. (1993) June. *Palaeogeography of an 'Ubaid archaeological site, Saudi Arabia.* Arabian Archaeology and Epigraphy Vol 2 Issue 2, pp. 69-147.

[cxix] Van De Velde, Thomas (2015). *Black Magic Bitumen.* Faculteit Letteren and Wijsbegeerte, Universiteit Gent, Gent. (Also referencing Thesiger 1994).

[cxx] Edens, Christopher (1992). *Dynamics of Trade in the Ancient Mesopotamian "World System".* American Anthropologist Vol 94, 118-139.

[cxxi] Verlag, Harrassowitz (2010). *The World of Berossos.* Durham: Hatfield College, Durham.

[cxxii] Espak, Peeter *Was Eridu the First city in Sumerian Mythology? (2015):* Estonian Science Council.

[cxxiii] Espak, Peeter *Was Eridu the First city in Sumerian Mythology? (2015):* Estonian Science Council.

[cxxiv] Safar, Fuad (1954). *Archaeological Finds of 1952 on Exhibition in the Iraq Museum, Baghdad.* Museum International Volume 7 1954 Issue 1, 33-36.

[cxxv] Jacobsen, Thorkild (1981). *The Eridu Genesis. Journal of Biblical Literature*, 513-529.

[cxxvi] Woolley, Leonard C. L. (1934). *Ur Excavation. Vol. II: pages 71-145 The Royal Cemetery. A report on the Predynastic and Sargonid Graves excavated between 1926 and 1931. Journal of the Royal Asiatic Society.*

[cxxvii] Haynes, John Henry (1900). *Nippur, Iraq expedition records*. Pennsylvania: University of Pennsylvania.

Chapter 6

[cxxviii] Loftus, William Kennett (1857). *Travels and researches in Chaldæa and Susiana; with an account of excavations at Warka, the "Erech" of Nimrod, and Shúsh, "Shushan the palace" of Esther, in 1849-52*. New York: New York, Robert Carter and Brothers.

[cxxix] Reade, Julian (1991). *Mesopotamia*. London: British Museum Press.

[cxxx] Leick, Gwendolyn (2009). *The Babylonian World*. Philadelphia: Routledge.

[cxxxi] Reade, Julian (1991). *Mesopotamia*. London: British Museum Press.

[cxxxii] Mark, Joshua J. (2011). *Uruk*. Ancient History Encyclopedia. *(Also referencing Reade 30).*

[cxxxiii] Bertman, Stephen (1987). *Doorways Through Time*. Tarcher.

[cxxxiv] Mark, Joshua J. (2011). *Uruk*. Ancient History Encyclopedia. *(Also referencing Pritchard, 167-172).*

[cxxxv] Kalyanaraman, Srini (2016). *Indus Script evidence validates maritime trade of Meluhha (Sarasvati civilisation) with Dilmun from 2500 BC*. www.academia.edu/26007634/Maritime trade of Meluhha.

[cxxxvi] Mark, Joshua J. (2011). *Uruk. Ancient History Encyclopedia*.

[cxxxvii] Kramer, Samuel Noah (1945). Enki and Ninhursag. *American Schools of Oriental Research*.

[cxxxviii] Mark, Joshua J. (2011). *Uruk. Ancient History Encyclopedia*.

[cxxxix] Mark, Joshua J. (2011). *Uruk. Ancient History Encyclopedia*.

Chapter 7

[cxl] Sanders, Nancy. K. (1962). *The Epic of Gilgamesh*. Online: Assyrian International News Agency.

Chapter 8

[cxli] Chew, Sing C. and Sarabia, Daniel (2016). *Nature-Culture Relations: Early Globalisation, Climate Changes and System Crisis.* Article; Department of Urban and Environmental Sociology, Helmholtz Centre for Environmental Research—UFZ, Leipzig 04105 Germany.

[cxlii] Annus, Amar *The God Ninurta – Chapter Three: Ninurta in Mythology.* In A. M. Mythology, Ninurta in Mythology (pages 109-186). state Archives of Assyria Studies XIV. (Also referencing Francfort 1987).

[cxliii] Re, Alessandro (2011). *Ion and Electron Microscopy for the Characterisation of Materials Determination of Provenance of Lapis Lazuli.* Torino: Università Degli Studi di Torino. (Also referencing Tosi 1974).

[cxliv] Lucy Blue, Kristian Strutt, Peter Sheehan, Peter Jackson, and Mark Beech (2013). *Developing an integrated policy for the maritime and coastal heritage of the UAE: a collaborative approach.* Seminar for Arabian Studies.

[cxlv] Masson, Charles (1844). *Narrative of Various Journeys in Baluchistan, Afghanistan, the Panjab, and Kalât.* London: Richard Bentley.

[cxlvi] Vidale, Massimo (2001). *Growing in a Foreign World: For a History of the "Meluhha Villages" in Mesopotamia in the 3rd Millennium BC.* Schools of Oriental Studies and the Development of Modern Historiography, 261-280.

[cxlvii] Cooper, Jerrold S.(1983). *The Curse of Agade.* Baltimore: Johns Hopkins University Press.(Also referencing Haywood Page 76).

[cxlviii] Udayashankar, Ramita. *Indus Valley Civilisation.* Academia.edu.

[cxlix] Giovanni de Feo (2020, February). *The Historical Development of Sewers Worldwide.* HAL Archives Ouvertes.

[cl] Gensheimer, Thomas R. (1984). *The Role of Shell In Mesopotamia: Evidence for Trade Exchange with Oman and the Indus Valley.* Paléorient, 65-67.

Chapter 9

[cli] Vidale, Massimo (2001). *Growing in a Foreign World: For a History of the "Meluhha Villages" in Mesopotamia in the 3rd Millennium BC.* Schools of Oriental Studies and the Development of Modern Historiography, 261-280.

[clii] Frankfort, Henri (1968). *The Birth of Civilisation in the Near East.* Barnes and Noble.

[cliii] Leick, Gwendolyn (2009). *The Babylonian World*. Philadelphia: Routledge.
[cliv] Woolley, Leonard C. L. (1934). *Ur Excavation. Vol. II: pages 71-145 The Royal Cemetery. A report on the Predynastic and Sargonid Graves excavated between 1926 and 1931*. Journal of the Royal Asiatic Society.
[clv] Bertman, Stephen (1987). *Doorways Through Time*. Tarcher.
[clvi] Curtis, John, and Roger Matthews (2012). *Mega-Cities and Mega-sites The Archaeology of Consumption and Disposal Landscape, Transport and Communication*. Proceedings of the 7th International Congress on the Archaeology of the Ancient Near East. London: Harrassowitz Verlag.
[clvii] Dixit, Yama (2014). *Decline of Bronze Age 'mega cities' linked to climate change*. University of Cambridge.

Chapter 10

[clviii] Chevalier, Nicole (2018). *France and Elam from The Elamite World*. Routledge.

Picture Credits

Page 1; Peter Smith Photograph of Ken Angus in Kuwait desert 2019.
Page 36, 66, 87, 93, 152, 264, Adapted Map Image of Coastlines of the Ice Age - Middle East; Map Porn, for interesting maps (reddit.com)
Page 43; Mesopotamian (Iraq) Marshes in 1974, before Saddam Hussein drained them as a punishment to the region's Marsh Arabs. : pics (reddit.com)
Page 66; Sheep grazing picture taken by Ken Angus in North Kuwait near Iraq border.
Page 77; www.nature.org/media/oceansandcoasts/mangroves-for-coastal-defence.pdf Natural mangrove in Senegal, by Wetlands International. Page 9.
Page 78; Post Glacial Sea Levels Rise; Sea Level Rise (antarcticglaciers.org).
Page 84; Persian Gulf Bathymetry and Tide Gauges PGS; Persian Gulf Bathymetry Maps|Persian gulf and strait of Hormuz bathymetry (persiangulfstudies.com).
Page 93; Flooded Forest, Tallowa Dam - Byron Bay Gallery Artist: Tommy Salmon
Page 94; Stock Image of Middle East from Space.

Page 95; Mesopotamia versus Egyptian Historical Chronology Bar Chart (Work In Progress). Prepared by Blazes And Amuzed; ap1rka9kdi241.png (2880×1540) (redd.it).

Page 187; Sculls decorated with plaster and shells; Copyright: Institute of Archaeology UCL. Creator; Whole Plate Negatives Art History 101 – Part IA: Prehistoric Era – 399 CE | Make Lists, Not War (wordpress.com)

Page 207; Çatalhöyük. Museum of Anatolian Civilisation, Ankara (photo: Nevit Dilmen CC BY-SA 3.)

Page 88; Çatalhöyük. Building 80 (photo: CC BY-NC-SA 2.0)

Page 89; Çatalhöyük the original drawings made by James Mellaart Photo by Behice Ozturk May 28th 2006.

Page 163; Göbekli Tepe gobekli-tepe-temple-mystery-night-sky.jpg (1330×700) (thetravelimages.com)

Page 190; Agriculture Area (Abdali) 2020 2 x Pictures taken by Ken Angus in North Kuwait.

Page 207; https://nationalgeographic.grid.id/read/132187193/ Working Swimming near reed beds.

Page 208; 2nd Image ;
http://worldtruth.tv/the-mesopotamian-venice-the-lost-floating-homes-of-iraq/

Page 208; 3rd Image;
https://www.meridelrubenstein.com/wp-content/uploads/2012/06/NATURE-IRAQ-2010.

Page 208; 4th Image; Daily Life in the Mesopotamian Countryside - History (historyonthenet.com).

Page 234; Plimpton 322 is Babylonian exact sexagesimal trigonometry - ScienceDirect Historia Mathematica Volume 44, Issue 4, November 2017, Pages 395-419.

Page 239; 1st Image; Sources of Water in Ancient Mesopotamia (sciencing.com)

Page 239; 2nd Image; Basra | Photo, Nature, Cover photos pinterest.com.

Page 239; 3rd Image; Basra | Photo, Nature, Cover photos pinterest.com.

Page 247; Shulgi of Ur - Ancient History Encyclopedia Foundation Figure of King Shulgi of Ur. By Metropolitan Museum of Art (Copyright).

Page 248; Ancient Southern Mesopotamia: Water and the Rise of Urbanism - Advanced Science News.

Page 249; 2 x images Southern Mesopotamia: Water and the Rise of Urbanism - Advanced Science News Canals and water supply in the Lower Euphrates valley.

Page 253; Layout of an Agricultural Cell in Southern Mesopotamia; (Adamo, 2020).

Page 257; mesopotania_irrigation.pdf Author By J. Nedelcu. A Levee with its Remaining Water being Divided into Multiple Irrigation Canals.

Page 258; Sluice Gate of a large stream; Lambert (2007) and (Adamo, 2020).

Page 259; Schematic layout of an agricultural complex in middle Mesopotamia; From Buccellati and (Adamo, 2020). https://www.researchgate.net/figure/Map-of-the-remains-of-major-irrigation-canals

Page 260; An example of a settling reservoir and complementary waterworks; (Adamo, 2020)

Page 261; Head Regulator of Nina-Gena Canal; (Adamo, 2020) Drawn by Steven Convery (2021)

Page 262; The dimensions of this regulator were 18 x 3 metres; Stienkeller and (Adamo, 2020)

Page 264; Map of the Remains of Major Irrigation Canals and Regulators Produced by Jacobson;

Page 264; 1st Image; A Plough and Seeder; Seeder Plough - WH 15 Sem 1:Mesopotamia GO (google.com)

Page 264; 2nd Image; ancient-mesopotamian-tools-4 | Mesopotamian Civilisation and Ancient Greece (wordpress.com).

Page 269; 3rd Image; Ancient Plough photos, royalty-free images, graphics, vectors and videos | Adobe Stock

Page 270; 1st Image; Carvings with Stories: a blog about woodcarving: July 2014

Page 265; 2nd Image; Mesopotamia Plough | Sutori

Page 280; Eridu, Sumer, The Reed Boat of the Cult Image of the God Enki, 3200 BC – Archaeology Illustrated Balage Balogh.

Page 281; a reedboat history (atlantisbolivia.org) length 55ft (16.5m) Breadth 16ft (4.9) Reed made hull made a journey in 2,000 AD of 2,850 miles. Proving long distance travel in Reed Made boats

Page 311; The Sacred Tree (Assyrian), embossed in Gold Gilt on a book cover (William Harris Rule. Doctor of Divinity. Oriental Records. Monumental. London. Samuel Bagster and Sons. 1877).

Page 316; ANE TODAY - 201709 - Rebuilding Eden in the Land of Eridu - (asor.org) Eridu First Temple Level XVI (Safar 1981)

Page 337 A clay Bullae with Tokens, excavated at the Tell of the Acropolis in the city of Susa, Elam. Uruk Period. Excavated between 1933-1939 by Roland de Mecquenem Public Domain. The Invention of Writing :: Proto-Cuneiform in the Uruk Period - Projeda (projectglobalawakening.com)

Page 339; Cylinder Seal; Sumerian Amazonite Cylinder Seal of King... (tumblr.com)

Page 346; A Proto Cuneiform Tablet from the Jemdet Nasr Period 3,100-2,900 BC probably from Uruk. Metropolitan Museum of Art.

Page 350;

https://www.academia.edu/15289406/Indus Script Hieroglyph multiplex on Al-Sabah Kuwait Gold Disc Meluhha

Page 361; 1st Image; Warka "The Lady of Uruk" Baghdad, Iraq - Circa 2002:: (100% royalty free) 30516661 | Shutterstock

Page 362; 2nd Image; Uruk Facade of Inanna's Temple; Facade of Inanna's Temple at Uruk (Illustration) - Ancient History Encyclopedia

Page 363; Uruk, Southern Iraq, The so-called "White Temple" 3000 BC – Archaeology Illustrated.

Page 365; A comparison of the polychrome geometric patterns painted on Egyptian "palace façades" / false doors with potential counterparts in Mesopotamia (hcommons.org) Figure 7.

Page 370; Kubaba; Kubaba The First Female Ruler https://thisissouthsudan.com/.

Page 441; A measured take on the Pylos Combat Agate – Ancient World Magazine.

Page 368; Before the Great Flood 8 Kings Ruled for 241,200 years, Says Ancient Text Curiosmos.

Page 461; Getty Image The 'Peace' side of the Standard of Ur, Southern Iraq, about 2600-2400 BC.

Page 461; Getty Image Side B of the Standard of Ur, Southern Iraq, about 2600-2400 BC.

Page 465; 1st Image; Queen Kubaba;

Queen Ku-Baba (sumerianshakespeare.com).

Page 370; 2nd Image; Sargon I Bust - Biblical Archaeology (Bible History Online) (bible-history.com).

CPSIA information can be obtained
at www.ICGtesting.com
Printed in the USA
LVHW080609210622
721685LV00004B/29